Cubase® 4 Power!

The Comprehensive Guide

Robert Guérin

THOMSON
COURSE TECHNOLOGY
Professional ■ Technical ■ Reference

ISBN-10: 1-59863-002-4
ISBN-13: 978-1-59863-002-2

Library of Congress Catalog Card Number: 2006907925

Printed in the United States of America

07 08 09 10 11 PH 10 9 8 7 6 5 4 3 2 1

Professional ■ Technical ■ Reference

Thomson Course Technology PTR, a division of Thomson Learning Inc.
25 Thomson Place
Boston, MA 02210
http://www.courseptr.com

Publisher and General Manager, Thomson Course Technology PTR:
Stacy L. Hiquet

Associate Director of Marketing:
Sarah O'Donnell

Manager of Editorial Services:
Heather Talbot

Marketing Manager:
Mark Hughes

Acquisitions Editor:
Orren Merton

Marketing Assistant:
Adena Flitt

Project Editor/Copy Editor:
Cathleen D. Snyder

Technical Reviewer:
Colin MacQueen

PTR Editorial Services Coordinator:
Erin Johnson

Interior Layout Tech:
Digital Publishing Solutions

Cover Designers:
Mike Tanamachi and Nancy Goulet

Indexer:
Kelly Henthorne

Proofreader:
Laura Gabler

Acknowledgments

Big thanks to Sang Hee Park, for all her support, gentle words of encouragement, love, and affection. I am truly blessed to share this path with you.

Thank you to Colin MacQueen: You have definitely elevated this book with your collaborative views, words of wisdom, and hard labor. Cathleen Snyder and Orren Merton, thank you for all the long hours spent going through this material and making sure I was happy with the result. Andy Shafran and Mark Garvey, for being there from the start and always there, ready to help at a moment's notice.

I would like to give thanks to Arnd Kaiser and Martin Gente at Steinberg, who have provided me with the necessary tools and help when needed, and to Athan Bilias from Yamaha for knocking on the right doors when it was time to get things moving in the right direction.

To all of you, *merci beaucoup*. Your help is truly appreciated, and this book would not have been possible without your support.

About the Author

A composer for the past 16 years and a music enthusiast since 1976, **Robert Guérin** has worked on different personal and professional projects, such as feature and short films, television themes, and educational and corporate videos. Composing, arranging, playing, recording, and mixing most of his material, he has developed working habits that allow him to be creative without losing his sense of efficiency.

As a professor, Robert has put together several courses covering a wide range of topics, such as computer software for musicians, digital audio technologies, sound on the Web, sound in multimedia productions, hard disk recording, and many more. He has been program coordinator at Trebas Institute in Montreal and a part-time professor at Vanier College, also in Montreal. Robert has developed online courses on sound integration in Web pages and has written several articles, tutorials, and software reviews for audio- and music-related online magazines.

This is Robert's fifth edition of *Cubase Power!* He has also written two editions of *MIDI Power!*, he co-wrote *Nuendo Power!*, and he has worked on a number of Thomson Course Technology PTR CSi CD-ROM products, such as *Sound Forge 7 CSi Starter*, *ACID 5 CSi Starter*, and *Cubase SX 3 CSi Starter* and *Master*.

To find out more about the author or to contact him, please visit this book's support site at www.wavedesigners.com.

TABLE OF Contents

Introduction

Cubase has been around for a while now. I remember using its ancestor, the Pro 24 software, on my Atari ST in 1987 to create musical arrangements for composition assignments during my university training years. Since then, many things have changed, and Cubase has made the transition from a MIDI sequencer to a Virtual Studio Technology (VST) software. This installment of Cubase grows on the knowledge Steinberg has acquired from years of user comments like yours and dedicated development teams. If you are new to Cubase, you can expect this software to help you through your entire musical creation process. If you are a veteran Cubase user, you will find many of the things you loved and a few new features, as usual, that have made their way into the standard music producer toolbox over the years. Hopefully, in both cases, this book will help you to get the most out of this great tool.

Like any software, as it allows you to do more things and do them in a more intuitive way, the learning curve becomes more and more abrupt. You will find extensive documentation on all available features found in Cubase on the CD-ROM provided with the software, but you will have to sift through thousands of pages of electronic documentation. For most users, this might seem like an overwhelming task. *Cubase 4 Power!* will provide you with the most important features and some lesser-known features in step-by-step examples, as well as online resources that complement this book.

Beyond describing the features of the program and how they work, I address through examples the "why" of using certain features and when they can become useful to you. All of the Cubase Studio 4 features are included in Cubase 4; for those of you who have this version of the software, this book should address your questions as well, but since this is a trimmed-down version of the application, some features described in this book won't apply to you. You can find a complete list of feature differences on Steinberg's website.

Since Cubase is also available in both Macintosh and PC versions in quite similar environments, it doesn't really matter which platform you are using—the way to use the features and functions will be the same. That being said, Mac users are *strongly* encouraged to purchase a two-button mouse. Although it is possible to use the Mac alternative Control-click for single-button devices, many of the features in Cubase are available through context menus, and the second button simply makes them easier and more convenient to access.

I offer you my years of experience working with the software, as well as my insight into some tips and tricks that have been very useful in getting the job done throughout these years. As a professor and program coordinator in sound design vocational schools in Canada, I have answered questions of many students who have wanted to work with this tool to create music. I have drawn from their most frequently asked questions and answered them in a way that I hope you will find enlightening.

Enjoy.

How This Book Is Organized

Because the feature set offered by Cubase is so vast and expansive, it would be impossible to write a book that covers all production styles and musical genres through specific examples in which all these features are described in the production context you would like to see. There are simply too many variables involved. Some of you might even find this book's approach too academic. Although this may be the case, understand that this book and Cubase are tools that will hopefully help you jumpstart your imagination. We can give you paint and a brush and show you creative techniques, but what you do with that is all up to you.

With this in mind, the book is organized into 39 chapters that address specific topics. The topics are laid out in a typical production workflow. Here's a summary of what you can expect to find:

- **Part I: Setup.** Chapters 1 through 5 address basic concepts related to digital audio, MIDI, and Cubase terminology. They also look at what needs to be done to connect peripherals to Cubase and to get Cubase to send its signal back to these peripherals. In other words, Part I covers getting sound in and out of Cubase and making sure your project is properly configured to handle these connections.
- **Part II: Recording.** Chapters 6 through 14 address recording preparations, monitoring setups through the Control Room Mixer, managing assets through the new Cubase management system called SoundFrame, configuring and using hardware and software instruments in a project, as well as recording both audio and MIDI data. We will also discuss the following main topics: the ReWire application, plug-in effects as inserts, audio content management through the Pool, and advanced recording options.
- **Part III: Navigation.** Chapters 15 through 18 address project navigation and functionalities, along with the most common operations performed in Cubase's main interface: the Project window. We will take a close look at the components and controls provided in the audio and MIDI tracks, which can easily be considered the two most important track classes in a Cubase project.
- **Part IV: Editing.** Chapters 19 through 24 address editing environments outside the Project window: the Sample editor for audio events, and the Key and Drum editors for MIDI events. We will also explore a number of editing features and commands found in the MIDI and Audio menus.
- **Part V: Arranging.** Chapters 25 through 30 address techniques and tools associated with organizing your content in a project—from setting up grids to move events in a project, to applying MIDI effects; from creating copies of an entire section of a project, to trimming two bars off the second chorus. We will explore Cubase's Play Order Tracks functionality, which makes it possible to build a project in a non-linear environment. Finally, we will look at tempo changing and synchronization functionalities available in Cubase.

- **Part VI: Mixing and Mastering.** Chapters 31 through 37 address using the Mixer panel, working with plug-in effect tracks and send effects, creating group channels for submixes, and cueing mixes along. This section also investigates Cubase's automation techniques and functionalities, surround mixing, and project audio export options.
- **Part VII: Managing.** Chapters 38 and 39 look at ways to customize Cubase to better fit your working style, as well as techniques to make a project more resource-efficient.

At the beginning of each chapter, you will find a summary of what you will be learning. You can read this book from beginning to end, or you can quickly jump to the topics that interest you the most if you are already familiar with some of the features discussed in a particular chapter.

Keeping the Book's Content Current

Everyone involved with this book has worked hard to make it complete and accurate. But as we all know, technology changes rapidly, and a small number of errors may have crept in besides. If you find any errors, have suggestions for future editions, have questions about the book or other topics, or simply would like to find out more about Cubase or audio-related subjects, please visit the support website at www.wavedesigners.com. Who knows–you might even find some additional bonus chapters there!

I } Setup

1 Basic Concepts

Before we begin our tour of Cubase, it is important to have a good understanding of this application and what it can do. Also, Cubase supports both MIDI and digital audio, so we'll make sure you understand the fundamental differences between these two types of music-making events, as well as some basic MIDI and digital audio principles.

Here's a summary of what you will learn in this chapter:

- How Cubase evolved through the years
- A brief introduction to MIDI fundamentals
- A brief introduction to digital audio fundamentals
- How sound is digitized and what the parameters are that affect the quality of your digital audio recording
- What the basic concept is behind 32-bit floating-point digital audio recording

What Is Cubase?

You can think of Cubase as a musician's toolbox with tools to record, edit, mix, and publish MIDI and audio information, as well as tools to convert MIDI into printable sheet music.

Since its beginning as a MIDI sequencer in 1989, Cubase has undergone many transformations. In 1996, Cubase became not only a MIDI sequencer, but also a full audio production tool, contributing in many ways to the development and democratization of the creative process that lies inside every musician. With the introduction of VST (*Virtual Studio Technology*), Steinberg made it possible to replace hardware devices with their software equivalents. While Cubase SX 3 introduced a comprehensive audio warping technology and pattern-based arrangement with Play Order tracks, Cubase 4 adds many workflow enhancements. It also introduces a set of brand-new media management tools, which will help any musician deal with the ever-growing number of media resources now available. To help you better understand this toolset, here's a look at the different areas Cubase covers:

- **Audio and MIDI recording environments.** Cubase records and plays back digital audio, MIDI, and effects parameter automation events.
- **Audio and MIDI editing environments.** Once audio or MIDI is recorded, you can edit these events using one of many editing windows available in Cubase.
- **Virtual instruments.** If you don't own external sound modules, Cubase provides the technology necessary to transform your computer into a "virtual instrument" through *VST instruments*. VST instruments are software synthesizers installed on your computer that use your audio interface to generate its sounds. You no longer need to purchase expensive synthesizer modules, since they are part of your "Virtual Studio" environment. Cubase 4 includes six instruments (four new ones).
- **Effects.** Cubase allows you to use its built-in audio and MIDI effects, add third-party effects, use effects already present on your computer, or even connect external effect devices. Effects allow you to process audio in a number of ways, such as controlling the dynamic and harmonic content of audio through compressors, filters, or other types of signal processing. Cubase integrates this potential within its Virtual Studio Technology and gives you the necessary tools to control every aspect effects can provide. Cubase 4 includes 16 real-time MIDI effects and 48 real-time audio effects.
- **Mixing environment.** While you're recording, editing, and manipulating MIDI and audio events, you can mix every track by using a virtual mixer not unlike its hardware counterpart. This virtual mixer accommodates as many inputs, output busses, effects, MIDI tracks, virtual instrument tracks, groups, and audio tracks as your project needs. Then, automate your mix easily and create complex mixes without leaving your computer. Connect one of several compatible hardware controllers to get a more interesting tactile experience during your mixing process. Cubase 4 introduces users to a studio control room–like interface, which makes recording live musicians and performing overdubs easier than ever.
- **Multimedia production environment.** You can synchronize your Cubase project to play back a digital audio file or incoming SMPTE/EBU timecode in multimedia or video productions, making it a great post-production environment for today's producers. Cubase now supports more import and export formats than ever, making it a great tool to prepare content for the Web, as well as for high-quality surround productions.

What Is MIDI?

The Musical Instrument Digital Interface (MIDI) represents two things: First, MIDI is a communication system used to transmit information from one MIDI-compatible device to another. These devices include musical instruments (keyboard controllers, samplers, synthesizers, sound modules, drum machines) and computers or other hardware devices, such as MIDI control surfaces or synchronizers. Second, MIDI represents the hardware—the ports and jacks found on all MIDI instruments and the MIDI cables that connect them together to allow the transmission of musical data. Each time a key is pressed or a wheel is moved on your MIDI controller, one or more bytes are sent out from this device's MIDI Out port. Other devices connected to that sending device are looking for those bytes to come over the wire, and the received MIDI event messages are then translated back into commands for the device to obey.

MIDI sends information at a rate of 31,250 bps (*bits per second*). This is called MIDI's *baud rate*. Because MIDI is transferred through a serial port, it sends information one bit at a time. Every MIDI message uses 10 bits of data (8 for the information and 2 for error correction), which means that MIDI sends about 3,906 bytes of data every second (31,250 bps divided by 8 bits). If you compare this to the 176,400-byte (or 172.3-kilobyte) transfer rate that digital audio requires when recording or playing back CD-quality sound without compression, MIDI may seem very slow. But, in reality, it's fast enough for what it needs to transfer. At this speed, you could transmit approximately 500 MIDI note events per second.

Anatomy of a MIDI Message

MIDI sends or receives the following information:

- Events related to your performance, such as a note played or released.
- Parameters for these actions, such as the channel setting. Each MIDI cable or port can support up to 16 channels of information, much like having up to 16 separate instruments playing at once.
- Wheels and pedal controls, such as pitch bend and modulation wheels or levers, sustain pedals, and switch pedals.
- Key pressures of pressed keys, also known as *aftertouch* information, sent by the controller keyboard or by the sequencer to a sound module. Note that not all keyboards support this function, but when they do, the information is sent as MIDI data.
- Program changes or patch changes, as well as sound bank selections.
- Synchronization for MIDI devices that have built-in timing clocks. These timing clocks may determine the desired tempo of a drum machine, for example. Through synchronization, MIDI devices can also follow or trigger other devices or applications, such as sequencers or drum machines, making sure each one stays in sync with the "master" MIDI clock.

- System Exclusive messages used to alter synthesizer parameters and control the transport of System Exclusive–compatible multitrack recorders.
- MIDI Time Code or MTC, which is a way for MIDI-compatible devices to lock to a SMPTE device—a translation of SMPTE timecode into something MIDI devices can understand.

MIDI transmits performance *data*, not sound. You can think of MIDI as an old player piano using a paper roll. The holes in the paper roll marked the moments at which the musician played the notes, but the holes themselves were not the sounds. MIDI information is transmitted in much the same way, capturing the performance of the musician but not the sound of the instrument on which he or she played. To hear the notes that MIDI data signifies, you will always need some kind of sound module that can reproduce the musical events recorded as MIDI data. This sound module could be an external synthesizer module, a sampler, a virtual synthesizer inside your computer software, or even the synthesizer chip on your audio interface. This is precisely one of the types of information Cubase allows you to work with—recording a musical performance through your computer, using a keyboard to trigger MIDI events, and using Cubase as the recording device *and* the sound generator, thus creating a virtual paper roll inside the application.

MIDI Connectors

MIDI devices come in many flavors, shapes, and sizes. Manufacturers have adapted the MIDI format to fit today's needs and market. Earlier devices would typically have either two or three MIDI-connector plugs: In and Out; or In, Out, and Thru. Two-port configurations were reserved for computer-related hardware (see the left side of Figure 1.1), as well as software-based synthesizers because the output connector could be switched within a software application. Soft-switching allows users to transform the MIDI output into a MIDI Thru connection. With time, a single USB port can now replace the need for two (more expensive to produce) MIDI connectors. As a result, many devices now communicate MIDI events to and from a computer workstation using a USB connector, which can be configured via the computer's operating system.

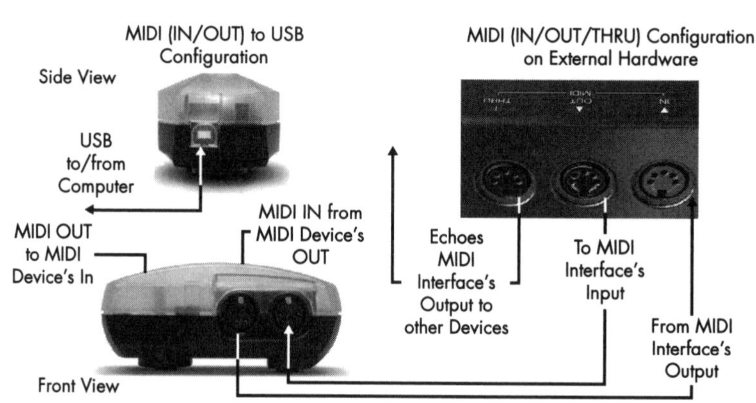

Figure 1.1
On the left is an example of a two-connector configuration typical of a USB-to-MIDI interface for computers. On the right is a typical three-connector configuration found on keyboards and sound modules.

MIDI Out

MIDI does not transmit sound over cables the way audio components in a sound system do. Instead, MIDI sends a message that contains an identifier portion and its associated parameters. For example, when you play a note, the identifier would be that this is a "note on" event, whose parameters would be the note number for the key you pressed, plus a velocity parameter indicating how hard you hit that note.

As you play on a MIDI keyboard or another type of MIDI controller, the internal processor in that device examines your performance, converting it into a stream of MIDI events that represent your actions. That information is sent out over the instrument's MIDI output to other synthesizers that reproduce the performance using their own sounds—and/or to Cubase in order to be recorded as part of your project.

A device's MIDI output will not echo (retransmit) any MIDI events received at its MIDI input. If you want to do this, you will need to use the MIDI Thru connector, which is described later in the chapter.

MIDI In

Many MIDI keyboards can be viewed as two machines in one (see Figure 1.2):

- **A sound module.** The part under the control of the onboard processor, the electronics that actually make the sounds.
- **A MIDI interface.** The computer processor that monitors the keyboard, front panel displays, and program memory to send events to the sound module or out through the device's MIDI ports.

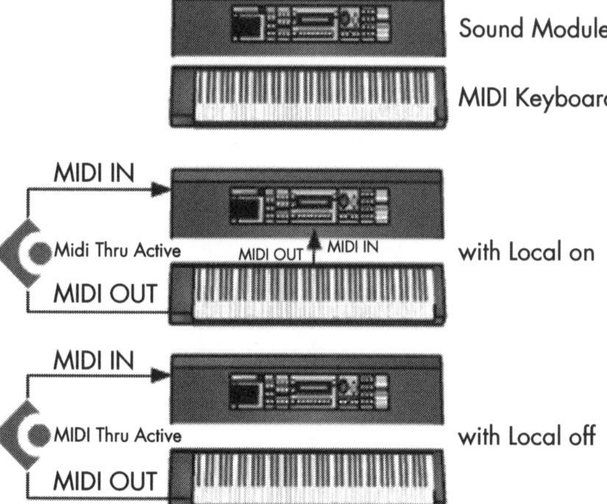

Figure 1.2
Configuring your keyboard's MIDI input.

The MIDI input receives incoming MIDI information and sends it to the instrument's processor, which will act upon it in much the same way as a performance on the instrument itself, such as pressing a key to play notes. It makes no difference to the sound-making parts of a synthesizer whether the command to play notes comes from a key press on the instrument's local keyboard or as a command from other MIDI devices and programs.

When you are working with a sequencer program such as Cubase, it is recommended that you set your MIDI instrument's local switch parameter to off because both Cubase and the local keyboard would be sending MIDI information to the sound module portion of your instrument if it is connected to Cubase through MIDI. When the local switch is enabled, your instrument plays sounds directly when you press keys on its keyboard; when the local switch is set to off, the instrument responds only to incoming events on its MIDI In port. In other words, setting it to off will disconnect the bridge between the actual MIDI playing surface (the keyboard) and the sound module part that allows you to hear the keyboard's sounds as you play the keys.

When using Cubase, you will use your keyboard or other MIDI controller to send MIDI to the host computer through the instrument's MIDI Out. As Cubase records the information you play, it can also send the information back out to your keyboard's MIDI In connector. If your keyboard's MIDI setting isn't set to Local off, the sound module portion of your instrument would play the sounds twice—once when you play the notes on your keyboard, and once when Cubase sends the MIDI information back to it. Note that this precaution also applies to MIDI controllers that serve as a tactile mixing interface when mixing in Cubase.

On the other hand, if you have a sound module without a keyboard, you will not need to take this precaution because there is no MIDI being sent to the device's MIDI input besides what is connected to this input.

MIDI Thru

MIDI Thru retransmits the MIDI data received at the MIDI input of a device so that it can be received by another device in a chain. An important concept to understand when putting together a MIDI-based music system is that anything played on a MIDI instrument goes only to the MIDI Out and not to the MIDI Thru. This third port is very useful when you want to avoid MIDI loops when hooking together your MIDI devices.

A MIDI loop occurs when MIDI information is sent from one instrument to another and ends up being routed back to the MIDI In initial instrument. This causes the instrument to play each note twice and, in some cases, causes a feedback of MIDI data that could potentially cause your sequencer to crash.

If you have a MIDI patch bay or a multiport MIDI interface—MIDI devices with multiple MIDI inputs and outputs called *MIDI ports*—you are better off using a separate MIDI output for each connected device, thus reducing the amount of information flowing through a single MIDI cable. Each MIDI port in a MIDI setup sends or receives up to 16 MIDI channels. For example, if you are using a MIDI interface with four MIDI ports, you will have four MIDI inputs and four MIDI outputs, and you will have independent control over 64 MIDI channels. If you do not own a multiport or MIDI patch bay, daisy-chaining MIDI devices using the MIDI Thru socket is your best bet (see Figure 1.3).

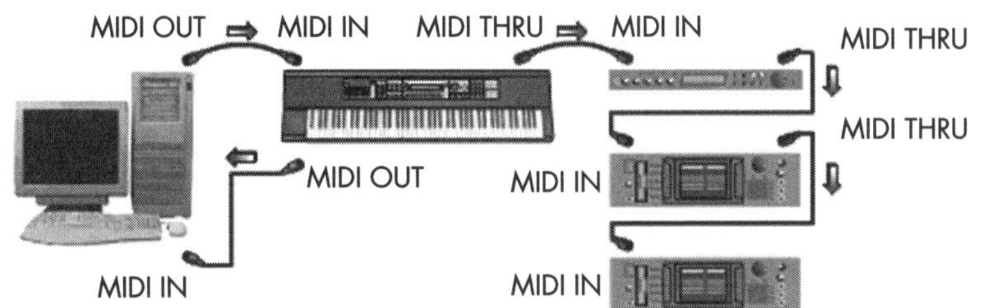

Figure 1.3
Using the MIDI Thru connector to hook together multiple MIDI devices.

A Brief Overview of Digital Audio

Understanding how sound is transformed into digital audio will put you in a better position to predict and control the result, as well as prevent potential problems associated with digital audio recording. This saves you time and most likely will produce better results.

Digital audio recordings, like analog audio recordings, are not all created equal. Recording with higher digital resolutions and superior equipment—through better analog-to-digital converters—in conjunction with the technology available in Cubase 4 will allow you to create better-sounding results. Let's look at how this works and how digital recordings are different from analog recordings.

What Is Analog Sound?

When a musical instrument is played, it vibrates. Examples of this include the string of a violin, the skin of a drum, and even the cone of a loudspeaker. This vibration is transferred to the molecules of the air, which carry the sound to our ears. Receiving the sound, our eardrums vibrate, moving back and forth anywhere between 20 and 20,000 times every second. A sound's rate of vibration is called its *frequency* and is measured in Hertz. (The human range of hearing is typically from 20 Hz to 20 kHz (kilohertz).) If the frequency of the vibration is slow, we hear a low note; if the frequency is fast, we hear a high note. If the vibration is gentle, making the air move back and forth only a little, we hear a soft sound. This movement is known as *amplitude*. If the amplitude is high, making the windows rattle, we hear a loud sound!

If you were to graph air movement against time, you could draw a picture of the sound. This is called a *waveform*. You can see a very simple waveform at low amplitude on the left in Figure 1.4. The middle waveform is the same sound, but much louder (higher amplitude). Finally, the waveform on the right is a musical instrument, which contains harmonics—a wider range of simultaneous frequencies. In all of these waveforms, there is one constant: The horizontal axis always represents time, and the vertical axis always represents amplitude.

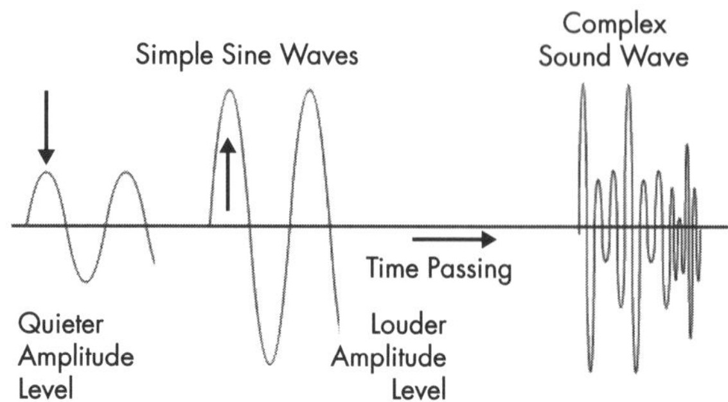

Figure 1.4
The vertical axis represents the amplitude of a waveform, and the horizontal axis represents time.

Real-life sounds don't consist of just one frequency, but of many frequencies mixed together at different levels of amplitude (loudness). This is what makes a musical sound interesting. Despite its complexity, every waveform can be represented by a graph. At any given time, the waveform has a measurable amplitude. If we can capture this "picture" and then reproduce it, we've succeeded in our goal of recording sound.

A gramophone record does this in an easily visible way. Set up a mechanism that transfers air vibration (sound) into the mechanical vibration of a steel needle. Let the needle draw the waveform onto a groove in tinfoil or wax. "Read" the wiggles in this groove with a similar needle. Amplify the vibration as best you can. Well done, Mr. Edison!

Instead of wiggles in a groove, you might decide to store the waveform as patterns of magnetism on recording tape. But either way, you're trying to draw an exact picture of the waveform. You're making an analog recording by using a continuous stream of information. This is different from digital audio recordings, as you will see later in this chapter.

The second dimension of sound is amplitude, or the intensity of molecule displacement. When many molecules are moved, the sound will be louder. Inversely, if few molecules are moved in space, the sound is softer. Amplitude is measured in volts because this displacement of molecules creates energy. When the energy is positive, it pushes molecules forward, making the line in Figure 1.4 move upward. When the energy is negative, it pushes the molecules backward, making the line go downward. When the line is near the center, it means that fewer molecules are being moved around. That's why the sound appears to be quieter.

Space is a third dimension to sound. This dimension does not have its own axis because it is usually the result of amplitude variations through time, but the space will affect the waveform itself. In other words, the space will affect the amplitude of a sound through time. This will be important when we talk about effects and microphone placement when recording or mixing digital audio.

But suffice it to say now that the environment in which sound occurs has a great influence on how we will perceive the sound.

What Is Digital Audio?

Where analog sound is a continuous variation of the molecules of air traveling through space, creating a sound's energy, digital sound consists of a discrete—noncontinuous—sampling of this variation. In digital audio, there is no such thing as continuous—only the illusion of continuum.

In 1928, mathematician Harry Nyquist developed a theory based on his findings that he could reproduce a waveform if he could sample the variation of sound at least twice in every period of that waveform. A period is a full cycle of the sound (see Figure 1.5) measured in Hertz. (This name was given in honor of Heinrich Hertz, who developed another theory regarding the relation between sound cycles and their frequency in 1888.) So, if you have a sound at a frequency of 20 Hz, you need at least 40 samples per second to reproduce it. The value captured by each audio sample is the voltage of that sound at a specific point in time. Obviously, in the 1920s, computers were not around to store the large number of values needed to implement this theory adequately, but as you probably guessed, we do have this technology available now.

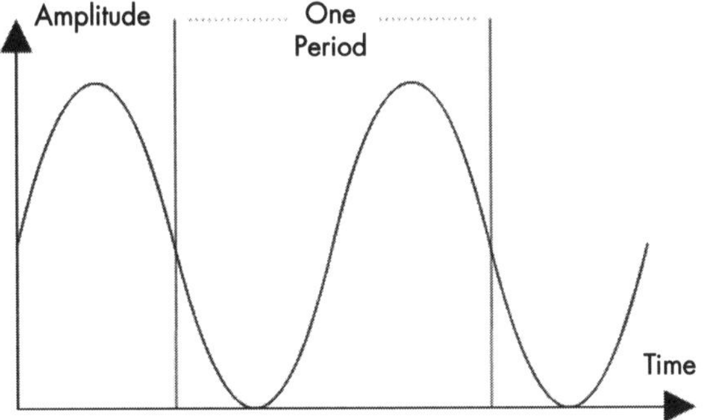

Figure 1.5
Each bit in a digital recording stores a discrete amplitude value. The frequency at which these amplitude values are stored in memory as they fluctuate through time is called the sampling frequency.

How Sampling Works

In the analog world, the amplitude is measured as a voltage value. In the digital world, this value is quantified and stored as a number. In the computer world, numbers are stored as binary memory units called *bits*. The more bits you have, the longer this number will be. Longer numbers are also synonymous with more precise representations of the original voltage values the digital audio was meant to store. In other words, every digital audio sample stores the value of the amplitude (or voltage) as a binary number. The more bits per sample, the more values you can represent. You can compare this with color depth in digital pictures. With 8 bits of color comes a 256-color palette; 16 bits of color (also known as *resolution*) can represent more than 65,000 colors. A 24-bit resolution offers more than 16.7 million colors, and so on. In sound, colors are replaced by voltage values. The higher the resolution (in bit depth—the number of bits per digital audio sample), the smaller the increments that can be captured and represented between these voltage values. If you were to calculate the distance between New York and Paris using the same accuracy as the one provided by a 24-bit digital recording system, you would be accurate within a foot (13.29 inches, or 0.34 meter, to be precise). That's an accuracy of 0.0000005%! It would be fair to assume that most high-resolution digital audio systems are fairly accurate at reproducing the amplitude variations of an audio signal.

Because the computer cannot make the in-between values, it jumps from one value to the next, creating noise-like artifacts, a kind of digital distortion known as *quantization error*. This is not something you want in your sound. So, the more values you have to represent different amplitudes, the more closely your sound will resemble the original analog signal in terms of amplitude variation. The sampling frequency (measured in Hertz) represents the number of times a voltage value is recorded each second, using bits to store this (voltage) value once it has been converted into a binary number. As with amplitude values in bits, the sampling frequency greatly affects the quality of your sound—in particular because it directly affects the highest frequencies that can be captured and played back. Because most audio components, such as amplifiers and speakers, can reproduce sounds ranging from 20 Hz to 20 kHz, the sampling frequency standard for compact disc digital audio was fixed at 44.1 kHz—a little bit more than twice the highest frequency produced by your monitoring system.

The first thing you notice when you change the sampling frequency of a sound is that with higher sampling frequencies—or greater numbers of samples per second—you get a sharper, crisper sound with better definition and fewer artifacts. With lower sampling frequencies (fewer samples), you get a duller, mushier, and less defined sound. Why is this? Because you need twice as many samples as there are frequencies in your sound, higher sampling frequencies allow you to capture higher harmonic components in the source audio—and that's where the sound qualities mentioned previously are found. When you reduce the sampling frequency, you also reduce the frequency bandwidth captured by the digital audio recording system. If your sampling frequency is extremely low, you lose not only harmonics, but fundamentals as well. And this will change the tonal quality of the sound altogether.

So how does this tie into Cubase? Well, Cubase is, in many ways, a gigantic multitrack sampler, as it samples digital audio at various sampling frequencies and bit resolutions. Whenever you are recording an audio signal in a digital format, you are sampling this sound. Cubase will allow you to sample sound at rates of up to 96,000 samples (96 kHz) per second and at resolutions (also known as *bit depths*) of up to 32 bits per sample. How high you can go will depend on the audio hardware installed on your computer.

About 32-Bit Recording

All professional audio hardware available today supports at least 16-bit resolution. Better-quality audio interfaces also support 20- and 24-bit resolutions. With the 16-bit resolution (see Figure 1.6), the vertical steps corresponding to voltage values are few and far between. In the 24-bit resolution, there are many more steps than in 16-bit recordings. In 32-bit, the binary word is twice as long, but as you will see in Table 1.1, instead of having 65,535 steps, you have more than four billion steps. Finally, in 32-bit floating-point resolution, you have more than four billion steps; however, they are not fixed, but variable points that adjust themselves according to the needs of the audio waveform. This dramatically increases the dynamic range (the range between the loudest sound before digital clipping and the minimum level) of a digital audio recording. On the minus side, it also increases the hard disk space required to record digital audio as well as processing time when applying changes, such as adding an effect to a sound. Ultimately, to record using precisions higher than 24-bit resolutions, you'll need a fast computer, a fast hard drive, and lots of memory, both in disk space and in RAM.

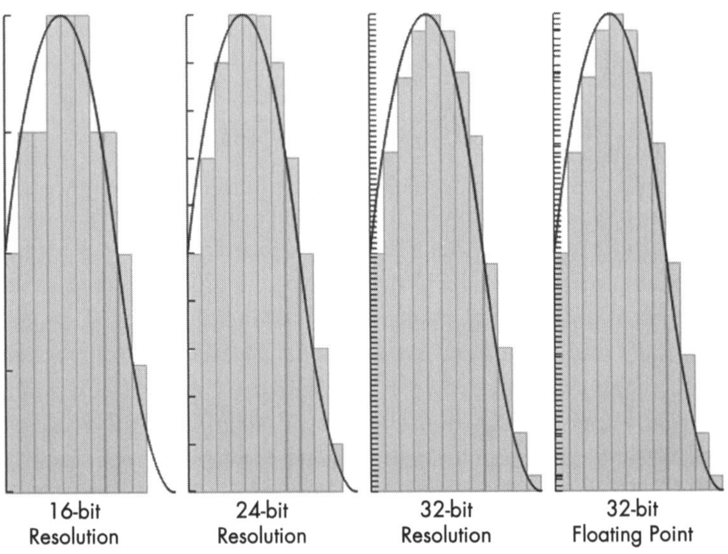

Figure 1.6
Understanding the importance of resolution (bit depth) in digital audio recording.

Table 1.1 illustrates the different values that can be stored in their respective resolutions.

Table 1.1
Minimum and Maximum Values for 16-, 24-, and 32-Bit Resolution Audio Signals

Resolution	Minimum Value	Maximum Value	Dynamic Range	Hard Disk Space (min/mono)
16-bit	-32,768	32,767	96 dBFS	5,168 KB
24-bit	-8,388,608	8,388,607	144 dBFS	7,752 KB
32-bit	-2,147,483,648	2,147,483,647	193 dBFS	10,336 KB

Recording audio up until now was limited to fixed integer values, as mentioned previously. With floating point, the computer adds a decimal value and can move that decimal point wherever it needs it to get greater precision. Here's an example: Suppose you have an analog signal coming in at 1.2245 volts. If you have a system that provides only two decimal points, your resulting value would be 1.23 or 1.22. In both cases, this would not be very precise, but it's as precise as the recording system could be. Floating-point technology simply adds a decimal value (up to seven) as needed, making the recorded value exactly 1.2245. This kind of technology yields a dynamic range of almost 200 dB! This dynamic range means that you can record a guitar passing through a plug-in effect and record the resulting waveform with great precision.

Remember that the bit depth (resolution) of the mixdown does not have to be the same as the recorded tracks. Cubase allows you to select a different format to mix down your tracks when you are finished working on them. This process happens because Cubase records in a format that is superior to the quality available on regular CD players. As a rule of thumb, always work with the best quality your entire system supports (all devices involved in the recording process especially), bringing down the quality to a more common 44.1-kHz, 16-bit format only when rendering a CD-compatible mix. As long as your hardware and software can handle it, go for it. But remember this: Audio CD format supports only 44.1-kHz, 16-bit stereo files. So, if you don't convert your audio beforehand, either in Cubase or in another audio-conversion application, you won't be able to write it in audio CD format unless your CD writing software specifically offers tools for converting source audio files from higher resolutions.

2 Cubase Terminology

One of the biggest challenges most musicians face when starting their journey into the music production arena is understanding how they can get the right signal to the right place. This might sound simple, but when you're working with four musicians in different rooms, some tracks may be recorded while others are played back, and signals coming from your computer may need to feed an external sound effect module, musician headphones, and studio monitors in a completely independent manner. Although tools such as Cubase provide a tremendous amount of flexibility and power when it comes to signal routing, it is easy to get lost in the possibilities if you don't understand the terminology and the routing concepts associated with this terminology.

This chapter lays down some of these issues and describes the concepts behind terms such as ports, inputs, outputs, and channels.

Here's a summary of what you will learn in this chapter:

- How MIDI and digital audio are handled inside Cubase
- How MIDI tracks, ports, channels, inputs, and outputs function
- What audio tracks, channels, inputs, and outputs are
- What the differences are between windows, dialog boxes, and panels
- What the Project window components are

Audio Connections

An audio connection creates a link between your audio interface's physical inputs and outputs inside Cubase. Before sound can reach Cubase, it needs to enter your computer through an audio interface. This audio interface is then identified by your computer's operating system through an ASIO driver, or optionally a Core Audio driver on Mac OS X. This driver is what Cubase uses to identify the inputs and outputs of the audio interface installed on your system. ASIO is the acronym for *Audio Stream Input/Output*, a technology developed by Steinberg that allows audio hardware to process and synchronize inputs and introduces the least amount of latency, or delay, between the inputs and the outputs of the audio hardware. You will find additional information about ASIO drivers in Chapter 3, "Setting Up Peripherals."

To understand the terminology used in Cubase, let's start outside your computer and move upstream into Cubase.

- The audio device *port* is where you make the physical connection to your audio interface—where you plug in your bass guitar, mixer, microphone, synth, or whatever. A device port can be an input or output on your audio interface. How many ports your interface has depends on the model itself and the number of physical ports it offers. You will need a minimum of one mono input and one mono output to get sound into Cubase and out of it, but if you plan to record live musicians, at least two inputs and four outputs are recommended.
- These ports are identified by the *audio device driver* installed on your system. There may be several types of drivers on your computer, but Cubase works best with ASIO on both Windows and Mac systems. The driver lets you tell Cubase which audio device to use. Once Cubase knows which audio device to use, it then displays the available ports mentioned previously.
- *Busses* are created to group together ports on an audio device to create mono, stereo, or, in Cubase 4, surround recordings. You can change the name of a bus to give it meaning inside your own studio setup, whereas audio devices and ports cannot be renamed inside Cubase. By selecting a mono input bus when recording, for example, you decide that the content will be recorded in mono (see Figure 2.1). By selecting a stereo output bus for a track, the same mono content plays through two output ports in mono. You can create multiple bus configurations using the same ports on your audio interface for different purposes, reducing the need for a complex patch bay to change how ports are used by Cubase.
- An *audio channel* is created in a Mixer whenever an audio, an effect, a VST instrument, or a group track is created. The audio channel offers controls over several audio-related and routing parameters. When you want to record audio on an audio channel, for example, you need to select which input bus to use as its source. The bus selection depends on where the sound source you want to record is actually connected. To monitor during recording, or to play it back, you need to assign the audio output from that channel to an output bus.

By creating connections, you can use the same physical connections in multiple configurations; for example, if your audio hardware offers four audio inputs, you can use either inputs 1 and 2 as a stereo input bus or two mono input busses. You could also create an external effect bus, using an additional output to send a signal to an external reverb or other device and two inputs to receive the stereo signal back from the effect device.

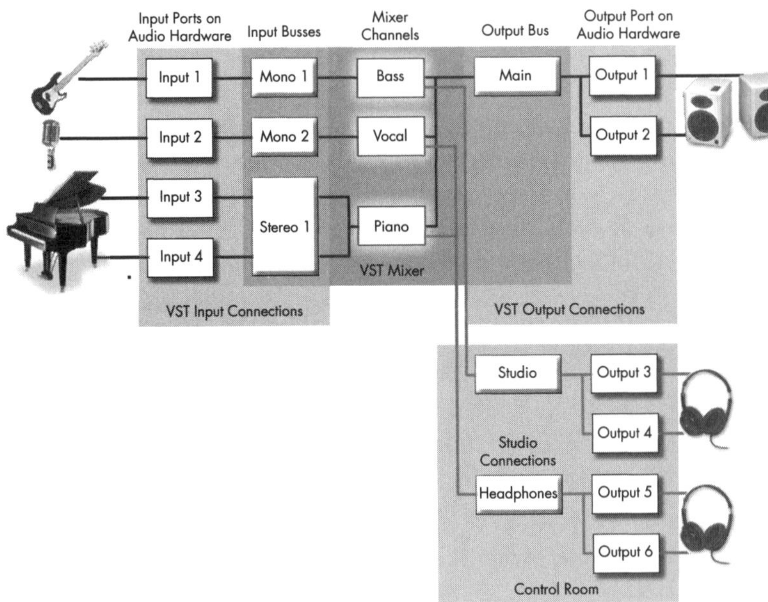

Figure 2.1
How Cubase routes audio from the input (left) to the output (right), using VST connections.

Bus configurations are saved with each project file, and you can also save them as templates to be recalled later. If you find yourself using certain configurations each time you begin a new project, then you can simply set the connections once at the beginning of a project. Cubase will save these connection configurations along with the project file so that you don't need to repeat the configuration every time you open the project, but you do need to create connections every time you create a new project.

Input Busses

An input bus is a bridge between the physical inputs of an audio interface and the source for the audio that you want to record onto an audio track (represented by a channel in the Mixer). By selecting an input bus, you also decide whether the audio track will record mono, stereo, or surround content, depending on how you configured this input bus in the first place. Cubase 4 allows you to adjust this level to prevent clipping or input levels that are too low, but you can also adjust the input level of a signal through the controls available on the audio interface's control panel or the output level of the device being recorded.

Output Busses

Output busses enable you to monitor the content of an audio track through one or several audio outputs on an audio interface and/or send the signal to an external hardware effect or a headphone amplifier. As with input busses, you can create multiple output bus connections, depending on your needs. You need a minimum of one master stereo output bus, but you can create as many output busses as you need.

Audio Track

An audio track in Cubase is similar to an audio track in an audio multitrack recorder. It has, however, the advantage of being either mono, stereo, or multichannel to support surround sound, depending on the configuration of the input/output audio busses you choose for it. You can create as many audio tracks as you need in Cubase. That said, there will be practical limits related to your computer's speed, disk access, or memory capacity, so working within these limits will be your only concern.

Your project's settings determine the audio properties of audio tracks (record format in bits per sample and sample rate in Hertz); however, the number of audio channels each track will support is determined when it is created. Cubase will ask you which configuration you want to use: mono, stereo, or one of many multichannel setups. This will ultimately influence your available choices for assigning input and output busses on this track later. For example, if you want to create a vocal track, you could typically create a mono track and then select a mono input bus.

As a rule of thumb, you should:

- Record mono signals on mono tracks using a mono input bus and monitor through a mono bus.
- Record stereo signals on stereo tracks using a stereo input bus and monitor through a stereo bus.
- Record multichannel signals on equivalent multichannel audio tracks using the same type of input bus and monitor through the same type of multichannel output bus.

Audio Channels

Whenever you create an audio track, a channel is also created in the Mixer (see the Strings channel in Figure 2.2, as well as in the Inspector area of a selected track (Project window) under the Channel section.

An audio channel in Cubase is similar to a mixer channel on a hardware mixer with some exceptions:

- If you set a track to record or play stereo or multichannel events, a single mixer channel will display information for all the subchannels that constitute its signal path. On hardware mixers, stereo channels often require two channel strips.
- Adding an FX channel or a Group channel track also creates its own channel in the Mixer.

Because this is a virtual mixing environment, the Mixer will change as you create more tracks in a project.

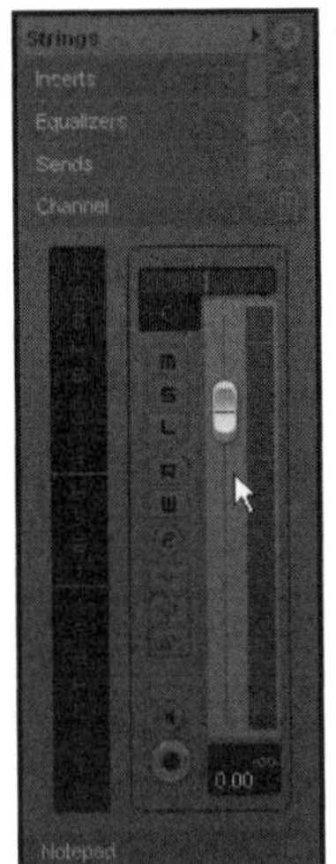

Figure 2.2
The Channel section in the Inspector area of the Project window (left) and the same channel in the Mixer (right).

MIDI Connections

Although MIDI and audio are different, the concept of connection, either hardware or software, to record or play back MIDI is similar to that of audio. Instead of an audio signal connected to an audio port that's associated with an input bus assigned as the source for a track, we have MIDI events coming from a MIDI port on the selected MIDI input channel for a MIDI track, which plays through a MIDI instrument (either a software-based virtual instrument or an external device connected to the selected physical MIDI output for the track).

MIDI Ports

A MIDI port is a hardware (physical) or software (virtual) point of entry or exit for your MIDI data. The number of physical MIDI ports that will be available is determined by your computer's MIDI interface. This might be a stand-alone MIDI interface or MIDI connectors included on the audio interface itself. If your interface has four MIDI inputs and four MIDI outputs, you will have four MIDI ports available for this interface in Cubase. On the other hand, if you are using Cubase to send or receive MIDI information to or from another application inside your computer, you will also be using virtual MIDI ports.

Why virtual? Because they do not require additional hardware. This is the case when you are using VST instruments (which will be discussed further in Chapter 9, "Using Instruments") or when using separate, third-party programs in conjunction with Cubase, such as Reason, GigaStudio, Live, or others. Whenever you load virtual instruments, they create virtual ports that can be addressed in Cubase much like external MIDI instruments that are plugged into your computer through an actual MIDI port. The virtual ports will, in other words, allow you to receive MIDI from these applications or send MIDI to them.

The MIDI port determines which physical or virtual MIDI socket the events on a MIDI track are coming from and going to (see number 4 in Figure 2.3). Each MIDI port can carry up to 16 independently addressable MIDI channels.

HOW TO

View/change a MIDI track's input and output port settings:

1. If the Inspector area is not visible, click on the Show Inspector button in the Project window's toolbar (see Figure 2.3).

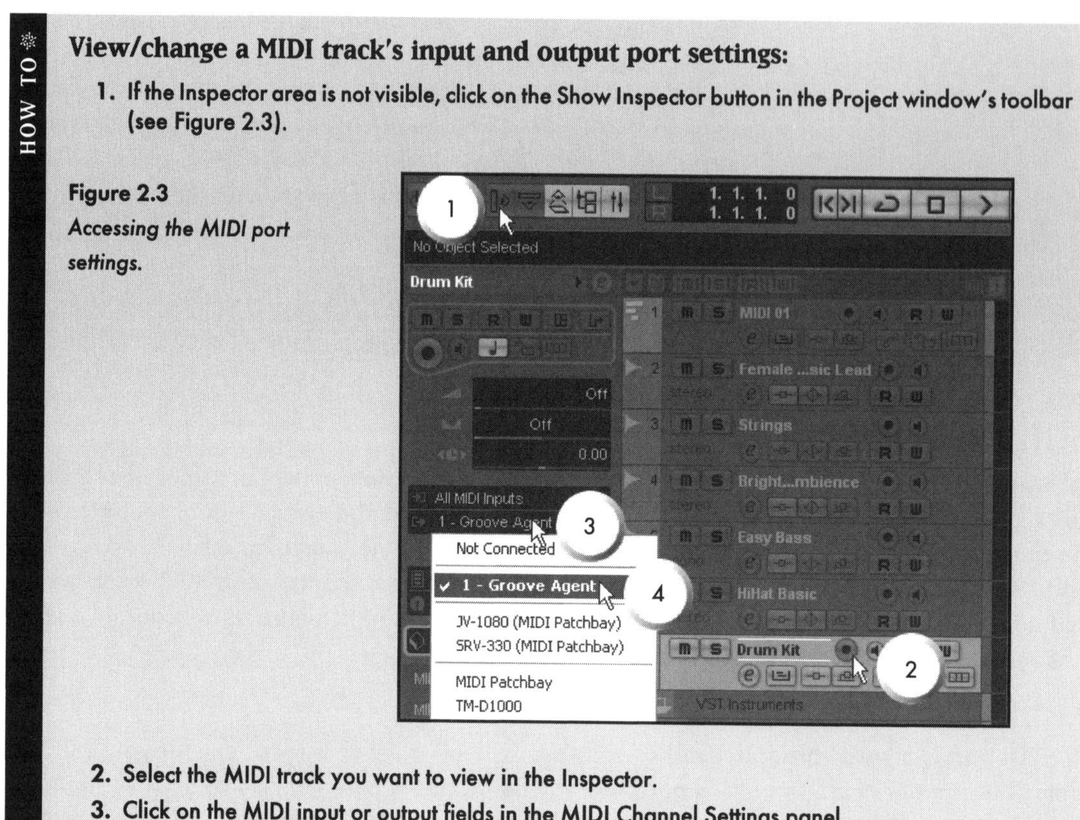

Figure 2.3
Accessing the MIDI port settings.

2. Select the MIDI track you want to view in the Inspector.
3. Click on the MIDI input or output fields in the MIDI Channel Settings panel.
4. Select the appropriate ports from the list. A check mark represents an active port.

Each MIDI track has its own MIDI input and output port setting. You can record MIDI from multiple MIDI sources directly in your project as long as you have a MIDI input device, such as a keyboard or other MIDI controller, connected to these input ports.

The available MIDI input ports that appear in your Track Input Port Selection field depend on which ports are currently set as active in Cubase's MIDI Device Setup window. This will be discussed later in this chapter.

MIDI Channel

Each MIDI port will support up to 16 simultaneous MIDI channels. The channel used by a MIDI device connected to the MIDI input has little effect over the result, unless the MIDI track's channel setting is set to Any, which implies that incoming MIDI events are re-transmitted to any channels at the output. As a result, incoming signals coming on channel 2, for example, would be re-transmitted on channel 2 as well. Otherwise, the MIDI track's channel setting re-transmits the events through the channel number you choose. It is the MIDI output channel you assign to the track that determines how the incoming MIDI data is routed and the resultant sound. For example, suppose you have connected a multitimbral instrument to the MIDI output port of this track. A multitimbral instrument can play one sound per MIDI channel. So you might configure a piano sound on channel 1 of this instrument, a guitar on channel 2, and a bass on channel 3. If you change the output MIDI channel on the piano track to channel 2, a guitar sound will play what the piano was previously playing.

Once your MIDI channel is selected, you can assign a patch to it, such as a bass, for example. This sends a MIDI Program Change message on the selected MIDI channel and output port for this track. Each MIDI channel playing over a device or virtual instrument plug-in has the capacity to play one MIDI program at a time. You can change the patch or preset along the way, but you can have only one patch or preset assigned to that channel at a time. In other words, you can have up to 16 sounds/patches/MIDI devices playing simultaneously on one MIDI port.

If you run out of MIDI channels for one MIDI port, you will need to use another MIDI port to play the MIDI events. Each virtual instrument loaded into a project will create its own virtual MIDI port, so running out of MIDI channels because of MIDI events is unlikely. Where it might become an issue is when you are using MIDI controllers that require several MIDI channels to transfer control data through a MIDI port.

In Figure 2.4, the MIDI In port is set to All MIDI Inputs, which implies that any device sending MIDI to Cubase will be recorded. The MIDI Out port is set to lm-7, which will send MIDI events being monitored through this track to this virtual instrument's MIDI port. Selecting a different channel in this case would not have any effect because the lm-7 is not multitimbral. However, changing the MIDI channel assigned to a device or virtual instrument that does support multiple channels would change the sound you hear playing your MIDI events.

Whenever the channel is set to Any, the MIDI channel assignment is determined by either the channel information recorded on the track or the channel information being sent by the input device connected to your MIDI interface, such as a MIDI keyboard or other controller, for example. Also, sending MIDI performance data on multiple MIDI channels simultaneously is common among MIDI guitar and drum set controllers, for example, since the type and density of MIDI data they create would be impractical on a single MIDI channel. MIDI channel "Any" would be a common recording choice for them.

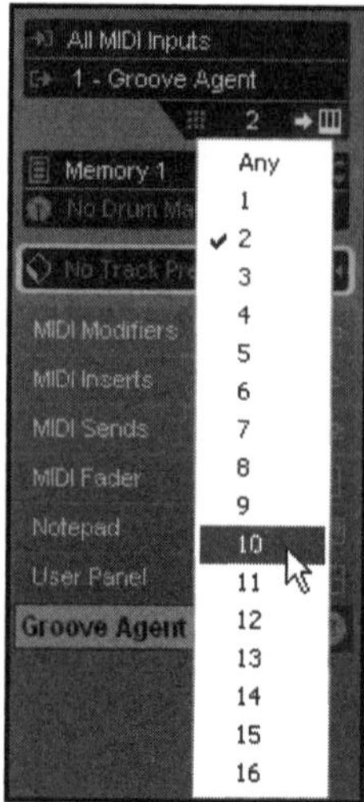

Figure 2.4
Selecting a MIDI channel for a MIDI track.

MIDI Track

A MIDI track most typically contains MIDI events for a single MIDI port. When you play on a keyboard, it sends out MIDI events on a MIDI channel that is recorded into a MIDI track. You then assign a MIDI channel and program number to that track to get the appropriate sound at the output, as mentioned previously.

Cubase doesn't replace the original MIDI channel information it records. It simply puts a filter at the output of the track that redirects the MIDI events to the selected MIDI port and channel for this track.

Each track has its own MIDI input and output port settings, as well as its channel setting. You can also record from multiple input sources and multiple channels simultaneously on a single track by selecting the appropriate settings for this track; however, it is recommended that you keep each musical part on a separate track for easier editing later. Because you can create as many MIDI tracks as you need in Cubase, you don't really need to worry about running out of them.

Mixer Channel

Creating a MIDI track also adds a MIDI Track channel to Cubase's Mixer panel. You can control MIDI parameters such as volume and pan (which are two types of MIDI controller messages), as well as mute or solo this track, and even insert MIDI effects. However, you can't perform any EQ or add audio plug-in effects to this type of mixer channel. Loading a virtual instrument as the destination for a MIDI track creates two channels: one MIDI channel for the MIDI events and automation found on the track and one audio channel for the virtual instrument's output, where you can add audio effects or equalization. Some virtual instruments offer multiple output channels. When this is the case, there will be as many audio channels created in the Mixer as there are output channels for this instrument. For example, you can enable up to 12 channels of audio in the Cubase Mixer by loading the Groove Agent 3 drum machine. The number of MIDI channels depends on the number of tracks you create to control the Groove Agent 3.

Cubase 4 also introduces instrument tracks, which provide a very convenient way of selecting a virtual instrument as a MIDI track's destination. As a result, a single instrument track is created in the Mixer channel, which combines the flexibility of MIDI recording with the power of audio processing. Instrument tracks are discussed further in Chapter 9, "Using Instruments."

Cubase Environment

Cubase uses a number of windows, dialog boxes, context menus, and panels to display settings and options. We will refer to these elements throughout this book, so to be sure you understand the terminology, here are some elements that set them apart:

- A **window** contains a toolbar at the top and sometimes a toolbar on one side. It may also have a local menu bar at the top of the window. You can edit information inside a window (as with other elements). You don't need to press any buttons to accept or apply changes made to windows. When you make changes to information within a window, the window is automatically updated.
- A **dialog box** appears when you want to apply a process or transformation that requires you to accept or apply this process. It is usually associated with a function, such as the Save function or a setting of some sort, such as the Metronome Setup or the Project Setup dialog box. When a dialog box is open, you most likely have to close this dialog box by accepting or rejecting the changes (via OK and Cancel buttons, for instance) before doing anything else in your project.
- A **panel** is similar in nature to a front panel of a device. Panels have controls or fields in which you can make selections. Panels do not have any menus or toolbars and do not have any confirmation or cancel buttons. An example is the Mixer panel, which enables you to mix channels, route signals, assign effects to channels, and modify their parameters, as well as perform other mix-related tasks.
- A **context menu** appears only through a right-click action on a PC or a Control-click action on a Mac. Context menus often provide a quick contextual set of options. As the name implies, the options found in this type of menu are context-sensitive, so right-clicking/Control-clicking over an audio track will reveal different options, depending on the object found underneath the cursor.

About Audio Terminology

To work with audio inside a Cubase project, it is important to understand the associated audio terminology. In Cubase, audio is referred to as *audio clips*, *events*, *parts*, *regions*, and *slices*. This section describes how, when, and why these terms are used.

Audio Clips and Audio Events

In the Project window, recorded audio is referred to as an *audio event*. In essence, when you edit an audio event inside Cubase, you edit the graphic representation of all or part of an actual audio file on your media drive (called an *audio clip*), without changing the original content of that file. When an audio clip is placed on a track in a project, it becomes an audio event. So the difference between an audio clip and an audio event is that the event has been positioned (either manually or through recording) in order to play at a specific time in the Project window's timeline, whereas clips don't have a playback time associated with them and are viewed outside the Project window, in the Pool, MediaBay, and SoundFrame Browser windows.

Audio Regions

Audio clips in the Pool also can contain *regions*. Regions can be created automatically when recording in Cycle mode, or you can create regions manually inside the Sample editor. Typically, regions represent a portion of an audio clip or audio event.

When placing an audio event that contains several regions in an audio track, it is possible to change which region will play without changing the event's location. You simply need to tell Cubase to play another region instead. For example, if you have recorded three takes of a solo performance in Cycle recording mode, each time the recording started a new lap, a region might have been created. (This depends on the recording preferences found under File (PC)/Cubase (Mac) > Preferences > Record > Audio Cycle Record Mode options.) You can later decide which lap you want to listen to by selecting which region is active (on top).

Audio Slices

Another type of event/region combination found in Cubase is called an *audio slice*. Slices are used with rhythmic parts, such as drum loops. You can create slices only inside the Sample editor window. Using the Hitpoints tool enables you to define where important beats or slices occur in rhythmic or percussive musical content. For example, you can cut a drum loop into individual hits. Each hit is what Cubase then calls a *slice*. Unlike regions, these slices do not appear in the Pool; however, when you place a drum loop sample containing slices onto an audio track, Cubase creates an audio *part* that holds this drum loop, and each event in the part corresponds to a slice of the audio clip. By dividing rhythmic audio events using slices, you can later quantize these events the same way you would quantize MIDI events. Furthermore, if you change the tempo of a project, the position of each slice's start point will be adjusted to maintain its relation to the beat. If an audio file containing a rhythmic loop is not time-sliced, changing the tempo would not affect the bar/beat location of this loop's start point, but the rhythmic accuracy would suffer because the tempo of the audio loop won't match the project anymore. If you take a look at Figure 2.5, you will see an audio part containing a sliced audio drum loop that has been placed on an audio track. The same content is represented in both portions of Figure 2.5; however, the top portion represents the slice locations when the project plays at a tempo of 159 BPM (beats per minute), whereas the bottom portion represents the same slices at 120 BPM. As you can see, the beats occur at the same location relative to the bar/beat grid, but there is space added between each slice when the loop is played at a slower tempo.

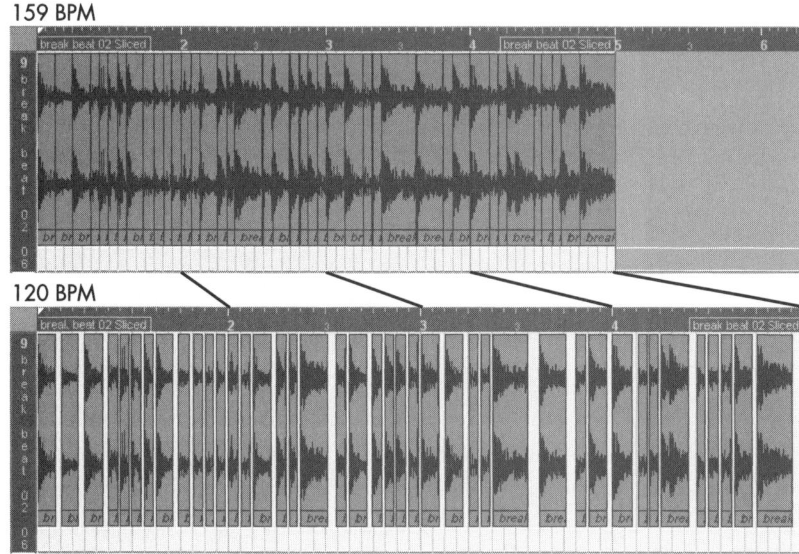

Figure 2.5
Example of a drum loop sliced using Hitpoints.

Audio Parts

Finally, you can have audio parts in your project. Audio parts are containers for audio events, regions, or slices. An audio part does not represent a recorded or imported audio event, but you can place audio events inside of a part. You also can convert an event into a part, and you can place additional audio events inside an existing part. In other words, audio parts are similar to MIDI parts in that they hold information that can be moved across other audio tracks or in time. Audio parts are useful when you want to move together multiple related audio events, such as the ones found when using slices.

Figure 2.6 is divided into three parts. On the left, you can see where to find the different types of audio terms mentioned in this section. In the center, you can see the hierarchy of relationships between these terms, and on the right, a diagram displaying how this hierarchy works in your project. By default, when you double-click an audio part in the Project window, it launches the Audio Part editor. Once a part is opened in the Audio Part editor, you can drag other regions, events, or sliced events into it. When you double-click on an individual audio event or a region inside the Audio Part editor or in the Project window, it launches the Sample editor. You can't drag anything in the Sample editor.

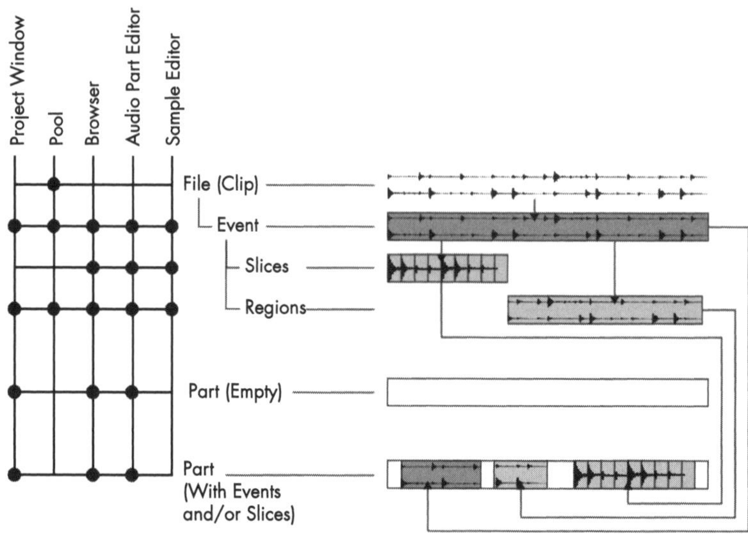

Figure 2.6
The audio terminology's hierarchy.

This hierarchy allows for nondestructive editing because what you normally edit is the audio clip, its associated event, regions, and slices, not the audio file itself. When a portion of the audio event is processed, Cubase creates an additional audio clip on the media drive containing the newly processed section of your audio. The audio parts containing references to processed audio material update themselves to correspond to this new link.

Destructive and Nondestructive Editing

Sometimes, we get musical ideas that require us to take risks or to try out things and listen to them to see how they sound. If you don't like how they sound, it's nice to be able to put things back the way they were. If only life could be so easy! Most of us have used the Undo command time and time again. When you are typing an e-mail to a friend, you can undo operations many times over until you get it right. However, if you save the e-mail, open it later to change things, and save it once more, you are replacing the original e-mail with a new copy unless you saved the new version under a different name.

Working with audio files is quite similar in the sense that a Cubase project offers you a way to reorganize the information inside the application without affecting the saved data on the disk. Furthermore, Cubase, unlike an e-mail text file, doesn't even change the content of the files it refers to unless you specifically tell it to. If you applied the same philosophy to editing e-mails, you'd have a document with text that doesn't change, but you could place this text anywhere you wanted inside the actual e-mail and then save the layout of the e-mail separately. In Cubase, the media files are called *clips*. These clips are on the media drive, usually inside a project subfolder appropriately called *Audio*. When you save a Cubase project file (with the .cpr extension), that file itself does not contain the audio, but merely links or references to the original audio clips. When you split an audio event and place it somewhere else in your project, you are changing the reference points found in the project file to the audio clip, but you are not editing or transforming the original clip in any way. The same applies to effects or volume changes you might add to a project; none of these transformations affect the original audio file. This type of editing is referred to as *nondestructive editing*.

If we push the editing further and decide to apply a time stretch, a normalize, or fade-out to a portion of an audio clip, Cubase still does not touch the original content of the file because it creates additional files inside the *Edits* subfolder of your project folder to store the result. If this is not enough to convince you that Cubase is a completely nondestructive environment, you also can use multiple undo levels through the History option in the Edit menu. In addition, the Offline Process History option in the Edit menu allows you to select processing you applied to an audio file—let's say, seven steps ago—and edit the parameters of that processing without affecting the other six steps you did after that... even *after* the Project file has been saved various times!

Destructive editing, on the other hand, has one advantage: It requires less space. Whenever you work on large files, every processed audio bit in your project is retained unless you decide to clean up the audio through another function, called Remove Unused Media, which is discussed later. Keep in mind that a project can grow quickly, and you should prepare sufficient media drive space when working with a digital audio multitrack project using high-resolution recordings. If space is not an issue, then enjoy the benefits of working in an environment that allows you to undo large numbers of steps that may have led your music in the wrong direction and to take creative risks with the audio files you record.

Working with Events, Regions, and Parts

As mentioned earlier in this chapter, Cubase uses different levels of audio references. The basic recording is saved as an audio file, which is referred to as an *audio clip* inside Cubase. An audio event is automatically created in your Project window once the recording is completed. Cubase also can create regions, which define portions of an audio clip that can be easily reused somewhere else in a project. You can also convert audio events into a region or a part. Because regions can be reused elsewhere and parts that contain more than one region or event make it easy to move a number of events at a time, you might find it easier in certain instances to convert your events into regions or parts. Each of these three types of audio objects offers different editing properties when placed on a track. Table 2.1 takes a look at how different these objects are.

Table 2.1
Differences Between Events, Regions, and Part Objects on an Audio Track

Events	Regions	Parts
You can modify the length of an event on a track, but you can't extend the event beyond the limit of the source disk file to which it refers.	You can modify the length of a region on a track and extend it beyond the original limits of the region itself, but not beyond the limit of the clip to which the region refers.	You can extend the boundaries of a part as much as you want because a part is simply a container that does not refer to a particular audio clip, event, or region.
Audio events have envelopes (fade-in, sustain level, fade-out). You can use these envelopes to control the level of the event. The envelope is locked with the event, so when you move the event, the envelope follows.	Audio regions also have envelopes (fade-in, sustain level, fade-out). You can use these envelopes to control the level of the event (see Figure 2.7). The envelope is locked with the region, so when you move it, the envelope follows.	Audio parts do not have envelopes associated with them, but the events and regions they contain have individual envelopes that can be edited inside the Audio Part editor.
The default editing window for events is the Sample editor. On an audio track, you can convert an event into a region or a part using the Events to Part option found in the Audio menu.	The default editing window for regions is the Sample editor. On an audio track, you can also convert a region into a part using the Events to Part command found in the Audio menu. Also, if you have resized a region in the Project window beyond the original region's boundaries, you can bring the region back to its original size using the Events From Regions command found in the Audio > Advanced menu.	The default editing window for parts is the Audio Part editor. You can dissolve an audio part containing several events and regions to create independent objects on a track using the Dissolve Part command found in the Audio menu.

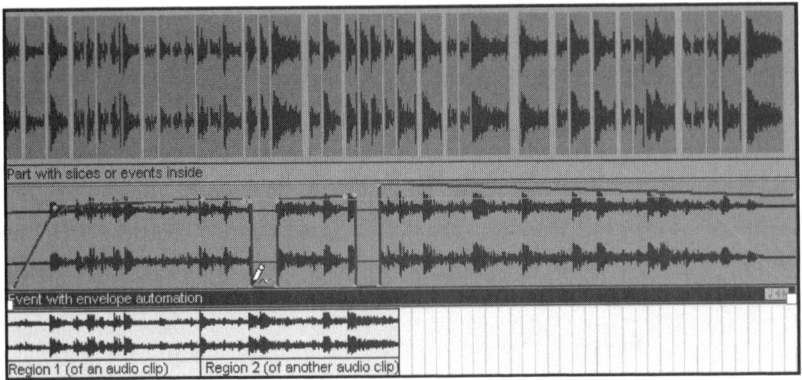

Figure 2.7
Comparing audio part (top), audio event (middle), and audio regions (bottom).

The Browser Window

When you want to see every type of event used in your project in a track hierarchy format, the Browser window is the tool for you (see Figure 2.8). This window is similar to the List editor described earlier in the sense that events are displayed in lists, but this is where the similarities end. Because the Browser window displays all types of events in hierarchical lists, it also implies that you can modify them by using the fields it displays for each type of data.

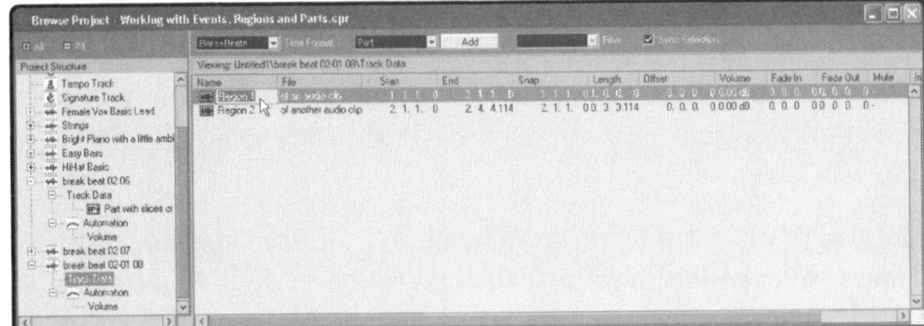

Figure 2.8
The Browser window.

Browser Window Areas

The Browser window is divided into left and right panes plus a toolbar. In the left area, called the Project Structure, you will find a tree with the file name for the current project as its root. Linked to the file are all the tracks available in the current project. In other words, each type of track currently present in your project is displayed here. If the track contains data (this could represent events, regions, parts, or automation parameters), it is displayed under the track's name. The details for the events or data found on a track are visible in the List area found on the right side.

The toolbar offers a few options:

- The **Time Format** field selects the time units used for displaying values in all relevant columns below.
- The **Add** button lets you add various types of events or objects, depending on what kind of item is currently selected in the Browser window, as shown in the pop-up field to its left. For example, when a MIDI track is selected, you can add a MIDI part; when a MIDI part is selected, you could add a program change or note event. When a marker track is selected, you can add a marker or cycle marker.
- The **Filter** drop-down menu selects the type of MIDI events you want to see when a MIDI Part is selected and filters out all others. For example, selecting the Controller option from this menu displays only MIDI controller messages found in the track, such as modulation or MIDI Pan and Volume.
- The **Sync Selection** check box is a convenient option that links selection of objects in the Project window with selections in the Browser window, and vice versa. If you want to troubleshoot an object in your project, you can open the Browser window and check this option. Next time you select an object in your project, when you open the Browser window, this object is displayed in the List area.

The List area on the right of the Browser adapts its content to the selected objects in the hierarchy structure on the left. For example, if you select an audio track on the left, icons for its track data and automation are displayed on the right. If you select a track event or automation type within these categories that appear beneath the track name in the Project Structure area, the details for it appear in the list on the right.

After you can see an event's details, you can make any modifications you want in the appropriate column. At the top of each column are the column headers. You can click and drag column headers to change their order. You can also click in a column header to make it the basis of the sorting order in this list. An arrow pointing up or down appears in the columns, indicating that it is the basis for an ascending or descending sort.

To expand the entire project structure or to hide the details in each track, you can use the +All/–All buttons at the upper-left corner of the window.

Understanding the Information

Although it is possible to add events in the Browser, because of its list nature, this environment is more appropriate when you are editing existing events. When you want to make changes to events in the Browser, it's important to understand what each column represents. In most cases, the column header describes this well. However, some column names might appear ambiguous. To clear that up, the following list describes the columns that aren't so obvious.

- **Snap column.** This represents the absolute position of the Snap-point for this object (audio event). This can be different from the start point because the Snap-point is used to adjust the position of an event with the grid setting of the project or editor. Changing this value does not change the position of the Snap-point in relation to the event's start but rather moves the Snap-point (and its event) to the location entered in this field.
- **Length column.** This represents the length of the event. Editing the value affects the length of the event, moving its end position, not its start position.
- **Offset column.** This represents the location in the audio clip that corresponds to the start of the event. This offset location value is found in the audio event or region and in the MIDI and audio part. When you change this value, the part or event stays in place on the audio track, but the content inside the part or event slides forward or backward in time with respect to its "container."

As for the other columns, you can change the values by entering data directly in the appropriate field.

Linear and Musical Timebases

When you are working with MIDI, audio, and video, some events are more sensitive to absolute time references, such as sound effects, ambiances, or Foley sound effects (such as footsteps), which occur at specific moments in time regardless of the tempo. Other events, such as the entrance of a sustained MIDI string sound, will be easier to position if they occur at bar 9 beat 1, for example. Both types of events are sensitive to timing, but not the same type of reference. Linear or time-based events should not be affected by tempo changes in a project because no matter which tempo the project plays at, they need to always occur at the same absolute time. Musical or tempo-based events, on the other hand, should still be able to match up to even bars and beats, no matter what fraction of a second the cue begins on. You can toggle the Timebase of a track from musical (the default Timebase, which is relative to bars and beats) to linear (absolute) in order to keep events on this track from shifting in time when the tempo of the project changes. Furthermore, if you want to lock all events on this track from being edited or moved by mistake, you can do so by using the lock button for that track in the Inspector or Track list.

HOW TO

Toggle the Timebase of a track:

1. Make the Timebase button visible in either the Track Settings in the Inspector or the Track Controls area.
2. Toggle the Timebase button (see Figure 2.9) to the desired Timebase setting.

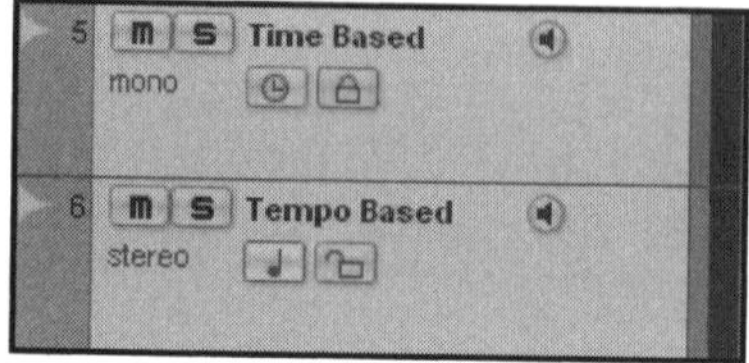

Figure 2.9
A linear and locked audio track above a musical and unlocked track below.

3 Setting Up Peripherals

Preparing your computer for Cubase means that your operating system, audio hardware, and MIDI interface are installed properly and configured for optimal audio operations. Running an application such as Cubase requires a stable computer environment and lots of available computer resources, especially when you are using effects and software instruments. Making these resources available to Cubase will help you get the most out of your working session. Operating systems are designed to look good and do many things. Consider changing your computer's configuration to emphasize performance rather than looks.

This chapter explores how to set up peripheral devices both inside and outside the Cubase environment.

Here's a summary of what you will learn in this chapter:

- How to choose the right driver for your audio hardware when working in Cubase
- The difference between hardware-specific ASIO drivers and generic ASIO drivers
- How to set up MIDI interfaces and drivers in your system
- How to set up MIDI ports inside Cubase
- How to set up remote devices inside Cubase
- How to set up audio ports inside Cubase
- The impact background processes have on Cubase performance
- The implications of loading other audio applications when running Cubase

HOW TO

Optimize Your System for Cubase Performance

Before you can do anything in Cubase, you must make sure that:

- Your software is properly installed on your system.
- You have a stable operating system.
- The latest drivers for all your peripherals are installed, including peripherals you think are not related, such as video and network drivers.

If you find that your computer crashes often for no apparent reason, be sure you have all the latest drivers installed for your peripherals. If that doesn't work:

1. Create a backup of the data on your computer.
2. Get and save all the latest drivers.
3. Finally, reinstall your operating system.

Starting with a clean slate reduces many problems and will improve your system's performance because with use it tends to clutter up with data, even after you uninstall software or peripherals. This may save you from experiencing problems later.

Audio Hardware and Drivers

Cubase handles both MIDI and audio recording, which makes it important to configure these peripherals appropriately. One of the most important steps in configuring audio and MIDI interfaces is to be sure you have the proper drivers installed on your computer.

Both Mac and PC users should always use the ASIO driver provided by the audio hardware manufacturer. Macintosh users can also use the Core Audio driver in order to use the computer's built-in audio for Cubase (although certain other audio devices can optionally be assigned for audio input/output via the operating system itself, in the Sound section of System Preferences. PC users can choose to use a generic ASIO driver provided by Cubase: ASIO multimedia driver. It goes without saying that trying to work with audio hardware in Cubase using a generic driver will not provide great performance because the drivers have not been specifically optimized to work with your interface. You can find a list of recommended audio interfaces offering ASIO drivers on Steinberg's Web site or by performing a search on Google.

ASIO Drivers

Audio interfaces with proprietary ASIO drivers are *strongly recommended* when you are using any Steinberg products. The smaller the latency, the shorter the time between what you record and what you hear back out through Cubase once the signal has been processed by the computer. High latencies are often troublesome when recording live material. There is always a delay when monitoring audio through software, and the greater the latency time, the more noticeable this delay will be. ASIO drivers have a short latency because they do not send the signal into the operating system before sending it to its outputs. Therefore, you can record music while playing back tracks without any noticeable differences. A typical latency for audio hardware using a dedicated ASIO driver should be around or below 10 milliseconds. Note also that latency affects the response time of VST instruments, the output and input monitoring in a channel.

Most professional and semiprofessional audio interfaces today support this format, but if in doubt, consult both Steinberg's Web site and the audio hardware manufacturer's Web site for information about ASIO compatibility.

ASIO DirectX Full Duplex Drivers

This section only applies to PC users who don't have an audio interface offering a dedicated ASIO driver. If this is your case, you will need to use Microsoft's DirectSound technology, which is part of DirectX.

The DirectX driver is included with your Windows operating system, and you can find free DirectX updates on Microsoft's Web site. Steinberg provides the ASIO DirectX Full Duplex driver on the Cubase installation CD. In the absence of a soundcard-specific ASIO driver, the ASIO DirectX driver provides the next best (but by far not the most desirable) solution. This driver allows Cubase to communicate with DirectX and allows full duplex with your audio hardware. Full duplex means that you can record and play back simultaneously through the audio hardware. In contrast, half duplex allows only one operation at a time: play or record. Because Cubase has to communicate with DirectX through the ASIO DirectX driver, and then DirectX communicates with the audio hardware, expect higher latencies when using this type of driver setup.

To set up this driver, you need to use the ASIO DirectSound Full Duplex Setup window to configure your audio hardware properly (see Figure 3.1). This window lists all DirectSound-compatible input and output ports on your system. Devices that are checked are available inside Cubase. You can find the ASIO DirectX Full Duplex setup utility in a special ASIO folder under the Cubase program folder. To launch it, simply locate its icon or alias and launch it from there.

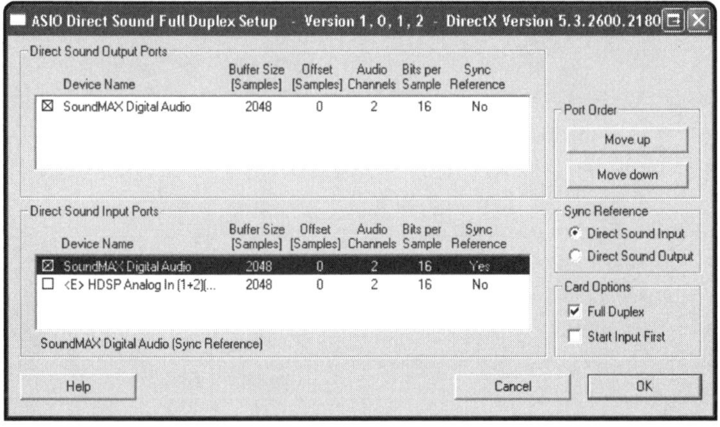

Figure 3.1

The ASIO DirectSound Full Duplex Setup dialog box.

HOW TO

Configure your DirectSound drivers:

1. Activate the device ports you want to use by adding a check mark in the box next to them.
2. To change the buffer size, double-click in the corresponding column and enter a new value. The buffer size is used when audio data is transferred between Cubase and the audio hardware. Larger buffer sizes will ensure that playback will occur without glitches with relatively larger numbers of tracks and plug-ins, whereas smaller buffer sizes will reduce the latency. The default buffer size appearing in this column should be fine in most cases; however, if you want to solve crackling sounds in your audio when using this driver, you can increase the buffer size by increments of 64 samples or greater.
3. To change the Offset value, double-click in the corresponding column and enter a new value. If you hear a constant offset (delay) during playback of audio and MIDI recordings, you can adjust the output or input latency time by using an offset value. In most cases, you should leave this at its default zero value. If you are noticing a delay at the output, increase the output offset, and if you are noticing a delay at the input, increase the input offset.
4. The Sync Reference option lets you determine how MIDI is synchronized with the audio. You can choose to synchronize MIDI to the audio input or audio output. This also determines which offset value you should adjust, as mentioned earlier.
5. The Card Options should be left with the Full Duplex option selected; however, if you are noticing problems while this is selected, you can check the Start Input First option.

MIDI Interfaces and Drivers

Most MIDI interfaces available today are installed in two simple steps—connect the device (don't forget the power supply, if required) and install its drivers on your computer. This is usually quite simple and is explained in the documentation that comes with your MIDI interface. Hardware specifics will not be discussed here because there are too many MIDI and audio interfaces out there to cover them thoroughly. But to make sure everything is set up properly, one good starting point is to verify that your MIDI port appears in your system configuration.

HOW TO

Verify installed MIDI ports (under Windows):

1. Right-click on My Computer and select Manage from the context menu.
2. In the Computer Management window, select the Device Manager entry under the System Tools.
3. Locate the *Sound, video and game controllers* entry and expand the list to view the items under this entry.
4. Double-click on your MIDI interface or audio hardware if you have a MIDI port on it to view its properties.
5. The device's Properties dialog box will appear. In the General tab, make sure the Device Status reads "This device is working properly." If not, click on the Properties tab.

> 6. **Select your installed MIDI port and click on the Properties button to see whether there are any messages warning you that the device is not installed properly or whether this device is in conflict with another peripheral.**

At this point, if you have not seen any question marks or exclamation marks next to your device, and if there are no indications that it is not installed properly, you should be able to use this port in Cubase. If, on the other hand, you have found a problem, you should try reinstalling the driver for this peripheral and following the installation procedure provided by your device's manufacturer.

Looking at Figure 3.2, if your device were not installed properly, you would see a red X or a question mark on the device's icon in the list. If the device is installed but is not working properly, an exclamation mark would appear over your device's icon in this same list.

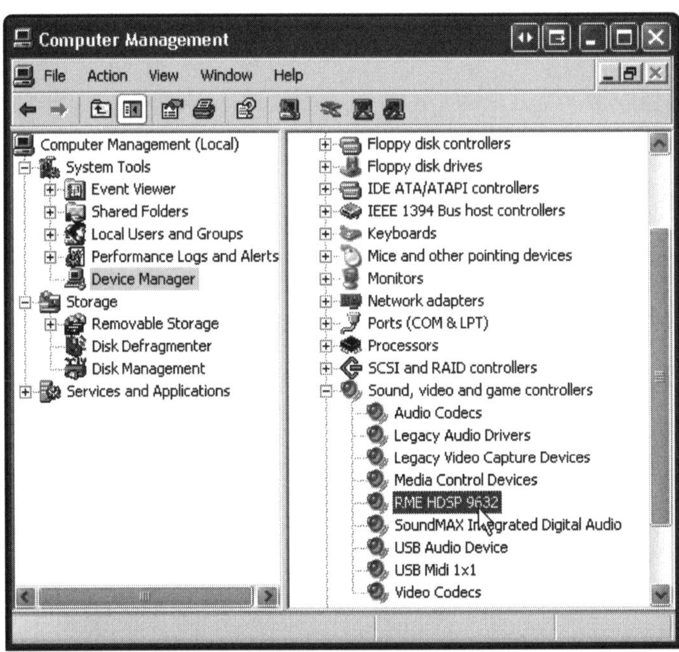

Figure 3.2
Windows XP's Device Manager dialog box.

You might want to consult your manufacturer's Web site for specific settings related to your MIDI or audio hardware device. This Web site will probably provide you with a driver update and tips on configuring your device with Cubase and other software.

HOW TO

Verify installed MIDI ports (under Mac OS X):

1. After installing any Macintosh drivers that were provided with your MIDI interface from its installation disk, open the Audio-MIDI Setup utility. The Utilities folder can be opened via the Go > Utilities menu command or by using the keyboard shortcut Shift+Command+U.
2. In the Audio-MIDI Setup utility program, an icon for your MIDI interface (or the MIDI interface features of your audio interface if a single device provides both functions in your setup) should now appear.
3. Now you need to indicate to the operating system what external MIDI devices are in your studio confirmation. Click the Add Device button in this utility's toolbar (see Figure 3.3).
4. Double-click the new device icon, and in its Properties dialog box, select the manufacturer name and device model from the preconfigured pop-up lists. If the device you want to add doesn't appear, simply type in this information, which can be edited at any time to make the naming conventions in your studio setup more self-explanatory.
5. If you are using a preexisting device definition, an appropriate icon and other information about this device's properties will be filled in automatically. Otherwise, the most important thing is to indicate on what MIDI channels the device can transmit or receive (many sound modules may not transmit on any MIDI channel at all, and some controllers don't respond to any incoming MIDI channels since they don't have any sound-generation capabilities) and whether it is strictly a General MIDI (GM)–compatible device. If the device responds to MIDI Timecode or MIDI Beat Clock (which is common for drum machines and some onboard hardware sequencers), this property can also be indicated here. You can also assign an icon, from the selection provided by the Macintosh operating system.
6. Arrow graphics at the bottom of the icons for your MIDI interface and each external MIDI device that you have defined indicate their available MIDI inputs and outputs. Click on these to drag virtual "cables" between the devices, to mirror how they are physically cabled together in your studio setup.
7. Your devices will now appear by name when you open the Cubase program and start selecting input sources or external output destinations for your MIDI tracks. One of the advantages of the preexisting MIDI device definitions is that they already come associated with patchname scripts (which allow you to specify program and bank changes by name, rather than by number). If a particular device in your studio doesn't appear in the preconfigured list, you may also be able to locate patchname scripts (a text file in XML format) on the Internet. The Macintosh forums at www.cubase.net are an excellent place to start, since a fairly sizeable collection of device maps and patchname scripts has been compiled there.

Setting Up Devices in Cubase

At this point, the audio and MIDI devices are properly installed on your system and you are now ready to tell Cubase which devices to use. The Device Setup, found under the Devices menu, lets you configure MIDI, Transport controls, remote control devices, video device drivers, and audio hardware, as well as VST System Link settings. VST System Link networks multiple computers

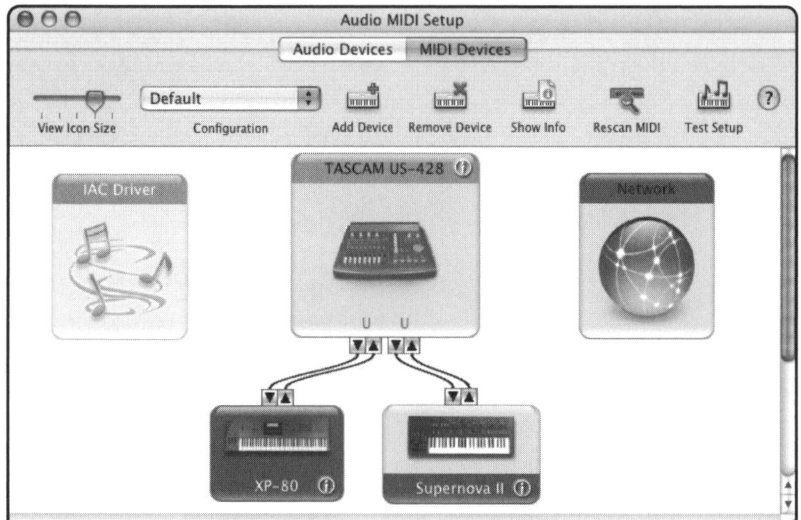

Figure 3.3
In Macintosh OS X, MIDI interfaces and external devices are managed using the Audio-MIDI Setup utility.

through a digital audio connection. In this chapter, we will discuss only the MIDI and audio settings and leave the other settings for later, as they become relevant to the topic under discussion.

> **USB and FireWire Devices**
> Always make sure your USB or FireWire devices are connected and powered up before launching Cubase; otherwise, the device will not show up in the Device Setup dialog box, and you won't be able to configure it or use it properly.

When you launch Cubase, it scans all installed peripherals and plug-ins—both audio and MIDI—in order to make them available in a Cubase project. All successfully recognized devices appear in the Device Setup dialog box. Selecting the appropriate entry in the Devices tree (see the left side of the dialog box in Figure 3.4) reveals this device's setup options on the right-hand side. Here, the MIDI Port Setup is visible.

Setting Up MIDI Ports

Because the MIDI devices appear at the top of the list, let's start there. MIDI ports connect external MIDI devices, such as MIDI keyboards, synthesizers, and multitimbral sound modules, to Cubase through your MIDI interface's MIDI Input port and transmit MIDI events to these devices through its MIDI Output port. The Device, I/O (input/output), and Port System Name columns display system-related information over which you have no control. However, the Show As, Visible, and In 'All Inputs' columns let you set up how these ports appear in a project.

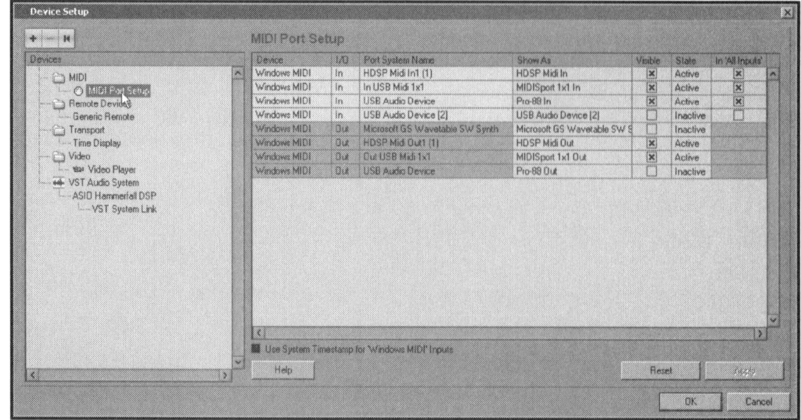

Figure 3.4
The Device Setup dialog box.

The Show As name displays how the MIDI port appears when selecting MIDI ports (see Figure 3.5). To rename a MIDI port, click in the Show As column and type a new name.

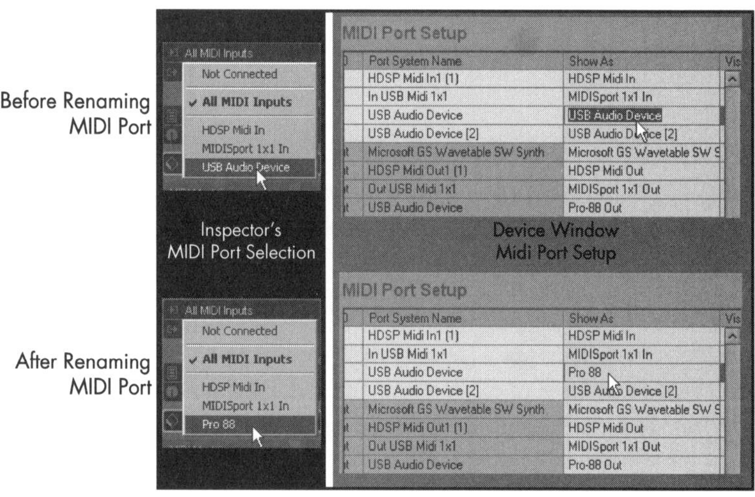

Figure 3.5
Renaming MIDI ports in the Device Setup dialog box.

The Visible option hides a MIDI port from the pop-up selector on MIDI tracks when it is not checked (see Figure 3.6).

Monitoring Active MIDI Ports

The State lets you know whether a port is currently active in your project. A port is active when a MIDI track is assigned to it, so avoid hiding MIDI ports that are active.

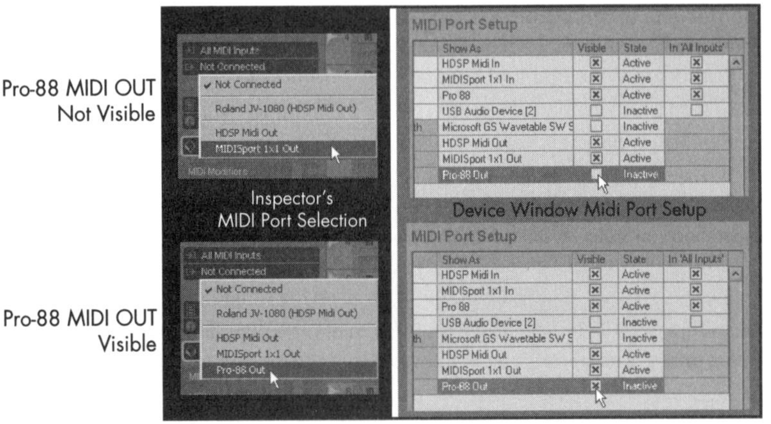

Figure 3.6
Hiding/displaying a MIDI port in the Device Setup dialog box.

The Inspector's MIDI Input selector for MIDI tracks offers an All MIDI Inputs choice. When this option is selected, the track records or echoes all MIDI events coming from all currently active MIDI inputs. Uncheck an input port here in Device Setup to filter it out from this ALL MIDI Inputs mode. For example, in Figure 3.7, the HDSP MIDI In is connected to a MIDI-enabled mixer, which sends MIDI events whenever a channel fader is moved. Because we don't want to record these events at this point in time, we can exclude it from the In 'All Inputs' group. Because All Inputs is selected by default when each new MIDI track is created, this will enable you to avoid having to change this setting every time in order to avoid recording events from this port.

MIDI Port Setup

	Show As	Visible	State	In 'All Inputs'
	HDSP Midi In	☐	Inactive	☐
	MIDISport 1x1 In	☒	Active	☒
	Pro 88	☒	Active	☒
	USB Audio Device [2]	☐	Inactive	☐
ith	Microsoft GS Wavetable SW S	☐	Inactive	
	HDSP Midi Out	☒	Active	
	MIDISport 1x1 Out	☒	Active	
	Pro-88 Out	☒	Inactive	

Figure 3.7
Excluding a MIDI port from "All Inputs" in the Device Setup dialog box.

Click the Reset button to make all ports visible and include all ports in the In 'All Inputs' column.

Setting a Remote Device

A remote device is a hardware device that can be programmed to offer a physical, tactile interface for Cubase's virtual controls. Remote devices come in many shapes, formats, and functions, and the setup options will vary from one device to the next. Without going into detail on how each remote is implemented inside Cubase, here's a look at how you can set up a remote control surface inside Cubase.

HOW TO

Install a MIDI remote control device:

1. Select the Device Setup option from the Devices menu.
2. Click the plus sign above the Devices list in the dialog box (see Figure 3.8).

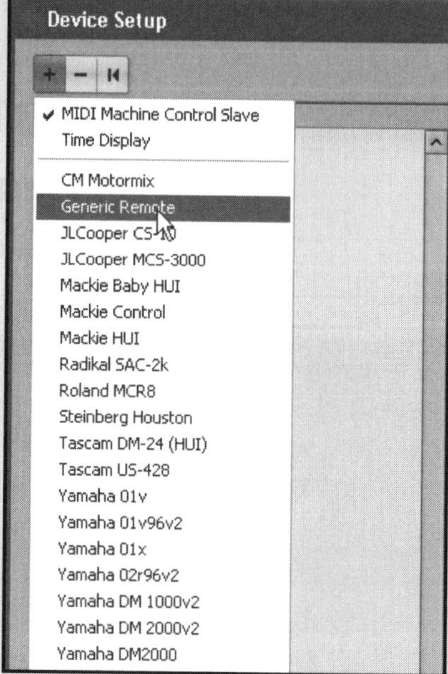

Figure 3.8
Adding a MIDI device controller to your device setup.

3. Select the appropriate device from the supported devices list. If your device is not in this list, select the Generic Remote device. The device is added under the Remote Devices folder in the Device Setup dialog box.
4. Select the device in the list.
5. Select the appropriate MIDI input and output ports connecting the controller to Cubase, and be sure these ports are well connected to this device.
6. Enable the Auto Select option if your device supports this option. (A channel is automatically selected when the corresponding fader on the remote is touched.)
7. Click OK when you are finished.

Once a remote is installed, its name appears in the Devices menu. In Figure 3.9, this device happens to be a Generic Remote. Selecting its name brings up the device's control panel. Use

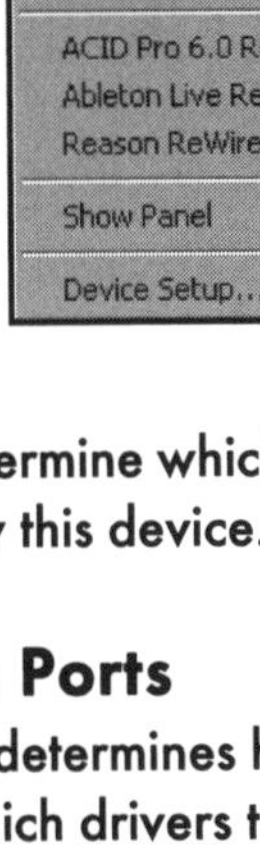

Figure 3.9
Displaying a remote device control panel.

the control panel to determine which Cubase virtual controls are affected by incoming controller messages generated by this device.

Setting Up Audio Ports

The VST Audio System determines how Cubase interfaces with your system's audio peripheral. You can tell Cubase which drivers to use and which ports should be visible, save these settings, and never worry about it again. On the other hand, you can change any of these settings when needed. Audio ports correspond to physical inputs or outputs. For now, remember that you will need to associate these ports with input and output busses later. When selecting the source or input for a track, you will be selecting the bus associated with the port, not the port itself.

HOW TO

Set up audio ports in Cubase:

1. From the Devices menu, select the Device Setup (if you are not already there).
2. Select VST Audio System in the list to view its properties (see Figure 3.10).
3. In the ASIO Driver field, select the appropriate driver for your audio interface. If you have a dedicated ASIO driver for your interface, it is strongly recommended that you use it. Cubase uses this driver by default (although on Macintosh your ASIO Driver selection may default to Built-In Audio), but it's always good to confirm this the first time you run Cubase after it has been installed.
4. Click Apply to update the ASIO driver displayed under VST Audio System if you've made any changes.
5. Select the ASIO driver to display its settings (see Figure 3.11).

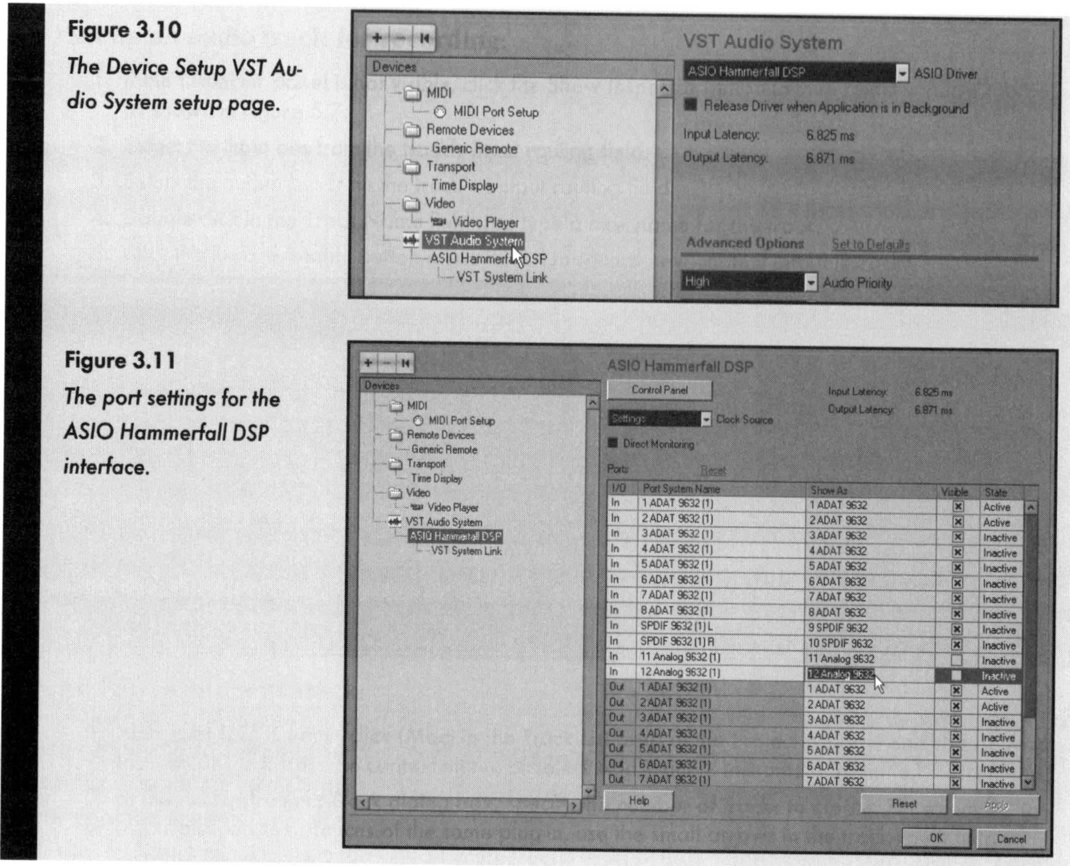

Figure 3.10
The Device Setup VST Audio System setup page.

Figure 3.11
The port settings for the ASIO Hammerfall DSP interface.

The number of columns in the table will always be the same, but the number of ports will vary from one device to the next. If you have more than one audio interface with ASIO drivers installed on your system, additional selections will appear under VST Audio System. Each has its own settings page.

As with MIDI ports described earlier in this chapter, the I/O column identifies whether the port is an input or output, while the Port System Name shows all the ports available in this interface. You can also rename the ports in the Show As column to change the way they appear whenever busses are created in the VST Connections panel. Notice how the ports in Figure 3.11 match the names in the drop-down list in Figure 3.12.

To hide certain audio ports when working inside Cubase, uncheck their Visible check box.

Ports that are not visible will not appear when you are associating ports to busses in the VST Connections panel later. You can change these settings at any time, but hiding ports that are

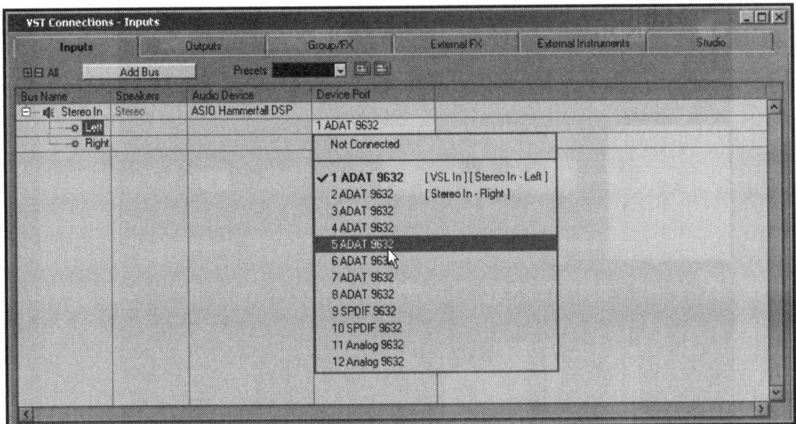

Figure 3.12
Selecting the renamed ports in the VST Connections panel.

currently used within a project will force Cubase to discard any routing information associated with this port. The State column plays a similar role as described for MIDI ports earlier in this chapter. Whenever an audio port is connected to a bus, its state will become active.

If you are using a dedicated ASIO driver, you can set the clock source of the audio device by clicking on the control panel in Windows or by using the pop-up Clock Source selector within the Device Setup dialog box on Macintosh computers. The clock source determines whether the sampling frequency (see Figure 3.13) of your audio peripheral is controlled by its own internal clock or some other external source. Once again, the number of settings found in this dialog box varies from one device to the next.

Set the clock source of your audio device to master (internal) when:

- You don't have any other digital audio devices in your studio setup.
- You want the clock of your audio device to serve as the master clock reference for other devices.

Set the clock source to slave/external sync or auto-sync when:

- You want the digital clock of another device to control your computer's audio hardware clock.

HOW TO

Adjusting the Buffer Size

For best results when playing VST instruments in real time or monitoring source audio through Cubase during the recording process, especially if you're applying plug-in effects, the input and output latency should be as low as possible. Latency won't affect the quality of the sound or the timing of a performance once it's inside a project, but with larger amounts of latency, you will hear a delay between what is being played back from Cubase and the part you're currently recording. This delay can throw off your timing while recording a performance.

Because latency is directly related to the Audio Buffer Size setting, increasing its size will also increase the latency. But to get rid of some crackling noise in the audio when working on projects with many audio tracks and/or a large number of plug-ins that may be taxing the processing power of your CPU, increasing the buffer size is the first thing to try. You can always reduce the buffer size later, if you need lower monitoring latency while recording performances with VST instruments or live audio, for example.

If you don't notice any changes in your audio after increasing the buffer size and you notice that your hard drive performance meter (press F12 to display) still indicates that your drive access peaks, you might need to get a faster drive or mix down some of the tracks to reduce the disk access. (Other possible causes of slow hard drive response are fragmentation or another program running concurrently with Cubase.) VST Performance meters are also found in the default Transport Control panel on the left.

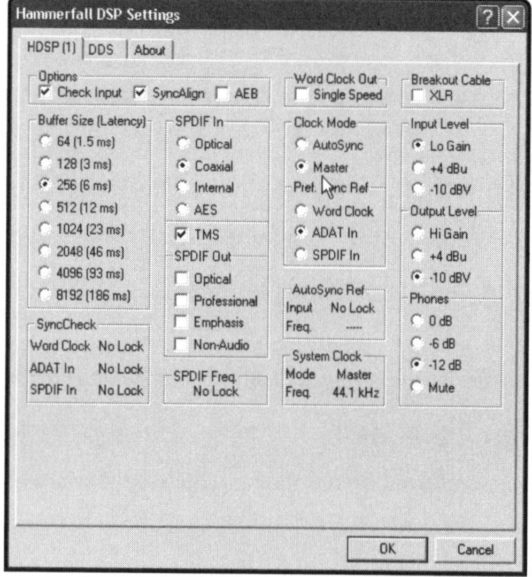

Figure 3.13
The control panel for the Hammerfall DSP-9632 from RME.

Running Other Applications Simultaneously

Most digital audio workstation applications, such as Cubase, require a lot of memory and CPU power. Running other applications simultaneously will prevent Cubase from using these resources.

Some background applications might start doing a hard drive scan in the middle of a recording. A good example of this would be Find Fast, an applet that comes with Microsoft Office, or a Norton AntiVirus system scan.

Background Processes

Any background applications that make intensive use of memory or hard drive resources should be disabled when using Cubase. A good rule of thumb for improving your performance is to not run *any* other nonessential applications while using Cubase. To find out which background applications are running on Windows XP, press Ctrl+Alt+Del to bring up the Windows Task Manager. For example, you can click on the Processes tab to view how much memory Cubase uses (see Figure 3.14).

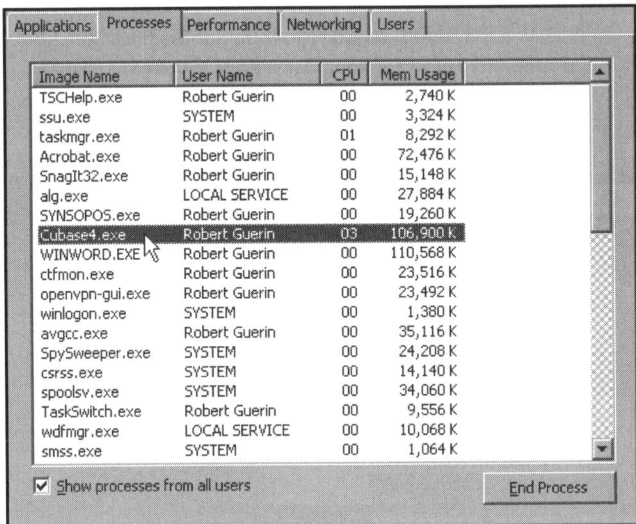

Figure 3.14
The Processes tab in Windows Task Manager.

You can end a process or an application (depending on whether the Applications or Processes tab is active) by selecting the item in the list, right-clicking on it, and selecting the appropriate option. Nothing you do in this dialog box can harm your system in any way. Note that once you reboot your system, the background applications that were running before you ended them will be back in business. So, changing the settings for these applications is a good idea. The more icons you have in the bottom-right corner of your taskbar (on a PC), the more applications that may be running in the background, using valuable resources. Be sure you keep those to a minimum. If you can, try to use a separate computer for your Internet activities. Antivirus utilities can use up to 30 percent of your system's resources.

If you are running OS X on a Macintosh computer, you can also view the active processes by accessing the Activity Monitor. You can access the Activity Monitor window from the Finder menu by choosing Go > Applications > Utilities Folder, then double-clicking the icon for the Activity Monitor program (see Figure 3.15).

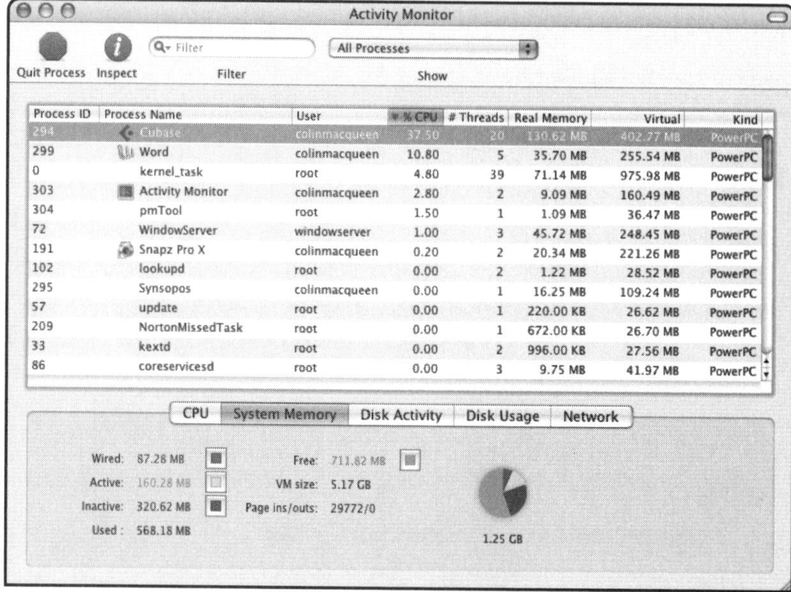

Figure 3.15
The Activity Monitor window on OS X.

There is a way to deactivate certain unnecessary applications to free up resources while running Cubase. The most effective way to do this is to choose any program that is loaded on the Dock, and then choose the File > Quit option. You could also do this in the Activity Monitor; however, you need to be very sure that you know exactly what you need to turn off.

Other Audio Applications

The situation is different if you try to run another audio-related application. To run other audio-related applications simultaneously with Cubase, you need audio hardware that provides a multi-client driver. A multi-client driver shares access to the audio hardware between audio applications. Think of it this way: A single-client access is like going to the grocery store and having only one cash register open. Everybody has to line up and wait their turn to pay for their groceries. A multi-client driver is like having two or three cash registers open so people can go to a second or even a third cash register if the first is busy.

When Cubase is loaded, it generally assumes control of the audio hardware, leaving it unusable for other applications that would also need it to run concurrently with Cubase, such as a third-party virtual sampler. If you don't have a multi-client driver, there are ways around this, but with some limitations.

Steinberg provides an engine developed by Propellerhead Software, called *ReWire*. ReWire lets you share audio resources between ReWire-compatible applications, such as Ableton Live, Propellerhead Reason, Cakewalk Sonar, Sony Media Software ACID, and so on. Working with ReWire applications is discussed in Chapter 11, "ReWire."

For other types of software, you will have to load this software first and set Cubase as your default sequencer from within the application's environment. After this has been configured, you can launch Cubase from within this application when needed. If you still have problems doing this, try disabling any audio outputs in that application that you intend to use in Cubase (for good measure, keep outputs 1 and 2 available for Cubase) and disabling audio inputs and outputs in Cubase that you want to use in the other application. By doing this, you are effectively assigning certain outputs of your audio hardware to Cubase and the remainder to the other application. You should also enable the Release Driver when Application is in Background option, found in the Device Setup dialog box under VST Audio System properties (see Figure 3.16).

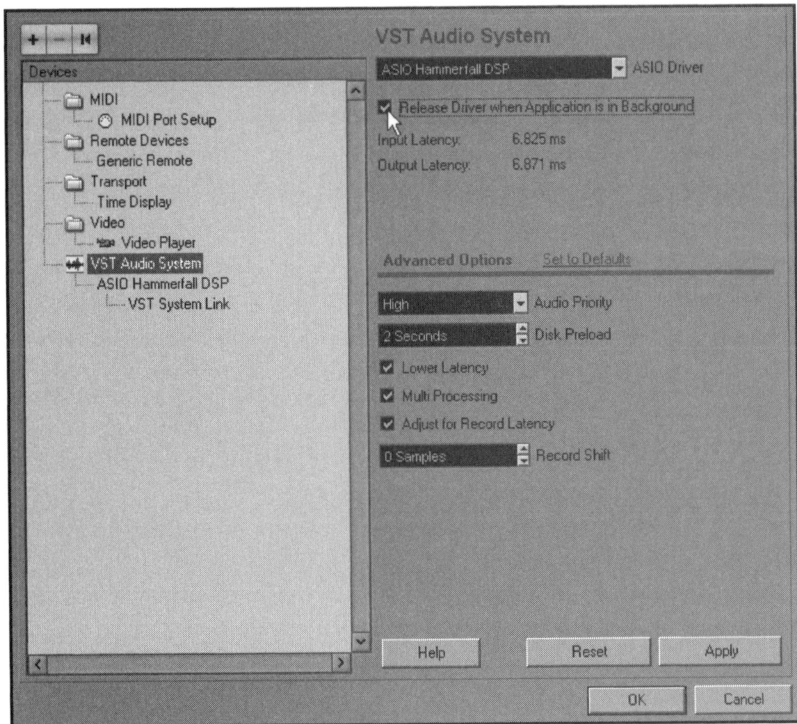

Figure 3.16
The Release Driver when Application is in Background option.

Running such a setup imposes a huge load on your computer resources, and you are also testing many compatibility issues between different software and hardware manufacturers. If you are experiencing difficulties, here are a couple of places to look for information:

- Visit Steinberg's Web site to see whether there is any additional information on the difficulty you are having.
- Visit your other software manufacturer's Web site; it also might have some answers for you.
- Check on your audio hardware manufacturer's Web site to confirm that you have the latest drivers for your audio hardware, and take a look at the support, troubleshooting, or FAQ section to find additional help.
- Use discussion forums (such as www.cubase.net and others) to share your problems with other users; there is a good chance that someone else has had the same problem and can suggest a workaround for you.

4 Monitoring Audio

What connecting a microphone to a preamplifier is to the hardware signal routing, making VST Connections is to Cubase's internal signal routing. In the first half of this chapter, we will discuss the former concept, and in the second half, we will discuss the latter. The signal path routing sometimes needs to change from one project to another, and your equipment might evolve over time. Setting up this equipment to fulfill your production needs is just as important as where the signal is or where it can be routed inside Cubase. It's about understanding how you can add a click track to a musician's headphones without sending it to the control-room monitors or to the audio track being recorded. It's also about enabling the producer to communicate with the guitarist in another room, without the drummer hearing what's being said. No matter what your signal routing needs are, VST Connections will make them happen.

Here's a summary of what you will learn in this chapter:

- How to monitor music productions through Cubase's VST audio engine
- How to monitor audio through an external mixer
- How to use direct monitoring mode to reduce latency effects
- How to make simple to complex hardware setup connections
- How to set up input and output busses
- How to set up group and plug-in effects busses
- How to set up external effect and instrument busses
- How to save VST Connections

Monitoring Methods

In this case, monitoring audio refers to listening to an audio signal as it enters the computer hosting Cubase, and as it exits Cubase to a monitoring setup. There are three basic audio monitoring methods when working with Cubase (see Figure 4.1): monitoring through Cubase, monitoring

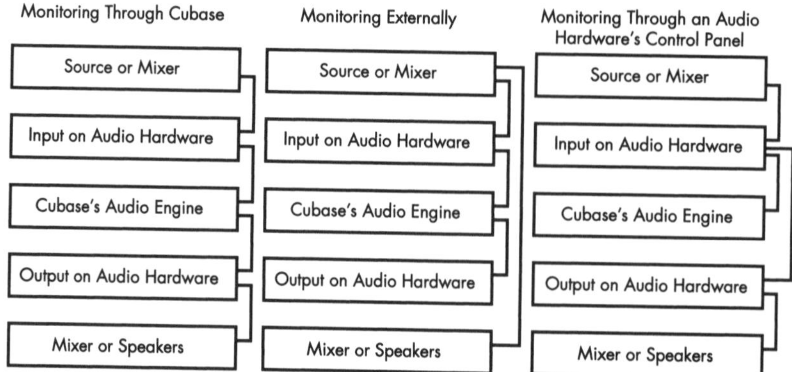

Figure 4.1
Different methods of monitoring audio.

through an external mixer, and direct monitoring, which is a combination of the two other methods.

Monitoring Through Cubase

When monitoring through Cubase, the signal enters the VST audio system, is routed and processed inside Cubase, and then is sent to the audio device's output port. For this to work well, you need an audio device with a low latency. Latency is the delay between the actual input signal and when it is heard coming back out through the audio hardware. The signal coming out of Cubase, once it has been processed, panned, leveled, and equalized, is delayed by the amount of this card's latency. With lower latencies, this delay will not be noticeable, but with higher latencies, it will definitely throw off someone trying to record a new track while listening to what has been previously recorded.

When you monitor sound through Cubase, there are four different monitoring preferences that influence when an audio track starts monitoring an incoming signal.

HOW TO

Set up auto monitoring preferences:

1. Select Preferences in the File menu (PC) or the application menu for Cubase (Mac).
2. Select VST at the bottom of the list on the left (see Figure 4.2).
3. In the right section, select one of the four auto monitoring options: Manual, While Record Enabled, While Record Running, and Tape Machine Style.
   - **Manual** monitoring enables you to switch to input monitoring by pressing the Monitor button in the track's channel mixer or the Mixer panel (see Figure 4.3). When this button is active, signals coming into Cubase are monitored through the Mixer panel, and then sent out to the channel's output bus. This is the default setting in Cubase.

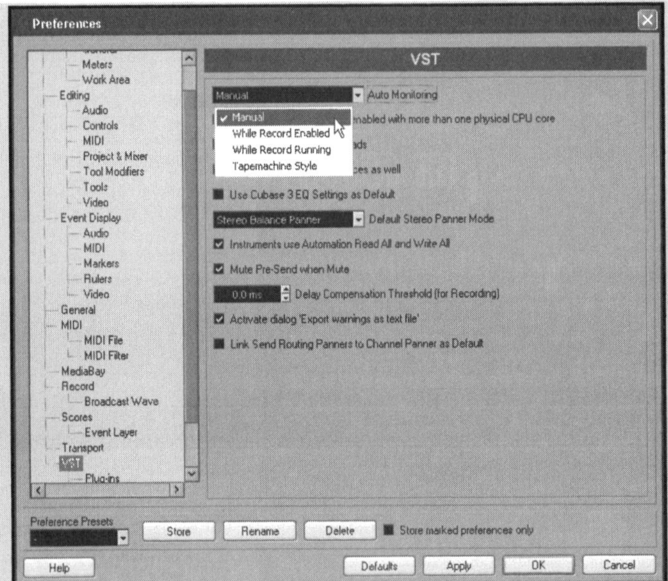

Figure 4.2
Changing the auto monitoring options in the VST Preferences.

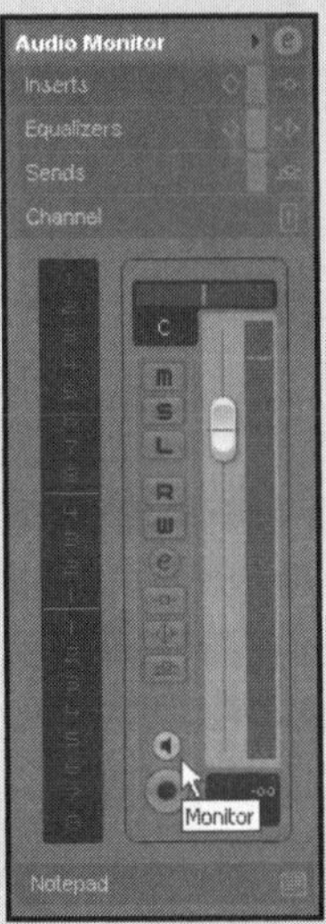

Figure 4.3
The Monitor button in the channel mixer.

- **While Record Enabled** switches the channel to input monitoring as soon as you enable the Record Enable button for this channel. This is the button below the Monitor button in Figure 4.3.
- **While Record Running** switches all the record-enabled channels to input monitoring when you click the Record button on the Transport panel.

- **Tape Machine Style** switches a selected audio track to input monitoring automatically when recording or when the project is stopped, but it will revert to output monitoring when you press Play. This mode is similar to traditional analog tape recorder behavior.

4. Click Apply, and then OK.

Monitoring through Cubase is the recommended mode because it lets you add processing and control the sound inside Cubase at every step of the production process.

Monitoring Externally

This monitoring technique implies the following setup:

- You are monitoring through an external mixer.
- What you are monitoring is routed and processed through an external mixer or an audio hardware mixer application, not inside Cubase.

Think of external monitoring as a direct output on a mixer—a point going back out right after coming into Cubase, but before any type of control or processing can occur. When monitoring through an external mixer, you should avoid also monitoring through Cubase simultaneously because you will hear two different signals with a delay between them. You can monitor an audio signal that has been previously recorded without any problem, but make sure to mute the track being recorded inside Cubase to avoid this double-monitoring problem when using an external mixer.

Direct Monitoring

Direct monitoring (with ASIO 2.0-compatible audio devices) controls the monitoring from the audio device's control panel. The options available to you will therefore be device-dependent. Cubase 4 users can also use the input bus faders to adjust input levels, but because the signal is sent back out right away, monitoring the input through the track's audio channel will not be possible. You can't apply processing, such as EQ or insert effects, and monitor these effects while recording when direct monitoring is active. The sound is sent directly to Cubase, but you are monitoring the input, not what's going into Cubase. In other words, you are monitoring the sound coming in through the audio device's Mixer utility, bypassing the VST audio engine that sends the signal into the Cubase Mixer for processing. This is an advantage when using audio devices with higher latencies, because you monitor what is coming into Cubase directly through your device's outputs, without adding any delay between the input and the output. On lower-latency audio devices, monitoring through Cubase is preferred because it gives you access to the controls and routing possibilities Cubase offers.

HOW TO

Enable direct monitoring mode:

1. Select the Device Setup option from the Devices menu.
2. Select the appropriate ASIO driver under VST Audio System.
3. Check the Direct Monitoring option in the ASIO driver settings page.
4. Click Apply, and then OK.

Hooking Up Your Equipment

There are many ways to hook up your equipment to your computer, and it all depends on what you want to do and what type of equipment you want to hook up. On this topic, there are two major problems you want to avoid:

1. Having too much sound–what is normally called a *feedback loop*
2. Having no sound at all

The following figures represent simple, yet effective ways to connect your equipment. Obviously, there are many more combinations, and you should try drawing out one for your own studio to help you organize your wiring effectively.

Figure 4.4 shows a modest digital audio/MIDI setup:

- MIDI events are sent to be recorded into Cubase from the keyboard (which is also a sound module).
- MIDI events can be echoed back to the keyboard's MIDI input via Cubase's MIDI Thru function, and its sound generation section will produce an audio signal in response to incoming MIDI events.
- You can monitor the audio from this external MIDI instrument/module through Cubase by creating an instrument track, selecting this module as the MIDI destination. We'll discuss how to connect such MIDI sound modules to Cubase later in this chapter.
- MIDI events generated by the keyboard can also be routed to VST instruments inside Cubase and monitored through any monitoring system connected to the output of your audio device.
- Depending on the number and type of audio ports available on your audio device, you could connect an acoustic instrument or a microphone as well.

Audio Input Levels

Remember that microphones require a low-impedance input. If your audio device offers only line-level inputs (often labeled +4 dBm or –10 dbV), then you need a separate microphone amplifier. Some line-level inputs on some professional audio devices use the same 3-pin XLR connector type as microphones.

> However, these are not suitable for directly connecting a microphone. For quality audio, you should also avoid using the "microphone" inputs with 1/8[dp] connectors on many consumer-type audio devices.

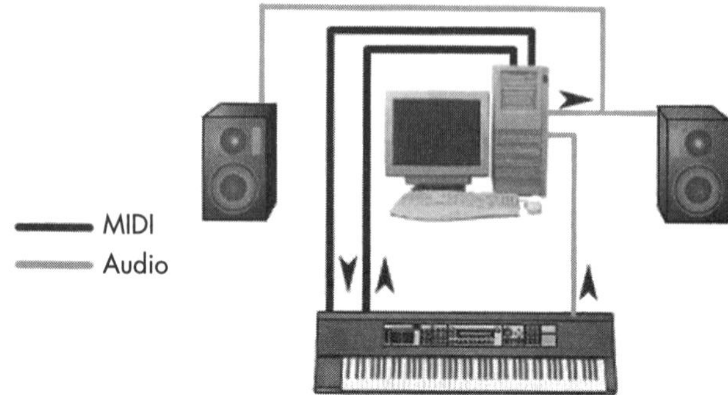

Figure 4.4
Simple setup without any mixer for single-source monitoring.

Connecting audio outputs from the audio device of your computer will depend on the monitoring system you are using.

- If you have powered monitors, you can hook up the audio outputs of your computer or keyboard directly to them.
- If you are using an amplifier, you send the signal to the amplifier first, and then distribute the audio signal from the amplifier to the speakers.

In Figure 4.5, a small desktop mixer has been added. You can also substitute the mixer for a multi input/output (I/O) audio device. Having several I/O will be necessary if you want to record and monitor several audio sources simultaneously (in this case, the keyboard and sound module). You can have as many audio sources as your mixer or audio device has inputs. There is not just one way to connect your studio setup. The idea is to get the audio flowing in the direction you need it to flow. If you only have one set of outputs on your mixer, use it to feed Cubase. You can use the output of Cubase to send a signal to your monitoring system. By doing so, you can monitor what's being recorded through the external mixer without running into a situation in which the signal being monitored is also being recorded at the same time. Most desktop mixers have separate volume controls for monitoring and master outputs. If this is the case, take the audio outputs of the computer and feed them into a separate pair of inputs that can be routed to a signal path that doesn't go back into itself (in this case, the computer), such as a tape return, for example. If you have direct outputs or busses on your mixer, use those to send the signal to your computer rather than using the main outputs. Always keep recorded events on a separate pathway from events being recorded.

Use the MIDI Thru of the keyboard to echo the MIDI output of the computer into other sound modules if you only have one MIDI port. MIDI events from your keyboard will be sent to Cubase,

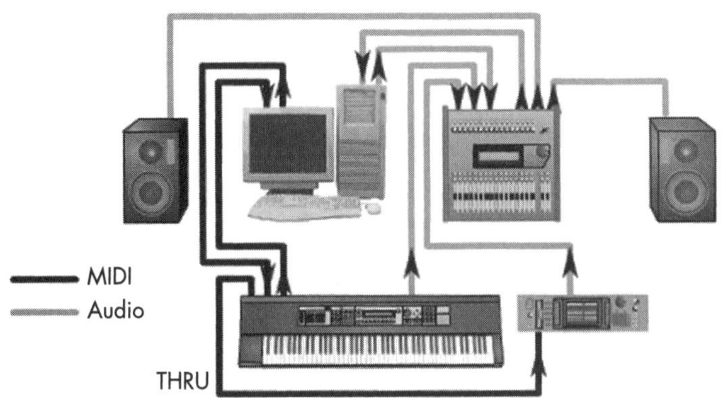

Figure 4.5
Simple setup with a desktop mixer for multiple-source monitoring.

and Cubase will send MIDI events back to the keyboard and the subsequent sound modules in the chain.

Figure 4.6 shows a setup using a multiple I/O audio device without the use of a mixer, where Cubase's virtual mixing environment is used to route audio signals. This does offer some flexibility; the routing scenarios will be limited by the number of I/O ports found on your audio device. If you are on a budget and can't afford a mixer, it's a good compromise.

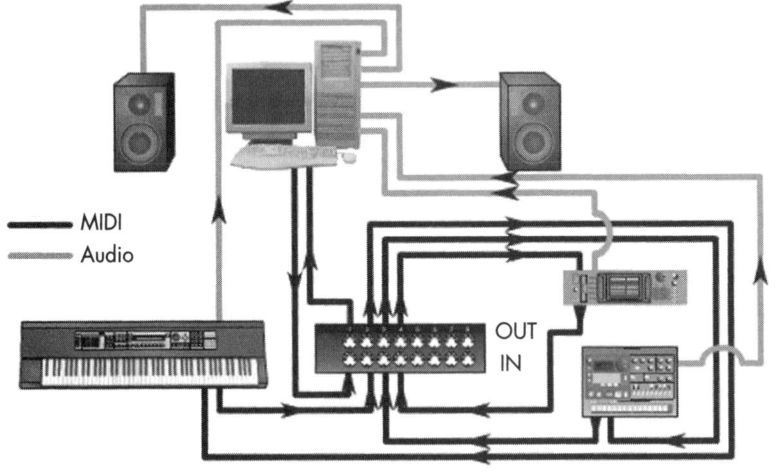

Figure 4.6
Setup for a MIDI studio using a MIDI patch bay and multiple input audio device without any mixer.

Send audio source outputs to separate audio inputs on the audio device, and a pair of outputs from the audio device to a monitoring system. A MIDI patch bay has been added to help with the MIDI patching, but this is not necessary. If you don't have a MIDI patch bay, you will need to send the MIDI Thru of your keyboard to the MIDI In of the sound module and the MIDI Thru of the sound module to the MIDI In of the drum machine (or other sound module), making the keyboard and computer front and center in your MIDI routing (keyboard's MIDI Out to computer's MIDI In, and vice versa).

Figure 4.7 shows a setup using a simple digital in/out audio device that sends and receives information through a digital connection with the digital mixer. As in Figure 4.5, you might want to use an extra pair of audio outputs to monitor the output from your computer without sending it back into the signal of the mixer, which otherwise could create a feedback loop.

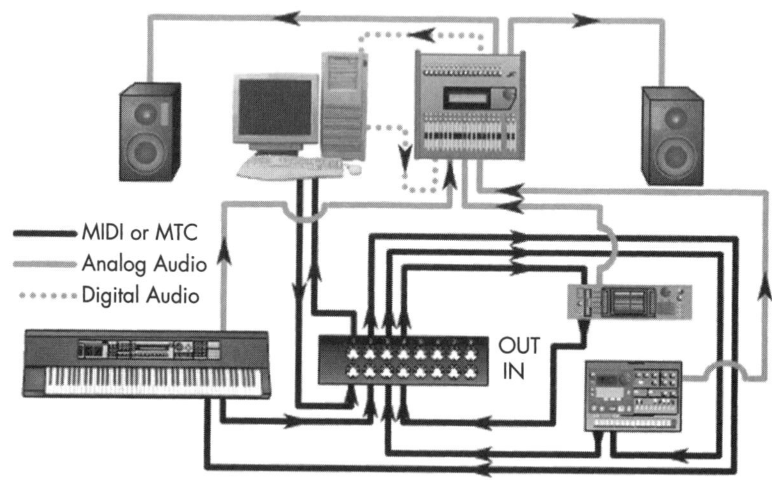

Figure 4.7
Setup for a MIDI or audio studio using a digital mixer and an audio device providing digital inputs and outputs.

Setting Up VST Connections

The concept of connections was introduced in Chapter 2 as a way to connect busses to ports—busses being what you select inside Cubase as the source or destination for audio. A bus can be mono, stereo, or multichannel. A port, on the other hand, is a single (mono) physical connection. By adding the concept of a bus to connections, Cubase makes it possible to use the same inputs and outputs for different purposes, offering much more flexibility in studio setups of any type.

Most of this discussion will center on options found in the VST Connections panel, which can be opened by selecting its name under the Devices menu or by pressing the keyboard shortcut F4.

The VST Connections panel offers six tabs: Inputs, Outputs, Group/FX, External FX, External Instruments, and Studio. The following sections describe the purpose of each tab and how to configure connections according to your needs. Because you need at least one output bus, you should configure the VST Connections before you begin a new project.

Input Connections

The first tab on the left in the VST Connections panel lets you create input busses manually or select them from a list of presets. Once busses are created, you can connect audio device input ports to these busses (see Figure 4.8). Input busses are used to record audio. You can create as many input busses as you need and in the desired channel format: mono, stereo, or multichannel. For example, if you do a lot of rock band recordings, you'll need a number of mono input busses for the bass, guitar, and vocals; a combination of mono and stereo busses for the drum kit; and possibly a stereo bus to record keyboards.

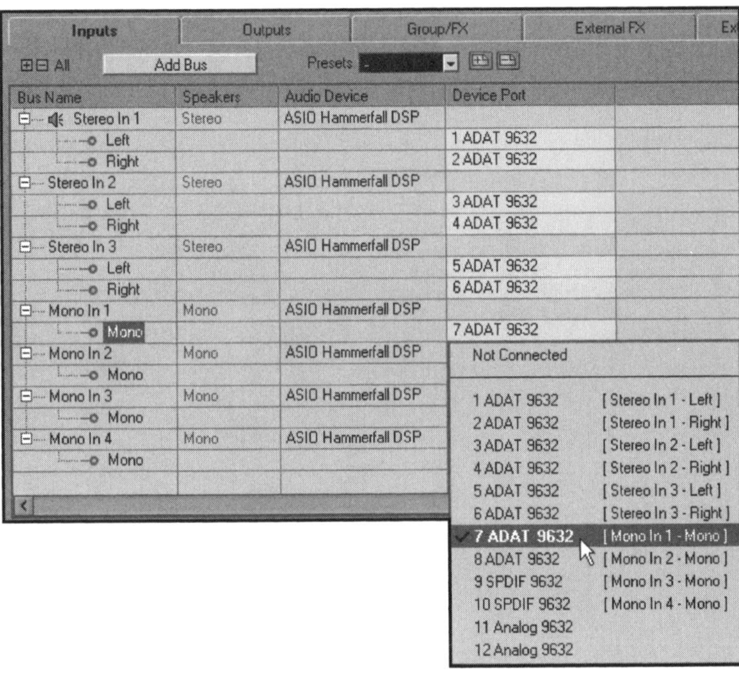

Figure 4.8
The Inputs tab on the VST Connections panel.

HOW TO

Create input busses:

1. Open the VST Connections panel (press F4 or select Devices > VST Connections).
2. Select the Inputs tab.
3. Click on the Add Bus button (refer to Figure 4.8).
4. In the Add Input Bus dialog box, select the bus configuration from the drop-down menu. For example, select Mono to create a bus for recording mono instruments, such as bass, vocal, trumpet, and so on.
5. Adjust the number of busses you want to create, if needed.
6. Click OK.
7. In the Audio Device column, select the audio device driver you want to use for this bus (see Figure 4.9). The names of devices that appear here will depend on your VST Audio System setting, as described earlier in this chapter.

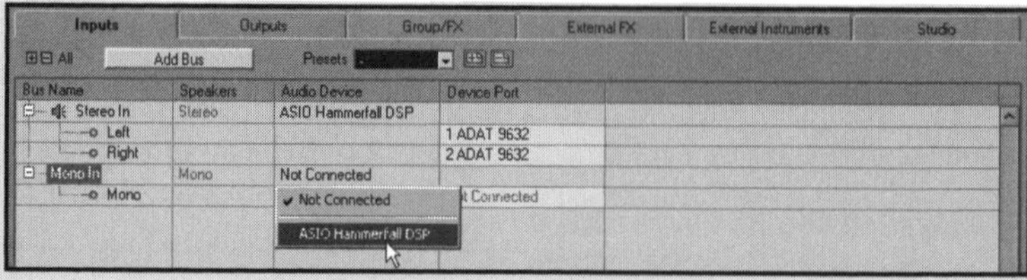

Figure 4.9
Connecting an audio device to a bus.

8. In the Device Port column, select the port on the audio device that you want to use for this bus. By assigning a device port to a bus, you effectively tell Cubase where the sound is coming from when you select an input bus on a channel's Input Bus selection menu.
9. Select the bus name, then click on it a second time to rename it if necessary. A rectangle appears around the name when you can edit it. The name you enter here appears in the bus selection menu (see Figure 4.10).

Figure 4.10
The Input drop-down menu, found in the audio track Inspector area, lists available busses.

10. Repeat these steps for each input bus you want to create.
11. Close the VST Connections panel when you are finished. Once the busses are created, the Speaker column in the VST Connections panel will display their configuration.

You also need to configure a studio connection to monitor samples being edited or monitor real-time exports. Follow Steps 7, 8, and 9 in the preceding list when you want to configure your studio bus in the appropriate tab on the VST Connections panel. You can't have more than one audition/studio bus per project.

Output Connections

The Outputs tab in the VST Connections panel lets users create output busses manually or select them from a list of presets. Once busses are created, users can assign audio device output ports to these busses. Outputs are used to monitor a track or channel's playback or to send the signal to an external multitrack recorder, for example.

HOW TO

Create output busses:

1. Open the VST Connections panel (press F4 or select Devices > VST Connections).
2. Select the Outputs tab.
3. From this point, follow Steps 3 through 10 describing how to create an input bus earlier in this chapter. The Transport panel provides a Click button, which is convenient when you need to generate a click track during the recording process. However, you might not want to send this click sound to all output busses. This is where the Click column comes in handy.
4. Use the Click column to toggle the click track on or off for each output bus.

When the Click function is enabled in the Transport panel (see Figure 4.11), busses with the word "Click" will echo the click track through the device port connected to this bus.

Figure 4.11
Click track assignment for output busses.

Group/FX Connections

The Group/FX tab lets you add group busses/channels that allow you to combine and control the main audio output from several other channels. You could apply the same EQ to the signal from all channels in that group, control their overall volume with a single fader, or control the position of an entire group through a single pan control. FX (short for *effects*) can be added to a project to process audio channels, such as adding a filter or reverb effect to one or several tracks. On traditional mixers, this type of effect is often called a *send effect*, as opposed to an *insert effect*. Send effects are called this because audio from multiple channels is "sent" through an FX bus to an effect. Use the Group/FX page in the VST Connections panel to keep track of these types of tracks in your project or add new ones. You can also create groups and effects from the main Project window as well, which is not the case with the rest of the connections in this panel. Look for additional ways to use FX channels in Chapter 32, "FX Channel Tracks," or create groups in Chapter 33, "Group Channel Tracks."

External FX Connections

If you have external effect units and would like to integrate them into your Cubase environment, use the External FX bus tab. For example, suppose you have a good analog preamp you like because it warms things up, and you wonder how it would sound on your mix. By creating an external FX bus, you can make the necessary connections. The External FX tab lets you connect Cubase to an external effect by configuring both the *send to effect* and the *effect return* pathway.

Once the connection between the external effect and Cubase is established, you can use external effects the same way you would use a VST plug-in effect inside Cubase.

HOW TO

Create an External FX bus:

1. In the VST Connections External FX tab, click on the Add External FX button.
2. In the Add External FX dialog box, type a name for the effect. In Figure 4.12, we've renamed the device to match the Roland reverb module connected to our audio ports.

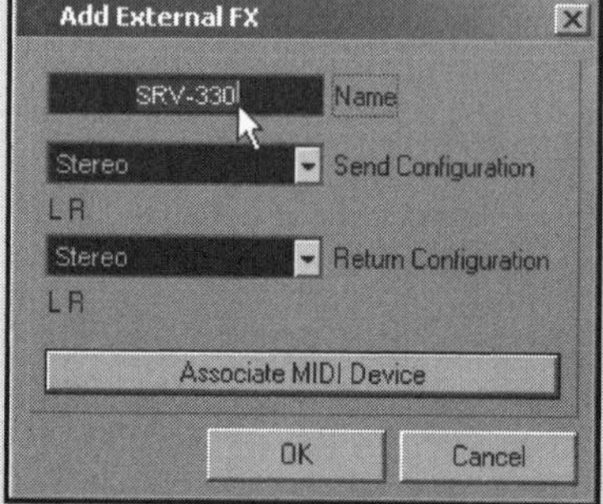

Figure 4.12
Renaming an external effect.

3. Select a Send and Return channel configuration. These settings depend on the external effect's input and output configuration and on the number of inputs and outputs available on the audio device. Quite often you might have a stereo pair going to an effect and a stereo pair coming back. Selecting a stereo configuration would be advisable in this case.
4. Click OK. The External FX bus name is visible in the FX Plug-in selection list whenever you want to use it (see Figure 4.13).

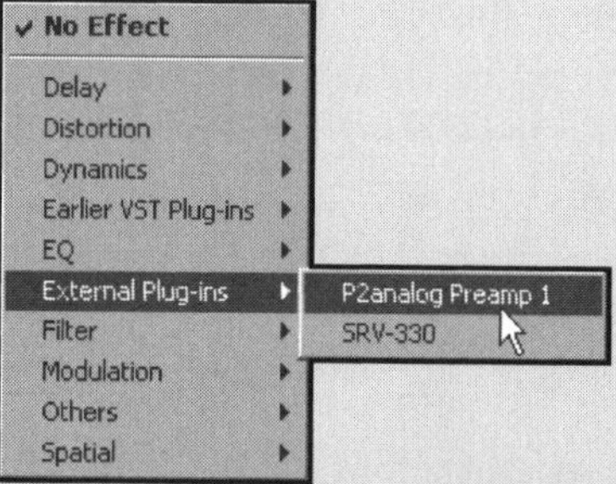

Figure 4.13
External FX as they appear in the plug-in effect list.

5. Set the Audio Device for both the Send and Return busses. Sends use audio outputs, whereas Returns use inputs. Once an output port is used by an Output, External FX, External Instruments or Studio busses, it can't be used as an External FX bus.
6. Adjust the Delay value, if necessary. The Delay value compensates in milliseconds for external devices that may have inherent latency once the signal returns. When using reverbs and delays, for example, it may be okay to leave this set to 0 ms. It would definitely *not* be okay to leave it at

0 ms for a compressor, a harmonizer, a preamp, and other time-sensitive processes in which the resultant delay would cause phase cancellation or other time-alignment issues.

Dealing with Audio Alignment Issues

When connecting external devices to Cubase through the External FX bus, understand that an audio signal gets sent outside Cubase, is processed by this external device, and returns inside Cubase before it is sent to the project's output. This little trip in the outside world can sometimes cause a time shift in the signal and potentially create time-alignment issues with the rest of your mix. This is due in part by the I/O conversion (if any) or the internal processing latency of the external device itself. When this is the case, use the Delay value to adjust the amount of delay needed to restore the timing of the signal. Adjusting the delay works better when the project is playing because you will hear the result of the change in value and the effect it has on the audio as it is moved in time to fit with the rest of your mix.

7. Enter the desired amount of Send Gain and Return Gain. The Send and Return Gain values let you adjust the gain level for the signal being sent to or received from the device.
8. If the external effect is MIDI-compatible and you want to associate a MIDI port with it, select an existing one from the MIDI Device column (see Figure 4.14) or create one if needed.

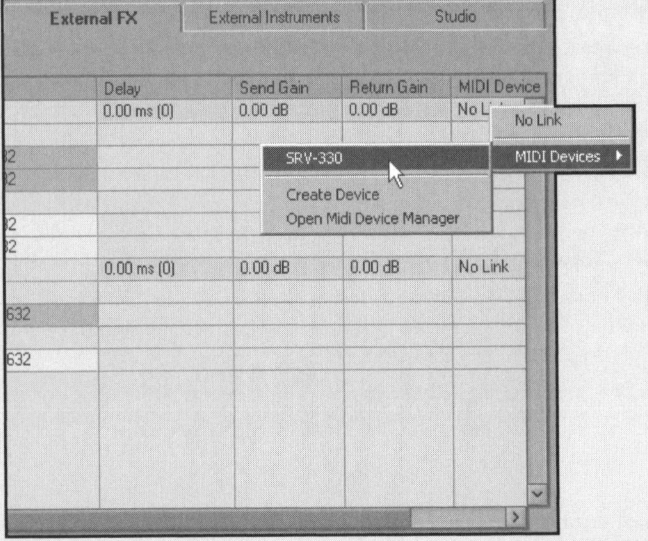

Figure 4.14
Connecting an external FX to a MIDI device.

Once an external effect device is connected to a MIDI port and properly configured in the MIDI Device Manager, you can record MIDI messages in Cubase and play them back to change presets or parameter values in your device. This is a very nice feature when you want to get the most out of your external devices.

Finding Existing MIDI Device Panels

You can find a number of preconfigured MIDI Device panels that can be downloaded—including various external effects units and digital mixers, which can be controlled via MIDI by logging into the Cubase Info Base or www.studioconnections.org from the Cubase.net Forum.

External Instrument Connections

Similar to external FX, the External Instruments tab, new to Cubase 4, lets you connect external hardware sound modules so that you can use them in your project as with any other virtual instrument. External instrument connections offer a very convenient way to set up MIDI and audio for these devices simultaneously in Cubase. Because you can save these settings to a template file, you won't have to redo the same setup steps every time you want to use your external MIDI gear in a new project.

HOW TO

Create an external instrument:

1. In the VST Connections External Instruments tab, click on the Add External Instruments button.
2. In the Add External Instrument dialog box, type a name for this effect.

   Because this name will appear in the instrument selection menu, it's recommended that you give it an easily recognizable name, such as "MOTIF ES8" if you own a Yamaha Motif ES8 synth.
3. Set up the instrument returns appropriately. These settings depend on the output configuration on your external device and the number of audio inputs on your computer you want to use for this setup. With many synths/samplers, a single stereo return should work fine. You can change this setting later, if necessary, by creating an additional instrument.
4. Click the Associate MIDI Device button and select an existing MIDI device. In order for the device's patchnames to show up in the Inspector, it is recommended that you create the MIDI device inside the MIDI Device Manager beforehand. For more information on how to install a MIDI device in the Manager, check out Chapter 9, "Using Instruments."
5. Adjust the Delay value, if necessary. As with an external FX, the Delay value compensates in milliseconds for external devices that may have inherent latency once the signal returns. Here again, we recommend that you start by leaving this value at 0 ms.
6. Enter the desired amount of return gain, if necessary.

   The Return Gain values let you adjust the gain level received from the device.

Once both MIDI and audio port connections are made, your external MIDI devices will appear in the VST Instruments panel and in the instrument selection field of the Add Instrument Track dialog boxs, as shown in Figure 4.15.

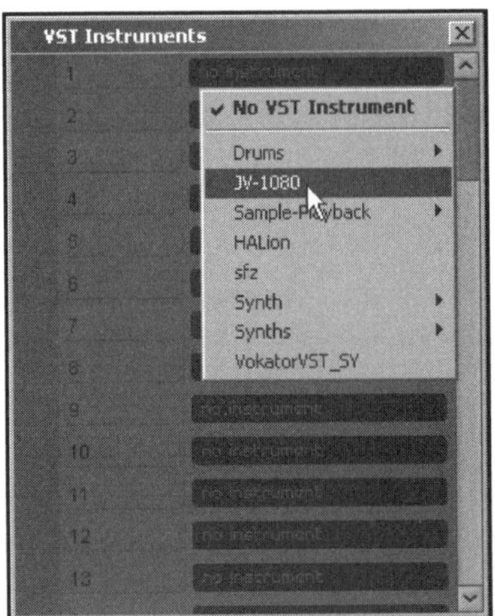

Figure 4.15
Selecting an external MIDI device from the VST Instruments panel.

Studio Connections

The Studio connection tab lets you configure a number of additional discrete cue mixes, from a control-room mono monitoring setup to a multichannel monitoring setup, headphone mixes, or a studio talkback microphone when you need to communicate instructions through a musician's headphones in a recording booth. In a simpler setup, cue mixes added in this tab allow you to cue sounds you're about to import to a project through a separate audio port, even though they haven't been assigned to a track yet. Think of it as creating a preview bus.

With that said, if you are using Cubase as a project or home studio production tool, have all your gear in a single room, and record most of your tracks while sitting in front of the computer, you probably won't need to create any studio connections. If this case applies to you, disable the Control Room Mixer by pressing the Disable Control Room button, as displayed in Figure 4.16. Disabling the Control Room Mixer is also recommended if you only have a stereo pair of inputs and outputs. When the Control Room Mixer is disabled, the audio generated when previewing files being imported to your project passes through the output bus.

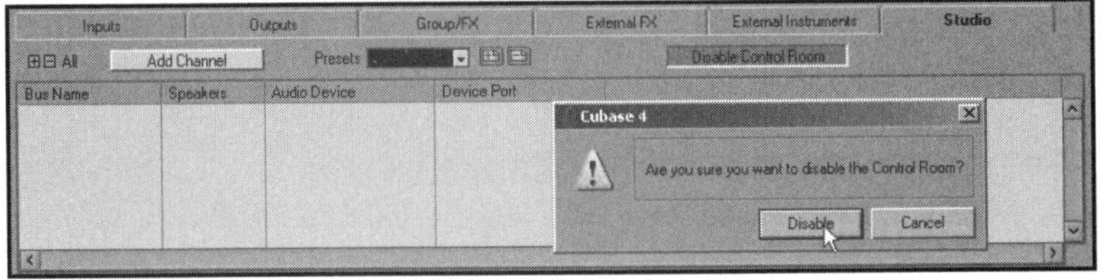

Figure 4.16
Disabling the Control Room Mixer.

For additional information about signal routing options associated with the different studio connections, check out the discussion of the Control Room Mixer in Chapter 6, "Control Room Mixer."

HOW TO

Create a studio connection:

1. In the Studio tab of the VST Connections panel, click on the Add Channel button.
2. From the pop-up menu, select the type of studio connection you want to create.
3. In the Add Channel dialog box, type a name for the studio connection and select the desired channel configuration.
4. Click OK.
5. Expand the channel to display the device ports connection assignment, as seen in Figure 4.17.

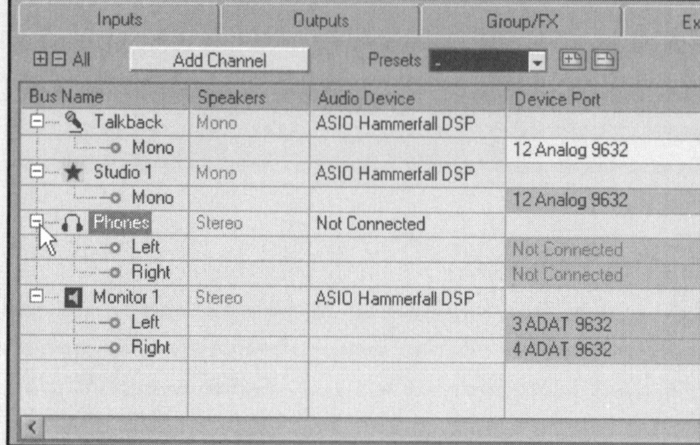

Figure 4.17
Expanding the connections to reveal device port settings.

6. Click in the Device Port column to assign this channel to unused audio ports.

Saving Connections

The connection settings discussed in this chapter can be saved and recalled later. Saving connections makes setting up work sessions a breeze. It's also convenient to save connections when the number of available audio ports is limited. The audio ports on your audio device become your patchbay, and Cubase handles all signal routing tasks internally. There are two ways to save connections:

- By setting everything up and saving the project as a template (File > Save As Template)
- By saving the connections as presets

Templates appear when you are creating a new project, as displayed in Figure 4.18. When a project is saved as a template, all connections are saved with templates. Create different connection configurations, using all your inputs to feed tracks when you know the project involves mostly live musicians in a studio. Save another template in which connections are optimized for projects with external effects and MIDI sound modules.

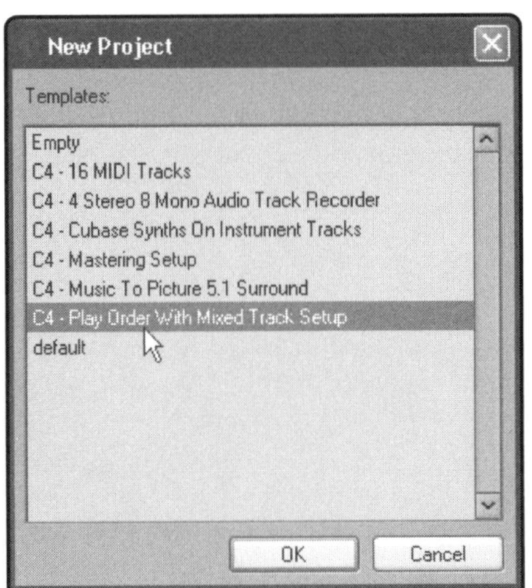

Figure 4.18
The New Project dialog box.

Saving connections makes it possible to change the signal routing inside the project without having to redo all your connections manually, as described in this chapter. Go from using a talkback microphone connected to an audio port A to an external input connected to that same port A.

To:	**Do:**
Save a connection preset	Click on the Store Preset button (1) in Figure 4.19 and give the preset a name in the Preset Name dialog box.
Recall a preset configuration	Select it from the Presets list (2) in Figure 4.19.
Delete a connection preset	Click on the Delete Preset button (3) in Figure 4.19.
Rename a connection preset	Double-click on the preset name (4) in Figure 4.19.

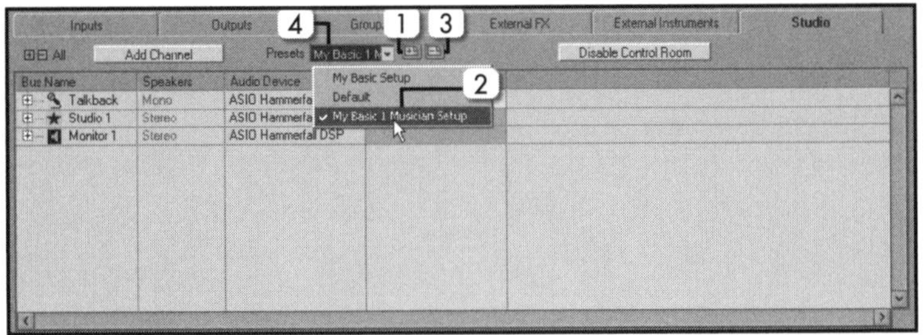

Figure 4.19
VST Connections: Connection preset tools.

5 New Project

Projects in Cubase 4 are the equivalent of documents in Microsoft Word, image files in Adobe Photoshop, or any other software-specific file format. A project holds all the information needed to recreate the work, with the exception of media files, which are saved as separate entities on your media drive and referred to by the project file when you are editing it.

In theory, you can have as many projects opened in Cubase as you want; however, in practice, your system's resources will most likely dictate how many projects you can load into memory simultaneously. The more tracks and plug-ins loaded into a project, the more memory it tends to use up in your computer.

DRAGGING EVENTS
When you have more than one Project window open in Cubase, you can drag events from one project to another.

By default, the first time you launch Cubase it prompts you to select a new project template (see Figure 5.1). Templates are simply project files that were saved as templates in the Cubase 4 program folder. To learn more about how to create templates, see Chapter 38, "Project Customization."

Here's a summary of what you will learn in this chapter:

- What a Cubase project file is
- How to create a new project
- How to set up a project's display, audio, and timecode properties
- How to create audio tracks
- How to set up audio tracks for recording

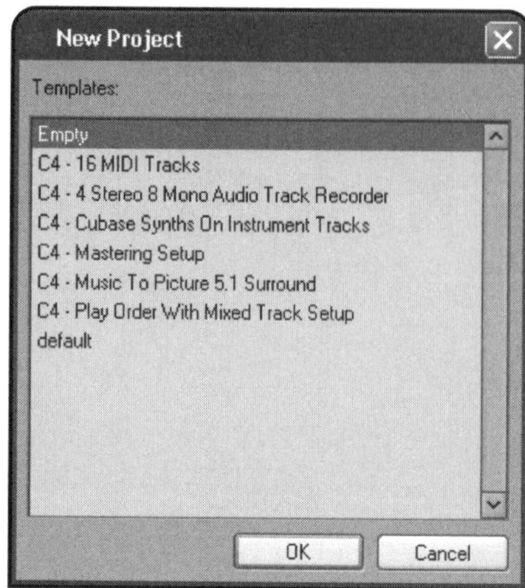

Figure 5.1
The New Project template selection dialog box.

- How to create instrument and MIDI tracks
- How to set up instrument and MIDI tracks for recording

Create a New Project

Each project is saved as a Cubase PRoject file (CPR file). Cubase projects contain all MIDI data, automation, plug-in effect settings and assignments, and overall mixer and connection settings. Although audio and video clips are not saved within the project file, the position and other playback parameters for audio events placed on the timeline inside Cubase tracks are also saved with the project file. When you reload a project file, it will find these media files where you left them. If you changed the media's location between saves, Cubase will prompt you for a new location before loading them in your project. Furthermore, if you delete a folder containing media files used in a project without backing them up beforehand, you will no longer be able to use this audio or video in your project, and Cubase will warn you that it could not load certain files.

Now that you understand the relationship between a project and its media files references, let's create a new project.

HOW TO

Create a new project:

1. Select File, New Project or press the keyboard shortcut Ctrl+N (PC)/Command+N (Mac).
2. In the New Project dialog box, double-click on the Empty project template or another project template of your choice. Cubase then prompts you to set the destination folder for the new project. This should be the location where you want to save your project file. Cubase automatically creates subfolders to store audio and other types of files related to this project.
3. Select the drive and folder inside that drive (if necessary). You may also choose to create a new folder by clicking on the Create button (see Figure 5.2). Give the folder the project's name. Doing so will make it easier to find later.

Figure 5.2
The Select Directory dialog box.

4. With the newly created folder selected, click OK to close the dialog box.

If you have chosen to create a new empty project, Cubase opens an empty Project window. If you have selected another template, it will automatically create a project with tracks corresponding to the template's default settings. For example, if you selected the Mastering Setup template, you'd get a single stereo audio track, as well as a marker track to navigate within the mastering project. Keep in mind that each project file should be saved in its own folder, and setting up projects should take place *before* you start recording any new content in them. So let's set up our project now.

Project Setup

The Project Setup dialog box contains four groups of settings: the start time and length of the project, the frame rate when working with video, the display format and its display offset value, and, finally, its digital audio properties. Although the length and display format won't affect the audio being recorded, the digital audio properties will determine how files are recorded onto your media drive. If you plan to do most of your work in 48 kHz, you should make sure your project is set up to record audio using this sample rate. This will also influence how files are imported into the project. For example, import audio files recorded at 44.1 kHz into a 48-kHz project, and Cubase will prompt you to convert the files to the project's sample rate before importing them.

CHANGING NUMERIC VALUES

Whenever you see numeric values—such as a time location or a volume level below a fader, for example—clicking on the value box to highlight it will allow you to change the value in one of several ways.

If you have a mouse with a scroll wheel, you can scroll forward to increase the value. When you point the pop-up arrow toward the top or bottom of a time display (see Figure 5.3), the cursor will change into a plus or minus sign; clicking when this pointer is displayed will increase or decrease the value by single units, while holding the mouse button down will scroll the selected value up or down. Finally, you can always type new values whenever a value box is selected and editable.

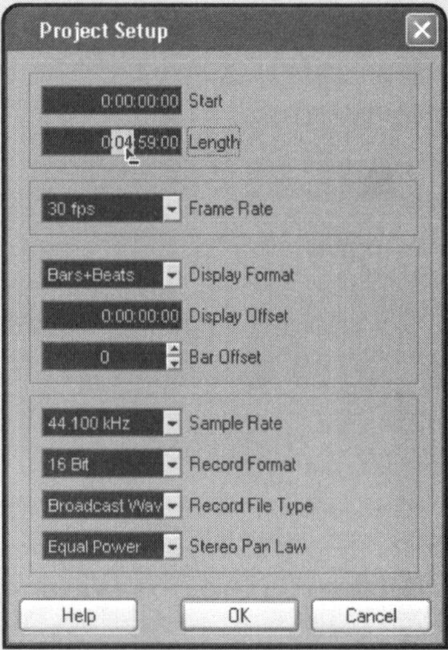

Figure 5.3
Reducing the selected value in a field by using the mouse button or scroll wheel.

HOW TO

Set up a project:

1. Press Shift+S (or choose Project > Project Setup) to open the Project Setup dialog box.
2. Leave the Start field at its default setting. If you want your project to start at a different time location, enter the proper value in this field in hours, minutes, seconds, and frames format. This adds the entered value to the time displayed in the project. For example, set the Start time to 01:00:00:00, and the project will begin at that time rather than at the usual 00:00:00:00.
3. Set the Length field to the approximate length of your project. Setting up the length influences the proportion of time displayed in the overview area of the current project and speeds up any freezing or rendering processes, which are discussed in Chapter 39, "Project Optimization."

4. If you are working with a video file or synchronizing to an external timecode provided by a video tape, set the Frame Rate field to this media's frame rate. This ensures that the timecode displayed in Cubase corresponds to the timecode format of the synchronizing media.
5. In the Display Format field, select Bars+Beats to determine how time is displayed on your project's Transport Control bar. You can change this later while working in your project.
6. The Display Offset value can be left at its default, in most cases. If you are synchronizing a project to an external video that starts at a frame other than zero—for example, if the tape starts at 01:59:45:00—you might still want the timeline display in your project to start at the position 00:00:00:00. Then you would set the Display Offset value at 01:59:45:00 for the start position (00:00:00:00) to correspond to this time.
7. Set the Sample Rate field to the desired rate (see Figure 5.4). Once you set a sample rate for your project, you will not be able to change it later because all the sounds in your project will have to be at this sample rate.

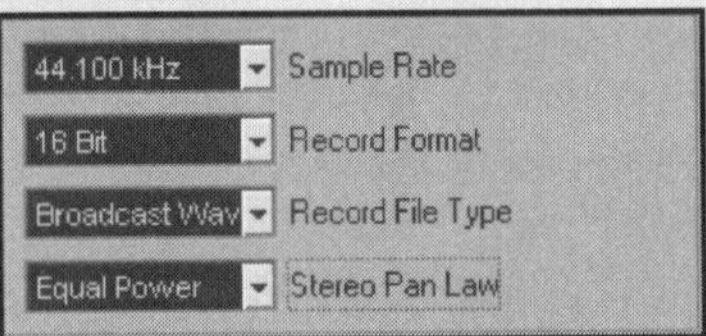

Figure 5.4
The digital audio project recording preference settings.

8. In the Record Format field, select the desired bit depth from the drop-down menu. You can select any resolution supported by your audio hardware. Unlike the sample rate, you can import or record audio files with different bit depths in a single project. However, the record format selected here will determine the number of bits per sample in any digital audio files created in this project by new recordings or other audio-related operations.
9. From the Record File Type field, select the desired audio file type. The Broadcast Wave File format is identical to the WAV format with one exception: It enters text strings that will be embedded in the audio files. These text strings can contain information about your project, its creators, and audio time stamping information. By using this file type, you don't have to enter this information later because it will be done automatically. Wave 64, on the other hand, is a Sony (formerly Sonic Foundry) proprietary format that supports files larger than 2 GB. Wave 64 files are better suited for live-concert recordings in surround format, in which file size can reach the limit of regular wave file capacity fairly easily.
10. In the Stereo Pan Law field, select the default –3dB from the drop-down field. When panning a channel, you want the left, center, and right pan positions to sound equally loud. Selecting 3 dB or 6 dB will ensure this. Otherwise, a setting of 0 dB will cause a channel panned to the center position to sound louder. When two similar signals are panned to the center, they double-up, causing the perceived loudness to be 3 dB louder than a single audio signal. For example, two trumpet players will be 3 dB louder than one trumpet player unless you pan both tracks hard left and hard right.
11. Click OK when you are finished.

Creating Audio Tracks

To record audio information in a project, you will need to start by adding audio tracks. When you add audio tracks to a project, you make a choice about how you want them configured. In Cubase 4, you can pick between mono, stereo, or multichannel tracks (up to six channels). Events recorded on a mono track are recorded in mono format, and events recorded on a stereo track are recorded in stereo interleaved format. *Stereo interleaved* means that both channels (left and right) are recorded into the same file. With multichannel tracks, the choice widens to include surround-sound formats such as LCRS (left, center, right, and surround), 5.0, 5.1, or one of many other multichannel formats, as shown in Figure 5.5.

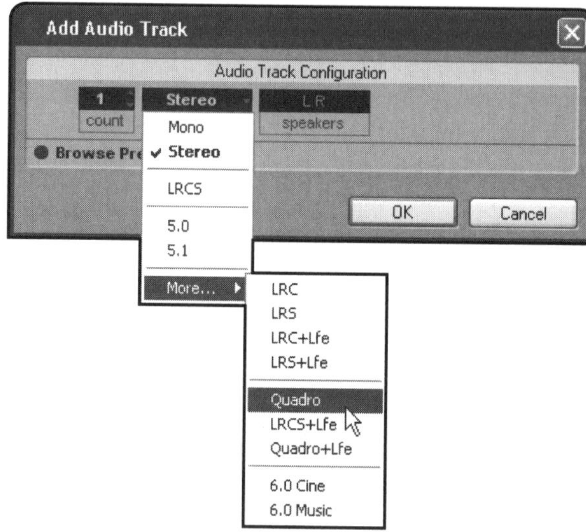

Figure 5.5
Multichannel audio track configurations.

After an audio track is created, you can record and import or move audio from the Pool into this track.

HOW TO

Add audio tracks:

1. Right-click (PC)/Control-click (Mac) in the Track List area of the Project window and choose Add Audio Track from the context menu, or select Add Track > Audio from the Project menu.
2. In the Add Audio Track dialog box, specify the number of tracks to create. For example, select the track count field and type 4 to create this number of tracks. Note that all of these tracks will have the same configuration.
3. Select a track configuration from the drop-down menu.
4. Click OK.

Setting Up an Audio Track

Once an audio track exists in a project, it can receive audio from a source, such as a mic, the audio of a keyboard, or the output of a turntable, and it can play existing audio events through an output bus. By default, audio tracks are labeled Audio 01, Audio 02, and so on. Naming a track makes it easier to manage and find its content later, as demonstrated in Figure 5.6, in which track 2 is named Audio 01 and track 3 is named more descriptively. More importantly, because audio files are given the name of the track where they were recorded, it makes sense to rename them before recording anything. Notice the audio event names on the right; they both correspond to their respective tracks.

Figure 5.6
Renaming an audio track.

Most of the operations described here take place in the Inspector panel of the Project window, as shown in Figure 5.7.

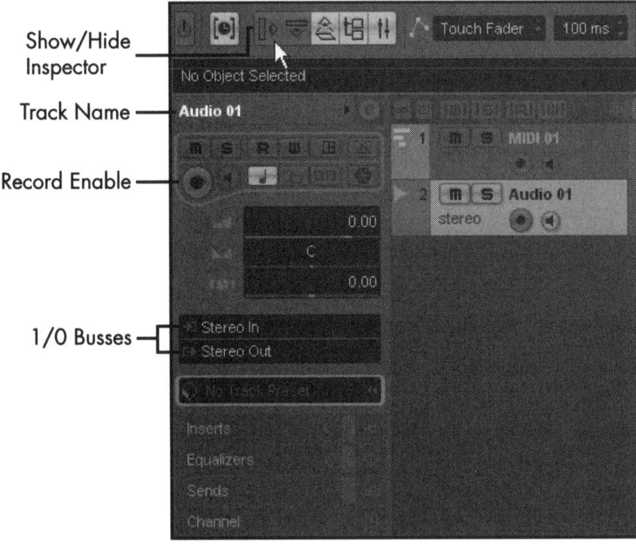

Figure 5.7
The Project window Inspector panel.

HOW TO

Set up an audio track for recording:

1. If the Inspector panel is not visible, click the Show Inspector button in the Project window toolbar, as shown in Figure 5.7.
2. Select the input bus from the track's input routing field.
3. Select the output bus from the track's output routing field.
4. Double-click in the Track Name field and type a new name for the track.
5. Click the Record Enable button if you intend to record new content into this track.

Creating an Instrument Track

As a composer, producer, or audio engineer, if you're not recording or importing audio in a project, chances are you're triggering synths, samplers, or a drum machine through MIDI. In Cubase 4, there are two ways to set up a MIDI track, and which one you choose depends on how you intend to use MIDI in the project.

One quick and easy way is to create an instrument track and assign any installed VST plug-in instrument or configured MIDI device as its MIDI destination.

HOW TO

Add an instrument track:

1. Right-click (PC)/Control-click (Mac) in the Track List area of the Project window and choose Add Instrument Track from the context menu, or select Add Track > Instrument from the Project menu.
2. In the Add Instrument Track dialog box, specify the number of tracks to create. For example, to use two separate instances of the same plug-in, use the small arrows in the track count field to increase the value to 2.

   Each instrument instance creates a track and its corresponding instrument channel in the Mixer, as shown in Figure 5.8.
3. Select the desired instrument as the track's MIDI destination. The list in Figure 5.9 displays the instruments installed on your computer.
4. Click OK. As a result, the instrument tracks are created, the plug-in instruments or external devices are automatically configured to receive any MIDI events being played from or coming through the track, and, finally, audio instrument channels are created in the Mixer panel (refer to Figure 5.8) for the output from the specified instruments.

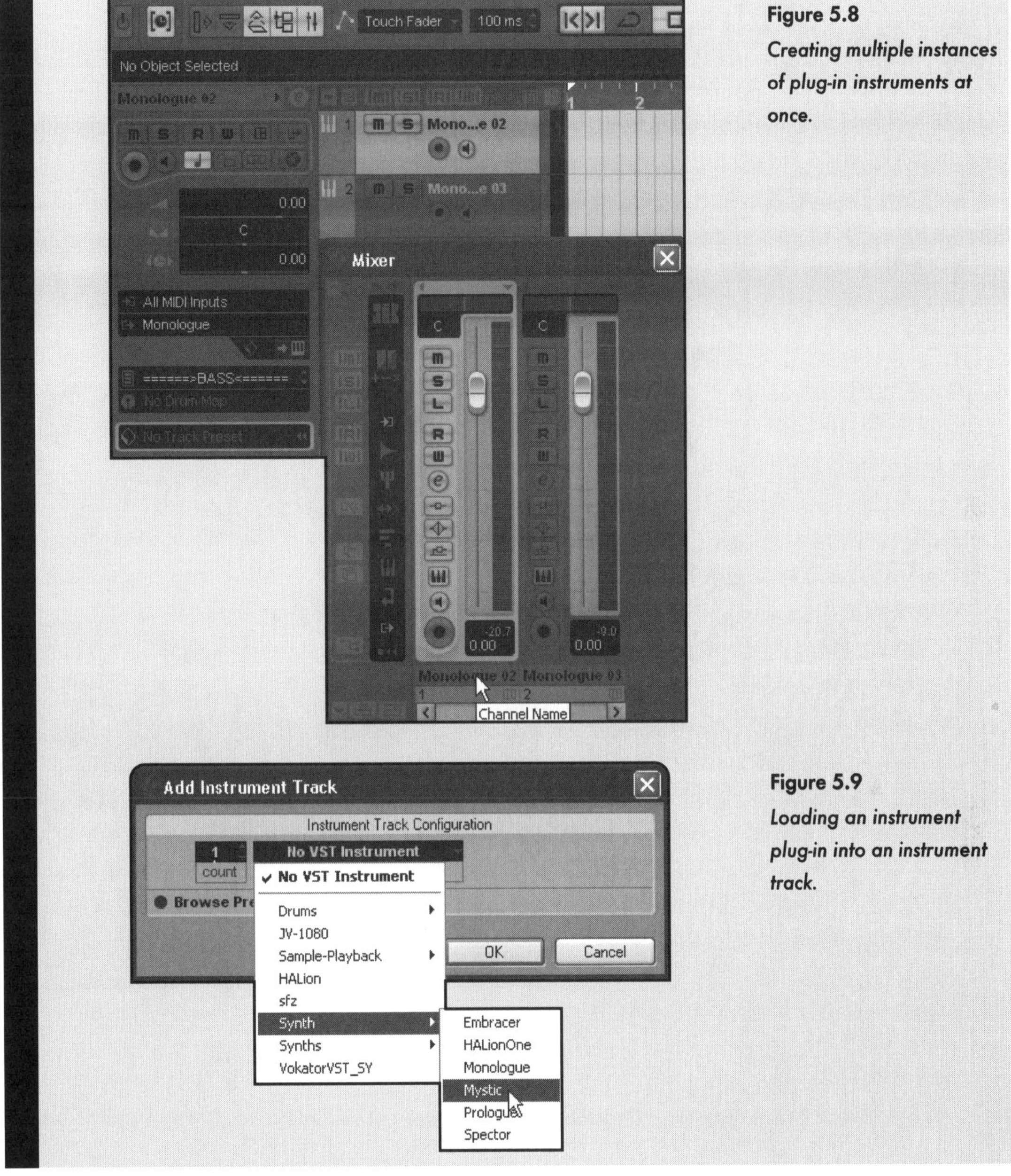

Figure 5.8

Creating multiple instances of plug-in instruments at once.

Figure 5.9

Loading an instrument plug-in into an instrument track.

Creating a MIDI Track

Create additional MIDI tracks to hold different MIDI events that will play through this same device or plug-in. This might be applicable when you need to use several MIDI channels playing through a single external multitimbral instrument, as demonstrated in Figure 5.10, or a single multitimbral plug-in instrument.

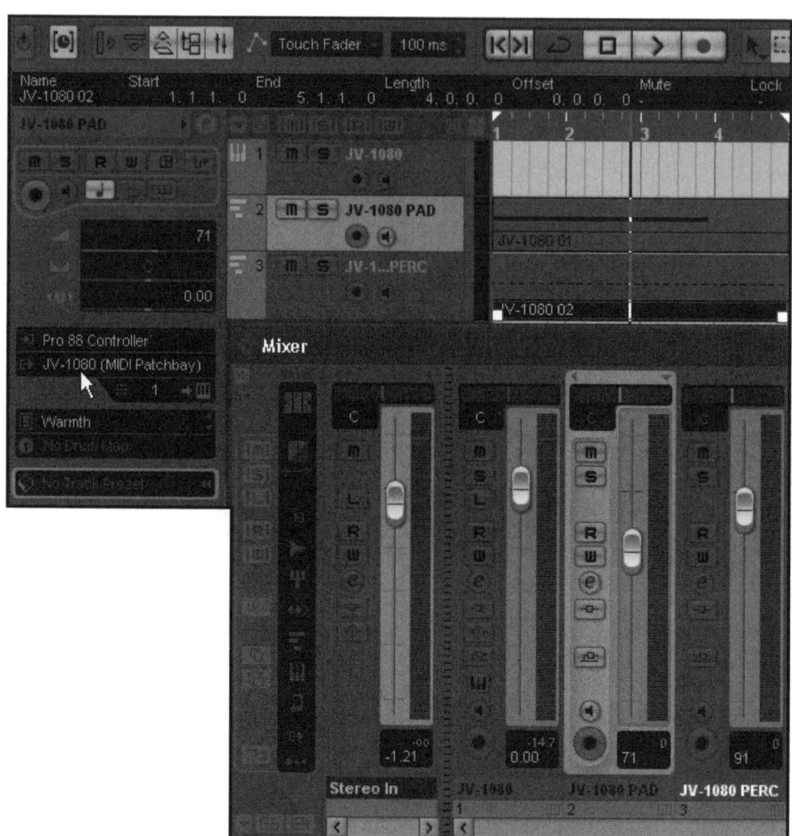

Figure 5.10
Two MIDI tracks playing through one external instrument.

> **HOW TO**
>
> ### Add a MIDI track:
>
> 1. Right-click (PC)/Control-click (Mac) in the Track List area of the Project window and choose Add MIDI Track from the context menu, or select Add Track > MIDI from the Project menu.
> 2. In the Add MIDI Track dialog box, specify the number of tracks to create. For example, to use two separate MIDI channels to separate a synth pad track from a percussion track playing through the same plug-in, increase the track count to 2.
> 3. Click OK.

Setting Up an Instrument Track

MIDI and instrument tracks share a content type: MIDI events. The parameters that can be changed are also quite similar—the input source, the output destination, and the program or patchname associated with the instrument's internal settings. In Chapter 12, "Insert Effects," you'll learn how insert effects can transform the sound of a MIDI instrument.

HOW TO

Set up an instrument track for MIDI recording:

1. Select the MIDI input port connected to your MIDI controller, or leave the MIDI input port set to All MIDI Inputs.
2. Select the MIDI output port, connecting to an external device or VSTi of your choice. The MIDI output determines what will actually generate the audio produced by MIDI events.
3. Configure the Bank and/or Program fields in the MIDI Settings section of the Inspector or in the Track List area, as shown in Figure 5.11. See Chapter 4, "Monitoring Audio," for more on creating the audio hookup to Cubase, and Chapter 9, "Using Instruments," for more on making your instrument plug-ins and external device patchnames available inside a project.

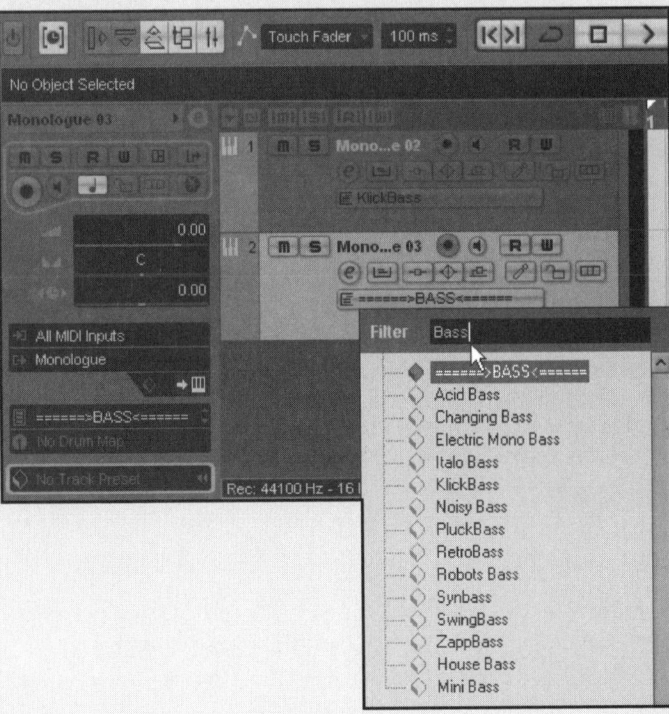

Figure 5.11
Selecting a Monologue preset from the instrument's patch selector.

4. Select the appropriate MIDI channel for the track's MIDI output, if necessary (see Figure 5.12).
5. Double-click in the Track Name field and type a new name for the track.

6. Click the Record Enable button if you intend to record new content into this track.

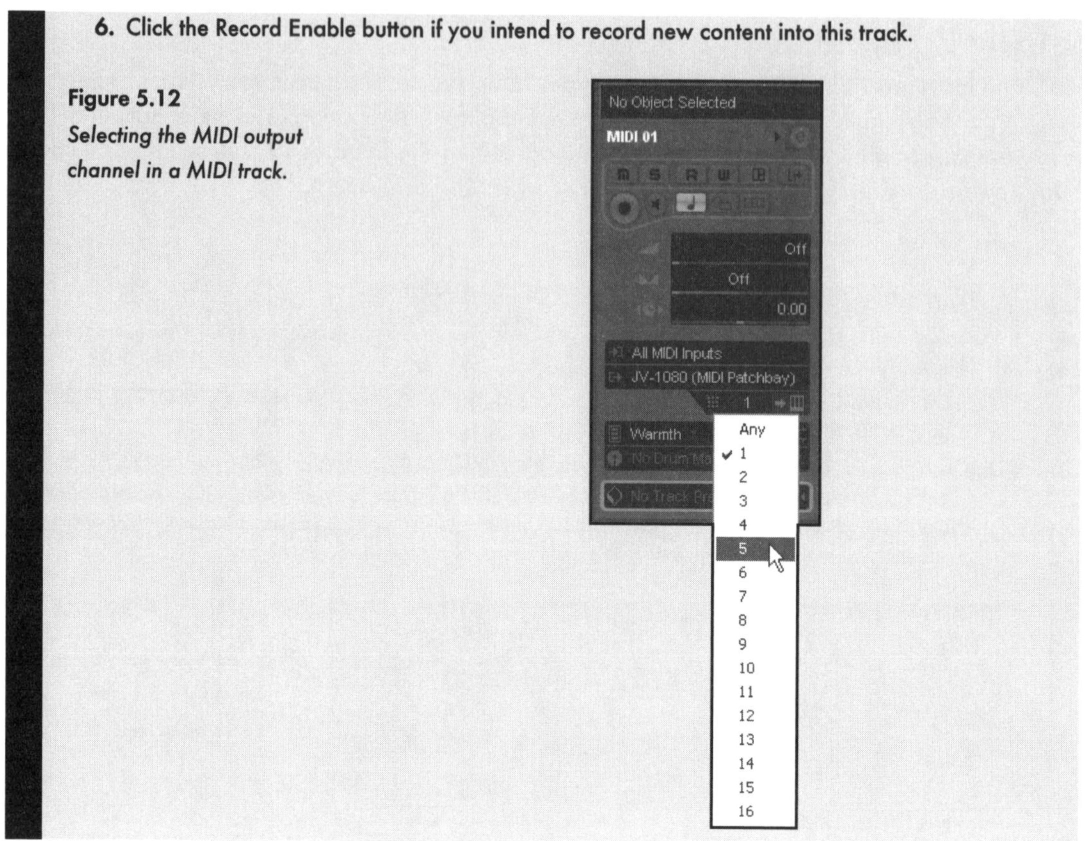

Figure 5.12
Selecting the MIDI output channel in a MIDI track.

II Recording

Control Room Mixer

Cubase 4 provides a new Control Room Mixer panel, which provides additional routing possibilities for users working in a studio with a recording booth and a separate control room. The Control Room Mixer is fully customizable and supports up to four separate studio cue mixes; four separate monitor mixes; six external inputs to route DVDs, DATs, iPods, and so on through your mixer without recording anything; one control room headphone mix; and a talkback channel to communicate instructions to musicians from the control room without having to walk over to the booth or yell your lungs out.

For project studio producers, the Control Room Mixer and its studio connections, combined with multi-I/O audio hardware for use with Cubase, provides a flexible monitoring system without having to use an external mixer.

Creating the studio connections is discussed in Chapter 4, "Monitoring Audio." This chapter discusses some of the applications and benefits associated with the Control Room Mixer panel and its Control Room Overview panel.

Here's a summary of what you will learn in this chapter:

- How the Control Room Mixer settings are represented in the Control Room Overview
- How to configure and monitor external input busses
- How to control room-monitoring options
- How to use the Listen Enable bus functionality
- How to use the control room's talkback functionality
- How to use the Dim button and Use Reference Level button
- How to display the Control Room Mixer extended panel
- How to add inserts to control room busses
- How to use studio sends to create discrete mixes

Project Studio Control Room

Before we begin discussing Control Room features, here are a few starter pointers:

- If you are monitoring through an external mixer, you do not need to turn on the Control Room Mixer (CRM) features. You can disable the Control Room functionalities by clicking on the Disable Control Room button in the Studio tab of the VST Connections window. Settings that are in effect when the CRM is disabled will be reestablished once it is enabled again.
- To avoid any routing confusion when using the Control Room Mixer (CRM), set all output busses to "Not Connected" or set the VST Mixer's main stereo output to act as the main mix on the CRM. You will be controlling what you hear in the control room through the CRM instead, which will provide you with additional monitoring and routing functionalities. Cubase displays the main stereo output bus corresponding to the CRM's main mix with a red speaker icon next to the connection's name in the VST Connections window, as shown in Figure 6.1. Right-click (PC)/Control-click (Mac) in the right column for another bus in the Outputs tab of the VST Connections window, and select the Set <*This Output's Name*> as Main Mix option if you ever need to use that bus as the main mix.

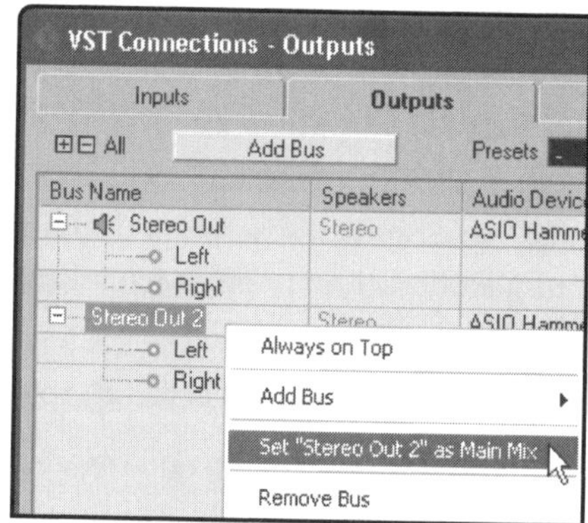

Figure 6.1
Setting the stereo outputs as the main mix.

- Like the Mixer, the CRM adapts itself to the connections created in the VST Connections. If you create a talkback connection, it will be available, but if you don't create one, those features will not be visible, as illustrated in Figure 6.2.
- In Cubase, the same audio ports can be used for different input and output busses, depending on your requirements at a given phase in the project. However, audio inputs and outputs used for studio connections can't be used for anything else. Once a port has been assigned to a studio connection, consider it unavailable. That's why you need an audio hardware

Before Creating a Talkback Connection

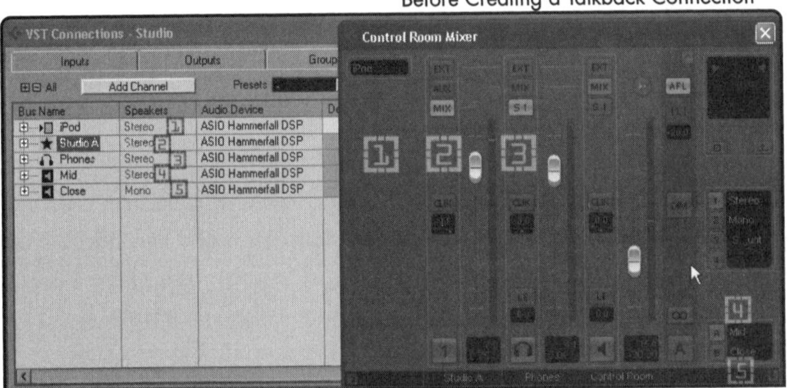

After Creating a Talkback Connection

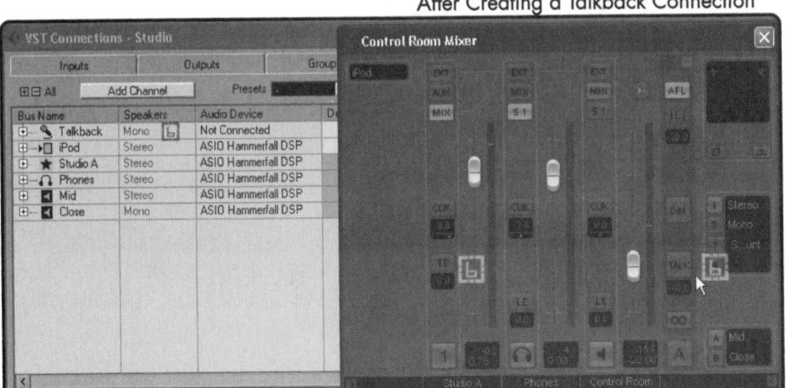

Figure 6.2
The Control Room Mixer with the studio connections, before (top) and after (bottom) creating a talkback connection.

device with multiple inputs and outputs to fully take advantage of the CRM features. There are a few exceptions to this rule. Using the same speakers in a stereo configuration and also in a surround configuration, with the same outputs on the audio hardware assigned to both monitor configurations, is one of those exceptions. Sharing the inputs between an input bus and an external input device is another exception in which using the same ports for both purposes makes sense when creating connections.

Here's a typical project studio example in which the CRM comes in handy. You're recording a guitar and vocal overdub tracks over a stereo mix of a groove a friend has sent on a CD, and you've loaded the audio mix in a track. The guitarist needs to hear this mix and a click track, but the vocalist wants to hear the mix without the click track. The guitar is connected to an external preamp, which feeds an input on the audio interface. The lead singer's microphone is also connected to an external preamp feeding another input.

Because this is a project studio, we'll assume everyone (musicians/engineer/producer) is in the same room, so monitoring is done through headphones during recording, but obviously, you should always make sure to listen to the recording through a monitoring system, not just your headphones. You'll need the following connections:

- Two mono **input busses**—one for the guitar and another for the vocals.
- One **monitor** connection to connect two audio output (stereo) ports on your audio hardware to control room monitors in the studio. If you need to mix for television and use additional nearfield monitors, create additional monitor connections in the Studio page of the VST Connections panel. Click the monitor switch in the Control Room Mixer, as shown in Figure 6.3, to switch between your main monitors and nearfield monitors at any point in time.

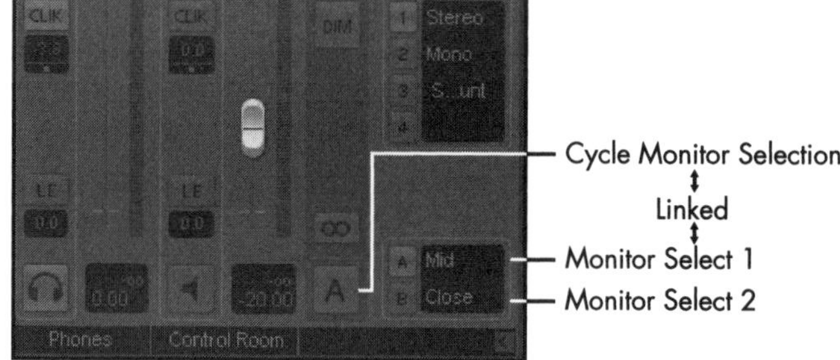

Figure 6.3
The Cycle Monitor Selection button in the Monitor channel of the Control Room Mixer.

- One **headphone** connection for the guitar/producer. The Phones connection is intended for the audio engineer in the control room. To create headphone or cue mixes for musicians in different recording booths, use the studio channels described later.
- One **studio channel** for an independent vocal headphone mixes. (The vocalist doesn't want to hear the click track.)

On the left of Figure 6.4 is the Control Room Overview panel of this setup, while the right side of the figure displays the setup's CRM. Let's look at the Control Room Overview (CRO) from top to bottom and describe what's happening. You can access the CRO through the Devices menu. The CRO displays all the external inputs and studio, monitor, and talkback connections available. When a connection has been created, the CRO displays it in a darker shade, as is the case for the first studio channel, the headphones, and the two monitor connections in Figure 6.4. The channel mixer is summed and sent to the active "studios," which in our setup are used to feed the signal to the singer's headphones. In the CRM, this channel is represented by the first channel on the left, labeled as "Singer HP Mix." The Mix button at the top of this channel also indicates that the signal monitored through this channel comes from the main mix. The Click (Activate Metronome Click) button in the center of the channel enables the metronome click for this

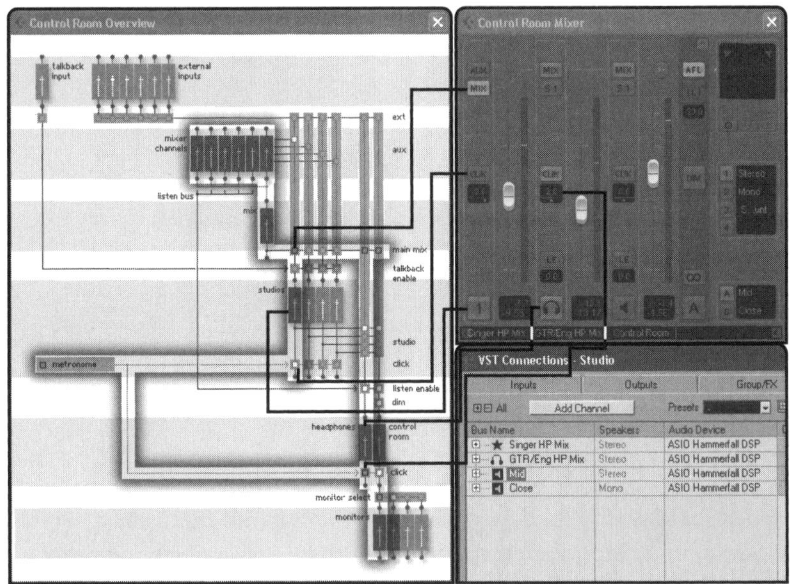

Figure 6.4
Example of a typical project studio Control Room Mixer setup.

channel, but here, it is disabled because the singer does not want to hear the click track. In the CRO, this is represented by the small white square below the active studios channel. Enabling the Click button in this channel or clicking to enable the corresponding small square button (labeled "click") in the CRO where the metronome line meets the studios line will offer the same result.

Moving along to the headphones at the bottom of the CRO display, in the second channel to the left of the CRM (labeled GTR/Eng HP Mix), you can see that it also monitors the main mix, but in this case, the Click button is enabled in both locations (the CRO and the CRM). That's because the guitarist wants to hear the metronome click along with the main mix.

HOW TO

Set up a metronome in the CRM:

1. Enable the Click button in the desired CRM channel.
2. Click on the Click Level display to adjust the volume of the metronome in this channel. As Figure 6.5 shows, a fader will pop up when you change the value.
3. Adjust the metronome's panning.
4. Press C to enable the metronome click in Cubase. The metronome control is also available in the Transport panel.

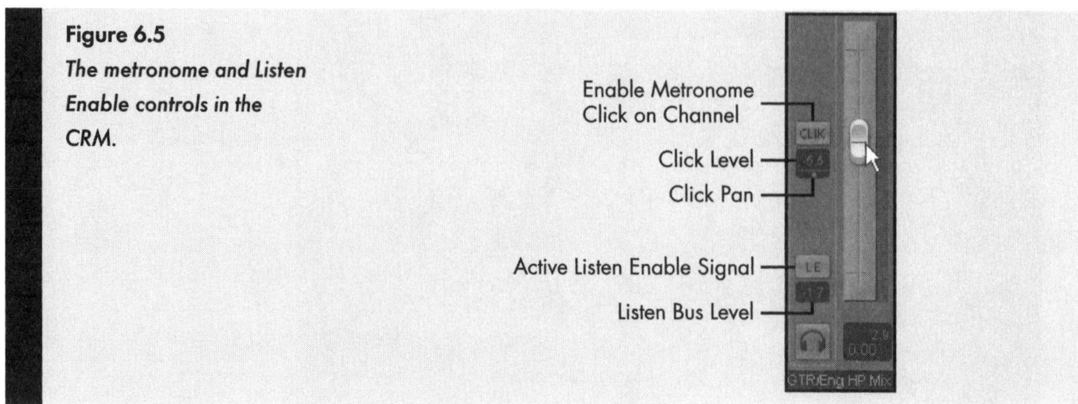

Figure 6.5
The metronome and Listen Enable controls in the CRM.

External Inputs

At the top of each CRM channel, as illustrated in Figure 6.4, is the Input Selector button, which controls the source of the audio signal entering each channel. When an external input is created, an additional EXT button shows up at the top. If more than one external input is created, you can click on the Show Left Strip button to expand the CRM's left strip, which reveals an external input selection, as shown in Figure 6.6.

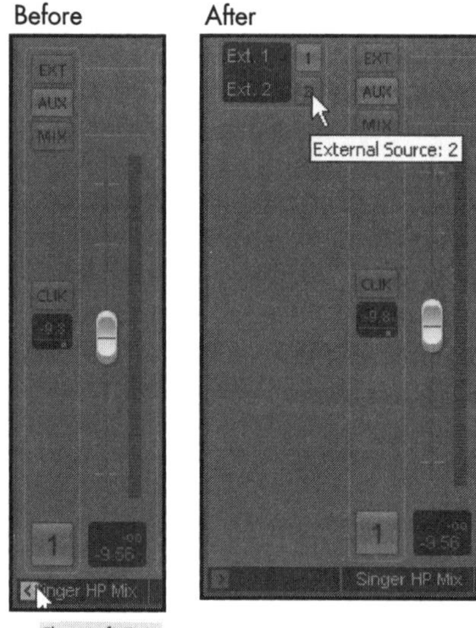

Figure 6.6
Expanding the left strip in the CRM.

Monitoring Options

There is also a similar strip on the right of the CRM that offers a number of monitoring options, which vary depending on the studio connections you have created (from top to bottom and left to right in Figure 6.7):

- Click on any speaker to mute all other speakers. (In a 5.1 surround configuration, the plus sign in the center allows you to solo the LFE channel.)
- Click on Cancel Speaker Solo to unmute all channels at once. There are also a number of additional solo functions depending on the active monitoring setup.
- Click any down-mix preset buttons to automatically switch between different down-mix options. A down-mix option lets you hear different mixes through the same monitors. For example, clicking on a stereo mix (the number 2 button in Figure 6.7) while monitoring in surround lets you hear how your surround mix will translate to stereo without having to switch monitors. This is very convenient when you are working with surround setups to verify whether the mix sounds as good in a stereo CD-type mix or a mono AM radio mix, for example. It's still a good precaution to take to avoid phase-shifting issues once the mix is down mixed. Clicking on the Down Mix preset button opens the settings panel for the MixConvert plug-in, where you can change the down-mix configuration if necessary.
- The monitor configuration reflects the selected down-mix preset mix configuration. Clicking on this button also changes the selected down-mix preset.
- The monitor selection lets you switch between the different speaker configurations (Monitor Connections) you have created. In Figure 6.7, there are three monitoring setups. Changing monitors lets you compare a mix as it sounds in mid-field monitors followed by nearfield monitors, for example. Once again, this is useful in multi-monitoring setups typical in mid to large studio facilities.
- The Cycle Monitor button displays which set of monitors is selected and can be used to cycle through them as well.

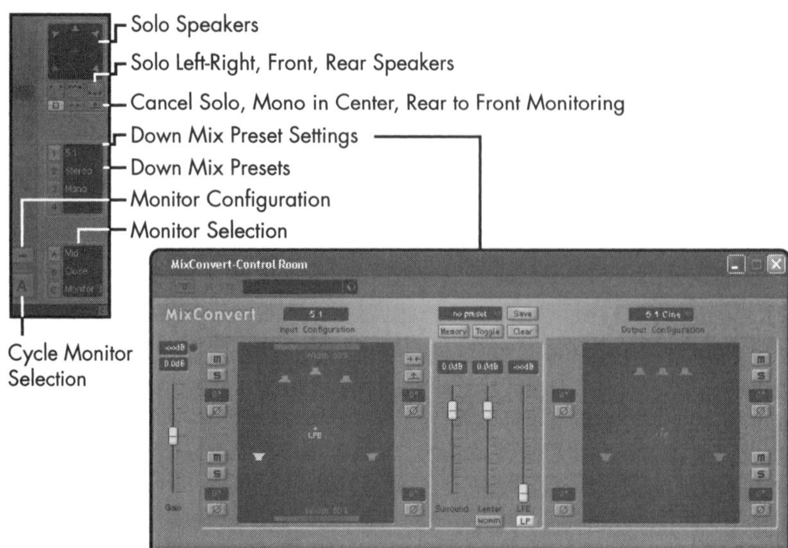

Figure 6.7
The monitoring options of the CRM.

Listen Enable Bus

The CRM's Listen mode lets you send the signal of all audio-related mixer channels that have their Listen button enabled to the control room monitors without interrupting the signal flow, overriding the normal signal being monitored. On many hardware consoles, this is also called the *PFL bus* or the *Pre Fader Listen bus,* because the levels that will be heard are unaffected by that channel's main volume fader. As you can see in Figure 6.4, the Listen bus bypasses the mixer's Volume Level control, the studio monitoring options, and the metronome options. When enabled, the signal is routed to this bus directly after the signal enters the channel, before any phase, trim, inserts, EQ, volume, or pan controls.

HOW TO

Use the Listen bus:

1. In the Mixer panel, enable the channels you want to include in the Listen bus, as displayed on the left in Figure 6.8. Note that you can disable all the listen-enabled channels by clicking the Deactivate All Listen button in the Mixer's Common panel, which is also reproduced in the CRM. In fact, this button appears lit whenever at least one channel is listen-enabled in the project.

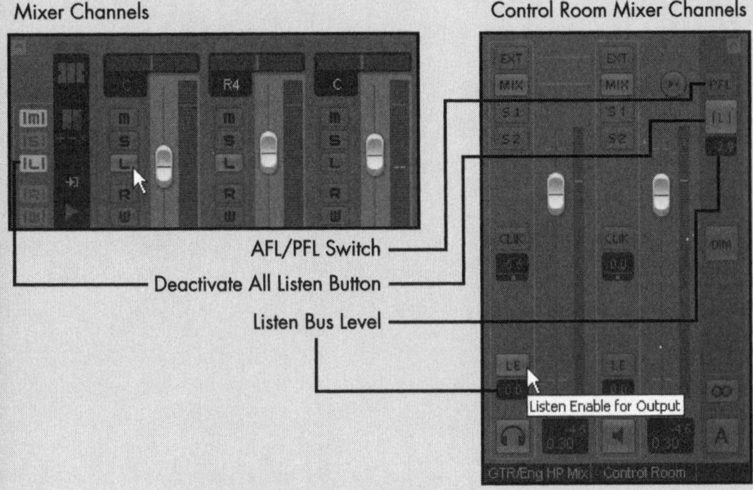

Figure 6.8
The Listen Enable functionality in the Mixer (left) and CRM (right).

2. In the CRM, click on the Listen Enable button found in any of the monitor channels or in the headphones channels. From this point on, all channels that have their Listen button enabled will be summed with the rest of the signal on the listen-enabled bus.
3. To switch the listen-enabled channels to After Fader Listen (AFL), click on the PFL button to enable the AFL mode. This button toggles between both modes.
4. To change the level of the summed LE bus, click on the Listen bus level value, and a fader will pop up.

Talkback Options

The CRM's Talkback mono connection provides a way to communicate with musicians in a different room through a studio connection, by connecting a microphone to one of the input ports on your audio hardware and creating a talkback connection in the VST Connections panel. Talkback options are displayed in the CRM only when a talkback channel has been created in the Studio tab of the VST Connections panel.

HOW TO

Use the Talkback functions:

1. Enable the Talkback button on each studio connection to which you want the talkback to be distributed. In Figure 6.9, the audio from the dedicated talkback microphone will be distributed to the Studio 2, but not to the Studio 1 connection.
2. Adjust the talkback level for each enabled studio connection.
3. Activate talkback functionality by pressing the Talk button.
4. Adjust the overall talkback level being sent to all studios.

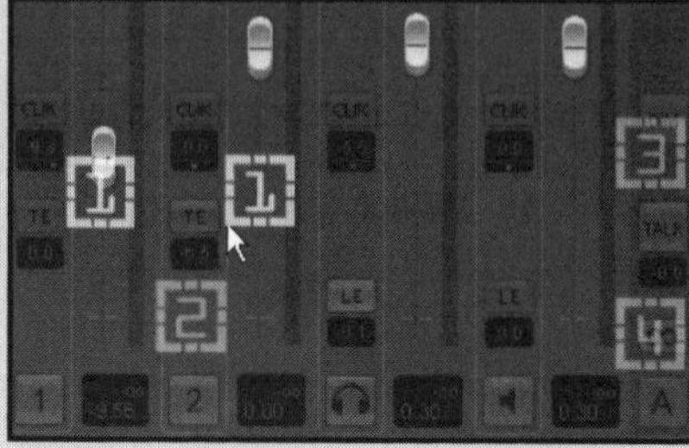

Figure 6.9
Enable the Talkback button on each desired studio connection.

Switching between Talkback Modes

The Talkback button has two modes. By default, clicking on the Talk button enables the talkback function, and clicking on it again disables it. This is called the *Latch mode*. You can also set the Talkback button to only be active when the button is pressed. In other words, the button doesn't latch; it simply switches to Talkback mode whenever you need it. Double-click once on the Talk button to toggle between the two modes. Manually enabling the Talk button is very convenient during a recording session when you just want to interject comments and you don't want to leave the talkback on by mistake.

Dim and Reference Levels

The Dim button, displayed in Figure 6.10, lets you quickly reduce the control room level by 30 dB without having to change the fader's position, which makes it very convenient when the producer wants to comment on a recording or mixing pass, and you want to make sure you heard the comments properly. Click the Dim button again to return the control room level to where it was. You can change the actual amount of reduction applied by the Dim button in the Preferences dialog box, on the Control Room page.

The reference level lets you set the control room monitoring level to a calibrated mix, essential to most film-dubbing stages. By default, this value is set to –20 dB, but you can change this value by setting the Control Room fader to a new level and holding down the Alt (PC)/Option (Mac) key when clicking on the Reference Level button. When the reference level is used, the button is lit.

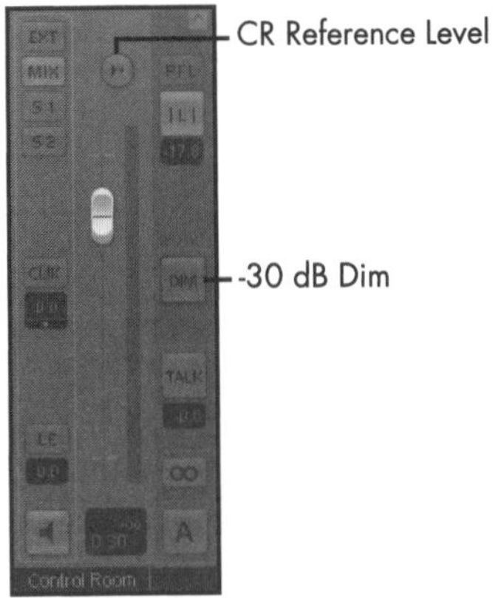

Figure 6.10
The Dim and Reference Level buttons.

Dim(d)CRM Extended View

You can add insert effects to all channels found in the CRM as well as display output level metering through the CRM's extended view. Click the Show Extended View button, as displayed in Figure 6.11, to display this panel. The Show Meters button toggles the display between inserts and output level meters.

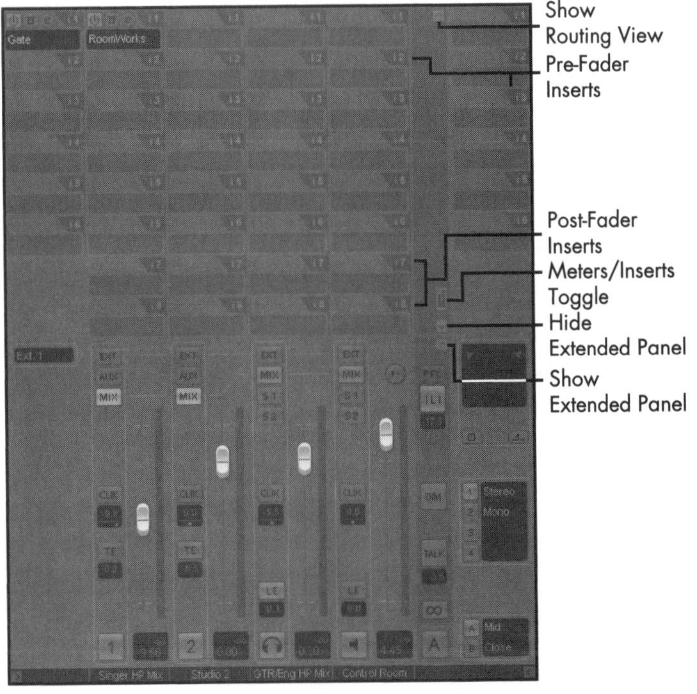

Figure 6.11
The CRM's extended panel.

As you can see, all channels can have up to six pre-fader inserts and, with the exception of external inserts and monitors, they also can have two additional post-fader inserts (numbers 7 and 8).

By default, the external input inserts are displayed, but you also can add inserts to the talkback connection. To do so, simply enable the Talk button. Cubase displays the talkback inserts where the external input inserts are currently displayed in Figure 6.11. The talkback connection can have up to eight inserts.

You will find more on using insert effects in Chapter 12, but understand that you can use dynamic inserts, such as a gate or compressor, on the talkback connection, for example, to protect your performers' ears or to reduce the noise level leaking when talkback is enabled, or to add some reverb to the mix sent to the singer in the example described at the beginning of this chapter.

Studio Sends

Studio sends are intended as discrete mixes that can be used to send a customized headphone mix through a studio connection. By creating a mix using studio sends, you can make sure the bass player hears the kick drum well without forcing the singer or pianist to hear the same mix. Like many functionalities available in the CRM, the number of studio sends available is tied to the number of studio connections you created, so you can have up to four studio send mixes or four discrete headphone mixes. The way studio sends work is very similar to the way FX channels work. However, FX channels are better suited to process audio being sent from a number of audio or instrument channels (with a reverb or delay send effect on one of their inserts, for example) and can be used outside the CRM. You'll find more on FX channel tracks in Chapter 32, "FX Channel Tracks."

HOW TO

Set up a discrete mix using studio sends:

1. In the Mixer panel (F3), display the extended panel.
2. In the extended panel's common area, click on the Show Studio Sends button. The studio sends controls will appear as displayed in Figure 6.12. In this example, only the first two studio sends are available, while the last two are grayed out.
3. Enable the studio sends for each channel you want to include in the mix.
4. Set the amount of signal sent from the channel to the studio connection by dragging the horizontal line displayed under the level value. You also can Alt-click (PC)/Option-click (Mac) on the value to use the pop-up fader.
5. Adjust the panning of the signal in the mix. As with the volume level, the pan value only affects the studio send mix.
6. By default, studio sends are set to Post-Fader, but to change the studio send level setting to Pre-Fader (so that its level will not be affected by changes to the channel's main volume fader), enable the option, as is the case in the Bass channel (Channel #4) of Figure 6.12.

In this example, the studio 1 sends are used to create a mix for the singer's headphones, so all channels have been enabled. Adjusting the level from each track creates an independent mix for this singer's headphones.

7. In the CRM, set the studio connection's source to AUX. From this point on, all signals being sent to studio sends 1 will be heard through the studio 1 connection. (In Figure 6.12, this connection is labeled Singer HP Mix.)

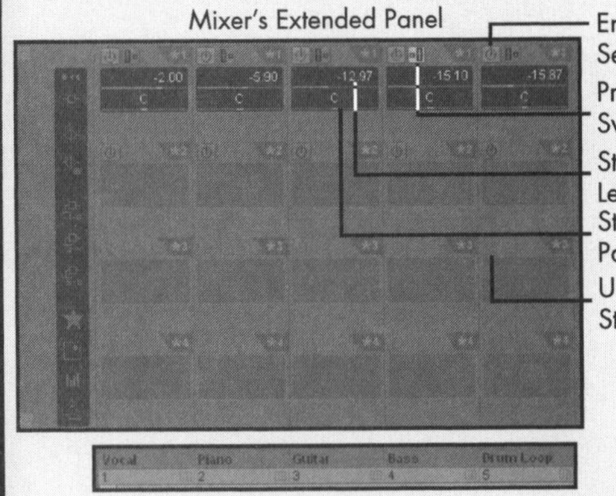

Figure 6.12
The Mixer's extended panel, displaying the studio sends setting.

Pop-Up Fader in the Transport Panel

To the extreme right of the Transport panel is a small fader, which mirrors the stereo output bus fader. Adjusting the level of this fader affects the audio level the same way as if you were to open the Mixer panel and adjust the stereo output bus fader. You should also see this control move if you have recorded any automation on this particular bus. When you click on this audio level control in the Transport, a larger fader will pop up to help you control the level (see Figure 6.13).

Figure 6.13
Audio-level control fader on the Transport panel.

7 SoundFrame

SoundFrame is a new resource management system built around the MediaBay, with the SoundFrame Browser and the Loop Browser being two close relatives of the MediaBay. SoundFrame provides a way to access all sorts of media files, such as track presets that set up your track with the best starting point to quickly get it sounding right. SoundFrame helps you manage everything from samples on a media drive to loops in your project, from reverb and instrument plug-in presets to search functionalities that let you find just the right drum groove to fit the project. Included in the SoundFrame is a tagging system that lets you associate attributes and categories with custom settings and presets. Combined with the powerful filtering options of SoundFrame, these tags can definitely help you find a needle in a haystack. Though the MediaBay, SoundFrame Browser, and Loop Browser all serve specific purposes for specific types of media, their functions are the same and their goals are common—to offer quick access to the right resources.

There are many points of access to SoundFrame tools, and most of them can be accessed when you are creating tracks or adding media content to a project, or by clicking on the SoundFrame logo displayed in Figure 7.1. Another common place for all things SoundFrame is the Media menu, where all the media-related windows can be accessed.

Figure 7.1
The SoundFrame logo.

Here's a summary of what you will learn in this chapter:

- How to use the MediaBay's browser to locate and manage folders containing media
- How to use the filtering options in the MediaBay's Viewer area
- How to use the Scope to preview media before importing it in a project

- How to update and populate media using tags or attributes
- How to customize the MediaBay, SoundFrame Browser, and Loop Browser to fit your needs
- How to add an instrument track to a project and preview presets before loading one in a project
- How to load and save VST presets
- How to load and save track presets
- How VST3-compatible plug-ins are different from other VST-compatible plug-ins

Shortcuts to Media

The easiest way to access the Media Browsers located under the Media menu is by using their key commands:

- F5: MediaBay
- F6: Loop Browser
- F7: SoundFrame Browser
- Ctrl+P (PC) / ⌘+P (Mac): Pool
- Ctrl+B (PC) / ⌘+B (Mac): Browser

Pressing any of these key commands will show or hide the corresponding window.

MediaBay

The MediaBay window (F5) represents the core of the Cubase SoundFrame system. The MediaBay holds four main areas: the Browser (1), the Viewer (2), the Tag editor (3), and the Scope (4), as illustrated in Figure 7.2.

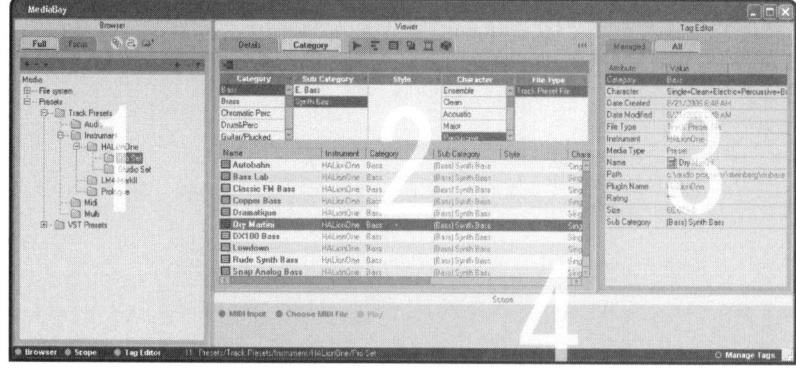

Figure 7.2
The MediaBay window areas.

Browser

The Browser lets you peruse folders where a number of resources can be stored for use in the current project. Its structure and functions are similar to other folder-browsing applications, such as Finder on a Mac or Explorer on Windows.

There are a few differences, however. For example, this Browser scans only for content that can be used in a project—in other words, compatible formats. These formats include a number of audio and MIDI file formats, as well as track presets (.trackpreset files), VST presets (.vstpreset files), Nuendo or Cubase project files, as well as video files such as QuickTime or MPEG. As the MediaBay scans the content of your computer, the colors of the scanned folders change from yellow when the folder hasn't been scanned, to red when the folder is currently being scanned, to a light grayish-blue, indicating the scan has been completed for that folder. Notice the different tints in Figure 7.3, between the Percussion Loops, Wood, and Samples folders in this tree. The status bar at the bottom of the window will display the folder currently being scanned and the number of compatible files available at this location. Selecting a new folder triggers the scan of this folder and all of its subfolders, until eventually all folders have been scanned. Scanning folders makes it possible to display relevant information inside them and index it properly, should there be any information.

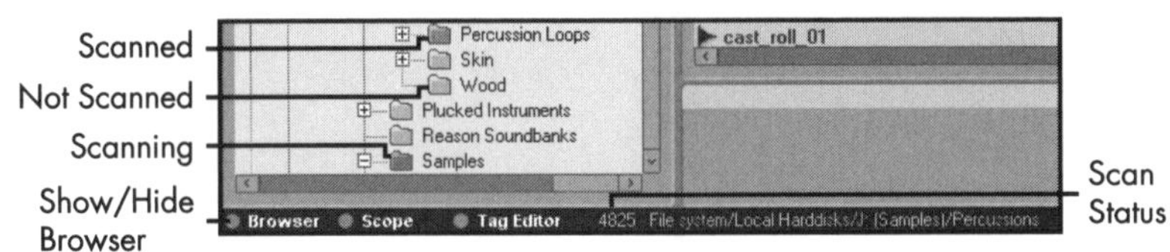

Figure 7.3
The Browser's scan process.

By default, Cubase automatically scans the selected folder for changes. Although this ensures the content is being displayed properly, the scan can take a bit of time when a folder contains a large collection of content, such as samples or loops. If you don't change the content of these folders on a regular basis, disabling the "Automatically Check Selected Folders for Changes" option by pressing its button at the top of the browser (see Figure 7.4) is recommended. You can hide the Browser area at any time from the bottom-left corner of the MediaBay window, as displayed in Figure 7.3.

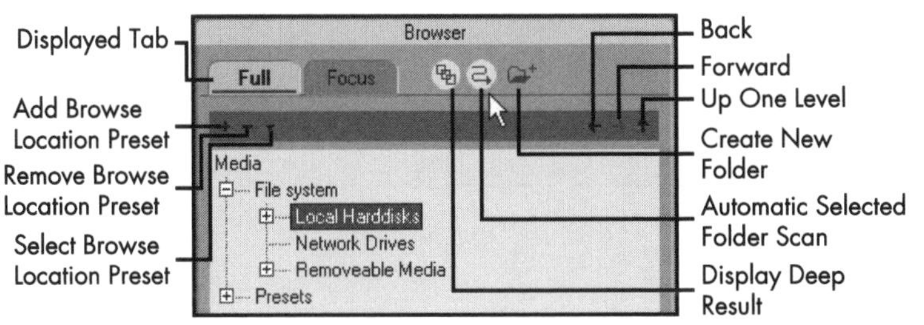

Figure 7.4
Browser navigational functionalities.

Use the Full or Focus tabs in the Browser to toggle the view between a full folder structure or a view focused only on the selected folder and its subfolder structure. The selected tab always appears in bold, and a bar appears across the tab (see the Full tab in Figure 7.4). Furthermore, you can recall specific locations by clicking on the Add Browse Location Preset button. Once a location is saved, it can be recalled from the Select Browse Location Preset drop-down menu. This offers a convenient way to create a list of commonly accessed locations. The browser also provides some Internet-like navigational features with the Back, Forward, or Up to Container Folder buttons. Use the Create New Folder button to open the Select Directory dialog box, where you can browse your computer's folder structure and create a new folder anywhere you want. Finally, when the Deep Result button is enabled, Cubase displays both the content of the selected folder and all of its subfolders in the Viewer area on the right (see the bottom part of Figure 7.5). When this button is disabled, the selected folder's subfolders (if any) and current content are displayed (see the top part of Figure 7.5).

Figure 7.5
Deep Results disabled (top) and enabled (bottom).

Deep Result Disabled: Viewer Displays Subfolders

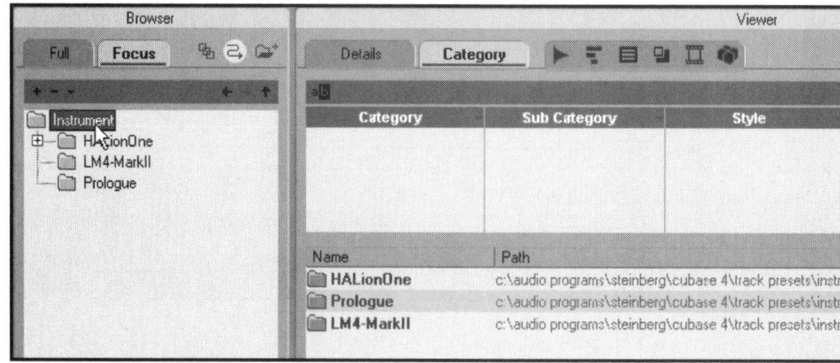

Deep Result Enabled: Viewer Displays Compatible Media Content Inside Subfolders

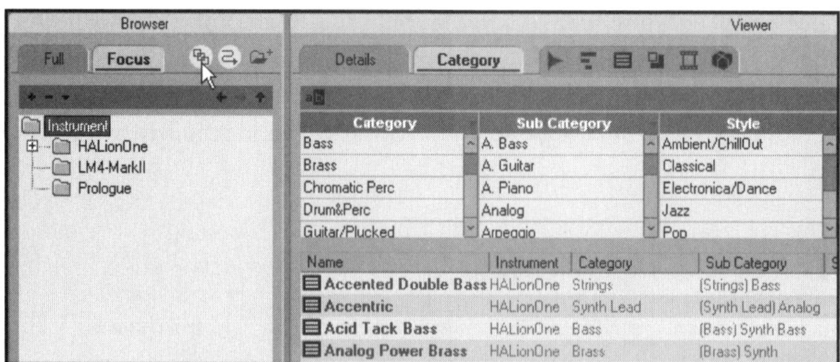

Viewer

The Viewer area of the MediaBay displays the content inside the selected folder in the Browser area, along with a number of filter and search functionalities that let you isolate the media you're looking for. Selecting the Details tab at the top-left of this area lets you create a detailed search string for various file attributes.

HOW TO

Perform a detail search in the MediaBay:

1. Click the Details tab in the Viewer area.
2. Select the attribute you want to isolate in your search from the Attributes drop-down menu, as shown in Figure 7.6. In this example, Cubase will look in the Name and Instrument attributes. Note that a list of frequently used attributes is moved to the top of the list for convenience.

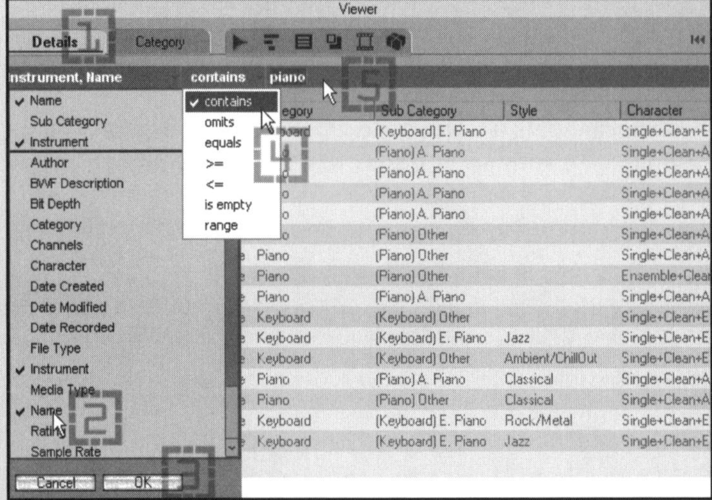

Figure 7.6
The Viewer's detailed search functionality.

3. Click OK when you are finished.
4. Select a condition from the next drop-down menu to the right. In this example, the search result will only display instruments and names that contain specific information.
5. The specific information should be typed into the field to the right of the Condition drop-down menu. In this example, the word "piano" is entered.

As a result, the Viewer displays only the names of instruments that contain the word *piano* in them.

Selecting the Category tab offers a different approach; this time, the search focuses on categories associated with the content. These categories are essentially tags or keywords associated with the SoundFrame-compatible media formats described earlier in this chapter. By default, Cubase displays five columns at the top: Category, Sub-Category, Style, Character, and File Type. As with the Details view, the content of the selected folder appears below these five columns, although here, selecting an entry in one of the columns hides any content that doesn't have this property. In Figure 7.7, the selected category is Bass. As a result, all bass sub-categories are displayed in the Sub-Category column, and only bass sounds are displayed. That's because the Category and Sub-Category columns are linked together. In this same figure, the filtering is pushed even further with the "E. Bass" sub-category selected, the "Rock/Metal" Style, and the "Clean" Character. In other words, all the media entries displayed correspond to these characteristics: clean rock/metal electric bass. When you are looking for a bass sound, this makes it much easier. The status bar at the bottom even shows you how many files are currently available in this selected folder. These columns act as an "And" condition in a query, and multiple selections in the same column act as an "Or" condition. For example, if the Brass and Bass categories were selected, the result would show all files in the selected folder with either a bass or a brass category associated with them. When you select the E. Bass sub-category, the query still displays the brass sub-categories, but since it's unlikely a file would have both Brass *and* E. Bass values, you end up with just electric bass-related files.

The area just above the filter column headers allows you to type a value. In Figure 7.7, the word "bass" narrows the search down to nine instrument presets with the word *bass* in the name.

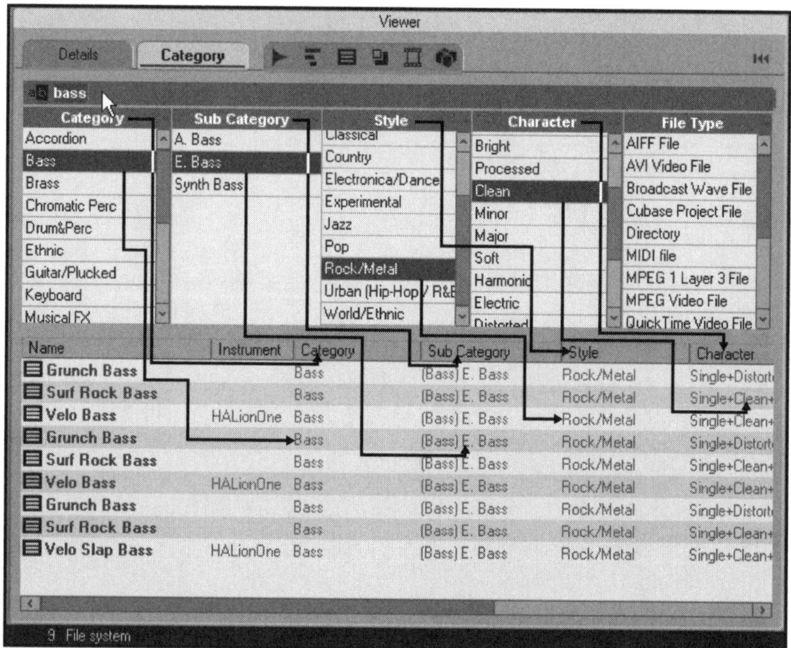

Figure 7.7

The Category filter options in the MediaBay's Viewer area.

Next to the Details and Category tabs in the Viewer area are six additional filter buttons representing, from left to right, audio files, MIDI, instrument presets, VST plug-in presets, video files, and Cubase or Nuendo project files. These icons match those displayed to the left of the file's name under the Name column in the Viewer, as seen in Figure 7.8. Clicking on one of these icons hides all other types of files from the media viewer.

No Filtering Applied

Track Preset Filtering Applied

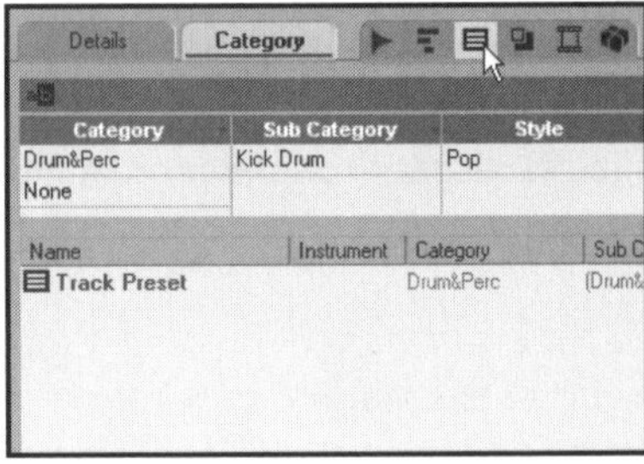

Figure 7.8
Media file types supported by SoundFrame: not filtered (left) and filtered to display only track presets (right).

Scope

The Scope section of the MediaBay window provides a way to preview selected audio or MIDI media and displays the options relevant to this media. Found under the Viewer area when the Scope radio button is selected, it displays a number of Transport controls and the preview level in the top part when an audio medium is selected, as represented in the top portion of Figure 7.9. Check the Auto Play button when searching for loops and media files to automatically play the selected audio. To hear the audio playing at the project's tempo, enable the Play in Project Context button next to it. When a MIDI file is selected, the Scope section of this window displays a number

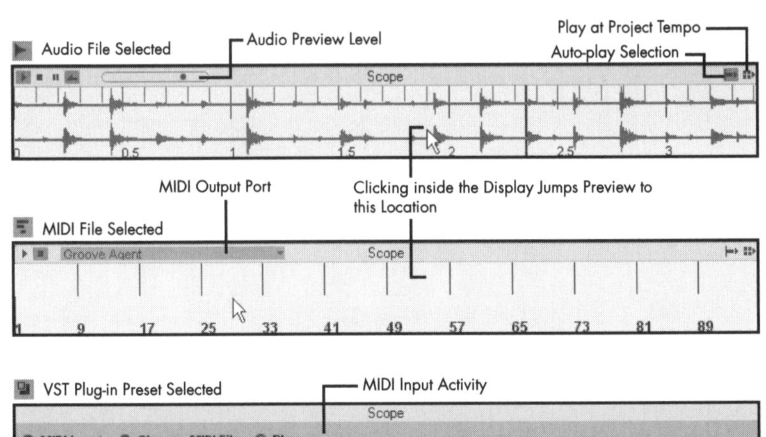

Figure 7.9
The Scope section of the MediaBay window.

of bars and a MIDI output port through which sounds are played. If you're looking for a VST plug-in preset, such as an instrument patch, you can specify how Cubase should preview these presets. Two choices are available: Either you enable the MIDI input, which sends MIDI events you play on a MIDI controller to the instrument associated with the preset so that you can hear the sound it produces, or you load a MIDI file into the MediaBay and press Play to trigger this file. In the latter case, Cubase plays the MIDI file in question through the selected VST plug-in using the selected preset settings.

The Scope section does not support previewing of video, track preset, or project files, but clicking inside the display does make it possible to jump to any point in the file when previewing content. To hide the Scope section, click its display radio button in the bottom-left of the MediaBay's status bar.

Tag Editor

The Tag editor area at the right of the MediaBay window offers two views: Managed and All. Both of these views display attributes associated with the currently selected media in the Viewer area of the MediaBay. In other words, tags are attributes that are inherited from the file itself, such as the bit depth, channel configuration, or sampling rate of an audio file, while user tags are attributes such as category, sub-category, style, and character that can be added to the file in order to be used in the Viewer's filtering functionality. Double-clicking inside a tag in the Value column (see the right column in Figure 7.10), such as the tempo or name of an audio file, allows you to enter new values for these attributes.

Figure 7.10
The Tag editor area.

Manage Tags

When you start working with the MediaBay or any other SoundFrame-related window, most of the tags displayed for category, sub-category, style, or character information will be from content included with your Cubase 4 installation disk, since most of the existing content on your system won't contain any of these tags yet. To add new custom tags or to make tags visible in specific areas of the MediaBay, you need to access the Manage Tags dialog box.

The Manage Tags dialog box displays tags listed alphabetically and three columns with check boxes, representing different MediaBay areas described earlier in this chapter. Tags can be text fields that contain words, numeric values with or without decimals, or yes/no values. This is represented in the Type and Precision columns. Selecting a media type at the top of the dialog box lets you manage tags for this type only. The plus and minus buttons (see the top of Figure 7.11) allow you to add or remove the selected tag from the list below, while the Restore button will reset the default tag properties.

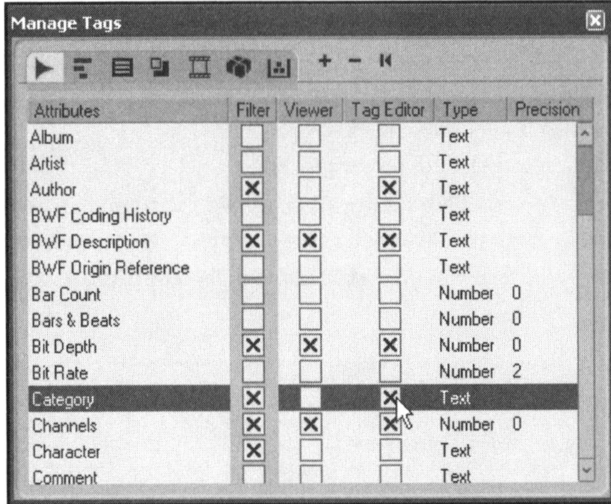

Figure 7.11
Managing tags.

> **HOW TO**
>
> **Display/hide tags in the Viewer (filter) or Tag editor:**
>
> 1. Click on the Manage Tags button in the bottom-right corner of the MediaBay window.
> 2. Select the type of media at the top of the dialog box.
> 3. Use the scroll bar on the right to locate the desired tag. Tags are listed alphabetically.
> 4. Add a check mark in the column corresponding to the area where you want to make the tag visible. For example, to make categories and sub-categories available in the Tag editor area, click in that column to the right of these tags, as shown in Figure 7.11.

HOW TO

Create a custom tag:

1. In the Manage Tags dialog box, click on the Add User Tag button.
2. In the Add User Tag dialog box displayed in Figure 7.12, type a name for the tag you want to add.
3. Select the appropriate tag type from the drop-down menu.
4. Click OK.

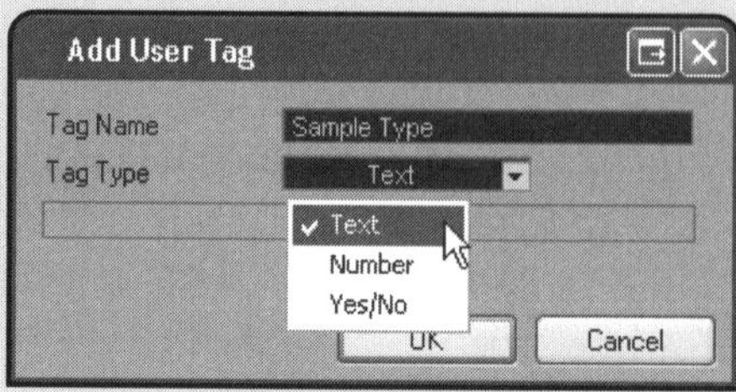

Figure 7.12
The Add User Tag dialog box.

HOW TO

Associate tags to audio and MIDI files:

1. Make sure the tag you want to associate with the media file type is visible in the Tag editor by checking its box in the Manage Tags dialog box, as described earlier.
2. Make sure the Tag editor is visible and select the Managed tab.
3. Select the media file in the viewer. You can Shift-click multiple contiguous files at once or Ctrl-click (PC) /-click (Mac) non-contiguous files to associate the same tags with all the selected files.
4. In the Tag editor area, select the value you want to associate with the selection, as shown in Figure 7.13.

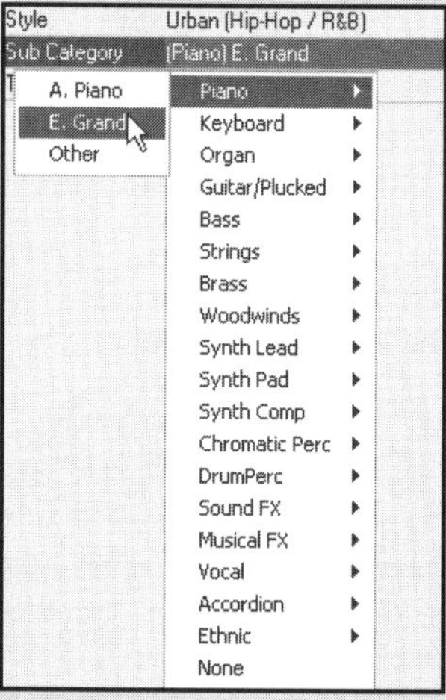

Figure 7.13
Associating sub-categories with custom media files.

5. Repeat this for each tag attribute you want to add to a file.

Sometimes, finding all the drum loops or piano sounds is not precise enough. That's when associating sound characteristics with media files, especially when dealing with large collections of samples, can be quite helpful. Sound characteristics are visible through the Character filter in the Viewer area or in the Tag editor if this tag has been made visible for the selected type of media. Sound characteristics can tell you whether the sample is part of an ensemble or is a solo instrument. They can also tell you whether the sample has been processed, whether it's an acoustic or electric instrument, whether the chord played is major or minor, and so on. It might take a while to get through your entire collection and add these values to your audio and MIDI files, but it will be worth the effort once you can quickly locate just the right sound and characteristic later.

HOW TO

Associate sound characteristics with media files:

1. Make sure the Character tag is visible in the Tag editor by checking its box in the Manage Tags dialog box, as described earlier.
2. Make sure the Tag editor is visible, and select the Managed tab.
3. In the Viewer, select the media file you want to associate with character values.
4. Double-click in the Character Value column to display the Edit Character dialog box, as shown in Figure 7.14.

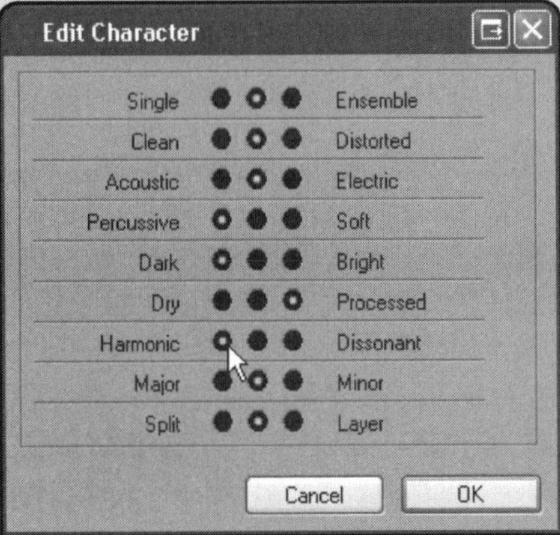

Figure 7.14
The Edit Character dialog box.

5. By default, all values are set in the center. To add a characteristic corresponding to the selection, click next to the value that applies to add that characteristic to the file. Characteristics are organized in pairs, and you can only have one of the two paired characteristics associated with a media file. For example, you can't have a sample or an instrument that is both dark and bright. But you can have a dark harmonic processed percussive instrument, as displayed in Figure 7.14.
6. Click OK when you are finished.

Customizing the MediaBay

All of the MediaBay sections can be customized. You can hide or display the Browser, Scope, or Tag editor sections by using the buttons found in the bottom-left portion of this window. The same overall functionalities can be found in the Loop Browser and SoundFrame Browser, allowing you to set up each of these windows to fit your needs and working habits. You can also resize each section of the window by dragging the divider lines, as illustrated in Figure 7.15, and you can change the order in which the tags (attributes) are displayed in the Viewer area by dragging the column headers into a different order, as illustrated in Figure 7.16.

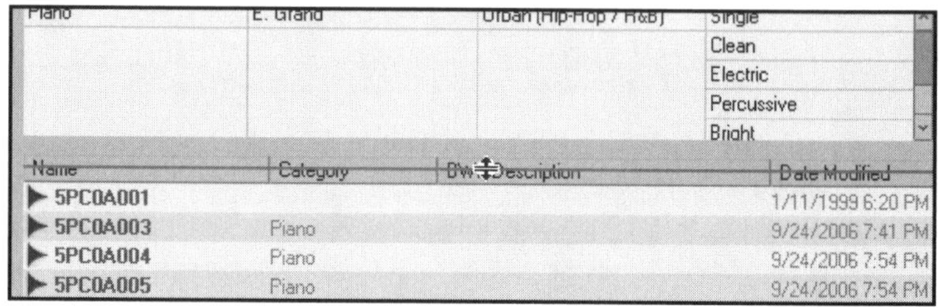

Figure 7.15
Resizing sections in the MediaBay.

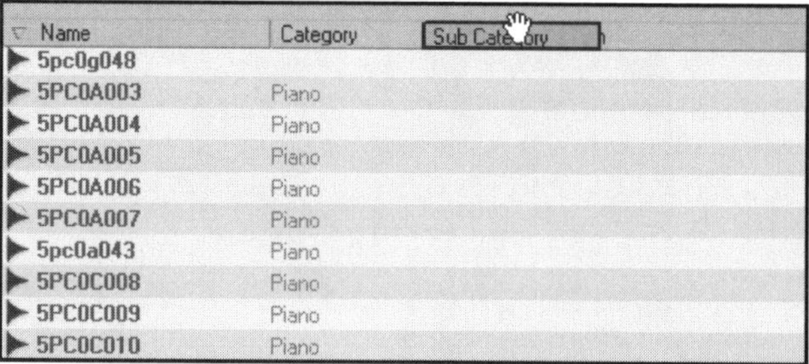

Figure 7.16
Changing the order of columns in the Viewer area of the MediaBay.

You can also customize which tags (attributes) can be filtered in the top of the Viewer area by selecting another value from any of the drop-down menus, as illustrated in Figure 7.17. This is very convenient when you start adding your own custom tags and you want to use them to find something.

Instrument Tracks

Instrument tracks provide a quick and convenient way to combine both the creative flexibility that MIDI events provide and the power that VST instrument plug-ins offer. You will learn more about setting up VST instruments and using external MIDI devices in instrument or MIDI tracks in Chapter 9, "Using Instruments," but for now, we'll look at how some of the SoundFrame features discussed previously in this chapter apply to instrument tracks.

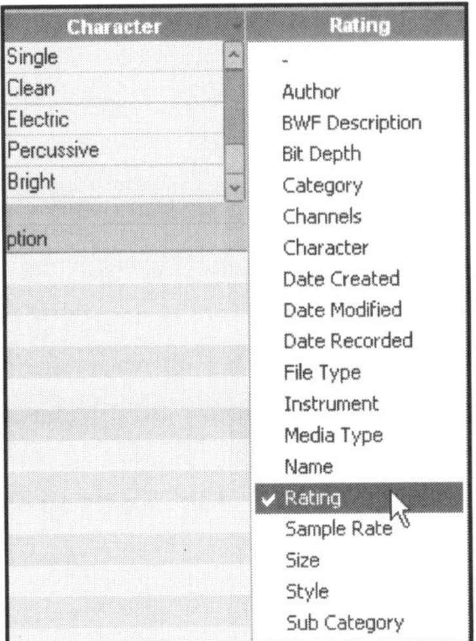

Figure 7.17
Changing the order of columns in the Viewer area of the MediaBay.

You can add an instrument track by selecting Project > Add Track > Instrument. By default, the Add Instrument Track dialog box appears, displaying the Browse Presets features. This is similar to the Viewer/Filter combination in the MediaBay, where the selected filter hides all values not corresponding to the current selection. In Figure 7.18, the filter displays only Bass patches for the Monologue VST instrument plug-in. To hear what this preset sounds like before loading the instrument plug-in, enable the MIDI Input button under the Viewer table or choose a MIDI file and click on the Play button to hear the preview. Once the appropriate instrument preset is displayed and selected in the Viewer, click OK to complete the process. As a result, the instrument track is created, its MIDI output is automatically routed to the VST instrument plug-in, the preset is loaded into the plug-in, and the track is ready to be used in a recording.

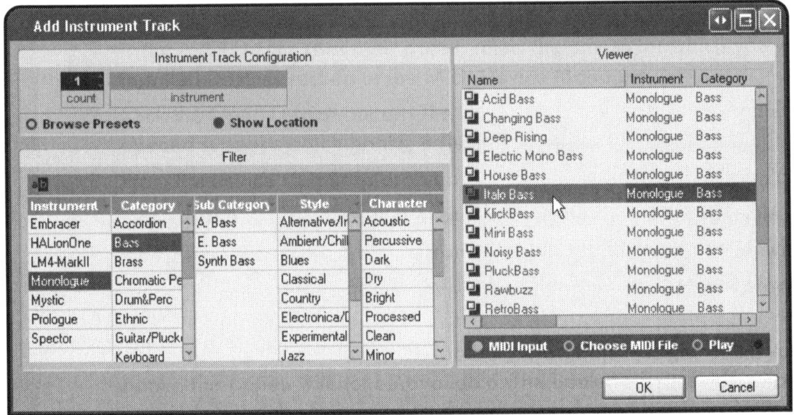

Figure 7.18
Using filters to find the right instrument preset.

VST Presets

VST presets are plug-in settings that can be stored and recalled at any moment. Because VST presets are compatible with Cubase's SoundFrame management system, you can associate a number of tags with them and access them wherever you find the SoundFrame logo. For example, when you load the MonoDelay VST plug-in as an insert on an instrument track, the MonoDelay panel appears by default. Clicking inside the preset Name field, as illustrated in Figure 7.19, opens up the Browser already focused to display only the presets for this plug-in, with the attributes (if any) associated with the presets found for this plug-in. In this example, none of the VST presets have any associated attributes, but the Viewer area does display all currently available presets for this plug-in. Selecting each preset changes the setting of the plug-in automatically, making it possible to preview the result if signal is passing through the plug-in as you select presets.

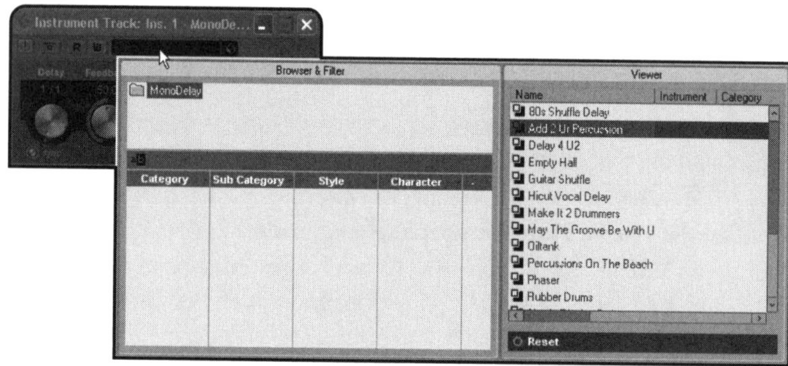

Figure 7.19
Selecting VST presets for a plug-in effect.

Presets included with Cubase offer a great starting point, but you might want to save your own customized presets as well. VST presets are stored as separate files and have the .vstpreset extension.

HOW TO

Save custom VST presets:

1. Click on the SoundFrame logo and choose Save Preset from the pop-up menu.
2. In the Save Preset dialog box, enter a file name for the preset.
3. To associate tags (attributes) with this custom preset, enable the Tag editor and choose the appropriate values next to the corresponding attribute.
4. Click OK when you are finished.

Note that all custom VST preset files are stored under the user's application data folder, but will appear in the MediaBay under the VST Presets node corresponding to the plug-in to which the preset belongs. In the example illustrated in Figure 7.20, these presets will show up in the MediaBay under the Presets > VST Presets > Steinberg Media Technologies > MonoDelay plug-in. To view or manage the files on your disk, you can right-click (PC) / Ctrl-click (Mac) over the desired preset name in the Viewer area of the MediaBay and choose Show in Explorer/Finder from the content menu, as displayed in Figure 7.21. Cubase will open the folder containing that file in an Explorer/Finder window. From there, you can rename the file or move it somewhere else if necessary. Copying a preset on a disk might come in handy when you work in different studios and sharing presets from one studio to another is essential.

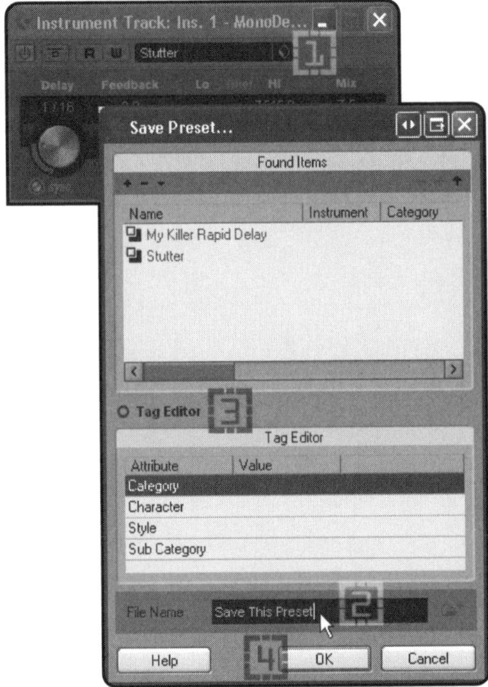

Figure 7.20
Saving VST presets.

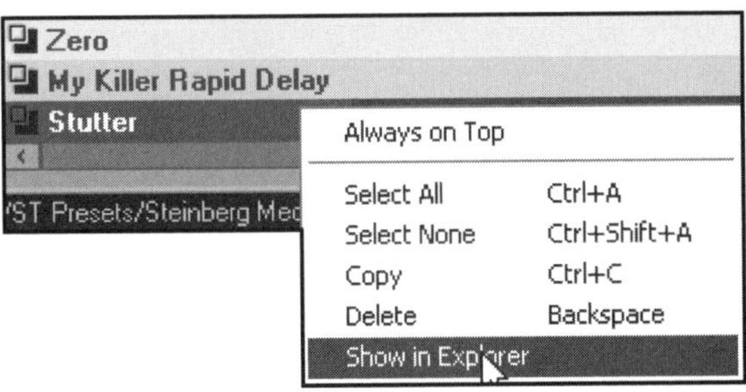

Figure 7.21
Accessing the location where preset files are saved.

Track Presets

Track presets offer similar functionalities as VST presets; however, in this case, the settings stored in this type of file aren't limited to a single plug-in. Think of a track preset as a track template holding a number of settings, including one or several track inserts preloaded with presets and/or EQ settings tailored to get you started quickly. You can also save volume, pan, input gain, and phase settings, along with audio track presets. Instrument track presets also save MIDI insert FX, track parameters, and input transformer settings, as well as VST instrument settings. In Figure 7.22, the Filter area allowed us to search for a lead male vocal audio track template with an EQ setup to get a good electronica sound out of it. Isolating this particular track preset was done simply by selecting the filter options we wanted to end up with. By selecting this preset, Cubase automatically creates an audio track loaded with a compressor, delay, mono to stereo, and reverb plug-in inserts displayed in the Inspector. The new track is also named after the preset, all of which takes some of the guesswork out and reduces initial setup time considerably. You can, of course, disable, unload, or tweak any of these settings and store them as your own.

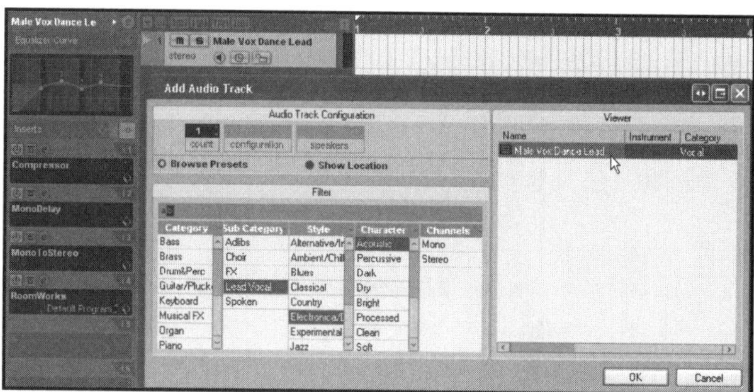

Figure 7.22
Creating a track using track presets.

HOW TO

Create a new track using track presets:

1. Right-click (PC) / Ctrl-click (Mac) in the Track List area or select Project > Add Track and choose an audio, MIDI, or instrument track to add. These are the only track classes that support track presets.
2. In the Add Track dialog box, make the necessary selection in the Filter area or choose from the list of presets available in the Viewer area. If the Filter and Viewer options are not visible, click on the Browse Presets radio button to enable them.
3. Click OK when you are finished.
4. Select the newly created track in the Track List area of the Project window to make its settings visible in the Inspector.
5. Customize the track's settings as needed.

HOW TO

Load a track preset into an existing track:

1. Start by selecting the existing audio, MIDI, or instrument track.
2. In the Project window's Inspector area, make the Track Settings section visible.
3. Click inside the Track Preset field, as displayed in Figure 7.23, to open the Apply Track Preset dialog box.

Figure 7.23
The Apply Track Preset field in the Inspector.

4. Browse or filter the list of presets as necessary.
5. Enable the Auto Preview option and start playback. Selecting a different track preset allows you to listen to the result of that selection on your track.
6. Press OK when you are finished.
7. Select the Inserts or Equalizer section in the Inspector to access the settings currently loaded in the preset if you want to modify them.

HOW TO

Save a custom track preset:

1. Select the track or tracks you want to save as presets.
2. Right-click (PC)/Ctrl-click (Mac) over the Track List area and select the Create Track Preset option from the pop-up menu.
3. Type a name for the preset in the File Name field.
4. Enable the Tag editor option if you want to associate tags (attributes) with this preset. It is strongly recommended that you tag everything as you save because this will make it easier to find what you are looking for later.
5. Click OK when you are finished.

About VST3

New to Cubase 4 is the VST3 plug-in format, which saves processing power by detecting silence and ultimately shutting down its processing during these periods to leave the resources available for other, more immediate needs at a given point in the project. VST3 plug-ins also adjust themselves to the channel's configuration. For example, adding a VST3 plug-in to a stereo channel will work just as well as using the same plug-in on a 5.1 channel.

8 Recording Audio

Without content, there is no project. Recording and importing audio represent the two most common ways to get content into a project. It used to be the musician's job to get the notes right, and it was up to the recordist or sound engineer to get the performance recorded properly. In today's computer-based production environment, chances are you'll be doing both jobs, playing the guitar with one hand, triggering the recording device with the other and singing your way to a perfect performance. Cubase is there to make your job look easy and to make you feel confident about getting the most out of a recording session. This chapter discusses setup options for optimal audio recording and explains the tools of the recording trade. You can also import audio, MIDI, and video in different formats using the import features included in Cubase.

Here's a summary of what you will learn in this chapter:

- How to configure the metronome
- How to set up Cubase to record digital audio
- How to use Cycle mode when recording audio
- How to create events and regions in recording sessions
- How to use stacked mode recordings and display lanes
- How to import different file formats into a Cubase project

Metronome and Tempo

Using a metronome, also known as a *click track*, provides a simple way to lay down some rhythmically accurate tracks. When editing a project later, you'll want to use the bars and beat markings the project provides as reference points to cut, move, copy, or resize events along the timeline. Using a click track or metronome makes it easy for a musician to fall into these subdivisions, especially in the absence of any other rhythmic guide track.

Click Settings

To help you keep the beat while you are recording, you can activate the Click button on the Transport panel, as shown in Figure 8.1. The Click button enables or disables the metronome click. To generate the metronome click, you can use a MIDI device, your audio hardware output, or both. When the metronome click is enabled, the word "click" is lit, and the field next to the button displays the word "ON."

Figure 8.1
The Click, Tempo, and Sync options on the Transport panel.

HOW TO

Configure the metronome settings:

1. Ctrl (PC) / (Mac)-click the Click button on the Transport panel, or from the Transport menu, select the Metronome Setup option. The Metronome Setup dialog box will appear, as shown in Figure 8.2.

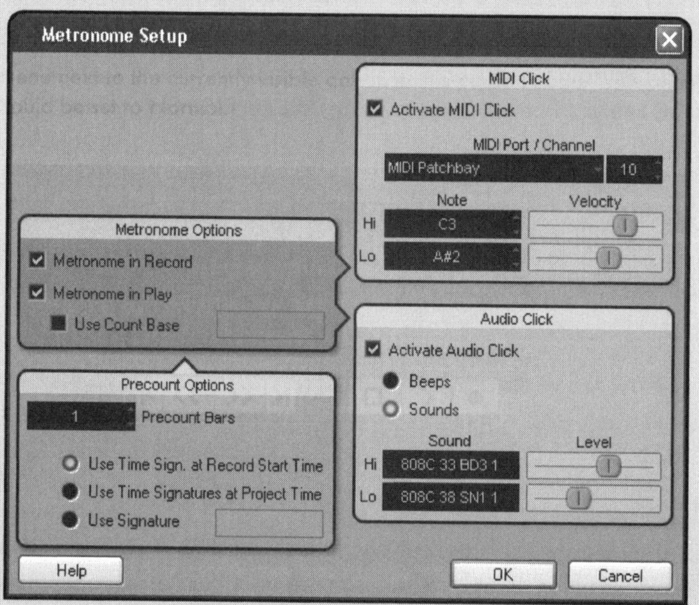

Figure 8.2
The Metronome Setup dialog box.

2. Check the Activate MIDI Click and/or the Activate Audio Click check boxes, depending on which type of click you want to hear. The MIDI click plays through a MIDI device or plug-in, while the audio click plays through an audio output.

3. If you've selected the Activate MIDI Click check box, make sure to select a MIDI port connected to a device that will play the MIDI click and an appropriate MIDI channel.

   You can change the MIDI note value of the high and low notes. High notes are played on the first beat of a bar, whereas low notes are played on the other beats. Finally, you can adjust the MIDI velocity of these notes in the same area.

4a. For the audio click, choose to hear beep sounds automatically generated by Cubase.

OR

4b. Select the Sounds radio button and load different click sounds for both Hi and Lo clicks by clicking inside the field to load your own custom metronome samples.

5. Use the corresponding level controls to adjust the volume for each sound if this is the case.
6. Set the metronome options by choosing the Metronome in Record mode if you only want to hear the click sound while in Record mode when the Click button is enabled, or the Metronome in Play mode to also hear the click sound during normal playback when the Click button is enabled.
7. If you want your metronome clicks on a different value than your time signature setting, such as every eighth note rather than every quarter note in a 4/4 bar, check the Use Count Base option and set the value using the up and down arrows to the right of this check box to adjust the beat subdivision for your metronome's click.
8. In the Precount Bars field, enter the appropriate number of bars you want Cubase to sound off before it actually starts playing or recording. This will have no influence on the metronome if the Precount button is disabled in the Transport panel.
9. The Use Signature option affects the time signature of the metronome's during the precount. This technique is convenient to hear a different time signature from the project's tempo track time signature. For example, if your project switches from a 4/4 to 3/4 time at the exact point you're punching in a new recording, you may want the count-in metronome to be in 3/4 as well. On the other hand, if you don't want to use the signature values associated with the tempo track of a project, enter a custom signature here. For example, it can sometimes be more natural to use a 4/4 count-in, even though the figure you're about to play is in 7/8.
10. When you have completed setting these options, click OK.

Tempo and Time Signature

The tempo of a project is counted in beats per minute (BPM) and determines the speed of the project. When the Tempo button is enabled, the tempo track controls the tempo of the project. Ctrl (PC)/ (Mac)-clicking the Tempo button opens the Tempo Track window, which is explained further in Chapter 29, "Tempo Track." When the tempo track is enabled, the project's tempo follows tempo changes in the tempo track. When the Tempo button is not active, as shown in Figure 8.3, the project tempo remains fixed at the tempo value entered in the Transport panel. To the right of the Tempo button, the project's current tempo and time signature are displayed.

HOW TO

Set a fixed tempo and time signature for the project:

1. Disable the Tempo Track button on the Transport panel.
2. Select the Tempo value box in the Transport panel and type a new tempo for the project. Once this value box is selected, you can also use the mouse scroll wheel to change the value.

   Note that entering a new tempo later on will override this tempo setting. If you want to change the tempo at a specific location in a project, use the tempo track instead.
3. Select the Time Signature value box in the Transport panel and type a new value or use the mouse's scroll wheel.

Figure 8.3
The project playing at a fixed tempo of 120 BPM.

Recording Audio

Make sure your audio connections are configured properly before going any further because you need to test them out as you read the information in this chapter. Your project settings should also be completed at this point, especially the sample rate. Check the Project Setup dialog box (the default key command is Shift+S) if you haven't done so already. All audio files in a project have to be recorded (or imported) at the same sampling rate. As a final checklist item before recording audio, make sure the digital clock of the audio hardware is set up correctly if you are using a digital input to record your audio. The digital clock defines the exact sampling rate (frequency) of the audio hardware. If the audio hardware is receiving its digital clock information from an external digital audio device, it should be set to match this device's sampling frequency.

HOW TO

Configure the digital clock on audio hardware:

1. Select the Device Setup option in the Devices menu.
2. In the Device Setup dialog box, select the ASIO driver entry below the VST Audio System option.
3. In the Parameter panel for the selected audio device, click the Control Panel button to access your audio hardware's configuration panel.
4. In your audio hardware's configuration panel, set the master clock (digital clock) appropriately. If the external device is set as master (or internal), set your audio hardware to follow the external device's digital clock by using the appropriate option for your card. (Consult your audio hardware's documentation if you are unsure which option it is.) It's preferable for your audio hardware's digital clock to control other devices rather than the reverse, in which case, the external digital audio devices need to follow your audio hardware's digital audio clock. You will find more information in Chapter 30, "Working In Sync."
5. When you are finished, close the audio hardware's configuration panel.
6. Back in Cubase, click Apply.
7. Click OK to close the Device Setup dialog box.

Should the Audio Hardware Follow or Lead?

If you don't have any digital connections with other devices in your studio setup, your audio hardware should always follow its own internal synchronization.

HOW TO

Record a single track of audio in Cubase:

1. Select the audio track where you want to record. You might have to create a track if none exists in the project. The audio track's configuration (mono, stereo, multi I/O) will determine the number of channels the audio file will have.
   Let's assume you've already gone through the steps found in Chapter 5, "New Project," and you have already created a track, renamed it, and armed it for recording (Record Enable button).
2. Enable the Monitor button to monitor the input level of the audio signal (see Figure 8.4).

Figure 8.4
When the Monitor button is active, the level meters become input level monitors.

3. Start playing as you would during recording to adjust the input level of the audio. The fader in the audio channel does not influence the input level; it only influences the output (monitored) level.
4. Adjust the input level by starting at the source of the signal. Control the level coming out of the instrument, adjust the level coming out of the mixer (if your signal passes through a mixer before heading to Cubase), or adjust the input level from your audio hardware's mixing applet if it allows this. Cubase 4 users can also adjust the input channel first because it offers phase reverse and up to 48.2 dB of gain or cut within the Mixer.

Adjust Your Source Levels First

The longer an audio signal chain is, the more likely it will pick up noise along the way. Increasing the audio's amplitude level later in the audio chain also increases any noise that has been added at previous points in this chain. As a rule of thumb, it's always better to increase a signal's amplitude at the source than at the input bus level (once it has already been converted or passed through electronic components).

5. In the Transport panel, select the appropriate recording mode. When recording audio, Normal is usually the appropriate choice.
6. To start and stop a recording at a specific point in time, position the left and right locators appropriately and enable the Punch-In and Punch-Out buttons on the Transport panel.

Avoid Recording the Metronome

To hear a metronome click while you are recording (but not in the recorded signal), be sure the metronome click is not somehow routed into the recorded signal. For example, this might occur because you are recording audio from a keyboard or MIDI sound module that is also the source for your MIDI metronome sound, or because the click sound has been inadvertently routed into your record input path via an external mixer. See Chapter 6, "Control Room Mixer," for more on this topic. You can configure your metronome click through the Metronome Setup dialog box. After your settings are made, close the dialog box and enable or disable the metronome click from the Transport panel. (The default key command is C.)

7. Place the project cursor at the position where you want your recording to begin.
8. Click the Record button and begin recording the audio.
9. Click the Stop button or press the spacebar to manually stop the recording if you haven't enabled the Punch-Out button.

Recording Audio in Cycle Mode

Working in Cycle mode allows you to repeat a section of your song over and over again. While this section plays, you can try different things and even record each lap through the repeated section. When you're finished, you can either try to reproduce the best ideas you had while practicing or edit together portions of the different takes if recording mode was enabled. That's the whole point behind cycle recording.

In Cubase, when you are recording in Cycle mode, you are looping a portion of the project timeline between the left and right locators. In Cycle recording mode, Cubase creates a single long audio file that contains events and/or region definitions associated with each lap. These takes are automatically numbered for you, although it is often helpful to edit their names afterwards. Whether events, regions, or both are created for each recorded lap depends on the current setting found in Cubase's preferences (see Figure 8.5).

Create Events

When you record in Cycle mode and create events, Cubase creates a single long audio clip, but each time a lap (a cycle) is completed, an event is inserted on the track. The event that appears when you stop recording is the one recorded during the last lap (or cycle). All the other events are still on the track, but in layers underneath this last event.

Because you can only hear one event at a time on a track, you need the To Front option found in the Project window's context menu, as shown in Figure 8.6. This option appears when you right-click (PC)/Control-click (Mac) over the overlapping events. You should create and work with events when you want to split up the events to create a composite version using parts of each take.

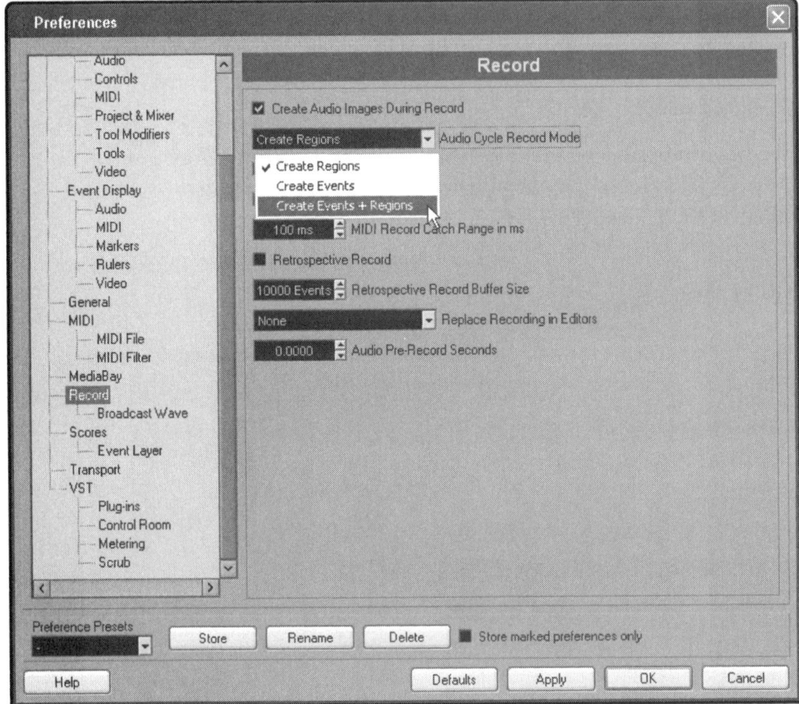

Figure 8.5
The Cycle recording mode options found in the Cubase Preferences dialog box.

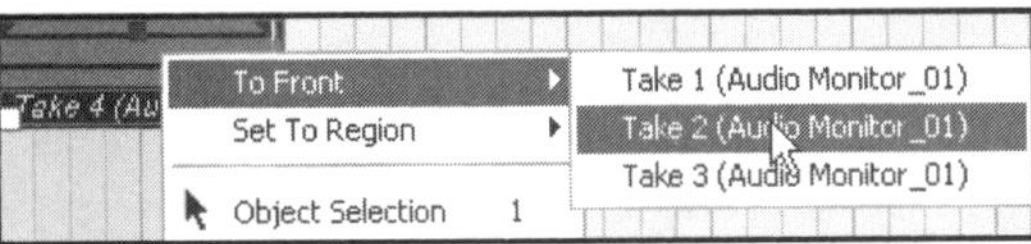

Figure 8.6
Select which take you want to bring to the front after a cycle recording.

Create Regions

When you record in Cycle mode and create regions, Cubase creates a single long audio clip where a region defines each lap (cycle). The difference here is that there is only one event on your track, but by using the Set to Region option (also displayed below the To Front option in Figure 8.6), you can choose which region you want to display in this event.

Because regions are created, you can also see the defined regions in the Pool (see Figure 8.7) and in the Sample editor. You should create and work with regions when you want to select an entire region as the desired take for the event.

Create Events and Regions

Finally, you can set Cubase to create both events and regions. This places a number of overlapping events on your track and creates identical regions in the Pool window. By doing this, if you decide

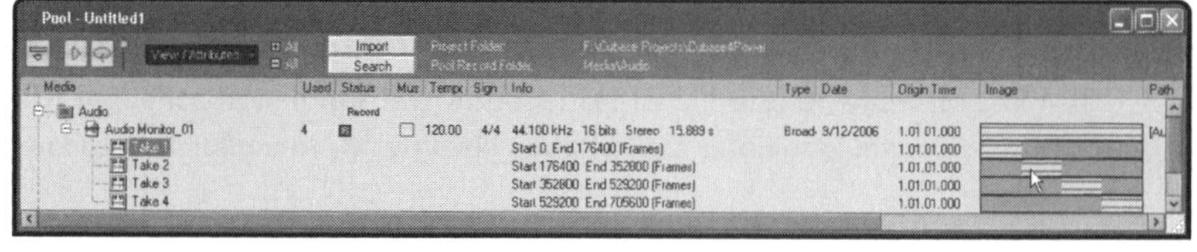

Figure 8.7
*The regions created during cycle recording are named Take *, where the asterisk represents the number of the lap/take.*

to go back to a take and modify it, you can place the region from the Pool onto a track. However, using both methods simultaneously for selecting takes during editing can become confusing, so pick one and stick with it.

When using the Scissors tool to split an event, you split all the overlapping events. Selecting an event in one portion and a region in another might not give you the result you were going for.

HOW TO

Change your Cycle recording mode preferences:

1. Select Preferences in the File (PC)/Cubase (Mac) menu.
2. Select Record in the Preferences dialog box.
3. Select the desired option in the Audio Cycle Record Mode drop-down menu (refer to Figure 8.5).
4. Click Apply and then OK to close the dialog box.

Stacked Cycle Record Modes

Cubase offers two Stacked Record modes that automatically create a MIDI part or an audio event for each completed lap when recording in Cycle mode. Each event is then automatically placed on its own lane inside the track, as shown in Figure 8.8. With Stacked mode selected, Cubase displays each recorded lap on its own lane in the track once recording is stopped. By default, Cubase mutes all lanes except for the lowest and most recently recorded lap. (When viewing track events in lanes view, the events or portions within them that are unmuted appear shaded in green.)

Stacked 2 cycle record mode is intended for MIDI/instrument tracks (since on audio tracks it behaves exactly like ordinary Stacked recording mode). In Stacked 2 mode, Cubase doesn't mute the previously recorded MIDI laps, so you can build on the content you recorded in each successive lap. Use this mode when you want to create a complex rhythm one lap at a time and you need to keep instruments (played in each lap) in separate parts or events. In Figure 8.9, the MIDI events on all three lanes will be heard, whereas the bottom audio lane on the lower audio track would still be the only one heard in Stacked 2 mode.

Figure 8.8
Stacked Cycle Record mode during MIDI (top track) and audio (bottom track) recordings.

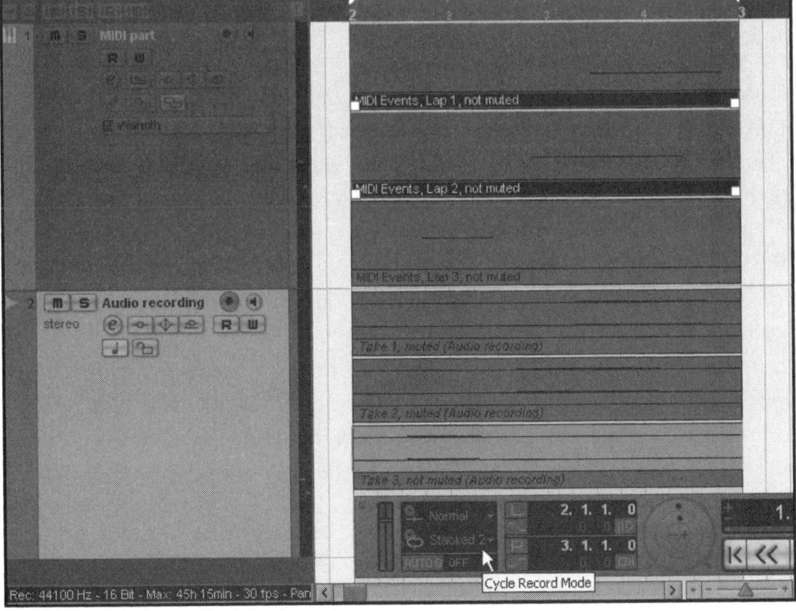

Figure 8.9
Stacked2 Cycle Record mode during MIDI (top track) and audio (bottom track) recordings.

To use Stacked modes, select the desired mode from the Transport panel before starting the recording process.

Manually Changing the Lane Display

Each part or event is placed on its own lane inside the track. Cubase automatically switches the lanes on when Stacked mode is selected, but if you need to turn lanes off or back on again, select the Lanes Fixed (or Lanes Auto, in MIDI tracks) option from the Lane Display Type button found in the Track Control area (see Figure 8.10). Once you have completed the editing process and want to hide unused lanes, set the lane display type back to Lane Off.

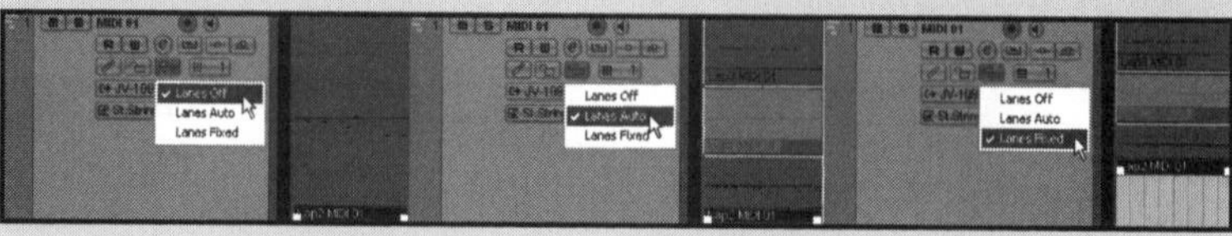

Figure 8.10
Change lane display types when using Stacked Cycle Record modes.

Importing Content

When working on a project, you not only can record events, but you also can import events that are already on your media drive or use content from another source. All the import functions of Cubase can be found in the File menu under the Import submenu.

As an alternative to using the Import submenu, it is possible to drag MIDI and audio files from your file management system directly into a project. Note that when importing an audio file, Cubase will prompt you to copy the file into the active project folder. It is recommended that you keep all your audio files inside this project folder and that you accept that a copy of the audio file be created there. You can always work with audio files from different locations on your hard disk, but keep in mind that backing up a project with all its associated files will be easier if you keep all content in one folder.

About Audio File Imports

Cubase supports many of today's common audio formats: WAV, AIFF, WMA (Windows Media Audio), or MP3 files, for example, can be dragged directly from folders in the Windows Explorer or Macintosh Finder onto a track or into the empty space below the last track in the Project window's event display area to create a new track. When importing WMA or MP3 files (which use audio data compression to reduce file size), Cubase creates a WAV or AIFF copy on your media drive, rather than using the source WMA or MP3 file directly. Just remember that WAV and AIFF files can be much larger than their WMA or MP3 counterparts.

You also can import ReCycle files, and Cubase will recognize any tempo and pitch metadata usually associated with ACID loops. ReCycle files are generated by the software called ReCycle, which was developed by Propellerhead. ReCycle cuts drum loops into smaller time slices to be reused as samples at different tempos without changing the pitch. This process is similar to the Hitpoint and Musical mode processes found in the Sample editor. Sony applications, such as ACID or Sound Forge, embed this time-slice information into standard WAV files as metadata.

This information is interpreted by Cubase, which makes it possible to match the loop's tempo to the project's tempo on the fly.

HOW TO

Import audio files:

From any folder in the Windows Explorer or Mac Finder, drag the compatible files into your project or into the Pool window of Cubase.

Alternatively, you can:

1. Select File > Import > Import Audio File.
2. Browse to the location of the file you want to import.
3. Select the file and click the Open button.

You can also import audio from inside the Pool window by selecting the Import button or by right-clicking (PC)/Control-clicking (Mac) in the Pool and selecting the Import Audio File option. When you import audio into a project, keep a copy of media files inside the audio folder of the project whenever possible to avoid mistakenly changing a sample that you might need for another project later.

About Audio CD Track Imports

You can grab audio tracks directly from an audio CD by using the Import Audio CD option in Cubase. There are two ways you can perform this task; which one you choose depends on what you want to do with these imported tracks. In both ways, the Audio CD Import window is the same; however, if you use the submenu option in the File > Import menu, the imported tracks automatically appear in your Project window starting at the project cursor's current location and on the selected audio track. If you don't have an audio track present, one is automatically created for you.

The second option is to import from the Pool by right-clicking (PC)/Control-clicking (Mac) inside the window and choosing the Import Audio CD option. In this case, the audio track is imported in the Pool only, and no events appear in the project's Event Display area. This might be the method of choice when you start building a Pool of good drum loops for your new project.

HOW TO

Import audio tracks from an audio CD:

If you don't want to place the content of an audio track directly in your project, skip to Step 3.

1. Create an empty audio track (for safety) and select it in the Track List area.
2. Position the cursor at the location where you want the event to be inserted.
3. Select Import Audio CD from the File > Import menu or right-click (Control-click on Mac) in the Media Pool and select the Import Audio CD option found at the top of the context menu.

4. The Import from Audio CD dialog box will appear, as displayed in Figure 8.11. Choose the appropriate drive containing the audio CD from which you want to import. This field is found in the upper-left corner of the dialog box.

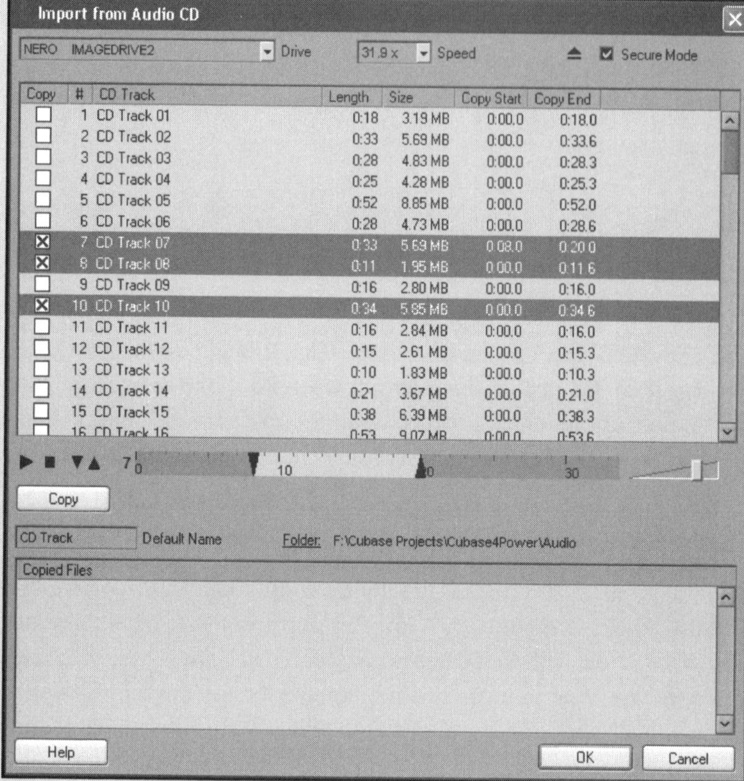

Figure 8.11
The Import from Audio CD dialog box.

5. Select the transfer speed you want to use to import these files. Note that faster speeds result in a faster transfer, but slower speeds limit the potential for errors that can occur during the transfer.

> **Previewing CD Tracks**
> You can preview a track before importing it by using the Play button in the lower-right portion of the dialog box.

6. Move the Grab Start and Grab End arrows found in the Track Display area below the Play button when you don't want to grab the entire CD track. This changes the value in the Grab Start and End columns in the Track Display above, allowing you to import only sections of the audio.
7. In the Grab column, select the tracks you want to import. Hold the Ctrl (PC)/ (Mac) key while you click on non-sequential tracks to select more than one track, or select the first track you want

to import, hold down the Shift key, and click the last track you want to import to select all the tracks in between.

8. Type a new name in the File Name field to give a different name to your tracks.
9. Click the Change Folder button to change the folder destination, browse your computer's hard drive, and select a new destination folder.
10. Click the Grab button at the bottom of the dialog box to begin the extraction process. The files will appear in the Grabbed Files section when the extraction is completed.
11. Click the OK button when you are finished.

Using Secure Mode

If you're running into read errors when importing content from an audio CD, try enabling the Secure Mode option, as shown in Figure 8.12. This mode takes more processing time, but it will help you get better results from a drive if it's having a hard time reading the data on a disc.

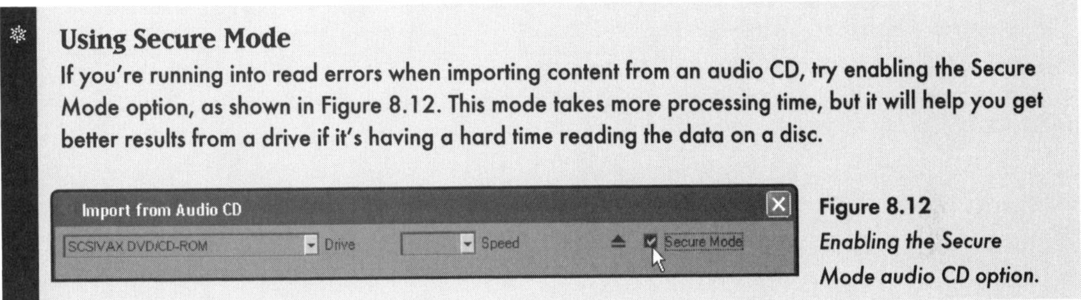

Figure 8.12
Enabling the Secure Mode audio CD option.

Importing Audio from Video Files

Sometimes all you need from a video file is its audio track, not the video track itself. If that's what you want, the Import Audio from Video File option will create a separate audio file from the selected video and place it in your project. The format of the audio file will be converted to the project's settings, and a copy of this audio track can be found in the project's folder. In other words, the original video file will not be used once you've imported the audio file from it.

About OMF

Cubase users can import (and export) files saved in OMF format. OMF stands for *Open Media Framework,* and it is a platform-independent file format intended for the transfer of digital media between different applications. Because this format is adopted by most professional video editing applications (such as AVID, After Effects, and Final Cut Pro, for example), exporting projects in OMF format makes sense if you expect to exchange them with one of these applications.

OMF files can be saved using one of two formats: 1.0 or 2.0. OMF files do not contain video media files, but references to external video files, so if you are working on a video project and an OMF file is sent to you, you will need to import its source video files into your project separately. The OMF file will include markers telling Cubase where the video file goes.

9 Using Instruments

Music is often created from performances played on acoustic or electric instruments. Synthesizers, which exploded onto the market in the '80s due to the arrival of MIDI, pretty much defined the sound of that decade. In the '90s, sampled loops were just as big, and they still remain an important part of the creative set of tools used by many musicians today. Today, the processing power provided by computers makes it practical to use virtual instruments that can be programmed to produce a wide variety of sounds, emulating classic synths or providing entirely new ways of creating sounds. The computer has become the new musical instrument. This chapter focuses on software-based instruments and describes how Cubase communicates with these plug-ins. It also discusses how to reproduce your MIDI devices inside Cubase in order to manage these devices without having to physically change the settings on the front panel of the device.

Here's a summary of what you will learn in this chapter:

- How to create and set up an instrument track
- How to create and set up an instance of a VST instrument
- How to load and save presets
- How to add a MIDI device in the MIDI Device Manager
- How to manage external MIDI device presets
- How to use installed devices in the Inspector
- How to use filter options to find the desired preset in the Inspector

VST Instruments (VSTi)

VST instruments (VSTi) are software-based synthesizers that use the ASIO 2 protocol to generate an audio output through the audio mixing/routing environment of the host program, which then sends this signal to the audio outputs of the computer's audio interface. These software instruments take the form of special audio plug-ins working within Cubase. They can be used to generate sounds triggered by MIDI events recorded in a project when the MIDI output of a track is routed into a VSTi plug-in that has been loaded in your project.

Using VST instruments opens up a whole world of exciting possibilities for any music enthusiast, as well as for hardcore music veterans. They are activated through the VST Instruments panel, which can be opened via the Devices menu or by pressing F11 on your computer keyboard. The VST Instruments panel (see Figure 9.1) is like an empty rack of instruments in which you load instruments as you need them. Each slot in the panel offers plug-in controls for the loaded instruments. Cubase comes with some VST instruments, but you also can install others; just follow the instructions provided by the plug-in manufacturer when you do so. It's recommended that you close Cubase whenever you install a new plug-in or VSTi.

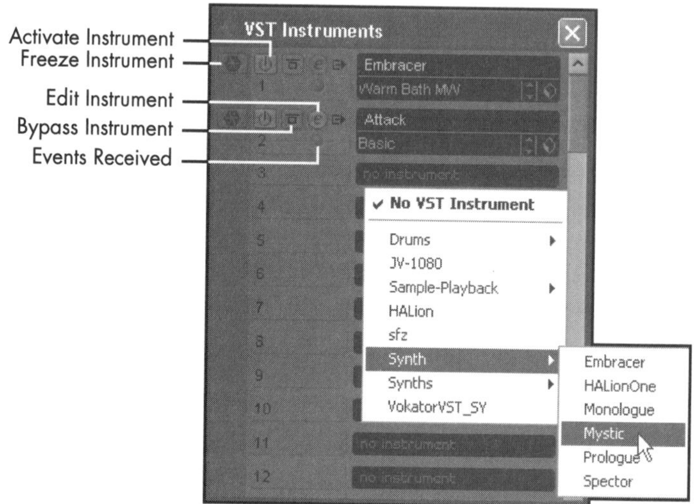

Figure 9.1
The VST Instruments panel.

A VSTi can be added to a project in one of two ways—by creating an instrument track or by creating an instance of a VST instrument in the VST Instruments panel and assigning it as the output destination for an existing or new MIDI track.

Setting Up an Instrument Track

When a VSTi is loaded into a project through creating an instrument track, it will be checked in the MIDI output selector for that track in the Inspector (as shown in Figure 9.2), and a stereo instrument channel for that VST instrument's audio output is added to the Mixer panel.

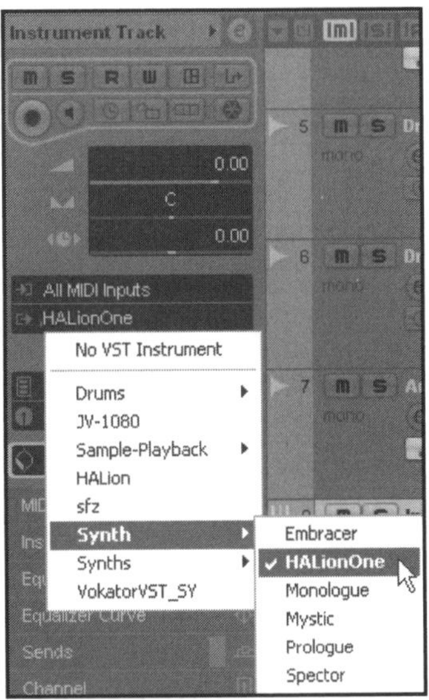

Figure 9.2
An instance of the HalionOne loaded into an instrument track.

HOW TO

Create an instrument channel:

1. Right-click (PC)/Ctrl-click (Mac) in the Track List area of the Project window.
2. Select Add Instrument Track from the context menu.
3. In the Count field in the Add Instrument Track dialog box, enter how many instances of a VSTi you want to create. Each instance loads in its own instrument track, with its corresponding stereo channel in the Mixer.

   By default, Cubase 4 enables the Browse Presets option, which displays a number of filter options below. These options are discussed in greater detail in Chapter 7, "SoundFrame." Here, we'll set up the instrument without loading any presets into it.
4. Disable the Browse Presets radio button, as shown in Figure 9.3.

Figure 9.3
The Add Instrument Track dialog box with the Browse Presets option disabled.

5. From the Instrument drop-down menu, select the appropriate VST instrument. This list contains all compatible VST instrument plug-ins installed on your system, along with external MIDI devices that have been configured through the MIDI Device Manager, discussed later in this chapter.

Cubase automatically creates the instrument track(s) per the number of instances you indicated in the Count field.

Table 9.1 describes a few advantages and disadvantages of creating instrument tracks this way:

Table 9.1 Advantages and Disadvantages of Using VSTi through Instrument Tracks

Advantages	Disadvantages
Offers the most convenient way to load a VST instrument plug-in into a project.	No support for multiple MIDI output channels.
No need to assign a MIDI output channel because it automatically routes MIDI events through the VSTi plug-in and its audio outputs.	No support for multiple audio output channels.
Creates a single channel in the Mixer instead of separate channels for the MIDI track and VSTi audio output, which makes it easier to manage.	When the plug-in offers multi-timbral support, loading multiple instances of this plug-in through the instrument track will use up more computer resources (both CPU and memory).
Both MIDI and audio inserts can be added to the same track in the Inspector.	

Setting Up a VSTi

If you want to use a single instance of a multi-timbral and/or multi-output instrument, you'll need to load the instrument in the VST Instruments panel first. By doing so, you can route any number of MIDI tracks to the same instance of the VSTi. Furthermore, if the VSTi offers multiple audio outputs, each of its active outputs will be visible in the Mixer panel as well as in the Project window inside the instrument's folder tracks. In this case, you will deal with separate channels in the Mixer—one MIDI channel for each MIDI track from which MIDI events are routed to the VSTi, and one instrument channel for each active audio output on the VSTi. Unlike instrument tracks, a VSTi loaded in the VST Instruments panel creates its own folder track where automation events are stored, as shown in Figure 9.4. VSTi Folder tracks do not contain any MIDI or audio events, but they contain all the automation associated with VSTi. (See Chapter 35, "Automation Techniques," for more on automation.) Table 9.2 offers a few advantages and disadvantages of loading a VSTi in a MIDI track. By comparing this with Table 9.1, you should get a good idea as to which technique is more convenient for your needs.

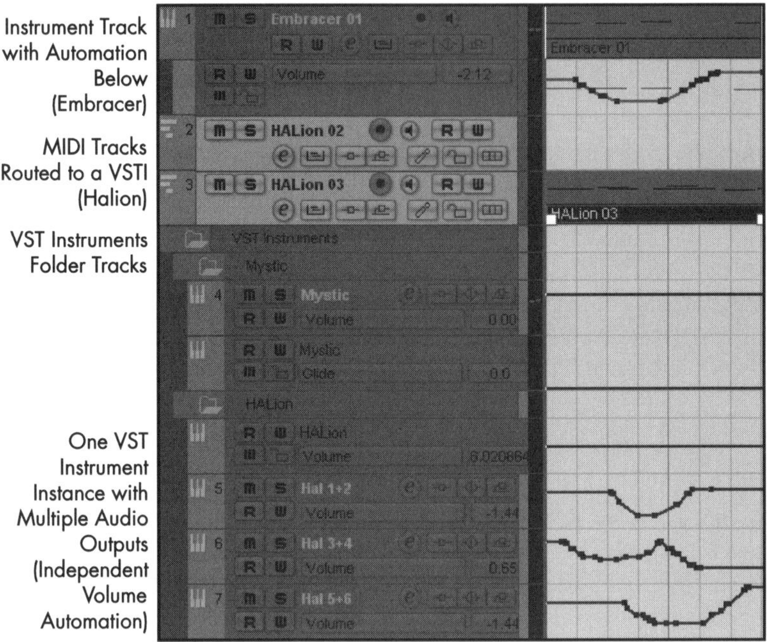

Figure 9.4
Instrument track (top) vs. MIDI+VST instruments (below).

Table 9.2 Advantages and Disadvantages of Using VSTi Through the VST Instruments Panel

Advantages	**Disadvantages**
Offers support for multiple MIDI output channels.	You must load the VSTi in the VST Instruments panel first, and then create individual MIDI channels that are routed to it.
Offers support for multiple audio output channels.	You must make the appropriate output settings for MIDI tracks as well as the VSTi channel itself.
Consumes fewer computer resources than a configuration using multiple instances of a VSTi.	MIDI/audio routing and representation can be confusing for beginners.
Each audio output from the VSTi can have its own EQ, inserts, and automation.	
Each MIDI track routed to the VSTi can have its own MIDI inserts, track settings, and modifiers, such as transpose or velocity compression.	

Let's set up a VSTi so that you can try it out (if you haven't done so already). The hardest part is choosing the sounds to use in the new project.

HOW TO

Set up a VSTi in a project:

1. Press F11 to open the VST Instruments panel, or select this option from the Devices menu.
2. From the VST Instruments panel, select the first available slot in the rack and click anywhere on the drop-down menu where it currently says "no instrument." This will reveal the installed VST instruments on your computer.
3. Choose a VSTi from the list to activate it. The blue active button next to the selected instrument reveals that this instrument is ready to be assigned to a MIDI track.
4. Cubase prompts you to create a new MIDI track to control this instrument. Click Create to create a new MIDI track. Cubase will automatically route this MIDI track's output to the VSTi and create a stereo audio channel in the Mixer for the audio output from this software instrument.

   Cubase opens the instrument's panel, where you can build a patch from scratch or select from the Preset selection field, as shown in Figure 9.5.

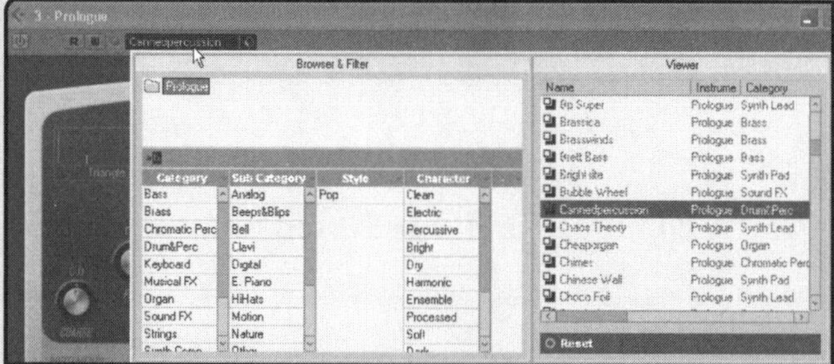

Figure 9.5
The list of presets available for the Prologue VSTi included with Cubase 4.

5. From the VST Preset selection field, use the filtering options described in Chapter 7 to find the appropriate preset, or select a preset from the Viewer table on the right. As you scroll down the list and select each preset, you can preview the result by playing a few notes on your MIDI keyboard or other controller.
6. When your selection has been made, close the instrument's panel to leave the instrument with these preset settings, or click outside the Preset selection box and tweak the instrument's controls to get the desired sound.

At this point, if you still can't hear anything, make sure the MIDI track's MIDI input selector is set to receive MIDI events from the port where your controller is connected and that the output of the audio hardware is connected to your monitoring system.

If you change your mind about the preset or sound on a VST instrument that is playing MIDI events received from one or more MIDI tracks, or you want to select a different VSTi preset, you can always use the Patch Selector field in the Inspector, as shown in Figure 9.6. Notice the Filter option above the list of available patches, which lets you enter a keyword or part of a patch name to display, filtering out all other patches. Filtering patch names doesn't affect the number of available patches; it simply makes it easier to find the ones you're looking for. On the other hand, if your intention is to modify the current patch or preset sound by editing one of the instrument's parameters, click on the Edit Instrument button to bring up the instrument's main editing interface.

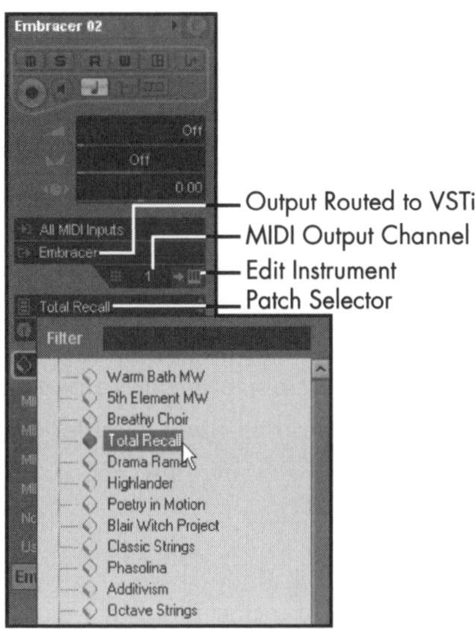

Figure 9.6
The Patch Selector field in a MIDI track playing through a VSTi plug-in.

To route MIDI events from additional MIDI tracks to the same VSTi, simply create additional MIDI tracks and select that VSTi in each track's MIDI output selection field, either in the Inspector or in the Mixer's routing panel, as displayed in Figure 9.7.

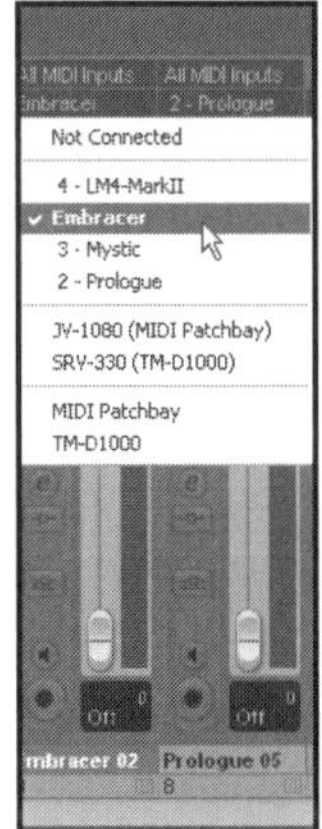

Figure 9.7
Routing a MIDI track through a VSTi in the Mixer's routing panel.

Some VST instruments support multiple audio outputs, which makes it possible to set up each of their output channels in the Mixer with different compression settings, EQ, or send effects, among other things. By default, Cubase 4 will enable the first stereo pair for a new VST instrument, but it is possible to enable as many audio channels as the VSTi supports.

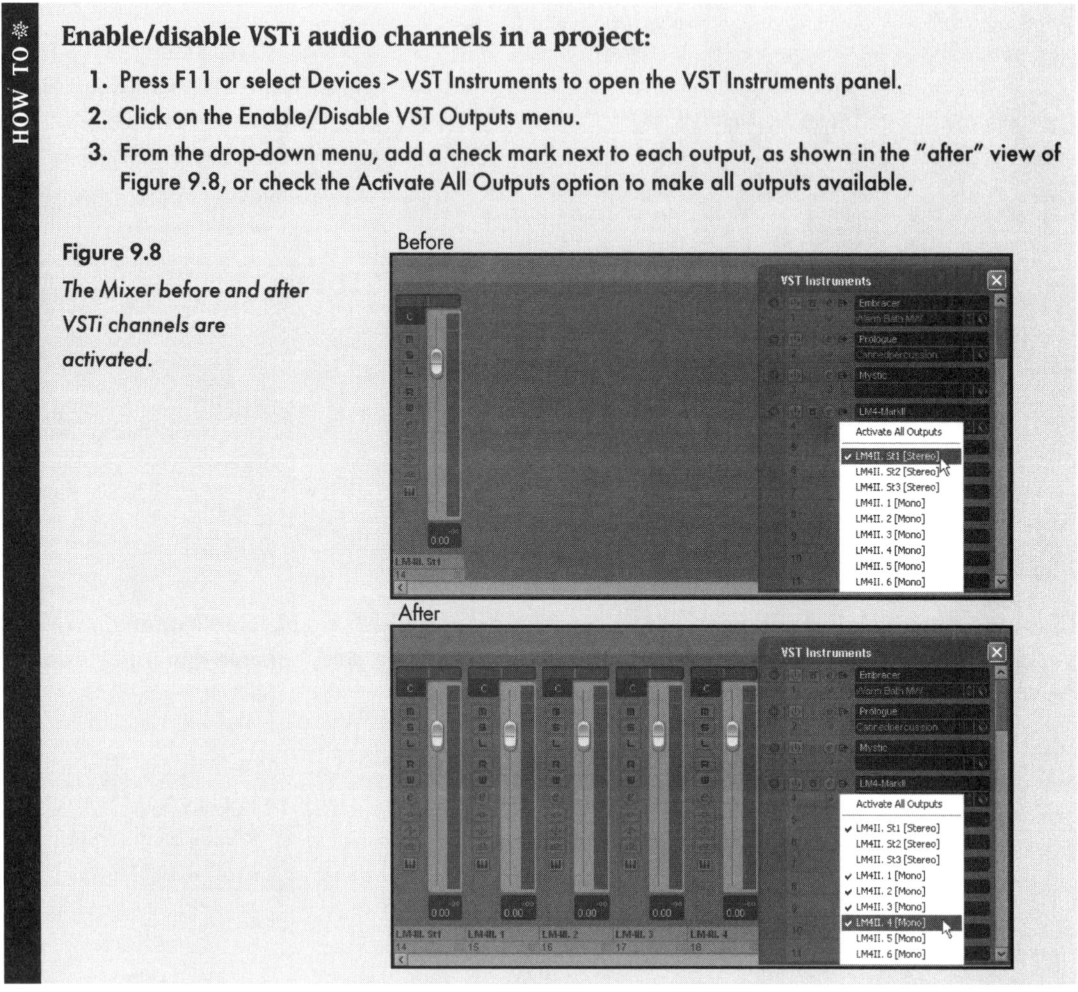

HOW TO

Enable/disable VSTi audio channels in a project:

1. Press F11 or select Devices > VST Instruments to open the VST Instruments panel.
2. Click on the Enable/Disable VST Outputs menu.
3. From the drop-down menu, add a check mark next to each output, as shown in the "after" view of Figure 9.8, or check the Activate All Outputs option to make all outputs available.

Figure 9.8
The Mixer before and after VSTi channels are activated.

When you create an instrument track or load a VSTi through the VST Instruments panel, it is active by default, but you can always deactivate a VSTi without changing its settings by clicking the Active button that appears next to its number in the VST Instruments panel (refer to Figure 9.1).

Using Presets

With most VST instruments, you also can create your own preset patches and save them for later use. Use the VST Instruments panel's Save Preset option to store custom presets and the Load Preset option to recall presets that were previously saved (see Figure 9.9). You will also find the same options at the top of the instrument's editing panel. For instruments (patches) and banks that were saved from previous versions of Cubase, use the Import FXP/FXB (Effects Patches/Effects Banks) option in the same drop-down menu to load these files with FXP or FXB extensions. Once loaded, these legacy formats can be converted into presets that can be loaded through the SoundFrame browser. Legacy instruments (.FXP) usually hold settings for a single sound, whereas banks (.FXB) hold a set of sounds, presets, programs, or instruments (depending on the name assigned by you or the manufacturer).

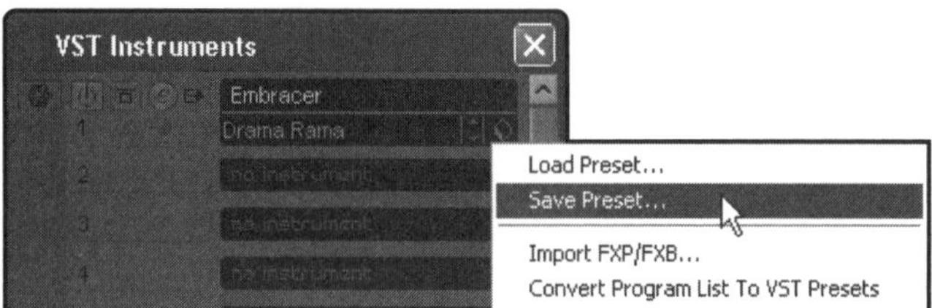

Figure 9.9
The plug-in's preset options in the VST Instruments panel.

VSTi and Latency

Because a VSTi plays through your audio hardware, latency plays a great role in how effective the instruments are on your system. Because latency introduces a delay between the time a key is played and the time a sound is heard from the VSTi, shorter delays make the experience more realistic. Your system needs to be configured properly, as outlined in Chapter 3, and always use the ASIO driver provided by the audio hardware manufacturer. If the latency is greater than about 25 milliseconds, you might find it disconcerting to play a VSTi, especially when you are playing parts with high rhythmic content, because there will always be a delay between the moment you press the keys on your keyboard and when you hear the sound. The smallest theoretical latency is 0 milliseconds, but in reality, you can expect at least a 1.5- to 3-millisecond latency, which is pretty good. For the best experience when playing through a VSTi, try setting your audio hardware driver preferences (if you have a dedicated ASIO driver for your audio hardware) and Cubase to have less than 10 milliseconds of latency.

> **Working with High-Latency Setups**
>
> If your audio hardware doesn't provide an ASIO driver with low latency, you can always monitor MIDI events through an external MIDI device temporarily while recording these events into a project. Once the events have been recorded, you can then reassign the MIDI output of the recorded track to the VSTi.

> That way, you don't deal with the latency delay during recording and, because latency does not affect the timing of your performance, the recorded events will be properly in sync with other events in the project. Obviously, this is just a workaround. Consider investing in an audio interface with low latency if you intend to use plug-in instruments on a regular basis.

The Device Manager

It is possible to create program changes or tell a MIDI track to play a specific program and bank from the MIDI Settings section of the Inspector and the Track List. When working with a VSTi, this is quite easy to deal with because when you select a VSTi as the MIDI output for the track, the track's settings display the available parameters for that instrument. So, for example, if you load the new Mystic VSTi, the Inspector will display a list of this plug-in's available presets when you click inside the Inspector's Program field.

Working with external MIDI devices is a bit trickier because Cubase can't see which device is connected to it. To access the functionalities provided by external devices inside Cubase, you need to add these devices to the MIDI Device Manager so that Cubase will know how and what to communicate with them. Many common MIDI device definitions are provided on the installation CD. You do need to install the devices in your personal setup through the MIDI Device Manager, to let Cubase know what is in your studio and how to address it properly.

When you open up the MIDI Device Manager for the first time, it will be empty because you have not defined any devices in your setup yet. You can access the MIDI Device Manager in a couple of ways:

- Select the MIDI Device Manager option in the Devices menu.
- Click the MIDI Device Manager button on the Devices panel if it is visible (Devices > Show Panel).

In Cubase 4, you also can use the MIDI Device Manager to create or edit existing panels, which are virtual representations of your external device. These panels are called *Device Maps* and they let you control specific parameters on your external device from within each Cubase project, without touching its front panel. Think of these device maps as customizable remote controls.

Adding a MIDI Device

After you have identified your external MIDI devices, you can proceed with their installation inside the MIDI Device Manager. We're going to look at how you can install an existing device definition in the MIDI Device Manager.

HOW TO

Add a MIDI device:

1. Open the MIDI Device Manager panel.
2. Click the Install Device button. The Add MIDI Device dialog box will appear, displaying a list of existing device definitions (see Figure 9.10).

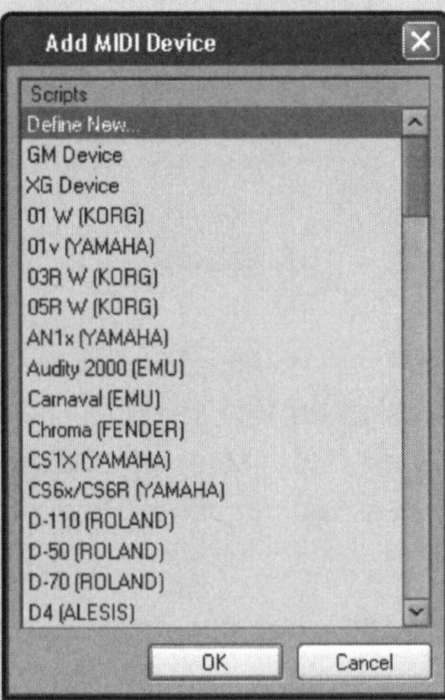

Figure 9.10
The Add MIDI Device dialog box.

3. Select the device you want to install and click OK. Your selected device will now appear in the MIDI Device Manager panel.
4. Select the device's name in the Installed Devices section.
5. Select the MIDI output to the right of your device in the center of the window, and select the port on your MIDI interface where this device is connected. When you select this instrument as a track's MIDI output, the device's name will appear along with the associated MIDI port used to connect Cubase to this device, as shown in Figure 9.11.

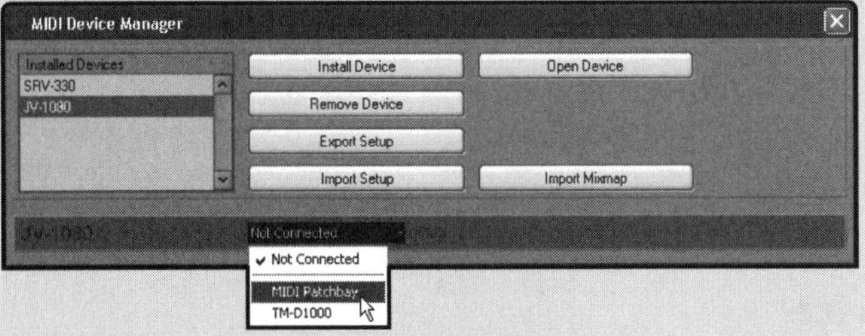

Figure 9.11
The MIDI Device Manager panel.

6. Repeat this operation for each MIDI-based external sound module in your studio.
7. Close the panel when you are finished. The changes remain in effect even when the window is not visible.

The name of each installed device appears in the MIDI output port selection menu with the MIDI port associated with it on the right, as shown in Figure 9.12.

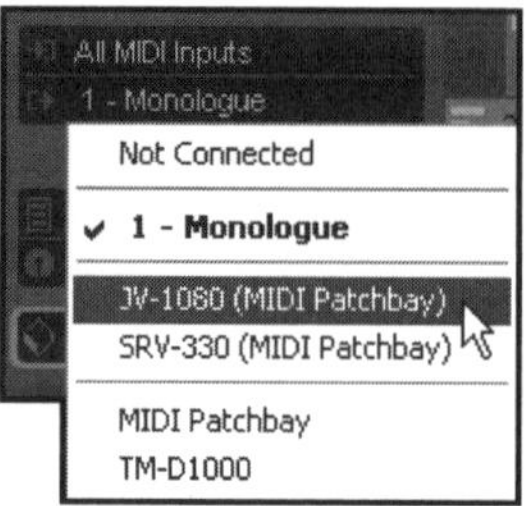

Figure 9.12
MIDI port selection field.

If your MIDI device is not included in the default list, you might have to create a definition for it yourself. Remember, however, that if you are using a MIDI sampler, creating such a device definition in the MIDI Device Manager is pointless because a sampler generally does not have a fixed set of programs it loads by default when turned on. In fact, that might be why your device is not listed in Cubase's list of devices!

With that said, if you *do* have a MIDI device with programs and banks that are not defined already in Cubase, or if you want to create a panel that allows you to send parameter change messages to any external device that supports MIDI, you can create your own MIDI device in the Device Manager. Because creating a device from scratch is intricately linked to the device in your setup, you need to refer to your owner's manual and the online documentation (under the "MIDI Devices and Patches" section) provided with Cubase to find out how to create your own custom device with patches, banks, and specific MIDI messages associated with those, as well as customized panels that appear in the User panel section of the Inspector.

> **Finding Resources on the Web**
> Before writing your own script or customizing an existing one from the installation CD, try searching on the Web. Google will certainly point you to sites that may already contain what you are looking for. Most of these sites offer free downloads. The Cubase.net Forum is also a good starting point for device maps and patchname scripts.

Managing a MIDI Device

After a device is installed, you can reorganize its Patch Bank list, export or import other devices, and rename items in the patch banks. For example, the Roland's JV-1080 patch list is organized in patches, performances, and drums. Inside the Patches folder, there are some 20 groups in which all the actual preset names of this MIDI device are found (see Figure 9.13). However, if you've ever used or seen the JV-1080, programs can also be grouped by type of sounds rather

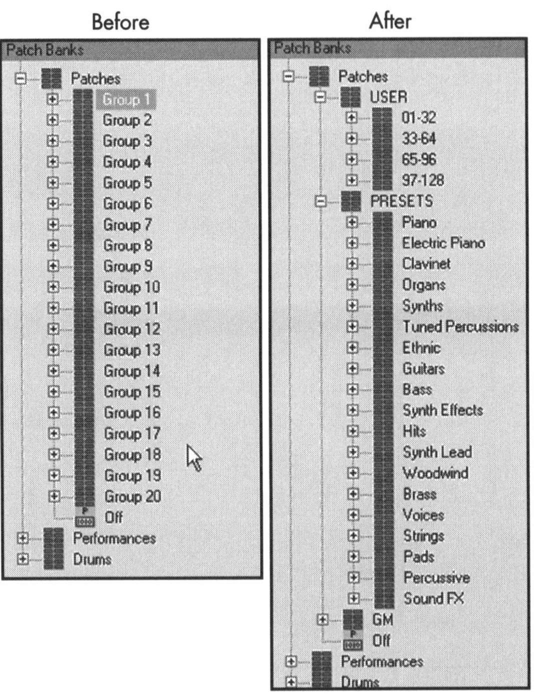

Figure 9.13
On the left, you can see the original Patch Bank list provided by Cubase; on the right, you can see the modified list that corresponds to the user's preferences.

than taking programs 0 to 31 and putting them in a group. So, you can start from the original instrument definition and create your own structure to better suit your needs. This makes it easier when you want to find the right sound for your track.

HOW TO

Add a patch bank to your device's setup:

1. In the MIDI Device Manager panel, select the device for which you want to add the content in the Installed Devices section of the MIDI Device Manager.
2. Click the Open Device button. The Device panel will open by default. When the device you just opened supports patch banks, a field will display this selection.
3. From the device's Options drop-down menu on the toolbar, select Patch Banks (see Figure 9.14).
4. In the device's Patch Bank mode, check the Enable Edit box to enable the Commands field to its left.
5. Select the Create Banks option from the Commands menu if this is what you want to do.
6. A new bank will be created, called New Bank. Double-click this new entry and type a new name for this bank.
7. From the drop-down menu in the toolbar, select Bank Assignment. If your device doesn't have patch banks, this option will not be available. The Bank Assignment function associates MIDI channels with specific banks. For example, if you have a drums bank, you might want to assign this to Channel 10 (see Figure 9.15). When you select this device as the MIDI output port from a MIDI track and

select Channel 10, the programs listed in the Inspector correspond to associated drum banks. Simply select the banks from the drop-down menu next to each channel to associate a bank with a channel.

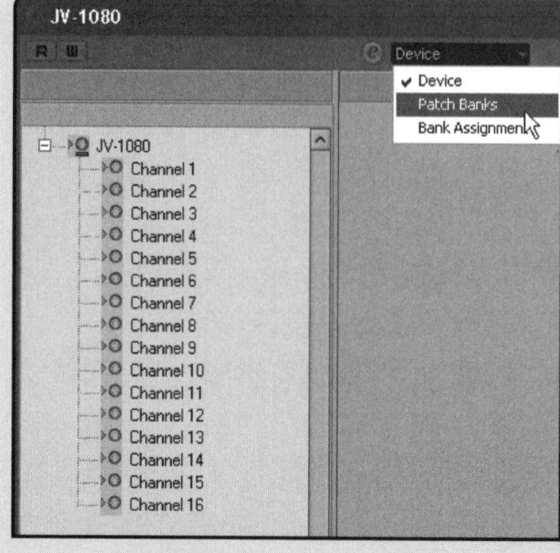

Figure 9.14
Accessing additional device-related options.

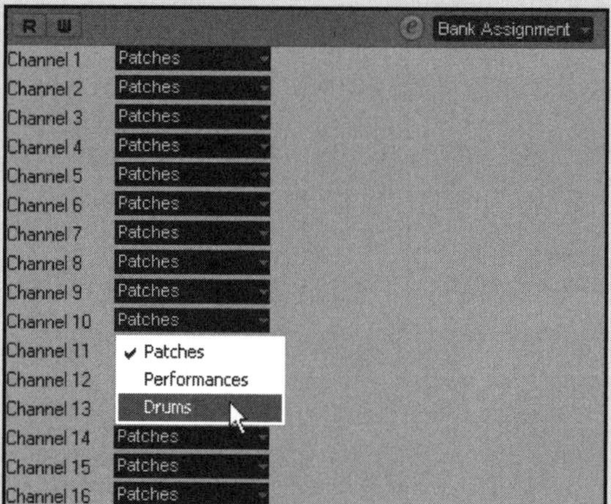

Figure 9.15
Assigning a patch bank to a specific MIDI channel.

If you want to add a bit more order in the presets listing, making them easier to find when the time comes, you can create folders for different types of presets, such as by putting all your piano-related sounds under a Piano group.

HOW TO

Add a preset or a folder to your device's setup:

1. In the Device panel, be sure the Enable Edit option is checked and that the toolbar displays patch banks.
2. Select the bank or folder in which you want to add the preset or (sub)folder.
3. Select the New Preset or New Folder option from the Commands menu.
4. Double-click the new entry to rename it.
5. If you have added a preset, you need to add the relevant program change information (a type of MIDI message) associated with your device in the Value column found in the right portion of this window. With previously created templates, you won't need to know which MIDI message corresponds to each patch/preset, but when you create a MIDI device from scratch, you will need this information from the MIDI Implementation section of your external MIDI device's manual.

To create more than one device preset at a time in the Device Manager, select the Add Multiple Presets option in the Commands drop-down menu.

When you select the bank or folder in which you have created multiple presets, you will find a list of preset names. For example, there can be 64 presets numbered from Patch 0-0 to Patch 0-7 for the first bank, then Patch 1-0 to Patch 1-7 for the second bank, and so on. Selecting any of these presets reveals (in the right side of the MIDI Device Manager panel) the actual MIDI message sent to the device.

If you made a mistake or you are not satisfied with an entry in the patch banks, you can simply click the entry and press the Delete key to remove it from the list. You also can change the order in which items appear and rearrange the list to better suit your needs.

HOW TO

Move an item in the list:

- Simply click and drag the desired entry to its new location. You also can move more than one item at a time by using the usual methods: Click the first entry and Shift-click the last item to select consecutive entries, or Ctrl-click (PC)/⌘-click (Mac) the different entries you want to select.

If you've made some adjustments to your MIDI device listings in the MIDI Device Manager patch banks, device panel, or Bank Assignment page, export these changes to a file so you can retrieve them later if you ever have to reinstall your software or simply use your device setup with Cubase in another studio.

HOW TO

Export a MIDI device setup file:

1. In the MIDI Device Manager panel, select the currently installed device setup you want to export.
2. Click the Export Setup button.
3. Choose an appropriate folder and name for your file.
4. Click the Save button. This will create an XML file.

HOW TO

Import a MIDI device setup file:

1. Open the MIDI Device Manager panel.
2. Click the Import Setup button.
3. Browse to the location of the file you want to import.
4. Select the file and click the Open button. This will add the device to your MIDI Device Manager panel.

Adding a new device to a setup does not change or influence how existing devices are handled, so you don't have to worry about messing things up by installing an additional device, even temporarily. You can always remove any device you no longer use or need.

HOW TO

Remove a MIDI device from the MIDI Device Manager:

1. Select the device in the MIDI Device Manager's Installed Device section.
2. Click the Remove Device button.

Using Devices in the Inspector

After you've installed devices in the MIDI Device Manager, you can use the Program field in the Inspector or the Track List area of a MIDI track to select a program by name. If you have created a panel or imported a device configuration that contains one or several device panels, you also can load these in the User panel area of the Inspector. When you select an entry in one of the aforementioned fields or in the device panel, Cubase sends the appropriate MIDI message to your external MIDI device in order for you to hear the appropriate sound from that device as it responds to incoming MIDI events.

HOW TO

Assign a program to a MIDI track:

1. Start by setting your MIDI track's output to a device defined in the MIDI Device Manager.
2. In the Track Settings section of the Inspector or in the Track Controls area, click the Program field (prg) to reveal its content (see Figure 9.16).
3. This field reveals the patch bank structure as defined in the MIDI Device Manager. Use the Filter field if you are looking for a specific name. In Figure 9.16 the name "piano" was entered, which reveals all the program names that contain this text.

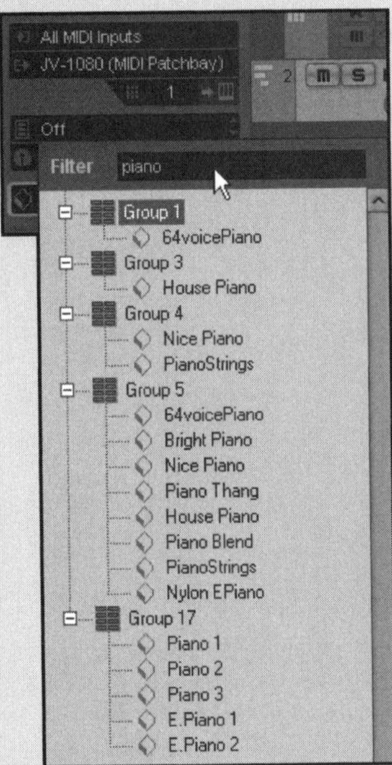

Figure 9.16
Using the Program field along with the Filter option to pinpoint the sounds you want.

4. Select the program by clicking on its name. When you do so, Cubase sends a MIDI message to your device on that track's selected MIDI channel, causing it to change its program. You can listen to the sound if you want or select another entry if you want to hear another sound.
5. Clicking once again on the selected sound or clicking outside this drop-down menu selects the sound and hides the menu once again.
6. Click on the User panel section in the Inspector.
7. Click on the User panel icon and choose the appropriate panel to display from the current list.

10 Recording MIDI

MIDI offers the possibility of capturing a set of performance events without recording the audio output of this performance. By recording MIDI events, you capture the essence of a musical performance, which can be later edited creatively or aesthetically, with great detail. Because the sound isn't part of what has been recorded, you can try a number of different sound, tempo, and pitch permutations. Although recording MIDI is often about recording note events, it's also about recording program changes, pitch bend values, or sustain pedal messages.

Here's a summary of what you will learn in this chapter:

- How to choose the appropriate Record mode
- How to use Cycle and Linear recording
- How to use and navigate with locators in a recording context
- How to use MIDI and audio activity meters
- How to record from single and multiple MIDI sources
- How to import MIDI files into an existing or new Cubase project

Record Modes

The Record mode section of the Transport panel enables you to set the Linear (top) and Cycle (bottom) record modes. The Linear record mode offers three options. Normal and Merge are the same for audio, but act differently with MIDI, and there is also a Replace option, as shown in Figure 10.1. All three options determine how Cubase will handle overlapping recorded events.

- **Normal** record mode means that when you record MIDI events over existing MIDI parts, Cubase will create a new part, which will overlap the existing MIDI part without changing the previous content or location of these parts. As for audio recording, it implies that a new event is created over the existing audio event.

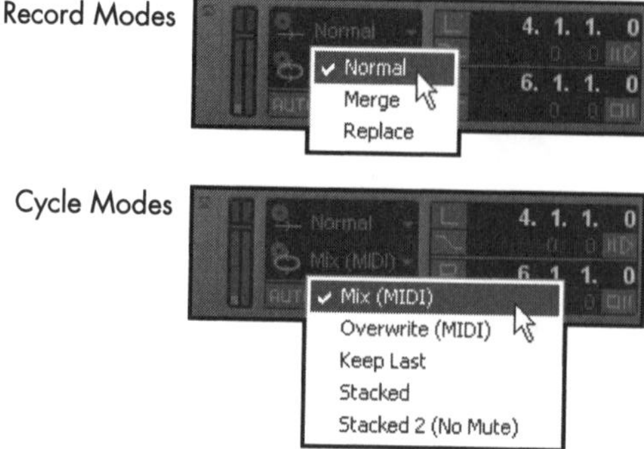

Figure 10.1
The Record mode options on the Transport panel.

- **Merge** record mode means that when you record MIDI events over existing MIDI parts, Cubase will merge the new content and the existing content into a new merged part.
- **Replace** record mode will remove any existing event or part over the period overlapping with a new recording on a specific track. This would have the same result as a typical punch-in/punch-out operation on a standard analog multitrack recorder.

HOW TO

Change the Linear record mode on the Transport panel:

1. Click on the drop-down menu next to the currently visible option in this portion of the Transport panel. (By default, this should be set to Normal.)
2. Select the desired mode.

The Cycle record mode offers five options, two of which only apply to MIDI recordings. These modes determine how MIDI and audio will be recorded during a cycle (looped) recording. A cycle recording occurs when the Cycle button is active on the Transport panel (see Figure 10.2).

Figure 10.2
Cycle mode option enabled on the Transport panel.

When you are in Cycle mode, Cubase continuously plays the content found between the left and right locators. Each time Cubase starts again at the left locator, it is called a *lap*. How the events are handled during a recorded lap depends on the currently active Cycle record mode. For audio cycle recordings, the way the events are recorded will also depend on the cycle recording preferences found in the Preferences > Record > Audio Cycle Record Mode options under the File menu (PC) or Cubase application menu (Mac). These preferences are discussed further in Chapter 14, "Advanced Recording Options."

The following two modes apply only to MIDI recording:

- **Mix.** Each time a lap is completed, the MIDI events recorded in the next lap are mixed with the events from the previously recorded lap. This is the perfect mode to build up a rhythm track, adding each musical part over the previously recorded one. All events are recorded inside a single part.
- **Overwrite.** Each time a lap is completed, the MIDI events recorded in the next lap will overwrite (replace) the events that were previously recorded. Use this when you are trying to get the perfect take in one shot. Just be sure to stop recording before the next lap begins, or your last take will be overwritten. If you stop playing at the end of a lap and stop recording in the middle of the next lap, without having played a note in that lap, you'll be okay. Overwrite will only "overwrite" when there are new events recorded during the current lap.

The following three modes apply to both MIDI and audio recordings, but are also found under the same Cycle record mode selection drop-down menu:

- **Keep Last.** This mode keeps whatever was recorded in the last *complete* lap. So if you start playing a lap but stop before it's done, it will not keep that lap. However, if you complete a lap and stop halfway during the next lap, the last completed lap will be the one kept, as with the Overwrite option. This is a good mode to use when you want to record different takes until you get the perfect one. The main difference with overwriting is that in the case of audio recordings, each lap you record is still available in your project. Depending on your audio cycle recording preferences, this may mean that Cubase has created regions each time a lap is completed, keeping the last region as the active and visible one onscreen.
- **Stacked.** This is a great way to use cycle recording when you are not as proficient as you would like to be with your playing skills. Every time you complete a lap, an event is created and Cubase continues recording, creating a new event on the same track, lap after lap, stacking up events, as illustrated in Figure 10.3. Once events are stacked, you will only hear the last one recorded, but you can use the best moments of each take to compile an edited version of the part you were trying to record.
- **Stacked 2.** For cycled audio recording, this is identical to Stacked mode, but for MIDI all the takes (laps) remain audible, without automatically muting previous laps as in normal Stacked mode.

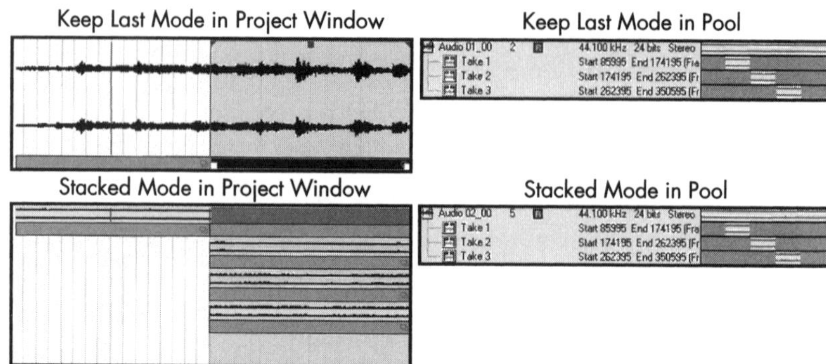

Figure 10.3
Comparing the Keep Last and Stacked Cycle recording modes.

HOW TO

Change the Cycle record mode on the Transport panel:

1. Click on the drop-down menu next to the currently visible option in this portion of the Transport panel, as shown in Figure 10.4.
2. Select the desired mode.

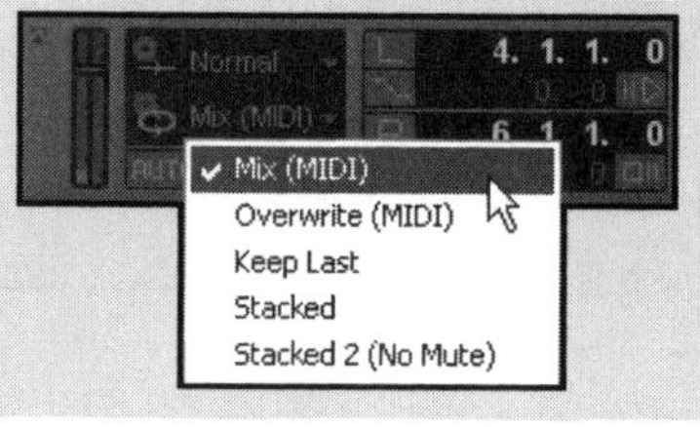

Figure 10.4
Cycle recording modes on the Transport panel.

Below the Linear and Cycle record modes, you will find the Auto-Quantize toggle button (AUTO Q). When this option is enabled (the button is lit, and the text next to the button reads "ON"), new MIDI recordings will automatically snap to the current grid and quantize values without additional steps. For example, use this option when you want to be sure what you record through MIDI is tight with the current groove of a song.

Left and Right Locators

The left and right locators are used to identify positions in the project timeline, which are used as boundary markers for cycle recording and as punch-in/punch-out markers during recording when these options are enabled. Locators are also used to define a cycle area during playback, and they play an important role in exporting audio mixdowns and many project-editing operations.

Locators appear in most content editing windows inside Cubase that display a Ruler bar—the Project window and the Key, Drum, Sample, and Audio Part editors. However, it's the Project window locators that are important to this chapter's MIDI recording topic. The Transport panel and the toolbar can also display the locators' positions, as shown in Figure 10.5.

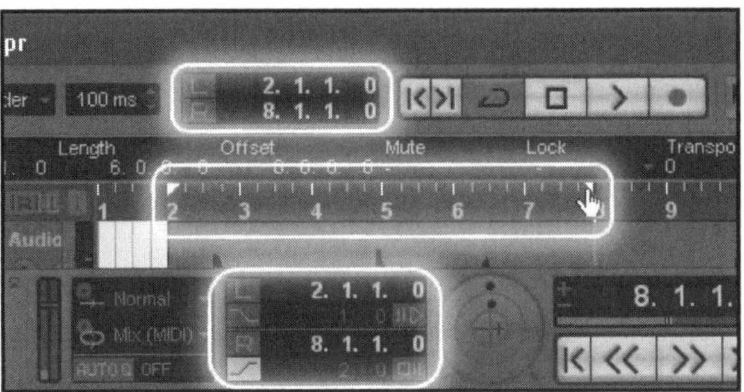

Figure 10.5
Locators in the toolbar (top), Ruler bar (center), and Transport panel (bottom).

HOW TO

Display locators' positions:

- In the toolbar: Right-click (PC)/Control-click (Mac) over an empty area of the toolbar and check the Locators option in the context menu.
- In the Transport panel: Right-click (PC)/Control-click (Mac) over the Transport panel and check the Locators option in the context menu.

You can quickly move the project cursor to the position of the left or right locators by clicking on the L or R buttons found at the left of the locator position fields in the Transport panel. Note that you can achieve the same thing by pressing 1 (for left) or 2 (for right) on the numeric keypad.

HOW TO

Change locators' positions:

- Move the cursor over the left or right locator handles in the timeline ruler. When the cursor changes into a hand, drag to the desired location.
- Ctrl-click (PC)/Option-click (Mac) in the Ruler bar to position the left locator at this location.
- Alt-click (PC)/-click (Mac) in the Ruler bar to position the right locator at this location.
- Above and below each digit in the numerical field for left and right locator positions in the Transport panel, there is a sensitive area. Clicking on this sensitive area will cause your cursor to change to an arrow with a plus or a minus sign. If you click above, the value will increase; if you click below, the value will decrease. Once a numerical field in Cubase is selected, you can also use the scroll wheel on your mouse to increase or decrease these values.
- Or, you can click on a value and enter a new position for it by using your keyboard.

You can also change the left and right locators' positions by using the position of the project cursor as a new left or right locator position.

HOW TO

Change a locator's position to the current cursor location:

- To set the left locator, hold the Ctrl (PC)/Option (Mac) key and click on the L button in the Locators display.
- To set the right locator, hold the Alt (PC)/ (Mac) key and click on the R button in the Locators display.

The Punch-In/Punch-Out and Pre-Roll/Post-Roll functions are discussed in Chapter 14, "Advanced Recording Options."

MIDI and Audio Activity Indicators

The MIDI activity indicator (see Figure 10.6) displays incoming (red) or outgoing (green) MIDI activity. The audio activity indicator displays incoming and outgoing audio (green for both) from and to external devices, as well as clips when they occur. A clip occurs when the digital signal is louder than 0dB Full Scale (or 0dBFS) on a digital audio system. If you're not hearing anything (MIDI or audio), try taking a look at these activity meters first. If you see activity here, then the problem might be outside Cubase. If you don't see activity here when you should, it's possible that Cubase is not receiving or transmitting MIDI or audio properly. Note that MIDI or audio metronome activity will not be displayed in these activity output meters.

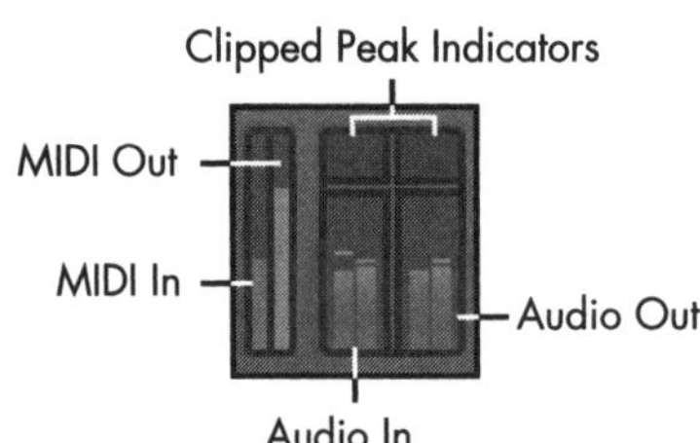

Figure 10.6
The MIDI activity input and output monitors on the Transport panel.

MIDI Activity Troubleshooting Tips

If you are not seeing any MIDI activity when sending messages from an external controller, be sure the selected MIDI track's MIDI Out and In ports are configured properly.

MIDI events sent to a VST instrument will not show up in the MIDI activity output monitors. However, if you are not seeing any MIDI activity when playing recorded MIDI events that are supposed to go to an external device, chances are this is caused by one of the following reasons:

- The tracks in your project contain no MIDI events.
- You have not set the track(s) containing MIDI events to play out through a physical MIDI port such as your MIDI interface.

For example, if your external instruments are not receiving MIDI data, try loading a virtual instrument (VST instrument) and routing your MIDI track to that VSTi's MIDI input. If you do hear the MIDI data playing through the VSTi, then try reassigning the previous MIDI output port to this track again. If you still don't hear MIDI coming from your external instrument, your problem is probably somewhere else.

- Be sure your MIDI connectors and cables are connected properly. If they are, try switching them around to see whether one of them is faulty.
- Are the MIDI ports you're trying to use properly configured in the Device Setup dialog box?
- Is your MIDI interface installed properly?
- Is the MIDI Thru active in Cubase? To check this out, look in the MIDI tab of the Preferences dialog box.

Recording MIDI

Recording MIDI performances makes it possible to edit any of the performance later, as well as process or edit the sound generated by the instrument playing the performance. It offers a very powerful creative tool.

Before recording MIDI, be sure the MIDI Thru Active option is selected in the MIDI tab of the Preferences dialog box. As you play into a MIDI track, the MIDI Thru function re-sends the MIDI information Cubase receives through that track's MIDI output destination.

HOW TO

Record MIDI events on one or multiple tracks:

1. Activate the Record Enable button on the MIDI track you want to use to record incoming MIDI events.
2. In the Transport panel, set the appropriate Record mode (Normal, Merge, or Replace).
3. In the Transport panel, set the appropriate Cycle mode (Mix, Overwrite, Keep Last, Stacked, or Stacked 2) if you want to record in cycles. In most cases, the Mix mode will work best.
4. Position your left and right locators appropriately. For example, if you want to record from bar 5 beat 1 to bar 9 beat 1, set the left and right locators to bar 5 and bar 9, respectively.
5. Activate the metronome click on the Transport panel to hear a click while recording.
6. Click the Record button on the Transport panel or press the asterisk (*) on the numeric keypad, and start playing. If you've enabled the metronome click, the precount value you've entered in the Metronome Setting dialog box determines how many bars of the metronome click sound you will hear before the cursor starts moving forward in the project timeline.
7. Click the Stop button on the Transport panel or press the spacebar when you're finished. If the Punch-Out button was enabled, Cubase should stop automatically when it reaches that location.

Recording Multiple MIDI Channels Simultaneously

When transferring a MIDI sequence from a hardware sequencer to Cubase, or when several MIDI controllers need to be recorded simultaneously, you will need to take additional measures to record MIDI events.

You can record all MIDI events on the same track and split up (dissolve) the events by channel later by setting the track's MIDI output channel to Any. This enables the incoming events to be redistributed to the output port without re-channeling the events to a single, common MIDI channel. You'll find out more about dissolving MIDI parts in Chapter 24, "MIDI Menu Options."

To record MIDI events on separate tracks (one per channel, for example) with a multiport MIDI interface, assign each track to a different input port.

Now that you've just recorded events on a track or multiple enabled tracks, you might want to record over a portion of this recording to correct errors that would take too long to edit in the editor. Or, maybe you just feel like recording over a portion of the track. In the previous steps, you were using the left and right locators as a point of reference to begin playback and recording, as well as to stop recording. You can also use the pre-roll value in the Transport panel to begin playback before you start recording and the post-roll value to have Cubase continue playing after you've stopped recording.

Importing MIDI Files

You can either import Standard MIDI files of Type 0 and 1 into an existing project or create a new project from the imported MIDI files. In a Type 0 MIDI file, all MIDI events in any channel are contained in one single track. After importing such a file, you need to make sure the MIDI track hosting this imported track is set to play out through *any* MIDI channels. A Type 1 file contains as many MIDI tracks as there are MIDI channels actually used in the file. Cubase creates a corresponding number of separate MIDI tracks to host the newly imported Type 1 MIDI file. When you import any MIDI file, it is imported at the beginning of the project.

HOW TO

Import a MIDI file in the existing project:

1. In the project's timeline, position the project cursor where you want the MIDI file to begin.
2. Select File > Import > Import MIDI File.
3. At the prompt, click the No button.
4. Browse to the location of the file you want to import.
5. Select the file and click the Open button.

This prompts Cubase to create the new MIDI tracks necessary to place the imported MIDI content in the current project.

Note that you also can drag and drop a MIDI file from any folder location on your computer directly into a Cubase project.

11 ReWire

ReWire is a software-based technology that lets you share application resources inside your computer—more specifically, ReWire-compatible ones. Developed by Propellerhead and Steinberg, most products sold by either company are compatible with this technology. Today, more and more third-party application developers have joined in by making their applications ReWire-compatible. This chapter looks at some setup tips when working with ReWire applications in a Cubase project.

Here's a summary of what you will learn in this chapter:

- How to use Cubase as a ReWire host
- How to set up a ReWire channel in a project
- How to use ReWire and VSTi (VST instrument) channels in the Mixer
- How to export ReWire tracks as audio files

ReWire Setup

What ReWire does is quite nice, and it's simple to use. It patches the outputs of one software application into the inputs of another software application and synchronizes their Transport controls. This has some similarities to using a VSTi, except that ReWire instruments or ReWire software applications are not running inside Cubase, as a VSTi is. Active ReWire channels appear as additional channels in Cubase's Mixer. This enables all ReWire-compatible applications to share the same audio hardware, assigning each ReWire instrument a different output if you want, and also providing a common Transport control and timing base; you can control playback for all applications from Cubase.

In other words, to use ReWire, you need to have ReWire-compatible applications installed on your system. Available ReWire applications appear under the Devices menu, as shown in Figure 11.1. For example, several ReWire applications, including Sony's ACID Pro 6, Ableton's Live, and Propellerhead's Reason, are installed on this system.

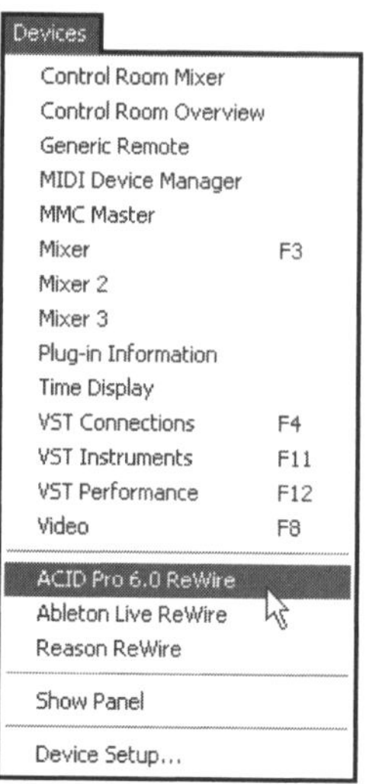

Figure 11.1
Available ReWire applications appear under the Devices menu.

HOW TO

Prepare Cubase for ReWire applications:

1. Launch Cubase first. It is important that your other ReWire applications are launched after Cubase so that they will start up in ReWire Slave mode; otherwise, both applications run independently. This can create conflicts when attempting to access the audio hardware and might prevent you from using either application.
2. Be sure the Release ASIO Driver in Background option is not selected in Devices > Device Setup > VST Audio System.
3. In the Devices menu or the Devices panel, select the installed ReWire application. The ReWire panel will appear, as shown in Figure 11.2. What appears in this panel depends on which ReWire-compatible application you're using. In this example, Ableton Live's panel is opened, offering a maximum of 64 channels.

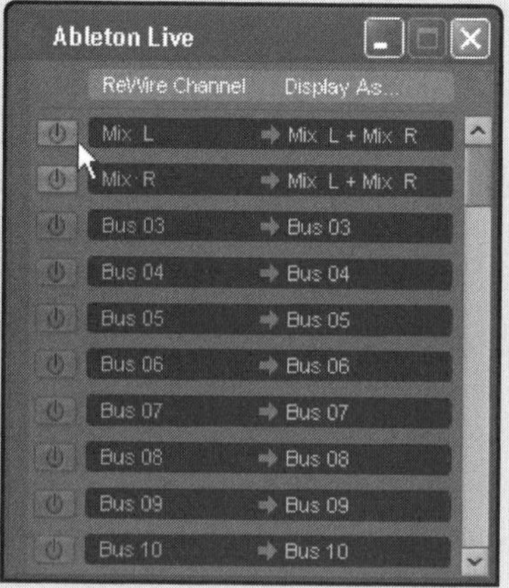

Figure 11.2
The ReWire panel; active channels appear lit.

4. Click the Activate button to the left of the channels you want to create inside Cubase's Mixer.
5. If you want to rename a channel, click in the Display As column and type the label you want to use.
6. Launch your ReWire application.

Each application can offer a large number of channels; so for a given project you will enable only the specific number of channels you want to stream between applications, because each active ReWire channel imposes an additional load on your system. Once a channel is enabled, a corresponding ReWire channel appears in the Mixer. ReWire-compatible applications support up to 64 channels, while ReWire 2.0-compatible applications support up to 256 channels. You can always enable *additional* ReWire channels in your project later if needed. At this point, we only enabled ReWire channels in Cubase, but in order to actually use the other application with Cubase, you'll need to launch it as well.

The order in which you launch ReWire applications is important because the first ReWire application will be considered the ReWire *host*. Each subsequent ReWire application you launch will run in ReWire *slave* mode. The audio properties and tempo setting of slaved applications will conform to the host's properties and settings. If you change the tempo in the slave application, Cubase will turn its tempo track off to follow this new tempo. In other words, to keep any tempo changes accurate in both applications, it's better to use the tempo track in Cubase to change tempos.

The audio output of any software instruments or events recorded in the slaved ReWire application becomes available in Cubase's Mixer; however, creating projects and using these applications will not be discussed here. You can find information about other ReWire applications–such as ACID, Reason, and Live–in other Thomson *Power* books and the *CSi* series of interactive CD-ROMs.

At this point, the Transport bars in both applications are linked. This means that you can start and stop playback within any ReWire-compatible application, and the others will follow. If you record events, they are recorded in the application that is active–in other words, the recording takes place in the application where you clicked the Record button. So, recording in each application is independent, but playback follows. If you use cycle playback or recording, all applications follow this loop. When you have a loop playing in Ableton Live, for example, this loop stays looped. As the ReWire host, Cubase always controls the tempo setting when the Tempo track is active. If you change the tempo in Cubase's Tempo track, the other applications follow its lead. If you are not using the Tempo track, you can change the manual tempo setting in either application, and the playback reflects it. When you start playback at 100 BPM in Live and the Tempo track in Cubase is not enabled to control the project tempo, both applications play at 100 BPM.

All ReWire channels that are not muted when you export your mixdown using the File > Export > Audio mixdown option are included in this output file.

One thing to look for is the sample playback rate. Be sure both applications are set to the same sampling rate. When the rates don't match, the ReWired application might not play at the right pitch.

When the ReWired application uses MIDI to trigger software instruments, you may need to create a MIDI track in Cubase and select the ReWire-compatible MIDI output port as its output. This will send the MIDI events from this Cubase track to the ReWire application in order for it to generate the sounds that will appear in the ReWire audio channel you have configured inside Cubase for the output from that ReWire application. On the other hand, if the ReWire-compatible application is strictly audio-based, using audio loops or events on tracks of its own, then simply activating the bus to which the audio is routed inside Cubase will do. For example, if you have audio tracks in a ReWire application that are coming out through its Main Mix bus, activating this bus inside Cubase (as in the example found in Figure 11.2) will cause any audio routed to that application's Main Mix to be sent (rerouted) into the Cubase Mixer's ReWire channel (see Figure 11.3).

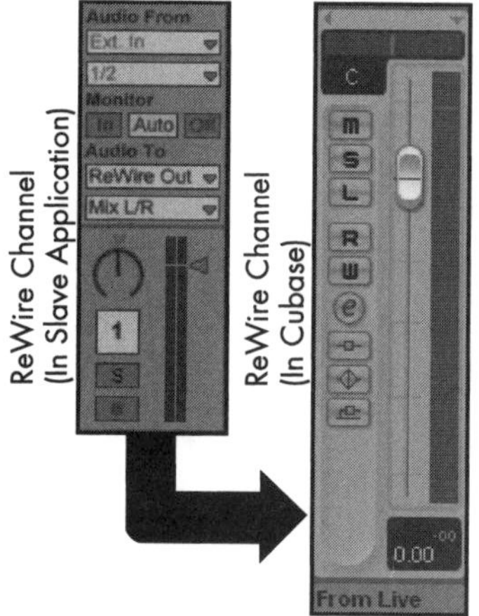

Figure 11.3
The audio in ReWire channels from the third-party application (left) is routed into a ReWire channel inside Cubase (right).

VSTi and ReWire Channels

We saw in Chapter 9 that you can use a VSTi either by loading it as you create an instrument track or by loading the VSTi in the VST Instruments panel and then selecting this VSTi as the output destination for one or more MIDI tracks. Figure 11.4 shows the latter case, with a MIDI track assigned to a VSTi. With ReWire 2.0 applications, such as Reason in the example found in Figure 11.5, a MIDI track can be routed through a ReWired MIDI output port. This allows you to send MIDI events from Cubase to a software instrument loaded in the ReWired application. Once the ReWired instrument receives the signal, you then need to route the audio output back to Cubase by enabling that channel, as described earlier in this chapter.

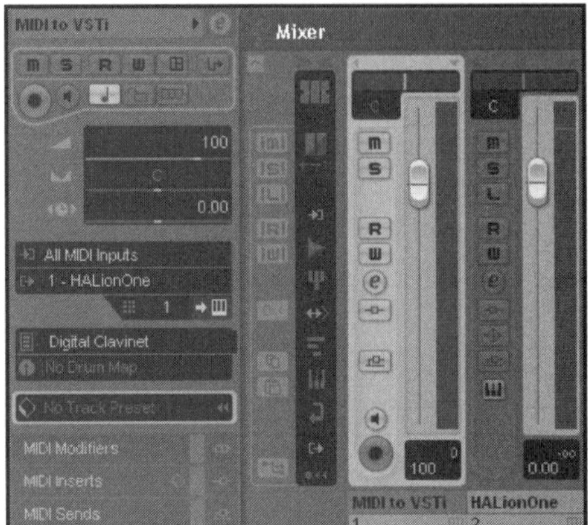

Figure 11.4
The Inspector showing the MIDI routing (left), and the Mixer showing both channels (MIDI on left and VSTi on right).

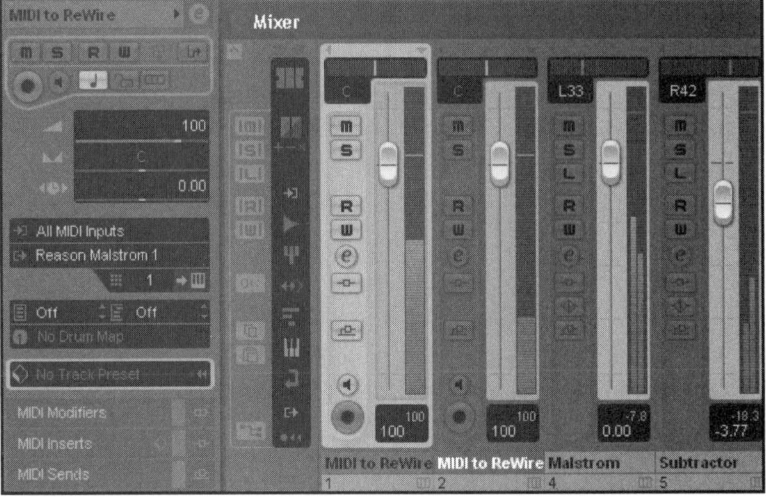

Figure 11.5
The Inspector showing the MIDI routing (left), and the Mixer showing both channels (MIDI on left and ReWire channels on right).

For the most part, audio channels representing audio tracks or the audio output from a VSTi or ReWire instrument are fairly similar. There are, however, some notable differences:

- You can't assign an audio input bus to an instrument, a VSTi, or a ReWire audio channel.
- There are no Record Enable buttons on these audio channels. Instrument channels do have a Record Enable button (see Figure 11.6), which will record MIDI events, but not audio.
- There is no Monitor button because there are no audio inputs to monitor. On instrument channels, the Monitor button lets you monitor or play MIDI events without having to record-enable the track. This is convenient when you simply want to play through the instrument while recording something else on another track.

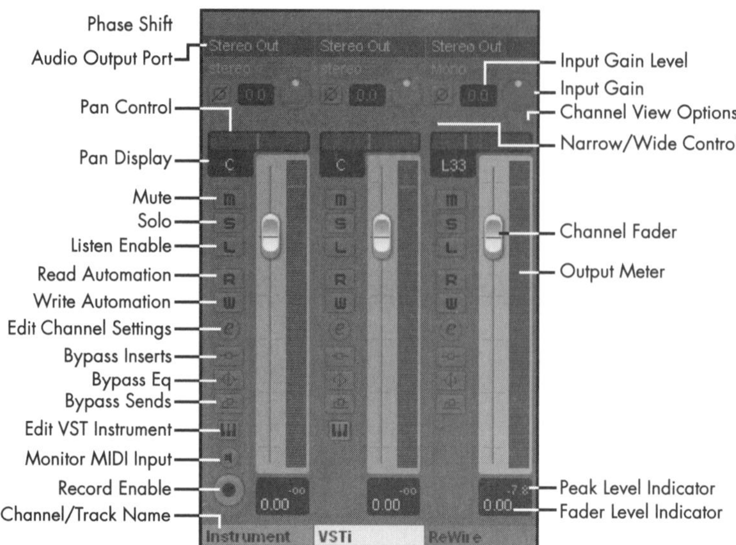

Figure 11.6
From left to right, an instrument, a loaded VSTi, and a ReWire channel.

- Below the Bypass Send Effect button on VSTi and instrument tracks is the Edit VST Instrument button that opens the VSTi interface for changing settings in the instrument. In contrast, because ReWire instruments are not inside Cubase, you need to access their host application to make changes to their settings.
- VSTi and ReWire channels have a separate button in the Mixer's Common panel on the left, allowing you to hide all instances of either type of channel from view.
- In the Mixer, there are distinct background colors behind the volume faders on Instrument and VSTi channels, ReWire channels, and audio channels.

Exporting VSTi and ReWire Channels

Because VSTi and ReWire channels are audio channels within Cubase's Mixer, they will be included in the audio mixdown when the File > Export > Audio Mixdown function is used. Make sure these tracks are unmuted if you want to include them in the exported audio file for your mixdown.

VSTi and ReWire devices can eat up resources from your computer; exporting those tracks as audio files might also let you unload them from memory to add more real-time inserts or FX channels. If this is what you need to do, always save your project with a different name to keep access to the original MIDI-based tracks and synth settings in the project.

HOW TO

Export a VSTi or ReWire channel:

1. Set the left and right locators at the start and end of the portion you want to export.
2. Take note of the VSTi or ReWire channel you want to export and solo the MIDI track you want to export.
3. Monitor the instrument's audio channel in the Mixer, adjust any settings to avoid clipping, and optimize the sound.
4. From the File menu, select Export > Audio Mixdown.
5. In the Export Audio Mixdown dialog box (see Figure 11.7), enter a name for the file.

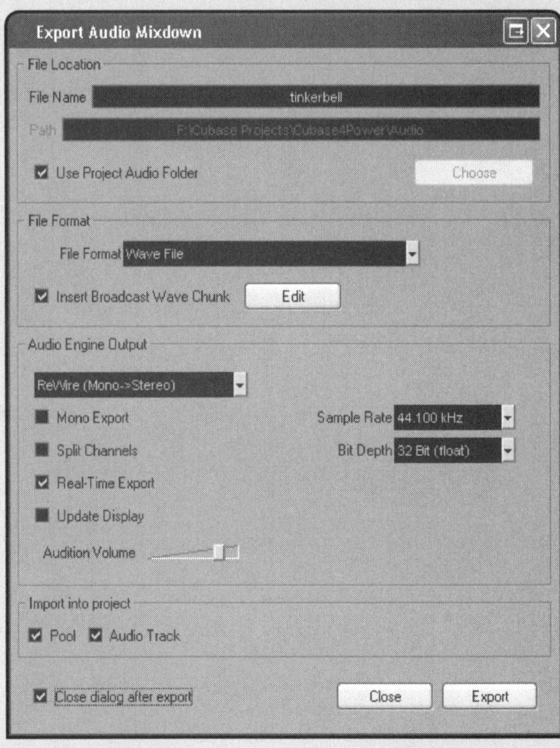

Figure 11.7
The Export Audio Mixdown dialog box.

6. Select a path (destination folder) for the file or enable the Use Project Audio Folder option to save the file in that location.
7. Select the file format. Avoid lossy compression types, such as MP3, WMA, and OGG, when exporting any audio that you want to use as part of a subsequent mixing or mastering operation in Cubase or some other audio program. Some file types offer additional attribute options when selected. Choose the desired attributes according to your requirements.
8. Choose the appropriate channel, resolution, and sample rate settings for the exported file from the corresponding drop-down menus. When exporting audio to integrate it back into a project, be sure these settings correspond to the current project settings.

9. From the Outputs drop-down menu, select the VSTi or ReWire channel you want to export. With some automated VST or ReWire instruments, you might need to export the information in real time to include all the parameters being automated in the export. Whether this is needed depends on the instrument itself. Please read the instrument's documentation to find out whether real-time export is required when exporting a MIDI track with parameter automation. If you did use any parameter automation for this VSTi, don't enable this option. In most instances, you *won't* need it, but if you run into problems, remember this warning.
10. Enable the Import to Pool and Audio Track options.
11. Click on the Export button when you are finished.
12. Enable the Close Dialog after Export option only if you don't intend to export another track.
13. Repeat for each ReWire channel you need to export.
14. When you are finished, you can unload the ReWire application from your computer's memory.
15. Delete all corresponding MIDI tracks, or even better, place them inside a folder track in case you want to try playing the same MIDI events through a different instrument later.
16. From the File menu, select Save As.
17. In the Save As dialog box, select a new name for this new copy of the project file in order to keep your original file intact, while using this "lighter" version for the mixing process.

For instrument tracks you can use the Freeze Instrument Channel functionality, which offers a number of convenient resource optimization options. You will find more on the Freeze options in Chapter 39, "Project Optimization."

12 Insert Effects

Inserts on traditional analog and some digital mixers are points in an audio channel strip where the signal can leave the channel, pass through an external (or built-in) effect, and then be re-introduced into the signal path of the channel. In analog audio scenarios, this excursion outside the channel provides an ideal technique to apply signal processing, such as compressors and other dynamics processors, equalization, or other types of effects required to process a single channel.

In Cubase, inserts play a very similar role, but because everything can occur in the virtual realm, the signal doesn't necessarily need to leave the channel. If you choose, it can be exclusively routed through software-based effects known as plug-ins.

Here's a summary of what you will learn in this chapter:

- The signal flow of insert plug-in effects
- How to use post-fader inserts
- How to add inserts to Control Room studio and headphone channels
- How to add inserts to Control Room talkback and external input channels
- How to load insert plug-ins into monitor channels

Audio Track Inserts

In Cubase 4, you can have up to eight insert effects per channel. The signal from an audio track is routed through each active insert effect, one after another. In other words, the output of one insert effect feeds the next one, and so on, from top to bottom. Generally speaking, effects such as compressors, limiters, gates (which are all dynamics processing effects), equalizers, and filter or modulation effects (such as chorus and flangers) are often used as inserts. On the other hand, effects such as reverbs and delays are often used as sends. Although Cubase already offers a dedicated four-band parametric EQ section on each audio-related channel type (which, in addition to audio tracks, also includes input and output busses, as well as instrument, VSTi, FX, and group channels), you might prefer loading a particular EQ plug-in in one of the track's insert slots, because you prefer its sound and the parameters it offers. If this is the case, inserts are where you would load such EQ and filter plug-ins.

As you can see in Figure 12.1, the signal enters the first six *pre*-fader inserts once it enters the channel and passes through the phase and trim control. The output level of the active effect in each insert slot determines the input level of the following insert in this chain. There is no control over the amount of output signal for the insert section as a whole. However, some plug-ins do offer their own output level control. After the signal passes by the access points for any sends sent to pre-fader (which are not affected by the track's main Volume fader), EQ section, level, and mute controls, it enters the two *post*-fader inserts.

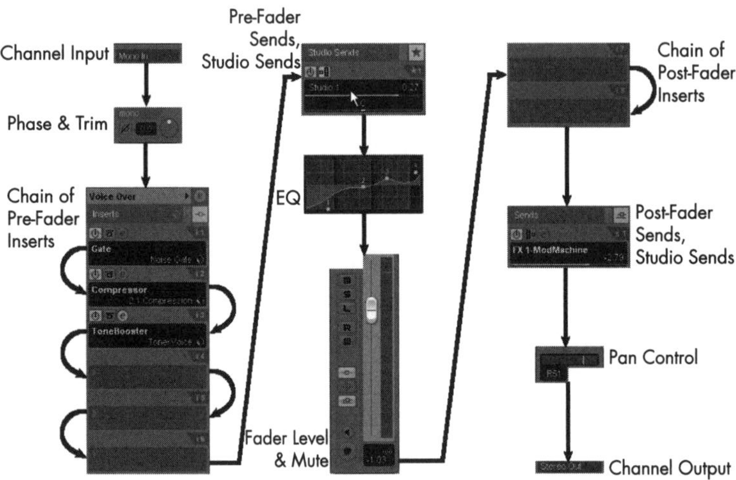

Figure 12.1
Audio signal path of pre- and post-fader inserts.

Because the first six insert slots are not affected by the track's main Volume fader, this is the best place to apply a compressor and control the peaks of a signal. You can then use the fader to adjust a signal that has already been dynamically controlled, allowing for greater flexibility and presence when needed.

Using Inserts 7–8 for Post-Fader Processing

Normally, when using inserts, the signal passes through the effect before the volume control (pre-fader) and before any EQ is applied to the track. However, with inserts 7 and 8, the signal is sent to the insert *after* the track's EQ section and its main Volume control (in other words, these insert slots are post-fader).

This type of insert is best suited for effects that should be applied *after* the track's volume and EQ settings. A good example of this would be final dynamic processing such as limiters or compressors during the mastering process or dithering processes. These would typically be applied as inserts 7 and 8 on the output bus for your mix.

Each insert effect slot has six controls:

- **The Activate/Deactivate Insert button.** The plug-in stops processing the signal when the inserts are turned off, but it retains all of its current settings.
- **A Bypass button.** Cubase continues to process the signal as it passes through the plug-in, but the channel's signal bypasses the plug-in's output.
- **An Edit button.** This will open the control panel for that slot's active insert plug-in.
- **A Plug-In Effect selection field.** This lets you choose from a list of installed plug-ins.
- **A preset selection field.** This displays the selected preset or lets you access Cubase's SoundFrame preset management system.
- **A cube-shaped preset management button.** This lets you load or store saved plug-in presets.

You also will find a number of controls in the title bar of this section that affect all inserts within it:

- The Bypass Inserts button bypasses the entire Inserts section on this track. As with the Activate/Deactivate button for each insert slot, this can be useful for comparing your track (with or without effects), without having to alter each individual effect. When the Inserts section is bypassed, a yellow rectangle appears at the location of the Bypass Inserts button.
- The Inserts title bar maximizes or minimizes this section of the Inspector, while the Show Active Inserts indicator displays whether any inserts are currently active this track. The default project color means that there are no active inserts on this track (even though some may be selected for the slot, but they may not be currently active), and turquoise means that there are active inserts.

On all track classes (including both audio-related and MIDI tracks), adding an insert effect, bypassing an individual insert, or bypassing the entire Inserts section is done exactly the same way.

When you work on a mix, it is important to understand that the more effects you have running in real time (online, as opposed to offline), the more processing power is required from your computer. With this in mind, it is highly recommended that you use the send effects (through FX channels) rather than using the inserts, if you're going to apply the same effect with the same settings to various tracks (typical with delay and reverb effects, for example). If you need to apply the same dynamic process on several channels, then route the output from all these channels to the same group channel by setting these channels' output to an available group channel (or creating one if necessary) and adding an insert effect to that group channel instead. By doing so, all channels routed to this group channel will be processed through the same plug-in with the same setting, and you will use fewer computer resources, which will allow you to save these resources for when you really need them.

Reducing Processing Power Needed by Using Sends Instead of Inserts

Each instance of an effect loaded into an insert effect slot on an individual channel uses the same processing power and memory as it does if it were loaded into an insert slot on a group or FX channel and used as the common destination for multiple sends from *multiple* source tracks.

To monitor how your computer is doing in terms of system resources, you can take a look at the VST Performance window or the Transport panel. The default key command to open the VST Performance window is F12. Macintosh users should reassign the keyboard shortcut for the Dashboard in System Preferences, which by default uses the F12 key. You also can open the VST Performance window from the Devices menu. It provides a tool for monitoring system performance, so that if necessary you can make changes to your project before your computer starts to become overloaded.

When you are finished tweaking the inserts on a track, you can always use the Freeze command to free up some resources by temporarily freezing these settings in place. To find out more on how to use the Freeze command on audio channels, take a look at Chapter 39.

Inserts on Control Room Connections

Cubase's Control Room Mixer provides additional monitoring controls, most of which also support the addition of processing through the use of insert plug-in effects. For example, you can add a limiter plug-in effect to a talkback, studio, or headphones channel in order to prevent any strong peaks from damaging monitoring equipment (or the ears of the musicians themselves!).

HOW TO

Add inserts to Control Room studio and headphone channels:

1. In the Control Room Mixer (CRM), expand the extended view.
2. Click on the Show Meters/Inserts button if the meters are currently displayed (see Figure 12.2) and select the Inserts section view from the pop-up menu.

Figure 12.2
Toggle the extended panel of the CRM between inserts and meters.

3. Select the insert you want to enable.
4. The control panel for this plug-in opens by default, so you can choose a preset from its preset menu and adjust its settings as needed.
5. Close the plug-in's control panel when you are finished.

HOW TO

Add inserts to Control Room talkback and external input channels:

1. Click on the Show Left Strip button at the bottom-left corner of the CRM to display these channels.
2. To view the talkback channel settings and its inserts in the extended panel, click on the Talk button of the CRM, as displayed in Figure 12.3.

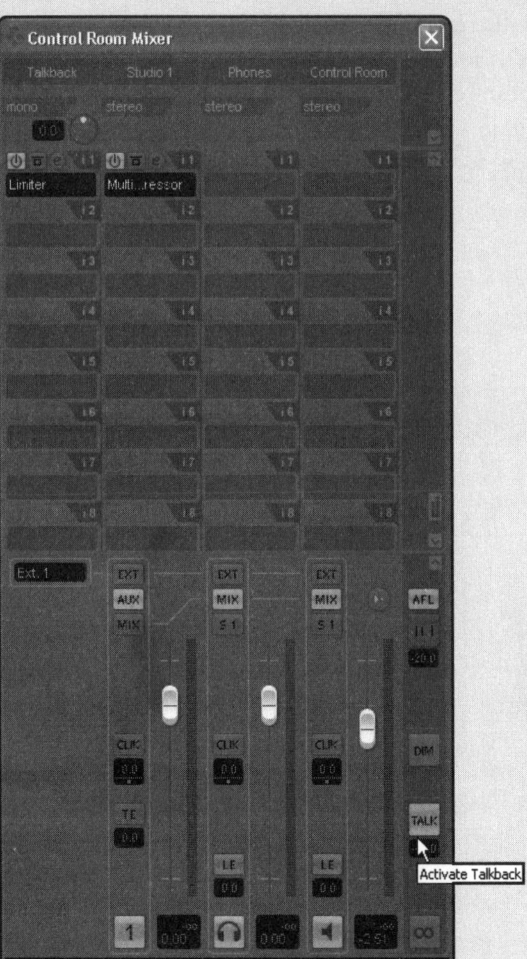

Figure 12.3
Switching between the talkback and the external inputs in the CRM.

3. Set up the inserts as discussed earlier in this chapter.
4. To switch back to the external inputs, deactivate the Talk button.

Loading Insert Plug-Ins into Monitor Channels

Click on the Show Right Strip button (a small arrow in the lower right-hand corner) to display the Monitor section, and repeat the same steps found here to load inserts in the monitor channels of the CRM.

The only difference in using inserts in the Inspector and working with inserts in the Mixer's extended panel for Cubase 4 users is that all the channels are side by side in the Mixer, making it easier to adjust the different settings of several tracks. Cubase Studio 4 users can use the Channel Settings window described in Chapter 18, "Audio Tracks." This won't allow you to see all the effects settings side by side in the same window either, but it does provide a bird's-eye view of all the effects (inserts, EQ, and sends) for a particular channel within a single window.

13 Pool

The Pool holds references to all audio and video clips used in a project. When you record onto an audio track, an event is created in the Project window, and a clip representing the audio file on disk appears in the Pool. When an audio file is imported, once again, an audio clip represents this file in the Pool. Each project has its own Pool (see Figure 13.1), which optionally can be saved separately so that its contents can be imported into another project. You also can open more than one Pool in a single project, allowing you to share Pool resources between projects. The Pool also enables you to view your audio clip references (called *events*) and corresponding regions. You can use the Pool to monitor, update, and manage these references.

Here's a summary of what you will learn in this chapter:

- How to access and use the Pool
- How to use the audio event preview functions in the Pool
- How to find audio files using the Pool's search functionality
- How to recover missing audio files with the Pool
- How to optimize the disk space used by the project's audio assets
- How to archive and export Pools from a project
- How the Pool can interact with a project
- How to use offline processes in the Pool

Pool Folders

There are three default folders in the Pool: Audio, Video, and Trash. Create any number of additional subfolders within these folders as you see fit, but you can't rename or delete these default folders. You can access the Pool by selecting its option in the Devices menu, by pressing the key command Ctrl+P (PC)/ ⌘+P (Mac), or by pressing the Open Pool button on the Project window's toolbar.

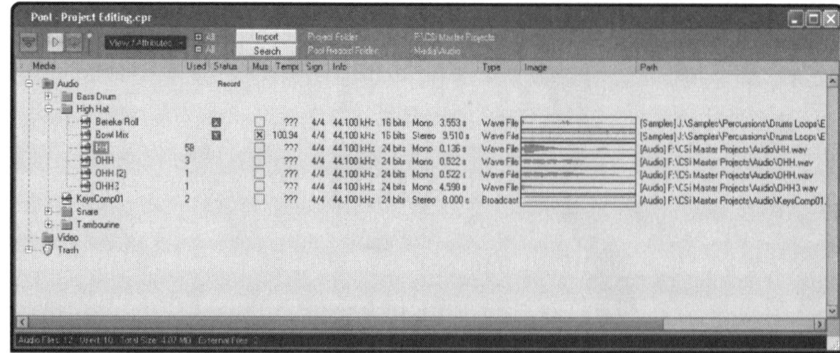

Figure 13.1
The Pool window.

The Pool Areas

The Pool is divided into two main areas: the toolbar and the main display area. A third, less obvious but very important area of the Pool is its menu options, found under the Media menu and through a right-click (PC)/Control-click (Mac). Most Pool operations are done through this menu. Enable the Show Info button (the first button on the left in Figure 13.1) to reveal the Info Line at the bottom of the Pool to view the current status information for your Pool, the number of files it contains, how many are currently used in this project, the total size of the Pool, and how many of the media files that it references reside outside the project's folder.

The next two buttons in the toolbar are used to monitor a selected event or region in the Media column below. The Play button starts/stops playback of the selected file. The Loop button next to it loops the playback, and the small fader adjusts the preview volume. This volume is linked to the main stereo output when the Control Room features are disabled or to the main Control Room monitors when this latter feature is enabled. To stop the playback, click the Play button again.

The View field customizes the Pool columns displayed below it. There are a total of 12 information columns available. Adding a check next to a name (by selecting it in the View drop-down menu) adds this attribute to the columns displayed in the Pool. Selecting the Hide All option hides every column to the right of the Media column.

Use the plus (+) All or minus (–) All button next to the View field to expand/collapse the tree found under the Media column. The Import button lets you import supported media files to the project's Pool. Cubase supports most audio file formats, as well as video files in AVI, QuickTime, WMV (Windows only), DV (Mac OS X only), and MPEG 1 and 2 format.

HOW TO

Import media files into the Pool:

1. Click the Import button in the Pool.
2. Browse the media drive to find the file you want to import. After a file is selected, preview it by using the Play button found below the File Display area in the Import Options dialog box.
3. Select the file and click the Open button to import it to the current Pool.
4. When the file you want to import is not currently inside the Audio folder of your project, Cubase prompts you to select different import options (see Figure 13.2). When the imported file does not correspond to the current project sample rate and bit depth, Cubase offers to convert these files. Audio files must have the same sample rate as the project, but can have different word lengths (also known as bit depths; the number of bits used for each sample).
5. Click OK when you are finished making selections to add the files to the Pool.

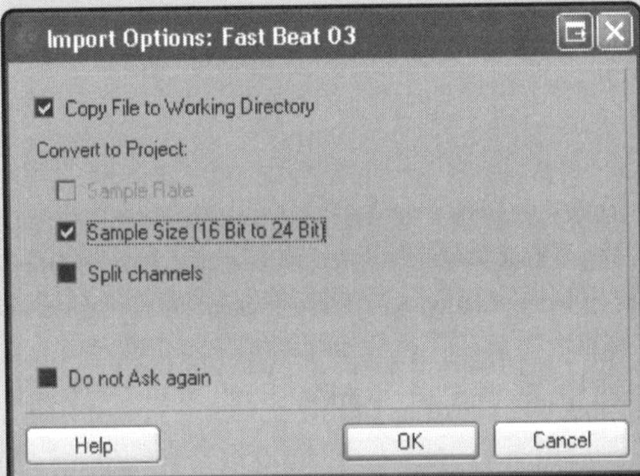

Figure 13.2
The Import Options dialog box.

The Search button, found below the Import button, opens the Search panel at the bottom of the Pool. The search parameters are similar to any search tool on your computer. For example, enter keywords or use wildcard characters to find multiple files whose names contain specific strings of characters. (See the example in Figure 13.3.)

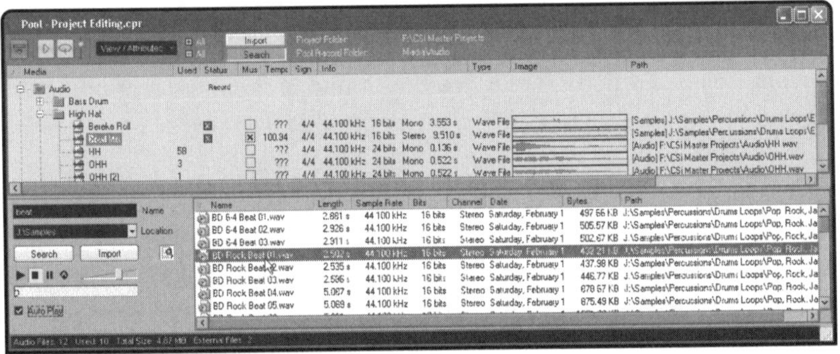

Figure 13.3
The Search panel found in the Pool when the Search function is activated.

HOW TO

Search for files to import:

1. Click the Search button in the Pool's toolbar.
2. In the Name field of the Search panel, type the name of the file you want to find. You can use wildcard characters to widen your search criteria.
3. In the Location field, select the drive or drives you want to look in or select a specific path to look in at the bottom of the drop-down menu.
4. Click the Search button. The search results will appear in the list to the right.
5. Enable the Auto Play check box if you want to automatically preview the files found by the search. To preview a file, select it in the list. If the Auto Play option is not activated, you can click the Play button below the Search button in this panel. You can also adjust the level of the preview by using the Preview Level fader.
6. To import the selected file or files, click the Import button.
7. Select the appropriate import options from the dialog box and click OK to import the files into the Pool.

To the right of the Import and Search buttons, you can see the project folder's path and its associated Pool Record folder. By default, the Pool Record folder is found inside the project folder and is called Audio; it can easily be backed up later with the rest of the project.

Directly below the toolbar are the column headers for each column in the Pool. Click on a header to sort the Pool's contents according to the information in this column if necessary. Columns used to sort information have a little arrow pointing up or down next to the column's header that indicates ascending or descending order. You also can drag the column headers horizontally to change the columns' order. The header is inserted to the right of the column found on the left edge of the header's border when dragged.

Understanding the Information

The Media column displays the names and types of media used in the project, as well as any folders that you might have created inside the Pool to organize your media files. There are three different icons displayed next to the name (see Figure 13.4), representing an event object, a region object, and a sliced event object. Region objects are positioned under the event object to which they refer. You can click on the plus sign to expand an event object to reveal its defined regions.

Folder

Record Folder

Event Object

Region Object

Sliced Event Object

Figure 13.4
Icons associated with different objects in the Pool window.

HOW TO

Rename objects in the Pool:

1. **Select the object you want to rename. A light blue box will appear around it.**
2. **Click again to make the blue box change into a frame, as shown in Figure 13.5.**
3. **Type in the new name for the object.**

Figure 13.5
Renaming an object in the Pool window.

The Used column displays the number of times the object in the row appears in the project. In other words, it displays how many times you've used it. Objects that aren't used anywhere in the project have no value in this column. Used sliced objects are incremented by the number of slices found in the object every time you repeat, copy, or duplicate the corresponding part in the Project window. For example, a drum loop divided into eight slices will display 16 in the Used column if this object is used twice in a project (two parts), even if these are shared copies of the same object.

The Status column offers information on the status of the objects inside your Pool. Table 13.1 describes each icon's meaning in this column.

Table 13.1
Understanding the Status Column's Icons

Icon	Its Meaning
Record	Represents the content found in the Pool's Record folder; found next to the Audio folder. If you create a folder in the Pool, you can click in the Status column next to this folder to make this the new Record folder. Subsequent recordings appear under this folder. This does not create a new folder on your hard disk, but it helps you manage the appearance of your files in the Pool. For example, you could create a folder for a vocal session called Vocals. When you click in the Status column next to this folder, the record icon moves next to it, and all recordings made from this point on appear in this Pool folder.
R	Represents events that have been recorded since the last time you opened the project, making it easy to find newly recorded material.
X	Represents events that are not located in the current Pool Record folder. These events might have been imported from another location on your hard disk. This occurs if you don't select the Copy to Project Folder option when importing them. In other words, if

Icon	Its Meaning
	you were to back up your project's folders, these files would not be included unless you use the Prepare Archive function described later.
	Represents events that have been processed offline. In other words, they consist of both references to the original clip and other portions that have been processed and saved in the Edits subfolder within your project's folder.
?	Represents files that have not been found when loading the project. You can use the Find Missing File function to scan these missing files. This is explained later in this chapter.
reconstructible	Represents files that have been processed in some way by using offline processes or effects and for which some of the processed portions have been lost or misplaced. Cubase displays this indication in the Status column when it can reconstruct the missing portions.

HOW TO

Create a folder in the Pool:

1. **In the Pool, select where you want the new folder to be created—under the Audio or Video folder or another previously created subfolder.**
2. **Right-click (PC)/Control-click (Mac) and select the Create Folder option. You also can find the same option in the Media menu.**
3. **Name your folder appropriately.**

The Musical column identifies samples that contain musical loops that have been detected when the file was imported or that you have identified in the Sample editor by enabling the Musical mode button. Clips that are in Musical mode will be time-stretched when the tempo of a project changes, without altering the pitch of the sample. A check in the Musical Mode column also will appear when you import ACID wave files, and Cubase will automatically adjust the tempo of the file to its current project tempo when you add the file into the project. Musical mode is discussed later in this chapter. The Tempo and Signature columns are also associated with the new Musical mode offered in this version of Cubase. You can toggle the Musical mode on and off for a sample by adding or removing a check mark in the option box.

The Info column displays one of two things—either the event's file format and length details or a region's start and end locations.

The Image column displays a graphical representation of the event or the region within the event's boundaries. You will notice that the contents of all the events are displayed within rectangles corresponding to the current width of the Image column; however, regions are represented as a proportion of this length. You can quickly preview any portion of an object's content by clicking on its image representation.

HOW TO

Preview an audio object using the Image column in the Pool window:

1. To begin playback, click anywhere in the image, as displayed by the pointer in Figure 13.6. Playback occurs from the clicked point until the end of the object or until you stop the playback. For more precision, drag the right edge of the Image column header to increase its width.
2. To skip to another portion of the same object, click approximately where you want to hear in the display before the preview ends.
3. To stop the playback, click beside the Image column next to the image, or click the Play Preview button in the toolbar.

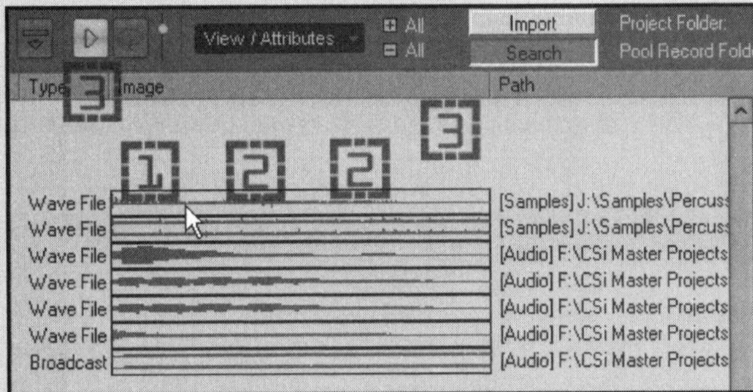

Figure 13.6
Preview navigation using the audio image.

Pool Functions

Generally speaking, the Pool is not something you worry about or use the most at the beginning of a project unless you begin the project by importing a whole bunch of audio files. When your project is taking shape, you will probably also want to organize your Pool to quickly find what you need, so managing content should be something to keep in mind here.

We've already discussed certain managing functions related to the Pool through the creation of folders in which to put additional media objects or through the renaming of existing objects. Let's take a look at other typical Pool functions, such as knowing what to do when an audio file goes missing or when the Pool starts getting messy and locating the files you need gets hard. Archiving a Pool for backup is also something to keep in mind to avoid losing precious work later.

Dealing with Missing Files

Deleting audio files by mistake or intentionally deleting them because you don't need them anymore are things that happen. When they do, Cubase might not be able to find files previously used in this project, especially if you forget to update your Pool before saving it. The file references in Cubase are now pointing to the wrong place. Whatever the reason may be for Cubase not finding missing files, when references to files need to be reestablished, use the Find Missing Files option from the Media menu. Missing files are identified with a question mark in the Status column.

HOW TO

Find missing files in the Pool:

1. From the Media menu, select Find Missing Files. The Resolve Missing Files dialog box will appear (see Figure 13.7).

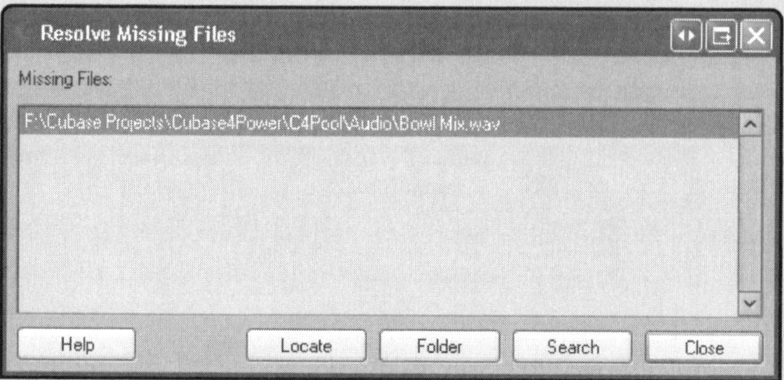

Figure 13.7
The Resolve Missing Files dialog box.

2a. To locate the files, click the Locate button.

OR

2b. To let Cubase look for the missing files, click the Search button, and then the Folder button, and choose the desired folder.

3. Depending on the option selected in Step 2, you are offered different solutions or results. However, if you have chosen the Search option, a new dialog box will appear in which you can change the name of the file you are looking for. Use this option when you remember renaming the file in the operating system after it was last saved with the Cubase project. Enter the new name in the appropriate field, and then click the Start button to begin the search process.
4. When the search successfully finds the missing files, select the file you want from the list displayed and click the Accept button. This updates the link to the file in your Pool to the new file.
5. If you don't want to do this every time, save your project at this point.

In the event that a file is missing, even after a search (or you don't want Cubase to keep referring to a file because you've erased it anyway), you can use the Remove Missing Files option from the Media menu. This affects any object in the Pool with a question mark in the Status column.

Optimizing the Pool

After five or six recording and editing sessions, or a long import session, hundreds of audio files can start piling up in the Pool. Optimizing the Pool lets you keep it organized so that files are easy to access. That's when you can create folders, drag and drop objects inside these folders, and organize your project's assets. When you delete events or regions from the Pool, they often end up in the Trash folder. This means that the files are still using space on your computer. Use the Empty Trash option in the Media menu to free up some of that media drive real estate. Cubase prompts you once again to make sure you really want to erase the files from the hard disk or only remove them from the Pool (see Figure 13.8). If you choose to erase the files, you cannot get them back because this function can't be undone. This is one of the only ways that you can erase audio clips from your drive within Cubase.

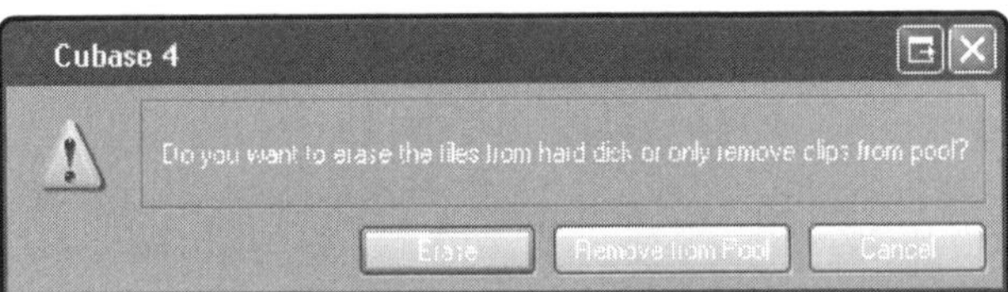

Figure 13.8
Cubase offers you a last chance to keep the files on the computer or completely erase them from your hard disk.

Besides the trash you've collected, there might be some files that were used at the beginning of your project, but aren't being used any longer. If you don't need them, you can use the Remove Unused Media option in the Media menu. This time, you are prompted to choose whether you want to remove these files from the Pool completely (although the source files will still remain on your media drive) or just send them to the Trash folder of the Pool. Removing files from the Pool when you are done with them doesn't erase them from the media drive. It is, therefore, recommended that you always use the Trash folder as a transitional stage when optimizing your Pool. When you are finished, the Media > Empty Trash command gives you the option to actually erase the source files for items in the Pool's Trash folder, which will free up space on the media drive.

Recording long segments often includes useless audio that takes up extra space on your media drive. Creating regions, resizing, or splitting events in the Project window to hide unneeded portions does not remove these portions from the source file on your media drive. Using the Minimize File option in the Media menu creates new copies of the selected files in the project, effectively removing any portions of the original file on the media drive that aren't used in the current project. It also initializes the offline process history for this file. However, bear in mind that the Minimize File command doesn't take into account how the affected files may be used in *other* Cubase projects! Before using this option, it might be advisable to consider another option available in Cubase that also enables you to minimize the file sizes of all audio clips for your project.

Use the Save Project to New Folder option in the File menu to save all the files referenced in a project, as well as the project file itself, to a new folder, minimizing the space used by the project. However, by doing this, you still have the original content in the original folder where you began the project. If you want to revert to this project at a later date, the files will still be there.

HOW TO

Minimize file sizes in your project:

1. Select the files you want to minimize in the Pool window.
2. Choose the Minimize File option from the Media menu.
3. When completed, Cubase prompts you to save the project so that the new file references take effect; click the Save button.

Archiving and Exporting a Pool

When you want to save a backup of your project or use it in another studio, it's important to have access to all the files that are used by the project. Saving the project using the Save command updates the project file, but doesn't copy any files that reside outside the project folder. Use the Prepare Archive option in the Media menu or in the Pool's context menu to copy all the audio clips used in your project to the audio project folder and freeze all offline processes that you may have applied to any audio files. Cubase automatically copies the content of the Edit folder into a backup folder, along with all files used by the project. After this operation is completed, simply copy the resultant project file, its Audio folder, and any video file referenced in the project to a backup CD, for example.

HOW TO

Prepare a project for backup:

1. Select the Remove Unused Media option from the Media menu.
2. Click the Trash button when you are prompted to choose between trashing and removing from the Pool.
3. Select the Empty Trash option from the Media menu.
4. Click the Erase button when you are prompted once again to remove whatever files are not used in the project and erase them from the drive. However, be very careful about this if you happen to be using any of these same files in other projects!
5. Select the Prepare Archive option from the Media menu.
6. Because this is a backup, you can opt to freeze the edits or not. If you choose not to, be sure to also include the Edit subfolder of the project folder when you copy it to the backup medium.
7. Save the project file.
8. When you are ready to back up your files, be sure to include the project file, its Audio subfolder, and the video files you might have used with the project on the backup medium.

If you are in the final stages of a project and you want to save a final version of the project files, repeat the previous steps with the addition of a couple more steps to save only the necessary material. Before heading on to Step 3 from the previous list, you can use the Conform Files option from the Media menu to change all audio files in your project. This converts all your files to the currently selected sample rate and word length (bit depth) for your project. You can use the Minimize Files option, as described earlier, to reduce each file to only its portions that are actually used in the project. Then proceed to Step 7 and use the Save Project to New Folder option in the File menu instead.

Working on game music often requires composers to create several projects, one for each scene in which you build loops for the scene. On the other hand, sharing the same sounds from one scene in a game to another is pretty common. Using the Export and Import Pool options saves the status of objects in the Pool and lets you retrieve them later in another project if needed. An exported Pool does not contain the audio media files because these are located in the Audio folder. Instead, it saves the *references* to regions, slices, and other Pool-specific settings, as well as to the source media files themselves. Exporting a Pool makes it easy to store drum loops and sound effects that have been edited and need to be shared between project files. Whenever you want to use these sounds later on, all you need to do is import that Pool into your current project.

HOW TO ❋

Export or import a Pool:

1. Prepare the Pool by making sure all your files conform to the project's format, removing or searching for missing links, and emptying the Pool's Trash folder.
2. From the Media menu, select the Export Pool option.
3. Type a name for the Pool.
4. Click the Save button.
5. To import the saved Pool inside another project, select Import Pool from the Media menu.

Pool Interaction

Now that you know how to get files into the Pool and sorted once they are in it, let's look at getting the content from the Pool into the project. The quickest and easiest way is to drag events from the Pool to the Project window, as shown in Figure 13.9. When you drag an object from the Pool into the Project window, the actual location of this object depends on two variables:

- The snap and quantize grid settings.
- The position of the snap point inside the audio event or region. Because the snap point can be anywhere within the event, when the Snap button is enabled it's the snap point itself that adjusts to the closest grid line in the Project window.

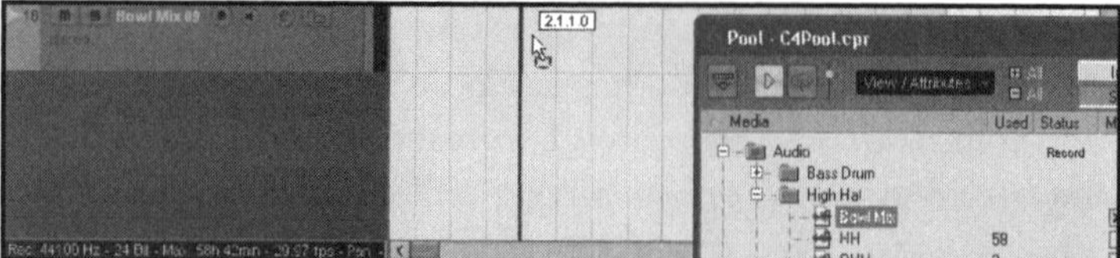

Figure 13.9
Dragging a region from the Pool to a track in the project.

The location displayed above the cursor as you move the selected object over a track indicates the snap or start position where this object will be inserted, depending on the two variables mentioned. When the blue line next to the cursor and location display the desired location, drop the object into place.

> **Dragging Events into a Project**
> Dragging an object from the Pool to the empty area below the last track in the Project window automatically creates a new audio track matching the sample's configuration. For example, dragging a mono event creates a mono track, dragging a stereo event creates a stereo track, and so on.

Create a new audio file from a region in the Pool window by highlighting this region and using the Bounce Selection option in the Audio menu. Choose an appropriate folder for the new file. Once saved, the new file will be added to the Pool as a new event.

Offline Processes in the Pool

When you apply any type of offline process (from the Audio > Process or Audio > Plug-ins menus) to an object inside the Pool, this processing affects the entire object. For example, if you apply a delay effect to a region, the whole region is affected. To process only a portion of a region, use these processes from the Sample editor's context menu instead. Offline processes in the Pool window can be viewed in the Offline Process History panel found in the Audio menu, as can processes applied in the Project window or Sample editor.

> HOW TO
>
> **Apply an offline process to an object from the Pool window:**
>
> 1. Select the object in the Media column.
> 2. From the Audio menu, select the process you want to apply.
> 3. Make the appropriate setting in the process's dialog box.
> 4. Click the Process button.

14 Advanced Recording Options

By default, Cubase is configured to work with the most commonly used and convenient settings. However, there will come a time when some of the recording options might not meet your needs, and a bit of tweaking will be required. This chapter addresses a number of MIDI-related settings that have a direct impact on the type of MIDI events entering or being played back by a project.

Most musical productions these days rely heavily on layers of musical elements and pristine performances.

Here's a summary of what you will learn in this chapter:

- How to change MIDI, recording, and Transport-related preferences
- How to set up MIDI filtering options
- How to use punch-in and punch-out overdubbing techniques
- How to use pre-roll and post-roll overdubbing techniques

MIDI Recording Preferences

MIDI recording preferences influence Cubase's behavior during the recording process, from converting the MIDI Out port into a MIDI Thru, to chasing MIDI controller events embedded in the MIDI track when the playback stops, to filtering certain types of MIDI messages. These preferences are found in several sections of the Preferences dialog box that is opened under the File (PC)/Cubase (Mac) menu. The default settings should work fine for most users. Once you've set any of your own preferences for the Cubase application, however, you won't have to change them before each new project or recording.

You can change preferences when the default settings are not convenient for you. For example, enable the Enable Record on Selected Track option in the Editing page of the Project & Mixer tab to quickly record on a track without having to manually arm it each time (see Figure 14.1).

In Cubase, only those tracks that are record-enabled will record events when the Record button is pressed on the Transport panel.

Figure 14.1
The Enable Record on Selected Track option.

In the MIDI page shown in Figure 14.2, enable the Reset on Stop option if you want Cubase to send a MIDI Reset message, which includes an All Notes Off message, whenever the Stop button is pressed. If MIDI notes on one of your synths regularly get "stuck" after you press the Stop button, try enabling this option. Perhaps a more useful option is the Insert Reset Events after Record feature, which adds a MIDI Reset message at the end of a newly recorded MIDI part to, for example, prevent a sustain pedal from still being in its "on" state when the next part in the same track begins. In the same page, the Length Adjustment option determines the amount of ticks to remove from a MIDI event when reproducing two consecutive notes on the same pitch and on the same channel. This adjustment ensures that there is a small space between these two MIDI events. Still in the MIDI page, the Chase Events options refer to how Cubase deals with MIDI controller events that have been recorded. For example, when you start playback somewhere in the middle of the Cubase project, will it look back to see whether there was a patch change prior to this point in the track, or will it simply play the notes, leaving whatever patch is currently selected on the affected MIDI device? By default it won't, but add a check mark next to the appropriate MIDI event type in the Chase Events list, and it will. Here's another example: You stop playback while the pitch bend value is not at zero, then you decide to move a few bars back. If the Chase Events option for Pitchbend is not enabled, the MIDI device will still be set at the last pitch bend value it received, and the note will sound out of tune. If pitch bend values are chased, Cubase sends the last pitch bend value preceding the new start position. If you start playback before any pitch bend was recorded, the value will remain as is.

In the Record page shown in Figure 14.3, the Snap MIDI Parts to Bars option causes Cubase to extend the beginning and end of newly recorded parts to the closest bar lines when you record on the fly from a location other than a bar's beginning. This makes it easier to move parts when editing them on a track; therefore, the option is checked by default. The Solo Record in MIDI Editors option record-enables any track that is opened in a MIDI editor, while preventing any other MIDI or Instrument tracks from also recording new events for as long as the MIDI editor is opened. The Retrospective Record field captures MIDI events you play on any record-enabled MIDI or Instrument track, even if you are not recording them. The number of retrospective events

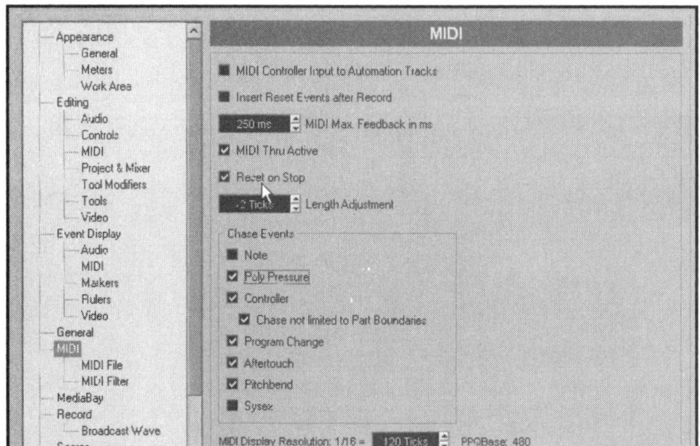

Figure 14.2
The MIDI preferences.

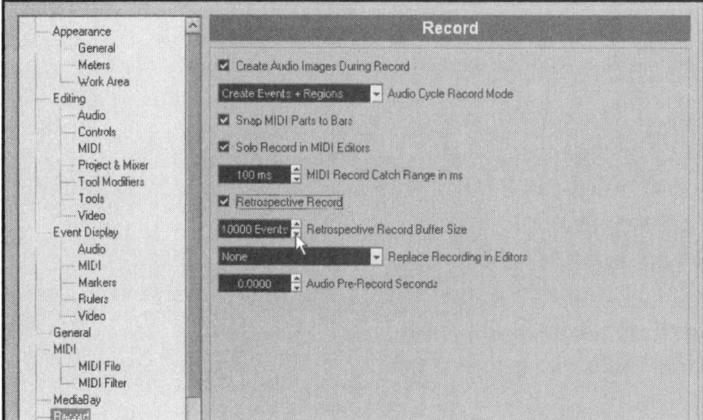

Figure 14.3
The MIDI Record preferences.

kept in memory is determined by the Retrospective Record Buffer Size field in this page of preferences.

In the Transport page shown in Figure 14.4, the Return to Start Position on Stop option returns the play line to the location from which it started when you last clicked Play or Record, rather than having it stay at its current stop location. Check this option when you're recording overdubs and you want the play line to always return to the same beginning point after each take. The Deactivate Punch In on Stop option disables the otherwise enabled Punch-In button whenever you click the Stop button or press the spacebar on your keyboard. Finally, the Stop after Automatic Punch Out option causes playback to stop automatically right after the project reaches the punch-out location or after the additional amount of post-roll time is played, if this setting is also enabled. A pre-roll and post-roll setting is enabled when you enter a time value for either of these fields in the Transport panel and when the Use Pre-/Post-Roll option is checked in the Transport menu.

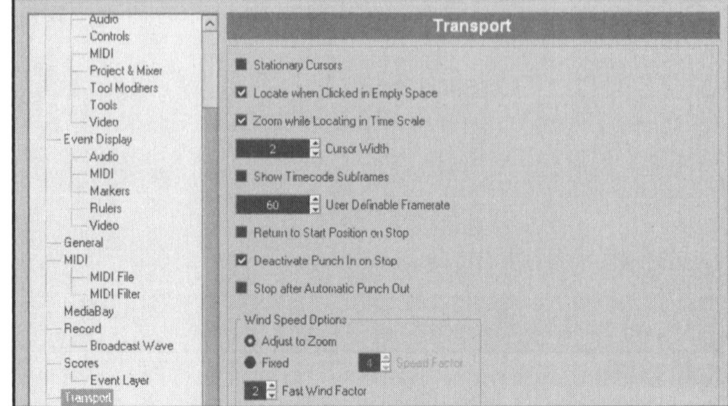

Figure 14.4
The Transport preferences.

MIDI Filtering

When recording MIDI performances, you are recording many different types of MIDI events. The Channel Voice MIDI message is often the most common type and includes Note On, Note Off, Program Change, and so on. You can record *all* MIDI messages or only specific MIDI messages, filtering other message types from the recording. In other words, you can choose which MIDI events you want to record. This can be useful when you want to avoid recording lots of useless data that might otherwise bog down your MIDI system. Also, some MIDI devices send events that might not be essential to your performance or even recognized by the device that you will use to play it back—polyphonic aftertouch data being one of the common examples. Cubase enables you to filter out these messages.

HOW TO

Filter MIDI events:

1. Select Preferences > MIDI Filter from the File (PC)/Cubase (Mac) menu.
2. In the MIDI Filter parameters, under the Record section, check all the types of events you do not want Cubase to record. Events of the specified types that are already recorded will continue to play back, even if you disable them for future recordings.
3. Under the Thru section, check all the types of events you do not want Cubase to echo to other MIDI devices. Previously recorded events of the affected types will still play back, but checked event types coming in from the MIDI input will be filtered out. In Figure 14.5, for example, Cubase records SysEx, or System Exclusive, messages, but does not transmit them to other devices.
4. In the Channels section, click the MIDI channels from which you do not want to record. In Figure 14.5, messages coming on Channels 11 through 16 will not be recorded.

5. Finally, if you want to add additional controller messages to the filtered list, use the Controller Selection field in the Controller section to scroll through the types of controller messages, and click the Add button to add them to your filtered list. Still in Figure 14.5, Portamento messages will be filtered out from recording.
6. When finished, click Apply and then OK.

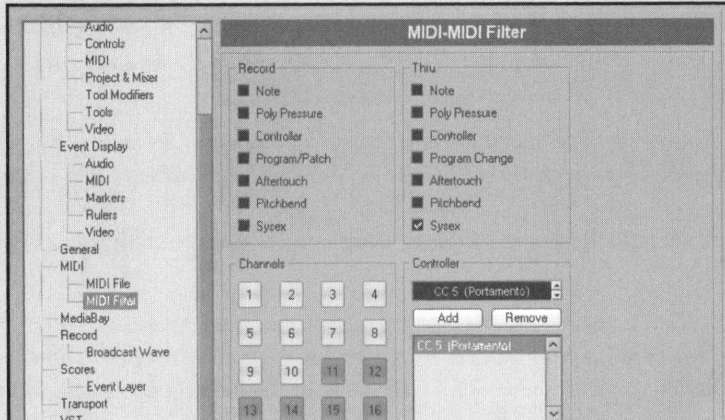

Figure 14.5
The MIDI Filter area in Cubase's Preferences dialog box.

As you've noticed in the previous steps, these settings are optional and, in most cases, filtering System Exclusive (SysEx) messages is all you need to do (and these, by default, are already filtered). On the other hand, you can deselect the SysEx filter if you want to save your external MIDI device's System Exclusive information into a project. You will find more on System Exclusive (SysEx) messages in Chapter 35, "Automation Techniques."

MIDI Filter parameters apply real-time input and recording on all MIDI tracks until you change the settings once again. You can, however, decide to filter out certain MIDI events or even convert them into other MIDI event types in a track in real time as you are recording. This is done through Cubase's Transformer.

The Transformer comes in two flavors—as a MIDI plug-in effect called *Transformer* and as a track input feature called *Input Transformer*. When you use the Transformer plug-in effect, it affects events that are already recorded on a track. In contrast, the Input Transformer transforms the events before they are even recorded into the track. You can access the Input Transformer's panel through its button in the MIDI Settings section of the Inspector, as shown in Figure 14.6.

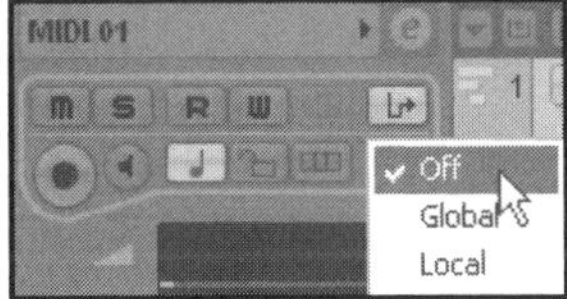

Figure 14.6
The Inspector's Input Transformer drop-down menu.

Using the Input Transformer

One very useful application of the Input Transformer consists of applying a filter to each MIDI track in order to transform the current Omni On Input mode of Cubase into an Omni Off Input mode.

The MIDI input port determines the source of incoming MIDI events, but not which MIDI channel triggers events on a specified MIDI track. In other words, your MIDI keyboard can send MIDI on any channel, and Cubase will play MIDI messages sent to all record-enabled tracks at the same time. As long as a MIDI track's input and output ports are set up properly, you can't control the channel to which a MIDI track responds, only the port.

Although this is fine in most cases, you might need to have control over which MIDI track plays back MIDI events on specific channels—for example, if you are using another computer to record a MIDI sequence and using Cubase simply as a rack of VST instruments. Without the possibility of selecting a MIDI channel for the input of each track, you would have to use one MIDI port per MIDI track to get Cubase to play more than one VSTi at a time.

To achieve this, click the Input Transformer button and select Local mode from the drop-down menu. Inside the Input Transformer's window, select Presets > Channel Filtering. Then select the channel number you want this track to let through, as illustrated in Figure 14.7. For each channel you need, create an additional track, add the Input Transformer, and set the filter to a different channel for each track. Both the Logical editor and the Input Transformer use similar controls. A template file is also available on your Cubase installation CD.

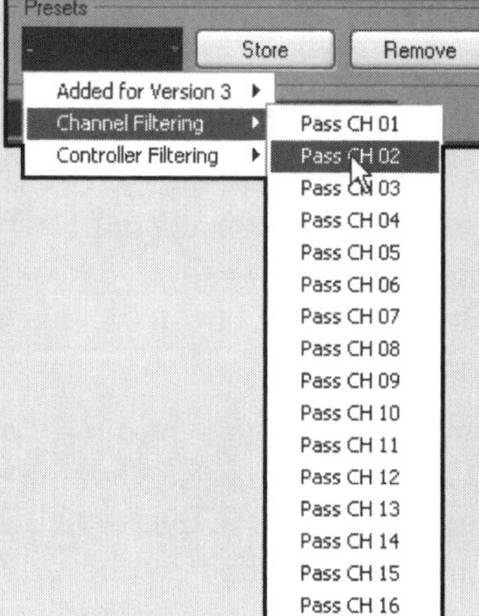

Figure 14.7
The Input Transformer presets drop-down menu.

Overdub Recording Techniques

Overdubbing is a recording term for the process of adding new recordings to previously recorded basic tracks. For example, the drums, bass, and rhythm (harmonic) guitar parts have been recorded, and you're about to lay down new lead guitar tracks in the existing project. Although recording sessions inside Cubase does not require the actual process of "dubbing" existing tracks from one tape to the next, as was the case when this term was coined, the process of overdubbing still requires some setup because you do want to hear what was previously recorded as you are recording new tracks. Because you can create as many tracks as you need during a recording session and you also can record in different modes—creating different takes in the same track—the next sections will focus on a specific overdubbing process—replacing a portion of a recording. This is also known as "punching in," which refers to the act of pressing, or punching in, the Record button at the exact time when the existing audio on a track should be replaced with new content being recorded.

To find out more on how to set up Cubase for an overdub recording session, review Chapters 4 and 6, which discuss a number of monitoring scenarios.

Transport Panel Recording Options

The Transport panel is a multitask floating panel. There are 11 areas on the Transport panel, each of which allows you to control an aspect of your session in progress. You can use the F2 key command to hide or display the Transport whenever you need it. To reveal or hide these different areas, right-click (PC)/Control-click (Mac) and check or uncheck the areas you need, as displayed in Figure 14.8. The pop-up menu is divided into four areas. The top options correspond to the 11 areas available in the Transport panel, and a check appears next to the ones that are enabled for display. Cubase provides a number of presets toward the bottom of the menu, and you can create your own by selecting the Setup option at the bottom.

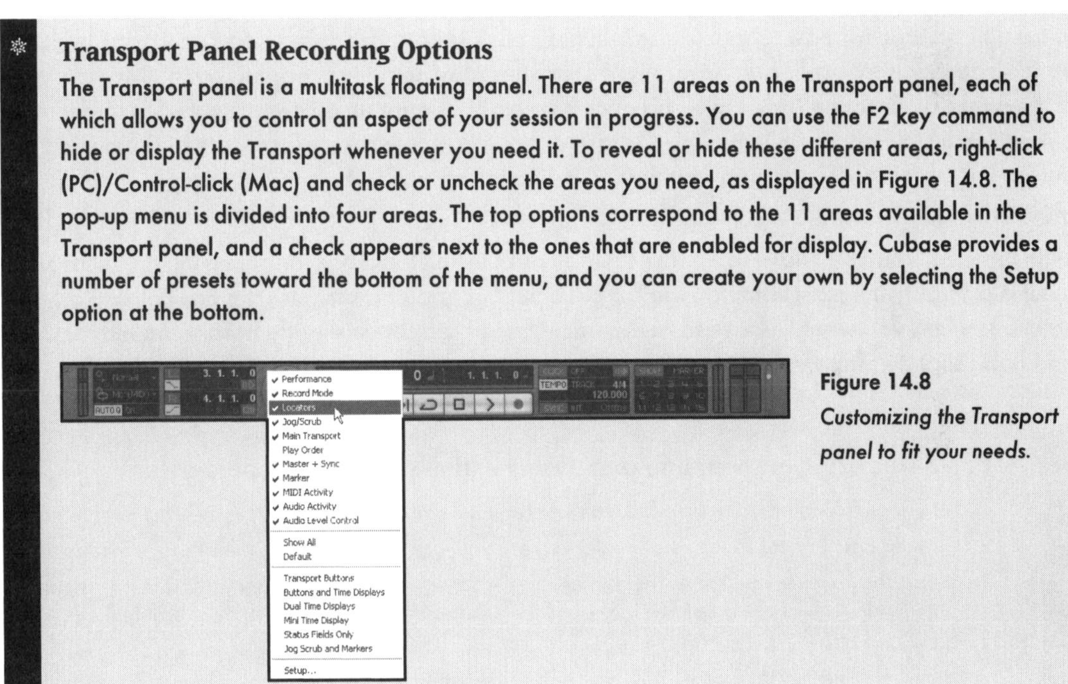

Figure 14.8
Customizing the Transport panel to fit your needs.

Punch-In/Punch-Out

Below the L and R in the Locator portion of the Transport panel are the Punch-In and Punch-Out buttons, which transform the left locator into a punch-in point (where recording will begin) and the right locator into a punch-out point (where recording will stop). For example, you could start playback at bar 1 of the project, but only record over the content starting at bar 3 and ending at bar 4 if your left locator is set at 3.01.01.000 and your right locator is set at 4.01.01.000 and the Punch-In and Punch-Out buttons are active (see Figure 14.9). This can be useful to replace events between these two locations (left and right locators) while making sure that content before or after this range isn't affected. Perhaps the most effective way to use the punch-in and -out is along with the Pre-Roll and Post-Roll Amount fields.

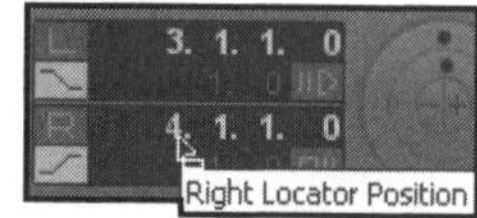

Figure 14.9
Setting the Punch options on the Transport panel.

Pre-Roll/Post-Roll

The Pre-Roll and Post-Roll fields at the right of the Punch-In and Punch-Out buttons allow you to enter a time value for how long Cubase will play back before dropping into Record mode at the punch-in location (pre-roll) and how long it continues playing after dropping out of Record mode at the punch-out location (post-roll). This allows you to configure an automatic punch-in and punch-out on a selected track, while having Cubase play back a few seconds or bars of the project before it starts recording, giving you time to prepare yourself to record the line you want to replace.

With this said, you don't *have* to use the Pre-Roll or Post-Roll functions for punch-in/-out recording, but it is probably the most common use for it. To put this another way, use the Pre-Roll or Post-Roll functions when you want Cubase to automatically start playback slightly before the left locator and finish slightly after the right locator.

HOW TO

Set up automatic punch-in and punch-out with a pre-roll and post-roll:

1. Set your left locator to the time location where you want to punch in to your existing events.
2. Set your right locator to the time location where you want to punch out of the Record mode.
3. Enable the Punch-In and Punch-Out buttons on the Transport panel. If you want Cubase to replace all existing events from a specific location forward, leave the Punch-Out button disabled.
4. Set a value for the pre-roll. This is the amount of time in bars or beats (depending on the ruler format displayed) that Cubase will play before the left locator. If this amount of time exceeds the amount of time from the left locator to the beginning of the project, Cubase will simply pause for the necessary extra amount of time prior to starting playback at the beginning of the project timeline. For example, if you enter a value of 10 bars and you want to punch in at bar 5, then Cubase will count five bars before bar 1 and will then start to play until it reaches bar 5, at which point it will go into Record mode.
5. If needed, set the post-roll time as well (found below the pre-roll time).

6. Disable the Click button in the Transport panel; otherwise, Cubase will use the metronome's precount setting rather than the pre-roll setting.
7. Enable the Pre-Roll/Post-Roll buttons on the Transport panel (see Figure 14.10).

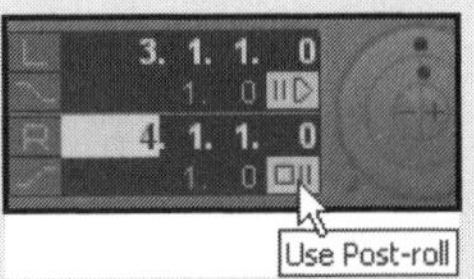

Figure 14.10
The Pre-Roll and Post-Roll functions enabled on the Transport panel.

8. If you want Cubase to stop automatically after the punch-out time, select File (PC)/Cubase (Mac) > Preferences from the Menu bar. Then select the Transport tab of the Preferences dialog box and enable the Stop after Automatic Punch-Out option.
9. Click Play or Record. Cubase will go into Play mode until it reaches the punch-in time, and then switch to Record mode. If you have enabled the Punch-Out button, it will revert to Play mode at that location. If you have checked the Stop after Automatic Punch-Out option, it will also stop playing after any additional amount of post-roll time value that you have entered.

III } Navigation

15 Project Navigation

The Project window represents the main view of a project; it is where most of the editing takes place—or at least where it all begins. Navigating from one part of the project to the other or focusing your attention on the first four bars of a chorus and then on the last eight bars of the second verse is something you will need to do quite frequently. Although repeatedly pressing the G key command to zoom out or the H key command to zoom in will work in some instances, there are more effective and elegant ways to move around in the project, which don't involve increasing your chances of getting carpal tunnel syndrome!

Here's a summary of what you will learn in this chapter:

- How to navigate using the overview rectangle
- Where to find different navigation menus in the Project window
- What the basics of the Project window's context menus are
- How to zoom into your work using the appropriate tool
- How to change the time format of the Transport panel
- How to use the jog, nudge, and shuttle features of the Transport panel
- How to identify the tools and functions available in the Transport panel

Changing Your Focus

Moving around in a project, finding what you want to edit, focusing on the task at hand, and then looking at the project in a more global perspective is as much a part of your work as editing MIDI and audio events themselves is. Changing your display and opening and closing windows is unfortunately part of the computer-based musician's reality. Having a large monitor display or two monitors side by side, displaying different parts of your desktop, is highly recommended, but this is not always a realistic solution. That's why it's important when you work on a project that you know and use shortcuts, which can quickly change your visual perspective to fit the task at hand inside the project.

Fortunately, Cubase offers many options in this respect, allowing you to get to what you need in different ways. The idea is not necessarily to use all these techniques, but to find out what is possible and to use a working method that makes it easy for you to quickly perform necessary tasks.

Using the Overview Panel

Although the Event Display area in the Project window can display a project from start to finish, most of the time, you will need to zoom in closer to have greater accuracy or to focus your attention on the section you're currently editing. The Overview panel gives you a way to always keep an eye on the entire project and the relation of the current Event Display within the project; this works no matter what your Project window's zoom level. When the Overview button is active in the Project window's toolbar, a white bar spanning the entire length of the Project window will appear. The total amount of time displayed in this overview depends on the Project's length value, which you can change in the Project Setup dialog box. The white bar depicts, from left to right, the "Mini Me" version of your project, tracks, events, or parts on these tracks. Besides displaying the content of your project, a blue box indicates the portion of the project that is currently visible in the Event Display area of the Project window. You can use this box to navigate throughout your project.

HOW TO

Navigate using the overview rectangle:

1. Draw a rectangle in the Overview panel to indicate the portion of the project's timeline you want to display in the event display portion of the Project window. Start the rectangle by clicking and dragging your mouse from the upper half of the Overview panel (where your cursor will display an arrow shape), as illustrated by the number 1 in Figure 15.1. The size of the rectangle determines the content displayed in the Event Display area.
2. To move the position of the rectangle without changing its size, click and drag inside the lower half of the blue rectangle, as illustrated by the number 2 in Figure 15.1. The zoom level will remain the same; however, you can use this technique to scroll in time throughout your project.
3. To resize the left or right border of the rectangle, causing the content to zoom in (when you reduce the box) or zoom out (when you enlarge the box), click and drag in the lower half of the left or right edge of the rectangle, as illustrated by the number 3 in Figure 15.1.

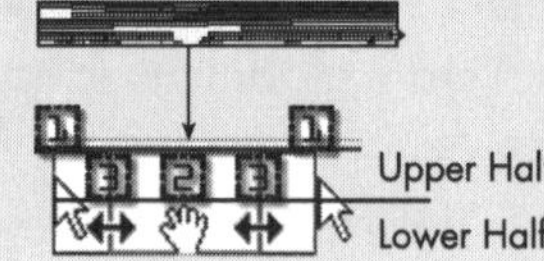

Figure 15.1
The Overview panel functions.

Using the Zoom Tools

There are a number of tools at your disposal to control the content displayed on your screen. Here's a look at these options. Note that each number in the list corresponds to the same number shown in Figure 15.2.

HOW TO

Zoom in to your work using the appropriate tool:

1. **The Zoom tool.** With this tool selected, you can use its "magnifying glass" cursor to zoom in on an area by drawing a rectangle around it. Holding down the Ctrl (PC)/ (Mac) key while using the Zoom tool allows you to zoom vertically and horizontally at the same time.
2. **The Event and Content Vertical Zoom bar.** This enables you to scale the vertical axis of the content within events or parts. Drag the handle up to enlarge the events within the event or part's vertical boundary, or drag the handle down to reduce the vertical scale of this content.
3. **The Zoom context submenu.** This submenu offers a variety of zooming options. (The Zoom submenu is found by right-clicking [or Control-clicking on Macintosh] in the Event Display area and scrolling down to the Zoom submenu options.)
4. **Track Scale pop-up menu.** This menu at the lower-right edge of the Project window sets the track height to a preset list of values or lets you enter how wide you want the tracks to be. Selecting the Zoom Tracks N Rows or Zoom N Tracks option brings up a dialog box in which you can type in the number of tracks you want to fit in your Event Display area. This menu is available by clicking on the down arrow found between the vertical scroll bar and the Vertical Zoom bar.
5. **The Vertical Zoom bar.** This zooms in (move downward) or out (move upward) vertically, affecting the height of tracks in your Event Display area. You can either drag the handle in the Zoom bar to get the desired height for each track or click on the arrows above or below to increase or decrease by one row at a time.
6. **The Horizontal Zoom bar.** This adjusts the portion of time displayed in the window. You can zoom in (move to the right) or out (move to the left) horizontally. You can either drag the handle in the Zoom bar to get the desired time frame inside the Event Display area or click the left or right arrows to increase or decrease by the time frame one step at a time.
7. **The Horizontal Zoom pop-up menu.** This enables you to select a preset amount of time, the space between the left and right locators, or any cycle marker and zoom in on it. You can also save a zoom level as a preset that you can recall later. For example, you can create two states–one for a larger perspective and another for a more detailed look at events or parts on your timeline. Then you can use this menu to toggle between the two (or more) zoom settings. Use the Add option to save the current zoom state to memory and the Organize option to manage the items available in this menu. This menu is available by clicking on the down arrow found between the horizontal scroll bar and the Horizontal Zoom bar.
8. **The Ruler bar.** This enables you to zoom in or out by clicking and dragging your mouse. Click in the lower half of the Ruler bar and drag your mouse downward to zoom in or drag your mouse upward to zoom out. Drag your mouse to the left to move back in time or the right to move forward in time. Your zoom always centers on the position of your mouse in the Ruler.

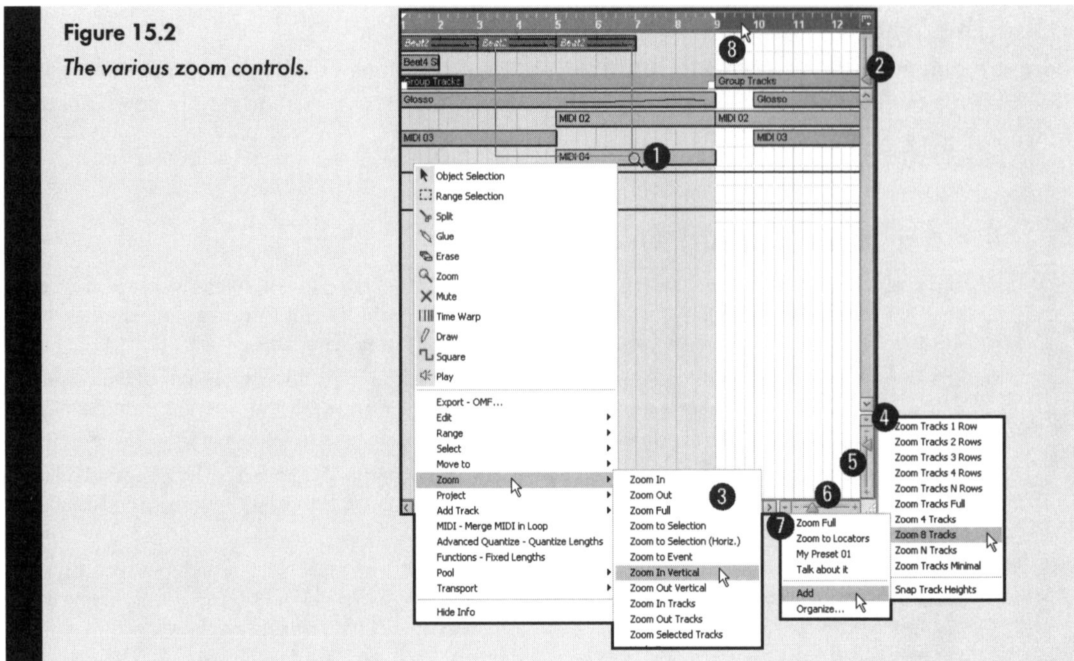

Figure 15.2

The various zoom controls.

The Transport Panel

The Transport panel is a multitask floating panel. There are 11 areas on the Transport panel offering access to different aspects of a project. Use the F2 keyboard shortcut to hide or display the panel whenever you need it.

Performance

The performance meter (see Figure 15.3) offers a smaller version of the CPU usage (left) and disk access (right) meters also visible in the VST Performance panel. (Press F12 to quickly access this panel.) When one of the two performance bars reaches the top and stays there, causing the

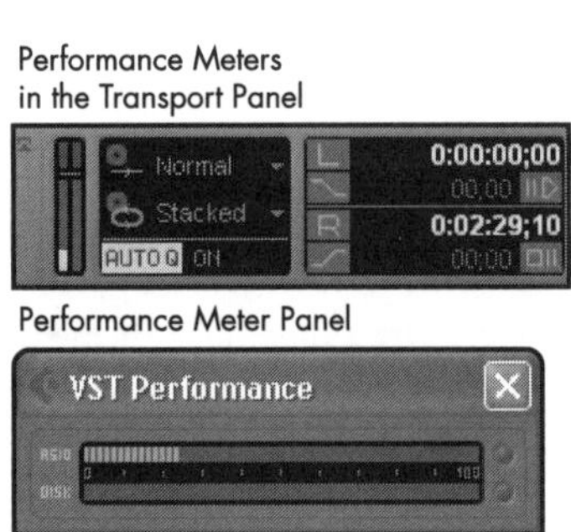

Figure 15.3

Performance meters.

red LED to light up in the display, you should think about reducing the load specific to that aspect of system performance. For example, VST effects and instruments can use up a lot of CPU power. Try freezing a track to free up some processing power (see Chapter 39, "Project Optimization," for more on this). If you have extensive disk access, try disabling audio tracks that are not currently in use. Simply muting tracks doesn't mean they are not read by Cubase; they will still make demands on available CPU power even though they are not heard during playback. Freezing and disabling audio tracks are discussed further in Chapter 39.

Shuttle, Jog, and Nudge

Cubase 4's shuttle, jog, and nudge wheels are useful editing tools that quickly move the cursor within a project while you are listening to the audio/MIDI. Here's an overview of these functions:

- **Shuttle wheel (outside ring).** Moving the ring to the right or the left causes the cursor to move forward or backward in time. The farther away from the center position you move the wheel, the faster the playback is. The maximum shuttle speed is indicated by the small markings on the lower half of the shuttle, on each side of the ring itself (see Figure 15.4). You can operate the shuttle wheel by clicking on the ring and moving your mouse to the left or right.

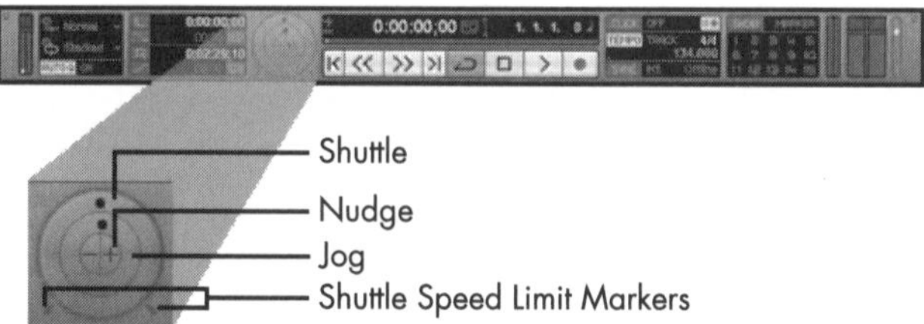

Figure 15.4
The shuttle, jog, and nudge functions on the Transport panel.

- **Jog wheel (middle ring).** Holding down the mouse button over the jog wheel and moving it toward the right or left in a circular motion makes the project cursor move forward or back in time. Unlike the shuttle wheel, you can turn the jog wheel as much as you want. This is a great tool to look for specific cues in a project, since you will hear your events under the playback cursor playing back at a speed and direction that's relative to how fast you rotate the jog wheel. (On tape recorders, this technique is known as "scrubbing.") Typically you would use the jog wheel when you are looking for something, going slowly over events. When you stop moving the mouse, playback stops.
- **Nudge frame buttons (inside the jog wheel).** These two buttons move your project one frame ahead (plus sign) or one frame behind (minus sign), no matter what your time display may be. The number of frames per second, however, is determined by your settings for this project in the Project Setup dialog box. Obviously, if you don't work with video, nudging the project cursor by a frame at a time may not be especially useful to you if you customarily deal with bars and beats.

Main Transport

The Main Transport buttons enable you to navigate through your project much like the Transport controls on an audio or video recorder. The upper portion displays the current location of the cursor in two customizable formats. Changing the format of the primary time display on the left will also change the time format in the project's Ruler—although afterwards you can also set the Ruler's time format independently without affecting this primary time display in the Transport. The secondary time format on the right does not have the same effect; it is there only to provide information about time and position in an alternate format. Between the two formats is a toggle button, which allows you to switch the position of the two currently displayed formats. In Figure 15.5, the time is displayed in bars and beats (left) and in timecode (right). The small plus and minus signs on the left of the time display allow you to nudge the position of the project cursor one unit at a time. Below the time display is a project cursor overview display (blue line), which enables you to monitor the location of the project cursor as your project moves along. You can click within the line to drag its cursor to any location you desire in the project's timeline, or simply click once anywhere in the line to make your project cursor jump to that location immediately.

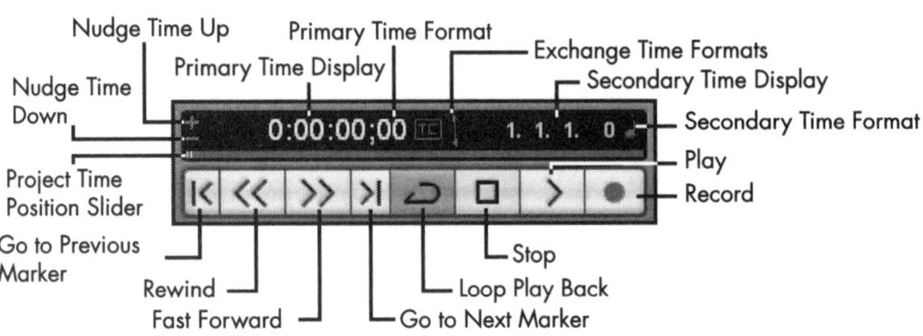

Figure 15.5
The Main Transport buttons and the project cursor location indicator.

HOW TO

Change the time format from the Transport panel:

1. Click on the time format icon (refer to Figure 15.5) to the right of the primary or secondary time display in the Transport panel to reveal a display format drop-down menu.
2. Select the desired time display format.

16 The Project Window

When you create a new, empty project, a blank project appears with no tracks. To add media content to this empty project, you need tracks that serve as containers for different media types, such as audio and MIDI events, automation, effects, and VST instruments. This chapter discusses track classes, the type of information each class handles, and how you can use the controls and parameters available in each class. We will also take a closer look at the different areas found in the Project window and how you can work with the information these areas provide. Most of your editing and production time will be spent between these areas.

Here's a summary of what you will learn in this chapter:

- How to recognize the Project window areas
- How and when to use the Constrain Delay Compensation function
- Where the different view switches are located
- How to use the different tools provided in the Project window toolbar
- How to set up snap and quantize functions
- How to quickly access options through the many Project window context menus
- How to add tracks to a project

Project Window Areas

The Project window is your main working area, and it is where events on a project's timeline are loaded. More than one project can be opened simultaneously, but only one can be active at any time. When you make a different Project window active (by clicking within it or selecting it from the Window menu, and then clicking its Activate Project button at the left end of the Project window toolbar), all other project-related windows also update their content to display the settings of this active Project window. The Project window is essentially divided into 12 main areas, each one of which provides some kind of control, function, or access to information within a project. Here's a list of the areas identified in Figure 16.1, to serve as a quick reference to all the components included in the Project window.

Figure 16.1
The Project window's main areas.

1. **Title bar.** Displays the current project's title.
2. **Toolbar.** Displays commonly used tools and can be customized by right-clicking on it (or Control-clicking on Macintosh) and selecting the tools you want to see or unselecting those you don't use. The default buttons visible in the toolbar are described in this chapter.
3. **Info Line.** Displays information on selected events in the Event Display area (see 9).
4. **Overview bar.** Displays an overview of the current project, the portion of this project currently displayed in the window, and serves as a navigational tool as well. You can quickly zoom to a specific section or move your point of view by using this area.
5. **Inspector.** Displays a series of settings for a selected track. Each track type will display different settings in the Inspector, and changes you make here are also reflected in the Mixer.
6. **Track List Header bar.** Controls global track states as well as Track List (see 7) display settings.
7. **Track List.** Displays all the track controls for all track types in a project. Tracks are stacked as rows in a column, and their order in a project can be moved using this area, which will also affect the order of their channel strips in the Mix window.

8. **Project Ruler.** Displays the main timeline for a project, as well as the left and right locators. You can't hide the Ruler, but you can change its format or use it to move your cursor in the timeline.
9. **Event Display.** The main work area where all events and automation are represented. The Event Display area lets you move and edit events, such as MIDI, audio, and automation recordings. Some edits can be done within this area, while others are done in separate editing windows.
10. **Scrolling controls.** Let you navigate within the project's timeline (horizontal) or tracks (vertical).
11. **Zoom controls.** Give you control over the time zoom level (horizontal zoom control), the track height (middle vertical zoom control), and the vertical scale of the audio and MIDI content displayed within the rectangles that represent events and parts on tracks (upper vertical zoom control).
12. **Project Properties and Status.** Displays the audio properties of the project, as well as disk space remaining for the current project location.

When more than one project is open within Cubase, a blue rectangular button found in the upper-left corner of the Project window indicates the active project. In Figure 16.2, the active project is currently displayed in the back, whereas an inactive project is displayed on top. Clicking the Activate Project button will make the top window active and automatically deactivate the background window. You can have many projects opened simultaneously, but only one can be active at a time.

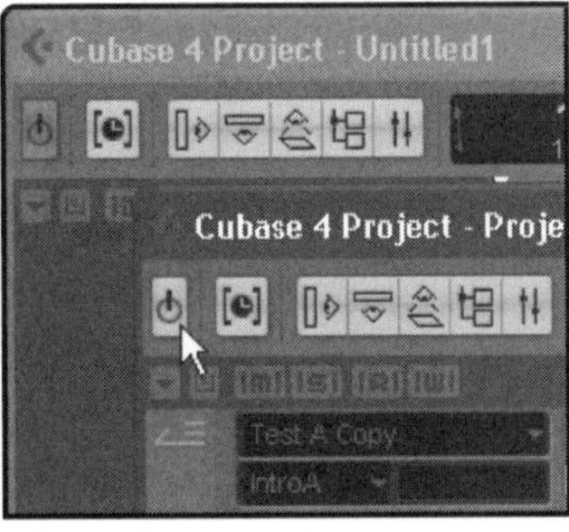

Figure 16.2
Active and inactive Project windows inside Cubase.

Constrain Delay Compensation

Use the Constrain Delay Compensation button (the first button on the left in Figure 16.3) whenever you need to reduce the latency caused by recording live audio through Cubase or playing VST instruments. If you don't hear any delay, leave this button deactivated. Cubase will automatically compensate for audio hardware and effect processing latency during playback or recording, to maintain more coherent time alignment between your tracks. This button works with the Delay Compensation Threshold setting found in the VST page of the Preferences dialog box. When this button in the Project window toolbar is active, any plug-in that has a delay longer than the Threshold value either will be turned off or will have its default automatic delay compensation disregarded temporarily. If you do activate the button to solve latency issues during live playback of VST instruments or recordings of digital audio tracks, remember to turn it off when you are finished.

Figure 16.3
From left to right: The Constrain Delay Compensation button, five View switches, and two Automation Mode menus.

View Switches

The View switches (see Figure 16.3) quickly display or hide certain areas of the Project window or open different windows easily from the Project window.

- **Show/Hide Inspector.** Shows the Inspector area of a selected track.
- **Show/Hide Event Information bar.** Shows information for a selected item in the Event Display area of the Project window. You can modify the values of selected objects using this bar—for example, names, positions, and durations for events and parts; various MIDI note parameters; values for automation breakpoints; and so on.
- **Show/Hide Overview.** Displays your entire project, spanning across your Project window. The current visible portion of your project is displayed by a blue outline in the Overview bar. The total time displayed in the overview depends on the Length field value in the Project Setup dialog box (Shift+S).
- **Open Pool.** Opens the project's Pool window.
- **Open Mixer.** Opens the project's default Mixer.

Automation Mode

In Cubase 4, you can select one of five automation modes, while in the Cubase Studio 4 version only Touch Fader mode is available. The first drop-down menu lets you select the active Automation mode, whereas the Automation Return Time field on its right determines the time it takes for the automated parameter to return to its original automated value after you release a control or the mouse button when overwriting existing automation. You will find more on automation modes in Chapter 34, "Recording Automation."

Transport

In Cubase 4, there are two sets of Transport controls. The Project window itself holds the same controls as the Transport panel, with the exception of the fast-forward and rewind buttons. While the Transport panel is a floating panel that you can move around or hide away, these Transport control buttons displayed in Figure 16.4 are integrated into the toolbar. If you don't want to see the Transport control buttons there, you could hide them from view in the Project window toolbar. To find out how to do so, go to Chapter 38, "Project Customization."

Figure 16.4
The Transport control buttons in the Project window toolbar.

Tools

In the middle of the Project window, you will find a series of tool buttons (see Figure 16.5) that you also can find by right-clicking (PC)/Control-clicking (Mac) anywhere inside the Project window.

Figure 16.5
The Tool buttons.

- **Object Selection.** This "arrow" tool selects events or parts by clicking on these events or by dragging a box over several events or parts when using the tool in Normal Sizing mode. The small arrow on the bottom-right corner of the button indicates that there is a pop-up selector for the different modes of this tool. There are three sizing modes available. Normal Sizing (the default mode) resizes the start or end position of an event or part. The Sizing Moves Contents mode moves the content inside the event in the direction of your resize while leaving the location of the surrounding event boundaries unchanged. The Sizing Applies Time Stretch mode time-stretches the events inside a part to correspond to the new duration of the event when resized. These modes are discussed further in Chapter 27, "Edit Menu Options."
- **Range Selection.** Make a selection of events over several tracks with this tool by dragging the mouse over the desired content. You can also select a specific portion within an event or part with the Range Selection tool. Once it has been selected, you can apply different range-specific editing processes, such as delete, cut, insert, or crop, to the selected range. These editing functions will also be discussed in Chapter 27.

- **Split.** Clicking events or parts anywhere in the event display area separates them into two segments, with the exact point of the split depending on the currently active snap mode and grid settings.
- **Glue.** Joins events or parts to the next event or part in the same track, creating either a continuous event (if you use glue after splitting an event in two) or a continuous part containing two or more events (if you glue either two nonconsecutive events or two parts together).
- **Erase.** Clicking with this tool erases events/parts from a track.
- **Zoom.** Zoom in to your project by dragging a box around the area you want to view more closely, or click to zoom in one step closer. Hold the Alt (PC)/Option (Mac) key while clicking (double-clicking will have the same effect) to zoom out a step.
- **Mute.** Mutes individual events or parts. This is an alternative to erasing them because muted events are not heard during playback; however, they can be "unmuted" later. This is different from the Track Mute button, which mutes *all* events on the track.
- **Time Warp.** Provides a way to insert tempo changes for musical events, to match up with video sequences, or tempo changes in a live recording. More on this in Chapter 29, "Tempo Track."
- **Draw.** This "pencil" tool can be used to create an empty part on a track, a series of envelope points for a volume curve associated with an individual event, or a series of automation points in any of the automation subtracks for tracks in the Project window (see Figure 16.6).

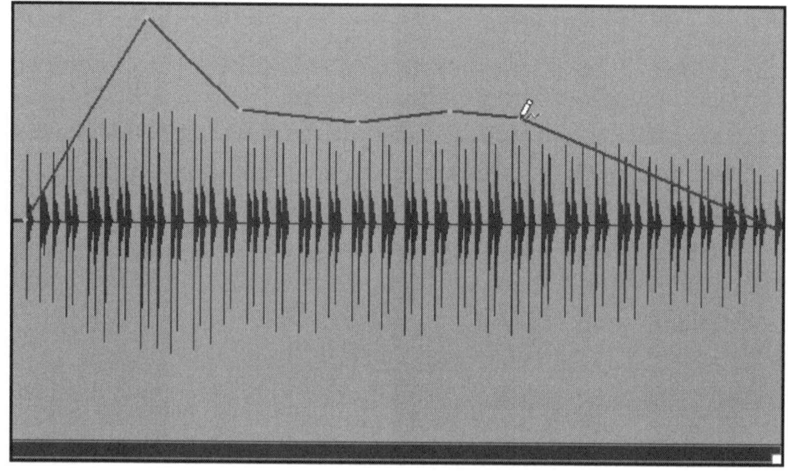

Figure 16.6
Creating an event automation envelope with the Draw tool.

- **Line.** Adds automation points in any automation subtrack. As with the Selection tool, a pop-up selector for the Line tool offers different operation modes. The Parabola, Sine, Triangle, and Square modes allow you to create different automation shapes, creating automation points that recreate the shape of the selected mode. For example, using the Line tool in Sine mode lets you create a panning automation shaped like a sine wave. These editing modes of the Line tool will also be discussed in Chapters 22, "Key Editor," and 34, "Recording Automation."
- **Play.** In the Play mode of this tool, you use the "speaker" icon of the Play tool to monitor a specific audio or MIDI event/part from the point where you click until the moment you release the mouse. In Scrub mode, you can drag your mouse back and forth over an event/part to monitor its contents. The direction and speed of scrubbed playback is proportional to the movement of your mouse as you click and drag with this tool.
- **Color.** Clicking with this tool assigns color to events/parts. The small area below this button with the "paint bucket" icon displays the last selected/applied color. You can change this color by clicking on its pop-up menu to select from a color selection swatch. Any custom colors applied to events with this tool will remain even after you change or add a color to an entire track. To remove the custom color of an event/part, reapply the default color (gray) to this event.

Autoscroll

When active (blue), the Autoscroll button (see Figure 16.7) follows the position of the project cursor in time as the project moves forward during playback, refreshing your display every time the project cursor moves past the right edge of the window.

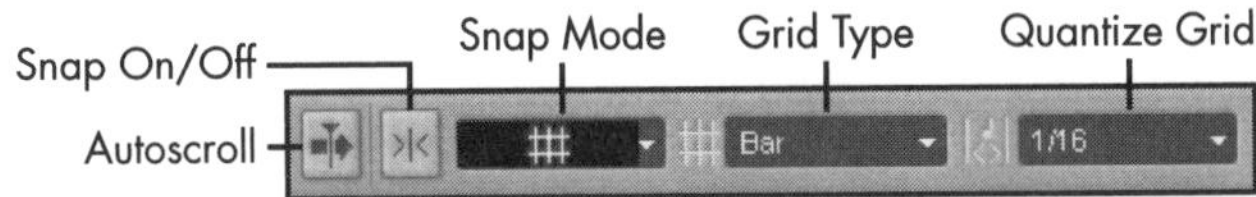

Figure 16.7
The Autoscroll, Snap On/Off, and Snap/Quantize buttons.

Snap/Quantize

You will be recording and editing events/parts in tracks and moving them around quite often. The Snap/Quantize buttons help you determine the accuracy of these movements by magnetizing the time increments on a grid, other events, the cursor, or any combination of these items. In other words, you can customize what is magnetized. When a grid is magnetized, you can even decide the precision of this grid.

On the Project window's toolbar, to the right of the Autoscroll button (by default), is the Snap On/Off button, which enables/disables the three fields to the right of the button. When it is enabled, movement of events/parts is restricted by the selected Snap mode—by default, a grid—found in the first of three fields to the right of the Snap On/Off button (refer to Figure 16.7). Cubase offers several modes from which to choose:

- **Grid.** When Grid is selected in Snap mode, the Grid Type and Quantize Grid fields become active. In Figure 16.7, the Snap mode is set to Grid and the Grid Type is set to Bar. In this setup, the start point of selected events/parts snaps to the closest bar when moving them along the timeline. (If the snap point within an event is at some point other than its beginning, that will be the actual point that snaps to the grid.) If your project displays time values rather than bars and beats, increments of milliseconds would be displayed in the Grid Type field rather than bars and beats. The Grid Type field always displays time units that are relevant to the project's main Ruler format. This makes it easy to snap events to any kind of grid, depending on the project at hand. Grid mode is the default Snap mode in Cubase. The Quantize Grid field is only relevant when the Ruler is set to Bars+Beats and the Grid Type is set to Quantize. When this is the case, the value in the Quantize Grid field will define the space between each gridline. In Figure 16.7, if the Grid Type was set to Use Quantize, the events/parts could be moved by increments of sixteenth notes.
- **Events.** The start and end of parts or events, as well as markers on marker tracks, become magnetized. So when you move a part, it will snap to the previous or next event as you move closer to it.
- **Shuffle.** This moves events/parts that are adjacent to other events/parts by switching places with them. In Figure 16.8, tracks 1 and 2 are before-and-after shuffle examples with two consecutive parts. Tracks 3 and 4 are before-and-after shuffle examples with four consecutive parts. As you can see, the Part 01 is being shuffled around in both examples. Shuffle mode is also very useful for editing voice-over narrations, since when you cut out any portion of the track's content, such as a false start by the narrator, the following material in the track will move up earlier in the timeline to close that gap.

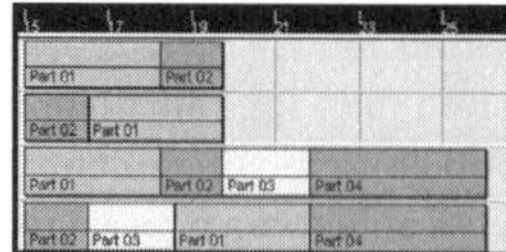

Figure 16.8
Using Snap in Shuffle mode.

- **Magnetic cursor.** The project cursor becomes magnetic. Moving an event/part close to it will cause it to snap to the cursor's position.
- **Combinations.** The other grid modes are combinations of the four modes described previously.

Quantize Values

Quantize values divide each bar in fractions equivalent to a note value. Typically, a 1/4 quantize value indicates that there will be a grid line at every quarter note. There are three groups of quantize value fractions: normal, triplet, and dotted. The normal fractions (1/2, 1/4, 1/8, 1/16, and so on) represent note values that can be divided by two. For example, there can be 4 quarter notes in each 4/4 bar, 8 eighth notes per 4/4 bar, and 16 sixteenth notes per 4/4 bar. Triplet notes can be divided by three. For example, a 1/4 triplet value means that you can have up to 6 quarter-note triplets per 4/4 bar, a 1/8 triplet value means 12 eighth notes per 4/4 bar, and so on. In other words, for every two notes in normal quantize value, you have three notes in triplet quantize value. A dotted quantize value represents one and a half normal quantize value. For example, three quarter notes are equal to two dotted quarter notes, or three eighth notes are equivalent to a single dotted quarter note.

In Figure 16.9, each row represents a different quantize setting within a single 4/4 bar. You can easily see the relation between each grid line from one quantize value to the next.

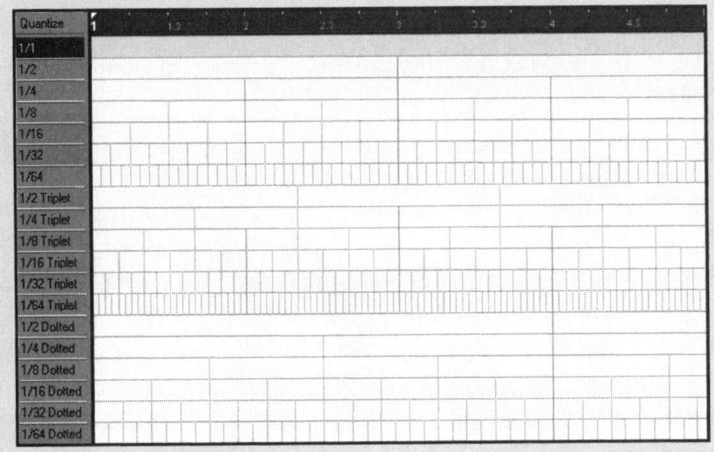

Figure 16.9
Example of quantize value lengths and grid size in a 4/4 bar.

Context Menus in the Project Window

In the Project window, as in many other windows in Cubase, you will find that right-clicking (Control+clicking for Mac users) in different regions will reveal a menu with a number of options related to the area in which you click. In many cases, these context menus allow you to choose options that are also available in the menu or toolbar of the Project window. However, having these options readily available in your workspace makes it easy to stay focused on a specific area and apply changes to events without having to move your mouse across the screen all the time.

You will learn more about these context menus as you learn how to edit events and work with a project. If you are a veteran Cubase VST user and are longing for the simple toolbox that was available through the right-click (PC)/Control+click (Mac), hold the Ctrl (PC)/ (Mac) key before accessing the context menu to only display the 12 tools available in the toolbar.

The Inspector

Use the Inspector to view or edit certain details pertaining to a selected track in the Project window. The information displayed in the Inspector is always relevant to the selected track class. For example, when a MIDI track is selected, the sections of the Inspector are displayed within up to seven different tabs: MIDI Track Setup/Name, Track Modifiers, MIDI Inserts, and so on. Each one of these sections allows you to hide or reveal settings that affect how the events on the track behave or play back. With the MIDI track example, settings in the Inspector's MIDI Modifiers tab are used to transpose all the events on the track. Other track classes—such as Folder Tracks, described in Chapter 39—do not have as many tabs in the Inspector area.

Nevertheless, all Track controls are accessed the same way in the Inspector, and some controls are common from one track type to the next. For example, the Read/Write Automation buttons are found in the Inspector, the Track List, and the Mixer panel, and they are common to MIDI, audio, group, FX, and instrument tracks.

Each Inspector section can be expanded by clicking on the tab that displays the section's title in the Inspector itself. When the Inspector area holds more than one section, each tab acts as a Fold/Unfold control button and is always visible. In other words, click on the tab for a section to view its parameters in the Inspector. Figure 16.10 reveals a folded and unfolded state of the Settings section of a MIDI track. The arrow in the Track Settings section (next to the track's name) pointing to the right in both examples lets you associate a color with the track. Associating a color with a track makes it easy to color-code tracks and organize them when the project becomes bigger. For track types that support insert and send effects, the symbol next to the corresponding section's title bar will be colored when any insert effect or send is active in that section (this is also the case with the MIDI Modifiers section, as shown in Figure 16.10). A similar color indicator appears on the EQ tab of any track that contains an active EQ setting. (An active EQ is displayed as green.) Finally, when a yellow rectangle appears to the right of the title of an Inspector tab, it indicates that the entire section is currently bypassed—this can be done with the Inserts State, EQ State, and Sends State buttons available in the Track List and Mixer window. Within each Inspector tab, you can also bypass an individual send, insert effect, or EQ setting to compare the effect these settings have on the track without having to reset all the parameters involved.

By default, when you click on one tab to expand that section of the Inspector, any other expanded section automatically folds itself. When a section is folded, all the settings you have made in that section remain intact, and bypass and assignment indicators remain visible.

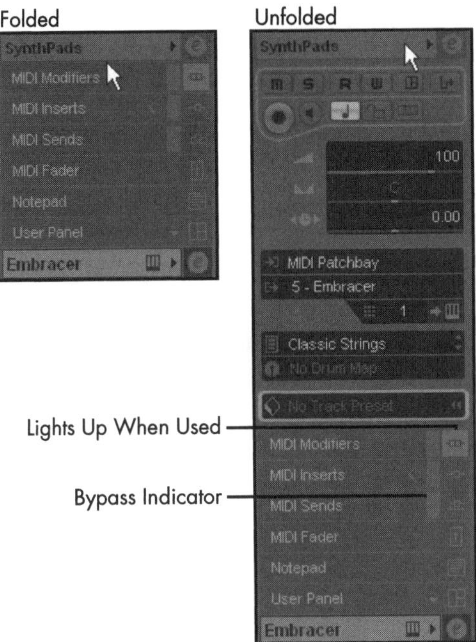

Figure 16.10
Folding and unfolding sections of the Inspector.

> **Viewing Multiple Sections of the Inspector Simultaneously**
> To maximize more than one section of the Inspector area at once, hold down the Ctrl (PC)/ (Mac) key as you click the tab for an additional section. You also can minimize all currently open panels at once by holding down the Alt (PC)/Option (Mac) key while clicking on any tab. Inversely, you can maximize all the sections at once by using the same key combination.

The Track List

Use the Track List area to view all tracks at once, to enable multiple tracks for recording, or to organize your material by type of content. Changes made in the Track List are reflected in both the Inspector and the Mixer. All events inside a track appear to the right of the track's position in the Track List. The content of each track in the Track List also differs according to the track's class. Recorded automation associated with tracks–such as volume or pan, for example–is saved in automation subtracks and moves along with the track whenever you move it inside a project. Each automation parameter can be viewed in its own automation subtrack. For example, if you automate the Gain, Frequency, and Q-Factor on one band of the StudioEQ plug-in, you would have three automation subtracks associated with the audio track where this insert resides. Finally, in the Track List area, you can also resize each individual track vertically.

HOW TO

Change the order of a track in the Track List area:

- Click and drag the track you want to move in the Track List area to its new location. As you drag, a red line will appear to indicate that Cubase knows you want to move this track (as shown in the first image on the left side of Figure 16.11). You can move more than one track at a time if needed. A green line indicates where the track would appear if you released the mouse (see the center image of Figure 16.11). In the right image of Figure 16.11, the HighHat track is moved between the Snare and RMFX tracks.

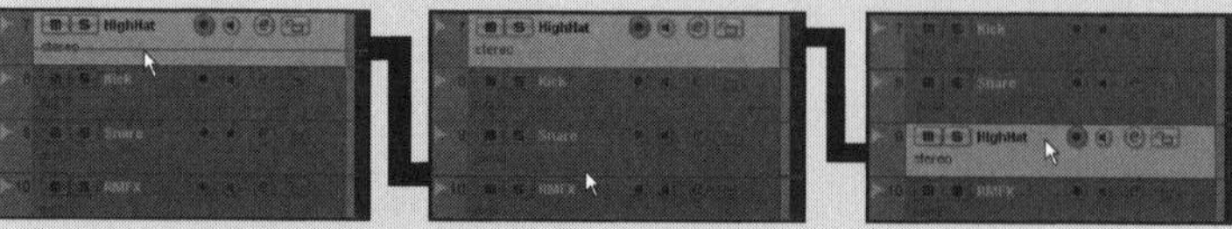

Figure 16.11
Changing the order of a track in the Track List area.

HOW TO

Reveal or hide automation subtracks:

1. Right-click the track you want to see in the Track List area.
2. Select the Show Used Automation option from the context menu. If you want the used automation visible for all tracks, select the Show Used Automation for All Tracks option instead.

Or

- Click the down arrow that appears in the bottom-left corner of the desired track in the Track List area to reveal its automation subtrack. At the top of Figure 16.12, clicking on the Show/Hide Automation button (a down arrow icon) reveals two automation tracks below. When you want to view more automation tracks, click the Append Automation Tracks button (a plus sign icon) found in the displayed automation track. Note that these buttons for opening and closing automation subtracks are only visible when your cursor rolls over the lower-left hand corner of each track/subtrack in the Track List.
- Click the Show/Hide Automation button again (which now displays an up arrow icon) to hide all automation or on the minus sign at the upper-left corner of an individual automation subtrack to hide it. Hiding automation subtrack(s) does not disable their recorded automation.

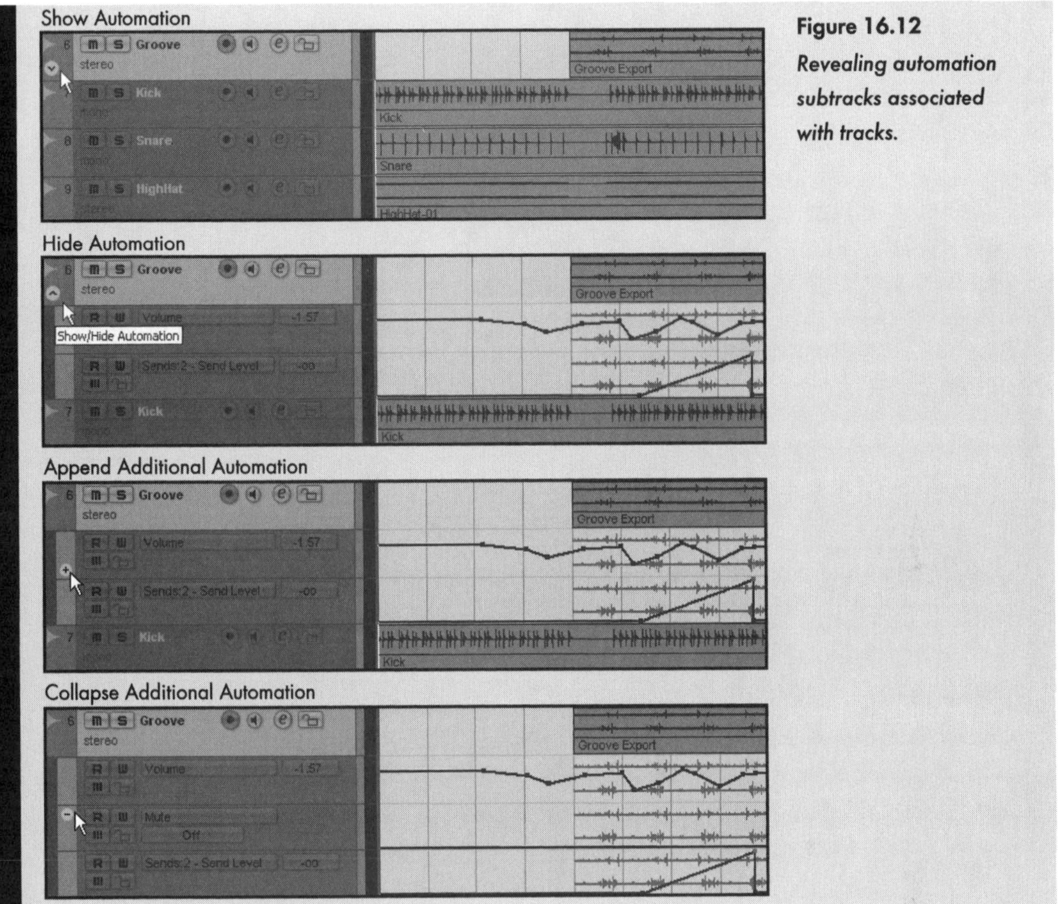

Figure 16.12
Revealing automation subtracks associated with tracks.

In each automation subtrack, you will find two fields. The first field indicates the automation parameter displayed in that subtrack. In Figure 16.12, these were Volume and Send 2's Send Level. The second field represents the value of the automation parameter at the current cursor location. You also can change the automation parameter displayed in the current subtrack without affecting any recorded automation if you wish.

HOW TO

Change the parameter displayed in an automation subtrack:

- In the automation subtrack, select the desired automation parameter from the Automation Parameter field. Parameters containing any automation events appear with an asterisk at the end of their names in this menu, as is the case for the Send Level in Figure 16.13.

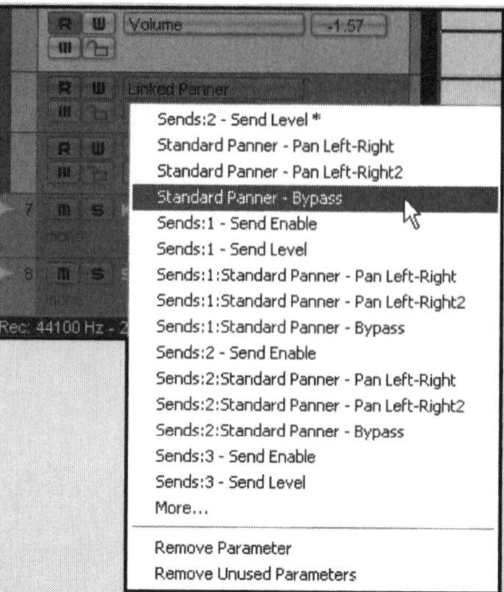

Figure 16.13

The Automation Parameter drop-down menu.

- **If the parameter you want to view is not in the drop-down menu, select the More option at the bottom of the menu. In the Add Parameter (see Figure 16.14) dialog, choose the automation parameter you want to display instead.**

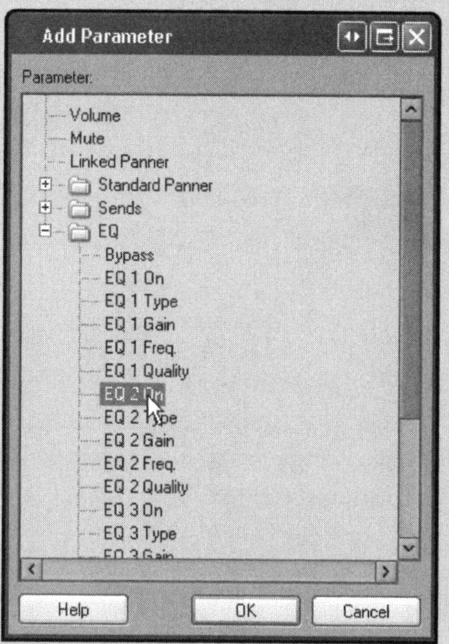

Figure 16.14

The Add Parameter dialog.

HOW TO

Resize an individual track's height:

1. Bring your cursor over the lower edge of the track you want to resize.
2. When your cursor changes into a double-headed arrow (see Figure 16.15), drag your mouse up to reduce the track's size or down to increase its size.

Before

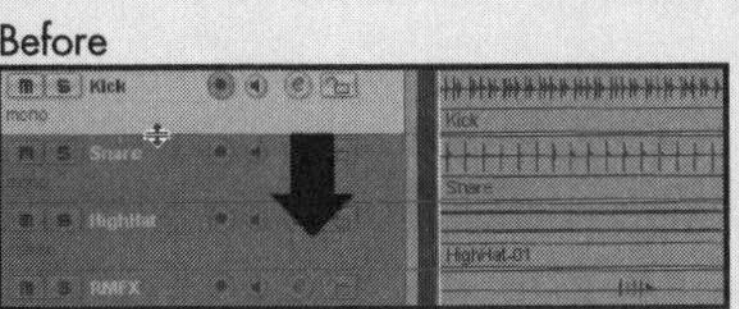

After

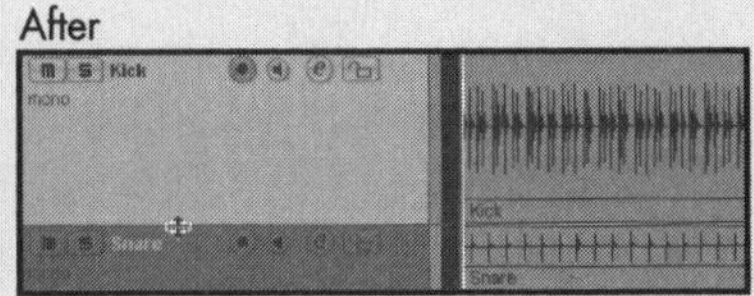

Figure 16.15
Resizing an individual track's height.

Resizing the Track List

You also can resize the entire Track List's width by dragging the right edge of the Track List area when your cursor changes into a double-headed arrow (see Figure 16.15). Moving the border to the left reduces the size, whereas moving it to the right increases the Track List's width. To adjust the *height* of all tracks simultaneously, hold down the Ctrl (PC)/ (Mac) key as you drag the lower border of any track.

The Event Display

The Event Display lets you edit and view parts, events, and automation information within the tracks in your project. Most of the work you do in this area is related to editing. We will discuss the functions and operations for the Event Display area in Chapter 27, "Edit Menu Options."

Track Classes

There are 10 classes of containers for events in a project. Each class can be added to any project as a track with its own set of controls. There is also an eleventh invisible track type automatically created with every project, and this is the Tempo track, which contains all tempo changes and time signature settings. Besides the Tempo track, here are the track classes available in Cubase 4:

- **Audio** tracks are used for audio events and automation. You can have an unlimited number of audio tracks per project (in theory).
- **MIDI** tracks are used for MIDI events and automation. They are also unlimited in Cubase 4.
- **Instrument** tracks provide a fast and convenient way to use VST instrument plug-ins in a combined MIDI/audio channel/track.
- **FX channel** tracks are used for audio plug-in effects. You can route audio to FX channel tracks by using Sends various other audio-related track types, in order to process their signal in

real time with insert effects you have placed on the FX channel track. You can create up to 64 FX channels in Cubase 4.

- **Folder** tracks are used to group together other tracks in the Project window, making it easier to work on projects with a great number of tracks. For example, use folder tracks to group different takes of a solo or multiple drum tracks. Some folder tracks are created automatically. For example, a VST instruments folder track contains all VST instruments that you add to the project.
- **Group channel** tracks are used to combine the signal from various tracks into a single channel. Use group channel tracks to create submixes where a common set of controls or insert points for effects for all the channels assigned to this group are needed. For example, you can have the track outputs for various backup singers assigned to the same group channel fader in the Mixer, where perhaps a compressor plug-in has been inserted. When you want the level of the background vocals to go down, reduce the level of this group channel, rather than reducing the levels of individual tracks. You can create up to 256 group channels in Cubase 4.
- **Marker** tracks are used to easily manage markers in a project. You can only create one marker track per project.
- **Play Order** tracks are used to create a playlist-type or pattern-like arrangement from previously created parts (musical sections) in a project. To experiment with an alternate arrangement, for example, instead of copying and pasting the content for each track belonging to a section of your song, create a Play Order Part that can then be added to a new location along the timeline. You can create one Play Order track per project.
- **Ruler** tracks are used to view the time displayed in a project's timeline. Create additional Ruler tracks when you need to view alternate time references, such as timecode, seconds, and bars and beats simultaneously with the main Ruler in the Project window.
- **Video** tracks are used to synchronize your music to a digital video file whenever this is needed.

Adding Tracks

When you start a new empty project, or you need to add an FX channel as a send effect destination, or you need to add a group channel that you will use to combine the audio signal from various other channels, or you simply need to organize existing tracks by placing them in a new folder track, adding tracks to a project is one of those inevitable steps you need to know how to do quickly.

HOW TO

Add a track to your project:

- Click Project > Add Track on the menu bar. From the Add Track submenu, select the type of track you want to add.
- Right-click (PC)/Control-click (Mac) anywhere in the Track List and select the type of track you want to add.

With both methods, the Count field in the resultant dialog box allows you to add more than one track of the same class simultaneously. You can't, however, add several tracks of different classes (or types) at once. Furthermore, if you want to load a track preset when creating audio, MIDI, or instrument tracks, you can click the Browse Presets option, as displayed in Figure 16.16. This option only displays track preset settings, which vary according to the track class.

Figure 16.16
The Add Audio Track dialog box without the Browse Presets option enabled.

Because audio, instrument, and Video track classes have been discussed in previous chapters and FX channel, group channel, play order, folder, and tempo tracks are discussed later in their own chapters, in this chapter we are left with Ruler and Video tracks to address. Let's take a closer look at these track classes and their specifics.

Ruler Tracks

Cubase 4 users have the ability to create various Ruler tracks in their projects to display the time scale of the project in other formats than what is shown in the main Ruler of the Project window. When working on a musical project, you might have the main Ruler display time as bars and beats, while another Ruler track displays minutes and seconds. When working on a video project, one Ruler might display bars and beats, while the main Ruler for the Project window displays timecode information. Ruler tracks do not have any controls available in the Inspector area, and are added in the same way as any other track in your project.

HOW TO

Change the format displayed in a Ruler track:

1. Click on the text icon in the Track List area (see Figure 16.17) that indicates this Ruler track's current time format.
2. Select the desired time format from the drop-down menu.

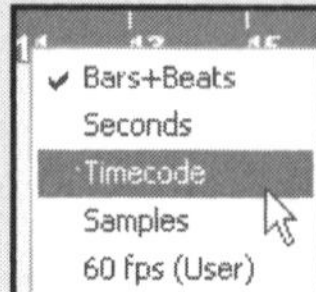

Figure 16.17
Changing the time format on a Ruler track.

Video Tracks

When you are working with video projects, currently it is very typical to work with a digital video file instead of synchronizing to a video tape deck via timecode. Cubase can load a compatible video file into a project and creates a Video track so that you can use this video file as a visual reference as you work. You can place more than one video file on one track, but you can't have more than one Video track per project.

Video editing options are fairly limited inside Cubase because it is not video-editing software. That said, you can cut, copy, paste, and resize audio files on a Video track. All versions of Cubase support QuickTime, MPEG, and AVI video. Macintosh versions of Cubase additionally support DV video files and can optionally play video out through their FireWire ports. PC versions additionally support WMV video files. PC users will probably find that using QuickTime as their video engine offers the best performance and flexibility, because the DirectShow video engine might not play files properly if you edit video events or place more than one video file on a Video track.

17 MIDI Tracks

In a Cubase project, the MIDI track class is for any type of MIDI events—from MIDI note events to controllers, such as velocity, modulation wheel, pitch bend, and so on. MIDI tracks also contain MIDI automation information for parameters such as pan, volume, or MIDI plug-in and send effects that might be assigned to a track. MIDI tracks also can contain MIDI filters and effects, such as MIDI compression, which are discussed in the next sections. All recorded MIDI events are saved as part of the Cubase project file itself. When you associate a drum map with a MIDI track, parts in that track will open in the Drum editor window by default, rather than in the Key editor window.

Here's a summary of what you will learn in this chapter:

- How to set your MIDI input port
- How to recognize the different functions associated with MIDI tracks
- How to recognize the different functions associated with MIDI channels
- How to change and access the MIDI Channel Settings panel
- How to convert instrument tracks playing external MIDI devices into audio tracks

MIDI Events in Cubase

When you record MIDI events, such as musical performances, through your MIDI controller, these events are stored in a part, which appears on the MIDI track's Event Display area in the Project window. You can have many parts containing MIDI events on your track, and parts can overlap each other on the track. Parts that are underneath other parts on the same MIDI track will still be active, and events inside them will still be heard when you play the track. You can compare a part to a container for MIDI events. In the case of MIDI, these containers can be stacked one on top of the other, playing either different drum instruments, different channels (if the MIDI track is set to play "any" MIDI channels, rather than just a specific one), or simply as part of your working process.

In the example in Figure 17.1, there are three different parts playing at the same time on the same track, creating a rhythmic pattern. These three parts could be playing events for different MIDI channels. However, you should know that when parts are stacked one on top of the other in a MIDI track, the only visible part is the one on top of the others. If all the parts are of equal length, this might lead to confusion because you will hear the parts playing, but won't see them unless you select all the parts by dragging the Selection tool around the visible part and then opening your selection in the MIDI (Key or Drum) editor.

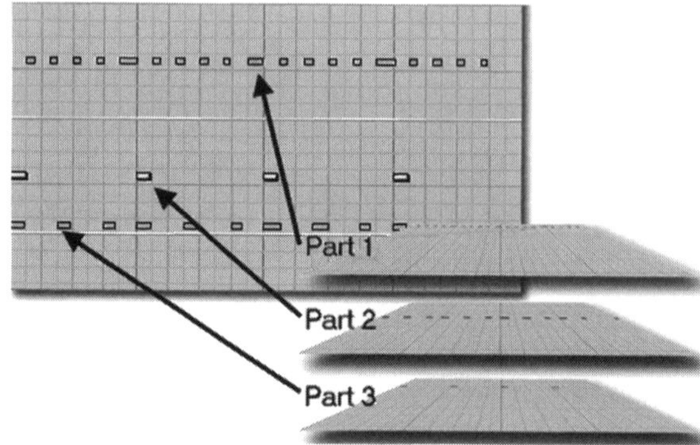

Figure 17.1
Overlapping MIDI parts on a MIDI track.

Setting Up a MIDI Track

Double-clicking in the empty area at the bottom of the Track List area offers the quickest method of creating a MIDI track in a project. You also can right-click (PC)/Control-click (Mac) in the Track List area and create either a MIDI or an instrument track. Both will offer similar MIDI settings; however, the instrument track will already be configured to play through a loaded VSTi.

On the other hand, to use a MIDI track, you must choose a MIDI input port and a MIDI output port for it. The MIDI input port receives incoming MIDI events on the track. For example, if a MIDI keyboard or other controller is hooked up to your MIDI input port A, you can set your MIDI track to All MIDI Inputs if you want any incoming MIDI ports to be recorded onto the selected track, or set the track to MIDI input port A to record events only from that MIDI controller.

HOW TO

Set your MIDI input port:

1. Be sure the MIDI Thru is active in the File (PC)/Cubase (Mac) > Preferences > MIDI option.
2. Select the MIDI track you want to set up for input.
3. Select the Track Settings section in the Inspector. The name of the track also doubles as the Expand button for the Track Settings section, as shown in Figure 17.2.

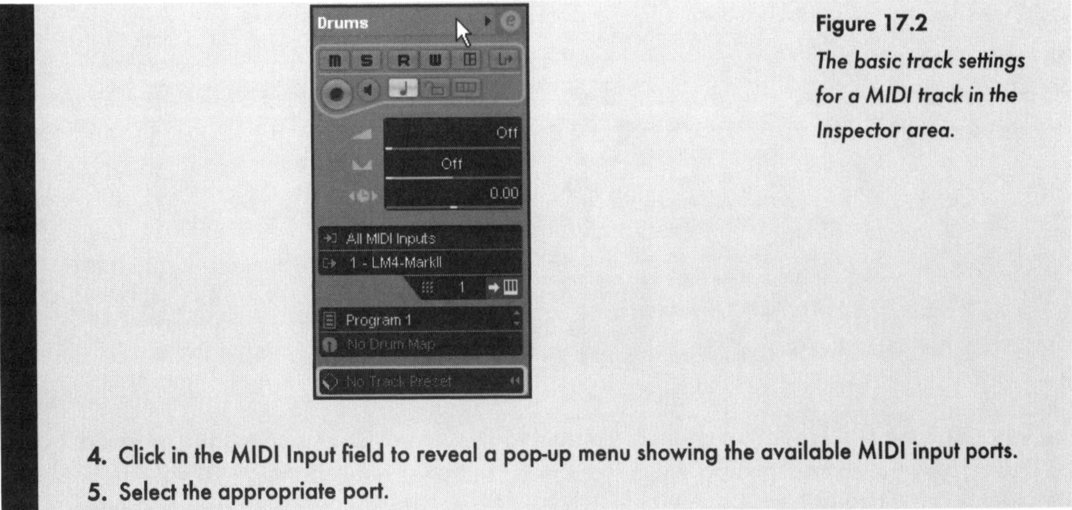

Figure 17.2
The basic track settings for a MIDI track in the Inspector area.

4. Click in the MIDI Input field to reveal a pop-up menu showing the available MIDI input ports.
5. Select the appropriate port.

Figure 17.3 gives us a look at each element found in both the Track Setting section of the Inspector and the Track List. Double-click on the track name to edit it, or click on it to reveal/hide the Track Settings section. Use the Track Color selector to assign a color to all events in a track when the Show Track Colors function is enabled. Click the Input Transformer button if you want to transform MIDI messages between the MIDI input and the track itself (thereby affecting what actually gets recorded). For example, you can use this to filter the MIDI input port's channels, allowing only the desired input channels to play through the MIDI output and be recorded for this track. Click the Record Enable button to arm this track for recording. When you press the Record button on the Transport panel, incoming MIDI events will be recorded on this track. Enable the monitor to hear incoming MIDI messages played through this track even when its Record Enable button is not active. Switch the track's time references for the events it contains between linear and musical Timebase using the Timebase button. When a track is displayed in musical Timebase, changing the tempo of the song readjusts the events in the part according to the new tempo setting. When a track is displayed in linear time, changing the tempo of the song does not affect the start position of the parts it contains. Lock your track from editing using the Lock button.

The Lane Display Type button enables a display mode where overlapping parts appear on several lanes inside the MIDI track. Clicking on this button reveals a menu with different lane display options. Fixed and Auto Lane display spread overlapping parts over the corresponding number of lanes. The Edit In-Place button expands the track to display a piano-roll style MIDI editor within the track that is very similar to the Key editor for MIDI events. This function is called "in-place" because it allows users to edit MIDI events directly in the Project window. A keyboard is also displayed along its left side, as is the case in the Key editor.

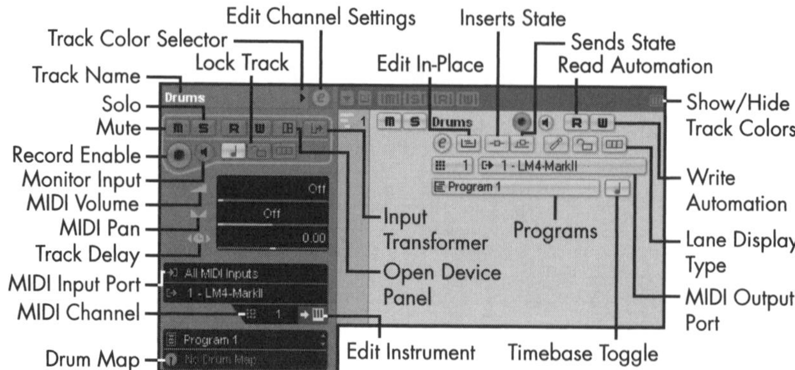

Figure 17.3
The MIDI track controls and parameters found in the Inspector and Track List area.

The Track Volume and Track Pan controls transmit MIDI Control Change message numbers 7 and 10 and display the corresponding values for these controller types if any MIDI volume or pan automation is active for this track. The track delay slider adds a positive or negative delay in milliseconds to your track. Events in a track with a negative delay play earlier, whereas positive values make them occur later in time. Track delays are great for offsetting a duplicate copy of a track that contains MIDI events. By assigning the duplicate track to another instrument and adding a slight delay, you can quickly get a thicker-sounding part. Try it with string parts, pads, and other parts that are not timing-sensitive.

MIDI events coming through the MIDI input port selection field can be recorded onto the track and/or monitored through its assigned MIDI output port. Note that the main Track Settings controls don't allow you to select which MIDI input channel passes through a MIDI track, but usually this is not a problem. If you *do* need to select which channel comes in, try the presets available for the Input Transformer. MIDI events that have been recorded on a track play through the devices or software selected in its MIDI output port field. You can also use the output port to monitor incoming MIDI events through some other port. When a VSTi is assigned to the track, the Edit Instrument button opens the control panel for that VST Instrument, which allows you to edit its parameters and settings. (MIDI tracks assigned to a physical MIDI output, any other non-VSTi-compatible MIDI port, or a ReWire MIDI output will not display the Edit Instrument button.) The MIDI output channel sets the MIDI channel used by the MIDI output port to play MIDI events on this track.

For any MIDI device that *hasn't* been configured through the MIDI Device Manager, the Bank Selector and Program Selector fields are used to send MIDI messages that change bank and program numbers according to your particular MIDI device's preset structure, as displayed on the bottom in Figure 17.4. Typically, programs are grouped in banks of 128 sounds each. (This is the maximum number of sounds MIDI can support.) To access sounds above this value, banks are created. You can access up to 128 banks of 128 programs using these settings. With some VSTi or MIDI devices that have been configured through the MIDI Device Manager panel (see the top of Figure 17.4), you can select the presets the instrument should play by name, using the Patch Selector drop-down menu, which then replaces the Bank and Program fields, and the names for the instrument's presets will appear in the Patch Selector, as shown in Figure 17.3. If the preset represents a drum kit, the Drum Map drop-down menu will associate a drum map with the MIDI events on this track. This is useful when you record a drum part on this track. You can also use the Drum Map setting in the Track List area.

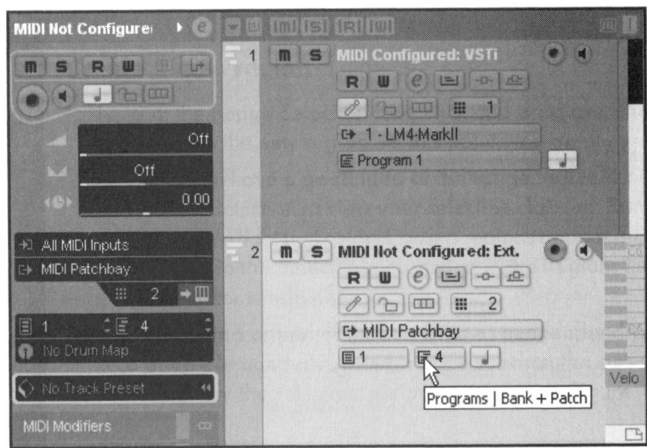

Figure 17.4
The MIDI track displaying a recognized (configured) instrument with Edit In-Place disabled (top) and an unrecognized (not configured) instrument with Edit In-Place enabled (bottom).

Moving to the Inspector's MIDI Fader controls, which are also found in the Track List and represented in Figure 17.3, the Inserts State button monitors the state of MIDI insert effects assigned to this track. The button is blue when any insert effect is assigned to the track, and a corresponding blue rectangular "active inserts" indicator appears in the title bar of the Inserts tab in the Inspector. Pressing this button in the Track List causes the MIDI to bypass all the inserts in this particular track, indicated by a yellow color on this button. There is also a dedicated bypass button for the Inserts section in the Inspector, just to the left of the active inserts indicator, which additionally turns yellow when a track's entire Insert section is muted via either of these methods. When the Insert section (or a specific insert within it) is bypassed, the MIDI events do not pass through the current inserts, but settings of these inserts remain untouched.

Similarly, the Sends State button found in both the MIDI Fader section and in the Track List (as displayed in Figure 17.3), monitors the state of MIDI send effects assigned to this track. The button is blue when any send effect is assigned to the track, and a yellow rectangle appears in the title bar of the Sends tab in the Inspector. Pressing this button in the MIDI Fader section of the Inspector or in the Track List will prevent the MIDI on this track from going out through the MIDI send destinations, but the sends settings remain untouched.

Finally, the track activity indicator at the right edge of the Track List (see the top track in Figure 17.4) monitors event activity on each track. In MIDI tracks, this may be any MIDI messages (note, controller, and SysEx if it is not filtered by Cubase). With audio tracks, this activity represents the playback level or the input level, depending on the track's monitor state.

Notepad

You can now add little bits of information to each track by using the Notepad section. Use it if you need to exit quickly and you just want to keep some notes on the current state of your project, describe which devices, settings, and connections were used for this track, discuss whether it was changed from its original setup, record names and phone numbers of your musicians or voice talent, and so on—anything you feel is worth writing down. If you save your file, only to reopen it in a few months, you might not remember what is what. The Notepad enables you to refresh your memory.

Simply type in the text field area. Any changes you make will be saved as part of the project file.

User Panel

The User panel lets you select any customized panels for external MIDI devices connected to this track's assigned output. In Figure 17.5, the custom panel offers an additional parameter slider that has been programmed to control the reverb level of the external synth connected to this track. Read the documentation provided with Cubase to find out more about creating your own device panel when you set up your studio's devices in the MIDI Device Manager.

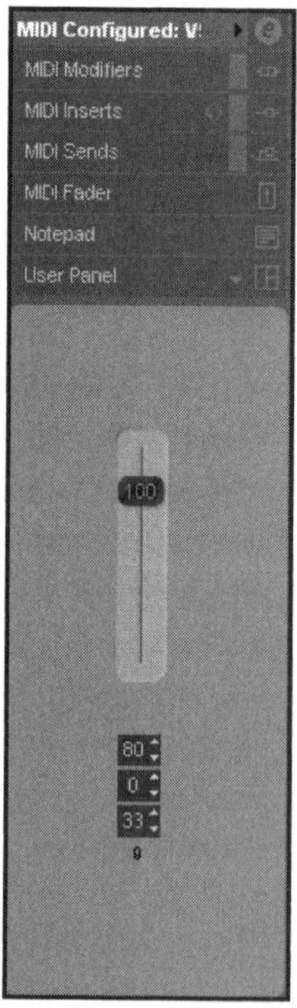

Figure 17.5
An example of the User panel in the Inspector.

Another useful application for the User panel is to create a control panel for a VSTi loaded in the track. By using the controls in the User panel, you don't have to open the VSTi's panel every time you want to change a setting or see the value associated with the parameter. If you use VST instruments quite frequently in a project and automate their parameters, User panels can be accessed quickly, just by selecting the track in the Project window.

When the output of a MIDI track is assigned to a VSTi, its name appears in the section at the bottom of the Inspector for that MIDI track, as displayed in Figure 17.6. Next to the instrument's name is the Edit VST Instrument button, which opens up the instrument's control panel and the Edit Instrument Channel Settings button, which in turn opens the VSTi's audio channel in the Mixer. You can add audio plug-ins to a VSTi's audio channel. This bar provides quick access to this channel, directly from any MIDI track that is assigned to this VSTi.

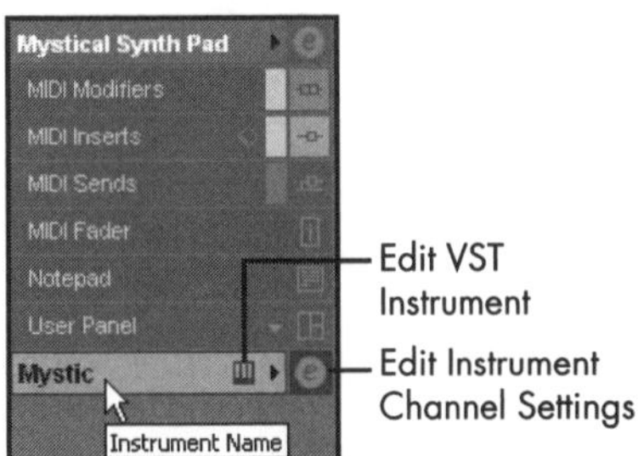

Figure 17.6
The MIDI Instrument section in the Inspector.

MIDI Channel

The MIDI Channel section (see Figure 17.7) offers many of the same options as you find in the MIDI Settings section of the Inspector area, as well as the Track List area for a MIDI track. It also mirrors the information you find in the Mixer panel for this specific track class, as well as most of the buttons that we have seen earlier in the Track List and Track Settings sections of the Inspector area. You can use this section to set the pan and volume levels of the device or VSTi assigned as the output destination for this track. You also can use this section to change or monitor which insert or send effects are active. Finally, below the Volume fader is the track's Name field, which you can use to rename the selected track.

A MIDI channel is added to the Mixer window each time you create a MIDI track in the Project window. While instrument tracks display MIDI settings in the Inspector, their corresponding channel in the Mixer displays the audio output of the VSTi instrument, rather than the MIDI controls found on a normal MIDI track (although you can choose to view the MIDI inserts for an Instrument channel in the Mixer window). A MIDI channel in the Mixer window displays an exact replica of the MIDI Channel section in the Inspector for a MIDI track with the exception of the View Options menu. The function of each control found in Figure 17.8 is described in the following list:

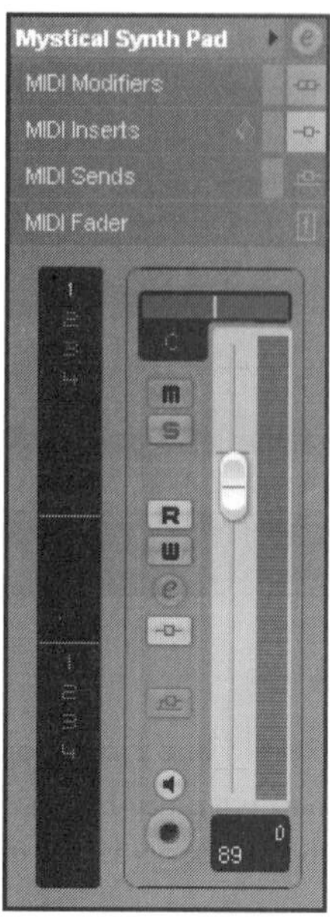

Figure 17.7
The MIDI Track Channel section in the Inspector area.

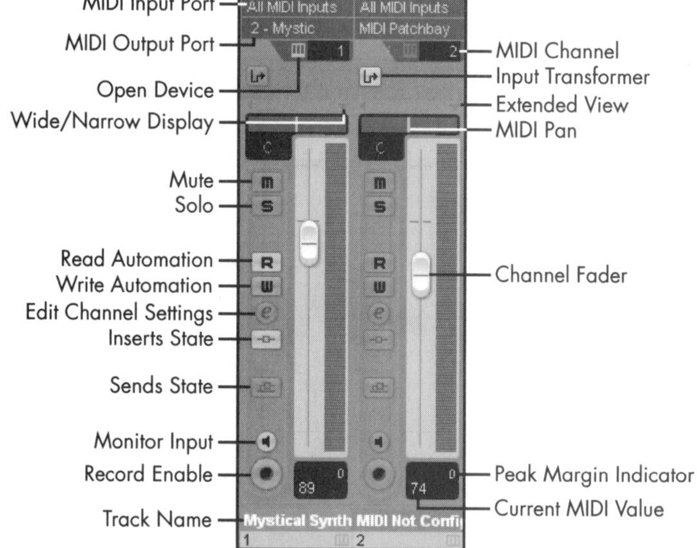

Figure 17.8
A MIDI channel in the Mixer window.

- **MIDI Input and Output port selection fields.** These allow you to choose the source and destination of MIDI events for this channel.
- **MIDI Channel selection field.** This allows you to choose the destination channel for your MIDI events.
- **Open Device button.** This opens the control panel for the VSTi and makes it possible to perform parameter changes to the instrument or loads and changes presets in the VSTi.
- **Input Transformer button.** This allows you to access the Input Transformer panel for the selected track.
- **Wide/Narrow toggle.** This toggles the channel's display between wide and narrow sizes. Making the channel narrow allows you to display more channels on the screen simultaneously, without affecting their properties. Some of the functions will be hidden when the track is in Narrow mode.
- **Extended View Type/Can Hide Option menu.** This offers you a way to change which panels are displayed in the extended panel of the Mixer for this channel only. It also makes it possible to enable the Can Hide property for the channel.
- MIDI **Pan control and display.** This displays a numeric and graphic representation of the Pan setting for this MIDI channel. Ctrl-clicking (PC)/-clicking (Mac) brings the pan back to its center position, which is represented by a C in the numeric display. On MIDI tracks, the Pan control actually corresponds to MIDI Controller #10.
- **Channel Setting Option buttons.** These are the same buttons found in the MIDI Channel section in the track's Inspector area. Whatever settings you made in the Inspector are displayed here and vice versa. These functions are Mute, Solo, Read, Write, Open Channel Editor Panel, Insert Bypass, Send Effect Bypass, Monitor (switches the track to input monitor mode), and Record Enable.
- **Channel Fader.** This controls MIDI Controller #7 (Volume), which can only be an integer value between 0 and 127. You should also be aware that the fader's default position is set at 100; holding down the Ctrl (PC)/ (Mac) key as you click on the fader's handle brings it back to this value. You also can hold down the Shift key while moving your fader for a finer level of precision. The level display on the right of a MIDI channel's fader, unlike the audio channels, does not represent the output level of the instrument. This level cannot be monitored because the sound of the MIDI instrument a MIDI channel is destined for is not monitored through the MIDI channel itself. In fact, this meter represents the velocity value of Note On and Note Off messages. Changing the volume level with the fader to the right does not, therefore, affect the level displayed in this bar, and no digital clipping can occur because of high velocities being monitored by this display.

- **Current MIDI value and Peak Margin Indicator.** Both fields display MIDI values. The first represents the current position of the MIDI volume fader, and the second represents the highest MIDI Note On velocity value.

MIDI Channel Settings

The MIDI Channel Settings panel offers a convenient way to edit all MIDI channel settings for a selected MIDI channel in a single window. You can access a Channel Settings panel through the Edit MIDI Channel Settings button in the Inspector's Channel section, in the Track List area, or in the Mixer window (see Figure 17.9).

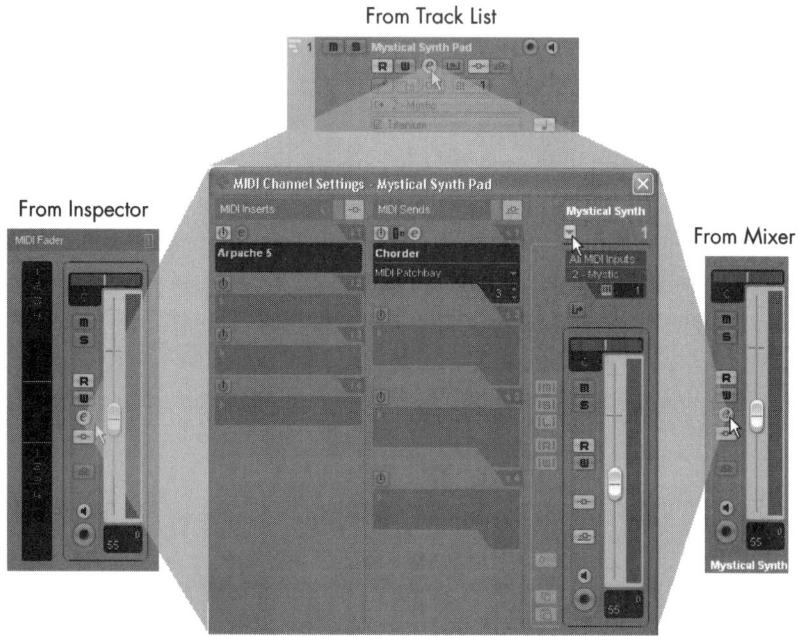

Figure 17.9
The Edit Channel Settings button.

The MIDI Channel Settings panel offers four areas (see Figure 17.9). Here they are from left to right:

- The MIDI Inserts display the current inserts settings for this channel. As with the MIDI channel settings, any changes you make here or in any other window in the project update this channel's settings in all windows.
- The MIDI Sends panel, as with the inserts, displays the current settings for this channel.

- The Common panel displays a number of options that affect all channels, even if they are not visible. For example, pressing the Mute button when it is active will unmute all currently muted channels in a project. More on the Common panel features in Chapter 31, "Mixer Panel."
- The MIDI Channel display offers settings identical to the ones found in the Mixer or Channel section of the Inspector in the Project window. Any changes you make here or anywhere else are reflected in all parts of the project.

Note that you can change the channel currently displayed in the MIDI (or audio) Channel Settings panel by accessing the drop-down menu in the upper-right corner of this panel (located under the cursor in Figure 17.9). This makes it easy to navigate or change the settings for different channels without changing your view.

You also customize this panel through the Customize View option in the context menu found in the title bar of the MIDI Channel Settings–right-click (PC)/Control-click (Mac)–as displayed in Figure 17.10. The Setup dialog box lets you hide or display panels and re-sort the order in which they appear. Clicking on the Save Preset button (a small diskette icon) allows you to save the current view and name it accordingly.

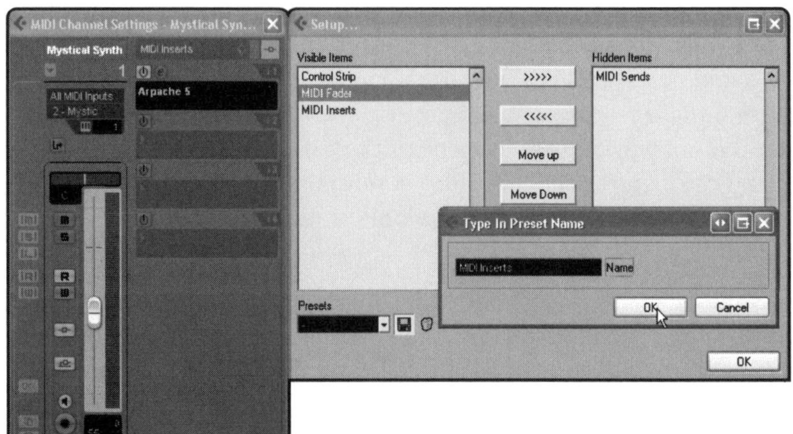

Figure 17.10
Customizing the Channel Settings panel.

Once you've saved a customized view of the Channel Settings panel, it will appear as a selection in the context menu, as displayed in Figure 17.11. To switch between different views, simply select the appropriate preset from the context menu.

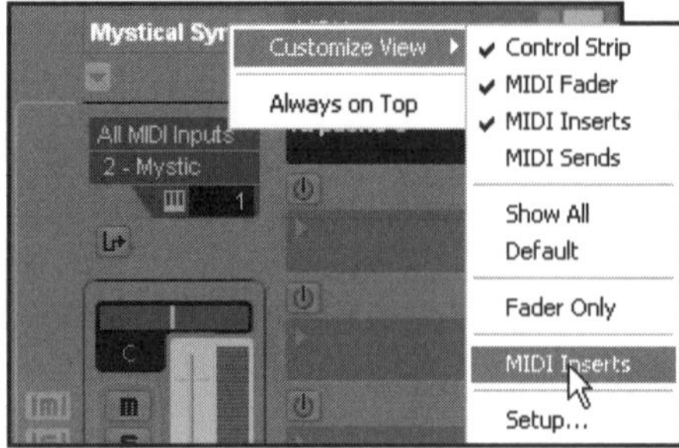

Figure 17.11
Selecting a saved customized Channel Settings panel view.

MIDI to Mixdown

MIDI provides a great way to lay down ideas and record music using synthesizers, samplers, and drum machines, among other things. However, distributing your work on a CD or through the Internet using MIDI files is not a practical solution. This is because even with the General MIDI standard (which establishes a common drum map and sequence of MIDI program numbers for instruments that support this standard), the sound quality will vary from one computer system to another, and audio CD players simply don't support MIDI. VSTi and ReWire instruments are also MIDI-based, so they won't work well outside the VST environment. So, at some point in the process you need to convert MIDI events into audio once you are satisfied with the tracks the way they are. Note that if you are using sounds generated by a synthesizer, a sampler, or any other sound-generating device based on audio hardware, or if you are using any software-based sampler that is not a VSTi within Cubase or ReWire-compatible, you often need to convert the output from these devices into audio files. This not only makes it easier to include them in your final audio mix without depending on the Real-Time Export option, but also ensures that their audio will be available in the future, even if the source device is no longer available or no longer connected to your studio configuration in the same way.

Before you can convert the audio output from an external MIDI instrument into an audio track, it's important to set up the connections properly in the VST Connections window, as described in Chapter 4. An external instrument connection ensures that MIDI events are sent to the external MIDI device and that its audio outputs are routed back to the project through instrument tracks, as displayed in Figure 17.12, and this is definitely the best way to set up your external MIDI keyboards and sound modules in Cubase. In this figure, the top of the Inspector displays the MIDI settings, while the Channel section displays the audio channels receiving the audio output from the MIDI device.

Figure 17.12
The audio and MIDI controls of an external MIDI device configured through the VST Connections window.

HOW TO ❄

Convert instrument tracks that are playing external MIDI devices into audio tracks:

1. Turn off the MIDI metronome, especially if the same device you are using to record generates that sound.
2. Set the left and right locators where you want the MIDI events to start and end being recorded as audio output from the destination device.
3. Solo the instrument track you want to record as audio. This ensures that the only signal being recorded comes from the part you want to convert.
4. From the File menu, select Export > Audio Mixdown.
5. Set up the File Location properties as desired in the Export Audio Mixdown dialog box.

6. Choose the desired file format for the file being exported.
7. In the Audio Engine Output options, select the output connected to your MIDI device. In Figure 17.13, the JV-1080 synth module's output will be recorded.

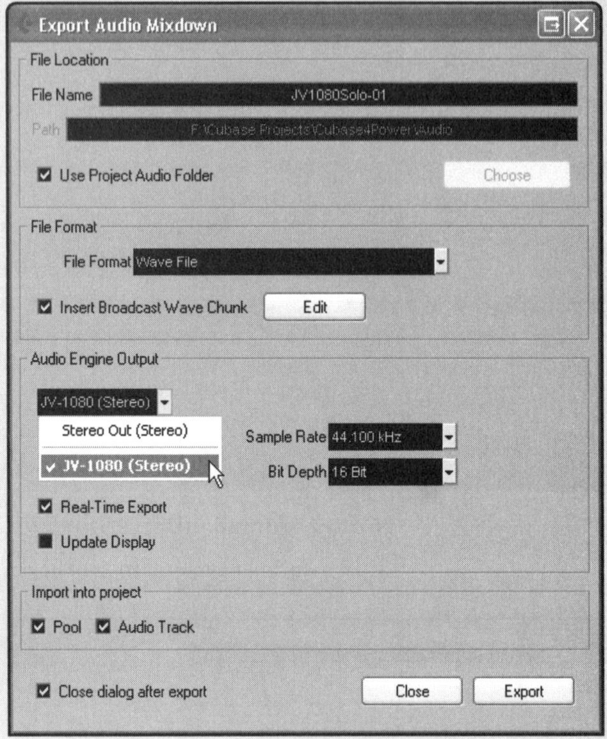

Figure 17.13
Setting up export options for external MIDI devices used in a project.

8. Because the audio comes from a hardware device outside of Cubase, check the Real-Time Export option and set the other Audio Engine Output options appropriately for your needs. If you intend to use this file in the current project, make sure the sample rate and bit depth match your project's audio properties.
9. Check the Import into Project options as needed. If you're simply converting the instrument tracks, both the Pool and Audio Track options should be checked.
10. Click the Export button when you are ready.
11. Repeat this process for other instrument tracks playing through external MIDI devices if necessary.

After you have completed the MIDI-to-audio conversion, you can drag all your instrument tracks into a folder track and mute them, listening to the newly rendered audio tracks for the remainder of this project. There might be volume changes between the original instrument tracks and the new audio tracks; when this happens, adjust the levels in the Mixer or record automation to restore the proper balance in your mix.

18 Audio Tracks

In a Cubase project, the audio track class can contain any type of audio events—from live audio recordings to looped samples, from rendered effect tracks to duplicated and processed audio tracks. Audio tracks can be automated and routed to various audio outputs, including studio sends and group channels. Each audio track in Cubase has its own dedicated four-band parametric equalizer section and can have up to eight inserts and eight sends for effects processing. Many of the controls found in audio tracks are similar to the ones discussed for MIDI tracks in the previous chapter and will behave in a way that should start to feel familiar to you by now. Also, audio, instrument, input, output, FX channel, and group tracks share many of the same basic controls. This chapter looks more specifically at the controls in the Project window's Inspector, but will also apply to the same controls when they appear in other windows.

While MIDI events are saved as part of the project file itself, audio events recorded into a Cubase project are stored in an Audio folder found inside the project's folder. It is also highly recommended to copy imported audio events to this Audio subfolder when importing them to the project to avoid having audio files all over the place. This will save you preparation time later when creating a backup of your project.

Here's a summary of what you will learn in this chapter:

- How to move and edit audio events or parts within audio tracks
- How to set up the Auto Fade options associated with audio tracks
- How to configure the input and output busses of an audio track
- How to display and change audio track settings through the Inspector sections
- How to use and adjust EQ bands in an audio track
- How to store, recall, and rename EQ presets
- How to adjust EQ settings using the Equalizer Curve
- How to customize the VST Audio Channel Settings panel

Audio Objects in Cubase

The audio track class is used to hold audio events, audio parts, and automation information. When you record audio on a track, an audio event is created in your project. Each audio track (or audio part within it) can only play one audio event at a time. This implies that if you overlap audio events, you only hear the topmost event at any given position. Changing the order of these events offers a way to control which event plays back on the track, as displayed in Figure 18.1. In the overlapping events found in the upper portion of this figure, Event A is in front (on top) and Event B is in back (behind). As a result, the track plays Event A until its end, and then plays Event B. The same events overlap in the lower portion of the figure, but this time, Event A is the one behind, while Event B is in front. You can change the order of these events by selecting the overlapping events, and then right-clicking (PC)/Control-clicking (Mac) over the selected events. From the context menu's To Front command, choose which of the overlapping events you want to place in front.

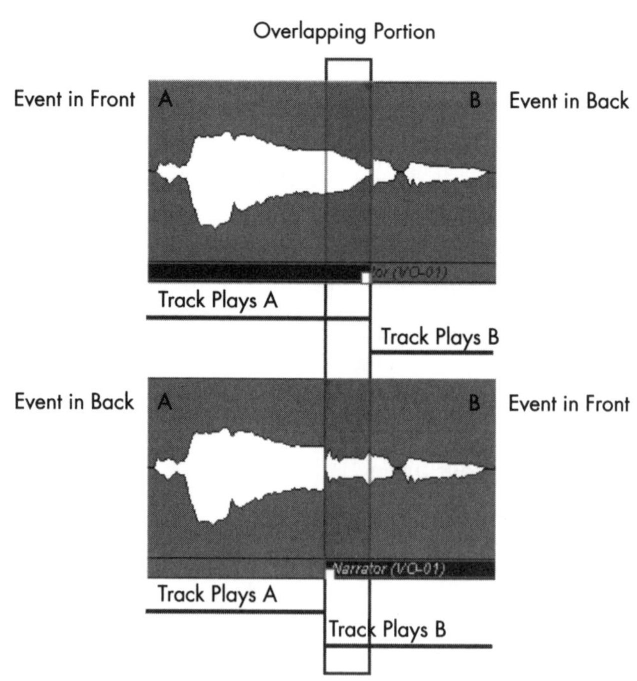

Figure 18.1
Changing the order of overlapping events on an audio track.

Audio tracks also make it possible to move recorded audio events along the project's timeline and edit any type of audio objects (events or parts) as needed.

Setting Up an Audio Track

Because audio tracks are very common to Cubase projects, they can be created in a number of ways and in various windows inside Cubase. For example, you can add an audio track through the Track List area's context menu, in the Mixer window's context menu, or by dragging an audio clip from the Pool or desktop to the empty area below the last track in the Project window's Track List. Once an audio track is created, its settings are available in the Inspector. Some of these settings are also mirrored in the Mixer window. For example, for each audio track in the Project window, an associated channel strip appears in Cubase's Mixer.

As you can see in Figure 18.2, the Audio Track Settings in the Inspector (on the left) and the Track List controls offer many of the same functionalities. Many of these have been described in Chapter 17; for example, the Mute, Solo, Read/Write Automation, Record Enable, Timebase, and Lock buttons play the same role in both types of tracks.

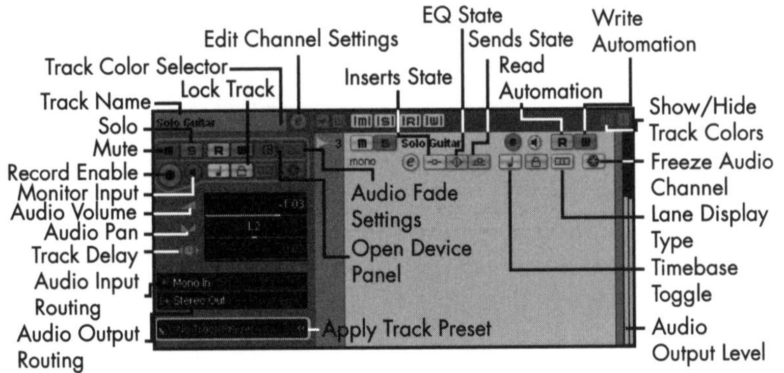

Figure 18.2
Many controls and parameters for audio-related tracks are found in both the Inspector and the Track List.

In the Channel Settings section of the Inspector for an audio track, the Auto Fade Settings button appears in the same location as the Input Transformer button on a MIDI track. The Auto Fades dialog lets you automatically create short 1- to 500-millisecond fades at the start and end of an event in order to reduce the possibility of clicks. This type of audio glitch can occur when an audio event ends or begins at a point where the audio waveform is not at a zero crossing (silence on the amplitude scale). The Auto Fade Settings can be customized for each track, or you can apply a single setting to the entire project through the Project > Auto Fade Settings menu. When the Auto Fade In, Auto Fade Out, or Auto Crossfades option is enabled for an audio track (see the check boxes in the upper-right corner of the dialog box shown in Figure 18.3), Cubase automatically applies the corresponding fade at the beginning or end of each event in real time. The dialog box also lets you choose the type of fade curve to apply. To use the dialog box's settings across all audio tracks, click on the As Default button. To return the current track's settings to the global defaults for this project, enable the Use Project Settings check box. Finally, although the Auto Fades dialog settings are similar to the Fade editor settings, Auto Fade lengths can't exceed

500 ms (half a second), whereas the Fade editor will apply the fade's settings over the duration of the event's fade, no matter how long it needs to be.

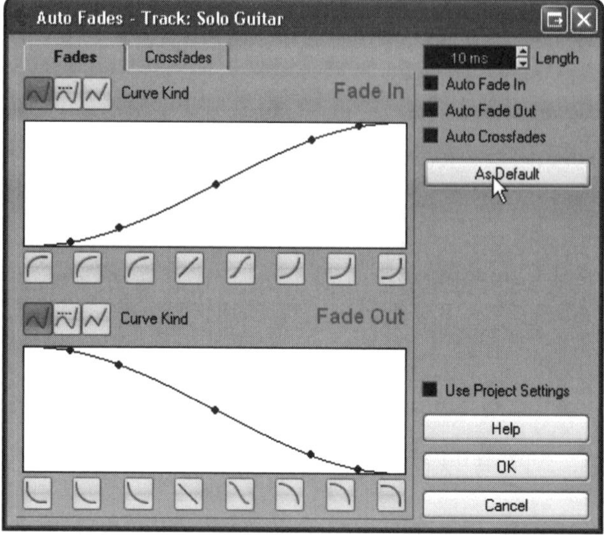

Figure 18.3
The Auto Fades dialog box.

The Freeze Audio Channel button is also available for audio (and instrument) tracks. For more on freezing audio tracks and how this function can help reduce the CPU load imposed by using real-time plug-in effects as inserts, take a look at Chapter 39, "Project Optimization."

The input routing pop-up menu in the Inspector lets you select the audio source for this track. This setting is particularly important when you are recording multiple audio sources, because it determines which track will record each input signal on your audio interface. The input busses available in this menu are those created previously in the VST Connections window. The audio output routing pop-up menu lets you select where the signal gets routed at the output of each track. Audio tracks can be routed either to output busses created in the VST Connections window or to group channels. If your project contains any group channels, a horizontal line in this pop-up menu will separate the output busses from the group channel assignments, as shown in Figure 18.4.

Figure 18.4
The output routing pop-up displaying output busses and group channel assignments for this audio track's output.

Inspector Sections

By default, the Inspector displays the audio settings at the top, followed by the Inserts, Equalizers, Sends, Channel, and Notepad sections. You can customize which sections the Inspector displays by right-clicking (PC)/Control-clicking (Mac) over a section's header. A context menu will reveal a number of additional sections, including an EQ Curve display, studio sends (which can be used to route the track to a headphone mix, for example), a graphic Surround Pan display, and a User Panel. All these sections share a few functionalities:

- Click on the section header to expand the section and reveal its controls, hiding all others.
- Hold the Ctrl key (PC)/ key (Mac) while clicking on a header to expand the section's controls without collapsing any other Inspector sections that are already open. For example, this will be particularly useful for keeping both the Equalizers and Equalizer Curve sections of the Inspector, discussed later in this chapter, open simultaneously.
- The Inserts, Equalizers, Sends, and Studio Sends sections offer a bypass button. This control lets you bypass these entire sections with a single click. The Track List, the Channel section of the Inspector, and the Mixer window also offer Insert, EQ, or Sends state buttons that perform a similar function for bypassing these entire sections on a channel. Whenever the bypass function is enabled, this button in the Inspector becomes yellow. An indicator at the right end of these same sections of the Inspector also indicates whether any insert, equalizer band, or send is currently active within them, as shown in Figure 18.5.

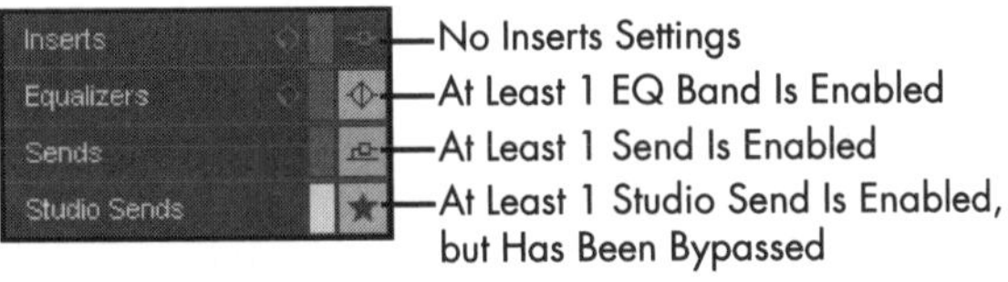

Figure 18.5
The Bypass and Show Active states features associated with the Inspector.

- The Inserts and Equalizers sections offer a Preset Management button that lets you load, save, or manage presets for these sections.

For more on the Inserts section, please take a look at Chapter 12, which is dedicated to insert effects.

Equalizers Section on Audio Tracks

EQ is part of the recording and mixing process in probably 99 percent of recordings today, and at some point in your creation process, you will find it to be a very useful tool. That said, it can be used correctively or creatively. Too much equalization, and you might lose the purity of a well-recorded original sound—then again, maybe this is what you were going for. You can use an EQ to increase or decrease specific frequencies to help the general quality of the sound, to correct certain flaws in the recording due to poor microphone placement or performance, to remove noise generated by fluorescent lighting or air conditioning, to reduce certain frequencies in a part so that it conflicts less with others in the mix, and in many more ways than this chapter allows us to mention. In Cubase, a dedicated EQ section for each audio-related track offers four bands of parametric EQ. (However, you always have the option to enable additional EQ or filtering via an insert plug-in effect, such as the GEQ-10 and GEQ-30 graphic equalizer plug-ins or the StudioEQ parametric equalizer plug-in provided with Cubase 4.) Note that MIDI channels do not have EQ controls, since only MIDI data passes through them.

Each EQ band gives you control over gain, frequency, and Q.

- The Gain control is the amount of gain or reduction that you apply to a frequency. You can boost or cut each EQ band by as much as 24 dB in either direction.
- The Frequency control determines what frequency is affected by your gain or cut. You can set each band to any frequency between 20 Hz and 20,000 Hz. Each channel offers four bands that can be set to different filter modes and independently enabled or disabled.
- The Q (*Quality Factor*) is the control you have over the slope of the range of frequencies that are boosted or cut around the center frequency of a band. The lower the numeric values for this field, the greater the width; the higher the numeric values for this field, the narrower the width. A narrow Q is useful for isolating a problematic frequency, such as a 60-Hz cycle, that is often associated with electrical equipment. A wide Q is useful to enhance or reduce a large area of the harmonic structure of a sound, such as boosting the high end of the sound.

Below the Track Inserts section is the track's Equalizer section (EQ). Each audio track you create has a four-band parametric equalizer (see Figure 18.6).

Most of the features for each EQ band are similar with the exception of the Hi and Lo bands. In the Hi band, setting the Q completely to the left creates a high shelf, which means that any frequency above the center frequency for this band is affected by the Gain control. Inversely, if the Q is set completely to the right, it creates a low-pass filter, where every frequency above the band's center frequency is reduced. For the Lo band, setting the Q completely to the left produces a low shelf and setting the Q completely to the right creates a high pass, as shown in Figure 18.7.

EQ1 and EQ4 bands share an identical set of features, while the EQ2 and EQ3 bands share a different set of identical features.

- **Low/High Pass I, II.** With mode I, the filter is unaffected by the Q value. The low pass filter usually associated with the EQ band 4 filters out the high frequencies, while the high pass filter usually associated with the EQ band 1 filters out the low frequencies. With mode II, a resonance filter creates a bump at the center of the band. The narrower the Q, the more pronounced this bump will be. See examples in the first two columns on the left and first two rows in Figure 18.7.

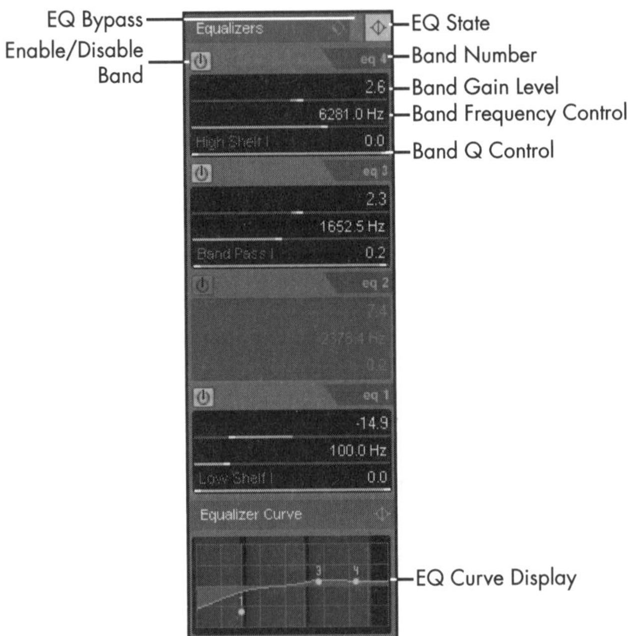

Figure 18.6
The Equalizer and Equalizer Curve sections from the Inspector.

- **Band Pass I and II (available on all four bands).** With the Band Pass II mode offering a slightly narrower resonance (or Q) at the center of the band's frequency. This is ideal in situations where a precise band filtering effect is required. Band Pass I mode will work well in most corrective EQ situations. See examples in the first two columns on the left and last two rows in Figure 18.7.
- **Low/High Shelf I, II, III, and IV (available on bands 1 and 4).** Each one of these shelves offers a different resonance "bump" or "dip" at the cutoff frequency point. A bump occurs when the resonance is applied in the same direction as the gain and a dip occurs when the resonance is applied in the opposite direction of the gain. Some of these differences will be more perceptible when using a very narrow Q. The narrower the Q, the greater the amount of "bump" or "dip" in the curve. The Low Shelf II has a "dip," and Low Shelf III has a "bump," while the Low Shelf IV offers a combination of both. See examples in the last two columns on the right and all rows in Figure 18.7.

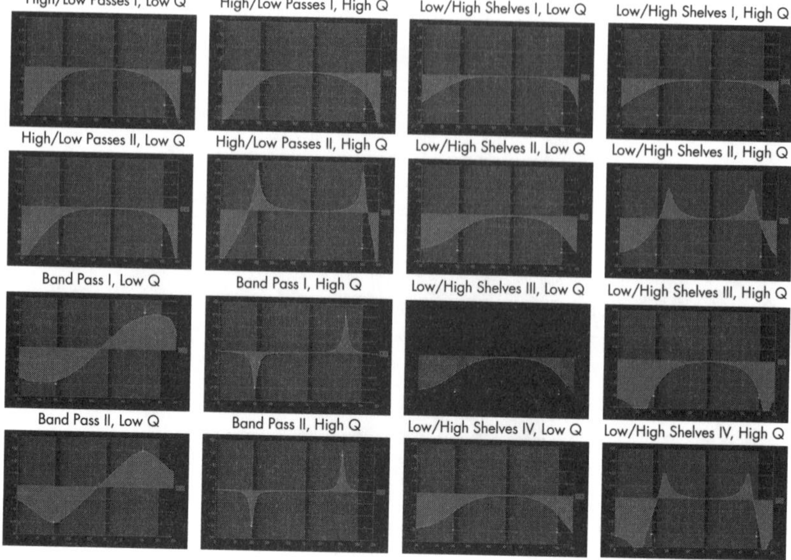

Figure 18.7
The different types of filters available in each audio channel EQ.

HOW TO

Adjust an EQ band from the Equalizers section for an audio track:

1. Make the Equalizers section visible for the track you want to adjust. (This can be done either in the Inspector or in the Mixer window.)
2. Enable the band you want to use, as shown in Figure 18.8.

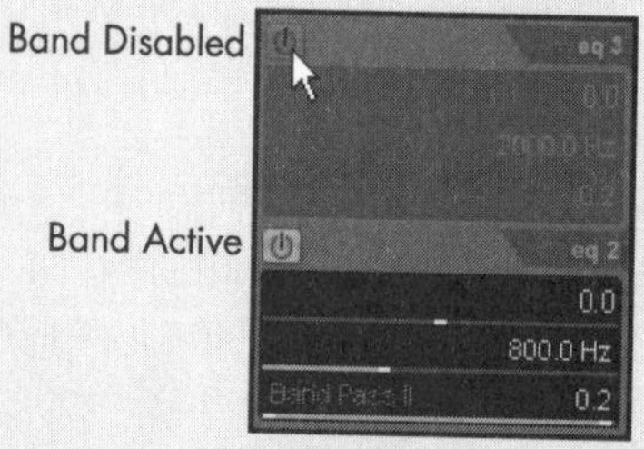

Figure 18.8
An EQ band needs to be enabled in order to affect the audio passing through it.

Band Disabled

Band Active

3. Find the frequency you want to adjust by dragging the slider bar under the numeric display of the frequency, by clicking on the frequency value and using your scroll bar to increase or decrease the value, or by double-clicking on the value and entering a new value between 20 and 20,000 (which corresponds to the range of each band).
4. Adjust the amount of gain boost or reduction you want to apply by using the Gain control values. You can adjust these values the same way you can adjust the frequency (as seen in Step 3). However, the minimum and maximum values for this field are +24 to –24 (which correspond to dB values of boost or cut).
5. Select the band's filter type from the EQ Band Type menu, as displayed in Figure 18.9.

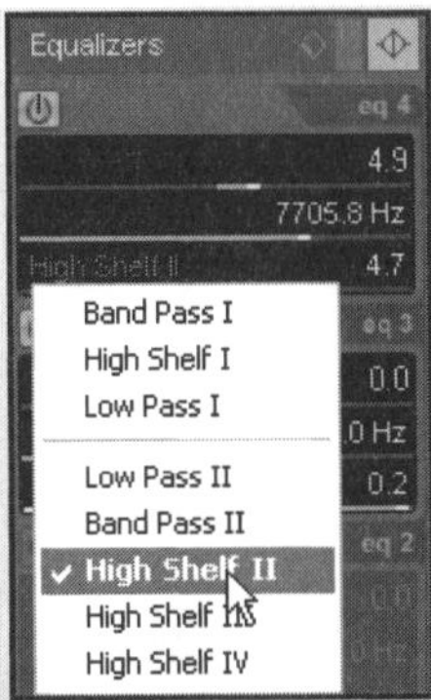

Figure 18.9

The EQ band's filter type.

6. Adjust the slope of the filter for this band by changing its Q value slider. On band-pass filters (the only mode available for EQ bands 2 and 3), at a given amount of gain increase or decrease, smaller Q values result in wider bands, whereas higher values result in narrower bands.
7. Repeat these steps for each band in your EQ.

You can bring back each value to its default position in the EQ by Ctrl-clicking (PC)/⌘-clicking (Mac) on the appropriate field. You also can do before/after comparison listening by deactivating an EQ band. This acts as a band bypass. When you deactivate an EQ band, its settings remain unchanged.

Reversing the EQ

Located to the right of the graphical display of the EQ in the Audio Channel Settings window (see Figure 18.10), you'll find the Inverse Equalizer button, which can be used to invert the gain value currently applied to each active band in your EQ. Click on this button while the Write Automation button is enabled and you can create some interesting filter effects.

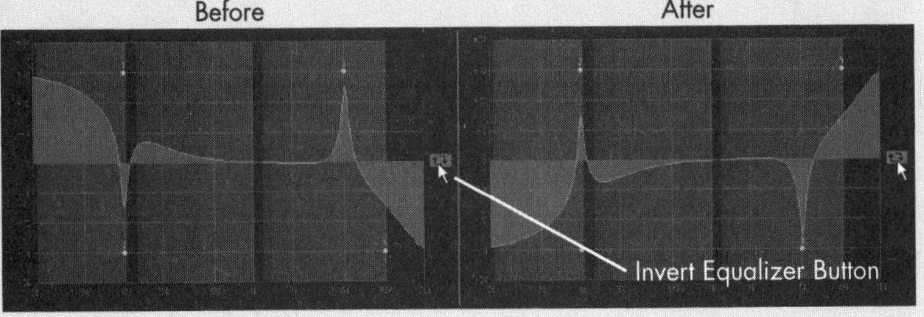

Figure 18.10

The Inverse Equalizer function.

Note that you also can adjust EQ settings (as well as inserts and sends) through the Mixer panel and the Channel Settings panel. To hear the sound without the EQ active, and to make sure that the settings you are applying actually help your sound, you can use the EQ Bypass button in the Channel section of the Inspector (or in the Track List or Mixer). Holding down the Control key

(PC)/⌘ key (Mac) as you click on any value slider in the EQ section will return it to its default position (no boost or cut, and a default frequency).

Using the EQ Curve Display

EQ curves can be edited either in the graphic display area provided by the Equalizer Curve section of the Inspector or in the Equalizers panel of the VST Audio Channel Settings window, which offers even more precision for these adjustments. Moving the handle for an EQ band left or right changes the frequency; moving it up or down adds or removes gain from that band. If no band control handles appear, it's because you haven't activated any bands. You can kill two birds with one stone by clicking on the green line that depicts the current EQ curve to activate the band corresponding to the frequency where you click. A control handle will appear, which you can drag to change where this EQ band's boost or cut will occur within the frequency spectrum of this audio track.

After you are happy with the results, you can store your settings for later use.

HOW TO

Store/recall/rename an EQ as a preset:

- Click the Preset Management button in the EQ panel. At the bottom of the pop-up menu, which includes many presets included with the Cubase program, select Store Preset.
- Click the Preset Management button and select a preset from the same menu, or select From Track Preset at the bottom of the menu to browse and extract an EQ preset from one of your stored track presets.
- Click the Preset Management button and select Rename Preset, type in a new name, and click OK when you are finished.

Equalizer Curve

The Equalizer Curve section of the Inspector area (see Figure 18.6) offers a graphical display, representing the current EQ settings for the selected audio track. (If you click the Edit Channel Settings button for any of the audio-related track types, the Channel Settings window also offers a larger version of this graphical display.) Each band is represented by a point along a centered horizontal line. This center line represents an EQ in its default state, which implies that no boost or cut has been made to the audio at the frequency. Frequencies are displayed from low on the left to high on the right of the display. The space above the centered line represents a gain boost, whereas the space under the centered line represents a cut.

Any changes you make in the Equalizer section are visible here, so you can use this area to quickly glance at the curve produced by your current EQ settings for this track. However, the EQ curve can also be used to change your EQ settings for the track graphically. Here's how:

HOW TO

Adjust the EQ settings using the Equalizer curve:

- **To add an EQ band:** Click where you want to add the EQ band on the EQ's curve. The band numbers correspond to their respective frequency ranges. This means that where you click in the display influences which band number appears. Remember that if you want to use a low-shelf, low-pass, high-shelf, or high-pass filter, you will need to click near the left or right extremities of the display, depending on the band you want to activate.
- **To change the gain without affecting the frequency:** Hold the Ctrl (PC)/ (Mac) key down while you drag the band's handle in the graphical display.
- **To change the frequency without affecting the gain:** Hold the Alt (PC)/Option (Mac) key down while you drag the band's handle in the graphical display.
- **To change the band's Q:** Hold the Shift key down and move your mouse up to increase the width of the Q (the Q value will actually go down), and move your mouse down to decrease the width of the Q (the Q value will actually go up).

Channel

The Channel section in the Inspector for an audio track offers controls over the track's audio signal path, which are also mirrored in the Mixer. Most of the controls found in Figure 18.11 are also mirrored in the Track List area.

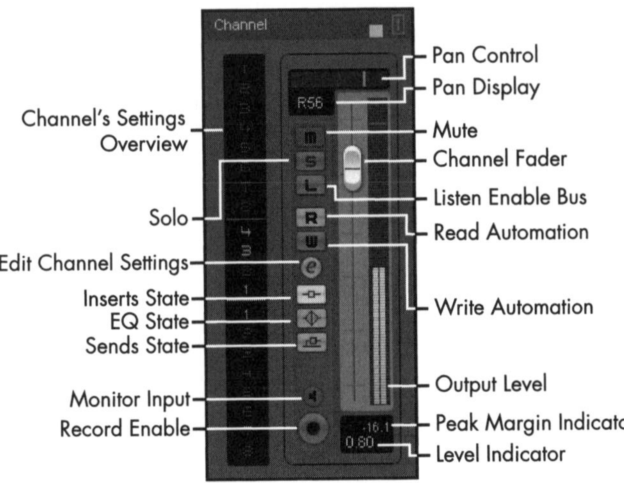

Figure 18.11
The Channel section of the Inspector.

Among the controls found in the Channel section of the Inspector are the Mute, Solo, Listen Enable, Read, Write, Edit Channel Settings, Inserts State, EQ State, Sends State, Monitor Input, and Record Enable buttons. Remember that when the Monitor button is enabled, the level indicator to the right of the channel fader becomes a pre-fader input level meter; changing the level of this fader will not have any effect on the input level. The settings overview panel on the left of the

Channel section displays active settings found in the channel. The eight numbers on the top correspond to the eight channel inserts (the last two of which are post-fader), the following four numbers correspond to the four EQ bands, and the last eight numbers correspond to the eight channel sends (each of which can be switched between pre- and post-fader modes). Clicking on any of the numbers currently illuminated will disable the corresponding setting.

The channel fader controls the output level of this channel (except when its Monitor button is enabled). As with many other controls in Cubase, to return the fader to its default 0 dB position, hold the Ctrl (PC)/ (Mac) key down as you click on it. If you want to move the fader by smaller, more precise increments, hold down the Shift key as you click and drag. This is useful when you want to create slow and precise fade effects with automation. The Channel Level numeric display below the fader tells you the position value (in dB) of this channel's fader. If you have a scroll wheel on your mouse, you can also adjust the selected channel's fader level by moving the wheel up or down.

Directly below the output level for the channel, the Peak Level indicator represents the distance between the highest audio peak in this track and the maximum digital audio level. This value resets itself as soon as you move the channel's fader or if you click inside the field. It's important to keep an eye on this margin because you don't want the audio on this track to go above 0 dB, but you don't want it to always stay very low when recording either. Ultimately, the Peak Level indicator should remain between −12 dB and 0 dB when recording.

Channel Settings Window for Audio Tracks

The Channel Settings window appears whenever the Edit Channel Settings button is pressed for any audio-related track in the Inspector, Tracks List, or Mixer window. This window shows all of that track's audio parameters, making it easy to perform detailed settings. The Channel Settings window displays by default four areas, but you can customize its contents to display up to eleven types of settings.

HOW TO ❄

Customize the Channel Settings window:

1. Right-click (PC)/Control-click (Mac) inside the Channel Settings window.
2. From the context menu, select the Customize View submenu and add a check to the section you want to display. This customized view for the Channel Settings window will be in effect for all audio-related track classes, including audio, instrument, input, output, FX channel, and group tracks.

Saving Views

From the context menu in the Channel Settings window, use the Setup option at the bottom of the Customize View submenu (Figure 18.12) to open the window's View Setup dialog box to save your favorite settings. Use the arrows in this dialog box to move channel settings back and forth between the columns for visible and hidden items, and use the Move Up and Move Down buttons to change the order in which these areas should appear. Once you are satisfied, click on the Save button (the floppy disk icon in Figure 18.13) and type in a name for your preset. Saved presets will appear in the Customize View submenu, where they can be quickly selected.

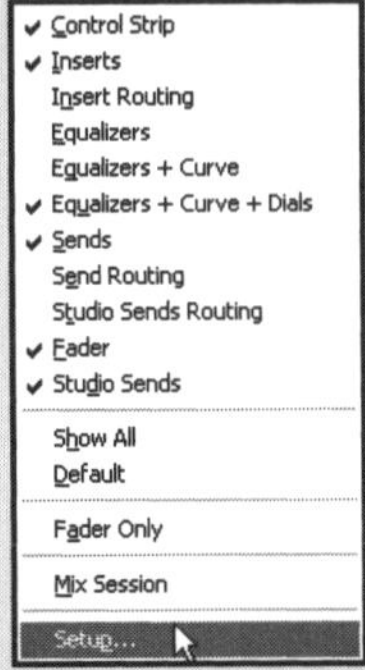

Figure 18.12
Custom View context menu options for the Channel Settings window.

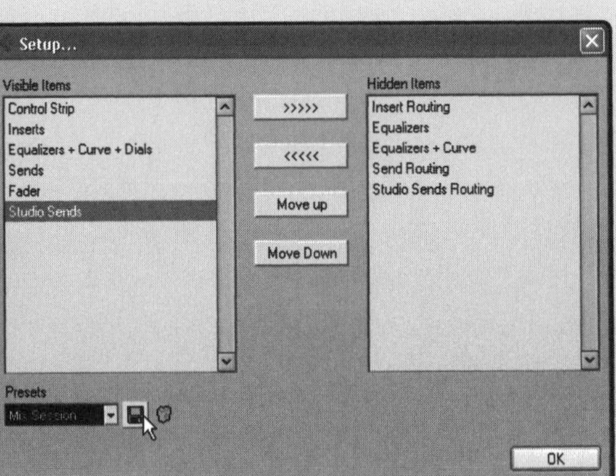

Figure 18.13
Saving a preset for the Channel Settings window from the Setup dialog box.

IV } Editing

19 Sample Editor

Cubase provides two audio editing environments (the Sample and Audio Part editors) and a number of audio asset management windows (the Pool and the MediaBay, SoundFrame, and Loop browsers), which manage media events, such as imported and recorded audio clips, as well as assets existing on media drives.

This chapter focuses on the Sample editor, which lets you edit recorded or imported audio, create regions and slices, and add special tempo markers to audio events to match their tempo with the tempo of a project by time-stretching samples in real time. This "warping" of time is similar to the MIDI Warp technique discussed in Chapter 29, "Tempo Track." Audio warping makes it possible to match the tempo of an audio event, such as a loop, to the project tempo without affecting its pitch. It also automatically adjusts the tempo of the audio event whenever the project tempo is changed, making audio events almost as flexible as MIDI events when it comes time to alter project tempos.

Here's a summary of what you will learn in this chapter:

- How to edit the boundaries of objects (events or regions) in the Sample editor
- How to cut, copy, or paste audio inside an event
- How to insert or remove silence inside an event
- How to create and edit regions inside the Sample editor
- How to edit a Snap-point's position
- How to create and edit Hitpoints
- How to create audio slices from Hitpoints
- How to create a groove quantize map from Hitpoints
- How to divide audio events at Hitpoints

Sample Editor Areas

The Sample editor is the editor associated with audio events; it opens any time you double-click on an audio event inside the Project or Pool window. The editor lets you perform different editing tasks in a nondestructive environment. You can create regions within an event, add effects, or edit an event by using offline processes and effects. The editor is divided into two areas—the Waveform Display area and the Regions List, displayed in Figure 19.1. It also displays a number of bars similar to the other editors—a toolbar, which includes various audio-specific tools; the thumbnail display, which provides a waveform overview of the entire event; the Info Line; the Ruler for the horizontal time scale; and the vertical Level Scale, which depicts amplitude. The following list describes the numbered areas in this figure.

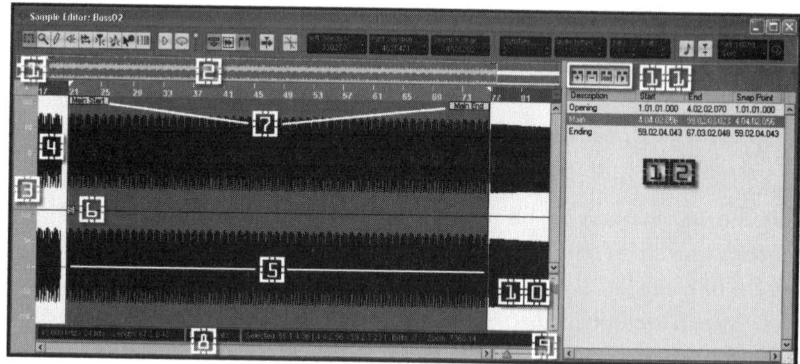

Figure 19.1
The Sample editor window.

1. The thumbnail display, an overview area that can be used to zoom and navigate within the audio event.
2. The currently displayed area in the overview area is displayed inside a box that can be used to resize or move the portion of this audio event or clip that is shown below in this editor's Waveform Display.
3. The Level Scale representing amplitude, which can be switched between decibel or percentage format.
4. The Waveform Display area.
5. The selected portion inside the Waveform Display area.
6. The Snap-point of the object (event or region).
7. Region handles that identify the start and end of a region inside an audio event.
8. The Info Line (status) area, which displays information about the sample being edited.
9. The Time Zoom slider.

10. The Amplitude Zoom slider.
11. The Region Option buttons (Add, Remove, Select, and Play Region).
12. The Regions List area, which displays existing regions that have been defined in the audio event or clip being edited.

Figure 19.2 displays the main tools found in the Sample editor. The first five buttons in the toolbar are used to perform different operations in the editor, such as selecting a range, zooming in or out, editing the waveform, performing audio playback, or scrubbing. We'll discuss these tools later, when we talk about the operations available in this window. Following these Sample editor tools are a set of buttons for Audio Warp tools:

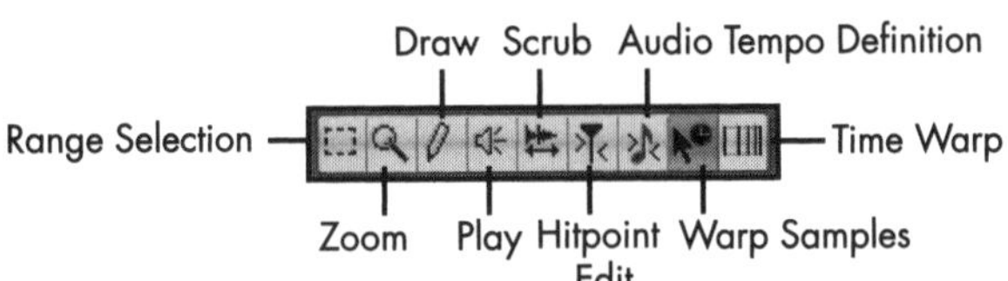

Figure 19.2
The main audio editing tools of the Sample editor.

- The **Hitpoint Edit** tool edits special markers that identify attack transients in an audio sample.
- The **Audio Tempo Definition** tool lets you adjust a "bars and beats" grid over the current sample. As a result, Cubase learns the precise tempo of this sample, which can then be time-stretched in real time to fit the project's tempo.
- The **Warp Samples** tool makes it possible to match time-based events to a tempo-based grid. As a result, you can correct the timing of an existing audio recording by dragging Audio Warp tabs within it from their current point in the timeline to the desired grid value. Cubase will time-stretch the sample in real time using one of several options.
- The **Time Warp** tool makes it possible to match a tempo-based grid to this time-based event.

We will get back to Hitpoint editing, the Audio Tempo Definition tool and its associated Musical mode option, and warping both samples and time in greater detail later in this chapter.

The Audition and Loop buttons, as displayed in Figure 19.3, have the same properties as in the Pool window. The small fader next to the Loop tool enables you to control the preview level when you are playing an event inside the Sample editor. Note that this preview level does not affect the level of the event in the Project window.

Click the Show Info button (see Figure 19.4) to display the Sample editor's Info Line. This displays information about the waveform or current selection below the Waveform Display, as seen in Figure 19.1. You can change the time units used for values represented in this bar by selecting a different format in the pop-up selectors at the right end of the Ruler or in the Info Line itself.

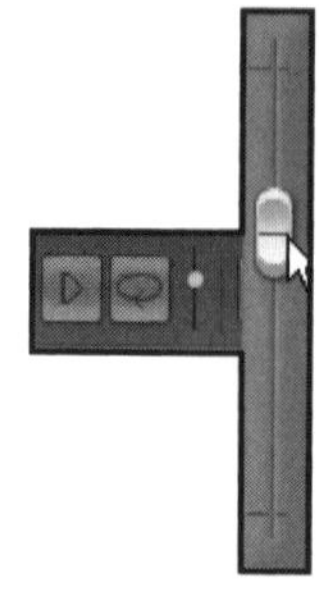

Figure 19.3
The Audition and Loop buttons in the Sample editor.

Figure 19.4
From left to right, the Show Info, Show Audio Event, Show Regions, Autoscroll, and Snap to Zero Crossing buttons.

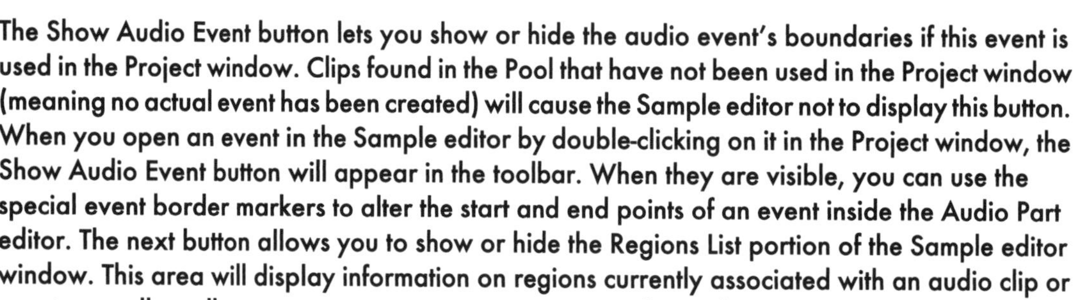

The Show Audio Event button lets you show or hide the audio event's boundaries if this event is used in the Project window. Clips found in the Pool that have not been used in the Project window (meaning no actual event has been created) will cause the Sample editor not to display this button. When you open an event in the Sample editor by double-clicking on it in the Project window, the Show Audio Event button will appear in the toolbar. When they are visible, you can use the special event border markers to alter the start and end points of an event inside the Audio Part editor. The next button allows you to show or hide the Regions List portion of the Sample editor window. This area will display information on regions currently associated with an audio clip or event, as well as allow you to create, remove, rename, select, edit, or preview regions.

HOW TO

Edit the start and end of an event in the Sample editor:

1. In the Sample editor's toolbar, enable the Audio Event button.
2. Select the Range Selection tool in the toolbar.
3. Click the marker for the start or end point of the event and drag it in the desired direction. For example, moving the start point to the right shortens the event, and moving it to the left lengthens it. Note that you can't extend these markers beyond the limit of the audio clip to which the event refers.

Changing these markers also affects the event as it appears in the Project window.

Using the Show Regions button reveals the Regions List and also displays region handles if there are any. This area enables you to create a region from a selection in the Waveform Display area, remove an existing region, select the highlighted region in the Waveform Display area, and play the highlighted region. If the Regions List area is not visible, you can use the Show Regions button in the Toolbar of this window. Unless you have recorded audio in Cycle mode with the Create Regions option enabled, events do not normally contain any regions when they are recorded or imported. It is through editing options or preference settings that regions are created or, as we see later in this chapter, through the buttons above the Regions List.

The Autoscroll button, located by default to the right of the Show Regions button, has the same property as it does in the Project window.

The Snap to Zero Crossing button forces any selection you make to move to the nearest zero crossing. Enabling this function is a useful way of being sure that regions you create or process will not begin or end at a position within the audio not corresponding to zero percent amplitude (silence). This helps in preventing clicks, pops, and other audio glitches from occurring due to sudden jumps in audio amplitudes at the beginning or end of a region.

The next set of buttons and subsequent fields in the toolbar are related to Hitpoints, Musical mode, and audio tempo definition, which are described later in this chapter.

Below the toolbar is the thumbnail display, which provides an overview of the current event loaded in the Sample editor. You can have only one event loaded in this editor at a time, so this overview displays only one event or several regions defined within this event.

The visual representation of the audio sample appears in the Waveform Display area. Cubase can display mono, stereo, and surround formats with up to six channels. The waveforms are displayed around a zero axis at the center of each waveform, which is also indicated in the vertical Level Scale along the left side of the Waveform Display. You can customize the elements displayed in this area by right-clicking (PC)/Control-clicking (Mac) in the Sample editor, selecting the Elements option at the bottom of the context menu, and selecting or deselecting elements found in this submenu. You also can change the Level Scale from percentage to dB display, or you can hide the Level Scale altogether by right-clicking (PC)/Control-clicking (Mac) in the button at the top of the Level Scale area itself (at the left end of the Ruler bar) and choosing the appropriate option in this context menu.

Basic Editing Functions

Use the Sample editor to cut, copy, and paste audio data. These basic editing functions are similar to any other type of application. For example, cutting and pasting audio can be summed up in four steps:

1. Use the Range Selection tool to select the desired audio.
2. Apply the desired function, such as Cut or Copy, from the Edit menu.
3. Position the cursor where you want to paste the audio.
4. Use the Paste command in the Edit menu.

You also can insert silence within an existing audio clip. This might be useful when you want to add pauses between specific audio content.

HOW TO

Add silence in an audio event:

1. With the Range Selection tool selected, drag a selection box over the area where you want to add silence.
2. Adjust the start and end points if needed by dragging the edge of the selection.
3. Select Edit > Range > Insert Silence. (This is also available in the editor's context menu or by pressing Ctrl+Shift+E (PC)/⌘+Shift+E (Mac).)

About Musical Mode

You also can use the Sample editor to define loop properties needed for Musical mode samples. Once Musical mode is enabled on a sample, its tempo becomes locked to the project's tempo setting. Cubase automatically time-stretches the loop to reflect any tempo changes that occur in real time. This type of feature is now commonly used in many loop-based composition tools, and using it in Cubase is pretty straightforward. Figure 19.5 displays a Musical mode–enabled audio sample in the Pool window.

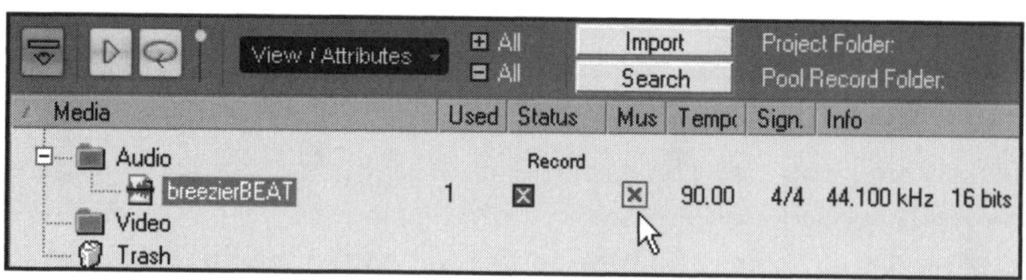

Figure 19.5
A Musical mode–enabled audio sample in the Pool.

We will further discuss how to quantize audio, tighten up the timing of a rhythmic part using Audio Warp tabs, and match an audio file's fluctuating tempo with the project's fixed tempo in Chapter 20, "Audio Processing Options."

Working with Regions

Regions enable you to define portions within an audio event that you can reuse several times in a project. For example, you could create regions from a 16-bar groove played by a drummer, naming each region appropriately: intro, beat, break, fill, and ending. Then drag the regions from the Regions List in the Sample editor into the Project window, just as you do when dragging objects from the Pool into the Project window.

HOW TO

Create a new region:

1. With the Range Selection tool, click and drag over the area in the Sample editor you want to include in the new region. At this point, you don't need to be precise.
2. When you have a good idea of the range, right-click (PC)/Control-click (Mac) and select Zoom > Zoom to Selection to view your selection close up. Range selections in the Waveform Display area appear in a light teal color. Existing regions appear in a darker shade of gray until they are selected (usually via the Select Region button in the Regions List), at which point they are displayed in an even darker shade of teal.
3. Edit the start or end of the selection as needed by dragging its edges. When the cursor becomes a double-headed arrow (which occurs when the cursor crosses one of the selection's edges), you can modify the selection without losing it (see Figure 19.6).

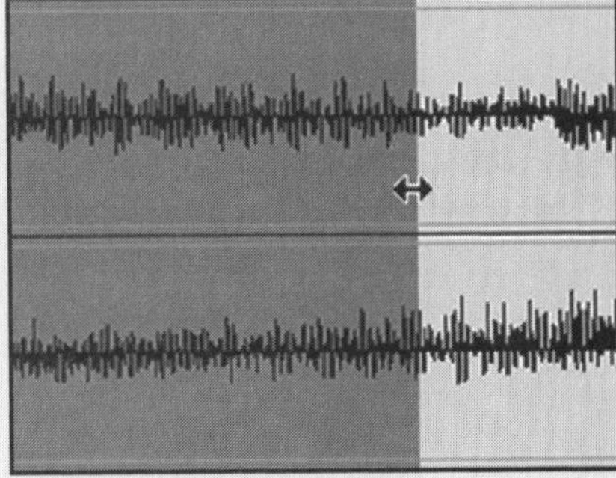

Figure 19.6
Adjust a selection by dragging the edges with the Range Selection tool.

4. Enable the Loop button and click the Audition icon (the "speaker" button) in the toolbar to hear the selection. Make any necessary modifications to your selection.
5. When you are satisfied with the selection, enable display of the Regions List if you haven't done so already.
6. Click the Add button.
7. Type a name in the Name field for your new selection.

Using the Snap to Zero Option

Keep the Snap to Zero Crossing button enabled to make sure the amplitude of the audio signal is at its lowest possible value (zero percent or minus infinity when displayed in dB) at the start and end points of the selections you make in the Waveform Display. This technique reduces the chances that glitches might occur during playback due to an abrupt change in amplitude. When the button is enabled, you will notice that the precise start and end points of your selection might skip over areas in the Waveform Display because Cubase cannot find a proper zero crossing in that portion of the audio.

HOW TO

Modify an existing region:

1. Click in the column to the left of the region you want to edit in the Regions List. This column does not have a name, but it enables you to move the content shown in the Waveform Display area to include this region.
2. Click the Select button. The region's start and end handles will appear.
3. Right-click (PC)/Control-click (Mac) and select Zoom > Zoom to Selection to center the selection in the display area.
4. With the Range Selection tool, drag the region's start or end handle to the new desired location.

You also can change the current region's start and end locations numerically by changing the values manually in the Start and End columns of the Regions List.

HOW TO

Add a region to a project from the Sample editor:

- Click in the empty column to the left of the Description column in the Regions List and drag the region to the desired location in the Project window.

The same rules apply here as when you are dragging files from the Pool window.

Snap-Point

Because audio events or regions don't necessarily begin at a specific quantize value, you can change the location of the sensitive area or "hook" within them that will be used for snapping them to the increments of the current quantize grid. This is called the *Snap-point*, and here in the Sample editor it is displayed as a vertical blue line, with an S in a box at the center of this line. In Figure 19.7, the left boundary of the event begins earlier than the point within it where the actual audio occurs. If this point within the event corresponds to a strong rhythmic division, you can drag the Snap-point there. As you drag the event within a track in the Project window or a lane in the Audio Part editor, the object snaps to the grid based on the location of this Snap-point, rather than the actual start position of the event that contains it. By default, Snap-points are placed at the event start point of audio events and regions.

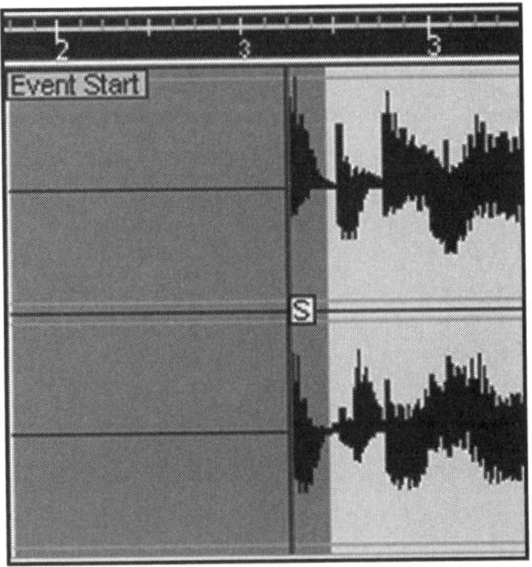

Figure 19.7
Example of an audio event's Snap-point.

HOW TO

Edit the Snap-point's position:

1. Open the event or region in the Sample editor.
2. Be sure the audio event elements are visible in the window. If not, select Elements > Audio Events from the editor's context menu.
3. Zoom to view the current Snap-point and the place where you want to reposition it.
4. For more precision, you can use the Scrub tool or the Audition icon (the "speaker" button in the Sample editor's toolbar) to find the exact place where the Snap-point should go.
5. Click and drag the S (in the box on the Snap-point line) and move it to the appropriate location.

Hitpoints

Hitpoints are also special markers that can be added to an audio event to, among other things, create audio slices or quantize templates known as "groove quantize maps." Use slices to extract individual sounds from a loop, replace certain slices, or move them around to create new variations. Even though their exact positions will automatically adjust to maintain their relative bar and beat locations, the pitch of slices is not affected by tempo changes in a project. Hitpoints use special markers to identify attack transients that are associated with beats in a rhythmic part. Later, you can use Hitpoint markers to slice up the event into separate beats, replacing a single audio event with a series of audio slices in an audio part.

Creating Hitpoints

Hitpoints are mainly used with drum loops, and the Attack Transient Detection tool helps you by analyzing the content for you. That said, to get the best results, you will often need to fine-tune the marker's location and make sure that your audio content is appropriate for Hitpoints. For example, audio with well-defined drum beats with high peaks and low valleys works better than sustained material. Also, drum beats that have a lot of effects, such as reverb or delay, are harder to slice accurately. If you want to use Hitpoints to create groove quantize maps, working with shorter one- to two-bar loops is ideal.

All the following operations assume you have already loaded the event into the Sample editor.

HOW TO

Create Hitpoints:

1. Select the Audio Tempo Definition tool to activate the appropriate fields (see Figure 19.8).

Figure 19.8
The Audio Tempo Definition tool.

2. Monitor the sample a few times to count how many bars and beats it has. This will help you later.
3. Enter the sample's time signature in the Signature field using the small arrows on each side of the field. Many contemporary drum loop samples in dance-oriented styles use a $\frac{4}{4}$ time signature.
4. Adjust the Bars and Beats fields to the corresponding values. For example, if your loop has eight beats, enter two bars (assuming the loop is in $\frac{4}{4}$ time). Cubase calculates the audio tempo for the sample automatically.
5. Enable the Hitpoint Mode button (see Figure 19.9).

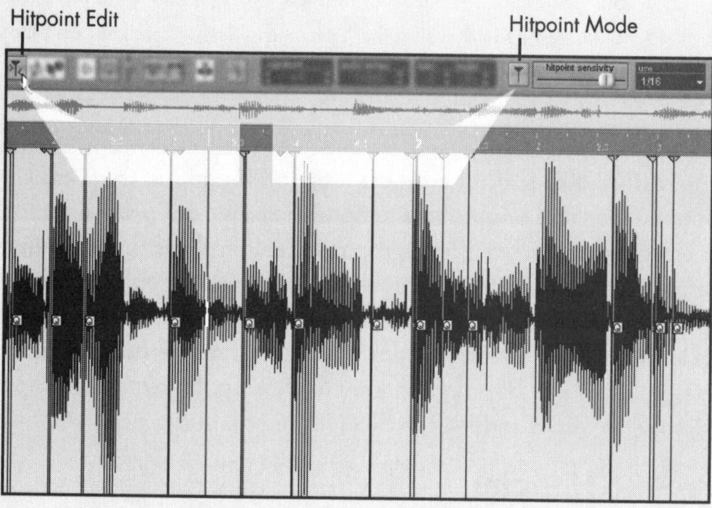

Figure 19.9
The Hitpoint-related tools.

6. Enable the Hitpoint Edit button. The Hitpoints Detection dialog box will appear, as shown in Figure 19.10.

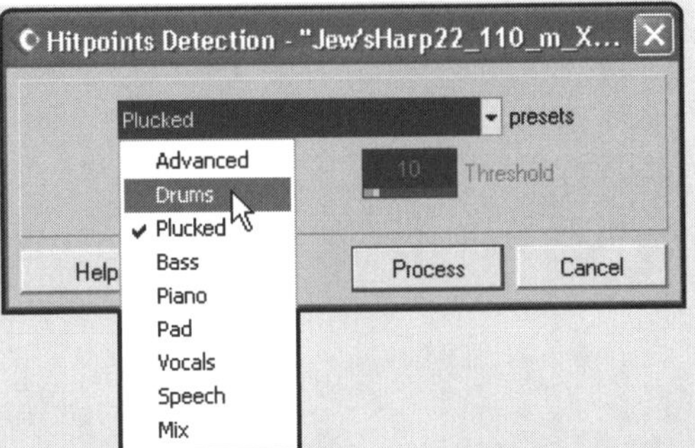

Figure 19.10
The Hitpoints Detection dialog box.

7. Select the appropriate preset for the current audio content from the drop-down menu. If you'd like to attempt to set the parameters on your own, select the Advanced preset and adjust the Sense and Threshold parameters accordingly. The Sense parameter affects how sensitive the detection is to attack transients, whereas the Threshold parameter determines how sensitive the detection is to low-level transients. Always start with the presets and tweak if necessary.
8. Click the Process menu to let Cubase detect the attacks and add Hitpoint markers to the sample. In some cases, the Hitpoints won't need any adjustments, but in most cases, you will need to fine-tune their positions before using them for other purposes.
9. Move the Hitpoint Sensitivity slider to the right to display a larger number of Hitpoints. The Use field lets you pick a predetermined beat subdivision if you already know that the loop is divided as such. For example, if there's a HiHat part in 16th-note subdivisions, select 1/16 in this field.

Zoom in closer in the Waveform Display to confirm that the transient detection has effectively placed the Hitpoint markers appropriately at each beat subdivision in the sample. The goal with Hitpoints is to separate each beat with a new sound into its own slice. Once Cubase knows how to interpret the beat rhythmically, you also can use the Hitpoint timing to create a quantize template known as a *groove quantize map*.

HOW TO

Edit Hitpoints:

1. Select the Hitpoint Edit tool in the toolbar (refer to Figure 19.9).

2a. Click between two Hitpoints to hear that audio slice (see Figure 19.11).

2b. Click on the Hitpoint's marker handle and drag it to move it.

2c. Hold the Alt (PC)/ (Mac) key and click where you want to add a Hitpoint. The cursor will become a pencil, and a new Hitpoint will appear at the location where you click.

2d. Hold the Alt (PC)/ (Mac) key and click on any existing Hitpoint marker handle to disable it. Alt-click (PC)/-click (Mac) on it again to re-enable the Hitpoint.

2e. Adjust the Q-point of Hitpoints, if available, by dragging the Q tab appropriately.

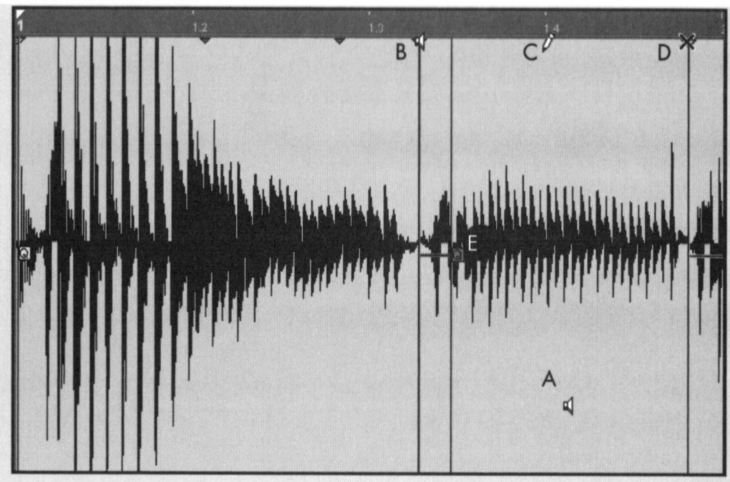

Figure 19.11
Editing Hitpoints in the Sample editor.

About Q-Points

Q-points are to Hitpoints what Snap-points are to events. They should be used whenever certain slices have slower attacks that often result in quantizing errors if the slices are later re-quantized. If Q-points aren't already displayed, in the File (PC)/Cubase (Mac) menu, select Preferences > Editing > Audio, and then check the Hitpoints Have Q-Points option.

Additional Hitpoint functions are located under the Audio > Hitpoints submenu. Here's a quick look at what you can do here:

- **Calculate Hitpoints** brings up the Hitpoints Detection dialog box, shown previously in Figure 19.10.
- **Create Audio Slices from Hitpoints** converts each portion of the audio between two Hitpoints into an audio slice. When placed on a track in the project, sliced audio events appear as audio events inside an audio part. As long as the timebase of the track stays set to Musical (rather than Linear), the precise locations of the slices within this audio part will be adjusted to maintain their current bar/beat locations if the project's tempo changes. The Musical mode also offers a similar option.
- **Create Groove Quantize from Hitpoints** uses the timing provided by the current Hitpoints to create a groove quantize map called "Groove." Groove quantize maps can be applied through the Quantize Setup dialog box (MIDI > Quantize Setup or Shift+Q). You could create a groove based on the drum loop's timing and apply the same feel to the MIDI bass line, for example.

- **Create Markers from Hitpoints** lets you convert existing Hitpoints into markers in a project.
- **Divide Audio Events at Hitpoints** creates an individual audio event for each slice, which will appear in the Pool. Use this option as a convenient way to create individual one-shot samples from events in the Pool. The Bounce Selection option found in the Audio menu would be the perfect companion to this Hitpoint option.
- **Reset Hitpoints** removes previously detected Hitpoints.

You can drag sliced events from the Pool into an audio track in the Project window. When you place a sliced event on an audio track, an audio part is automatically created, containing the corresponding slices inside this part. From this point on, when you double-click to edit the slices in the part, the Audio Part editor will open. This allows you to move the slices around in the part, apply a different quantize setting, or reorganize your loop to create variations of it.

After you've placed a sliced event on a track, you might notice that changing to a slower tempo than that of the original loop might create audible gaps between each slice. You can solve this problem by using the Close Gaps function, available in the Advanced submenu of the Audio menu. This function also can be used in other instances; however, this is probably the best use for it. As Figure 19.12 displays, the small gaps that were opened between each slice as the result of this slower tempo are removed after Cubase time-stretches each slice to compensate for the missing audio content. Note that extensive use of this function over very large gaps alters the sound quality of your audio content, so you should use it on small gaps only.

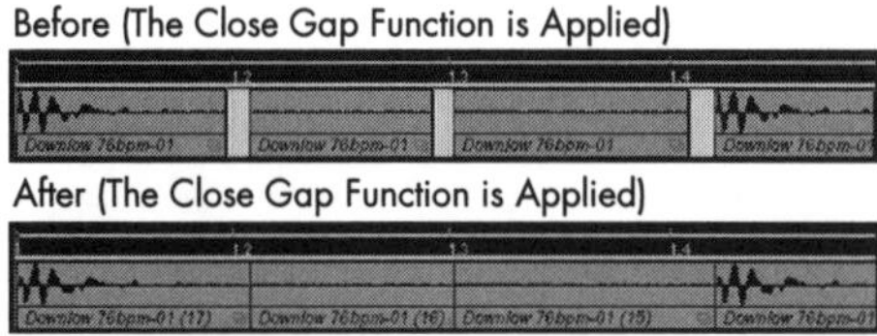

Figure 19.12
A before-and-after look at how the Close Gap function affects slices.

HOW TO

Close gaps between slices in a part:

1. Select the audio part(s) in the Project window.
2. From the Audio menu, select the Advanced > Close Gaps option or select the equivalent in the display area's context menu.

20 Audio Processing Options

In this chapter, we look at offline audio processing inside Cubase and at some of the advantages this provides over using plug-ins for real-time processing when you need more effects than your computer can handle. Offline and online processes offer identical parameters and results; however, offline processes are rendered to a temporary file. Cubase then reads this temporary file instead of calculating the effect each time. This technique lessens the load on the computer's resources. When processes are online, they are processed in real time, which lets you change their parameters or their importance in the mix and hear these changes immediately.

Freezing real-time processes as temporary files on a media drive is another alternative meant to reduce the processing load on tracks that have been set up properly but require Cubase to process them in real time along with all other tracks in a project. You can freeze VST instruments, instrument or audio tracks, or edits on certain events, as well as real-time time-stretching and transposing when using Musical mode on several loops. This is discussed further in Chapter 39, "Project Optimization."

Here's a summary of what you will learn in this chapter:

- How to enable Musical mode on audio events in the Pool or Sample editor
- How to transpose Musical mode audio events in a project
- How to lock the audio tempo to the project's tempo using Warp tabs
- How to quantize audio events using Warp tabs
- How to use Time Warp with audio events
- How to use audio processes found in the Audio menu
- How to use the recovery tools found in the Offline Process History panel
- How to use the recovery tools found in the Edit History panel

Audio Time Stretching

The audio warping features in Cubase let you match a time-based sample to a tempo-based grid. As a result, you can get a drum loop to match the tempo changes in a project, or correct timing errors in an audio recording, or tighten the kick of a drum by shifting it closer to the project's feel through quantizing or time warping without ever editing the original media file on the drive. All these processes are performed in real time and affect the timing of audio events as they are played back within tracks. They also make some significant demands on your CPU's processing power. All the operations described in the following sections assume that you have already loaded the audio event into the Sample editor.

Musical Mode

Enabling the Musical mode for audio events lets Cubase adjust an audio loop's tempo to the project's tempo in real time and without affecting the pitch, if necessary. Whenever the tempo in the project is different than the tempo displayed next to a Musical mode–enabled event, this audio media is automatically time-stretched to match the current project's tempo. Musical mode works best with "loopable" audio events, or at least events that start and end on a beat.

HOW TO

Enable Musical mode on audio events in the Sample editor:

1. Enable the Audio Tempo Definition tool, as displayed in Figure 20.1.

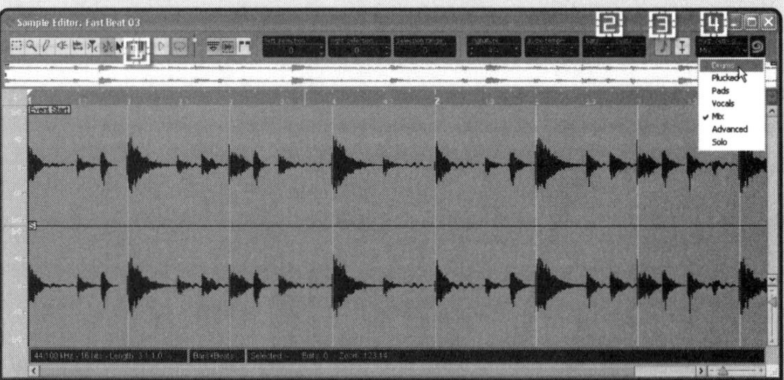

Figure 20.1
Musical mode options in the Sample editor.

2. Enter the appropriate number of bars and beats (if necessary) in the corresponding fields of the Sample editor's toolbar. Cubase automatically will display the audio tempo for this event.
3. Enable the Musical mode button.
4. Set the Warp Setting field to the most appropriate time-stretching algorithm for this audio content. The Warp icon lights up whenever the current event is time-stretched in real time. To customize the warp settings, choose the Advanced option to access the Advanced Warp Settings dialog box. Once the custom settings are made, click OK to accept.

Once the Musical mode is enabled for an audio event, you'll notice in the Pool (see Figure 20.2) that a check mark now appears next to it in the Musical Mode column, and the Audio Tempo column displays the original tempo you have assigned for this event. Cubase uses this tempo setting to calculate the amount of time-stretching it will apply for the event to match the current tempo at any given position in the project timeline. Drag the event from the Pool into the Project window or use one of the Insert into Project options found under the Pool menu, and the event will fit in the right number of bars and beats, no matter what the tempo may be.

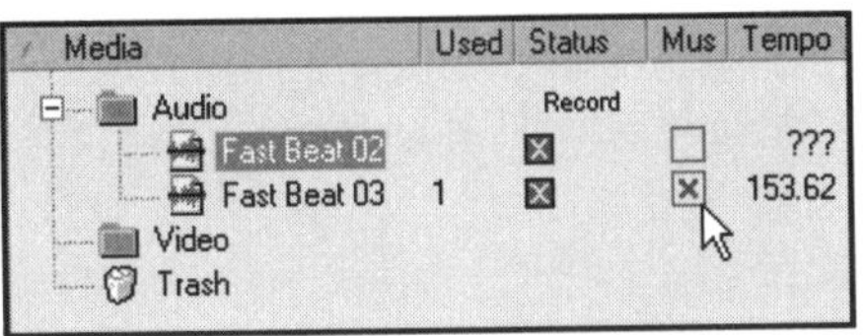

Figure 20.2
Musical mode settings displayed in the Pool.

You also can use the Musical Tempo Definition tool in the Sample editor's graphic display area to position the musical bars/beats gridline over the audio event if you are unsure about the number of beats it contains, but you are certain that the beat does not change tempo. If the first bar, or start of the looping area, is not at the beginning of the sample, move the bar 1 marker by clicking and dragging inside the graphic waveform display to the location corresponding to the first downbeat in your sample, as displayed in Figure 20.3.

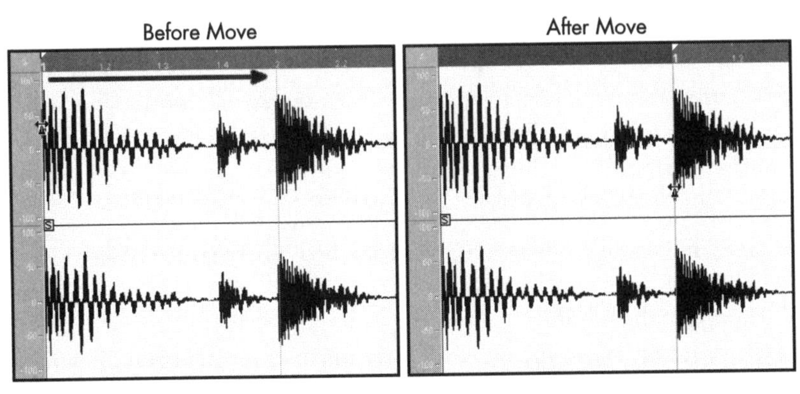

Figure 20.3
Adjusting the Ruler to match the beat of an event in Musical mode.

You can pitch-shift events when they are in Musical mode, to match the key signature and the tempo of your project. For example, create new harmonic variations by using a rhythm guitar loop and transposing different occurrences of the same event.

HOW TO

Transpose Musical mode events in a project:

1. Select the Musical mode-enabled audio event in the Project window that you want to transpose.
2. Make the Info Line visible in the Project window (if it is not already visible) and click in the Transpose or Fine Tune field. Each value in the Transpose field represents one semitone, and each value in the Fine Tune field represents one cent (100 cents = 1 semitone).
3. Use the mouse scroll wheel (or up and down arrows on your computer keyboard) to increase or decrease the value, or type in the desired value for this parameter.

Only the selected audio event is transposed by this setting in the Project window. Its tempo remains the same due to the tempo already defined for this event, whereas the Warp Setting preset field determines how time-stretching is applied in real time to this event during playback.

Importing ACID Loops

Whenever audio loops containing ACID properties or any other commercially available loops with embedded tempo and pitch information in them are imported into a project, Cubase automatically enables the Musical mode for these audio clips in the Pool and sets the tempo according to these properties. As a result, the events within these loops always follow the project's tempo when placed on an audio track.

Warp Audio

Use Warp Audio to change the timing of a recorded audio event, such as a bass that occasionally drifts away from the drummer's timing or a live recording where the song begins at 109BPM, then goes up slightly to 114BPM, and ends at 112BPM. Although these instances occur quite frequently and may be fine in many situations, the Warp Audio functions are intended for times when you need to have a steady BPM or a tight bass/kick combo. Also, when the tempo is not constant within an audio event, using the Audio Tempo Definition tool won't identify the tempo changes appropriately.

Once Warp tabs are added along the sample to identify where the first beat of each bar occurs—this is not a necessity, but using the first beat of each bar is a good place to start—the Audio Warp feature uses this local tempo map to extrapolate the necessary time-stretching required so that the sample's tempo between two Warp tabs always matches the project's tempo. When used with MIDI, this function is called Warp Grid (Musical Events Follow), which is discussed in Chapter 29, "Tempo Track."

You also can fix rhythmic imperfections or just change the rhythmic content of a drum loop, for example, by adding Warp tabs to a Musical mode-enabled event. Always proceed by defining the audio tempo, enabling the Musical mode, and finally applying the Time Warp tool, as demonstrated here.

HOW TO

Lock an audio event's tempo to the project's tempo using Warp tabs:

1. Be sure the project's tempo is roughly set to match the audio event being edited. For example, if the event's tempo fluctuates between 109 and 114BPM, the project's tempo should be within this range.

> **Time-Stretching Limitations**
>
> Although time-stretching can help match the varying tempo of a freely recorded audio event to a somewhat static tempo of a project, applying extreme time-stretching percentages will degrade the audio content's quality. It is advisable to find out what the original tempo of the event is using either the Beat Calculator or the Musical mode, as described in this chapter, to set the project's tempo to a BPM value in the same vicinity. For example, setting the project's tempo to 120BPM while the original sample plays between 90 and 95BPM does not necessarily represent a successful use of audio warping. The intention of this feature is to fine-tune and tighten rhythmic inaccuracies, not to apply large amounts of time-stretching over the entire event.

2. If the event does not begin on the first downbeat, before going any further you should edit the event in the Project window or move the Event Start handle in the Sample editor so that it does. (Enable the Show Audio Event button in the Sample editor's toolbar if these handles are not already visible.) Matching the start of the event with a recognizable downbeat will make it easier to locate more accurately the first beats of each subsequent measure.
3. Select the Time Warp tool.
4. Locate a moment in the audio event where the beat doesn't fall where it should according to the tempo grid, and click in the graphic display to add a Warp tab before this event (see the top lane in Figure 20.4). Where to click depends on the content; if you are trying to tighten the bass line here and there, monitor the audio event using the Play tool. When you need to straighten out a longer live recording, placing a Warp tab every two, four, or eight bars might be sufficient.

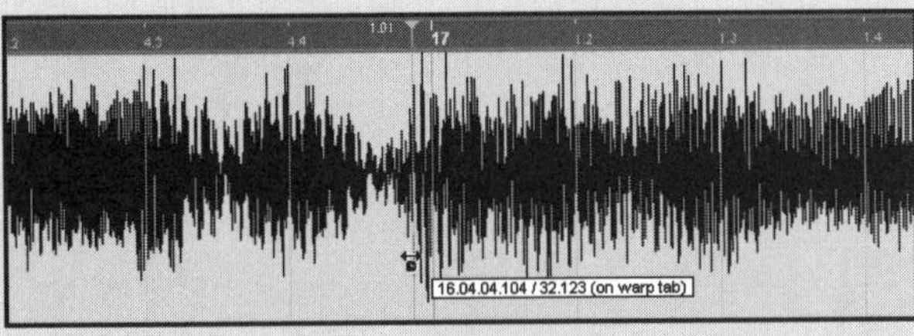

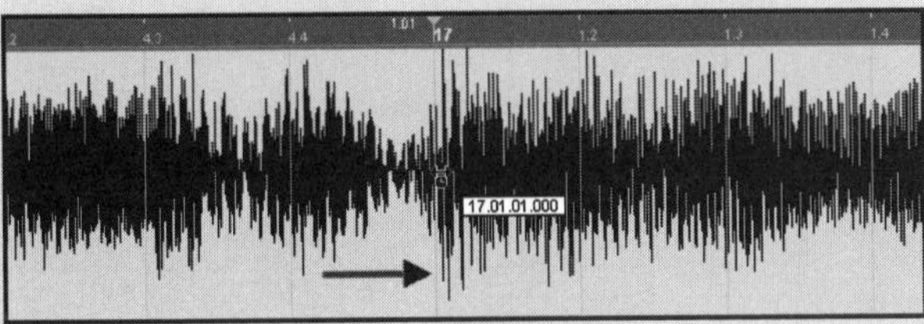

Figure 20.4
Using Warp tabs to adjust timing of audio events.

Changing the Ruler's Display Format

If the Ruler does not display bars and beats, now is a good time to change this using the Ruler's display settings drop-down menu, found at the right of the Ruler in the Sample editor.

5. Click on the Warp tab's line to grab it, and drag the line toward the desired gridline along the timeline (measure 17, bar 1 in the bottom lane of Figure 20.4). Note that you can complete steps 4 and 5 in a single step by clicking to insert the marker, then dragging to move it to the appropriate location along the tempo gridline.
6. Repeat this process inside the event if necessary. Each marker appears with an interpolation value in yellow, next to the Warp tab's handle, and the audio content is automatically stretched to match the content between Warp tabs to the current grid. The Warp icon to the right in the toolbar will appear lit, indicating that Cubase will time-stretch this event in real time.

Creating Warp Tabs from Hitpoints

Using a combination of Hitpoints and Warp tabs, you can requantize an audio event in Musical mode to match up with a new Quantize Setup grid nondestructively. Creating Warp tabs from Hitpoints provides an alternative if you don't want to slice the event. With this method, however, the quantizing is processed in real time using the Warp tabs.

HOW TO

Quantize audio events using Warp tabs:

1. Select the Audio Tempo Definition tool.
2. Enter the appropriate information in the Musical Control fields (signature, audio tempo, bars, and beats).
3. Activate the Musical mode button.
4. Enable the Hitpoints tool.
5. In the Audio menu, select Hitpoints > Calculate Hitpoints.
6. Adjust the Hitpoints calculated by Cubase, to identify significant musical elements in the current loop. If Q-points are present, quantizing will be applied to their location and not the Hitpoints when both don't occur at the same moment.
7. In the Audio menu or the Pool's context menu, select the Realtime Processing > Create Warp Tabs from Hitpoints option.
8. Close the Sample editor.
9. Select the event (or occurrences of the event) in the Project window. Each occurrence of the event in a project can be quantized independently in real time.
10. Open the Quantize Setup dialog box from the Project window's toolbar, or pick an existing preset from the drop-down menu.
11. From the Audio menu, select the Realtime Processing > Quantize Audio option to apply the current quantize settings to the selected audio event. You also can find the same option in the Project window's context menu.

When you open the quantized audio event in the Sample editor, you will notice how Cubase shifted the Warp tabs according to the Quantize setting you have applied, as shown in Figure 20.5.

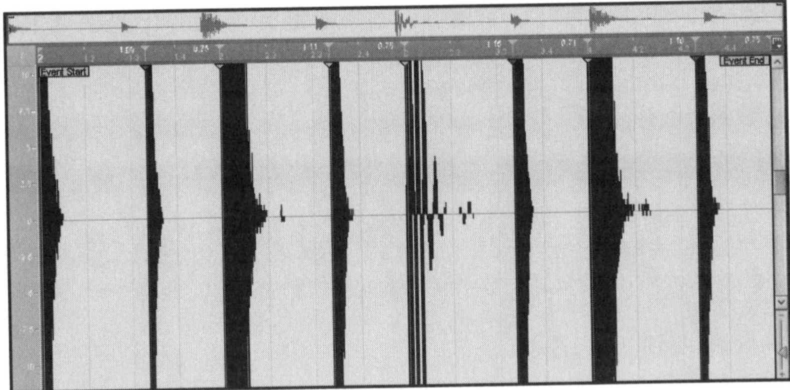

Figure 20.5
Using Hitpoints converted into Warp tabs to quantize audio.

Time Warp

While the previously described techniques provide a way to make linear time-based audio events more flexible when used within a musical tempo-based grid, Time Warp makes the tempo grid itself more flexible, allowing you to add tempo changes so that it matches up with the unprocessed audio. When Time Warp tabs are added, tempo curve points (tempo changes) are added to the tempo track to make this match between the audio event and the tempo work.

Earlier we discussed the example of a long live recording in which the tempo changed along the way. Quite often this tempo variation enhances the musical dynamic, so you might want to keep this variation as part of the emotional content of the project. When this is the case, warping samples of an audio event to even out the tempo might not be the best choice. Using Time Warp instead will let you keep these variations, while still enjoying the benefit of an accurate bar/beat grid for editing, Transport functions, and Marker locations.

HOW TO

Use Time Warp with audio events:

1. As with the Warp tabs, if the event does not begin on the first downbeat, edit the event in the Project window or move the Event Start handle so that it does before going any further. (Enable the Show Audio Event button if these handles are not visible.) Matching the start of the event with a recognizable downbeat makes it easier to locate more accurately the first beats of each subsequent measure.
2. Click along the gridline where the event should occur and drag the grid over the location in the audio event where this event actually occurs (see Figure 20.6).

3. **Repeat this along the file wherever the audio event and its tempo grid are out of alignment. Each handle added creates a new tempo curve point in the tempo track.**

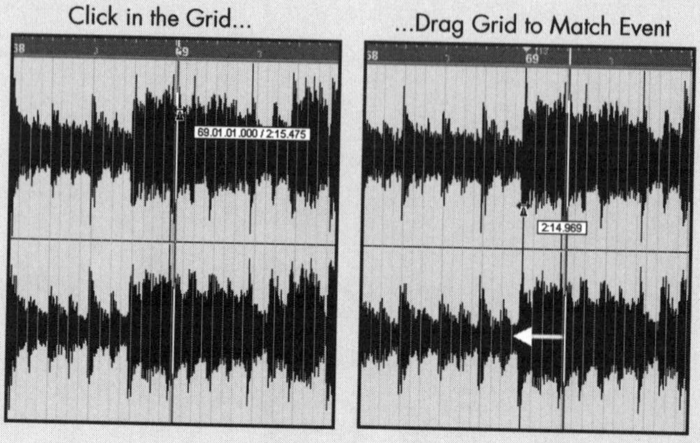

Figure 20.6
Add Time Warp tabs in an audio event.

Click in the Grid...

...Drag Grid to Match Event

Editing Audio and Time Warp Tabs

Here are a few additional operations to help you deal with unwanted Audio Warp or Time Warp tabs.

- **To move the location of a tab:** Click on the tab and drag it to the desired location. This operation has no effect on the time-stretching properties or grid location.
- **To delete a tab:** Hold down the Shift key and click on the tab.

Audio Processing Options

Audio processing, as with audio fades, can be applied to audio in two different ways: You can apply effects in real time that affect the entire track, also known as *online processing*, or you can apply processing that alters the content of the audio events played back by Cubase, also known as *offline processing*. In the former case, to automate the effects, you can change their parameters. In the latter case, effects are calculated beforehand. The end result of the audio event may be the same in terms of sonic qualities, but an *offline* effect is not using up the computer's CPU time each time the file plays. Processing audio offline offers a less CPU-intensive method of processing audio because the CPU doesn't have to process the audio every time you press Play. When using an *online* effect on a track, the audio passing through an insert, send, or main bus effect is processed by your computer in real time. The effect itself is not saved to an audio file, although the effect's parameters are saved as part of your project. Every time you play the project, the computer has to process all the active effects. This is why you can change parameters easily. On the other hand, it can add a serious load on your computer that can slow it down to a grind when your real-time processing needs exceed the computer's capabilities.

Processing files offline, replacing the affected portion of an audio event with the processed version, and saving this alteration as part of the project file create the effects without changing the original audio file's content and do not require any processing time during playback because the files are simply read from the media drive. The disadvantage is that you cannot automate this kind of processing by using automation in real time. There are many instances, however, in which automation is not needed. When you want to match the amplitude of an audio clip's amplitude by using a normalize process or add an effect to a portion of an audio clip, event, region, or slice, processing this portion and writing the effect to a file might be more effective than using real-time effects, not to mention it would reduce the load imposed on your computer. Pitch-shifting and time-stretching operations are notoriously heavy consumers of computer resources, so using them in offline processes is highly recommended, especially on slower computers or very process-intensive large projects.

You can apply real-time effects and processes through the insert effects and FX channels (a special type of audio track intended as a send destination, where you have enabled one or more insert effects). You can apply processes and plug-in effects through the Plug-Ins or Process submenus found in the Audio menu or through the same submenus in the Project window's context menu.

Using Audio Processes

In audio terminology, any effect applied to an audio signal is referred to as *audio processing*. However, in Cubase, the commands found in the Audio > Process submenu relate to more basic audio transformations, rather than reverb, chorus, and delay effects. Such processes can be found under the Audio > Plug-ins submenu, where there are many comparable offline processing options using the VST plug-in effects installed on your system. Although we can't go into all these options (which are immensely useful for applying layers of special effects on specific audio selections within a track, for example), bear in mind that many of the same basic dialog-box options apply.You can apply processing to an entire audio event or region in the Project window, or just to a portion selected within it using the Range Selection tool. You can also apply processing on individual audio events seen within the Audio Part editor. Selecting an event or a region in the Pool applies the processing to the entire selected object. Finally, you can apply a process specifically to a selected portion of an event or a region in the Sample editor. In all these situations, offline processing can be applied either via the Audio > Process submenu or via the Process submenu of that window's context menu.

Because some objects may be shared (used more than one time in the project's timeline), when applying a process to one of them, Cubase asks whether you want to create a new version or change all the instances of this object throughout the project's timeline. If you opt to create a new version, the selected object is the only one affected by this process, and the processed version of the object replaces that instance of the original content in the Project window (but not on your media drive; the results of online processing are always stored in your project's Edits subfolder). If you want all the shared instances of this object (event or region) to change, then you can select the Continue button (see Figure 20.7). This replaces the currently selected object rather than creating a new version, which causes all shared occurrences to change as well in the project.

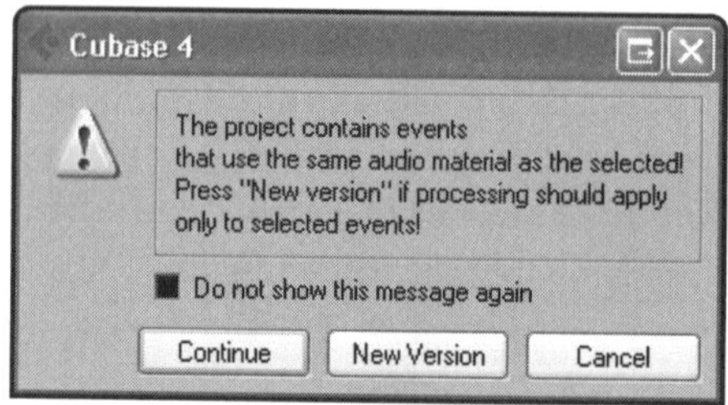

Figure 20.7
Cubase can replace the selected object or create a new one.

Pre- and Post-CrossFade Options

In some processes, you will find a Pre-CrossFade or Post-CrossFade option when the More button is enabled in the process's dialog box. These options enable you to apply the process gradually over time (pre-crossfade) and end the process also gradually over time (post-crossfade). As displayed in Figure 20.8, starting at the beginning of the selection, this process would take 301 milliseconds before being completely implemented, and it would start reverting from processed signal to non-processed signal over the last 870 milliseconds of the selection. So, if this were applied to the Gain process, for example, it would take 870 ms to reach the Gain setting in the Process window and would go back to the original gain over the last 310 ms of the selection being processed.

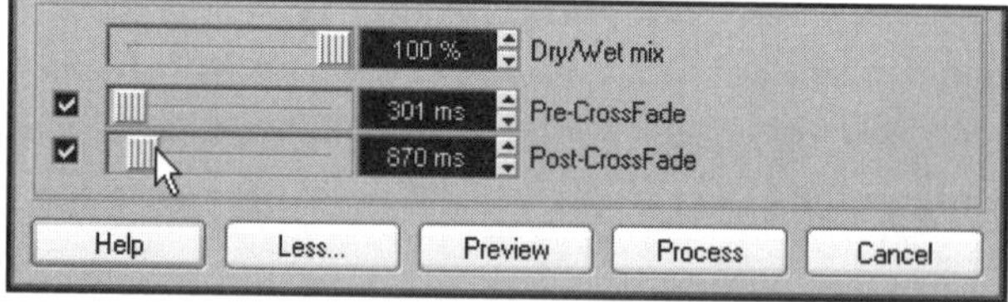

Figure 20.8
The Pre- and Post-CrossFade options.

Check the options you want to apply after setting the parameters to the desired value. The Dry/Wet mix value determines the proportion of unprocessed sound (dry) versus processed sound (wet) in the resultant audio. To hear only the processed effect, leave this mix value at 100%, but for a more subtle effect, adjust it as necessary. If you don't want to display this section of the dialog box (although any options enabled within it will still be in effect), click the Less button.

Gain

The Gain process increases or decreases the audio level within the currently selected object or objects. Moving the slider to the right adds gain, whereas moving the slider to the left reduces it.

You also can enter the desired amount of change in the Gain field by typing in the appropriate value. When you click the Preview button, Cubase indicates whether this gain change causes the object to clip (digital distortion caused by the amount of gain change exceeding the maximum permitted level), as displayed in Figure 20.9 If this occurs, reduce the gain until Cubase displays "No Clip Detected."

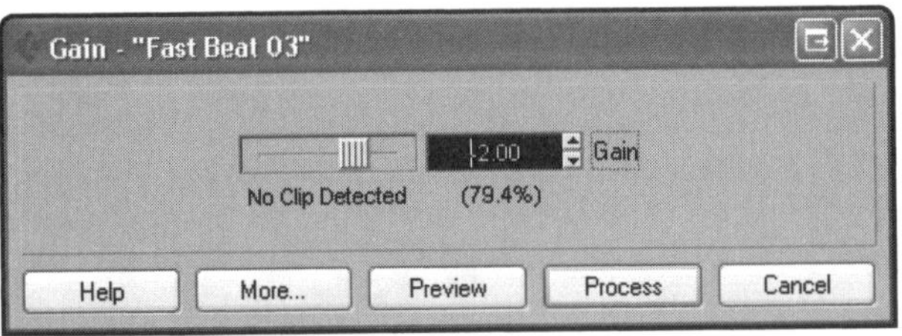

Figure 20.9
The Gain dialog box.

Merge Clipboard

This process merges audio content that has been previously copied to the clipboard into the currently selected object. Besides the Pre- and Post-CrossFade options that are revealed if you click the More button in this dialog box, the Merge Clipboard process (see Figure 20.10) allows you to specify a mix ratio between the audio selected for processing and the audio on the clipboard through a percentage slider. On the left side, you can see the proportion of the original (selected) object, and on the right side, you can see the proportion of the audio previously copied in the clipboard.

Figure 20.10
The Merge Clipboard dialog box.

Noise Gate

The Noise Gate process (see Figure 20.11) silences any portions of an audio signal that are below the specified threshold level. Imagine a gate that opens when a signal is strong enough (above threshold) and closes when it isn't (below threshold). You can use this to silence portions of an audio signal during relatively silent passages. For example, you can use a noise gate to remove a guitar amplifier's humming noise from your recording during passages where the guitar player is not actually playing any notes. A noise gate does not remove this noise when the guitarist is playing because the signal will most likely be loud enough to pass the threshold, but the noise at that point should be less noticeable because it is masked by the guitar sound. If the noise level is too loud even when the guitarist is playing, you should consider using a noise reduction plug-in or rerecording this part.

The attack time controls how long it takes for the gate to open, letting the sound through, and the release time controls how long it takes to close after the signal goes below the threshold level. The minimum opening time defines the minimum amount of time the signal has to be over the threshold before the gate can close again and can be useful if you discover after using this dialog box's Preview button that many brief transients in the selected audio are causing the gate to "flutter" open and closed.

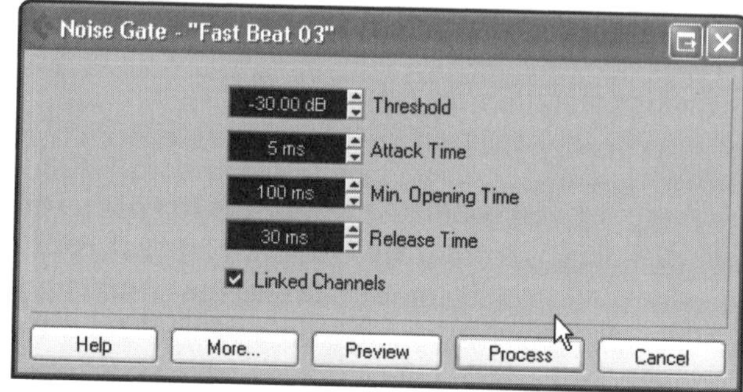

Figure 20.11
The Noise Gate dialog box.

Normalize

Normalizing an audio signal affects its overall amplitude level by adjusting its highest peak to the value set in the Normalize process dialog box (see Figure 20.12). It is similar to the Gain process in the sense that it acts on the level of the signal, but instead of calculating the level generally, it brings these levels up in proportion to the highest peak found in the signal, making sure that there is no clipping in the signal as a result of the level change. You can set the level value you want to assign to the highest peak level in this object by adjusting the slider or entering a value in the Maximum field.

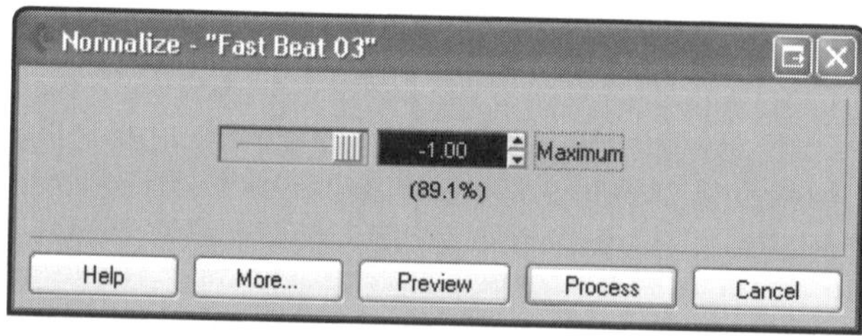

Figure 20.12
The Normalize dialog box.

Phase Reverse

Reversing phase, or polarity, does not change the shape of a sound file, but it changes the direction this shape takes. For example, the slopes going up will now go down and vice versa. In practice, this function is only rarely required, since each channel in Cubase has an "Input Phase" button (in the Mixer or VST Audio Channel Settings window) that is generally a more efficient way to accomplish such a fix. If you can barely hear the signal, then you might have phase cancellation occurring. In Cubase, you can reverse the polarity of both channels in a stereo file, or only one or the other. You should preview the result before applying this process (see Figure 20.13). When you mix different sound files that contain the same audio content captured by microphones at different distances, phase cancellation can occur. The most common examples are probably snares being captured from above and below or guitar amps from the front and back. This can sometimes produce a hollow sound as different frequencies in its harmonic spectrum are reinforced or cancelled out, known as *comb filtering*. Inverting the waveform on one of the files can prevent this phase cancellation from occurring. In other words, if the phase of the current audio file does not sound correct, changing its polarity via this Phase Reverse process might fix the problem. A good way to detect this problem is to occasionally monitor the audio in mono.

Figure 20.13
The Phase Reverse dialog box.

Pitch Shift

The Pitch Shift process can either change the pitch of the selection by a fixed amount throughout its duration or vary the amount of pitch change over time by using an envelope that determines how and when the pitch is shifted upward or downward.

At the top of the Transpose tab in this dialog box (see Figure 20.14), you will find a keyboard layout that can help you set the relationship between the pitch of the original audio content and the pitch-shifted version. In this example, the fundamental pitch or "root note" of the original content is D3, so this note is selected as the pitch-shift base area and appears red on the keyboard display. Clicking another note changes the pitch-shift settings automatically to match the value needed to get this pitch. In this case, B2 is pressed and displayed in blue on the keyboard. If you want to create a chord effect, creating several pitch shifts simultaneously, you can enable the Multi Shift check box, which adds other notes to the process. Remember that if you also want the root note to be included in the multi-shifted signal, it must also be selected (highlighted in blue). You can use the Listen Key or Listen Chord button to hear the notes you selected.

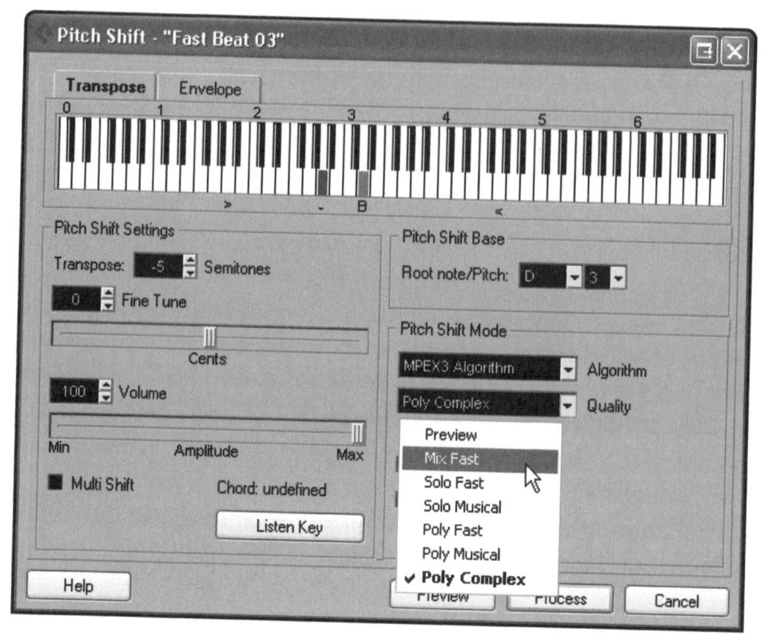

Figure 20.14
The Pitch Shift process's Transpose tab.

> **Using Real-Time Pitch Shifting**
> You also can pitch-shift events that are in Musical mode. If this imposes too much of a load on your CPU, you can freeze the real-time processing. Select the transposed event, then in the Audio menu, select Realtime Processing > Freeze Timestretch and Transpose.

The Pitch Shift Mode area sets accuracy values. Select the most appropriate quality for the content being pitch-shifted. If you are shifting vocal content, you should check the Formant Mode option, which helps to preserve the resonant qualities associated with the original, unshifted voice.

Keeping the Time Correction option enabled changes the pitch without altering the duration of the shifted content. If this option is disabled, events shifted upward play faster, and events shifted downward play slower.

Clicking the Envelope tab at the top of the dialog box reveals the envelope settings for this process (see Figure 20.15). Using an envelope rather than a keyboard changes how the affected audio selection is shifted over time. In this example, the Pitch Shift Settings Range field is set to two semitones, which means that at the upper limit of the display area, events are shifted upward by this amount, and at the bottom, they are shifted downward. The Transpose and Fine Tune fields represent the currently selected handle's value, in semitones and cents (1/100ths of a semitone). In this figure, the handle directly under the cursor is transposed upward by 13 cents. So, using these settings, the pitch shift on the first portion of the audio gradually rises to 13 cents of upward pitch shift during the first part of the selection and gradually ramps down until dipping to a downward pitch shift on a particular note, as can be seen in the grayed-out waveform beneath the pitch-shift envelope. The Pitch Shift Mode options are identical to those in the Transpose tab.

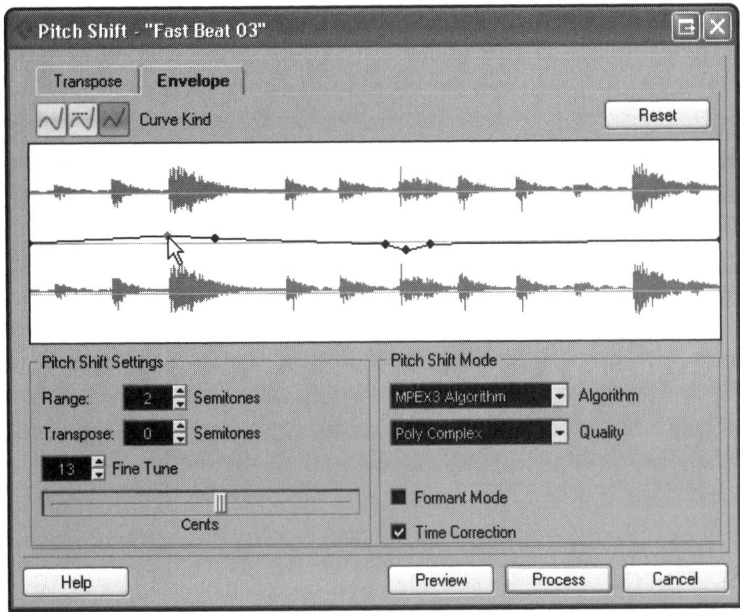

Figure 20.15
The Pitch Shift process's Envelope tab.

HOW TO

Apply a Pitch Shift to a selected object:

1. Select the desired object.
2. Select the Pitch Shift process from the Process option in the Audio menu.
3. Make the appropriate adjustments in the dialog box. To preview the result, click the Preview button.
4. When you are satisfied with the settings, click the Process button.

DC Offset, Reverse, and Silence

These three processes offer very different results; however, they do not offer any settings. The DC Offset process removes any audio signal offset that might be present in your audio signal. In Cubase 4, it might be a good idea to look at the statistics of a file (Audio > Statistics). If you need to remove a DC offset, run the process on the file. The Reverse process simply reverses the data horizontally, making it sound as if it is playing backward. The Silence process brings all the samples in a selection to a zero value, creating an absolute digital silence.

Stereo Flip

The Stereo Flip process (see Figure 20.16) can only be applied on stereo audio objects because it manipulates the stereo channels of the selected audio clip or event (including regions or other selections within an audio event). You have four modes available in this process, which appear in the Mode field. For example, you can merge both channels to create a mono file or subtract the left channel from the right channel to get a karaoke-like effect (since any signals, like a typical lead vocal, that are equally present in both channels will be cancelled out). Note that if you want to apply the basic mode here, Flip Left-Right, to an entire *track* rather than just a specific audio event or other selection, this is more efficiently accomplished by simply enabling the Dual Combined Panner view and dragging the left and right channel panners to their opposite sides.

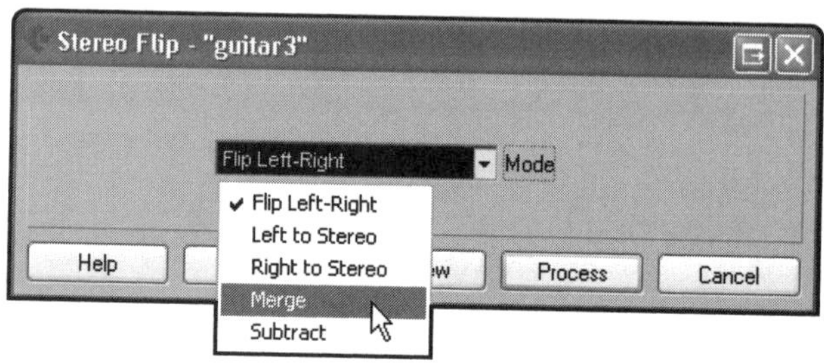

Figure 20.16
The Stereo Flip dialog box.

The Offline Process History

When you apply a process or plug-in to an audio object or a portion of an object through offline processing, an entry is made in this event's Offline Process History. Remember that offline processes mean that the effect is not calculated during playback (online), but on a "one-shot" basis that actually creates new audio data to contain the result (offline). Each process is displayed on its own row in the Offline Process History dialog box. You can decide to modify the settings of any process that appears here, even if there are subsequent offline processes in this list.

For example, you can select a previously rendered Normalize process and change the peak value. If a process has no parameters to modify (for example, the Reverse process), clicking the Modify button simply displays a warning telling you this process cannot be modified. You also can replace one previous offline process with another. For instance, you could select the Reverse process and select another process in the drop-down menu below the Replace By button (see Figure 20.17). The new process's dialog box will appear. Once replaced, the old process is removed from the list, and the new process takes its place. Before letting you replace a process, Cubase asks you whether this is what you really want to do. Finally, you can remove a process from the list entirely by selecting it and clicking the Remove button, no matter where it is in this list, as long as you haven't applied resampling or time-stretching processes, which affect the overall number of samples (and ultimately this event's position in the project). For example, in a list of four offline processes, you can select the third one and change it without affecting the first or second one. The fourth is updated accordingly. With Cubase 4, you also can use the Offline Process History dialog box with any plug-in effect applied through the Audio > Plug-ins submenu.

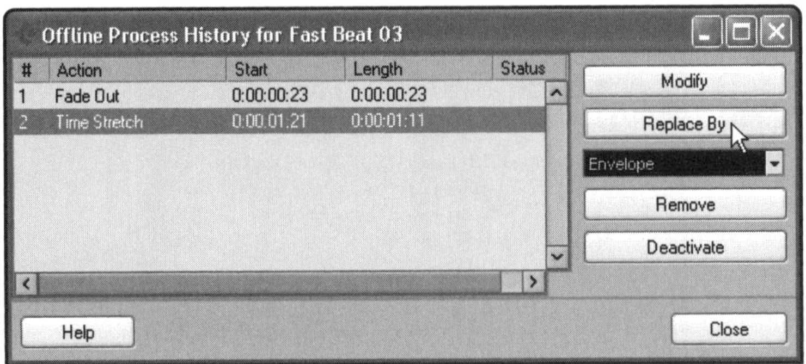

Figure 20.17
The Offline Process History dialog box.

HOW TO

Modify, replace, or remove an action from the Offline Process History:

1. Select the event containing offline processes you want to modify.
2. From the Audio menu, select the Offline Process History option.
3. Select the process you want to modify (step 4a), replace (step 4b), or remove (step 4c).

4a. Click the Modify button and edit the parameters inside the process's dialog box, and then click the Process button to update the Offline Process History dialog box.

4b. Select the new process you want to use instead of the currently selected one in the drop-down menu below the Replace By button, click the Replace By button, make the necessary adjustments in the process's dialog box, and click Process to update the Offline Process History dialog box.

4c. Click the Remove button to remove this process from the list.

5. When you have completed modifying, replacing, or removing the processes, click the Close button.

Because the history of each offline process is saved with the object affected, you still have access to this history after you close Cubase and reload the project into memory. This is not the case for the Edit History panel, described in the next section.

The Edit History

When you apply a transformation, such as deleting an object, moving, and so on, each action is saved in a list, which enables you to undo an unlimited number of actions. You can do this by using the Undo function in the Edit menu if you only have a few steps to undo; however, if you want to look at all the steps and undo a whole bunch in one go, you can use the Edit History dialog box, which is opened via the Edit > History command (see Figure 20.18).

This dialog box displays actions on the left and the target object for each action on the right. The latest actions appear at the top of the list, and the earliest ones at the bottom. The list is separated

Figure 20.18
The Edit History dialog box.

by a horizontal blue line. Clicking on this line and dragging it down creates a selection. All the actions that are included in this selection will be undone. This means that you can undo from the last edit to the first one, unlike in the Offline Process History panel, in which you can edit any single action within the list.

You should know that when you save and close your project, the Edit History panel is reset and is not available until you start editing again. However, only saving your current project without closing it doesn't clear out the contents of the Edit History.

21 Editing MIDI Events

The Project window's In-Place editor and the Key editor window offer two similar MIDI editing environments. Although the following discusses the editing functions of the In-Place editor, unless otherwise specified, these functions also apply to the Key editor. The main difference is how you get to the editors. With the In-Place editor, click on the Edit In-Place button found in the Track List area of the Project window, as shown in Figure 21.1; to open the Key editor, double-click on an existing MIDI part (unless a drum map has been assigned to that track, or some other has been selected as the default MIDI editor in Preferences).

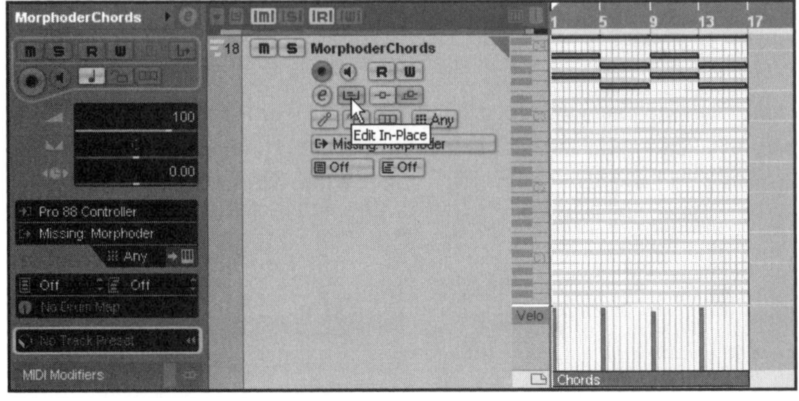

Figure 21.1
The In-Place editor.

Here's a summary of what you will learn in this chapter:

- How to select and edit MIDI events in the In-Place editor
- How to mute/unmute, merge, and resize one or more notes or controller events

- How to create notes using the Draw tool or insert events using the Line tool
- How to create a ramp of MIDI events using the Sine, Triangle, or Square tool
- How to edit events using the Info Line
- How to view and edit MIDI Control Change messages using the MIDI Controller Lane in the In-Place editor

In-Place Editor

Most of the In-Place editor tools are available in the Project window's toolbar, but many of the functions are applied through the context menu of the editor when right-clicking (PC)/Control-clicking (Mac) over the Event Display area. In the upper portion of this context menu are shortcuts to the tools available in the Project window's toolbar, and in the lower portion are shortcuts to various operations available in Cubase's menus. Furthermore, an additional local toolbar is displayed when the In-Place Toolbar icon is pressed, a small gray triangle in the upper right-hand corner of this track's Track List entry, as displayed in Figure 21.2. This local toolbar disappears automatically once you click anywhere in the In-Place editor area on this track, but if you hold down the Alt (PC)/Option (Mac) key as you click the In-Place Toolbar icon, it will stay in place as a floating toolbar.

Figure 21.2
The In-Place editor toolbar.

Editing MIDI events is not unlike editing text in a word processor. For example, if you want to copy, cut, or move a group of events, you need to select these events first, and then apply the desired operation to these selected events. That's when you use the Object Selection (arrow) tool.

HOW TO

Select MIDI/audio events:

- Single event: Just point to and click on it.
- Group of events: Click and drag a selection box around these events, as demonstrated in Figure 21.3.
- Multiple nonconsecutive events: Hold down the Shift key while selecting the additional events.
- All the notes on the same pitch in a part: Hold down the Ctrl (PC)/ (Mac) key and click on the corresponding pitch in the Keyboard Display area to the left of the Event Display area.

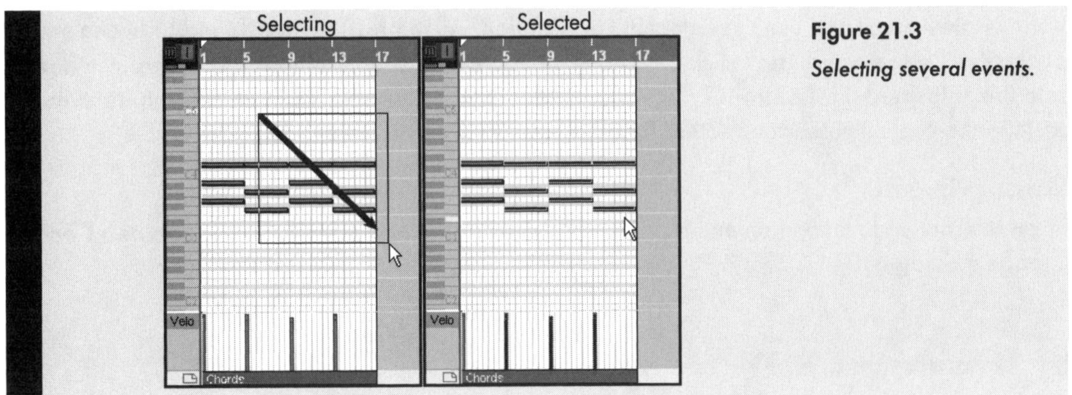

Figure 21.3

Selecting several events.

After events are selected, apply the desired functions. For example, you might want to move a group of notes to somewhere else in the part. If you want to keep the beginning of this group of notes aligned with a quantize grid, enable the Snap to Grid button and set the quantize grid to the appropriate value. To move one event, you simply need to click and drag it to its new location. To move several events, select them as mentioned previously, and then click and drag one of the selected events to the new destination. You can move both notes and Control Change values this way, *provided that the appropriate Controller Lane is visible and you hold down the Alt (PC)/ Option (Mac) key as you select and drag events in the Controller Lane*. If you move the velocity value of a note, you will also move the note. To lock pitches in place as you move notes in time or to change the pitch without changing the timing, hold the Ctrl (PC)/ (Mac) key down as you drag the notes. If you start moving the notes horizontally along the time axis, the pitch will be locked, and if you start moving the notes vertically along the pitch axis, their original time positions will be locked. You also can move selected notes by using the up and down keys on your keyboard or by using the Transpose Notes button on the toolbar.

Again, as with text in a word processor application, when you want to paste events to a new location, you need to select them, cut or copy to place these events into the clipboard, decide where you want to put them by placing your insertion point (in Cubase, this is the project cursor), and then apply the Paste command. As with the Project window, it is possible to hold the Alt (PC)/ Option (Mac) key down as you drag selected events to copy rather than move them. You will see a small plus sign (+) appear next to your arrow as you move the mouse. If you hold down the same key (Alt or Option) as you drag parts or events horizontally by their bottom-right corner in the Project window, the cursor displays a pencil, and they will be copied instead of moved to the new time location.

Cubase offers additional functions that make editing MIDI easier. For example, you can use the Select options in the editor's context menu or in the Edit > Select submenu to define what you want to select. Using this method, position the left and right locators across two bars, click in the

Note Display area, and use the Select in Loop option. All the MIDI events found between the locators will be selected; now click on a controller event and repeat these steps. This includes both the notes and the Control Change messages within this range. You can copy these events, position the project cursor at another location, and then paste the events.

Muting Events

As an alternative to muting an entire track, you can also mute selected events (notes and Control Change messages).

HOW TO

Mute/unmute one or several events:

- Select the events to mute with the Selection tool and press the Shift+M key command or select the Mute option from the Edit menu. Press Shift+U to unmute selected events.
- Or, select the Mute tool and click the desired notes. Click once more on muted notes to unmute them.
- Or, select the Mute tool and drag a selection box around the events you want to mute. All events within the box's range will be muted. Select in the same way muted notes to unmute them.

Splitting and Resizing Note Events

Splitting and resizing note events is handy when you need to modify the length of MIDI notes within a part or need to bring the end of a MIDI note inside the right boundary of a part. These operations also can be applied to a single note, a group of selected notes, or a range of notes in a MIDI editor.

HOW TO

Resize a note or a group of notes:

1. Select the note(s) using the Object Selection tool.
2. Bring the arrow over the start or end of the notes you want to resize. The arrow will turn into a double-headed arrow (see Figure 21.4).

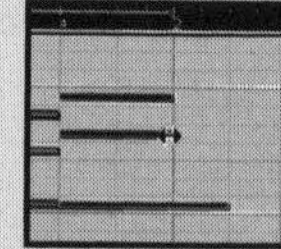

Figure 21.4
A double-sided arrow indicates that the cursor is over the start or end of this note event.

3. Click and drag the edge to the desired length. The precise increments as you resize will be determined by the quantize grid setting if it is enabled. Hold the Ctrl (PC)/ (Mac) key while resizing to override this grid setting temporarily.

Using the Nudge Palette and Transpose Palette

When resizing a good number of events, use the Nudge Palette tools to resize selected events instead. Select the events that need resizing, and use the appropriate Nudge tool to resize. By default the Nudge palette is not visible. To display it in the Project window's toolbar, right-click (PC)/Control-click (Mac) in the toolbar and check its option. The Nudge palette lets you precisely adjust durations and start times of events based on the Snap settings. In the top-left corner of Figure 21.5, the Nudge tools and the In-Place editor's Transpose palette are shown.

The Transpose palette lets you shift the pitch of events by one half-step (semitone) or an octave (twelve semitones) at a time. To toggle its display on or off in the toolbar for the In-Place editor or any other MIDI editor, right-click (PC)/Control-click (Mac) in the toolbar and select that option.

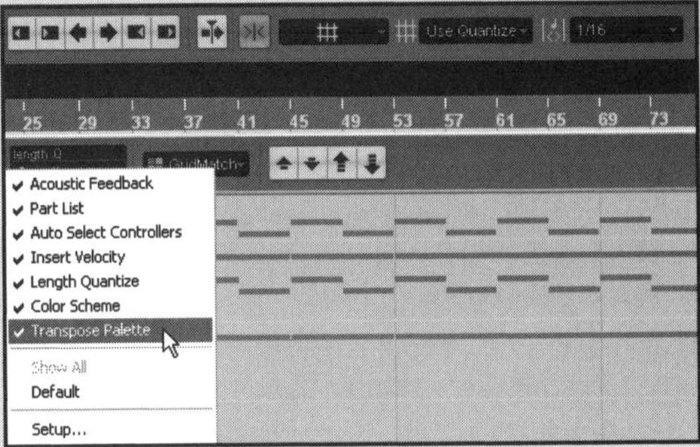

Figure 21.5
Displaying the Nudge tools in the In-Place editor's toolbar.

There are four ways you can split note events, and the quantize grid setting influences precisely where the split occurs in all methods:

- Use the Scissors tool at the desired location on single or selected notes.
- Use the Split Loop function in the Edit menu or context menu, which splits selected notes at the current left and right locator positions.
- Use the Split at Cursor option in the Edit menu or the context menu to split all note events that cross the current position of the play cursor.
- Hold down the Alt (PC)/Option (Mac) key as you click notes with the Selection (arrow) tool to split them at the point where you clicked. If more than one event is selected, all events will be split.

Merging Note Events

The Glue tool is the Scissors tool's counterpart. It joins the note you click with the following note of the same pitch or merges the selected event with the next one in time. Use it when you've split a note by mistake or you need to join two or more notes into one.

HOW TO

Merge note events:

1. Select the Glue tool from the toolbar or in the context menu.
2. Click the first note you want to glue.
3. Click again to glue the current note to the next note of the same pitch. For example, in the bottom part of Figure 21.6, the note to the right would be joined with the note on the left.

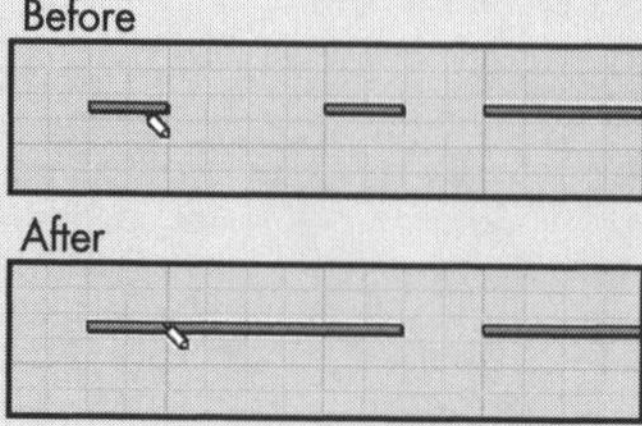

Figure 21.6
A before-and-after look at the Glue tool in action.

Using the Draw Tool

The Draw (arrow) tool in the In-Place and Key editor windows and the Drumstick tool in the Drum editor window offer similar functions. The difference with the Draw tool is that dragging a note determines the length of that note, whereas the Drumstick tool repeats the event using the quantize value to determine the spacing and the insert length value to determine the length of each event in the Drum editor window. Another difference is that the Line, Parabola, Sine, Triangle, Square, and Paint tools in the Key editor can be used to add note events in the Event Display area, whereas these tools are only available to modify Control Change values in the Controller Lanes of the Drum editor.

HOW TO

Create notes using the Draw tool:

1. Set the quantize grid and length values appropriately. The length determines how long each note is, and the quantize grid determines the spacing between the notes.
2. Select the Draw tool from the toolbar, or right-click (PC)/Control-click (Mac) in the editor to select the Draw tool, or use the key command (by default, this is the number 8 in the Key editor).
3. Adjust the Insert velocity setting in the toolbar to the desired value.
4. Click where you want to add a note. Each click adds a note with a length corresponding to the length value in the quantize length setting. Click and drag to draw longer notes instead. Their length increases or decreases by quantize value increments as you drag. In contrast, when adding notes using the Drumstick tool (in the Drum editor), dragging the drumstick to the right creates *additional* Note On events instead, at intervals set by the quantize grid and with individual note lengths determined by the current setting in the Drum editor's Insert Length field.

In Figure 21.7, the quantize grid is set at eighth-note intervals; the length for each note inserted is set to sixteenth notes. This means that when you click to insert a note, it appears at eighth-note intervals and is 1/16th note in length. Each inserted note has a Note On velocity of 79, as defined in the Insert Velocity field. In the upper two parts of this figure, you can see how these settings influence how notes are added when either clicking near the quantize gridlines or clicking and dragging across several gridlines. In the lower two parts, you can see the same operation, but with the Drum editor equivalent of the Draw tool, which is the Drumstick tool (when using the same grid and quantize settings).

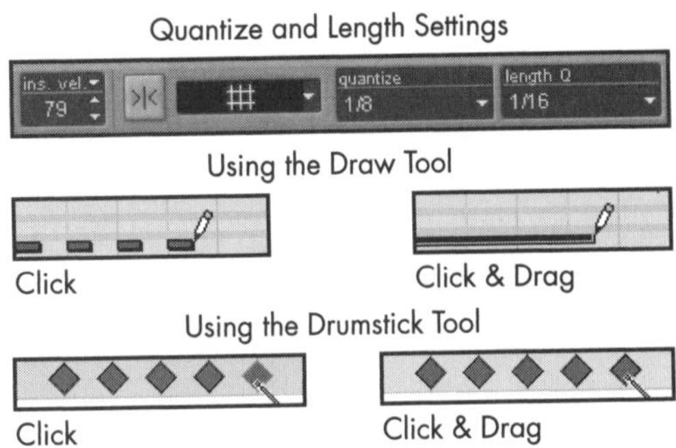

Figure 21.7
Adding note events in the Key and Drum editors by using the Draw or Drumstick tool.

Events are always created with the same MIDI channel as the part you are editing. After you have inserted notes using the Draw tool, you can modify their length by clicking on the existing note and dragging it farther to the right to lengthen the note or dragging it to the left to shorten the note. Remember that note lengths always snap to the next quantize grid value when Snap is enabled in the editor's toolbar.

The Draw tool can only lengthen the end point of an existing event. To modify the start point of a note, use the Selection tool, as described in earlier sections of this chapter.

Using the Line Tool

The Line tool, like the Draw tool, can be used to insert both note and controller events. Each shape under the Line tool offers its own characteristics. The most common use for the Line tool is to edit Control Change information, creating MIDI ramps, such as pan effects or fade-outs. Here's a look at these tools and their capabilities.

Moving the mouse up and down with the Paint tool adds notes on different pitches, whereas moving the mouse left and right adds them at different points in time. When dragging to create note events, the Paint tool is different from the Draw tool because it adds a note each time your cursor crosses a gridline. Both tools work the same when you are inserting Control Change events.

The Line tool draws a line across the Note Display area or the Controller Display area to create a series of events along the line. In the case of notes, these will be created at an interval, length, and velocity determined by the quantize setting. Figure 21.8 displays such lines: In the left half, note events are added, and in the right half, controller (Control Change) messages are added. In the case of controller events, you also can use the Line tool to edit existing controller messages to create a linear ramp.

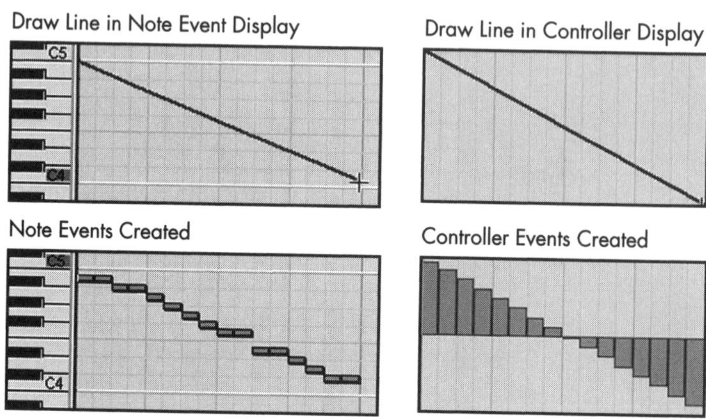

Figure 21.8
Adding note and controller events using the Line tool.

HOW TO

Insert events using the Line tool:

1. Set the quantize values appropriately. You also can leave the Snap off; however, a greater number of events will be generated, which can create a bottleneck in your MIDI stream if combined with other dense MIDI tracks.
2. Select the Line tool from the toolbar or the context menu.
3. Click where you want the line to begin. To move this point after clicking (but before releasing the mouse button to actually create the new events), hold the Alt+Ctrl (PC)/Option+ (Mac) keys down until you are satisfied with the start location.
4. Drag the mouse where you want the line to end, and release the mouse button to add the events.

The Parabola tool is similar to the Line tool except that it draws a parabolic ramp rather than a linear ramp (see Figure 21.9). Inserting events or modifying existing events using this tool is done in the same way as with the Line tool, with the following additional options:

- While still dragging this tool (before releasing the mouse button to create the new events), press the Ctrl (PC)/ (Mac) key to change the type of parabolic curve that will be created.
- As with the Line tool, you can hold down the Alt+Ctrl (PC)/Option+ (Mac) keys while still dragging, to move your start point to a new location.

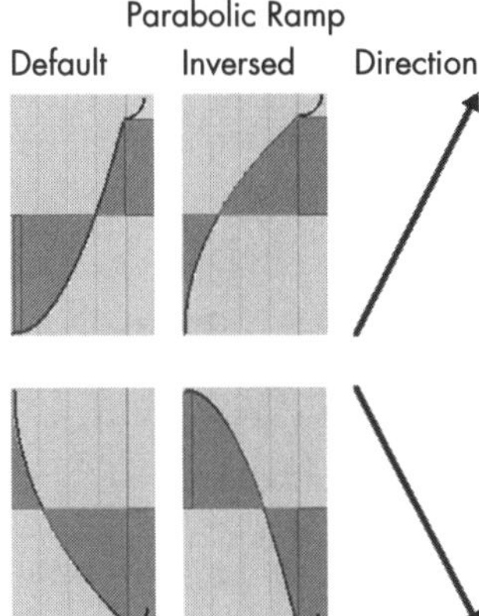

Figure 21.9
The different parabolic ramps available when using the Parabola tool.

The sine, triangle, and square ramps have similar options. However, as you drag to create these shapes, the farther you drag the mouse cursor away from the center point where you first clicked, the greater the amplitude of the shape will be. A small movement upward, for example, will create a small variation in note pitches or controller values. Dragging your mouse downward from the start point inverts the shape of the "waveform" you're using to draw.

HOW TO ❋

Create a ramp using the Sine, Triangle, or Square tool:

1. Select the appropriate tool from the toolbar.
2. Set the quantize grid if you want to use this setting to control how many and where the events will be created. For a smoother curve or change, disable the Snap to Grid option.
3. Click where you want to start inserting the events and drag the mouse to the right.
   - To adjust the frequency of the shape you are drawing, hold down the Shift key as you move the mouse left or right to adjust its period to the desired length. When you are satisfied with the period of the waveform, release the Shift key and finish dragging the mouse to the desired end location for the entire shape.
   - Try holding down the Alt (PC)/Option (Mac) or Ctrl (PC)/ (Mac) key while dragging the mouse to obtain different behaviors. Experiment on an empty track with different grid settings or without the Snap mode enabled.
   - Hold down both Alt+Ctrl (PC)/Option+ (Mac) keys after you've started drawing the new shape (but before releasing the mouse button to create the new events) to drag the start point and entire shape to a new location.
4. Release the mouse button at the desired end location to insert events corresponding to the current shape setting.

Zooming

In MIDI editors (In-Place, Key, Drum, and List), the zooming functions are similar to those found in the Project window, with the exception that you do not have a Presets menu next to the horizontal or vertical scroll bar. However, you do have access to the Zoom submenu options in the context menu or in the Zoom submenu of the Edit menu.

You also can use the Magnifying Glass tool on the toolbar to draw a selection box around the range you want to zoom into. Clicking inside the editor with the Magnifying Glass tool zooms in one step at a time, and Ctrl-clicking (PC)/-clicking (Mac) zooms out one step at a time. The data can be zoomed vertically and horizontally at the same time by holding down the Ctrl (PC)/ (Mac) key while dragging the Zoom tool over the desired area.

The Info Line

The Info Line is your greatest ally to determine the start position or the velocity value of an event. Use the Info Line to modify the start, end, length, pitch, velocity, channel, and note-off velocity parameters of any selected events by clicking in the Value field below the parameter's name to change its value. Use the scroll wheel of your mouse (if you have one) to change the value, or enter a new value using your keyboard. When more than one event is selected, the parameter values are displayed in yellow. You can change parameters of multiple selected events in one of two ways—either set them all to a single new (absolute) value or make the specified adjustment *relative* to the current values for that parameter in each event. By default, parameters on multiple selections change relatively; however, holding down Ctrl (PC)/ (Mac) causes the parameter value to become absolute. For example, if you have a G4 with a velocity of 64 and a C5 with a velocity of 84 selected, the pitch field in the Info Line displays the C5's parameters. Table 21.1 shows how this works.

Table 21.1
How Relative Editing of Multiple Selected Events Works in the Info Line Compared to Absolute Editing

Original Parameters (Pitch/Velocity)	Value Entered	Change When Relative (Default)	Change When Absolute (with Ctrl/ Key Pressed)
C5/64	D5/84	D5/84	D5/84
G4/104	See above	A4/124	D5/84

MIDI Controllers

Editing MIDI Control Change messages as they appear in the Controller Lanes is similar to editing note events. However, because the quantize grid setting influences the frequency at which these events are inserted when creating new Control Change messages (with the exception of velocity values, which are spaced according to the positions of their respective MIDI note events), it is important to be sure that this quantize configuration is set appropriately for the task at hand.

When you edit Control Change messages, it is important to understand the following principle. When you delete a Control Change message, the value preceding the deleted message becomes the currently effective value for that controller until another Control Change message of this type is reached. For example, if you have three sustain pedal values of 127, 0, 127 (on, off, on), and you decide to delete the second value, then you only have two values of 127 in your lane (see Figure 21.10).

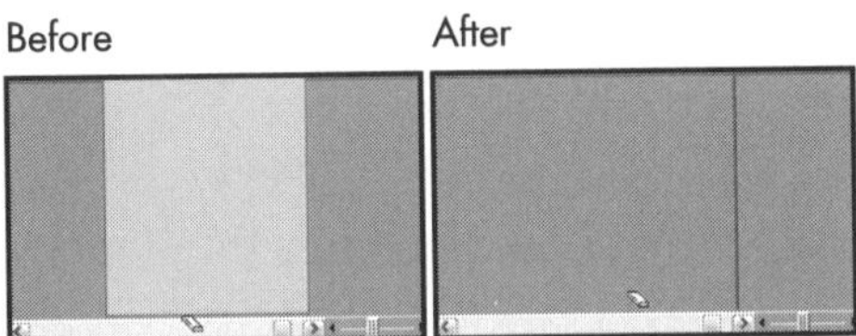

Figure 21.10
A before-and-after look at what happens when you remove intermediate values in Controller Lanes.

In the In-Place editor, you can change the controller displayed by choosing a new controller type in the pop-up menu at its lower-left corner, as shown in Figure 21.11. Controller types for which there are actually recorded events in this track are displayed with an asterisk after their name, as is the case with the Velocity and Sustain controllers in this example. Changing which controller is displayed doesn't change the recorded events in any way. To display/edit more than one controller at a time, use the Key editor instead.

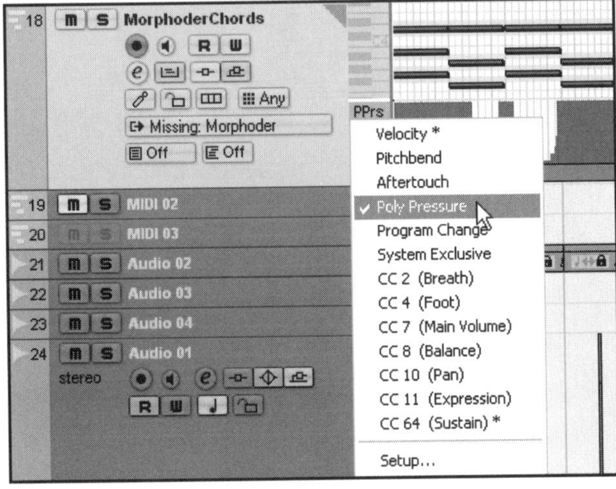

Figure 21.11
Changing the Control Change message displayed in the In-Place editor.

22 Key Editor

There are six MIDI-related editors to choose from in Cubase. The Key editor uses the piano roll analogy, in which events appear as horizontal rectangles within a strip moving from left to right as you play the events. The vertical axis represents the pitch, and the horizontal axis represents the timeline of the event being edited. For example, the start of the MIDI part(s) currently being edited is always on the left of the piano roll, and the end of a part appears on the right of the piano roll. This editor also enables you to edit Control Change messages on separate lanes below the Piano Roll view. The Key editor is the default editing environment for MIDI tracks that are not associated with drum maps.

Most of the editing techniques associated with the Key editor are also available through the In-Place editor in the Project window; however, the Key editor does offer a few additional features, such as multi-event and multitrack MIDI editing, as well as the ability to edit multiple lanes of Control Change events simultaneously. Finally, the Key editor also supports step recording for those hard-to-play passages or complex rhythmic patterns.

Here's a summary of what you will learn in this chapter:

- How to use the different tools in the Key editor to edit MIDI events
- How to use the different display options, such as auto scroll, chord scheme selector, or chord symbol and note
- How to adjust the velocity of inserted events
- How to adjust the positioning of events using Snap and Quantize features
- How to record MIDI events using step recording and real-time MIDI input
- How to create a playback loop within this MIDI editor, independently from the project's playback or locator positions
- How to add a Controller Lane to the Key editor
- How to edit more than one event and track at a time

Editor Toolbar

There are many ways to edit MIDI events inside MIDI parts. If you want to select, move, copy, or erase note events and Control Change events within a MIDI part, you can use the In-Place editor (see Chapter 21). On the other hand, if you want to edit several MIDI parts at once, if you need to add events that cross the boundary between two MIDI parts, or if you would like to move or copy parts while they are being edited, use the associated MIDI editor (Key or Drum). All editors have context menus available through a right-click (PC)/Control-click (Mac) with the same tools found in the toolbar. Finally, you can always use key commands to switch from one tool to another. (See File > Key Commands for a complete list.)

Solo Editor and Acoustic Feedback

By default, the first two buttons on the left of the toolbar are the Solo editor and Acoustic Feedback buttons (see Figure 22.1). The Solo editor button mutes all MIDI parts not currently loaded in the Key editor. The Acoustic Feedback button plays notes when they are selected with the Selection tool or when moving a note in time or to different pitch values. This is basically the MIDI equivalent of the audio Scrub tool. Hold down the Ctrl (PC)/⌘ (Mac) key to hear all notes playing at the same time as the note you are selecting.

Figure 22.1
The Solo editor, Acoustic Feedback, and Show Info buttons.

Show Info

The Show Info button toggles the Info Line on and off. Use the Info Line to enter numeric values directly in the appropriate field of selected events. For example, select a note event and change its length numerically by clicking in the Length field, as shown in Figure 22.2, or quickly transpose a series of selected note events by changing the value in the Pitch field. Every selected note will be transposed by the specified amount relative to the pitch initially displayed in this field.

Figure 22.2
The Info Line in the Key or Drum editor.

> **Using the Scroll Wheel**
>
> When a value field is selected in the Info Line, you can use the scroll wheel on the mouse (or up/down arrows on your computer keyboard) to increment or decrement values.

Tool Buttons

Next is a series of 10 tools for applying various editing operations to MIDI events found in your editor (see Figure 22.3). These tools are similar to those found in the Project window, but they offer editor-specific characteristics.

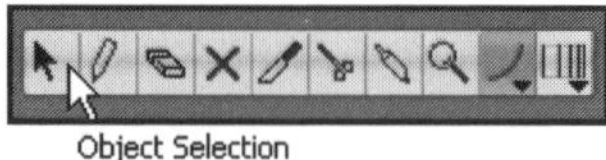

Figure 22.3
The Key editor tools, from left to right: the Object Selection, Draw, Eraser, Mute, Trim, Scissors, Glue, Zoom, Line, and Time Warp tools.

- **Object Selection.** This "arrow" tool serves to select and resize events. Use this tool to move, copy, and select a range of events or to change the start or end position of existing events in your editor.
- **Draw.** This "pencil" tool adds events by drawing them one by one inside the Key editor or modifies existing note and controller events in a freehand style.
- **Eraser.** This tool allows you to erase events by clicking on them. If multiple events were previously selected, they all can be erased by clicking on any one of them with this tool.
- **Mute.** An alternative to the Eraser, this tool mutes a note so that you don't hear it, but it does not erase the note. This provides a way to mute certain events that you're not sure you want to get rid of, but that you don't want to hear right now. Click and drag over a selection with the Mute tool to mute all events within the selection.
- **Trim.** This tool modifies the length of one or several events by trimming off the end (by default). If you hold down the Alt (PC)/Option (Mac) key, before using this tool, the beginning of the note is trimmed instead.
- **Scissors.** This tool splits selected events at the split mark. Exactly where the split occurs is determined by the Snap and Grid modes.
- **Glue.** This tool glues two notes of the same pitch together. More specifically, when they are playing at the same pitch value, it glues the event that follows to the precedent event that you click on.
- **Zoom.** This tool allows you to magnify your view of the content by dragging a box around it. You also can elect to click on a particular note to zoom in on it.

- **Line.** This tool performs as a multifunction tool in two modes. The Line mode allows you to draw a series of events in the shape of the tool (you can switch between line, parabola, sine, triangle, and square) or to shape controller information in one of these shapes as well. Paint, the last mode in its pop-up selector, allows you to insert multiple notes by dragging the cursor across the note display area in a freehand style.
- **Time Warp.** This tool creates tempo changes in the tempo track to match recorded musical events. Note that the Time Warp tool available in the Project window, the Sample editor, and the Audio Part editor all play similar roles—they help composers in the task of matching absolute, linear time (seconds, frames, and samples) with relative, musical time (bars and beats). However, Time Warp is applied differently to MIDI than it is to audio. You will find more on this tool in Chapter 29, "Tempo Track."

Autoscroll

Continuing our trip along the default toolbar, the next button toggles the Autoscroll function on or off in the Key editor (see Figure 22.4). When enabled, the window follows the project playback cursor. When disabled, events in this MIDI editor can be edited during playback without your worrying about the content of the window automatically scrolling to follow the playback position.

Figure 22.4
The Autoscroll button.

Auto Select Controller

This button is very useful when you are editing MIDI Control Change messages and moving them around (see Figure 22.5). When this button is enabled in the Key editor's toolbar, selecting and moving note events also selects and moves any Control Change events with the identical start time.

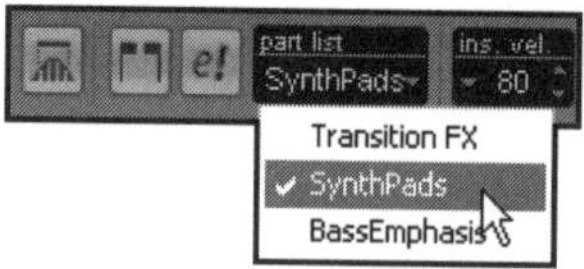

Figure 22.5
The Auto Select Controller, Show Part Borders, Edit Active Part Only, Part List, and Inserted Velocity fields.

Part Editing Options

The next two buttons and the drop-down menu offer editing options related to editing multiple MIDI parts that have previously been selected in the Project window simultaneously inside the Key editor. Use the Show Part Borders button to display each MIDI part's border limits inside the Key editor. When enabled, you will see a start and end handle for each MIDI part that is currently open in this MIDI editor. Clicking and dragging either one of these handles will modify the part's borders in the Project window as well.

The Edit Active Part Only button works well when you have opened several MIDI parts simultaneously in the Key editor. Enable this button and select the MIDI part from the Part List drop-down menu to apply changes or edits only to selected events in this active part. For example, if you do a Select All function followed by a Delete function with the Edit Active Part Only option disabled, all events in all the MIDI parts currently open in the Key editor will be deleted. If the Edit Active Part Only option is enabled and the SynthPads part, for example, is selected in the part list, then only the events found in that active part will be deleted.

Insert Velocity

The Insert Velocity field sets the default velocity value of notes that are manually added into this MIDI editor with the Pencil, Draw, or Line tool. You can change this value in one of three ways:

1. Click in the field and type in the desired value.
2. Click on the up or down arrow next to the current value to increase or decrease the value.
3. Select one of the preset values available in the Ins. Vel. drop-down menu associated with the Ins. Vel. field itself.

You can use the Setup option at the bottom of this menu to change the values it offers. You can also configure key commands to select among these values as you insert new note events with the Pencil or Line tool.

Snap and Quantize

The Snap and Quantize fields in the Key editor are similar to the ones found in the Project window. Activate the Snap button (the first button on the left in Figure 22.6) to make the fields to the right of this button active. The selected Snap mode determines how the Snap and Quantize functions will work. The Quantize field determines the grid's spacing and influences many operations inside the MIDI editors. For example, setting your grid to 1/32 note allows you to move, cut, and insert events at thirty-second note intervals. In other words, the grid Quantize setting prevents you from moving, cutting, or inserting events at positions other than the one defined by the field.

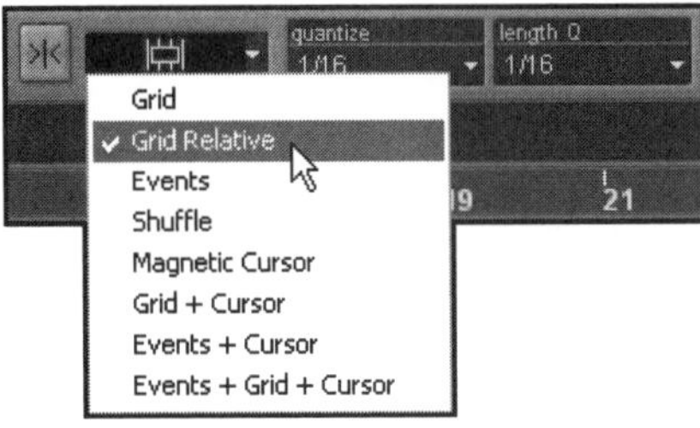

Figure 22.6
The editor's Quantize settings.

The Length Q field determines the length of inserted events in the Key editor. For example, if you set the length to ½, clicking in the display with the Draw tool will add a half-note to the part. When using the step-recording technique covered in detail later in this chapter with a Quantize value of ¼-Note and a Length Quantize value set to Quantize Link, all notes are inserted at quarter note intervals and will be of quarter note length. The Insert Velocity field, on the other hand, determines the velocity of Note On events that are added with the Draw tools.

Step Input of MIDI Events

Step Input is a boon for the rhythmically challenged—those less-than-proficient keyboard players who have great ideas but just need some help entering them into a sequencer. It's also great for creating rhythmically complex patterns, such as machine-like drum fills using sixty-fourth notes at 160 BPM, no matter what your skill level with the keyboard or other MIDI controller. Step Input may also be useful for musicians who can't enter MIDI events in their computers using VSTi in real time, because their sound card's latency is too high. No matter what the reason, step recording lets you enter notes or chords one by one without worrying about timing.

Table 22.1 describes the function associated with each of the Step Recording buttons (also shown from left to right in Figure 22.7).

Figure 22.7
The Step Input buttons.

Table 22.1
The Step Input Buttons on the Editor's Toolbar (from Top to Bottom in This Table)

Button Name	Button Function
Step Input	Enables or disables the Step Input recording mode. Whenever this button is activated, the Autoscroll function is disabled.
MIDI Input	When this button is enabled, you can select a note and assign it a new pitch by playing a new note on your keyboard or another MIDI controller.
Move Insert Point	Adds the played event at the position corresponding to the next quantize value following the playback line, pushing any subsequent existing events to the next quantize value (when this option is enabled). When the Move Insert Point option is disabled, events added using Step Input mode are added at the current position of the Step Input cursor, leaving previously recorded content in place. See Figure 22.8 for an example of how this works.

Button Name	Button Function
Record Pitch	Allows you to use your MIDI keyboard or another controller to reassign the pitches of existing events, advancing one note at a time through the existing MIDI note events in this editor as you play notes on your MIDI controller.
Record Note On Velocity	When enabled, the Note On velocity values of the notes you play in Step Input mode are recorded. When disabled, the velocity assigned to the note you record is fixed by the Velocity field in the toolbar. When Record Note On Velocity is enabled, pressing lightly on your keyboard adds notes with low velocity values, whereas pressing harder adds a higher velocity value to the notes recorded through the step recording method.
Record Note Off Velocity	Record Note Off velocities are notes entered in Step Input mode—otherwise these are set to a fixed value.

Original Events

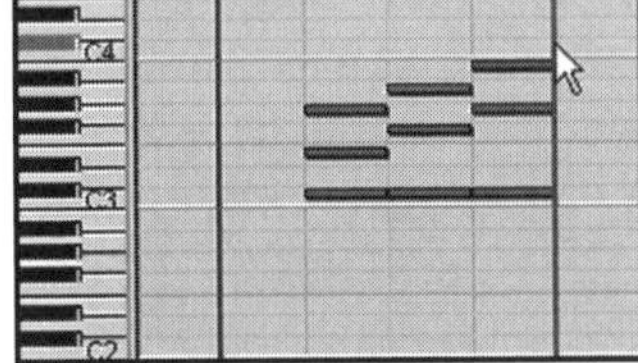

Insert Button Disabled

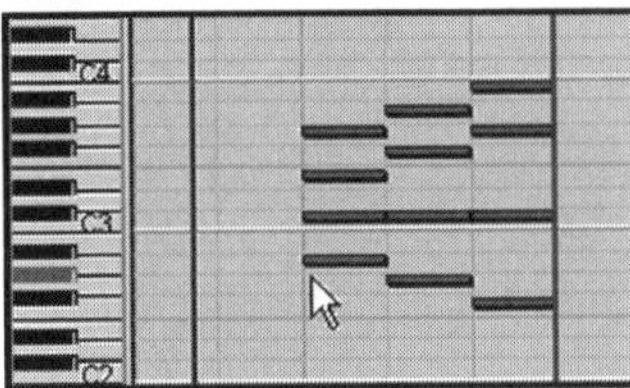

Insert Button Enabled

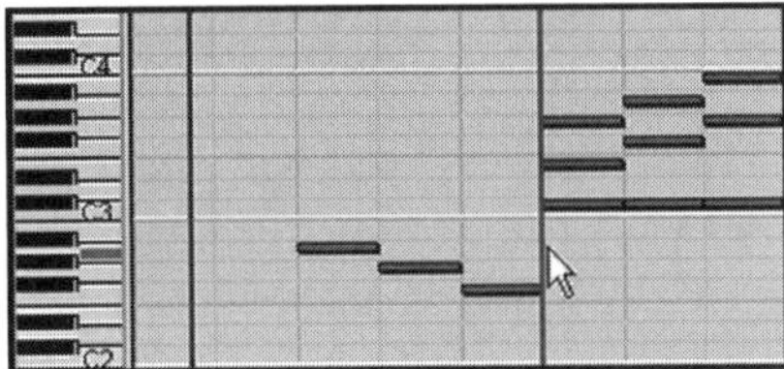

Figure 22.8
An example of the Insert button's effect on events recorded in Step Record mode.

Mouse Position

The top portion of this field displays the current location of your mouse cursor in the vertical or pitch axis (see Figure 22.9), whereas the bottom field represents the horizontal time position of the mouse cursor (or your Step Input cursor, if that mode is currently active)—in bars and beats, minutes and seconds, samples or timecode, depending on the current time units displayed in the Key editor's Ruler. Use these fields to guide you when adding events with your mouse.

Figure 22.9
The Mouse Position display field.

Independent Track Loop

The Independent Track Loop controls discussed here consist of an on/off toggle button and a start and end point setting for the loop itself. The Independent Track Loop creates a loop with the MIDI events found in the current MIDI editor, between the start and end locations that you set in these fields. When this feature is enabled, pressing the Play button on the Transport panel will cause the project to play normally, but the events inside the MIDI editor that are defined in the loop will cycle independently. For example, set this function so that the events playing a drum rhythm in the current MIDI editor loop from bar 1 to bar 3 (see Figure 22.10). This function creates an independent mini cycle loop within your MIDI editor, just as the left and right locators create a cycle in the Project window. Both are independent from one another. The only dependency is that when the cycle in the Project window is turned on and reaches the end, both cycles will go back to the beginning together.

Figure 22.10
The Independent Track Loop tools.

Color Scheme Selector

The Color Scheme Selector field is a visual aid that does not affect anything in the Key editor other than the colors that are displayed in it. You can choose to give a different color to the different Note On velocities (shown in Figure 22.11), pitches, MIDI channels, or parts. How you choose to use this coloring tool depends on what you are editing. For example, if you are editing events from multiple MIDI channels in a single window, you might want to select the Color by Channel option. On the other hand, if several parts are selected and opened in the Key editor, selecting the Color by Part option might make more sense.

Figure 22.11
The Color Scheme Selector field and the Chord/Note display.

Other Toolbar Items

There are three additional sets of tools available in the MIDI editors that are not displayed by default: the Nudge palette, Transpose palette, and Open Device button. To learn more about customizing toolbars (by right-clicking within them on PC, or Control-clicking on Mac), please consult Chapter 38, "Project Customization."

The Nudge palette offers a convenient way of bumping the position (in time) of selected events according to the current quantization grid. From left to right (see Figure 22.12), these buttons are:

- **Trim Start Left.** This moves the start position one quantize value to the left.
- **Trim Start Right.** This is the same as Trim Start Left, except it moves the start to the right.
- **Move Left.** This moves the entire selected event (or events) to the left (earlier in time) without affecting the event's length.
- **Move Right.** This moves the entire selected event (or events) to the right (later in time) without affecting the event's length.
- **Trim End Left.** This moves the end position of the affected note event(s) one Length Quantize value to the left. Changing the Length Quantize value field (Length Q) will influence the size of each increment.
- **Trim End Right.** This is the same as Trim End Left, except it moves the end of the affected note event(s) to the right instead.

Figure 22.12
The Nudge and Transpose palettes and the Open Device button.

The Transpose buttons from left to right transpose selected events one semitone (one half-step) up or down and one octave (12 half-steps) up or down.

When a MIDI track is assigned to a VSTi, events recorded on this track will play through the sounds generated by this VSTi. The Open Device button opens that VSTi's control panel to make changes to the parameters of this software instrument.

Key Editor Display Areas

The Key editor offers two main display areas—one for MIDI note events and another for Control Change messages. In the Note Display area, a keyboard appears vertically along the left edge. The Ruler spanning from left to right represents the time at which events occur. You can change how time is displayed by right-clicking (PC)/Control-clicking (Mac) in the Ruler and selecting one of the many display formats available or by selecting the desired format from the Ruler Format selection menu found at the right of the ruler itself.

> **Using the Ruler to Control Zoom**
>
> In the Key editor (as well as in all the other windows), when you click in the lower half of the ruler and drag your mouse up or down, you zoom out or in, respectively, centering your display on the position where you clicked to start the zoom. Holding down your mouse and moving it left or right moves the window and the project cursor in time. When you release your mouse, the project cursor snaps to the closest quantize value (if the Snap is active).

The Controller Display area is a customizable portion of the window that displays one or more controller types, such as volume, pan, expression, pedal, pitch bends, and so on. Using multiple controller lanes gives you a better view of the MIDI messages associated with the part you are editing (see Figure 22.13).

> HOW TO
>
> **Add a Controller Lane to the Key editor:**
>
> 1. Right-click (PC)/Control-click (Mac) anywhere within the Key editor.
> 2. From the context menu, select the Create New Controller Lane option at the bottom of the menu.
> 3. From the newly created lane, select the controller name you want to display from the drop-down menu at the left margin of the lane. Controller types for which there are actually recorded events in the current part are identified by an asterisk (*) at the end of their name.

If the desired controller is not displayed in this list, select the Setup option at the bottom of the drop-down menu. There are two areas inside the Controller Menu Setup dialog box: the In Menu area and the Hidden area.

- **To add a controller to the menu:** Select it from the Hidden area and click the double-arrow button below the area.
- **To remove a controller from the menu:** Select it from the In Menu area and click the double-arrow button below the area. Click OK when you are finished adding or removing controllers from the menu, then select the new controller to add its corresponding lane.

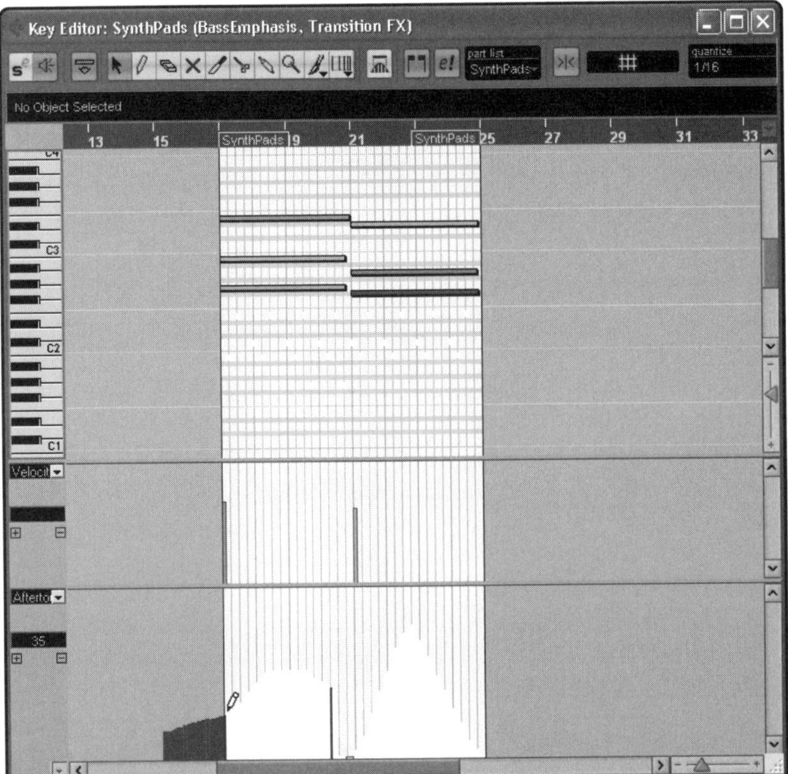

Figure 22.13
The Key editor with the note display area on top and two Controller Lanes below.

- **To remove a Controller Lane:** Select the Remove This Lane option at the bottom of the same context menu you used to add a new lane.

Control Change messages seen in the Controller Display area are represented by blocks, whereas note velocity values are represented by lines and are aligned with their corresponding MIDI note events. Moving a note moves its associated velocity value, but doesn't move any Control Change messages, unless the Auto Select Controllers button is enabled in the window's toolbar. The field below the controller's name represents the value of the controller if you were to add this value at the current cursor position. The Quantize value, when active, will affect the distance between each added or recorded Control Change message. If a quantize grid is set to ½-Note, controllers can be added at half-note intervals. To enter a greater number of Control Change messages, disable the Snap mode or set the Quantize value to a smaller value. More Control Change messages create smoother changes, but they also create greater numbers of MIDI events that can bog down the MIDI at the port's output. This is especially true when you are using lots of MIDI in your project.

Using Step Input

As mentioned earlier in this chapter, the Step Input functions are available in the toolbar of the Key and Drum editors. When the Step Input mode is enabled, a new insert cursor (a vertical blue bar) appears in the note display area. Keep an eye on the location of this line because events that are inserted appear at the gridline immediately to the right of this insertion point. You can move this line by clicking inside the note display area at the location where you want to insert new events in Step Input mode.

HOW TO

Record MIDI in Step Input mode:

1. In the Key or Drum editor, enable the Step Input button in the toolbar. All the Step Input buttons should automatically be activated, with the exception of the MIDI Connector.
2. Enable the Snap button and select the Snap mode.
3. Set the Quantize grid and the Length Quantize value, which determine how far apart and how long the events will be.
4. Position the Step Input cursor at the point where you want to begin recording by clicking inside the note display area of this MIDI editor.
5. If you do not want to use the Note On velocities you actually play as you step-enter these new MIDI note events, disable the Record Note On Velocity button and set the Insert Velocity field to the desired velocity.
6. Play a note or a chord on your keyboard or other MIDI controller. The notes you play determine the pitch and velocity (if that option is enabled) being recorded as you step-enter new notes, but the position in the timeline is determined by the insertion point and the Quantize Grid setting.
7. To move the Step Input cursor forward or backward, use the left and right arrows on your keyboard or click within the note display area. The insertion point where the notes will be added is displayed in the Mouse Time Value field in the toolbar of this editor.
8. To insert an event between two other events, activate the Insert Mode button in the toolbar of this MIDI editor, position your insert point (blue line) where you want to insert a note or a chord, and simply play the note or chord. To insert a note without moving the content found to the right of this location, disable the Insert Mode button on the toolbar.
9. When you are finished, don't forget to turn off the Step Input button; otherwise, Cubase will continue to insert events that you play on the keyboard in this part.

Editing Multiple Tracks

You can edit more than one track (of the same class) simultaneously in any of Cubase's MIDI editors by selecting parts on different tracks in the Project window and opening them in one of the MIDI editors. All selected tracks will be available within the MIDI editor. Editing several tracks together can be useful to compare events on different tracks in a single editing window. If you select a MIDI track associated with a drum map along with others that have no drum map assignment, the MIDI events for this track are displayed as normal MIDI events without the drum mapping information. In other words, if you want to edit multiple drum-mapped events, select only tracks that contain a drum map association.

When different colors are assigned to parts in the Project window, these same colors will be visible on their corresponding note events that you see in the MIDI editor.

HOW TO

Edit more than one track at a time:

1. In the Project window, click the first part you want to edit in a track.
2. Shift-click the next part you want to edit in another track or, with the Object Selection tool, drag a selection box over the range of parts you want to edit simultaneously.
3. Press Ctrl+E (PC)/⌘+E (Mac), or select the Open Key (or Drum) editor command from the MIDI menu, or double-click on any of the currently selected parts.

The editing window will appear with events from multiple tracks displayed, as shown in Figure 22.14. The active part is displayed with its part color and black borders around each of its events in the window of the MIDI editor. The title of the MIDI editors window also reflects which part is currently active. The other parts are visible, but inactive and displayed as gray events.

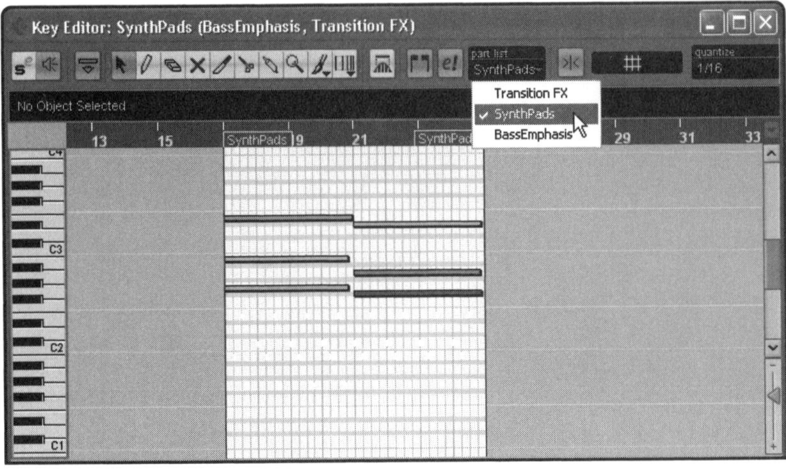

Figure 22.14
The Key editor when several parts are being simultaneously edited.

23 Drum Editors

The main advantage of MIDI over audio can be summed up in one word: flexibility. You can modify any musical or nonmusical parameter when a performance is recorded as MIDI events. Using virtual instruments, musicians also can produce and transform a wide variety of sounds and musical elements. The MIDI editors in Cubase offer full control over every aspect of MIDI events. This is, after all, where Cubase earned its first stripes as professional software, and it continues to do so by offering different editing environments to reflect the versatility MIDI offers when it comes to its editable parameters. Once the editing is completed, converting MIDI into audio for the final mixdown is usually needed—especially when external MIDI modules are involved.

Here's a summary of what you will learn in this chapter:

- What the different areas of the Drum and Key editors are
- How to load a drum map and assign it to a MIDI track containing a drum part
- How to create or customize a drum map

Drum Editor

What you have just read about the Key editor applies for the most part to the Drum editor as well. The Drum editor window gives individual controls over a set of parameters for up to 127 percussive instruments. One of these parameters is the quantize value, which can be set globally for the entire part or individually for each instrument assigned to a pitch in a drum patch. For example, set a different quantize value for the kick drum and the hi-hat when you step record. The quantize value determines the spacing between each manually entered event. When the General Quantize button is disabled, the individual quantize settings take over. When the General Quantize button is enabled, the quantize value set in the toolbar dictates the quantize grid for each instrument in the part.

Try this by creating a drum track. Set the quantize value for the kick drum to quarter notes and for the hi-hat to sixteenth notes. Disable the General Quantize button in the toolbar. Now, use the Drumstick tool to draw events on these instruments by simply dragging from left to right within their rows. You will see that MIDI note events are added on every quarter note for the kick, and on every sixteenth note for the hi-hat, as displayed in Figure 23.1.

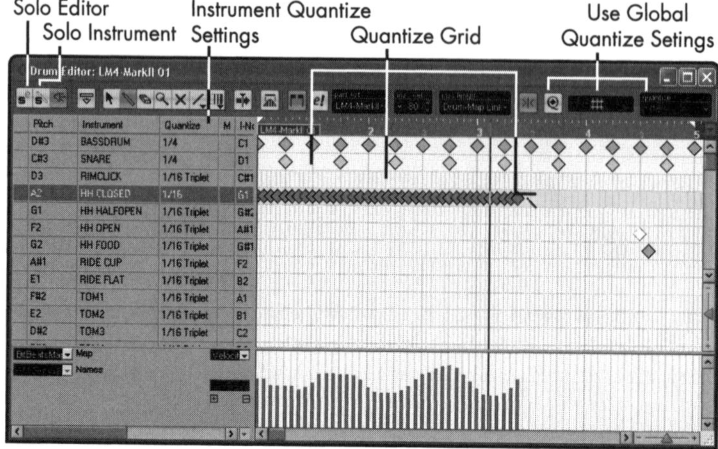

Figure 23.1
The Drum editor.

Click on an existing event to remove it. Setting an individual quantize value for each instrument in a drum track replaces the note lengths that will appear for this MIDI part in the Key editor. Most percussive sounds need to have precise trigger timings rather than precision in their durations, so when using drum maps, you don't usually extend the length of MIDI note events. With the exception of some samplers, most instruments play drum sounds until the end, and the MIDI Note Off event's position has little or no effect, no matter how long you hold the note. Unlike a guitar or keyboard note, the position of the attack, or Note On event, is more relevant in this case than the actual end of the event. As a direct result of this, there are no Scissors or Glue tools in the Drum editor.

To open a MIDI part in the Drum editor, either select the Drum editor from the MIDI menu once the MIDI part is selected or assign a drum map to the track you want to associate with this MIDI editor, as displayed in Figure 23.2.

Drum Editor Display Areas

As with the Key editor, the Drum editor is divided into task-specific areas. In this case, it is divided into five areas. The Solo Instrument button lets you solo a specific instrument within the Drum editor. The Drum Sound list and its columns replace the keyboard display of the Key editor. The number of columns displayed here depends on the drum map associated with the track (see Figure 23.1). This represents individual parameters for instruments that are defined in your drum map.

Figure 23.2
Assigning a drum map to a MIDI track.

Below the instrument list, in the left corner, are the Map and Name fields. The Map field selects a map from the Drum Map list or sets up a new drum map if you haven't already done that. The Name field selects from a drop-down menu the names of instruments associated with different pitch values. So this field is grayed out when a drum map is selected.

If you drag the vertical divider line that separates the drum sound list from the Note Display area toward the right, you will reveal some of the columns that might be hidden in the drum sound list. It can have up to nine columns, each representing a control parameter for an instrument. You can reorder these columns by dragging their headers, but we will list them here in their default order.

- The first unnamed column lets you select and monitor the instrument associated with this pitch. Selecting an instrument reveals its Note On velocity in the Controller Lane.
- The Pitch column represents the pitch associated with a particular instrument. This cannot be changed because most instruments are already preprogrammed to play a certain instrument on an assigned pitch value.
- The Instrument column represents the name of the sound associated with this row's pitch. Each drum map has its own set of instruments. These can be renamed or dragged into any order that makes editing more convenient as you work.
- The Quantize column represents the quantize value setting for each instrument. You can change this setting by clicking on the current value and selecting a new one. You also can change all the instruments' quantize value settings simultaneously by holding down the Ctrl (PC)/ (Mac) key as you make your selection. The list that appears offers the same options as the Drum editor's Quantize Grid drop-down menu.

- The M column controls whether an instrument is muted. To mute an instrument, click in its instrument row in the M column. To unmute that instrument, click in the M (or Mute) column next to that instrument once again.
- The I-Note column stands for the Input Note value or the note as recorded from the controller keyboard or drum machine, which we discuss when we cover the Drum Map feature in the next section. You can use the scroll wheel on your mouse to change this value (or the up/down arrow keys on Macintosh), or you can simply click in the field and type in a new value.
- The O-Note column stands for Output Note and represents the note at which the sound you want to map will be played back. By default, the O-Note is the same as the I-Note, but the ability to remap each input note to a different output note is an essential aspect of using drum maps. Again, this is discussed in the next section. You can change the value in this column in the same ways as the I-Note column.
- The Channel column sets the MIDI channel assigned to the instrument in a specific row. Each row in the drum map can be routed out to a different MIDI channel. You can change the value in this column in the same ways as described for the I-Note and O-Note columns.
- The Output column allows assigning each instrument (row) in this drum map to a different MIDI output port. To change the output, click the appropriate row in the Output column and select a new MIDI output from this column's pop-up menu. Each note in a drum track could be assigned to a different instrument. For example, you could have the kick drum assigned to an external GM device, the snare to an LM-9 VST Instrument, and so on.

To the right of the drum sound list is the Note Display area (see Figure 23.1). The vertical axis represents different instruments or pitches, according to the information found in the drum sound list on the left and the timeline, which appears with smaller divisions per the current quantize settings. The rectangles that represent MIDI note events in the Key editor are replaced by diamonds here in the Drum editor, each of which represents a Note On event. Notes are exactly aligned with the quantize grid when a vertical gridline crosses the diamond in its center.

Below the Note Display area are the Controller Lanes. Whereas the Key editor displays the velocity of every note in this area, the Drum editor only displays velocities for events in the currently selected instrument (row). In Figure 23.1, the currently selected drum instrument is the closed hi-hat. Therefore, the velocity values you see in the Controller Lane at the bottom of this editor represent velocities for the Note On events of this instrument only. For every other type of Control Change message, the editor behaves the same way as in the Key editor described earlier.

Working with Drum Maps

Depending on the manufacturer and model, MIDI instruments may use a wide variety of different MIDI note values for similar drum sounds. For example, one MIDI device's drum setup could use all the notes in a C scale to map its drum sounds, whereas another might use every chromatic note to map its drum set. One device might use C1 and D1 for its basic kick and snare sounds, while another uses C1 and F1 for the same purpose. This is fine when you know which note is playing which sound. But what if you want to try a different drum set or drum machine? Do you need to rerecord all your beats because C1 is not the bass drum anymore? That's when drum mapping becomes very handy.

As you read earlier in this chapter, the Drum editor displays Input and Output Note columns. These columns can remap recorded notes. By remapping the recorded kick-drum part from C1 to C3, for example, you can keep the recorded performance playing properly without permanently altering the MIDI events it contains. Cubase comes with ready-made drum maps on its CD; before you start creating your own drum map, check your CD or your Drum Maps folder if you have installed these on your computer. The Internet, in particular the forums at www.cubase.net, can also be a useful resource for finding drum maps for your particular MIDI device.

A drum map is essentially a list of 128 sound names associated with a pitch, Note In event, and Note Out event. You can assign one drum map per track. For obvious reasons, if you use two tracks with the same MIDI output and MIDI channel, you can have only one drum map assigned to that MIDI device/VSTi plug-in. Finally, you can assign only one Note In instrument per note name or note number, but you can have more than one Note In assigned to the same Note Out.

Each note in a drum map corresponds to a pitch value. Each pitch value (note number) can be associated with an instrument name, such as Kick Drum 1, Snare, Hi-Hat, and so forth. You can then assign the played note to that named instrument, which in turn is associated with a pitch, such as C1 (or note number 36). For example, you could create your perfect drum kit layout in which you position the instruments the way you want them on the keyboard (or other MIDI controller). Take, for example, the left portion of Figure 23.3. This could be a permanent drum layout setup used as a template for all drum parts, based on your favorite drum setup. From this point forward, all drum sounds can be remapped to correspond to this template. In the drum map on the right, the bottom half does not need remapping because the sounds in this setup are positioned to play the same input and output notes. This changes when you get into the cymbal sounds. Where you want the Ride 1 sound, the current drum setup plays a Crash 1, and your Ride Cymbal 1 sound is associated with another pitch. The solution: Remap the I-Note in the drum map of the currently loaded instrument to C#4 and the O-Note to D4. This way, you can play the

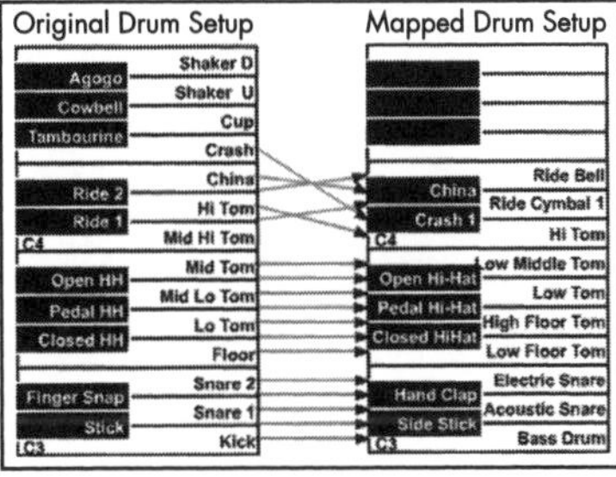

Figure 23.3
Example of a drum map in action.

C#4 to hear the ride cymbal. Because the C#4 is associated with the D4 pitch value, a D4 is actually recorded onto your MIDI track. Now, if you have a D4 recorded on your track, which in this drum map is a Ride Cymbal 1, what happens when you load another drum kit where D4 is a cowbell? Let's say that your ride is now on E5—all you need to do is set the O-Note of the pitch D4 to E5, and you will hear the ride sound once again.

HOW TO

Load a drum map and assign it to a drum track:

1. In the basic track settings section of the Inspector for this MIDI track, click in the Drum Map field and select the Drum Map Setup option. The Drum Map Setup dialog box will open.
2. In the Drum Map Setup dialog box, click to open the Functions drop-down menu and select Load, as displayed in Figure 23.4.

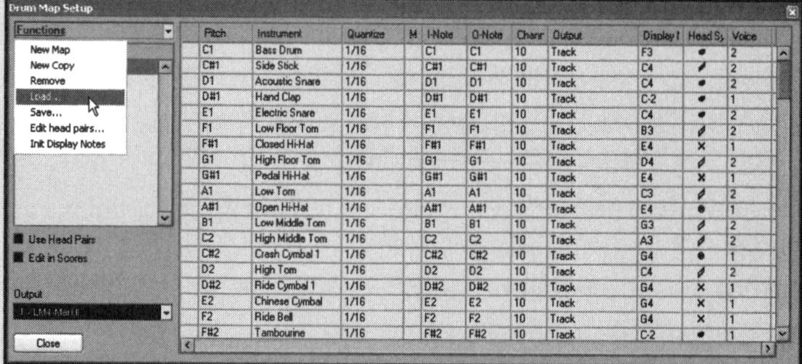

Figure 23.4
The Drum Map Setup dialog box.

3. Browse to the folder containing the desired drum map file (*.drm), select it, and click the Open button.
4. Select the newly loaded drum map from the Drum Map list.
5. In the Output field below the Drum Map list, select the default MIDI port associated with this drum map.

Or:

1. Assign the generic GM Map to the MIDI track containing the drum parts.
2. Double-click on a part in the Event Display area for this track in the Project window to open it in the Drum editor.
3. From the Drum editor, below the drum list, select the Drum Map Setup option.
4. From this point forward, follow Steps 2 through 5 from the previous list.

As mentioned earlier, you can customize drum maps. The editing process takes place inside the Drum Map Setup dialog box.

HOW TO

Create/customize a drum map:

1. Load the VSTi that will actually play the drum sounds or select the appropriate drum patch on the external MIDI device that is connected to the designated MIDI output port/channel.
2. From the Drum Map Setup dialog box, select New Map from the Functions drop-down menu.
3. Select the new map in the Drum Map field to rename it, as displayed in Figure 23.5.

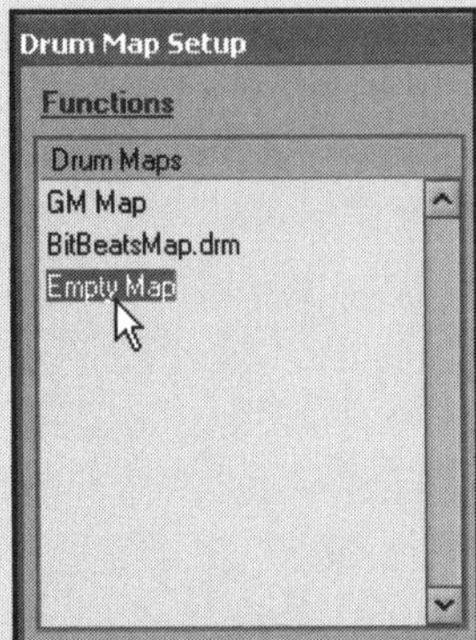

Figure 23.5
Selecting the new empty drum map in the Drum Map Setup dialog box.

4. Next to each pitch in the list of instruments, enter an appropriate instrument name.
5. Adjust the Quantize, the I-Note, the O-Note, the Channel, and the Output fields, if needed.
6. Repeat these steps for all the sounds available in your drum kit.
7. Click the Save button when you are satisfied with your current settings.
8. Name the file and browse to the location where you want to save the file, then click Save again.

To remove an unneeded drum map, select it and click the Remove button in the Drum Map Setup dialog box.

24 MIDI Menu Options

The MIDI menu is divided into five sections. The first section lists a number of commands that open different types of MIDI editing windows. In the second section, a number of quantizing options are listed, which can be used to modify the timing of MIDI events. This chapter mainly discusses the commands found in the third section, which offer a number of specific MIDI editing features that aren't handled by any MIDI editors because they are MIDI-part and Project window-specific. The fourth section relates mostly to the Logical editor functions. Finally, the last section is basically a MIDI reset function, which acts as a panic button on a MIDI patchbay, sending out All Notes Off and Reset Controllers messages on all MIDI output ports and channels. You can use this when you experience stuck notes after recording, playing, or editing a track.

Here's a summary of what you will learn in this chapter:

- How to transpose selected events using the MIDI Transpose command
- How to use the Merge MIDI in Loop command
- How to dissolve a MIDI part
- How to perform an O-Note conversion
- How to use a MIDI function

Transpose

The Transpose command in the MIDI menu enables you to perform three types of transformations to the pitches of MIDI note events. You can apply these transformations individually or combine them if you want to experiment a little:

- Use only the Semitones field if you simply want to shift the pitch of all currently selected MIDI events by the same amount. Unlike the Transpose field in the Inspector (which applies this transformation in real time), this command changes the MIDI note numbers of the events themselves.
- Use the Scale Correction fields to change the tonality of a line or harmonic part. Indicating the Root Note and Current Scale for the selected events tells Cubase how to interpret the source MIDI notes. Set the desired values for the New Scale and Root fields, and Cubase will adjust the notes appropriately to match the nearest pitch in the destination scale. If a value has also been entered in the Semitones field above, however, that pitch shift is applied *before* this scale correction step.
- Use the Keep Notes in Range fields to force all affected notes (after transposition and scale correction are applied, if you have selected those options in this dialog box) to remain within a restricted range. All notes outside this range are octave-transposed to fit within the pitch limits set by the Upper and Lower Barrier fields. For example, if the selected events contain a G6 (either in their untransposed state or as the result of operations in the first two fields of this dialog box) and your lower and upper barriers for the target pitch range are C2 and C5, respectively, that G6 would be transposed to C4, the nearest octave transposition for a G that will fall within the target range.

HOW TO

Transpose selected events using the MIDI Transpose command:

1. Select one or more MIDI parts or specific events inside a MIDI part that you want to transpose.
2. From the MIDI menu, select the Transpose command.
3. In the Transpose dialog box (see Figure 24.1), set the desired options.

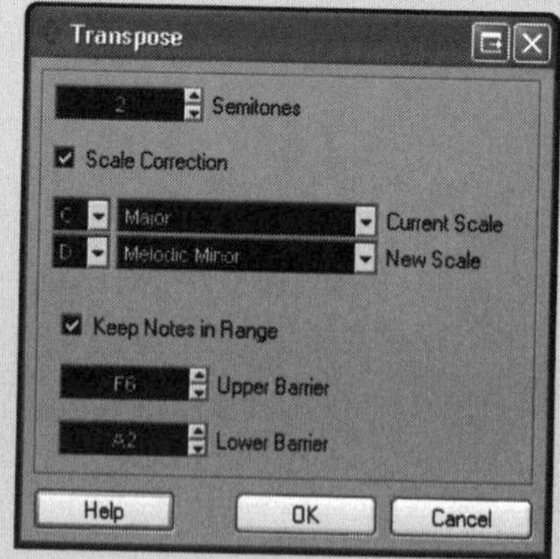

Figure 24.1
The dialog box for the MIDI menu's Transpose command.

4. Click OK to apply your changes.

Merge MIDI In Loop

Suppose you've applied different MIDI effects to a MIDI or instrument track as inserts or sends, and you've assigned different track parameter values to a MIDI part. When you are trying to edit certain details, you realize that the details you want to edit are transformed—or generated—in real time by the various settings you have assigned to this track. If you want to create a new version of the MIDI track, containing events that reflect the results of all MIDI effects and parameters you've previously assigned, you can use the Merge In Loop option found in the MIDI menu. Here's an example: You've recorded a piano accompaniment and played certain chords. Afterwards, you've applied the Track FX MIDI effect to adjust the notes in these chords to a different scale. When listening to your new chord coloring, you like the result, but you'd like to change a note in one of the chords so that it fits better with the rest of the arrangement. But because this is a real-time effect, you can't really change a note that you didn't play to begin with. That's when the Merge MIDI In Loop option comes in handy. The new merged track (containing the results of your real-time effects and parameters) can then be edited, and new track parameters or MIDI effects assigned to it. You will probably also want to merge all real-time MIDI effects and track parameters with recorded events before exporting MIDI parts to MIDI files to be used in another application.

HOW TO ❋

Use the Merge MIDI In Loop option:

1. Start by identifying the MIDI events you want to merge. This can be a MIDI part on one track or several MIDI parts on several tracks assigned to various MIDI channels.
2. After you've identified what you want to merge (or freeze), set the left and right locators to include this content.
3. Mute any other MIDI track you don't want to include in this process.
4. If you want to keep the original content intact, create a new MIDI track.
5. If you have chosen to create a new MIDI track for the merged destination, select it in the Track List area; otherwise, select the desired destination track (which might be the same track as the original content).
6. From the MIDI menu, select the Merge MIDI in Loop option. The MIDI Merge Options dialog box will appear, as displayed in Figure 24.2.

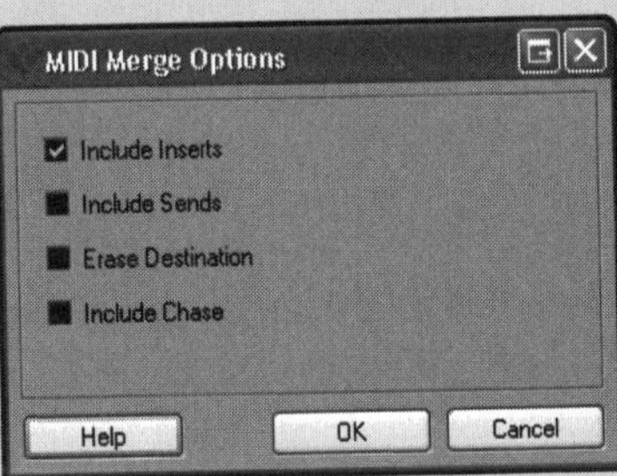

Figure 24.2
The MIDI Merge Options dialog box.

7. You have four options to enable or disable. The Include Inserts and Include Sends options convert any MIDI messages generated by these MIDI effects into MIDI events in the new merged part, which can be edited further if necessary. If you have selected a track that already contains MIDI events as the destination track for this command, you can choose to erase its content by checking the Erase Destination option. If you do not check this option, the new MIDI part will appear on top of any overlapping MIDI parts that already exist on the destination track. Finally, if you want to include Conrol Change values that are in effect prior to the selected range of events in the source track, such as program changes or pitch bend information, check the Include Chase option.
8. Click OK after setting your options.

Dissolve Parts

Suppose you have a MIDI file that you want to import into Cubase. You do so by using the Import MIDI File command (described later in this chapter), only to realize that this file contains only one track with all the different channel information and events on this single track. If you look at the example in Figure 24.3, the first track named Original contains MIDI events for three distinct MIDI channels. After applying the Dissolve function, three additional tracks appear below, each containing the program change messages, volume and pan settings, and MIDI events corresponding to each MIDI channel in the original multi-channel MIDI file.

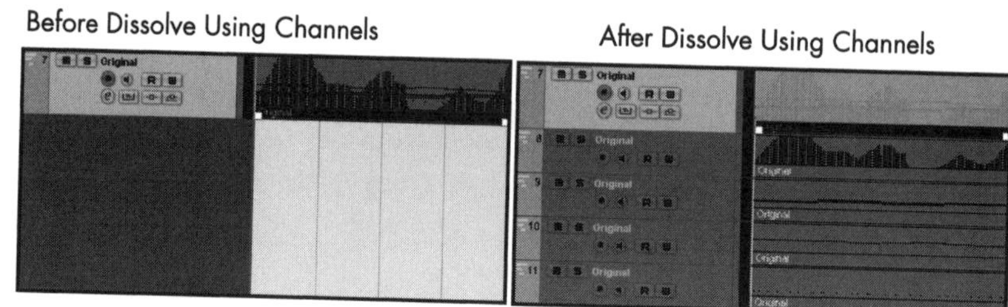

Figure 24.3
The first track has been dissolved into three tracks.

Similarly, you might record a drum pattern in Cycle mode using the LM-7 VSTi drum instrument, adding drum or percussion elements to your pattern every time the cycle repeats until you get a complete pattern. This is probably the simplest way to create a repeating MIDI drum part. But after all these percussion elements are recorded, they all end up in the same MIDI part. If you wanted to assign a MIDI insert or send effect specifically on the snare drum, this could only be done if each sound in the drum part is on a separate MIDI track. Because your drum figure is already recorded, you can use the Dissolve Part command and select the Separate Pitches option instead of the Separate Channels option. In Figure 24.4, the first track corresponds to the original drum loop. The following tracks contain the MIDI note events for each pitch actually used in the selected MIDI part (in this case, each MIDI note represents one sound of the LM-7 drum kit). By separating each drum sound to its own MIDI track, you can assign different MIDI effects to each piece of this virtual drum kit while still using only one instance of the VSTi as the MIDI output port for all of them. This also allows you to render each MIDI track as a separate audio track so that each drum instrument can be treated independently.

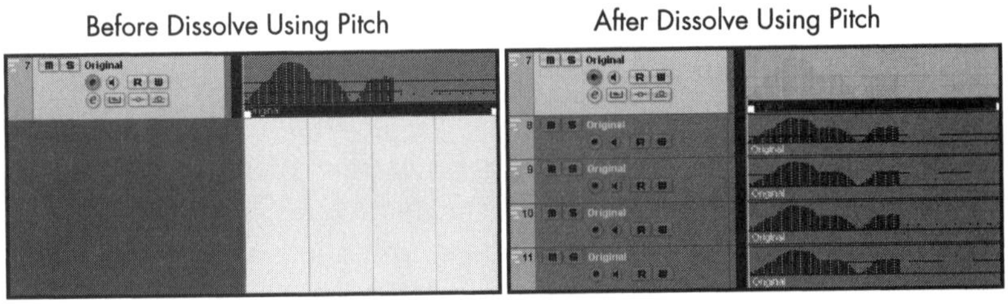

Before Dissolve Using Pitch

After Dissolve Using Pitch

Figure 24.4
An example of a dissolve by separating pitches.

HOW TO

Dissolve a MIDI part:

1. Select the MIDI part you want to dissolve.
2. In the MIDI menu, select the Dissolve Part option.
3. If the selected part contains MIDI events for more than one MIDI channel, Cubase offers you two choices: Separate Channels or Separate Pitches (see Figure 24.5). Select the appropriate option. On the other hand, if there are only MIDI events for one MIDI channel in the selected part, you can only separate pitches.

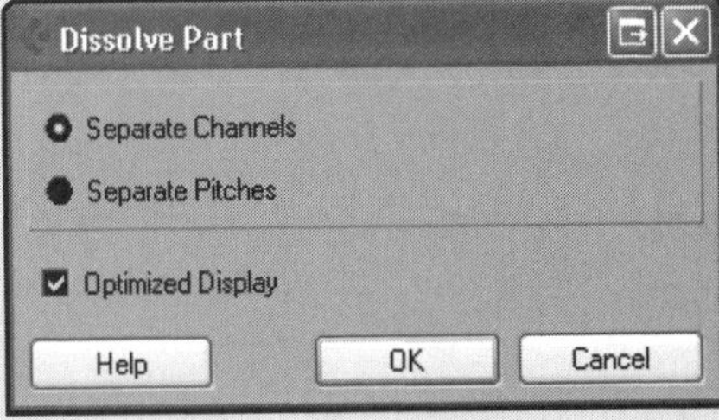

Figure 24.5
The Dissolve Part dialog box.

4. Click OK to continue.

Note that the original track is automatically muted after being dissolved.

O-Note Conversion

The concept of the O-Note command is directly related to drum maps; this function only becomes active when a MIDI part associated with a drum-mapped MIDI track has been selected. Drum maps use three specific note names to identify a drum instrument: the pitch, the I-Note (input note), and the O-Note (output note). The pitch is associated with a drum instrument and cannot be modified. So, a C1 can be associated with a kick drum, for example. The I-Note is the note you play on your MIDI controller to trigger a specific instrument. In practice, playing a C1 note should trigger a kick drum because that's what is loaded for this MIDI note number in the destination instrument. The O-Note is the note sent out by the drum map when that I-Note is received. In theory, the I-Note and the O-Note are usually the same.

Why all these note names? Well, sometimes you might want to reorganize which note triggers which instrument to lay out the drum kit more efficiently on your keyboard. This can make it easier, for example, to play a drum part on notes you are accustomed to using, even when the currently selected VSTi or external MIDI module uses some other mapping for its drum sounds. That's when you start playing with the drum mapping in Cubase, changing the I-Note and O-Note values. As long as your MIDI part plays through this drum map within Cubase, you are fine, but if you want to convert this to a *non*-drum-mapped track to export your file as a MIDI file, you need to convert the drum map appropriately so that the MIDI note events in the result correspond to the output note currently being played by the drum map. And that's when you need to use the O-Note Conversion tool. This permanently converts the MIDI note number values according to whatever O-Note mapping is currently in effect. This allows you to play the part afterwards as a regular MIDI track (without any drum map) while still hearing the appropriate sounds played by the drum kit for which this MIDI track is intended.

HOW TO

Perform an O-Note conversion:

1. Select the MIDI part(s) with drum maps in effect that you want to convert.
2. From the MIDI menu, select the O-Note Conversion command.
3. A warning message might appear; click Yes if you want to proceed anyway or Cancel if you are not sure this is what you want to do.

About MIDI Functions

The commands in the Functions submenu of the MIDI menu play a similar role to MIDI track parameters. However, there are different reasons that would motivate you to use a MIDI function rather than a real-time setting in the track parameters. For example, track parameters affect all events (parts) on a given track, whereas MIDI functions can be applied to selected parts in the Project window or selected events in any MIDI editor window. Another example is that the results of parameter settings do not show up in the MIDI editor, whereas MIDI functions actually change the appropriate value in the actual MIDI events, therefore making their results visible in the MIDI editor. In other words, if you want to try things out before committing to them, you can use the track parameters, but when you want to alter the track's MIDI events permanently, you are better off using the MIDI functions.

Most of the commands in the Functions submenu are self explanatory. For example, Delete Doubles deletes any duplicate MIDI events within the current selection (two notes starting at the same time and at the same pitch). Some of these functions display a dialog box, whereas others perform their task without needing additional input.

HOW TO

Use a MIDI function:

1. In the Project window, select the parts you want to edit, or, if you don't want to affect all the events in the part, open the MIDI part in one of the MIDI editors and select the events you want to edit.
2. In the MIDI > Functions submenu, select the MIDI function you want to apply.
3. Change any values needed in the dialog box if one shows up and click OK to complete; otherwise, the function is automatically applied.

V } Arranging

25 Quantizing Your Events

Quantizing makes events cling to a virtual grid. As you record MIDI performances, notes might be recorded a little bit before or after a beat. Humans are not as steady and consistent as the timing in Cubase, nor would we want them to be when it comes to the music's feel. To make events fall more closely into place and on the beat, you can use the Quantize function to nudge MIDI events to their nearest increment on a time grid, according to the current quantize value. For example, setting the quantize value to quarter notes (¼) will make all recorded notes cling to quarter notes. Setting the quantize value to a lesser note value splits the grid into smaller, more precise subdivisions.

Quantizing MIDI events affects the way MIDI events are played back, but it does not alter the recorded material. It merely acts as an output filter, while the original position values are usually stored with the project regardless of the undo history list. If you desire, the Freeze Quantize function will permanently replace the original timing of the MIDI events with their quantized locations. After the quantization is frozen and the original timing is replaced, you can still re-quantize MIDI events to some other quantize groove or setting. However, the original position of frozen events is lost, being replaced by the quantized position of these events at the moment when the MIDI > Advanced Quantize > Freeze Quantize command was applied.

Here's a summary of what you will learn in this chapter:

- How to set up an appropriate Snap mode
- What the quantize parameters are
- How to save, rename, or delete a quantize setting to or from a preset list
- How to apply an automatic quantize value during the recording or editing process
- How to apply a quantize method to selected events
- How to undo quantization on selected events
- How to create a groove quantize preset based on selected MIDI events

Quantize Methods

The basic quantize method consists of moving the start of an event to the closest time increment on the quantize grid and is called *over quantizing*. Cubase offers four quantize methods, applying a different quantize rule each time for more control.

As displayed in Figure 25.1, the same original content (found in the upper-left corner) has been altered with different quantization methods. All these examples use the same eighth-note quantize grid.

- **Over quantize method.** This moves the start position of the event to the closest quantize grid setting.
- **End quantize method.** This moves the end position of the event to the closest quantize grid setting.
- **Length quantize method.** This does not affect the start position, but adjusts the duration of each MIDI note event to match the value of the quantize grid setting. In the example in Figure 25.1, each note is $\frac{1}{8}$ note in length.
- **Iterative quantize method.** This is a looser version of the over quantize method because it moves the start position of an event only a certain percentage of the distance toward the nearest increment on the quantize grid, as indicated in the Iterative Strength field in the Quantize Setup window. Iterative quantize uses the current location (this could be the quantized location) of the event rather than its original location (unquantized location). You can therefore quantize an event and then requantize it differently using the iterative quantize method.

The Quantize Setup window offers a beefed-up version of the over quantize method with controls over a number of different parameters that help make the quantized events sound more natural. This window gives you the opportunity to move an otherwise pretty square and static grid around, changing its reference points by different increments. Here are the controls you have over the grid in the Quantize Setup window (see Figure 25.2):

- **Grid** pop-up. This sets the quantize reference value for the grid. The values displayed in the Grid pop-up menu represent note subdivisions, as seen in Chapter 16.
- **Type** pop-up. This modifies the note value selected in the Grid field between straight, dotted, and triplet, which was also discussed in Chapter 16. So, for example, selecting the eighth-note value in the Grid pop-up and the triplet type creates a gridline every $\frac{1}{8}$ triplet.
- **Swing slider.** This shifts the position of a straight grid type, displacing the upbeats (that is, every second instance of the specified note value) to a slightly later position in order to produce a swing or a shuffle feeling. This works best when the Tuplet field is set to Off. As you can see in Figure 25.2, the Swing slider is set at 54%. If you look at the graphic grid

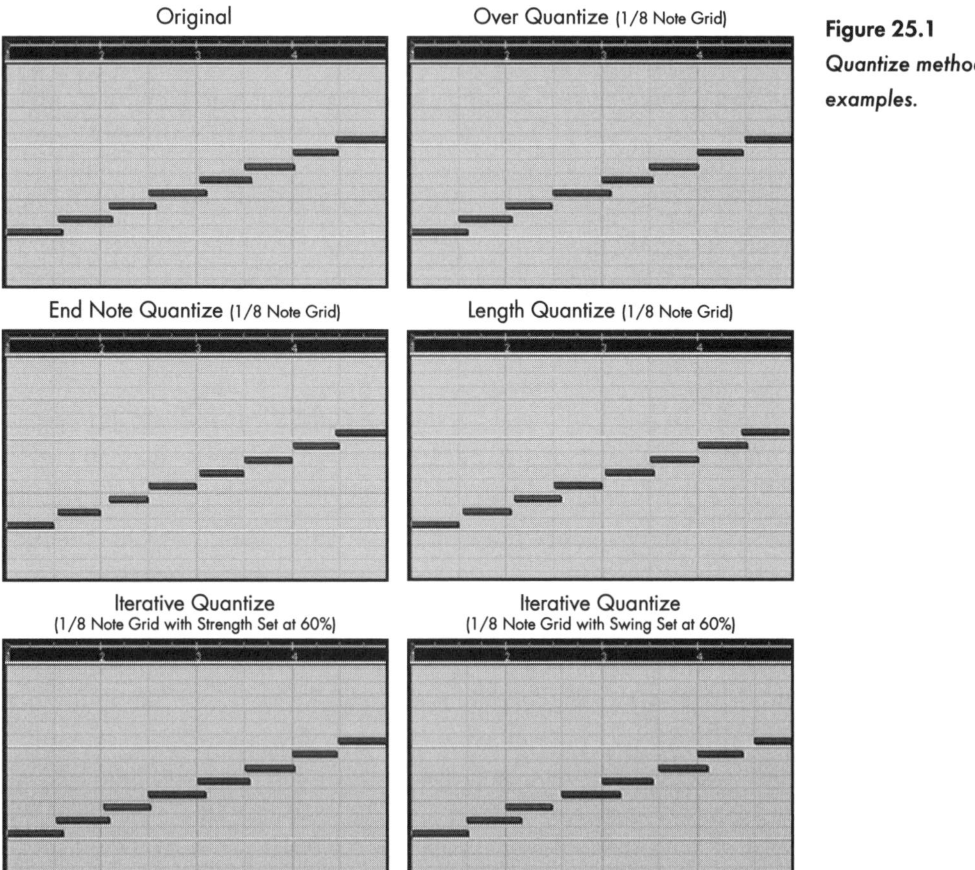

Figure 25.1
Quantize method examples.

display in the middle of the Quantize Setup window, the actual straight $\frac{1}{16}$ grid is shown in thin gray vertical lines, whereas the grid according to the current swing settings is indicated by the bold blue lines at the bottom of this same grid display.

- **Tuplet field.** This further subdivides the note value currently selected in the Grid field, to accommodate other rhythmic groupings that aren't binary (multiples of two), including triplets (which can already be selected more easily in the previously mentioned Type selector), quintuplets, septuplets, and so on. For example, selecting a Grid value of ¼ notes with a Tuplet value of 5 creates a grid of ⅛-note quintuplets—since there will be five grid subdivisions in the space of every ¼ note.

- **Magnetic Area slider.** This sets the area that note events must fall within in relation to the current grid setting in order to be affected by the quantization operation at all, by creating a magnetic field around each increment of the quantize grid. Quantization pulls any note events within that magnetic area toward the corresponding gridline, while events beyond that distance from the grid increment are not affected. The magnetic area is represented by a pale blue shaded area around the previously mentioned thick blue lines that represent the current quantize grid increments in this window's grid display.
- **Grid Display.** Found in the center of the Quantize Setup panel, this shows the result of your settings in the Grid Quantize area above. The entire display area represents a single $^4/_4$ bar.
- **Presets area.** This allows you to select different quantize presets that are stored on your computer and create or remove your own presets. You can also create "groove" quantize templates from audio loops, which will be discussed later in this chapter.
- **Non Quantize field.** This establishes an area around the center of each increment on the quantize grid, within which note events are *not* affected. Each tick value represents $^1/_{120}$ of a sixteenth-note. In other words, any note already found within this range is left un-quantized, creating a more human-like (read "looser") feel to the quantization. In this case, quantization would be applied only to notes whose position is outside of the non-quantize area that surrounds each grid increment.
- **Random Quantize field.** This is another feature that enables you to humanize the effect of quantization by adding small, random amounts of variation to the resultant position of the quantized notes. In Figure 25.2, the Random Quantize field adds or subtracts up to six ticks from every note that is affected by the quantization.
- **Iterative Strength field.** This sets the strength level of an iterative quantize method. With higher percentage values, events are moved closer to the nearest grid increment as specified by your current quantization settings. With lower percentage values, events are not moved as close to the grid setting, allowing for more variations. In other words, 0% strength would not move the notes at all, while 100% moves them all the way to the grid increment, as in normal over quantize mode.

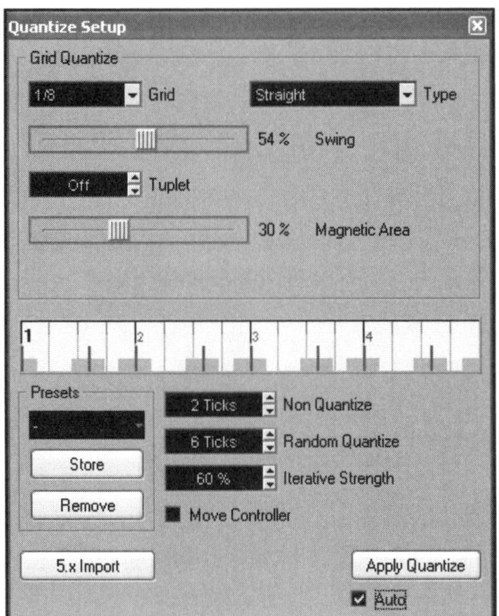

Figure 25.2
The Quantize Setup panel.

Setting Up a Quantize Grid

We've discussed how quantize grids work and looked at how you can magnetize different elements in the Project window using various Snap modes. Some Snap modes don't take the grid into consideration and therefore won't be affected by the currently selected Quantize Type; however, the Grid Type (in the Snap Mode field) not only affects movement of events, but also influences where parts are created and where markers will be placed. In other words, selecting an appropriate Grid and Quantize Type for the task at hand will help you get the result you want more effectively. For example, if you enable the Snap Grid mode and assign musical bars as your Grid Type, when you create a new part using the Draw (pencil) tool or when you record an event, the newly created part or recorded event will start at the closest bar from its beginning and will end at the closest bar after you stop recording or let go of the Draw tool. In such an example, as you create parts or events, their length could only be increased or decreased by one bar at a time. Here's another example: If you're working with a video file and you only want to create events that begin or end on a frame change, you can change your Ruler to display timecode and select the appropriate value in the Grid Type—in this example, one frame. By doing so, whenever you record a new event or draw in a part to hold events (MIDI or audio), it will begin and end only at the same moment a frame ends and another one begins.

HOW TO

Set up an appropriate Snap mode:

1. Enable the Snap On/Off button.
2. Select the appropriate Snap mode. For example, select Grid.
3. Select the appropriate Grid Type. For example, if you choose Grid and the Ruler format is set to Bars+Beats, you could select Bar, Beats, or Use Quantize. If you choose Use Quantize, you will additionally need to select an appropriate Quantize Type to complete the setup.
4. If you choose the Use Quantize Grid Type, select an appropriate Quantize Type note value (or custom groove template) for your grid.

If in the Snap mode selector you choose Events, Shuffle, or Magnetic Cursor rather than Grid, the quantize value has no effect when you resize or move events.

Quantize Parameters

Because the quantize setting influences how events are quantized, no matter which method you use, it's a good idea to start by setting up how you want Cubase to quantize these events before applying a method. This is especially true with the auto-quantize method.

HOW TO

Set up quantize parameters:

1. Select Quantize Setup from the MIDI menu to open the Quantize Setup window (as shown in Figure 25.2). If you already have a preset saved, select it from the Presets drop-down menu. Otherwise, complete the following steps.
2. From the Grid drop-down menu, select a grid value. Which one depends on the content you want to quantize.
3. From the Type drop-down menu, select a type setting. Straight is the most common grid type.
4. If you want to use tuplets, use the up or down arrow to the right of the Tuplet field to select the appropriate tuplet number. A tuplet is a beat subdivision that is greater than four, such as a quintuplet, in which five notes are played within a quarter note. Otherwise, leave this field displaying the Off selection.
5. If you want to create a Swing or Shuffle feel, click and drag the Swing slider to the right. Higher percentages result in more pronounced swing or shuffle feels.

Monitoring Quantize Setup Changes Before Applying Them

Check the Auto check box in the Quantize Setup window to monitor changes you make before applying them. When you click Play, you will hear the effect of the quantize settings as you change them in the panel without committing to them. This dynamic preview, however, is only available with MIDI events. You can apply a quantize setting to audio events or audio slices inside a part, but changing the quantize setup only affects the audio when you click the Apply button in the Quantize Setup window.

6. Set the Non Quantize value appropriately by using the up or down arrow. Remember that events within this range are not affected by the quantization.
7. Set the Random Quantize value appropriately by using the up or down arrow.
8. If you want to use the iterative quantize method (which, like Over Quantize, is available as a command under the MIDI menu), set the strength value by using the appropriate field in the Quantize Setup panel. The higher the value, the more its effect resembles that of the over quantize method (and at 100% strength is identical).

Now that you have set up your quantization properties and saved them as a preset that you can use later, you can use existing custom or default presets or delete presets you no longer use or need. Remember that a song's feeling is greatly influenced by its rhythmic definition. This definition is the result of rhythmic consistency throughout the instruments, the parts, and the project itself. Saving your own presets for quantize settings and reusing these presets throughout a project can help achieve this consistency.

HOW TO

Save a quantize setting to a preset:

1. Click the Store button in the Quantize Setup window to create a new preset.
2. Double-click the new preset to rename it. The Type In Preset Name dialog box will appear (see Figure 25.3) with the default name given to your preset.
3. Type in the new name and click OK to close the dialog box.

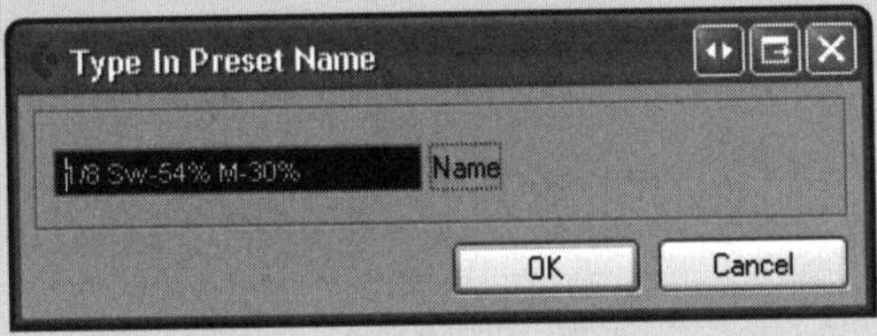

Figure 25.3
The Type In Preset Name dialog box.

HOW TO

Remove a quantize setting from the preset list:

1. From the Quantize Setup window's Presets drop-down menu, select the preset you want to remove.
2. Click the Remove button.

Applying Quantize

You can apply a quantize setup in a variety of ways. Here are a few that you can try out.

- Apply a standard over quantize method to already recorded events. Depending on which window is open when you click Apply, this method shifts the start position of selected events to the closest gridline set in the Project window or the current MIDI editor.
- Apply an automatic quantize value during the recording process. This records the note events exactly as you play them, but automatically adjusts their positions in the resultant MIDI part according to the quantize settings of your project. In other words, you can still unquantize events that were recorded with the Auto-Quantize (the AUTO Q button in the Transport panel) feature enabled.
- Use the Quantize Setup panel, which gives you more control over the effect quantization has on your recorded MIDI note events. For example, using the different parameters available in this panel, you can adjust the strength of the quantization, the swing factor, and the magnetic area of the grid, as well as create a grid for more complex rhythmic values, such as quintuplets and septuplets.
- Use the Quantizer, a MIDI plug-in, or a track's insert or send effect.

HOW TO

Apply an automatic quantize value during the recording process:

1. Choose the appropriate Grid Type and Quantize Grid or Quantize Setup Groove preset.
2. Enable the Auto-Quantize (AUTO Q) button on the Transport panel.
3. Start the recording process.

HOW TO

Apply an automatic quantize value during the editing process:

1. Open the MIDI part you want to edit in the MIDI editor.
2. Open the Quantize Setup window and choose the appropriate quantize settings.
3. Check the Auto option in the Quantize Setup window. Any changes you make in the Quantize Settings window from this point forward affect the events in the MIDI editor.

HOW TO

Apply a quantize method to selected events:

1. Choose the appropriate quantize setup or quantize grid setting.
2. Select the events or parts you want to quantize.
3. Press the Q key on your computer keyboard, or select the appropriate method you want to use from the MIDI menu: Over Quantize (Q on your computer keyboard), Iterative (Alt+Q on PC, Option+Q on Macintosh), or Quantize Ends or Quantize Lengths (in the Advanced Quantize submenu).

Within MIDI editors, you can also quantize the length of MIDI events using the Length Quantize drop-down menu in the MIDI editor's toolbar to apply the specified length value to the currently selected MIDI note events.

HOW TO

Undo quantization on selected events:

1. Select the events or parts you want to unquantize.
2. From the MIDI menu, select Advanced Quantize > Undo Quantize.

Creating Groove Quantize Presets

Cubase also offers the possibility to create a customized quantize setting, which is extracted from the rhythmic content of previously recorded MIDI events. For example, you might record a drum part and get just the groove you are looking for. Because the rhythmic "groove" of the percussions and drum parts is usually something you would want to apply to other musical parts, you can convert the MIDI groove you played into a reusable groove template (called a groove quantize map) that can be applied to other MIDI parts.

HOW TO

Create a groove quantize map from MIDI events:

1. In the Project window, select the MIDI part containing the groove you want to save. Note that the groove quantize map will only contain the MIDI events' rhythmic and velocity information.
2. Select from the menu bar MIDI > Advanced Quantize > Part to Groove.

When you create a groove quantize map, it will appear in the Presets drop-down menu of the Quantize Setup window. Once a groove quantize map is selected, the Quantize Setup window will offer a different set of controls from those described previously in this chapter for ordinary quantization.

- **Position.** Think of the position parameter as being like the iterative strength, where the position percentage represents the strength of the quantization from the groove's source. The difference between the normal iterative strength value and the position is that the latter influences the groove quantization applied *after* a possible pre-quantize setting (see below).
- **Velocity.** This indicates what percentage of the groove quantize map's velocity levels is applied to the velocity of the selected events. With higher values, the resultant velocities are closer to the groove quantize map than to the original. With lower values, velocities are not changed as much, with no change if the value is set at zero.
- **Length.** This indicates what percentage of the groove quantize map's length values is applied to the selected events' recorded length. With higher values, the resultant lengths are closer to the groove preset's length than to the original. With lower values, lengths are not changed as much, with no change if the value is set at zero.
- **Prequantize.** This quantizes events to a selected note value *before* applying the groove quantize map to increase the rhythmic accuracy of the events.
- **Maximum Move in Ticks.** Ticks are the smallest time increments inside a Cubase project. This parameter determines the maximum distance a MIDI event will be allowed to move from its original recorded position.
- **5.x Import.** This allows you to import groove quantize presets from Cubase VST 5.x versions.

Inside the MIDI editors, you apply a groove quantize map as you would apply any another quantize type—by selecting the desired events and then selecting that groove quantize map in the toolbar's quantize type field.

26 MIDI Track Effects

MIDI track effects allow you to transform MIDI events in a track in real time, without changing how the events were originally recorded. In other words, a MIDI track effect transforms the track's events on their way out to the MIDI output port. Imagine you're looking at your reflection in a distorted mirror at the county fair. You do not actually have a big head, small neck, big belly, and small legs, as seen in the reflection. You simply appear like that in the mirror. This chapter discusses the MIDI Modifiers, MIDI Inserts, and MIDI Sends sections of the Inspector area—all of which transform the data going out, giving you a transformed stream of MIDI events. Because MIDI track effects don't affect the source MIDI events in the track, these modifications do not appear in the MIDI editors. Also, keep in mind that MIDI track effects applied through the Inspector affect all the parts on a track.

Here's a summary of what you will learn in this chapter:

- How to use the MIDI Modifiers section of the Inspector for a MIDI or instrument track
- What the role of MIDI effects is
- How to add or edit MIDI inserts in a MIDI or instrument track
- How to bypass one or several MIDI inserts or MIDI sends
- How to assign a MIDI plug-in effect as the destination for a MIDI send

MIDI Modifiers

The parameters found under the MIDI Modifiers section provide a convenient way to try out things without changing the original MIDI messages, because you can bypass these parameters at any time by activating the Bypass button next to this section's name in the Inspector (see Figure 26.1). As soon as any parameter is modified in the MIDI Modifiers section, the indicator in the upper-right corner of the MIDI Modifiers section turns purple. When you click Bypass button for the entire MIDI Modifiers section (to the left of the Active MIDI Modifiers button), a yellow rectangle in this button indicates that this section is bypassed. Whenever you bypass the MIDI Modifiers settings, the track will play the MIDI events on the track as if there were no MIDI Modifiers applied to the track. This is very useful when you want to do a comparison listening of your events.

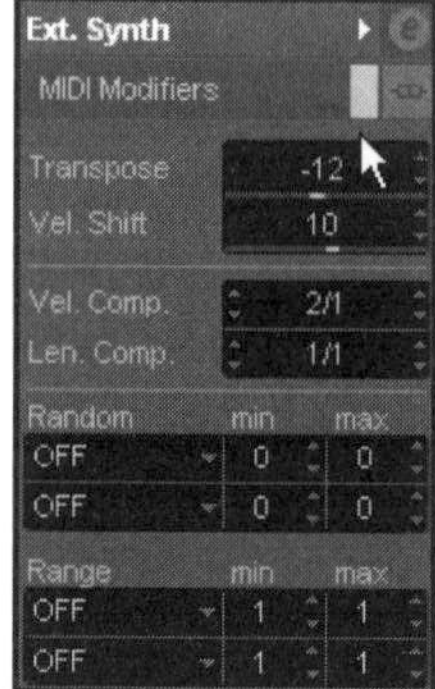

Figure 26.1
The MIDI Modifiers section.

The Transpose field enables you to set a value between −127 and +127. Each value corresponds to a semitone below or above the current note. Positive values shift notes higher; negative values shift notes lower. The Transpose setting in the Inspector affects all the notes found on this track. If you want to try changing the pitch of a song to find out whether you can sing it better in another key, this is a great tool to use.

The Velocity Shift field sets a value between −127 and +127 as well; however, in this case, these values add or remove that value from the Note On velocity of all MIDI events on the selected track. For example, adding a value of 10 causes all MIDI events to play at their recorded velocity plus 10. When most of what you recorded is great, except that the MIDI events were recorded slightly too soft (low velocity) or too loud (high velocity), use this to alter the overall velocity of your recorded events. You might also find this is a quick fix when you change the destination patch or MIDI device for a track and discover that the originally recorded velocities are too high or low for the sound that is now playing these MIDI events.

The Velocity Compression field uses a proportion, which compresses or expands the velocity of MIDI events on a track by the corresponding multiplication factor. This factor is defined by a numerator (left value) and a denominator (right value). The resulting fraction is applied to the Note-On velocity level of all the MIDI events on this track. You can see an example of this in the first and second rows of Table 26.1.

Table 26.1
How Track Parameters Affect MIDI Events

Track Parameter	Note 1	Note 2	Note 3	Note 4	Comment
Before Filters					
Velocity Value	50	70	35	100	Recorded velocities
Vel. Comp. (1/2)	25	35	17	50	Velocities heard after compression
Vel. Shift (+50)	50	50	50	50	Added to the previous velocities when heard
After Filter	75	85	67	100	Resulting velocity that can be heard

The Length Compression field also uses a proportion, which compresses or expands the length of MIDI events on a track by the corresponding multiplication factor. This factor is also defined by a numerator (left value) and a denominator (right value). For example, a factor of 2:1 means that all notes will be of double length, and a factor of 1:3 means that all notes will be one-third their original lengths. Note that this does not affect the start point of these events in time, only their lengths.

Below the Length Compression field are two Random generators with their corresponding fields. These two fields act independently from one another and serve to introduce random values to the position, pitch, velocity, or length of MIDI events on this track. This can be useful with clear rhythmic or melodic parts rather than with tracks containing long sustained notes. In other words, the randomness is more obvious when events occur more often. Under each Random generator is a field that lets you choose what type of randomly generated value you want to add (position, pitch, velocity, or length). You can then set a minimum and maximum value for these random values. A wider range between the minimum and maximum values creates a more pronounced effect, whereas a smaller range creates a more subtle effect. With the position and length selections, you can set the minimum and maximum values from −500 ticks to +500 ticks, respectively. For the pitch and velocity, you can set these values between −120 and +120. (This corresponds to semitones when used with pitch.) Note that velocity can't be outside the range of 0 and 127, no matter what values you set here; Cubase won't let you set any minimum value here to a higher value than the maximum.

At the bottom of the MIDI Modifiers section are two Range fields with associated minimum and maximum values that work just like the random minimum and maximum fields. However, in this case, the Range fields (as the name suggests) are used to set a range for which events are included or excluded from processing. There are four Range modes:

- **Velocity Limit.** Use this mode when you want all notes to play within a certain velocity range. Any note with a Note On velocity outside the range is either brought up to the minimum value in the range if it is below this value or brought down to the maximum value in the range if it is above this value. Any other velocity values (which are found within the defined range) play unchanged.

- **Velocity Filter.** Use this mode when you want to isolate only notes that have Note On velocities within a certain velocity range. Notes outside that range, either above or below, are simply not played back.
- **Note Limit.** Use this mode when you want all notes to be within a range of notes. Note values that are below or above this range are transposed an octave up or down, as appropriate, in order for their resultant pitches to be within the range. If your range is too narrow (i.e., if it spans less than an octave) and notes still can't fall within it after transposing an octave up or down, they are transposed to the center note value found within your range. For example, with a Note Limit range between C4 and G4, A4 is transposed to an E4 since no A is available within the range.
- **Note Filter.** Use this mode when you want to isolate only notes within a certain range. Notes outside the range are filtered out (not played back).

Customizing the Inspector

You can customize the sections displayed in the Inspector by right-clicking (PC)/Control-clicking (Mac), inside the Inspector over an existing section header, as displayed in Figure 26.2. Adding a check mark next to the entry in this context menu will display the corresponding section. Use this customization to hide sections you don't use often and display those you use regularly. Hiding a section does not affect any settings within it (or the rest of the Inspector settings).

To save your custom Inspector view, use the Setup command in the context menu.

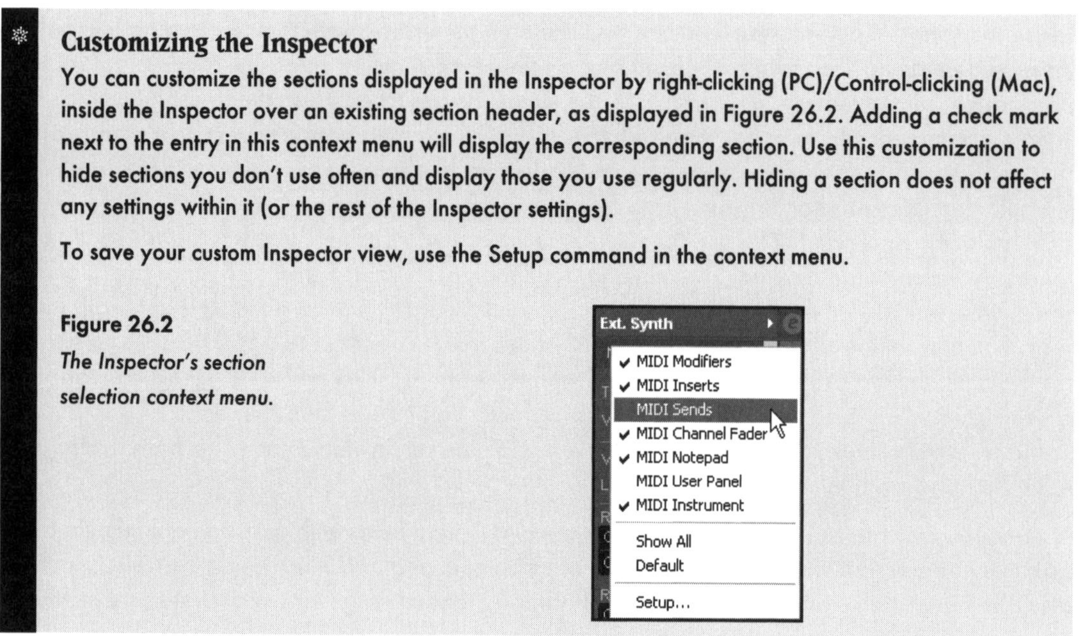

Figure 26.2
The Inspector's section selection context menu.

About MIDI Effects

You may already know about audio effects and how you can use them to make audio tracks sound better or different. In this respect, MIDI effects are similar to audio effects. However, the process is quite different with MIDI than it is for audio. When you apply a MIDI effect to a MIDI track, you are not processing the sound generated by the MIDI device (a VST instrument or hardware sound module, for instance). In fact, you are using a process that operates in real time as it transforms or adds to the MIDI events recorded on your track (or passing through it from its input) in real time, as do the options in the MIDI Modifiers section of the Inspector. For example, when you are adding a MIDI delay to your MIDI track, Cubase generates additional MIDI messages to simulate an echo effect by using MIDI notes. Because these effects are playing in real time, just like audio effects, you can rest assured that the recorded MIDI events on your track are not modified in any way except at the insert point or send destination where the MIDI effect actually does its processing.

If you are using an instrument track, you can combine both types of effects—audio and MIDI. This gives you even more flexibility in your creative process. A MIDI effect can be applied to any MIDI track in two ways: through MIDI inserts and MIDI sends. On the other hand, instrument tracks playing through a VSTi plug-in or an external MIDI device configured through the VST Connections window can also be processed using MIDI inserts, but not MIDI sends. Both MIDI inserts and MIDI sends transform the MIDI events in real time according to the settings found in the MIDI effect.

MIDI Inserts

The MIDI Inserts section adds a MIDI plug-in effect to your MIDI or instrument track. When you are using a MIDI plug-in effect as an insert, you are sending the track's MIDI events through this effect. This effect then generates the necessary MIDI events through the MIDI output port of the track containing the effect. It is the destination VSTi or external sound module's job to actually play the resulting MIDI effect along with the original recorded MIDI material in this track. You can have up to four MIDI insert effects on each MIDI track. When a MIDI insert effect is selected from the drop-down menu in each of the track's insert slots, a control panel opens up to reveal its settings. Once closed, you can access the insert's control panel by clicking on the Open Inserts Settings button above the appropriate insert. You also can force Cubase to open the parameters of a MIDI effect in their own window if, by default, they open in the Track Inserts section, as is the case with the Quantizer plug-in (see Figure 26.3). Do this by Alt-clicking (PC)/Option-clicking (Mac) on the Edit MIDI Effect button. Here are some of the things you can do with MIDI inserts:

HOW TO

- **Add a MIDI insert effect.** Select a MIDI effect from the drop-down menu in one of the four insert slots.
- **Edit a MIDI insert effect's parameters.** Click the Open Inserts Settings button (see Figure 26.3).
- **Bypass an individual MIDI insert.** Deactivate the plug-in effect you want to bypass by clicking the Activate Insert button. By default, an effect is activated as soon as you select it from the drop-down

menu. By deactivating it (see the Quantizer in Figure 26.3), you can do a comparison listening without having to reset your effect each time.

- **Bypass all MIDI inserts from playback.** Click the Bypass Inserts button at the top of the MIDI Inserts section. The MIDI Inserts section's top-right corner will turn yellow, indicating that the effects are bypassed. Because you can always see the top part of the Track Inserts section, you can easily change the status (active or bypassed) of your inserts by using this bar.

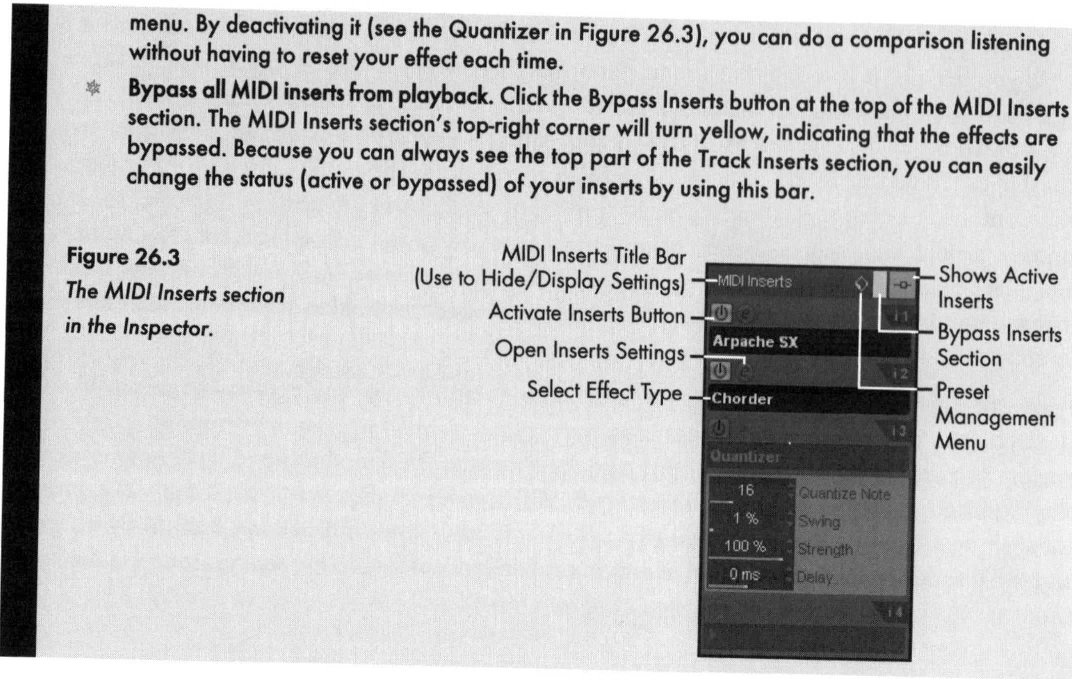

Figure 26.3
The MIDI Inserts section in the Inspector.

When you assign a MIDI plug-in effect to an insert slot, it affects the events sent to the MIDI output port of this track, as displayed in Figure 26.4. On the other hand, if you want to use one device to play the original content and another to play the processed information, you can use a MIDI send.

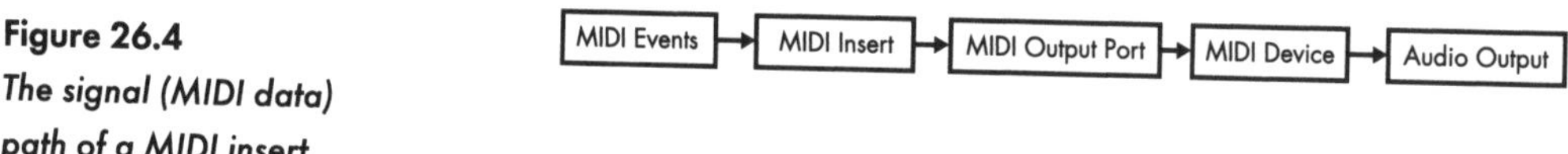

Figure 26.4
The signal (MIDI data) path of a MIDI insert.

MIDI Sends

The main difference between MIDI inserts and MIDI sends is that sends allow you to route the processed MIDI events generated by the MIDI effect to a second MIDI destination. MIDI track sends offer an additional setting for MIDI output ports and MIDI channels. As you can see in Figure 26.5, the signal can be routed to two different outputs. In other words, if you don't need the effect to play through a different MIDI port and channel, use the track insert. However, if you want your effect to play through some other port and channel, or you want to send the MIDI events before or after the volume control setting of the MIDI track, use MIDI sends instead of inserts.

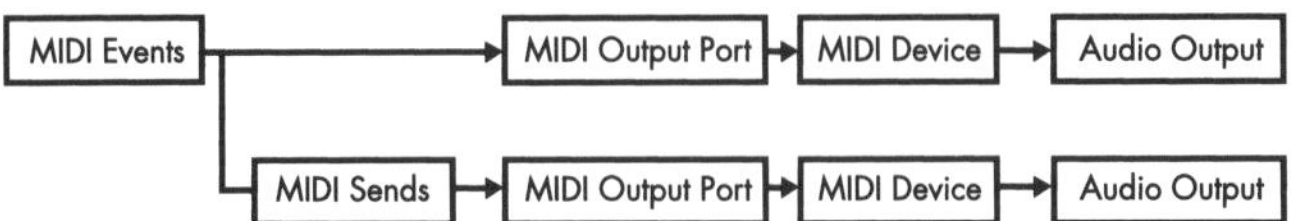

Figure 26.5
The signal path of a MIDI track send.

The options for the MIDI sends are fairly similar to the ones in the MIDI inserts section (see Figure 26.6). In addition to the options explained earlier, below the Select Effect Type field, you will find the MIDI Send Output Port selector that lets you choose the appropriate MIDI port that will be the destination for MIDI events generated by the MIDI effect, along with a MIDI channel setting. The Pre-/Post-MIDI Modifier toggle button lets you choose whether the MIDI events sent to the MIDI send output include the parameters found in the MIDI Modifiers section (the default Post- setting) or exclude them (Pre- setting).

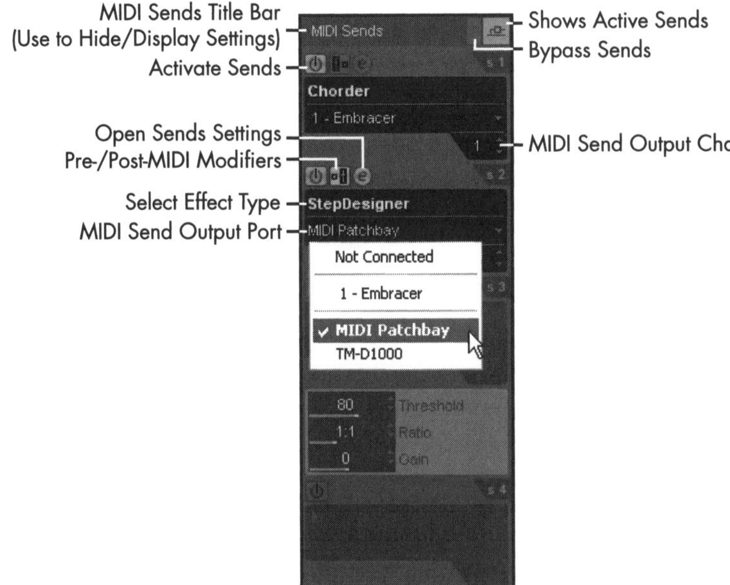

Figure 26.6
The MIDI Sends section in the Inspector.

HOW TO

Assign a MIDI plug-in effect to a MIDI send:

1. Unfold the MIDI Sends section for the selected MIDI track.
2. From the MIDI Effect Type drop-down menu, choose an appropriate effect.
3. In the selector below the MIDI Effect Type field, choose an appropriate MIDI port for the output of the MIDI effect. This affects where the MIDI events generated by the effect will be sent.
4. Next to the output port, select an appropriate MIDI channel for playback.
5. Select Pre- or Post-fader mode, according to your preference.

27 Edit Menu Options

Capturing performances and editing the audio and MIDI data inside the events to make them sound better is one thing, but organizing events inside a project's timeline or tracks offers perhaps the most flexible way for a producer to build (and rebuild) entire projects. Creating different mixes, versions, and styles is only possible if the events can be edited in time as easily as building with blocks in a Lego set. Splitting events and parts to move content around or having an event repeat 16 times are just two examples of this chapter's topics.

Here's a summary of what you will learn in this chapter:

- How to use the cursor location to split selected events
- How to split events to create movable blocks of music
- How to move and copy blocks of content defined by a locator range
- How to crop content inside a project
- How to insert additional empty time in a project
- How to use different Cubase-specific cut, copy, and paste functions
- How to resize objects and understand sizing options
- How to shift content inside events or parts
- How to mute objects
- How to lock objects in the timeline

The editing options inside the Project window are available in three places—in the Edit menu, through the Project window's context menu in the Edit submenu, and finally, through the editing tools found in the toolbar. This is where you find the basic cut, copy, and paste options, which work the same way as they do in any other application. In addition, you find other options specifically designed to give you more control over project-editing tasks.

Splitting

There are several options at your disposal when you want to divide objects in the Project window. The simplest and most common option consists of clicking the Scissors tool on an existing event. The exact position of the split is determined by the Snap's Grid settings if they are active or by the location of your click.

Split at Cursor

Sometimes it's easier to use the project's cursor position to determine where the split occurs, such as when you need to split all the events across all tracks in a project.

HOW TO

Split selected objects at the cursor's location:

1. Position the cursor at the desired location.
2. Select all the objects crossing the cursor at this location that you want to split. All non-selected objects will not be affected.
3. From the Edit menu, select the Split at Cursor command, as illustrated in Figure 27.1.

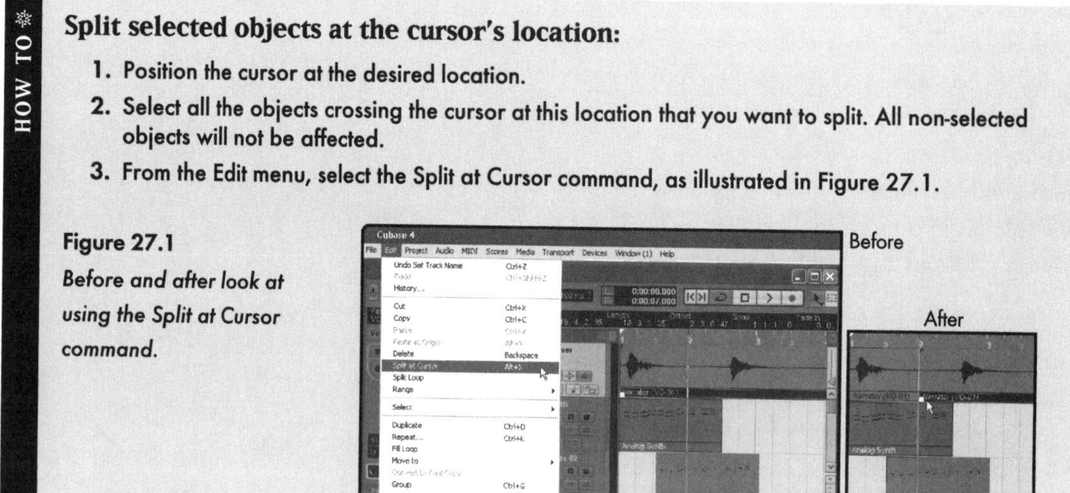

Figure 27.1
Before and after look at using the Split at Cursor command.

Split Loop

Use the locators' positions to determine where a split will occur when you want to create a loop with the objects (parts or events) between the locators' range. After these objects are split, for example, at bar 5 and bar 9, you can select only the objects that occur in this range and copy them elsewhere.

HOW TO

Split objects at the locators' position using Split Loop:

1. Position the left and right locators at the desired positions.
2. Select the objects you want to split.
3. From the Edit menu, select the Split Loop command. Selected objects crossing the left or right locators are split as displayed in Figure 27.2.

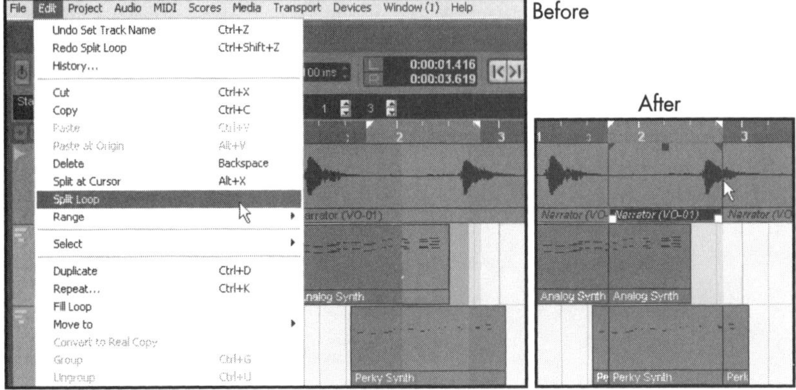

Figure 27.2
A before and after look at the Split Loop function applied to the locators' range.

Split Range

Using the Range tool with the Range > Split command, you also can achieve an effect similar to the Split Loop option. In this case, however, all the objects within the selected range would be split at the start and end positions of the selected range, instead of the range between the locators. The effect of the Split Range command is shown in Figure 27.3.

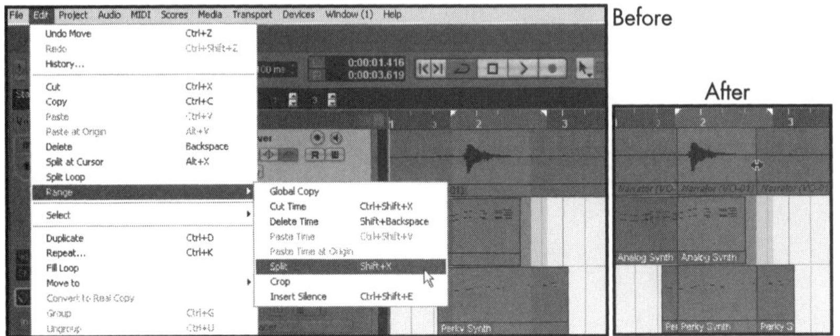

Figure 27.3
A before and after view of the Split Range function.

HOW TO

Split a range of selected objects:

1. Select the Range Selection tool.
2. Click in the upper-left corner where you want your range to begin and drag over the range and tracks you want to include in this range.
3. In the Edit menu, select the Range > Split command.

Range Crop

Another quick way to split objects is to use the Range > Crop command. Select the objects and range you want to keep, and all the rest will be removed (see Figure 27.4). This technique offers a quick way to build game scene soundtracks, where you build a score around prerecorded elements common to the entire game, but rearrange and crop only the content you want to keep for the current scene.

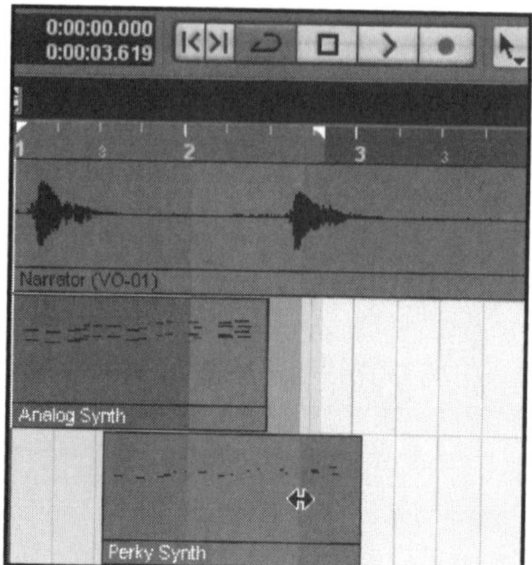

Before

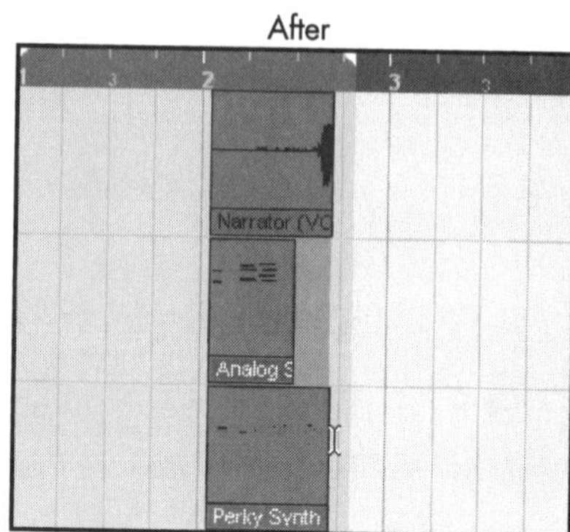

After

Figure 27.4
A before and after look at the Range Crop command applied to a selected range.

> **HOW TO**
>
> **Set the Range Crop command to a desired range:**
>
> 1. Select the Range Selection tool.
> 2. Click in the upper-left corner where you want your range to begin and drag over the range and the tracks you want to include in it.
> 3. In the Edit menu, select the Range > Crop command.

Insert Silence

The Insert Silence command in the Edit > Range submenu performs various tasks, depending on the tool used to make the selection prior to launching this command. With the Range Selection tool, all objects within the selection are moved to the end point of the selected range (see Figure 27.5). This technique is useful when you want to insert time in the middle of recorded events, but you don't want to apply the change to all tracks. On the other hand, to insert silence or add time at any point in the project over all tracks, click the Object Selection tool, set the locators' positions appropriately, and use the same Insert Silence command (Ctrl+Shift+E (PC)/ ⌘+Shift+E (Mac)). All events are split at the left locator position and moved after the right locator position, inserting silence in the range between both locators.

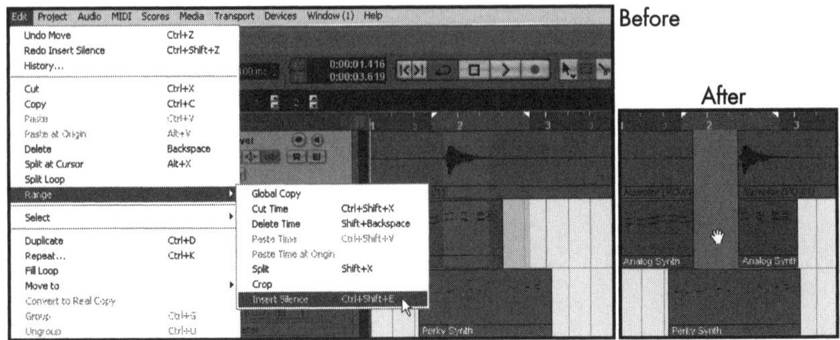

Figure 27.5
A before and after look at the Insert Silence command applied to a selected range.

Conversely, if you want to remove the time, including events recorded within this range, you can use the Delete Range command from the Edit > Range submenu. This deletes events within a selected range and deletes the time, moving all events following the range to its start point.

Pasting Functions

Using the Range Selection tool or a combination of the Object Selection tool and the locators, you can copy the content found inside a designated range and paste it back into the project using four different pasting commands: Paste, Paste at Origin, Paste Time, and Paste Time at Origin.

In Figure 27.6, the top track displays a highlighted selection made with the Range Selection tool. This selection was then copied to clipboard (Edit > Copy or its keyboard shortcut). With the project cursor position always at bar 4, here's what happens depending on the Paste function used:

- Using **Edit > Paste**, the clipboard content gets pasted after the cursor position without moving the content that follows further along the timeline.
- Using **Edit > Paste at Origin**, the clipboard content gets pasted at the same place in time. Use Paste at Origin to copy or move content from one track to another without changing its position in the timeline. Content following the newly pasted clipboard content does not move either.
- Using **Edit > Range > Paste Time**, the clipboard content gets pasted after the cursor position, moving the content that follows further along the timeline.
- Using **Edit > Range > Paste Time at Origin**, the clipboard content gets pasted at the same place in time, pushing the content that follows the newly pasted clipboard content further along the timeline.

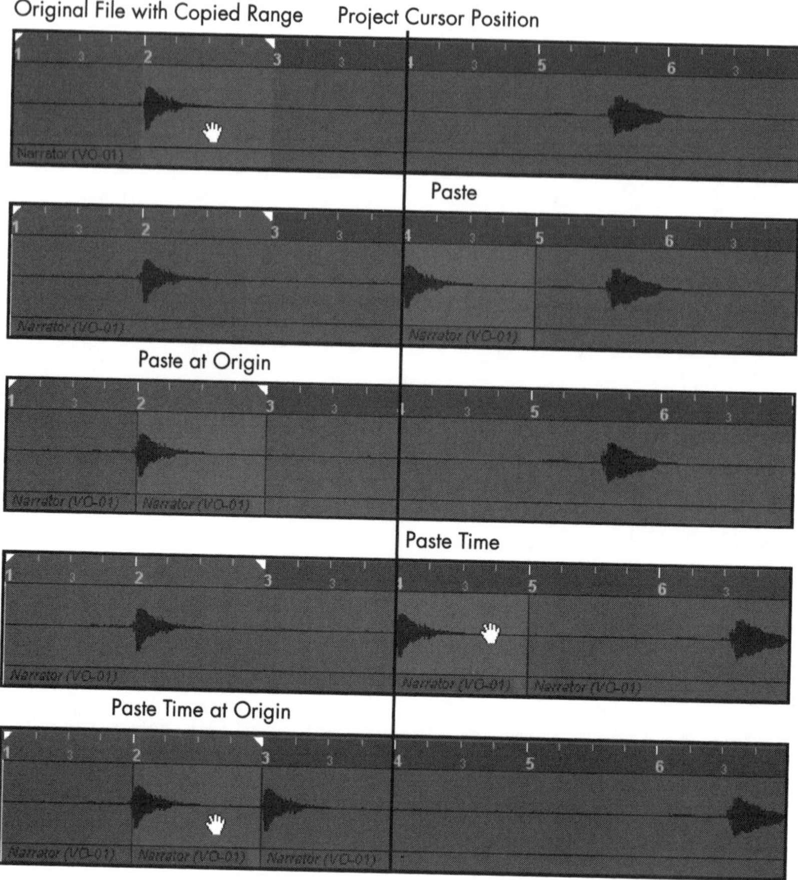

Figure 27.6
Differences between paste functions.

Copying

Cubase offers the standard copy/paste combination when you need to copy certain selected events from one location to another. Once again, content can be selected with the Range or Object Selection tools. For more specific copying applications, Cubase offers a variety of functions tailored to music production.

Duplicate

Use Duplicate from the Edit menu to make a single copy of selected events or parts. The start time of duplicated events occurs immediately following the end time of the selected object(s) being duplicated.

Figure 27.7 displays different results from a Duplicate action. In the top row, a single event is selected with the Object Selection tool and duplicated. As a result, the duplicated event begins immediately after the previous one ends. If you're working with loops, it makes sense to adjust the length of events with the Snap's Grid mode enabled. By doing so, you can avoid creating duplicate copies that aren't aligned with the tempo grid if the event happens to be slightly longer than the grid size. In the middle row, two events are selected with the Object Selection tool and duplicated. As a result, the duplicated events begin where the entire selection ends. Finally, in the bottom row, the Range Selection tool was used to highlight a range that overlaps multiple events, and the range was duplicated. The duplicated range begins where the previously highlighted range ends.

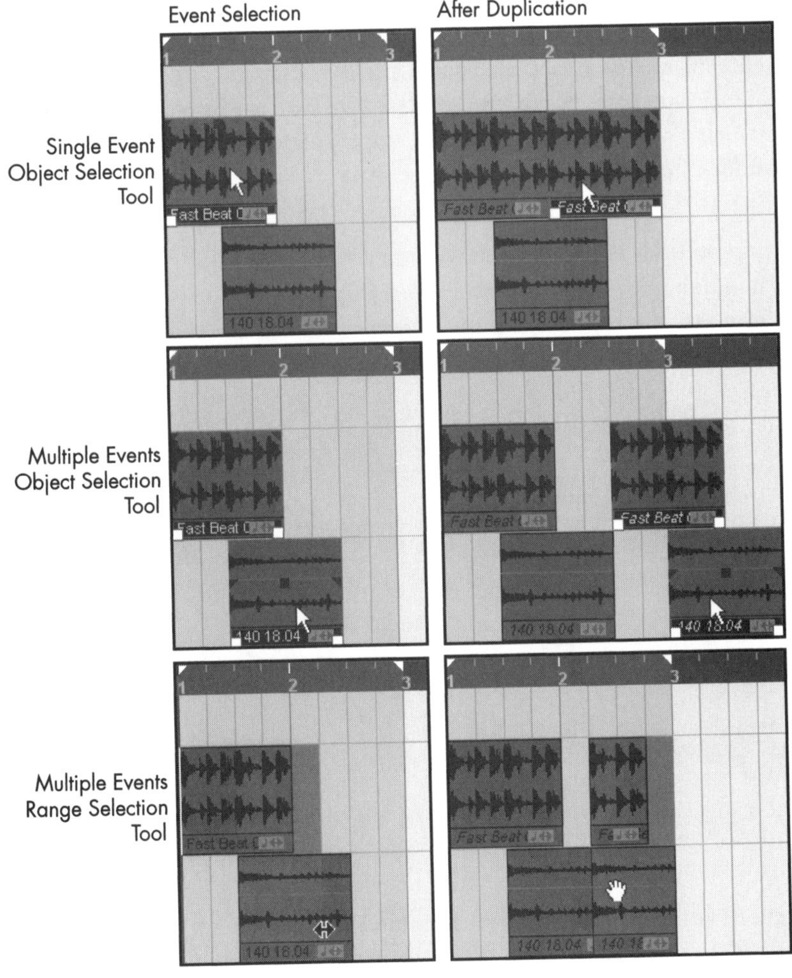

Figure 27.7
A look at the Duplicate command while using the Object and Range Selection tools.

HOW TO

Duplicate objects using the Object Selection or Range Selection tool:

1. Select the appropriate tool (Object Selection or Range Selection).
2. Select the objects or range you want to duplicate.
3. From the Edit menu, select the Duplicate command, or press Ctrl+D (PC)/⌘+D (Mac).

Repeat

To make more than one duplicate of a range or object selection, consider using the Repeat command from the Edit menu. This is a great way to repeat looped material several times instead of copying it over and over again. When repeating entire objects, you can share the copies, so when you edit one of the events, all shared repeated copies are automatically updated to reflect those edits. If you want to edit only one copy of the repeated material without affecting the others, either create real copies in the first place, or select the shared copy you want to edit and transform it into a real copy using the Edit > Convert to Real Copy option.

Cubase asks how many copies you want to make of the selected objects or range. If you are repeating objects, you will also be asked whether you want to create shared or real copies. The Repeat option follows the same behavior as described for the Duplicate option. In Figure 27.8, the repeated events start where the previous event ends. The copy at bar 3 has also been converted to a real copy, while the first two are shared instances. In Figure 27.9, the portion outside of the selected range is not repeated. Also, Cubase always assumes you want to create real copies when you use the Range Selection tool to repeat content.

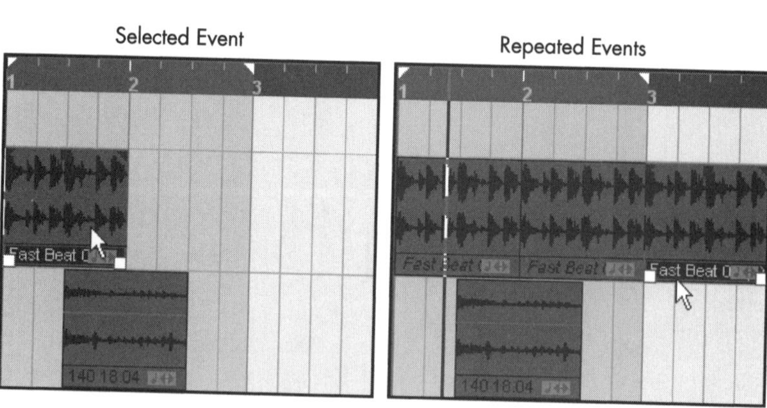

Figure 27.8
A before and after look at the Repeat function when using the Object Selection tool to select the content you want to repeat.

When using the Repeat function, you also will notice that the positions of the left and right locators have no effect on the placement of the repeated material. On the other hand, the Grid

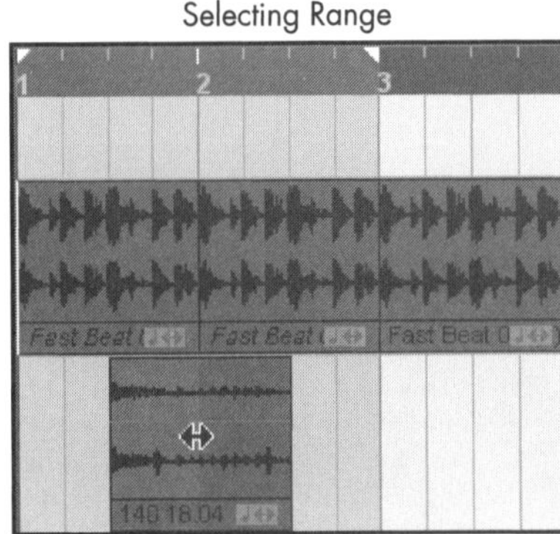

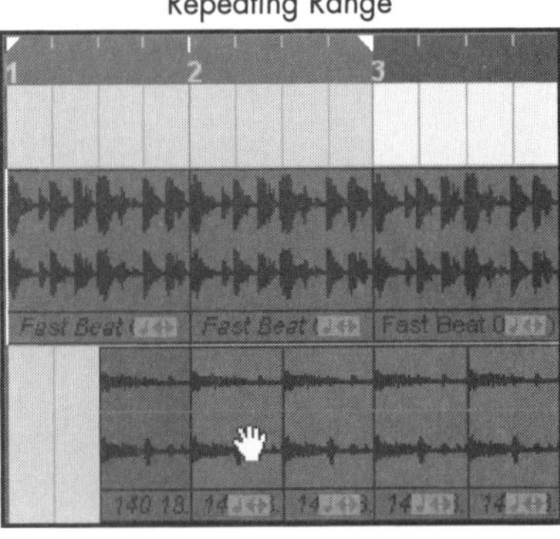

Figure 27.9
A before and after look at the Repeat function when using the Range Selection tool to determine the content you want to repeat.

mode settings for the Snap function play a role in where your repeated objects appear if you have selected objects that do not start or end exactly on grid increments (for example, bars and beats).

HOW TO

Repeat selected objects or ranges over time:

1. Select the appropriate tool (Object Selection or Range Selection).
2. Select the objects or range you want to repeat.
3. From the Edit menu, select the Repeat command or press Ctrl+K (PC)/⌘+K (Mac).
4. Enter the number of times you want this selection to be repeated.
5. If you have selected objects rather than a range, check the Shared Copies option if you want to do so.
6. Click OK.

Fill Loop

Another variation on copying events is offered through the Fill Loop function, which allows you to specify a cycle region between the left and right locators in which events will be repeated. If the last repetition of these events doesn't fit completely inside this area, it can be trimmed to fit within the range defined by the locators.

As with the Duplicate and Repeat options, you also can use the Range Selection tool to highlight the range that will be used to fill a loop section. This is a great way to create a section structure inside a project in which all selected objects are repeated until they arrive at the right locator position. In Figure 27.10, the top row displays a selected event occurring on bar 2. Once the Fill Loop function is applied, even the first empty bar is filled. In the third row, the Range Selection tool was used to make a selection that is repeated throughout the range between the locators (bottom row).

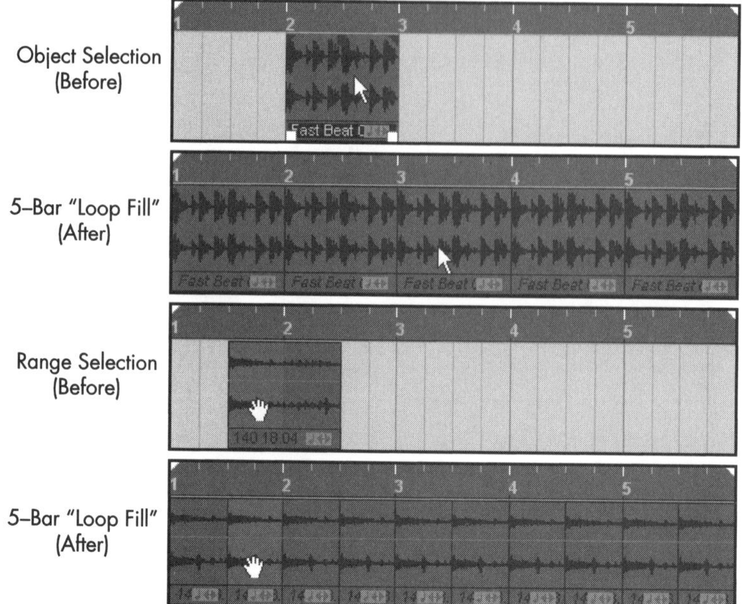

Figure 27.10
A before and after look at the Fill Loop function.

HOW TO

Fill an area with selected objects using the Fill Loop option:

1. Select the appropriate tool (Object Selection or Range Selection).
2. Position your left and right locators at the locations where you want the looped repetitions of the current selection to begin and end.
3. Select the objects or range you want to use in the fill.
4. From the Edit menu, select the Fill Loop command.

Alternate Fill Option

You also can copy looping content in the Project window by using the Object Selection (arrow) tool to drag the lower-right corner handle of a part while holding down the Alt (PC)/Option (Mac) key. Each copy snaps to the end of the previous event/part. While holding down the Alt/Option key, this tool's cursor turns from an arrow into a pencil, as displayed in Figure 27.11, indicating that the Fill option is active.

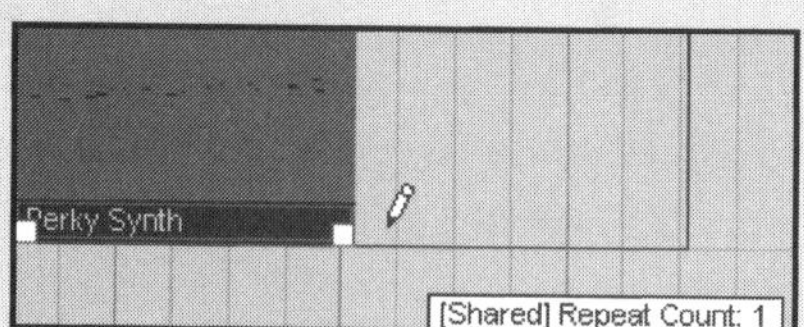

Figure 27.11
Using tool-modifying keyboard shortcuts to copy events.

Resizing Objects

Sizing or resizing an object makes it possible to adjust the start and end times of the object without affecting the media file itself. Think of sizing an object as a way to define which portion of the object plays in the project. Different objects have different sizing restrictions. For example, you can resize an audio event, but not beyond boundaries of that event's source audio file. The same restriction goes for audio regions: You can expand the event containing the audio region in the Project window beyond the region's boundaries, but not beyond the original clip's boundaries. In terms of audio or MIDI parts, you have no such restrictions because a MIDI part does not actually refer to any content; it only acts as a container for content. That being said, you might want these objects to react differently to the sizing you apply. The Object Selection tool has three resizing modes: Normal Sizing, Sizing Moves Contents, and Sizing Applies Time Stretch.

Normal Sizing

Normally, when you change an event's length by moving its start or end point, the content within the event stays in place and only the start or end point moves, as illustrated in Figure 27.12. Moving the end of the MIDI part in this case (middle segment) moves the end point back in time, whereas moving the start point later in time causes the events occurring before the new start point to be ignored during playback. But the events that were playing during bar 3 in the original version are still playing at bar 3 in the resized version.

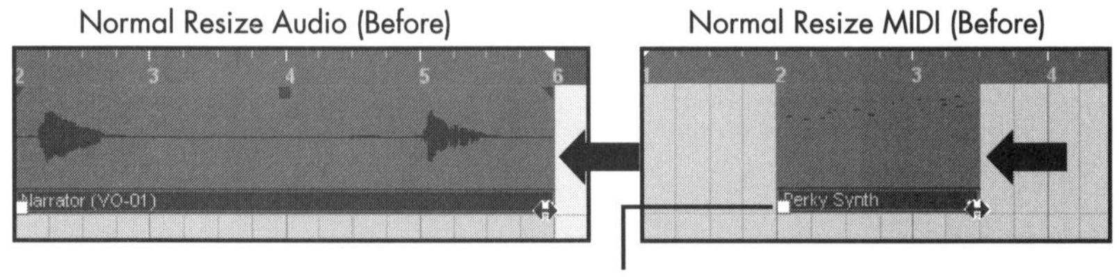

Figure 27.12
Normal sizing audio (left) and MIDI (right).

HOW TO

Resize objects (events or parts):

1. In the Project window's toolbar, select the Normal Sizing mode of the Object Selection (arrow) tool (a.k.a. the Normal Sizing tool).
2. Select an object to view its resizing handles.
3. Drag the handles in the desired direction.

Sizing Moves Contents

In other instances, you also might want to move the content inside of the object (event or part) when resizing it. The top row of Figure 27.13 displays the original content. The start handle of the audio event is moved forward in time (bottom row), moving the content forward as well, while the end point remains unchanged. The end handle of the MIDI part is also moved forward, unwrapping the MIDI events recorded earlier in time. This is done when the Sizing Moves Contents mode is selected from the Object Selection tool's pop-up menu.

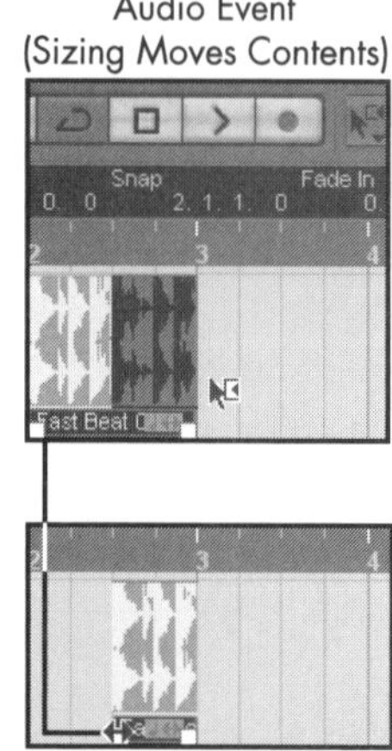

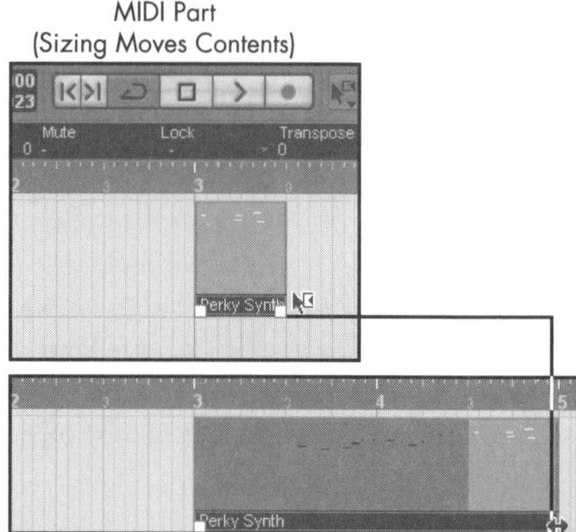

Figure 27.13
Resizing an event using the Sizing Moves Contents mode of the Object Selection tool.

HOW TO

Resize objects while moving their contents:

1. In the Project window's toolbar, select the Sizing Moves Contents mode from the Object Selection tool's pop-up menu.
2. Select an object to view its resizing handles.
3. Drag the handles in the desired direction.

Sizing Applies Time Stretch

The final resizing mode available in the Object Selection tool's pop-up menu enables you to time stretch objects so that the duration of the events inside is adjusted to fit the new object's size. This stretching can be applied to both audio and MIDI events. Figure 27.14 displays both types of events being stretched. In the top portion, MIDI events' note length values are adjusted to fit within the new proportion. If you stretch in a proportion that changes the quantizing of events, you might have to do a bit of editing inside the MIDI editor to get the MIDI events to work with the quantize grid. In other words, if you don't want too much hassle with this, try stretching in a proportion that is suitable to the time subdivision currently used in your project.

Original MIDI Events Before Sizing

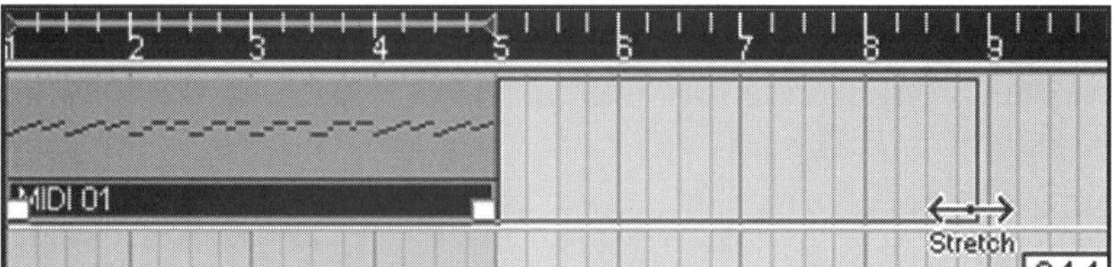

Time-Stretched MIDI Events: Using the Sizing Tool

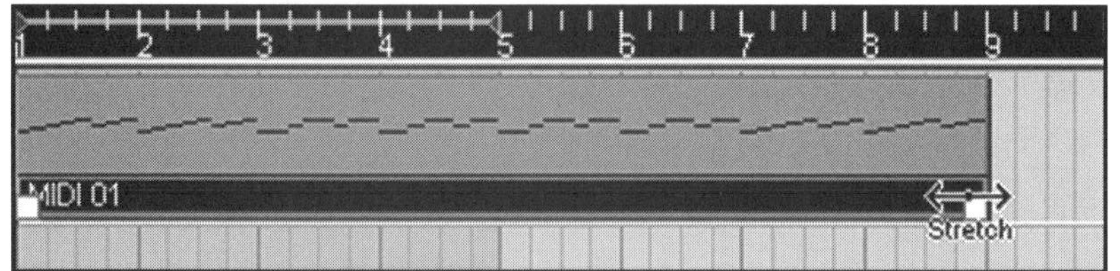

Original Audio Event

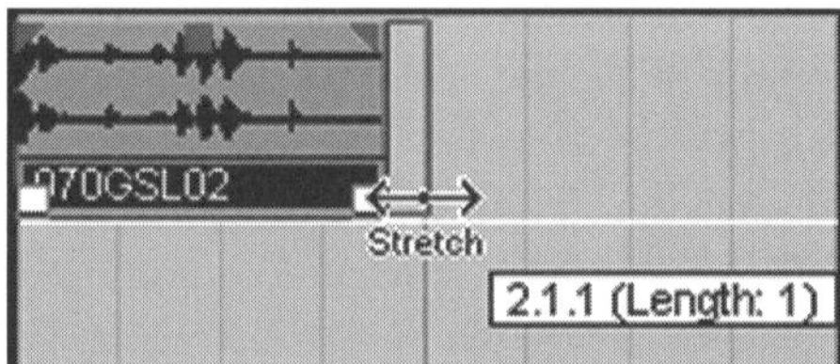

Time-Stretched Audio Event: Using the Sizing Tool

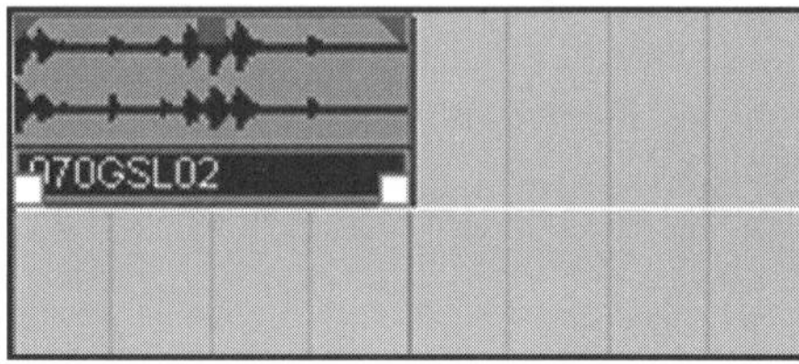

Figure 27.14
Resizing an event using the Sizing Applies Time Stretch mode of the Object Selection tool.

Using this option on audio is a great way to make a drum loop, for example, fit inside a specific number of bars—especially when the tempo difference is minimal. If you look at the audio example in Figure 27.14, you can see that the original content is less than one bar long. Stretching it allows you to loop it an even number of times using the Fill Loop or Repeat options described earlier in this chapter. You can select the algorithm and quality applied to audio through the File menu (PC)/Cubase application menu (Mac) > Preferences > Editing Audio > Time Stretch Tool fields. The option you select in this dialog box is applied to all audio events that are stretched using this tool, and the best algorithm for a specific task will depend on the nature of the source material.

HOW TO

Stretch the content of an object while resizing it:

1. In the Project window's toolbar, select the Sizing Applies Time Stretch mode from the Object Selection tool's pop-up menu.
2. Select an object to view its resizing handles.
3. Drag the handles in the desired direction.

You should know that applying a large proportion of time stretching on an audio file will probably create some major artifacts in the resultant sound . For natural-sounding results, avoid using time stretch in a proportion greater or less than 25 percent of the original content's length. For MIDI events, there are no such time-stretching limitations. The positions and durations of MIDI events are simply recalculated.

Shifting Events Inside an Object

Adjusting the timing of two takes can sometimes be daunting, and moving the start and end points of an event is not always desired. That's when shifting events inside an object (an event or MIDI part) without moving the object's boundaries comes in handy. Shifting the content inside the event is done by offsetting the position of the audio clip inside the object's start and end points, as illustrated in Figure 27.15. You also can shift MIDI events inside a MIDI part. In both cases, there is only one condition that applies: The object in which the events are found has to be smaller than the events themselves. For example, if you have MIDI events at bar 1, beat 1 and bar 3, beat 4 within a MIDI part that spans from bar 1 to bar 4, you cannot shift these events inside because the container covers the same area as the events inside the container.

Original Audio Event

Contents Shifted Forward in Time

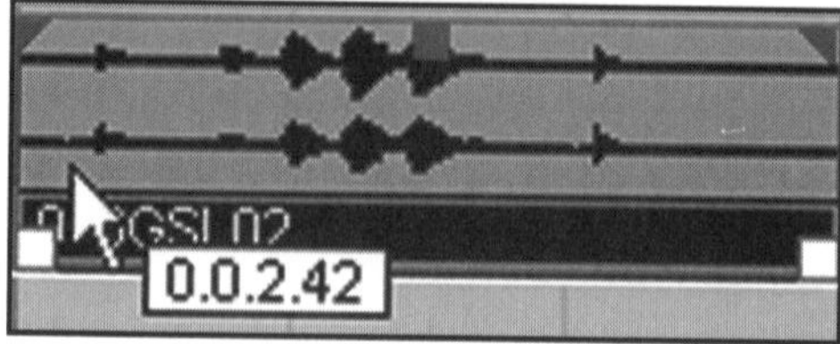

Figure 27.15
Shifting events' position within an object.

HOW TO

Shift events inside an object:

1. In the Project window's toolbar, select the Object Selection tool.
2. Select the object you want to shift.
3. Hold down the Ctrl+Alt (PC)/⌘+Option (Mac) keys as you click and drag the content within this event or MIDI part to the left or right.

You can use this technique creatively by shifting a drum loop, for example, trying out different beat combinations when playing a shifted event along with other events in the same timeline.

Muting Objects

When trying out ideas inside the Project window, you might want to mute a track by using the Mute button found in the Inspector and Track List area. However, if you only want to mute a number of events, you can do so by selecting these events followed by the Mute option found in the Edit menu. The default key command to mute events is Shift+M. After an object is muted, you can unmute it using the Shift+U key command or by selecting the Unmute option—also found in the Edit menu.

Lock

If you've worked hard at positioning events in the timeline, you can lock them in place to prevent time-consuming mistakes. When an object is locked, a tiny lock icon appears in the bottom-right corner of the object next to the end point handle. You can lock selected events by using the Lock option in the Edit menu [Ctrl+Shift+L (PC)/⌘+Shift+L (Mac)]. After objects are locked, you cannot move or edit them from the Project window. To unlock objects, select the corresponding option in the Edit menu or press [Ctrl+Shift+U (PC)/⌘+Shift+U (Mac)].

28 Play Order Track

When working on a project, we often find ourselves reorganizing the order in which sections of a song play in order to create variations or simply to find which arrangement works best. A Play Order track lets you create building blocks called *Play Order Parts* inside a project. Think of Play Order Parts as patterns, or regions inside a project defined by start and end points. Once these Parts are created in the Play Order track, you can create an order for them to play in, repeating each part as many times as needed and rearranging the order in which the parts (patterns) play. This playlist of Parts is called a *Play Order List*.

Here's a summary of what you will learn in this chapter:

- How to save a project before using Play Order functions
- How to enable the Play Order mode
- How to create and manage Play Order Parts
- How to populate a Play Order List
- How to manage Play Order Parts inside a Play Order List
- How to navigate a Play Order project
- How to convert a Play Order project into a linear project

Creating a Play Order Project

A Play Order project is not different from a normal Cubase project. But just as you would save a copy of a project and use an alternate version to create musical notation, for example, it makes sense to work on a copy of an existing project to create an alternate version of its arrangement. Furthermore, to create several versions (arrangements) of the same project, it's always easier when you can start fresh with the original project. It is not necessary to use the File > Save Project to New Folder option because different arrangements can share the same media files. You can use the Save Project to New Folder option when you are satisfied with the current play order arrangement and you are ready to flatten the play order. But we'll get back to that later in this chapter.

Once you've saved the project and renamed it, you are ready to start working with the Play Order features. The first step in building a Play Order arrangement is to create a Play Order track. As with the creation of all track classes in Cubase, this is done by right-clicking (PC)/Control-clicking (Mac) in the Track List area or by selecting Project > Add Track. In both cases, you then select the Play Order Track option. Just like Marker or Video tracks, you can only have one Play Order track per project. With the Play Order track created, the next step consists in making the Play Order controls visible in the Transport panel if they aren't already.

HOW TO

Make the Play Order controls visible:

- **In the Transport panel:** Right-click (PC)/Control-click (Mac) in the Transport panel and enable (check) the Play Order option in the context menu.
- **In the Project window toolbar:** Right-click (PC)/Control-click (Mac) in the Project window's toolbar and enable (check) the Play Order option in the context menu.

Displaying the Play Order controls, as illustrated in Figure 28.1, reveals a number of navigational controls specific to the Play Order track. Here's a quick overview of what each of these controls does:

- The Play Order Mode button switches Cubase's playback mode from Linear (reads from left to right) to Play Order mode (beginning of playlist to end of playlist).
- The Play Order List selection field lets you choose which list to play and displays its name.
- The Play Order Part selection field lets you choose which part inside a list to play and displays its name.
- The Current Repeat selection field lets you choose which repetition of a part inside a list to play and displays a small square for each programmed repetition of a part inside this list.
- The Next Play Order Part button lets you move to the next part in the list.
- The Previous Play Order Part button lets you move to the previous part in the list.
- The First Repeat of Play Order Part button moves the play cursor to the first occurrence of the part in the list.
- The Last Repeat of Play Order Part button moves the play cursor to the last occurrence of the part in the list.

For any of these controls to work, the Play Order Mode button needs to be activated (it appears as orange when it is active), and in order to activate the Play Order mode, you need to define

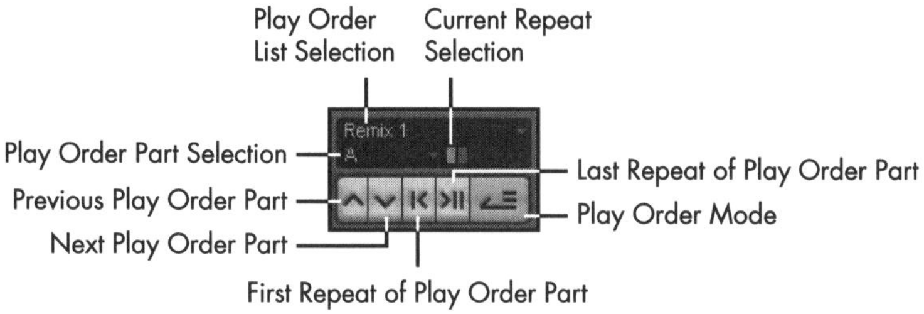

Play Order List Selection
Current Repeat Selection
Play Order Part Selection
Previous Play Order Part
Next Play Order Part
First Repeat of Play Order Part
Last Repeat of Play Order Part
Play Order Mode

Figure 28.1
The Play Order controls.

some parts and add them to a list before Cubase can move its cursor from one pattern (part) to the next.

Play Order Part

Play Order tracks, Lists, and Parts offer a way of creating different arrangements within the same project file. Play Order Parts represent an area or region within a project. Organizing the order in which these parts play back, you essentially get a Play Order List. Let's take a look at how you can create Play Order Parts to use in Play Order Lists.

HOW TO ❋

Create a Play Order Part:

1. In the Project window, enable the Snap mode and set the Snap and Grid types as desired. For example, if you don't plan to create parts smaller than bars, set the Snap type to Grid and the Grid type to Bar.

2a. Inside the Play Order track, use the Draw (pencil) tool to click and drag, highlighting a range for the new Play Order Part that will be created.

OR

2b. Position the left and right locators at the desired start and end positions in the timeline, then use the Object Selection (arrow) tool to double-click inside the Play Order track, creating a new Play Order Part inside this range.

HOW TO ❋

Rename a Play Order Part:

1. Select the part in the Play Order track.
2. In the Info Line, click where the current name appears and type a new name for the part.

You can resize a Play Order Part by dragging its start and end handles in the Play Order track, and you can move the part wherever you need it to be in this track.

Play Order Editor

You can access a special Play Order editor by clicking on the corresponding button, as shown in Figure 28.2. This editor, shown in Figure 28.3, displays a toolbar with the Play Order Transport controls, which duplicate those found in the Transport panel and the Project window toolbar. To the right of the controls are a number of additional Play Order function buttons to rename the current list; create a new list; or copy, delete, or flatten the selected list. We'll discuss flattening the Play Order List a bit later on in this chapter.

Figure 28.2
The Open Play Order editor button.

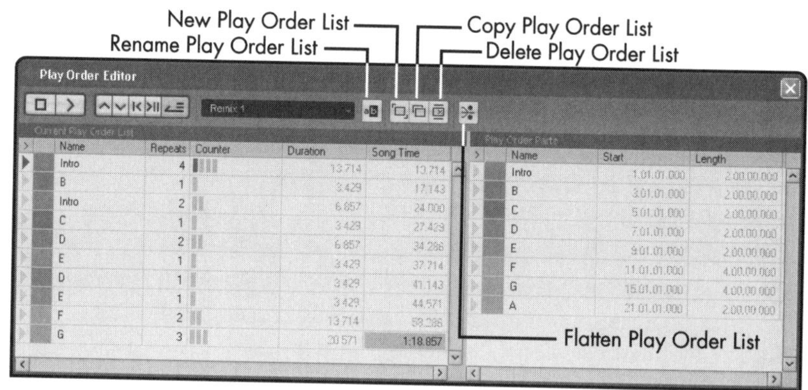

Figure 28.3
The Play Order editor.

The Counter column displays how many times the part has played already, whereas the Duration and Song Time columns automatically calculate the time it takes to play each row in the Play Order List sequence. The Song Time offers a convenient way of calculating the list's time duration.

Populating a List

Below the Toolbar are two areas. On the right are the building blocks for the Play Order List—the Play Order Parts. These parts were created in the Play Order track, as discussed earlier.

HOW TO

Add a Play Order Part to a list:

- Click and drag the Part's name into the left area to add this part to the Current Play Order List, as displayed in Figure 28.4. A horizontal blue line in the List area indicates where the Part you're dragging will be inserted. Dragging the same part (for example, part G, over an existing instance of part G) in the list will increase the number of repetitions for this part in the list area.

- In the Inspector, drag the part's name from the Play Order Parts area where you want to add the part in the Play Order List area. Once again, a blue line in the List area indicates where this part will be inserted.
- Double-click on a part in the Parts area to insert it at the bottom of the active list. To increase the number of times the part is repeated, double-click on the same part several times. You also can specify the number of repetitions of a part by typing a specific value in the Repeat column of the Play Order List itself.
- Double-click on any part in the Play Order track to insert it at the bottom of the active list. To increase the number of times the part is repeated, double-click on the same part several times.

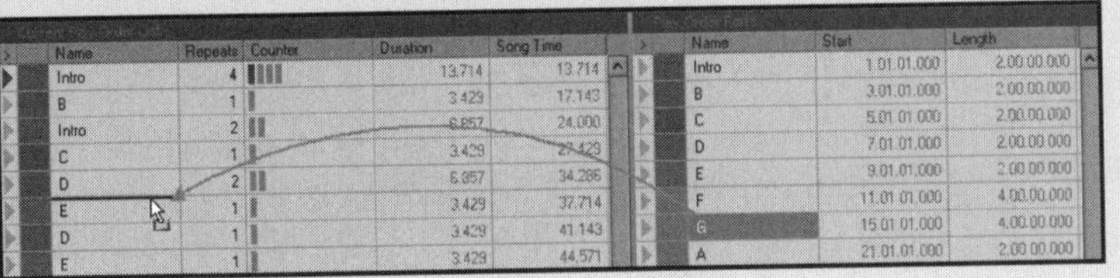

Figure 28.4
Adding Parts to a list in the Play Order editor.

When playing the project in Play Order mode, the List reads the Parts in the Play Order List from top to bottom. Clicking the Activate Play Order Mode button will disable the normal Linear playback mode of the project and enable this pattern-based Play Order mode.

Navigating the Play Order List

Once you have started populating the list with parts and you have enabled Play Order mode, you can play the list from any point. The starting point is always displayed in the Play Order controls described in Figure 28.1. Select a different part, or click inside any counter display to move the play line to that specific point inside the list during playback.

Clicking small triangles to the left of the parts in the list area (both in the Inspector and Play Order editor) immediately skips the project's playback to that location, making it convenient to test how well one part flows into the next. How you choose to use this navigation depends on how you choose to use the Play Order functions.

Creating Order

You can change the order of parts in a list the same way you can rearrange tracks in a project: by dragging the part's name to its new position in the list. Once again, a blue line displays where the part will be inserted. To remove an entire row from a list (which includes all the part's repetitions), right-click (PC)/Control-click (Mac) over the desired part in the list and choose Remove Selected from the context menu.

Managing Lists

Each project supports multiple Play Order Lists, making it easy to try different versions or structures of the same project. This section describes a few functions associated with Play Order Lists. All of these functions are available in both the Inspector's Play Order track drop-down menu, shown in Figure 28.5, and in the Play Order editor, using the buttons shown in Figure 28.3.

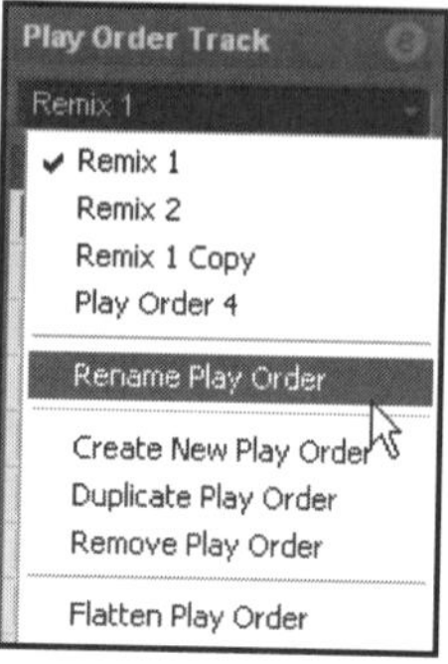

Figure 28.5
The Play Order track's list management options found in the Inspector.

HOW TO

Manage lists:

- **Rename a list:** Click on the Rename Current Play Order option (the current List is always the one displayed) and type a new name for the List in the dialog box. Click OK when you are finished.
- **Create a new list:** Click on the Create a New Play Order button or select this option from the Inspector.
- **Remove a list:** Click on the Remove Play Order button or select this option from the Inspector.
- **Duplicate a list:** Click on the Duplicate Play Order button or select this option from the Inspector. This option is convenient when you want to keep the current List's structure but you would like to experiment with some variations.

Flattening a List

The Flatten Play Order function lets you convert the Play Order List into a linear version. By doing so, Cubase converts the list, rebuilding your project according to the indications found in the List. When the process is complete, all names and settings remain the same, but their content in the track display area represents the new arrangement. Any section of the original project that was not included in this list will have been erased. That's why it is *strongly recommended* that you save your project before flattening the Play Order List, using the Save Project to New Folder option. Saving to a new folder will automatically save all content referenced inside the project and will optimize it as needed. If you do not save your project before flattening it, you will lose all other Play Order Lists in your project because once your project is flattened, the Play Order track is removed as well, as shown in Figure 28.6. The flattened result includes all automation associated with each part that was in the Play Order List.

Before Flattening

After Flattening

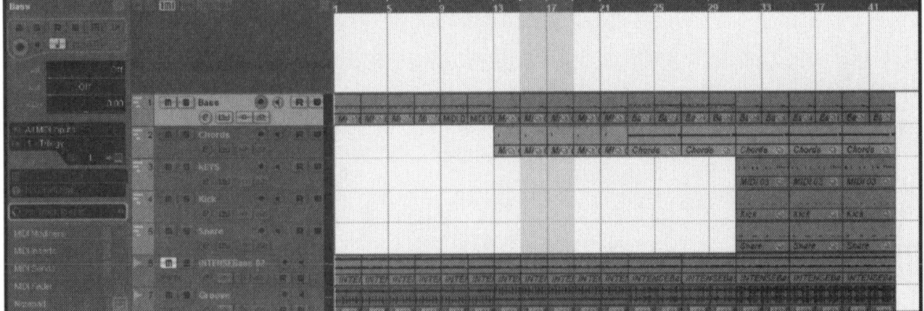

Figure 28.6
A project containing a Play Order List (above) and after it has been flattened (below).

HOW TO

Flatten a Play Order List:

1. Make sure a safety copy of the project containing the Play Order Lists has been saved.
2. From the Inspector's drop-down menu or the Play Order editor, select the list you want to flatten.
3. Click on the Flatten Play Order button or select this option from the Inspector.
4. Save the new flattened project.

29 Tempo Track

The tempo track in Cubase stores project tempo and key signature changes. The tempo track is the only track that doesn't really show up in the Project window's Track List area. Adding tempo changes to a project to slow down or speed up the beat is an essential feature in much non-pop music, but DJs using Cubase to create a track also can use this feature to gradually accelerate the tempo from one section to another. Changing the time signature also offers a convenient way to create a break in the rhythm or when adapting a song with multiple time signature changes inside a project.

Here's a summary of what you will learn in this chapter:

- How to add tempo changes or time signature changes using the Tempo Track editor
- How to edit tempo changes or time signature changes using the Tempo Track editor
- How to add tempo changes using the Time Warp tool
- How to edit tempo changes using the Time Warp tool

Tempo Track Editor

Because the tempo track is not visible in the Project window, to access it, you need to either Ctrl-click (PC)/-click (Mac) on the Tempo button found in the Transport panel, select the Tempo Track option in the Project menu, or press the default key command Ctrl+T (PC)/+T (Mac). All of these actions will open the Tempo Track editor. Let's take a look at the features found in this window.

The top toolbar in the Tempo Track editor (Figure 29.1) offers the following tools:

- The **Activate Tempo Track** button is lit when it is enabled, meaning that Cubase will follow any tempo changes found in the tempo track. When the tempo track is disabled, you can manually set a different tempo in the Transport panel's Tempo field, providing a way to set a slower tempo for hard-to-play passages when recording in MIDI, for example. When the tempo track is disabled, the word "Fixed" appears next to the Tempo toggle button in the Transport panel, indicating that tempo changes in the tempo track are not in effect. (The default manual tempo setting is 120 BPM.) Furthermore, whether you are using the tempo track or a manual tempo setting, the Tempo field in the Transport panel will always display the current setting at the playback cursor's location, both during recording or playback and when the Transport is stopped. The time signature changes in the tempo track will still take place as usual, even if the tempo track is disabled, as you will still need these to record events at the proper bars and beat locations.

- The **Object Selection**, **Eraser**, **Zoom**, and **Draw** tools perform the same functions as they do in other editing environments.
- The **Auto Scroll** and **Snap** buttons offer the same functionality as their Project window counterparts.
- The **Tempo** field displays the tempo value of a selected tempo event in the tempo display area below. When a tempo event is selected (see Figure 29.1), use the up and down arrows to the right of the field, type in a new tempo value, or drag any tempo event handle to a new position to change its tempo value or time location.
- The **Curve** field selects how the tempo changes between two selected tempo values. You will not be able to use this field if you don't have at least two tempo points selected. You can choose either Ramp or Jump. When a ramp is created, the tempo will move gradually from one point to another, as displayed between bars 17 and 25 in Figure 29.1. When a jump is created, the tempo will stay the same until the next tempo change, at which point it will jump abruptly to the next tempo value in the line, as displayed between bars 1 and 9 and 9 and 17.

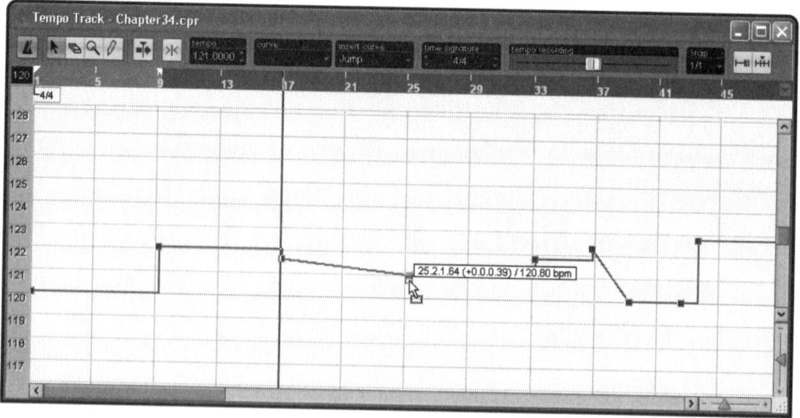

Figure 29.1
The Tempo Track window.

- The **Insert Curve** field determines how the following tempo changes will relate to previous tempo change values along the tempo line. As with the Curve field, you can choose either Ramp (gradual change of tempo from one point to the next) or Jump (sudden change at the location of the new tempo change). Note that if the Snap mode is on, the precise position where tempo changes can be entered will be determined by the Snap mode's Grid and Quantize settings, which are set in the Project window.
- The **Signature** field changes the value for the selected time signature event, in the horizontal Signature area below the Tempo Track editor's ruler.
- The **Tempo Record** slider allows you to record tempo changes in real time by moving the slider to the right to go faster or to the left to go slower while the project is playing. Hold down the Shift key while recording tempo changes to get more accurate (finer) control over this slider's values.
- The **Snap** field acts like a Quantize grid for tempo changes added with this editor's pencil tool. The selected value determines how the precise positions of individual tempo events are adjusted when you move them or add new ones or determines the frequency at which the new tempo changes get created as you drag with the pencil.
- The **Process Tempo** button opens the Process Tempo dialog box (see Figure 29.2), which lets you specify a time range to let Cubase determine the right tempo setting to fit this range within a given time. Enter a desired length or end time in the appropriate field, depending on whether you need the project to last a certain amount of time or whether you need the project to reach the end point at a certain time. Click the Process button to let Cubase calculate the rest.

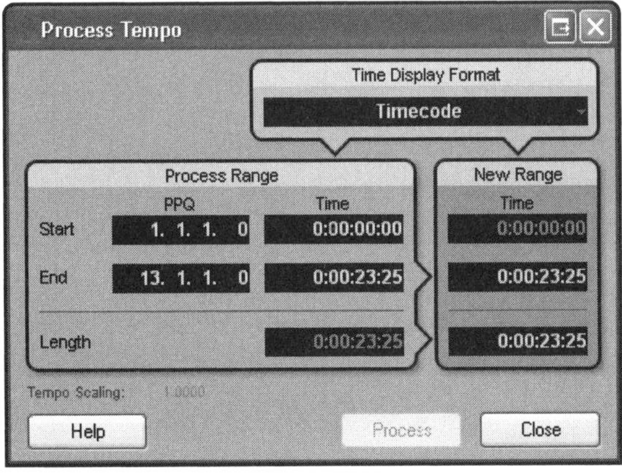

Figure 29.2
The Process Tempo dialog box.

- The **Process Bars** button opens the Process Bars dialog box (see Figure 29.3), which lets you add or remove bars (time) by defining a range through the Start and Length fields and then selecting the appropriate action from the Action field.

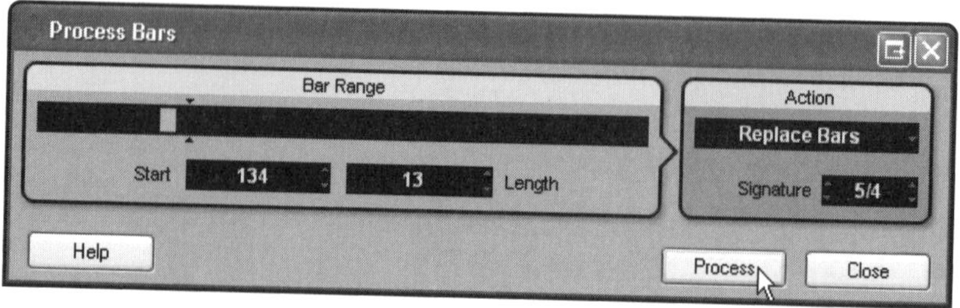

Figure 29.3
The Process Bars dialog box.

Below this editor's toolbar is its Ruler, which offers similar functions to Ruler bars in other windows.

The Time Signature area displays the time signature events in your project. When you start a new project, by default you will find a single 4/4 time signature event at the beginning of this bar. You can add several other time signature events along the project's timeline, which will adjust the spacing between bar numbers to reflect how these time signature events affect the number of beats in each bar.

The main area of the Tempo Track editor is, of course, the Tempo Display area. This consists of a tempo ruler displayed vertically along the left side of the window and an area where tempo change events appear along the tempo line. Each tempo event is represented by a square handle. When you insert a new tempo event, this line will connect it to existing tempo events on either side of it according to the current Curve and Insert Curve settings.

In the lower-right corner are the horizontal and vertical zoom bars, which enable you to adjust the zoom level for the timeline displayed in the Tempo track, as well as the tempo precision displayed in the tempo ruler, respectively.

HOW TO

Add a tempo change:

1. In the tempo track, click on the Draw tool in the toolbar.
2. Select the desired option in the Insert Curve field.
3. Activate the Snap button if you want the position of newly created tempo events to be adjusted per the Snap mode's current Grid setting. It is recommended that you enable the Snap button if you want tempo changes to occur at the beginning of musical bars.
4. Position your cursor at the time and at the tempo height you want to insert the tempo change. You can use the Cursor Location field to the left of the Ruler to guide you along the vertical tempo value axis.

HOW TO ❊

Add a time signature change:

1. In the tempo track, click on the Draw tool in the toolbar.
2. Click inside the horizontal Time Signature area at the location where you want to insert a time signature change. This adds a time signature using the current value displayed in the Signature field. For obvious reasons, time signature events can *only* be inserted at bar divisions.
3. With the new time signature still selected (a red square appears around the selected time signature), use the toolbar's Signature field to enter the values for the time signature you want to add at this point.

If for some reason you change your mind about any tempo change event, you can move one or several selected tempo events to a new tempo value or time location.

HOW TO ❊

Move a tempo or time signature event:

1. Select the Object Selection tool from the toolbar.
2. Click on the tempo or time signature event you want to move and drag it to the desired location.

You also can move multiple tempo change events simultaneously by dragging a box to select them. Selected tempo event handles will appear in red, as will the lines between them.

If you want to change the curve type between two or more tempo events, you can select the desired tempo event handles and then select the desired value in the Curve field. For example, if you have selected three tempo events, with a jump curve between the first and second events and a ramp between the second and third events, selecting a ramp will create a ramp between the first and second, leaving the curve between the second and third intact. Note that the line segments for jump curves between tempo events are blue, while ramp curves dark green.

HOW TO ❊

Erase tempo or time signature events:

- With the Object selection (arrow) tool selected, click on the tempo or time signature you want to erase and press Delete or Backspace. To erase several events, simply drag a box over the desired tempo or time signature events and use the Delete or Backspace key.
- Or select the Eraser tool and click on the events in the tempo track.

Time Warping

The Time Warp feature in the Project window provides a way to match musical (tempo-based) references to linear (time-based) references by adding special markers where you want both references to align. As a result, warp markers are added with tempo values that make it possible for this match to occur. For example, you can use the Time Warp tool to add tempo changes based on a track that was recorded freestyle (without a metronome), that will follow the MIDI or audio events within that track. Once the start point is determined, create tempo changes that will make bars in the project match up to the recorded events in the track. Because time warp markers are locked to the tempo-based Ruler (bars and beats), this Ruler "warps" to match the linear or time-based Ruler. This process is similar to the Audio Warp functions provided in the Sample editor in the sense that they both offer ways to match MIDI, audio, and video references together. The main purpose for warping the grid is to make the tempo warp to match a more static media reference. The main purpose for audio warping is to make the media reference to match an existing project tempo. For more information on audio warping, take a look at Chapter 19, "Sample Editor."

When using the Time Warp tool, the tempo value of the last tempo event (before the new tab's position) is adjusted accordingly. The Ruler bar will turn orange when the Time Warp tool is selected, and inserted tempo changes appear as markers along this bar (see Figure 29.5). There are two Time Warp modes—the default Warp Grid mode transforms the tempo grid into an elastic grid that lets you set the location of bars and beats in relation to absolute time. This is great to match a tempo grid to an existing audio track with changing tempos, as shown in Figure 29.4.

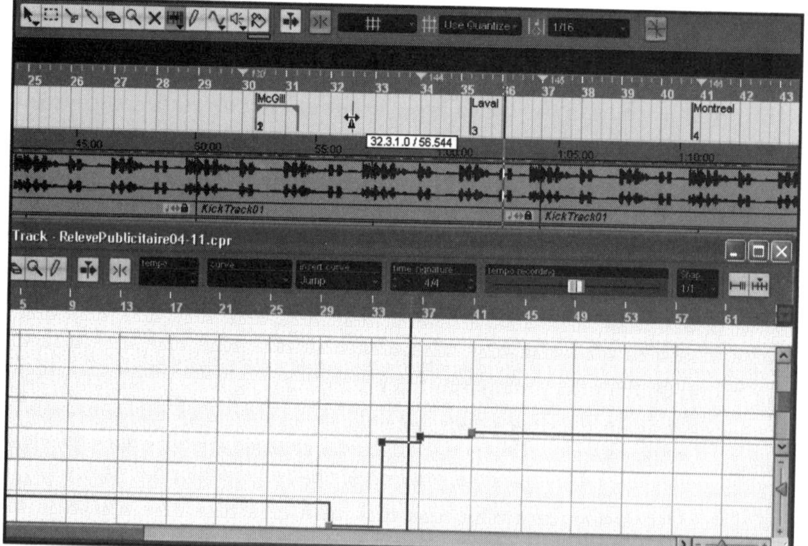

Figure 29.4
Tempo warping in Warp Grid mode.

HOW TO

Add a tempo change using the Time Warp tool:

1. Enable the tempo track; the Time Warp tool does not work when the tempo track is not enabled.
2. Enable the Snap function in the Project window and set your Snap mode appropriately. Depending on the grid and quantize types you choose, this forces tempo changes to occur on bars, at the cursor's location, or at an event's start point.
3. Select one of the two Time Warp modes from the toolbar.

3a. Select the default Warp Grid mode to keep musical events in their current location along the tempo grid and only adjust the tempo to match them. You also can convert all events into linear (time-based) events temporarily while placing musical (tempo-based) tempo match-up points;

OR

3b. Select Warp Grid (musical events follow) mode to adjust all tempo-based events to match existing time-based events, such as video tracks or time-sensitive audio events, accordingly.

4. Click and drag the tempo reference (bar or beat gridline, as shown on the left in Figure 29.5) to the desired time reference or time-based event. This can be done within the Project window or any other editing window in your project.
5. When you are satisfied with the location of the tempo change, release the mouse. You will see a tempo change marker appear in the Ruler bar with the BPM value rounded off to the closest integer value. In the image on the right in Figure 29.5, the MIDI beginning at bar 11.1 now coincides with the sound effects at the beginning of Scene 66 as a result of using the Musical Events Follow mode.

Figure 29.5
Using the Warp Grid (musical events follow) mode to add tempo changes.

Here are a few additional techniques for working with the Time Warp tool:

- To only affect the timing of a specific time range, use the Range Selection tool to define this time selection prior to using the Time Warp tool. Clicking to the left of the selected range only affects the tempo before the start point of the range. Clicking inside the selected range affects the tempo inside the range, adding a tempo change at the start, the end, and the point where you click. Clicking to the right of the selected range (or after) only affects the tempo after the end point of the selected range. If no tempo events were present, a new tempo change will be added at that point to reflect the time warp entered.
- When using the Time Warp tool inside an editor, a tempo event will also be added at the start location of the event or part in the Project window, if there isn't one there already.

- To manually add a tempo event at the current tempo value in order to lock all previous tempo events in place, hold down the Shift key while the Time Warp tool is selected and click where you want the tempo change to occur. The cursor will change into a pencil, and a tempo change will be inserted at the point where you clicked.

HOW TO

Erase a tempo change using the Time Warp tool:

- While the Warp Grid mode is selected, hold down the Shift key while clicking on an existing tempo event in the Ruler bar.
- Open the Tempo editor, select the tempo event, and delete it or click on it with the Eraser tool.

After the Time Warp tool is selected, you can see the tempo changes in the Ruler bar and move these tempo changes around by dragging their markers to a new location. You will notice that the cursor changes to a pointing hand as you hover over a tempo change marker.

Warping Inside Editors

Working with the Time Warp tool inside editors is similar to working with the Warp tool in the Project window. Inside MIDI and Audio Part editors, the time warping process is identical to the process in the Project window, with Warp Grid and Warp Grid (musical events follow). When working with warp inside MIDI or Audio Part editors, Cubase adds a tempo change event before and after the event in the Project window to prevent events following this event from being moved from their current location.

The Warp modes in the Sample editor are divided into two tools. The Musical Events Follow mode becomes the Audio Warp tool; the Time Warp tool temporarily switches the audio sample into linear time, and you can add tempo changes as previously described in the Project window or other editors.

30 Working in Sync

Synchronizing Cubase to other devices is often an important part of a project, but for many, it is probably the most feared and misunderstood aspect of it. Synchronization is often something we have to deal with, but we resist because it can lead to all kinds of problems. On the other hand, once the tools are understood, synchronizing can save lots of time and aggravation when working in any context that requires some device—hardware or software—to synchronize with another. Working in sync today implies making two computers work hand in hand, making an external video playback device control the playback position inside Cubase, or making a digital clock send the appropriate timing information to another digital clock. It also implies that you can match MIDI tempo changes with audio tempo changes, match scene changes in a video with sound effects, and so on. In this chapter, we will discuss synchronization options within Cubase that facilitate such tasks.

Here's a summary of what you will learn in this chapter:

- The difference between a Word Clock, a SMPTE timecode, and a MIDI clock
- How and when to use a specific timecode
- How and when to use a MIDI clock
- What MIDI Machine Control is and how you can use it
- Why digital clocks are important when you are using digital audio devices
- How to use audio warp markers to adjust audio files and match their tempo to a project
- How to synchronize devices by using different synchronization methods
- How you can deal with events that need to stay synchronized to absolute time references, whereas others are synchronized to bars and beats at the current tempo
- How to work with online video files

About Word Clock, SMPTE, and MIDI Clock

Before we start looking at how Cubase handles synchronization, it is important to understand the different types of synchronization, the terminology, and the basic concepts behind these terms. The idea behind synchronization is that there will always be a master/slave (sender/receiver) relationship between the source of the synchronization and the recipient of this timing reference. There can only be one sync master, but there can be many devices slaved to this master. There are three basic concepts here: SMPTE timecode, MIDI Clock, and Word Clock.

Timecode

The concept behind timecode is simple: It is an electronic signal used to identify a precise location on time-based media, such as audio, videotape, or digital systems that support timecode. This electronic signal then accompanies the media that needs to be in sync with others. Imagine that a postal worker delivering mail is the locking mechanism, the houses on the street are location addresses on the timecode, and the letter has matching addresses. The postal worker reads the letter and makes sure it gets to the correct address the same way that a synchronizing device compares the timecode from a source and a destination, making sure they are all happening at the same time. This timecode also is known as SMPTE (*Society of Motion Picture and Television Engineers*), and it comes in three flavors:

- **LTC (Longitudinal timecode).** This is also used to synchronize video machines, but contrary to VITC, it also is used to synchronize audio-only information, such as a transfer between a tape recorder and Cubase. LTC usually takes the form of an audio signal (which is modulated in order to encode the timecode information) that is recorded on one of the tracks of the tape. Because LTC is an audio signal, it is silent if the tape is not moving.
- **VITC (Vertical Interval timecode).** This is normally used by video machines to send or receive synchronization information from and to any type of VITC-compatible device. This type of timecode is best suited for working with Betacam and other professional video decks (both analog and digital). Since by definition VITC encodes the timecode information into the video signal itself, this type of timecode is generally not applicable when syncing audio-only devices. VITC timecode information is recorded as part of the video signal in an unused line, which is part of the vertical interval. It has the advantage of being readable when the master playback video deck is paused or when jogging and nudging its transport back and forth (while LTC timecode, being an audio signal, is only readable by the slaved device during normal playback).
- **MTC (MIDI timecode).** This is normally used to synchronize audio or video devices with MIDI devices, such as sequencers. MTC is essentially SMPTE (time-based) mutated for transmission over MIDI.

Each one of these types of timecode uses an hours: minutes: seconds: frames (and often subframes) format.

Frame Rates

As the name implies, a *frame rate* is the number of frames a film or video signal has per second. It is also used to identify different timecode uses. The acronym for frame rate is "fps" for *frames per second*. There are different frame rates, depending on what you are working with:

- **24 fps.** This is used by motion picture films, and, in most cases, will not apply to you unless you have a film projector hooked up to your computer running Cubase to synchronize sound.
- **25 fps.** The PAL (*Phase Alternation Line*) video standard used in Western Europe, Asia, and Australia, as well as parts of Africa and South America; and the SECAM/EBU (*Sequential Color and Memory/European Broadcast Union*) video standard used in France and ex-Soviet bloc countries, as well as parts of Asia and South America, both operate at 25 frames per second. If you live in those areas, this is the format your television, VCR, and DVDs use. A single frame in this format is made of 625 horizontal lines. In countries where the video standard is 25 fps, many users will use this frame rate even on audio-only projects. Among other things, unlike the frame rates associated with NTSC video, at 25 fps conversions between frames and minutes/seconds are extremely simple, since every frame corresponds to exactly 40 milliseconds.
- **29.97 fps.** This is also known as *29.97 nondrop* and may also be seen as 30 fps in some older two-digit timecode machines (but is not to be mistaken with real 30 fps timecode; if you can't see the 29.97 format, chances are the 30 format is its equivalent). This frame rate is associated with the NTSC (*National Television Standards Committee*) video standard used mostly in North America, Mexico, Japan, and South Korea, as well as parts of Central and South America. If you live in this area, this is the format your television, VCR, and DVDs use. A single frame in this format is made of 525 horizontal lines.
- **29.97 fps DF.** This is also known as *29.97 drop frame* (hence the "DF" at the end). This also can be referred to as *30 DF* on older video timecode machines. This is probably the trickiest timecode to understand because there is a lot of confusion about the drop frame. To accommodate the extra information needed for color when this format was first introduced, the 30 fps rate of black-and-white television was slowed to 29.97 fps for color. Though it is not an issue for most of you, in broadcast, the small difference between real time (also known as the *wall* or *house clock*) and the time registered on the video can be problematic. Over a period of one SMPTE hour, the video is 3.6 seconds or 108 extra frames longer in relation to the wall clock. To overcome this discrepancy, drop frames are used. This is calculated as follows: Every frame 00 and 01 is dropped for each minute change, except for minutes with 0s (such as 00, 10, 20, 30, 40, and 50). Therefore, two frames skipped

every minute represents 120 frames per hour, except for the minutes ending with zero, so 120 – 12 = 108 frames. Setting your frame rate to 29.97 DF when it's not—in other words, if it's 29.97 (nondrop)—causes your synchronization to be off by 3.6 seconds per hour. While for short-duration and industrial video many facilities will use the *non-drop* version of 29.97 fps timecode just to make time calculations simpler, for any piece that is going to broadcast or is of longer duration, drop-frame is the norm.

- **30 fps.** This format was used with the first black-and-white NTSC standard. It is still used sometimes in music or sound applications in which no video reference is required.
- **30 fps DF.** This is not a standard timecode protocol and usually refers to older timecode devices that were unable to display the decimal points when the 29.97 drop frame timecode was used. Try to avoid this timecode frame rate setting when synchronizing to video because it might introduce errors in your synchronization. SMPTE does not support this timecode.

Using the SMPTE Generator Plug-In

The SMPTE Generator is a plug-in that generates SMPTE timecode in one of two ways:

- It uses an audio bus output to send the generated timecode audio signal (LTC) to an external device. Typically, you can use this mode to adjust the level of SMPTE going to other devices and to make sure that there is a proper connection between the outputs of the audio hardware associated with Cubase and the input of the device for which the SMPTE was intended.
- It uses an audio bus output to send a timecode signal that is linked with the play position of the project currently loaded. Typically, this tells another device the exact SMPTE location of Cubase at any time, allowing it to lock to Cubase through this synchronization signal.

Since this plug-in is not really an effect, using it on a two-output system is highly inadvisable because timecode is not what you could call "a pleasant sound." Always use an audio output that is not used for anything else, or at least one channel (left or right) that you can spare for this signal. Placing the SMPTE Generator on an empty audio track is also necessary because you do not want to process this signal in any way; otherwise, the location information embedded within this audio signal will be compromised.

HOW TO

Use the SMPTE Generator plug-in:

1. Create a new audio track if necessary or select an existing empty one.
2. Open the track's Inserts section in the Inspector.
3. From the Plug-Ins Selection drop-down menu, select the SMPTE Generator.
4. Expand the Audio Setup section in the Inspector.
5. Assign the channel containing the plug-in to an output bus that isn't already used to transfer audio. If you don't have an unused bus, see whether you can use one side in a left/right setup and then

pan the plug-in on one side and whatever was previously assigned to that bus to the other side. For example, use a bass on the left and the SMPTE Generator on the right.

6. Click the Edit Plug-In Settings for this insert. The SMPTE panel will appear, as shown in Figure 30.1.

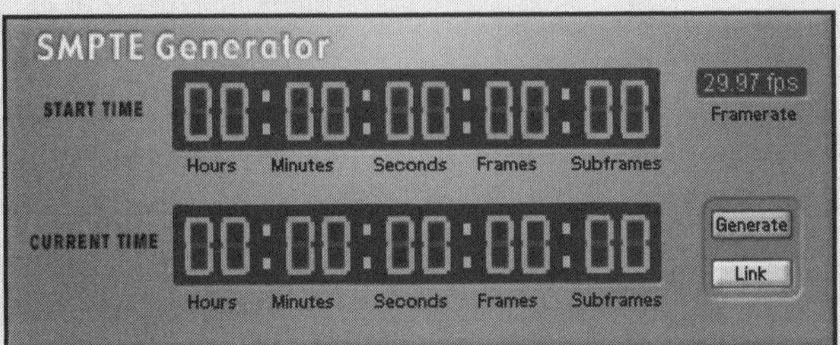

Figure 30.1
The SMPTE Generator panel.

7. Make sure the Frame Rate field displays the same frame rate as your project. You can access your Project Setup dialog box by pressing Shift+S to verify whether this is the case. Otherwise, set the Frame Rate field to the appropriate setting.
8. Make the connections between the output to which the plug-in is assigned and the receiving device (which will be "slaved" to the LTC timecode received from Cubase).
9. Click the Generate button to start sending timecode. This step verifies whether the signal is connected properly to the slaved device.
10. Adjust the level in either the audio channel containing the plug-in or on the slaved device's end. This receiving device must receive an undistorted signal in order to lock properly.
11. After you've made these adjustments, click the Link button in the Plug-In Information panel.
12. Start the playback of your project to lock together the SMPTE Generator, the project, and the slaved device.

MIDI Clock

MIDI Clock is a tempo-based synchronization signal used to synchronize two or more MIDI devices together with a beats-per-minute (BPM) guide track. As you can see, this is different than a timecode because it does not refer to a real-time address (hours: minutes: seconds: frames). In this case, it sends 24 evenly spaced MIDI clock pulses per quarter note. So, at a speed of 60 BPM, it sends 1,440 clock pulses per minute (one every 41.67 milliseconds), whereas at a speed of 120 BPM, it sends double that amount (one every 20.83 milliseconds). Because it is strictly tempo-based, the rate of MIDI Clock signals always varies according to the tempo of the master tempo source.

When a sender sends a MIDI Clock signal, it sends a MIDI Start message to tell any slaved devices or programs to start playing a sequence at the speed or tempo set in by the master. When the master sends a MIDI End message, the slaved device or program stops playing its sequence. Up until this point, all the slave can do is start and stop playing MIDI when it receives MIDI Start and MIDI End messages. If you need to tell the slaved sequence *where* to start within its own sequence (especially when you start playback on the master somewhere in the middle of the song, for example), the master MIDI device has to send what is called a Song Position Pointer message, telling the slave the current location of the master's song position. The slaved device or program then uses the MIDI data to calculate the appropriate position to start playback in relation to the MIDI Start message received from the master.

MIDI Clock should be reserved for use between MIDI devices only, not for audio. As soon as you add digital audio or video, you should avoid using MIDI Clock because it is not well-suited for these purposes. Although it keeps a good synchronization between similar MIDI devices, synchronizing digital audio requires much greater precision. Video, on the other hand, works with location references based on absolute time instead of BPM, making MIDI Clock unsuitable for this type of work.

HOW TO

Synchronize a Cubase with a MIDI Clock—compatible device:

1. Ctrl-click (PC)/-click (Mac) on the Transport panel's Sync button, and select Sync Setup from the Transport menu.
2. In the Synchronization Setup dialog box, check the MIDI Clock Destination port, as displayed in Figure 30.2. Cubase will send a MIDI Clock message on all checked ports.

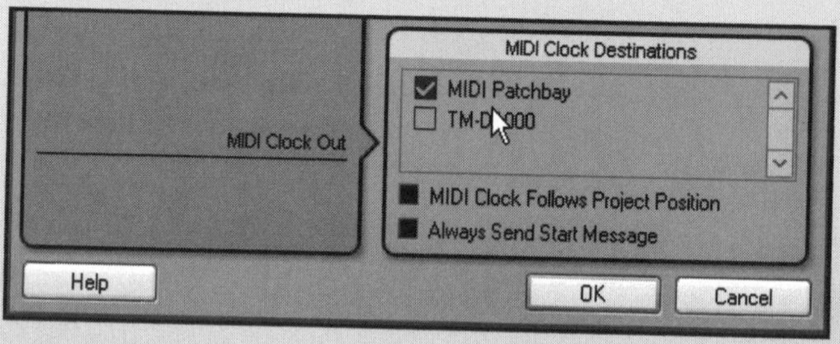

Figure 30.2
The MIDI Clock settings in the Synchronization Setup dialog box.

3. Check the MIDI Clock Follows Project Position and the Always Send Start Message options to enable these options. For example, if you need the MIDI device to follow a looped playback in your project rather than simply playing from a start point until the playback stops, enabling the Project Position option helps.
4. Click OK when you are finished.

MIDI Machine Control

Another type of MIDI-related synchronization is MIDI Machine Control (MMC). The MMC protocol uses System Exclusive messages over a MIDI cable to remotely control disk-based recording systems and other machines used for recording or playback. Many MIDI-enabled hardware devices support this protocol.

MMC sends MIDI to a device, giving it commands such as play, stop, rewind, go to a specific location, punch-in, and punch-out on a specific track.

To make use of MMC in a setup in which you are using a multitrack tape recorder as the master and Cubase or some other audio/MIDI program as the slave, you need to have a timecode (SMPTE) track on the master device sending timecode to a SMPTE/MTC interface (converter). This then sends the converted MTC to Cubase so that it can stay in sync with the multitrack recorder. Both devices are also connected through MIDI cables. It is the multitrack that controls Cubase's playback position, not vice versa. Cubase, in return, can transmit MMC messages through its MIDI connection with the multitrack, which is equipped with a MIDI interface. These MMC messages tell the multitrack to rewind, fast-forward, and so on. When you click Play in Cubase, it tells the multitrack to go to the position at which playback in Cubase's project begins. When the multitrack reaches this position, it starts playing the tape back, sending timecode to Cubase, which then syncs with the multitrack.

Digital Clock

Digital clock is another way to synchronize two or more devices together by using the sampling frequency of the master device as a reference. This hardware-level type of synchronization is often used in conjunction with the positional reference provided by MTC in a music application such as Cubase to lock both audio hardware and MIDI devices with video devices. Many studio configurations use a central, master clock source (Big Ben, Aardsync, etc.) that is the word sync master for audio interfaces on the computer and/or digital tape devices. In other cases, one may choose to sync the computer's audio interface to some external device such as a digital multitrack or a more sophisticated unit that does continuous resync (e.g., Digital Timepiece, Sync I/O) in order to continuously adjust the hardware clock timing reference to variation in the incoming timecode. Digital clock is by far the most precise synchronization mechanism discussed here. Because it uses the sampling frequency of your audio hardware, it is precise to 1/44,100 of a second when you are using a 44.1-kHz sampling frequency (or 0.02 milliseconds). Compare this with the precision of SMPTE timecode (around 33 milliseconds at 30 fps) and MIDI Clock (41.67 milliseconds at 120 BPM), and you quickly realize that this synchronization is very accurate. However, it is important to understand that Word Clock (also known as word sync, or simply digital clock) is simply a hardware-level timing reference—in relation to the sample rate—but contains no positional information that would tell the slaved device *where* to start playing its content back in relation to the master.

When you make a digital transfer between two digital devices, typically the digital clock reference of the sending device should send to the receiving device. Failure to do so results in signal errors and will lead to signal degradation. Often, when recording audio from an S/PDIF, AES/EBU, or ADAT source via a digital input, you will lock your computer hardware to the sample rate of that incoming digital signal. When a device is slaved to incoming Word Clock (a type of digital clock) sent by another device, it will follow that timing reference for digital audio playback rather than its own internal sample clock.

A Digital clock can be transmitted on one of these cables:

- **S/PDIF (Sony/Phillips Digital Interface).** This digital audio connector format is probably the most common way to connect two digital devices together. S/PDIF connectors have RCA or optical connectors at each end and carry digital audio information with embedded digital audio clock information. You can transmit mono or stereo audio information on a single S/PDIF connection.
- **AES/EBU (Audio Engineering Society/European Broadcast Union).** This is another very common type of digital connector format used to transfer digital information from one device to another, especially on more high-end audio devices. AES/EBU uses an XLR connector at each end of the cable. Like the S/PDIF format, it carries the digital audio clock embedded in its data stream. You also can transmit mono or stereo audio information on this type of connection. Because AES/EBU connections use balanced XLR connectors, they are less susceptible to digital errors that could create clicks, but because AES/EBU connections are more expensive, you won't find them on low-cost equipment.
- **ADAT (Alesis Digital Audio Technology).** This is a proprietary digital audio connector format developed by Alesis that carries up to eight separate digital audio signals and Word Clock information over a single, fiber-optic cable. If your audio hardware provides ADAT connectors, use them to send and receive digital clock information from and to an ADAT-compatible device.
- **TDIF (Tascam Digital Interface).** This is a proprietary digital audio connector format developed by Tascam that provides eight channels of digital audio in both directions. It also carries clocking signals that are used for synchronizing the transmission and reception of the audio; however, it does not contain Word Clock information, so you typically need to connect TDIF cables along with Word Clock cables (see the next item) if you want to lock two digital audio devices using this type of connection.
- **Word Clock.** A digital clock is called *Word Clock* when it is sent over its own cable. Because Word Clock signals contain high frequencies, they are usually transmitted on 75-ohm coaxial cables for reliability. Usually, a coaxial BNC connector is used for Word Clock connections.

To transfer digital audio information in sync from one digital device to another, all devices have to support the sampling rate being sent by the master device, unless you have a more sophisticated sync setup that converts different sample rates via multiple Word Clock (or AES/EBU-S/PDIF) connectors. This is particularly important when you are using sampling frequencies other than 44.1 or 48 kHz, which are pretty standard on most digital audio devices.

When you synchronize two digital audio devices, the digital clock might not be the only synchronization clock needed. If you are working with another hard disk recorder or multitrack analog tape recorder, you may need to send transport controls to and from these devices along with the timing reference generated by this digital clock, and of course you still require a positional reference so that the slaved device knows where to start playback. This is when you have to lock together both the digital clock and timecode. Again, do not attempt to use MIDI Clock for synchronizing with digital audio. The next section discusses different possibilities and how to set up Cubase to act as a master or slave in the situations described previously.

When you are doing digital transfers between a digital multitrack tape and Cubase, it is important that both the Word Clock (digital clock) information for timing and the timecode information for position be correlated to ensure a no-loss transfer and that for every bit on one end, there's a corresponding bit on the other. This high-precision task can be performed through ASIO Position Protocol (APP).

APP uses the ASIO driver provided for your audio hardware and a compatible APP digital device. In this type of setup, the ADAT provides the master (sender) Word Clock and the timecode information to Cubase. The ASIO 2.0–compatible driver of your audio hardware simply follows this information and stays accurate to the last sample.

Resolving Differences

Cubase offers solutions for most synchronization situations. If you have an ASIO 2.0–compatible driver for your audio hardware and an ASIO 2.0–compatible external device, it allows you to have a sample-accurate synchronization of the sample clocks in your devices, and it also provide a Positioning Protocol that calculates the relation between the Word Clock reference and the location information carried by timecode, to offer stable synchronization as you play longer durations and skip around within the project. If your external hardware does not support ASIO 2.0, use MIDI Time Code as your synchronization method instead. You might want to consult your manufacturer's documentation in regard to ASIO 2.0 implementation to find out more about the possibilities it has to offer.

Internal and External References

Because Cubase offers very stable synchronization, consider using this as your source, making it the master for other devices. But in the real world, this is not always possible. Cubase can be the slave, master, or both simultaneously. Depending on your audio hardware, it's possible for Cubase to receive a sync signal from a master sync device and send this sync signal to another slave device, regenerating the sync information for a stable synchronization.

You need to keep two important factors in mind when working out synchronization between devices, especially when you connect multiple devices using digital connections, such as the ones mentioned earlier in this chapter:

- What device is responsible for the digital clock information? In other words, who will be sending its Word Clock information to others? If you don't have any digital connections in your studio, chances are your audio hardware is the master. If this audio hardware is connected to any other device through a digital connection, you need to look at how it is connected and how it is set up. How devices are interconnected digitally influences how digital audio flows between these devices (see Figure 30.3).

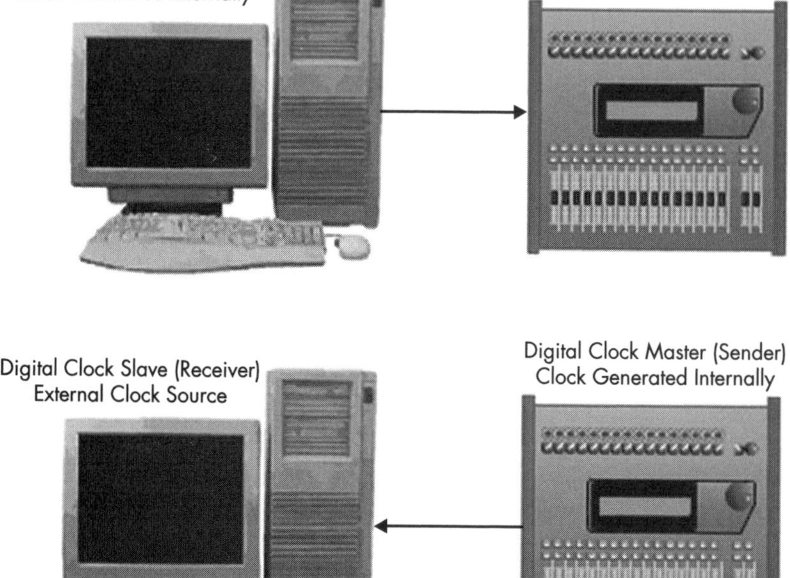

Figure 30.3
Top: The computer is master (sending), while the other device is slaved (receiving). Bottom: The computer is slaved to the other device.

- Where does the time-related (such as timecode and positioning) information come from? If you are working with a SMPTE timecode coming from a video deck or multitrack tape recorder, chances are you need to slave Cubase to these devices (set it to follow received timecode information). How devices are interconnected with a timecode reference influences who controls the transport and location functions.

These are two synchronization issues that are often misunderstood, but are essential in today's digital studio. So, let's first determine whether you need to worry about digital synchronization between the sample clocks in the audio devices used in your studio configuration, and then we'll look at timecode synchronization.

1. Does your computer's audio interface provide a digital connection of some sort (S/PDIF, ADAT, TDIF, AES/EBU, or perhaps a separate Word Clock connection)?
   - *Yes it does, but it's not being used* (or) *No, it doesn't.* Then your computer's audio interface is the digital clock (or sample clock) master (sender).
   - *Yes, it does provide a digital connection and it is being used.* Read the following question.
2. Is your computer's audio interface set to follow its internal Word Clock, or is it set to follow an external Word Clock source (or a digital audio connection that carries Word Clock information embedded along with the audio samples)?
   - *My audio interface's sample clock is set to internal.* Then your computer's audio interface is the digital clock master (sender). You should be sure other devices are set to follow (receive) this digital clock reference. This is done through your audio interface's control panel. Figure 30.4 shows an example of an audio interface control panel; however, yours might differ, depending on your audio interface model, manufacturer, and driver version.

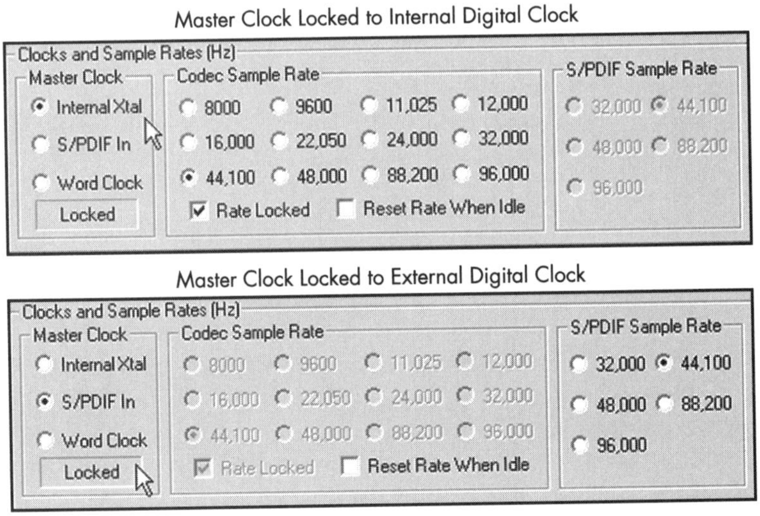

Master Clock Locked to Internal Digital Clock

Master Clock Locked to External Digital Clock

Figure 30.4
Setting up your audio hardware's Word Clock source in the audio hardware's control panel.

   - *My audio interface's sample clock is set to follow an external clock.* Then your audio interface is slaved to an external sample clock reference, and you should be sure that it is locked to this sample clock. This is done through your audio interface's control panel, as well as in the digital clock control settings on the master external audio device. It is important that the Digital clock master is connected with the Digital clock slaves at all times.

After you've established that the proper digital connections are made and that the master/slave relation has been established for Word Clock, you can configure the second step in the synchronization setup: Who controls the timecode? Let's look at some potential setups.

Setting Up Synchronizations

Inside Cubase, the synchronization options are in the Synchronization Setup dialog box, found under Transport > Sync Setup or by Ctrl-clicking (PC)/⌘-clicking (Mac) on the Sync button in the Transport panel. Let's take a closer look at Figure 30.5.

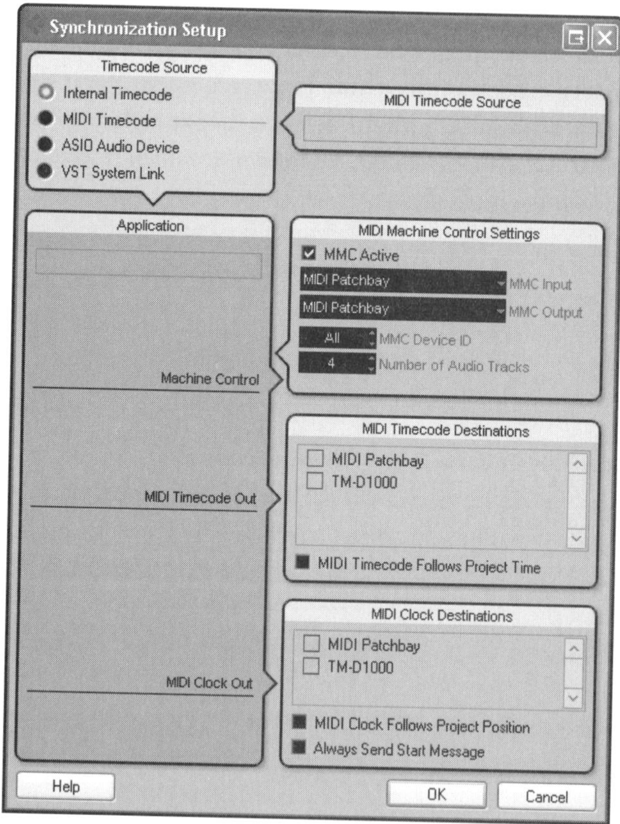

Figure 30.5
The Synchronization Setup dialog box.

- **Timecode Source.** This selects the source of your timecode. If Cubase is not receiving timecode from any other devices or if Cubase *is* the source of timecode, this option, by default, is set to Internal. Otherwise, you can select the appropriate timecode source. When slaving

Cubase to MIDI Timecode, select the MIDI input on which the MTC arrives. In some configurations, a single unit may act both as the MIDI interface and SMPTE/MTC synchronization peripheral.

- **Application fields.** This sets both the Drop Out Time and Lock Frames options whenever MIDI Timecode is selected as source, as shown in Figure 30.6. The dropout time is a frame value. When you are receiving timecode from a tape recorder or video deck, degradation of the timecode signal might occur, leaving the timecode unreadable for a number of frames. If this is the case, Cubase might stop playing, and then start again when it begins to receive legible timecode again. To avoid this problem, you can raise the amount of dropout time tolerated by Cubase before it stops playing. If your timecode is really bad, you might want to consider rerecording the timecode track rather than setting this option high because the shift in timecode between the estimated timecode (the one estimated by Cubase estimates while the incoming timecode signal has dropped) and the real timecode when it starts arriving from the master again might create undesired effects. The Lock Frames option represents the number of frames Cubase needs to receive before it starts playing after locking to that timecode. If you have many events to chase, such as program changes and mix automation parameters, you might want to set this to a higher value in order for all the data to load and play properly when Cubase starts playing. On the other hand, if you don't have that many events to chase, you can set this to a lower setting.

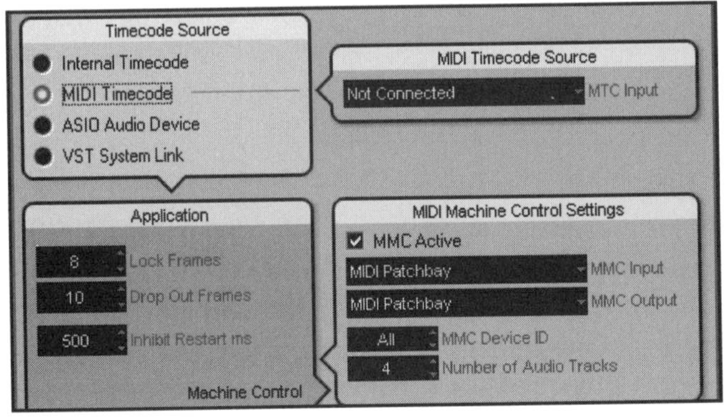

Figure 30.6
The application options when Cubase receives timecode from an external source.

- **MIDI Machine Control Settings.** When enabled, this lets you assign the MIDI port needed to receive and transmit MMC, as described earlier. In the event that you have connected Cubase to an MMC-compatible device, you need to select both the MIDI input and output ports that communicate the MMC information to and from this device in the appropriate fields of this section.

- **MIDI Timecode and MIDI Clock Destinations.** These enable the MIDI outputs Cubase should use to send these types of signals to other devices. If you have a drum machine or hardware sequencer that can only receive a MIDI Clock, for example, select the MIDI output connected to that device.

HOW TO

Set up synchronization properties:

1. Open the Synchronization dialog box: Ctrl-click (PC)/⌘-click (Mac) on the Sync button in the Transport panel or select Sync Setup from the Transport menu.
2. Select the appropriate timecode source for your project.
3. If you have selected MIDI Timecode as your timecode source, select the MIDI input port on which the MTC arrives.
4. If your project requires that you connect with a MIDI Machine Control–compatible device, select this option and set the appropriate MIDI output port to send and receive the MMC.
5. If you have other devices connected to your computer that require Cubase to retransmit synchronization signals to them, such as MTC or MIDI Clock, select the appropriate MIDI output ports.
6. For now, you should leave the options (Drop Out Time and Lock Time) in the Synchronization Setup dialog box at their default values. In the event that you need to change these values due to a bad timecode coming from a tape recorder or another source, you may access this dialog box and adjust the values until the timecode locks properly.
7. Click OK to close the Synchronization Setup dialog box.
8. Activate the Sync button on the Transport panel if the Timecode Source is not set to Internal Timecode. Cubase will now wait for an incoming timecode signal from the specified source. If you assigned an MMC, MIDI Clock, or MTC MIDI output, Cubase will automatically generate the necessary signals.

Synchronizing Cubase

Let's take a look at getting Cubase to synchronize with other devices. Figure 30.7 displays a simple setup in which a video player sends SMPTE information (most often LTC, since synchronization peripherals for this method are less expensive than VITC devices) to a MIDI interface with the capacity to act as a SMPTE-to-MTC converter, relaying the MTC to Cubase. In this setup, you should set the sample clock of your audio hardware to Internal and set the timecode source to MTC, being sure to select the MIDI input port on which the MTC arrives.

If, for some reason, the digital mixer or another digital device connected to your computer has to be the sender Word Clock, be sure your audio hardware follows the incoming clock by setting its digital clock source to External (this might be an S/PDIF, an ADAT, an AES/EBU, or a separate Word Clock connection–see Figure 30.8). Consult your audio hardware's documentation to configure it appropriately.

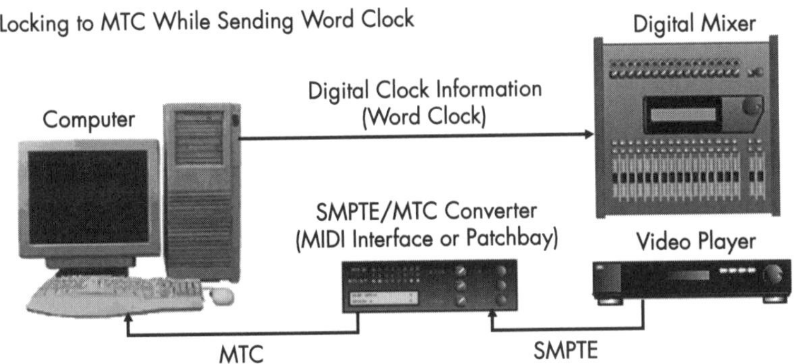

Figure 30.7
Simple synchronization diagram.

In Figure 30.8, Cubase locks to both the incoming MTC source (location information) and the Word Clock information coming from a synchronizer with *continuous resync* or *resolving* capability. This synchronizer can correlate both timecode and Word Clock together, making it the unique source feeding Cubase. This type of setup helps in keeping a simple, yet stable synchronization between devices. It also enables you to hook up other digital devices to the synchronizer in an effort to ensure that the source of the Word Clock information and MTC all come from one source. In this case, as in the previous example, Cubase's synchronization option should be set to follow an MTC source, and your audio hardware should be set to follow an external digital clock (slaving to it).

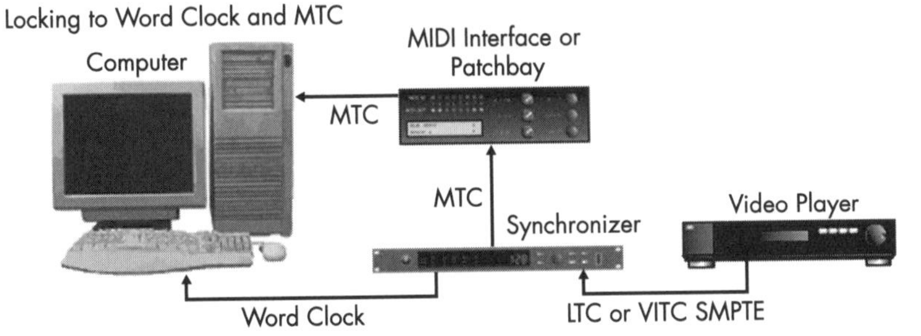

Figure 30.8
Another simple synchronization diagram.

In Figure 30.9, things might look complicated, but you can break this down one item at a time. This setup displays possible interconnections, in which different synchronization protocols are transmitted and received at once.

Let's start with the drum machine. In this setup, Cubase is connected through its MIDI interface to a drum machine, sending a MIDI Clock synchronization signal to it. For the drum machine to lock with Cubase, you need to check the appropriate MIDI output port to send MIDI Clock in the Synchronization Setup dialog box. You also need to set your drum machine to receive incoming MIDI clock pulses; otherwise, it does not respond to this signal.

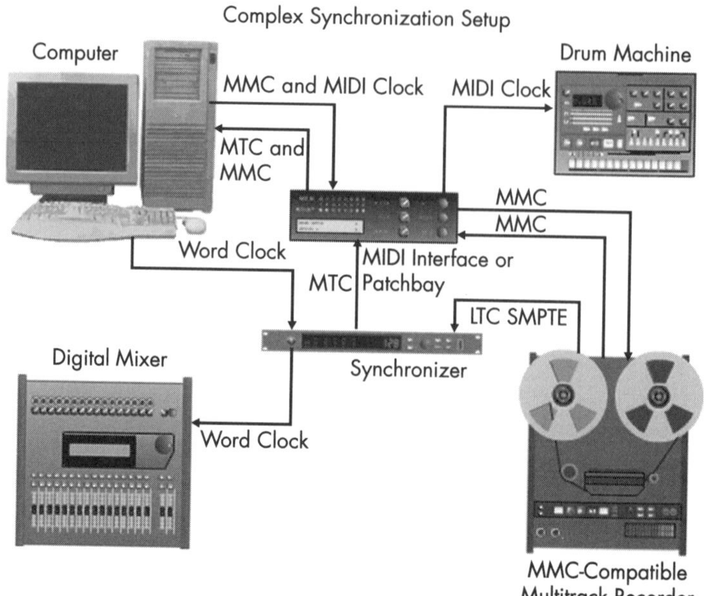

Figure 30.9
A more complex studio setup involving different types of simultaneous synchronization.

Below the drum machine is a multitrack tape recorder with a compatible MIDI Machine Control (MMC) interface. By connecting both the MIDI input and output to your computer's MIDI interface, you create the necessary MIDI bridge between Cubase and the tape recorder, as described earlier in the MMC section. But for MMC to work, the tape recorder has to send out timecode information to the computer. This is done through the LTC (SMPTE) signal being sent to the synchronizer. The synchronizer converts the LTC into MTC, sending it to the computer. Note here that if all you have is a tape recorder and a computer, you don't need the synchronizer in between, but you still need a SMPTE-to-MTC converter. In either case, for the timecode source in Cubase to read the incoming MTC signal, the MMC option needs to be selected, and the appropriate MIDI input and output ports receiving and transmitting the MMC information also need to be selected.

So, in this setup, Cubase's timecode source is external, yet it still generates a MIDI Clock to slave the drum machine to the project's location and tempo setting. The tape recorder provides the timecode source. The MMC provides the transport controls, but it is Cubase that controls the MMC. The computer's audio hardware provides the Word Clock along with the MIDI Clock. Finally, Cubase converts the timecode from the tape recorder into MIDI Clock and Song Position Pointer information, which then controls the drum machine. It is important to understand that the synchronizer in this example correlates or "resolves" both the Word Clock reference and SMPTE/MTC location information, in order for the synchronization to work properly even over extended periods of time.

VI Mixing and Mastering

31 Mixer

The Mixer in Cubase offers an interface that resembles a typical mixing console. This Mixer contains a replica of the channel settings previously described in other chapters of this book. So, why this fancy mixing window? Because it's convenient to have all mixing channel controls for each track next to each other once you've finished the recording and editing process. You can now focus on making each track sound better, both in itself and as a part of the project. A virtual mixer makes it easier not only to see the settings applied to all your tracks, but also to automate the mix for an entire project, as you will see later. A mixing environment is all about flexibility, accessibility, and your personal aesthetics when it comes to how music or sound appeals to your ears. The last part is yours to develop; fortunately, Cubase offers both flexibility and accessibility.

Here's a summary of what you will learn in this chapter:

- How to recognize the different areas of the Mixer panel
- How to save channel settings and apply them to other channels inside the Mixer panel
- How to customize the Mixer to fit the tasks at hand
- How to use groups to create submixes and to monitor mixes
- How to find input and output busses in the Mixer and how to use them
- How to use the Can Hide functionalities of the Mixer

Mixer Areas

Although the main purpose for the Mixer panel is to offer a single interface to control all channels in a project, as displayed in Figure 31.1, the Mixer offers more than just individual channel controls, which are mirrored in the Inspector and VST Channel Settings panel. To control the appearance and behavior of all the channel strips inside the Mixer, Cubase provides three additional areas that add even greater power to this panel's interface.

- The **Common panel**, located on the left of the Mixer, displays a series of controls that affect all channels in the Mixer.
- The **Extended Mixer** displays insert and send effect settings, EQ settings for audio and group channels, output levels, and an overview of settings applied to a channel.
- The **Routing panel** displays input and output bus assignments and controls for each channel in the project.

Figure 31.1
The Mixer panel.

Common Panel

The Common panel found on the left of the Mixer (see Figure 31.2) controls global settings for this Mixer panel, as well as for its appearance and behavior. This section includes a look at each item in the panel from top to bottom.

When you need to have an overview of all EQ, send, or insert FX settings, or you want to see which effect is loaded where, the Show Extended Mixer button (see Figure 31.3) offers a way to reveal the extended portion of the Mixer. When the extended portion of the Mixer is visible, click the Hide Extended Mixer button to hide it. You can use this minus sign to hide the extended portion of the Mixer.

Figure 31.2
The Common panel found on the left of the Mixer panel.

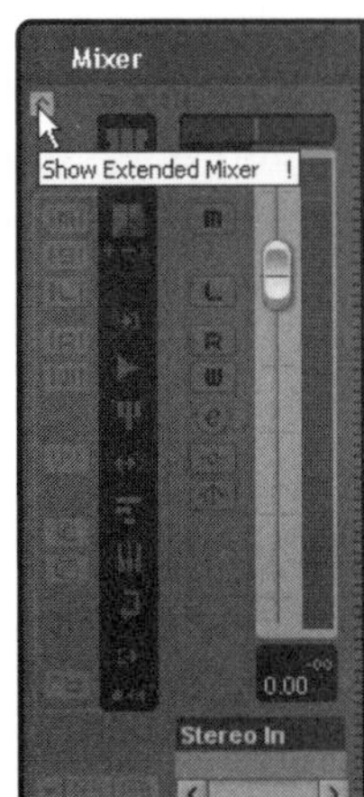

Figure 31.3
The Show/Hide Extended Mixer button.

All Wide/All Narrow buttons make all channels in the current Mixer wide or narrow, respectively. The same settings appear individually on each channel, enabling you to make them narrow or wide independently. But when you click here (see the cursors in Figure 31.4), all channels change to wide or narrow at the touch of a button. When a channel is displayed in Narrow mode, all of its functions remain active; however, some of the controls are hidden, allowing more channels to fit on your desktop. This becomes convenient when you are working with a project that has more channels than can fit in your current desktop resolution.

Figure 31.4
The All Wide and All Narrow buttons.

Store View and Remove View buttons let you save a set of Mixer display options as a preset and retrieve them later from the Select Channel View Set menu (see Figure 31.5). Creating your own presets enables you to customize the Mixer to display the information you need to see for specific tasks, such as audio recording, mixing, or any other task you frequently need to perform in this window.

HOW TO

Store a channel view set:

1. Set up the Mixer view options appropriately so that they display the information to which you want to have quick access.
2. Click on the Store View button.
3. Enter a name for your preset—for example, Audio EQ if you chose to display only audio channels with their EQ settings displayed in the extended panel.
4. Click the OK button.

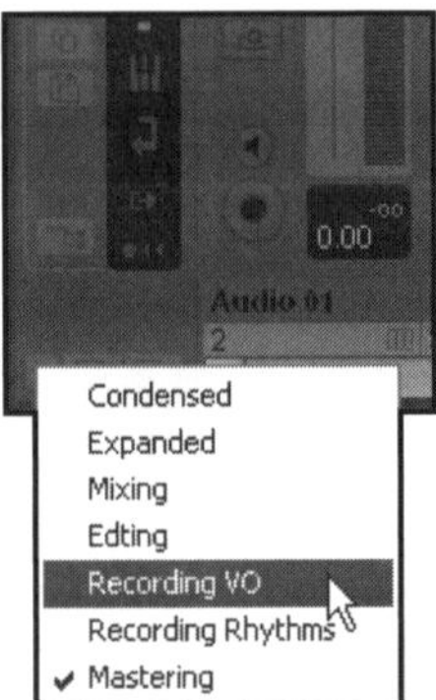

Figure 31.5
Selecting a Channel View Set in the Mixer.

Remove a channel view set:

1. Select the view from the Select Channel View Set menu.
2. Click on the Remove View button.

You can use up to three different Mixer panel configurations with Cubase. Take advantage of this feature to organize your mixing environment in a way that suits you best. For example, you can choose to display all MIDI channels in one Mixer and audio channels in another. Access the additional mixers through the Devices menu.

The global Mute, Solo, Listen, Read, and Write buttons in the Common panel resemble those on individual channels. Although changing one of these buttons on an individual channel won't affect the others, changing the state of one of these buttons in the Common panel toggles that function off for *all* channels available in the Mixer panel. Whenever one or more tracks in the Mixer panel is muted, the global Mute indicator button in the Common panel is lit, as shown in the "before" portion of Figure 31.6. Clicking this global button in the Common panel cancels all current mute settings, unmuting all channels in the project (see the "after" portion of Figure 31.6). The Listen and Solo buttons play a similar role in the sense that they are lit when one or more tracks is in Solo or Listen mode. Clicking the corresponding global button in the Common panel then deactivates the solo or listen monitoring for all channels in the project. The global Read and Write buttons in the Common panel can be used to activate or deactivate the read or write automation status on all channels. If one or more channels is already in Read or Write mode, the Mixer panel is lit as well to indicate that a channel is currently actively reading or ready to write automation.

The Show VST Connections button (see Figure 31.7) does the same thing as the VST Connections option found under the Devices menu; it brings up the VST Connections window, allowing you to make modifications to the current input and output bus configurations.

Before

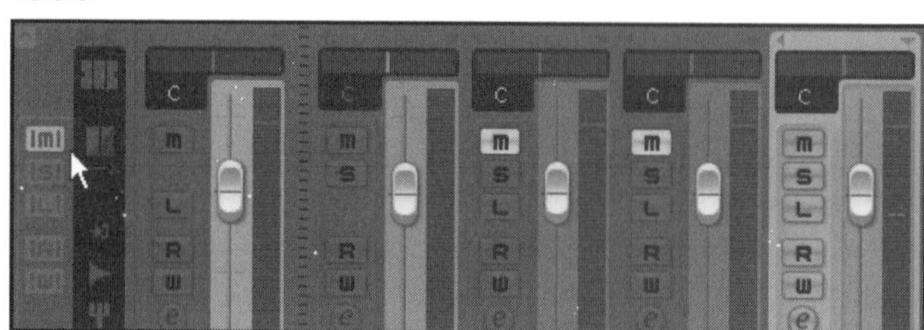

After

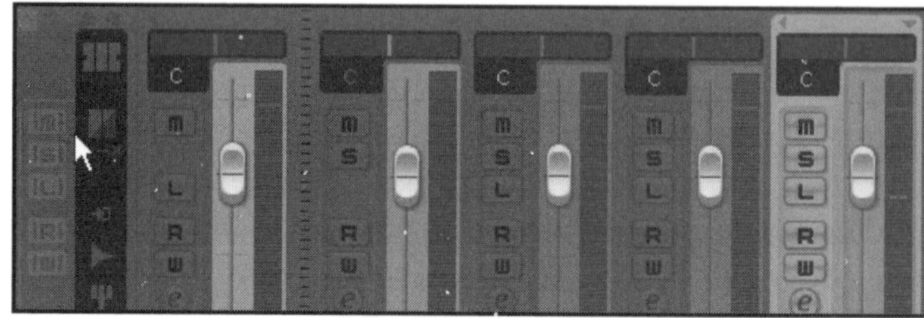

Figure 31.6
The common buttons for Mute, Solo, Listen, Read, and Write functions in the Mixer panel.

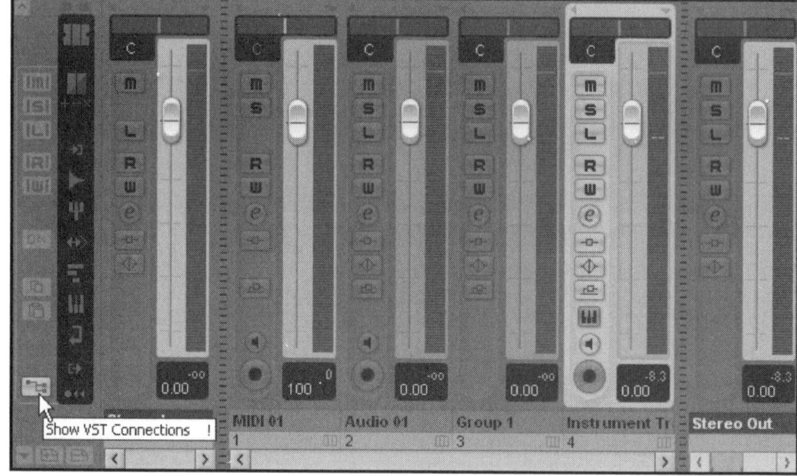

Figure 31.7
The Show VST Connections button.

The Reset Mixer/Reset Channels button (see Figure 31.8) resets all the channels or only the selected channels in the Mixer. When you reset a channel, you deactivate all solo, mute, EQ, insert, and send effect settings. The Volume fader also is set to 0 dB (that is, no gain change applied to the source signal) and pans to center position.

If you want to copy the settings of a selected track to another, you can use the buttons and menu found at the bottom of the Common panel (see below the Reset Mixer button in Figure 31.8). For

Figure 31.8
The Reset Mixer/Reset Channels button above the Copy/Paste Selected Channels buttons.

example, if you want to have the same EQ, insert, and send settings on several vocal tracks, you can make the settings on a first channel, and when you are satisfied with these settings, you can copy and paste them to one or more channels. Subsequently, all the channels to which you copied these settings will be the same.

HOW TO

Copy a channel's settings to another channel:

1. Adjust the settings of the channel you want to copy.
2. Be sure this channel is selected in the Mixer, as shown in Figure 31.9.
3. Click the Copy Channel button. The Paste button will become active.
4. Select the channel to which you want to paste the copied settings.
5. Click the Paste Settings button in the Common panel.
6. You can repeat this paste operation to any number of channels by selecting the channel and clicking the Paste button again.

Figure 31.9
A selected channel (left) compared to a non-selected channel (right).

The buttons found in Figure 31.10 will hide from view all channels of this particular class in the Mixer panel. These are, from top to bottom: input busses, audio channels, group channels, ReWire channels, MIDI channels, plug-in instrument channels (such as VST instruments), plug-in FX channels (send effects), and output busses. Hiding a class of channels does not influence the output, but it does make it easier to navigate the Mixer when the project has a large number of channels and you need to work on a specific class of channels.

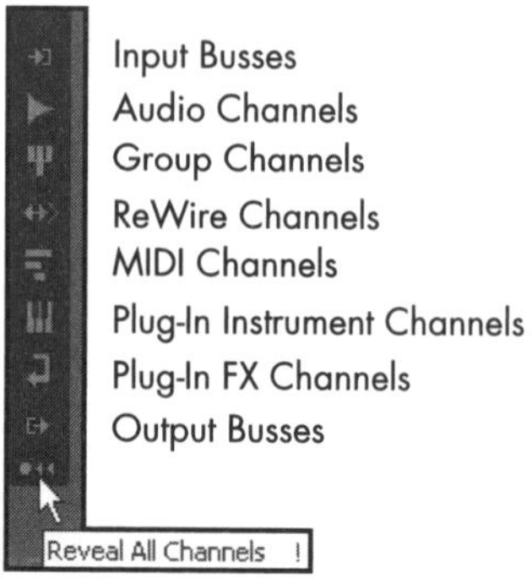

Figure 31.10
The Show/Hide Channel buttons.

> **About Command Target**
>
> It is possible to assign key commands to Mixer-related tasks, such as bypassing all inserts, for example. Although this may be convenient, what's even more convenient is the option to exclude all input busses, the currently selected channels, or all output busses from these key commands.
>
> To exclude inputs from key commands, enable the left button. To only apply key commands to selected channels, as shown in Figure 31.11, enable the center button. Finally, to exclude output busses, enable the right button.
>
> These settings also influence the Remove "Can Hide" from Target function. For example, if the Command Target is set to Exclude Outputs, the outputs will be locked out of the Can Hide status.
>
> 
>
> **Figure 31.11**
> *The Command Target buttons in the Mixer's Common panel.*

Extended Common Panel

The Extended panel is visible to Cubase users when clicking on the Show Extended Mixer button at the left edge of the Common panel. When the Mixer is in extended mode, the corresponding portion of the Common panel reveals an additional set of options (see Figure 31.12).

The difference once again is that when you click one of these view options in the Common panel, all channels in the current Mixer will display the same type of information. For example, clicking

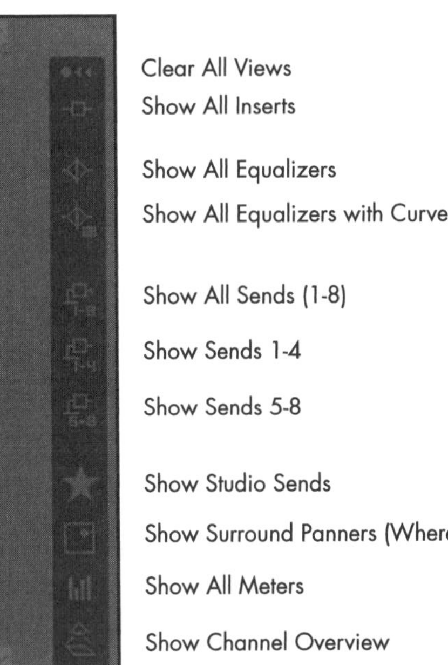

Figure 31.12
The extended portion of the Common panel in the Mixer panel.

the Show All Inserts button in the Common panel switches the display format of all channels to show insert settings in the extended portion of the Mixer. You can, however, change the displayed extended panel for a specific channel by selecting a different display option for this channel. As with the options found in the lower part of the Common panel, the global options here can also be set independently for each channel in the Mixer.

Note that changing the display format for Mixer channels does not in any way change their settings—it only affects the type of information that is displayed.

Depending on which option you choose to view in the extended Mixer area, different panels will appear, as shown in Figure 31.13. For example, there are no MIDI EQ settings in the Extended panel.

When you choose to display the EQ for other channels, the MIDI channel's Extended area keeps displaying whatever was there before you chose the extended EQ display. The MIDI insert's Extended panel displays the four insert settings. Each insert has the following functions:

- Enable/disable the insert
- Open the insert's edit window
- Select the MIDI insert effect

Audio inserts have the same controls as the MIDI inserts; however, the list displayed in the Insert Selection menu is different.

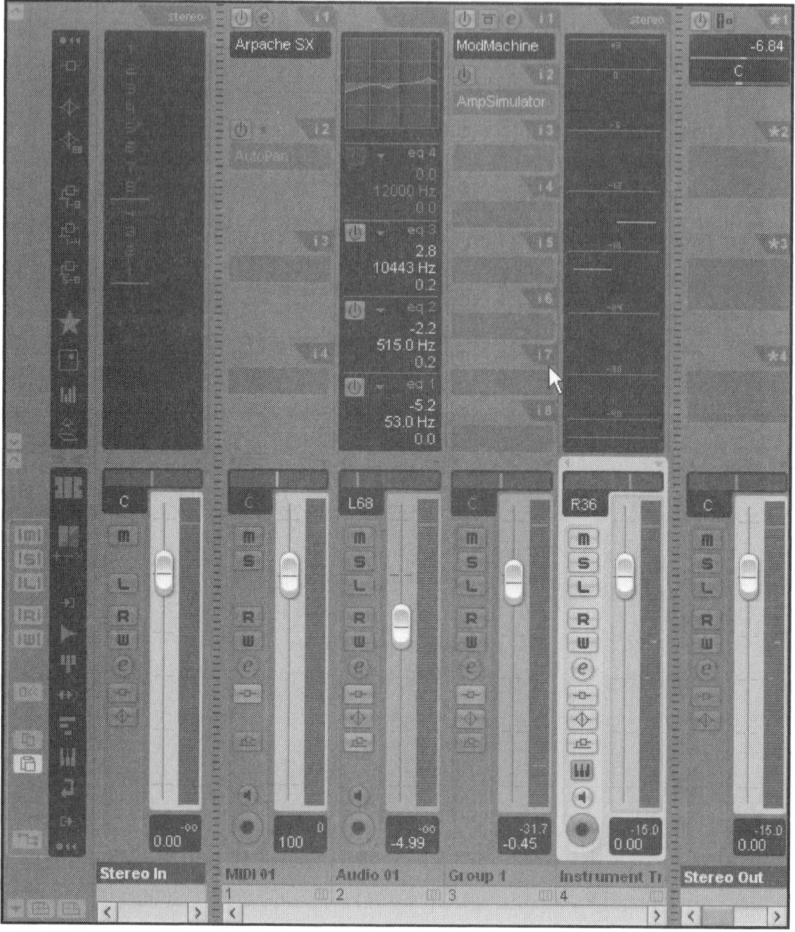

Figure 31.13
The Mixer's Extended panel.

Both extended EQ display options offer the same controls in different display options.

- An On/Off button to enable or disable the EQ band
- A gain control (top slider)
- A frequency control (second slider)
- A Q setting (third slider)

The MIDI sends in the Extended panel display the following settings for each of the four send effects:

- An On/Off button to enable or disable the MIDI sends

- An open effect's Editing panel button
- A pre- or post-fader selection button
- An effect selection menu
- A MIDI output port selection menu for the output of the effect
- A channel setting for the output of the effect

The audio sends offer the following controls:

- An On/Off button to enable or disable the sends
- An open effect's Editing panel button
- A pre- or post-fader selection button
- An effect selection menu
- A send to effect level (represented by a slider)

The settings displayed in the Extended panels are the same settings that are available in the Inspector area of each track, and you can click on the **e** button (Edit Channel Settings) next to the channel's Level fader to open that channel's additional settings panel.

Routing Panel

The Routing panel, found at the very top of Cubase's Mixer, lets you choose the input and output busses for audio channels and input and output MIDI ports for MIDI channels.

If you don't see the Routing panel, click on the Show Routing button in the upper-left corner of the Mixer (see the left side of Figure 31.14). To hide the panel once again, click on the Hide Routing button (see the right side of Figure 31.14). This is a great panel to set up multiple track inputs when you are recording bands instead of going through the Inspector area. In the end, working preferences or the types of projects you work on will determine whether this tool is for you. Knowing it's there when you need it is still a good thing.

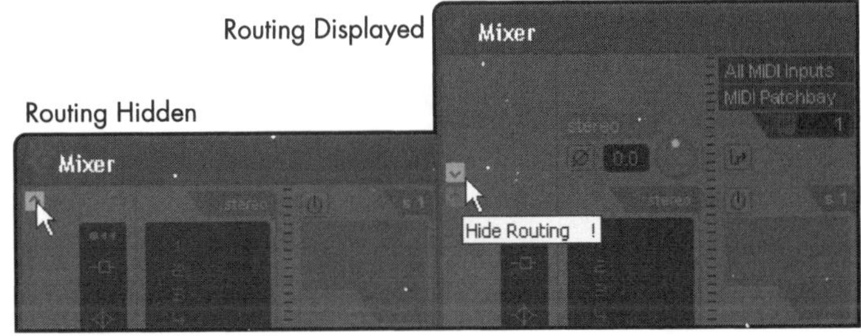

Figure 31.14
The Routing panel found in the Mixer panel.

Working with Mixer Settings

Besides Mixer channel views, described earlier in the "Common Panel" section, there are a few other Mixer settings you can save. After a setting is saved, you can load it later, applying these saved settings elsewhere in the Mixer. These options are available by right-clicking (PC)/Ctrl-clicking (Mac) over any channel in the Mixer (see Figure 31.15). The settings you save are those of the currently selected channel. Similarly, the Load Selected Channels option loads the saved Mixer settings in all selected channels. Saving selected channels also allows you to store bus routing.

The Save/Load All Mixer Settings function saves all the current audio channel settings so that you can retrieve them later by using the Load All Mixer Settings function. To load saved Mixer settings, you simply need to select the appropriate channel, select the load setting option desired, look for the file on your media drive, and load it in the Mixer panel.

In the same menu (see Figure 31.15), you also have the option to link or unlink channels. When channels are linked, the volume, EQ and send effect settings, and bypass insert and bypass send effect settings you apply to one channel also affect all the other channels linked to this one.

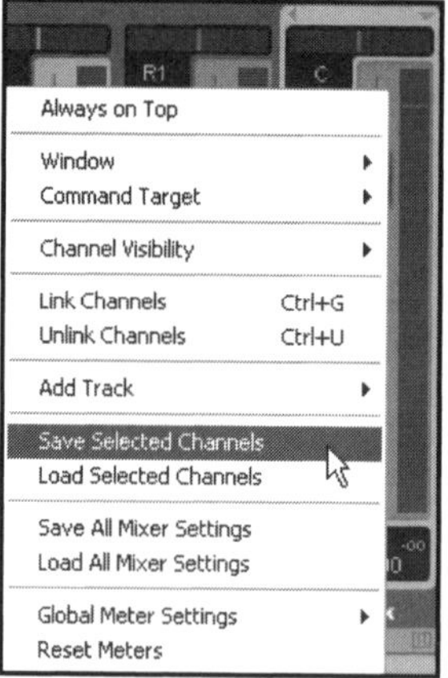

Figure 31.15
The context menu options available in the Mixer.

HOW TO

Link or unlink channels in the Mixer panel:

1. Select the first channel you want to link.
2. Shift-click on the other channels you want to link with this first channel.
3. Right-click (PC)/Ctrl-click (Mac) over one of the selected channels.
4. Select the Link Channels function from the context menu.
5. To unlink the channels, select one of the linked channels, and then select Unlink Channels from the same context menu.

Using Hold Peak

You can enable/disable the Hold Peak option by clicking inside the VU meter of any channel inside the Mixer.

Adding Tracks Inside the Mixer

Add tracks to a project from within the Mixer by selecting the Add Track option in the Mixer's context menu. The track is added to the right of the currently selected track.

Channel Settings Panel

The Channel Settings panel offers a convenient way of editing all channel settings in a single window. You can access the Channel Settings panel from the Project window through the Edit Channel Settings button in the Inspector's Channel section, in the Track List area, or from the Mixer panel (see Figure 31.16).

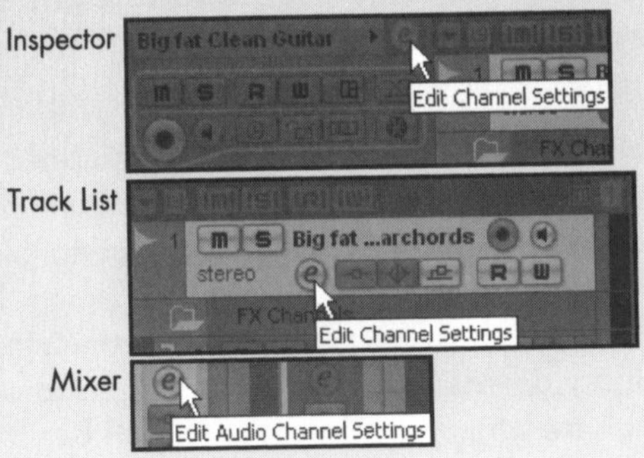

Figure 31.16
The Edit button opens the Channel Settings panel.

Output Bus Channels

The number and type of Output Bus channels available in the Mixer correspond to the Output Bus channels previously created in the VST Connections panel. How you use these outputs is contingent upon the project at hand and the number of available outputs on your audio hardware. Depending on how you set up your system or how many separate audio outputs your audio hardware offers, you will generally use the two main outputs of your audio hardware to monitor your project in stereo. If there are more than two outputs (and probably inputs) on your audio hardware, you can use these as additional output busses. These could be used to feed an external effect processor, a headphone amplifier, another recording device, or a multispeaker monitoring system typical in surround systems. For more on this, take a look at Chapter 6, "Control Room Mixer."

Each output bus created in the VST Connections panel appears when output bus channels are visible in the Mixer. You also can change or create bus output configurations through the VST Connections panel. (F4 is the default key command to access the panel.) If your audio hardware only offers a stereo output pair, then creating a single stereo output bus and perhaps two mono output busses should be enough because you can't separate the signal on its way out anyway (besides the two mono signals). If you want to group a series of channels and control or process their combined audio signal as one subgroup in the Mixer, you should use a group channel rather than a bus.

Output busses, like other audio channels, can also have up to eight different assignable inserts, but have no sends. Assigning effects to output busses can be useful when you want to optimize the overall level of a project with compression/limiting or some other dynamics processing, apply dithering to reduce the bit-depth of your project's audio output from 32 (or 24) to 16 bits per sample, or simply add a subtle reverb to the entire mix. Then again, output busses don't have to be used only for mixing purposes, as mentioned earlier. The last two insert effects on Cubase 4—inserts 7 and 8—are post-fader, contrary to the typical pre-fader insert configuration. As mentioned in the following tip, dithering plug-ins (or corresponding hardware inserts) should always be the last insert effect in the chain, placed in post-fader insert slot 7 or 8 on the final output bus for your mix.

When a project's sample record format is set to 32-bit floating point, you don't need to worry about digital clipping on audio channels after the channels are recorded and there was no clipping at the input. That's because the processing inside Cubase is done using this 32-bit (floating point) format, which makes it very difficult to actually produce digital clipping. However, after the signal is sent to the output, it is converted to the audio hardware's format. In many cases, this is 16-, 20-, or 24-bit. Because of this binary downsizing, digital clipping becomes a very real possibility if the clip indicator lights up below one of the output (or input) bus channels (see Figure 31.17). Avoid any clipping, especially when you are preparing a final mix from output busses. The remaining controls in the output bus channels are the same as in any other audio channel.

Preparing a 16-Bit Mixdown

If you are preparing your project for a final CD mixdown and you want to convert the files from 32- or 24-bit to 16-bit resolution (required for most CD burning programs that don't offer their own dithering options for source files at higher bit depths), you should apply the UV22 dithering plug-in effect as your last insert effect for the output bus containing the audio content, in one of the post-fader insert slots 7 or 8.

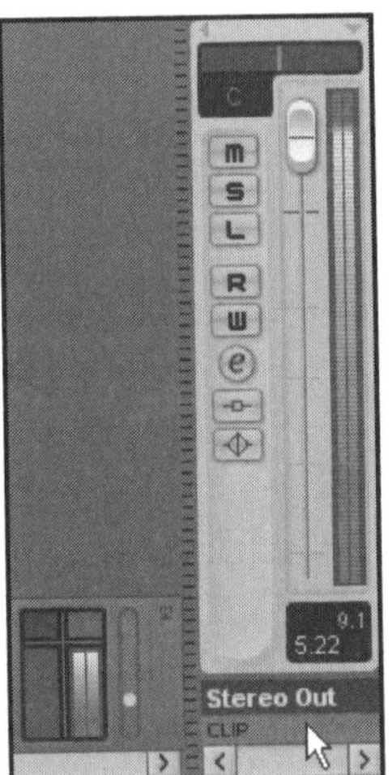

Figure 31.17
Clipping can be seen on this Output bus channel.

You can send any audio channel (disk audio, VSTi, ReWire, and group channels) to any active bus or group channels, as shown in Figure 31.18.

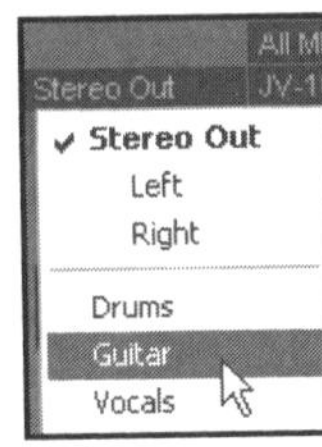

Figure 31.18
The Mixer's Output Bus selection menu.

Input Bus Channels

The input busses are the entry point equivalent of their exit point counterpart—the output busses. As such, they also offer the same controls inside the Mixer with one difference—you can't solo an input bus.

You can use input busses in Cubase to monitor the signal as it enters the inputs of your audio hardware and adjust its level accordingly. After an input or output bus is active, it becomes available at the top of the audio channels.

HOW TO

Change the physical input or output assigned to a bus:

- In the VST Connections panel, select the appropriate bus, and select the desired input or output path on your audio hardware from the available selections in the Device Ports column.

Renaming Busses

You also can rename busses inside the Mixer by selecting the current bus name at the bottom of its channel strip, as shown in Figure 31.19, and entering a new name for this bus.

Figure 31.19
Renaming a bus in the Mixer panel.

Can Hide

With a hardware mixer, hiding what you don't need is not an option. But in Cubase's Mixer, nothing could be simpler. When working with large projects, the number of channels displayed in a Mixer can become overwhelming. The ability to hide things can also be useful when working with ghost tracks, or tracks that you use to place events temporarily, but that are not part of your mixing process. Hiding them from view makes it easier to focus on the tasks at hand. Ghost tracks are simply audio or MIDI tracks that contain shared copies of events in another track for doubling parts or performing alternate processing. Sometimes ghost tracks are simply the disabled original audio track you're keeping as a reference. We discussed the Common panel's Hide buttons, but hiding all audio channels or instrument channels might not be what you had in mind. One way to deal with this is to use the Can Hide functionality, which allows users to flag certain channels as "hideable." Once a channel is flagged as a Can Hide channel, clicking the Mixer's Hide Channels Set to "Can Hide" button hides this and all channels from view. Hidden channels still play unless they were muted before they were hidden. Because this process is twofold, we'll start by looking at how to set this Can Hide flag.

HOW TO

Set individual channels to Can Hide:

- Click on the Channel View Options menu, as shown on the left in Figure 31.20, and select the Can Hide option. This menu displays more options when the extended panel is visible.
- Alt-click (PC)/Option-click (Mac) on the Can Hide State button, as shown on the right in Figure 31.20

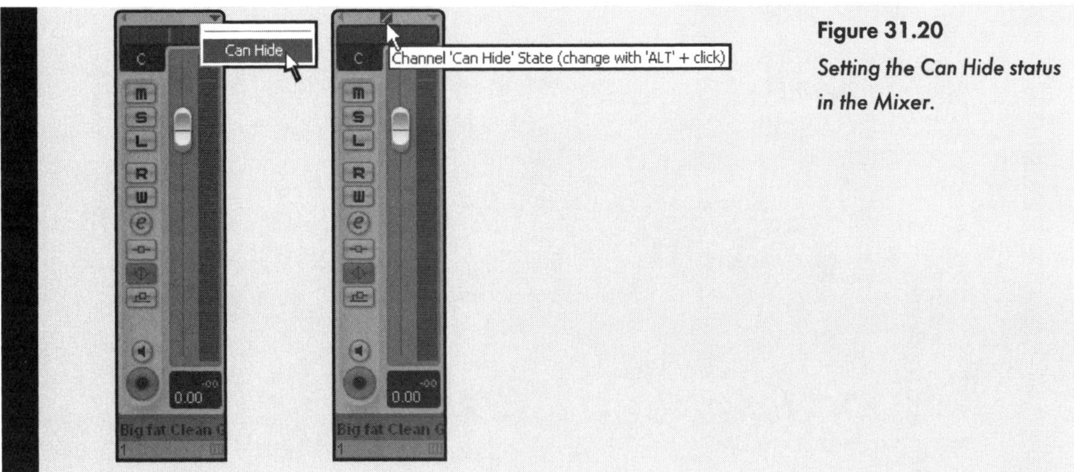

Figure 31.20
Setting the Can Hide status in the Mixer.

The Hide Channels Set to "Can Hide" button found in the Common panel of the Mixer, along with the three symbols below it, are part of a Can Hide set of features available in the Mixer's Channel menu. The main Hide Channels button hides all channels that are flagged as Can Hide. You can unhide all channels by disabling this button.

HOW TO ❊

Set a selection of channels as Can Hide:

1. Set the Command Target button to Selected Only.
2. Select the channels you want to set as Can Hide. Hold Ctrl (PC)/ (Mac) down when clicking on channels to select as many channels as you want.
3. Click on the Set Target Channels to Can Hide button (see Figure 31.21).

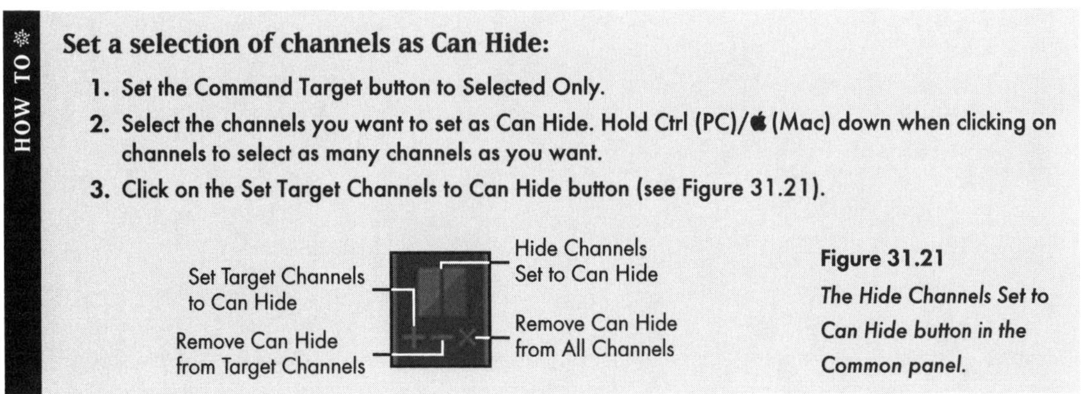

Figure 31.21
The Hide Channels Set to Can Hide button in the Common panel.

Use the other Can Hide functions to remove the Can Hide flag from selected channels or from all channels at once.

32 FX Channel Tracks

FX channel tracks are similar to auxiliary returns on a hardware mixer or console. On hardware mixers, aux returns are often used to incorporate the output from external effect modules into the mix. Although they also can be used this way in Cubase, more often the effects are actually software plug-ins on the FX channel itself. You can add up to 64 FX channels per project in Cubase, and each of them can hold a chain of up to eight plug-in effects. Because FX channels offer an independent volume control, it would be easier to increase the level of a delay while fading out the audio channel to emphasize the effect in the mix, for example. Audio signals can be routed to FX channels using the send controls available in every audio, instrument, group, or ReWire channel. Without any source signal routed through it via sends from other channels, the FX channel will be silent.

Here's a summary of what you will learn in this chapter:

- How to create an FX channel
- How to work with sends
- How to use FX channels as a send destination
- How to bypass FX channels and send destinations

FX Channels Options

The main purpose of FX channel tracks is to process audio sent from several channels simultaneously by passing the combined signal through the same audio plug-in. How much processing is applied to each audio channel passing through the plug-in is determined by one level, and how much processing is heard in the mix is determined by another independent level control. In comparison, an audio insert effects on each source channel can only process the audio signal of the channel where they reside, and the options for adjusting the mix level between the source and processed signals are a bit more limited. The perfect example for an FX channel is when you need to add some reverb to drum tracks, where each drum instrument has been recorded on a separate track. To make all the instruments sound like they were recorded in the same room or environment, a common reverb applied to these tracks makes more sense than loading multiple instances of the same reverb as inserts on each drum channel. This would not only take more time to set up, but it would reduce the number of insert slots available, increase the resources required to process each signal individually, and force you to update effect levels in every channel whenever a change is required.

At its core, the FX channel track in Cubase is very similar to a group channel or an audio channel. It offers the same volume, pan, mute, and solo controls, but it also offers a few distinct features of its own. You can't choose the input bus for an FX channel track because it receives its signal exclusively via sends from other audio channels (which include group and instrument channels, but not their MIDI counterpart). This also means that you can't record any audio into an FX channel track, but you can certainly record the output of an FX channel track. Because the main purpose of an FX channel track is to provide effects to audio from other channels in your project, the sends from an FX channel cannot be routed to another FX (or group) channel.

HOW TO

Add an FX channel track to a project:

1. Right-click (PC)/Control-click (Mac) in the Track List area of the Project window and select Add FX Channel Track from the context menu. You can select the same option from the Project > Add Track menu.
2. In the Add FX Channel Track dialog box (see Figure 32.1), select a track configuration from the drop-down menu. This determines how the effect will process the signal going through it. Keep in mind that most current plug-ins are configured for stereo audio processing.

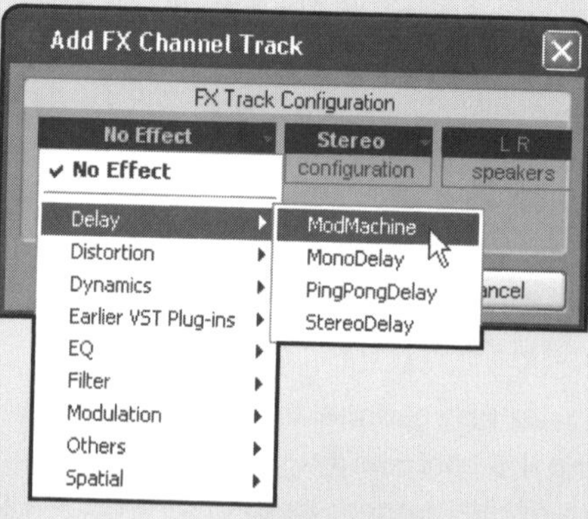

Figure 32.1
The Add FX Channel Track dialog box.

3. Select the desired plug-in from the drop-down menu. If you are not sure which plug-in you want to use at this point, you can leave the plug-in field set to No Effect and change it later. This will simply create an empty FX channel, which can also serve to send an audio signal to an external source.
4. Click OK.

As shown in Figure 32.2, the controls found in the FX channel's Inspector area are also mirrored in the Mixer and the VST Channel Settings panel.

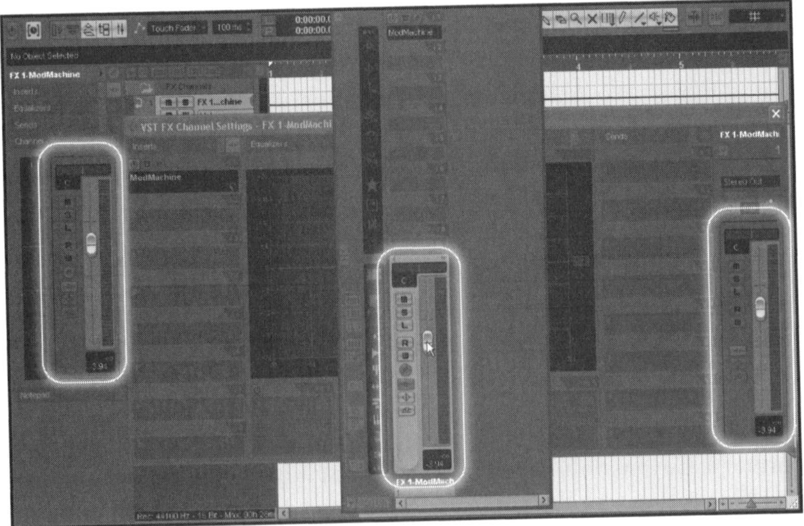

Figure 32.2
The Inspector, Channel Settings, and Mixer view of an FX channel's track controls.

Audio Track Sends

FX channels receive their input from other channels through the Track Sends feature. The term *sends* comes from the fact that, in addition to the channel's main output assignment, you are also "sending" the signal to another destination. Send controls are completely independent from each other and from the main channel controls. That's why they are so convenient.

Take a look at the Send controls in Figure 32.3 to understand how to use them. In the Sends section of audio and MIDI tracks, the Show Active Sends indicator lights up whenever one of the eight sends in the track is active. To the left of the "Show Active Sends" is a button that lets you

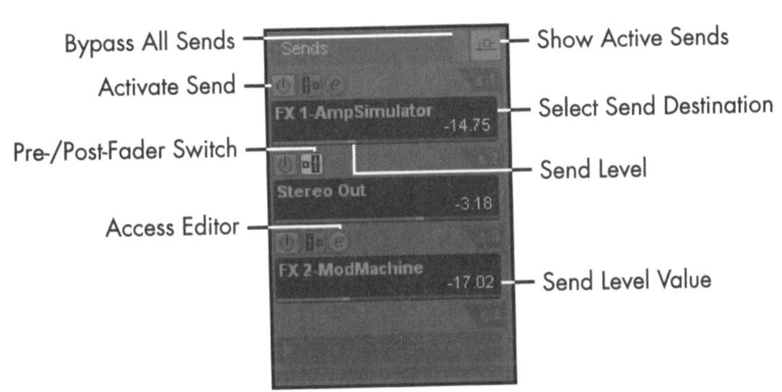

Figure 32.3
The first four audio-track sends.

bypass all sends at once without changing any settings in this section. When all the sends are bypassed, you will see a yellow rectangle next to the sends' turquoise Show Active Sends display. To bypass a single send, simply deactivate it. Deactivating the track itself will also disable its sends.

For each audio-track send, there are three buttons above the Select Send Destination field—the Activate/Deactivate (or Bypass) button, the Pre-/Post-Fader toggle button, and the Access editor button, which (unless the send destination is an output bus for physical outputs on your audio hardware) opens the panel for the plug-in insert in slot 1 of the destination track, where you can change parameter settings. Below these three buttons is the Select Send Destination field, which displays the name of the send destination when one has been assigned. Send destinations can be FX channels, output busses, or group channels.

If a send destination is an output bus to physical audio ports, the button is inactive, as it is while the destination FX/Group channel has no plug-ins. The Access editor button is only active if the destination channel has an insert plug-in effect in slot 1 (i.e., if slot 1 is empty, the button is inactive *even if the destination channel has active plug-ins in its other slots*).

To assign a send to any destination, this destination has to exist beforehand. Changing the name of the destination track alters the name that appears here. Once a destination has been assigned, sending a signal to this destination is done by dragging the Send Level bar or by entering a numeric value in the Send Level value field. This controls how much signal from this track you want to send to the selected FX channel track. Audio sent to an FX channel track (which then routes the signal through audio plug-in effects inserted into its signal chain) is processed at the level at which it is received. The more signal you send to the effect, the more processed sound you will hear for this audio signal. The idea is to give you control over how much processed signal you want to hear for each individual track without having to load multiple instances of plug-in effects to the source tracks.

You can only have a total of eight send destinations per audio track, but you can create up to 64 FX channels. This means that the send destinations from each channel can be completely different from the others. For example, you might have 10 FX channel tracks, in which audio track 1 uses sends 1 through 4 and audio track 2 uses sends 1 through 4 as well, but in both cases, the signal might be sent to different FX channel tracks altogether, with track 1 going to FX channel tracks 1, 2, 3, and 4 and track 2 perhaps sending its signal to FX channel tracks 3, 5, 7, and 9.

HOW TO

Send an audio track to an FX channel track:

1. Unfold the Sends section in the Inspector area of the audio track, open the VST Channel Settings, or display the Extended panel of the Mixer to select Sends from the Mixer's Common panel.
2. Select the desired send destination in the drop-down menu, as displayed in Figure 32.4. You can also send an audio signal to a group channel (if one exists) or an output bus.
3. Activate the sends.

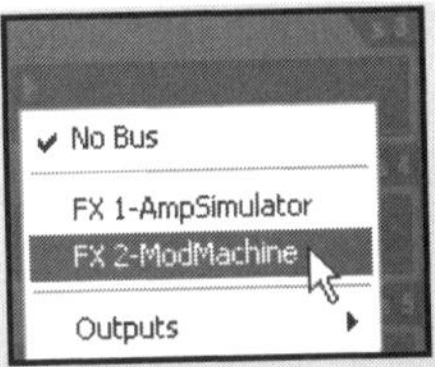

Figure 32.4
The Select Sends Destination menu.

4. **In the Sends section of the audio track, select Pre- or Post-Fader, as desired.**
   You can see how the signal is routed in Figure 32.5. In Post-Fader mode, the signal sent to the effect is taken after the audio track's channel volume level and volume settings.

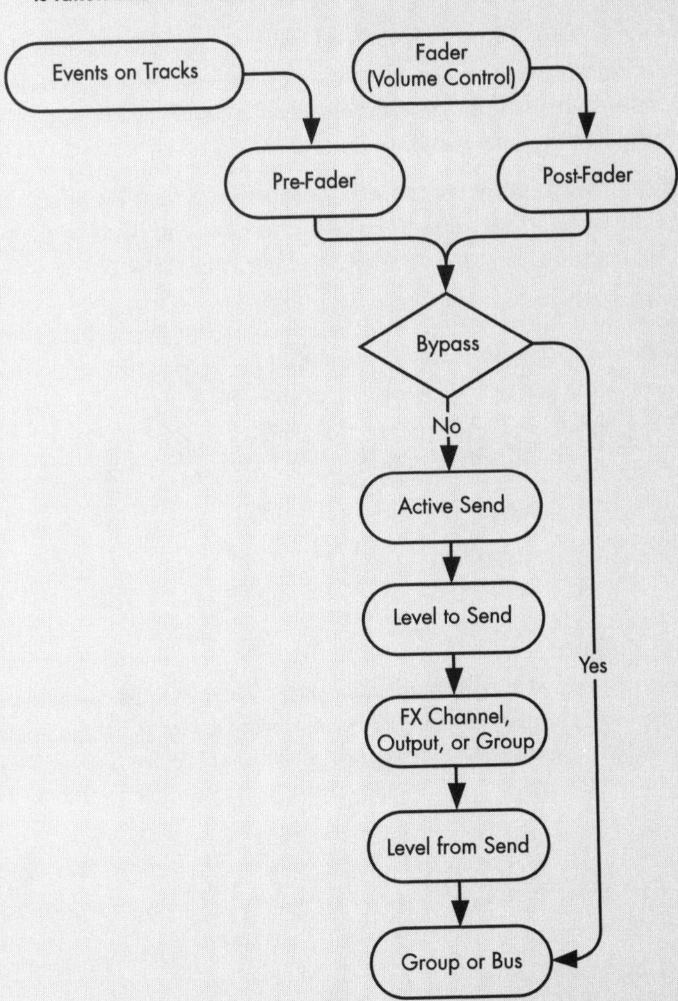

Figure 32.5
The audio send signal path diagram.

5. **In the Sends section of the audio track, raise the level sent to the effect until the desired effect is reached.**

Adjusting the Overall Level of an FX

To adjust the overall level of the effect in the mix, you can simply adjust the FX channel's volume level. Changing this level affects the signal from all audio tracks that are being routed through that FX channel.

After completing these steps, you need to fine-tune both the level being sent to the FX channel from each source channel and the level returning to the mix from the FX channel until the appropriate blend is found.

To send the signal from one track to more than one send destination, repeat the same steps mentioned earlier in this section for another send destination. Unlike insert effects, each send effect is processed in parallel, not in series. The slot numbers used for each of the eight potential sends from a channel do not influence the end result.

As you can see in Figure 32.5, there are many places where you can bypass an effect. The following sections describe the differences between each one and how you can use them.

HOW TO

- **Bypass/activate the signal sent to all send destinations in a track.** Use the Bypass button found in the Sends section's title bar (in the Inspector area of the audio track).
- **Bypass/activate the signal sent to one send destination in a track.** Use the Bypass/Activate button found above the name of that send destination (which in the case of FX channel destinations will display the name of the effect in its first insert slot) in the Track Sends section in the audio track's Inspector area.
- **Bypass all the tracks sent to the same effect.** Use the Bypass button found on the FX channel Track List or in the FX channel's settings.

Sending a Signal Outside Cubase

You also can use sends to route your signal to additional output busses on your audio hardware. This might come in handy when you want to process the signal with a hardware device rather than a plug-in, as well as for creating additional cue mixes and broadcast feeds if you are using the Cubase Studio 4 version (Cubase 4 already provides the Studio Sends for this specific purpose when the Control Room Mixer is enabled).

To route your signal through a piece of hardware outside Cubase using sends, create a new external FX connection in the VST Connections panel. After the connection is created, select the corresponding external FX from the FX selection menu.

This works better if you have a spare set of outputs (more than two) on your audio peripheral that can be dedicated as a send-to-effect bus.

FX Channel through VST Connections

For projects involving many FX channels, adding and managing this type of channel can be performed inside the VST Connections panel, which is accessible by pressing the key command F4 in the Mixer panel's Common panel, as shown in Figure 32.6, or inside the Devices menu. The VST Connections panel provides a few easy ways to create FX channels, rename them, and change their output settings within a few clicks.

Figure 32.6
The Mixer's Show VST Connections button.

HOW TO

- **Add an FX channel.** Click on the Add FX button or right-click (PC)/Control-click (Mac) in the Bus Name column and choose Add FX Channel from the context menu, as displayed in Figure 32.7.
- **Remove an FX channel.** Right-click (PC)/Control-click (Mac) over the bus name and select Remove Channel from the context menu.
- **Change the output of an FX channel.** Click in the Output Routing column next to the desired FX channel and choose another output bus from the context menu.

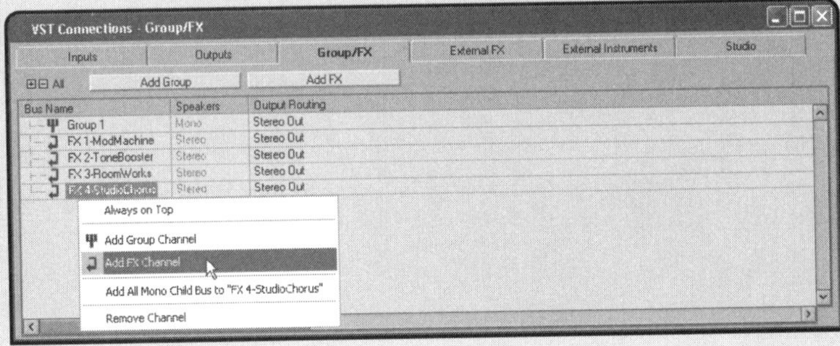

Figure 32.7
Adding FX channels in the VST Connections window.

33 Group Channel Tracks

A group channel track offers a way to assign the output of different audio channels to a common set of controls. By adding automation or effects to this group, you affect the summed output of all audio channels assigned to this group. For example, if you don't have a multiple-output soundcard, you could assign the audio outputs from various tracks to several group tracks and use these groups as submixes. Typically, you could send all the drum and percussion tracks to one group, all the backing vocals to another group, and the strings (if you have violins, violas, cellos, and contrabasses, for example) to another group. Then, if you want to increase the level of the string section, all you have to do is raise that group channel fader, rather than raise the individual audio channel faders for each string instrument.

Here's a summary of what you will learn in this chapter:

- How to create a group channel track
- How to use a group as a submix group fader
- How to use a group as a monitor mix (for Cubase Studio 4 users)

Anatomy of a Group Track

Group tracks do not contain any audio or MIDI events; as a result, in the Project window, group tracks display only relevant automation information, as shown in Figure 33.1. The Inspector for a group track offers similar controls to an audio track with a few exceptions:

- You can't record on a group track, so it has no Record or Monitor button.
- Group tracks are summing busses, taking their input from other channels assigned to them. As a result, you won't find any input selection fields. You can, however, assign the output of the group to a desired bus (or even another group channel).
- There are no track presets available for group tracks.

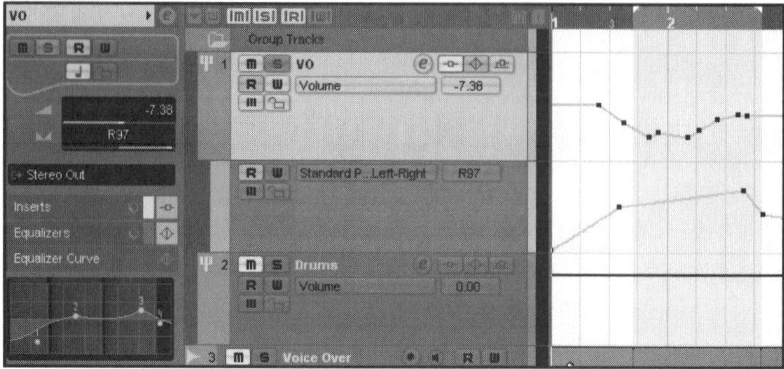

Figure 33.1
Group tracks in the Project window.

Group Channels

When a group track is created in the Project window, a group channel also is created in the Mixer. Groups are used as summing outputs only; you can assign other channels to play through them and then process all the channels sent to a particular group with one single set of controls. For example, if you have multiple tracks for the microphones on your drum kit, you can assign all these individual tracks to play through a stereo "drums" group channel and instantiate a limiter as an insert effect on this group channel. This limiter is thereby applied to the entire stereo drum submix, ensuring better control over the sum of all your individual drum instruments. In this example, applying limiting to the group channel does not prevent you from applying individual dynamic controls or EQ settings to each channel that has been routed to the group channel. Moreover, when you want to change the overall level of the drums in your mix, you will only need to adjust the group channels's level instead of all individual volume levels for each drum microphone channel.

Using Group Channels

A group channel appears in the Mixer whenever a group track is created in the Project window. After a group track is created, you can assign the output of other tracks to it in the Inspector or the Mixer window. Group channels are useful for creating submixes, in which the output from a series of related tracks are summed together. You can then use the group's fader as a general level control for all tracks routed to it, as displayed in Figure 33.2.

You can create a group channel track in a number of ways:

- In the VST Connections window (F4), select the Group/FX tab and click on the Add Group button.
- In the Project window, right-click (PC)/Control-click (Mac) in the Track List and select Add Group Channel Track from the context menu.

Figure 33.2
A group channel (left) with various audio channels routed to it in the Mixer window.

- In the Mixer window, right-click (PC)/Control-click (Mac) anywhere and select the Add Track > Group Channel command from the context menu, as shown in Figure 33.3.
- From the Project menu, select Add Track > Group Channel.

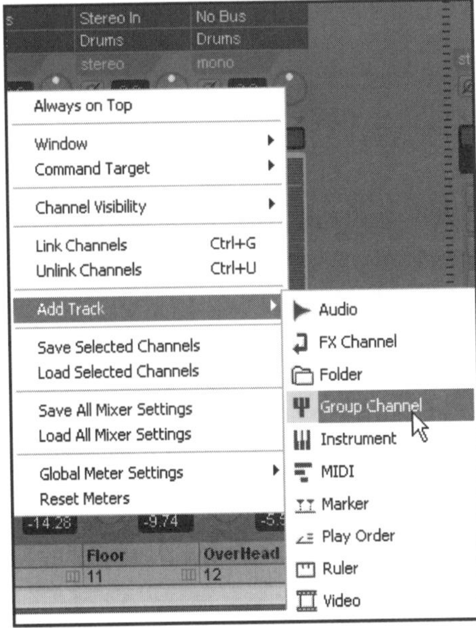

Figure 33.3
The Mixer's context menu displaying the Add Track submenu options.

HOW TO

Use a group as a submix group fader:

1. Create a group channel track in the Project or Mixer window.
2. Name this group appropriately. In Figure 33.4, the group track is labeled as "Drums." The group's name will appear in the pop-up selector when you select an output destination for any audio track or channel (see Figure 33.5).

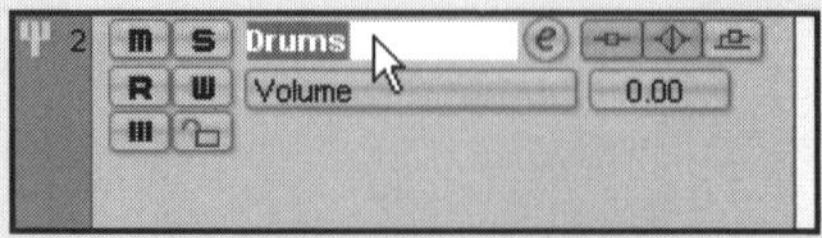

Figure 33.4
Naming a group track in the Track List area.

Figure 33.5
Selecting a group as the output for a channel.

3. In the Output Bus selection field found in the Channel Settings panel of the Inspector (see Figure 33.5), or in the Mixer (Cubase 4 users only), select the group's name from the channel's Output Selection field (where you can see "Drums" in Figure 33.2).
4. Repeat Step 3 for all the channels you want to send to this group or any other group channel.

Groups as Monitor Mix (Cubase Studio 4)

Now that you have assigned the outputs from various audio or VSTi channels to the same group channel, you can either adjust their relative levels individually or use the group channel's fader to adjust the overall level being sent to the master output bus.

While Cubase 4 users can make use of the Control Room Mixer to create a headphone monitor sub-mix, Cubase Studio 4 users can create a monitor mix that can be sent to any external devices, such as headphone amplifiers, effects, or other recording devices, by using one of the send effects. Instead of sending the signal of this channel to an FX channel, you can route the signal to a group channel, and then assign the output of this group channel to another available bus. Using this method allows you to send each channel to two sets of outputs (see Figure 33.6), giving you an independent control over levels being sent to each output. Note that you need at least two sets of outputs on your audio hardware to use this effectively.

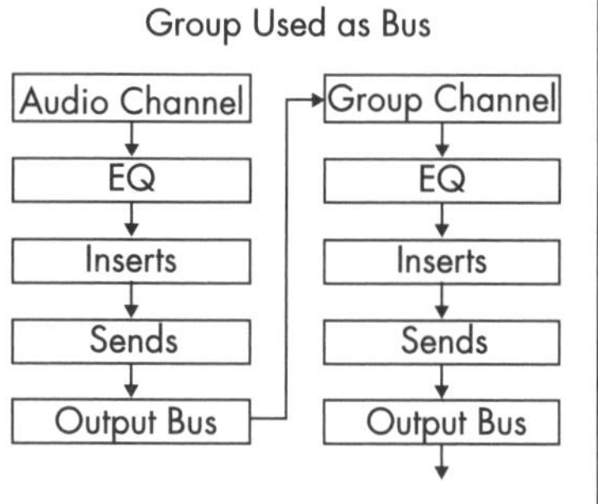

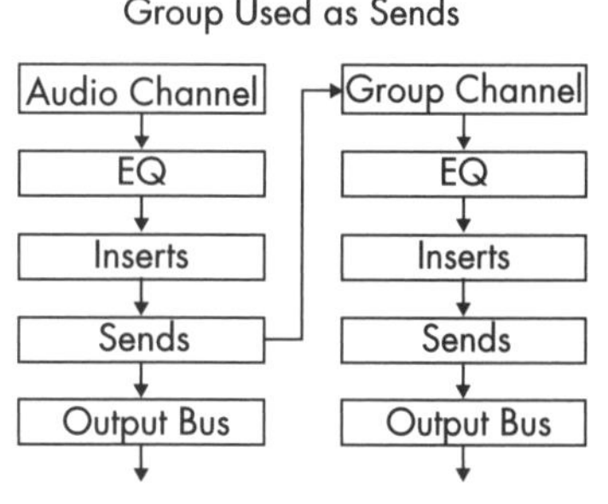

Figure 33.6
Using the group channels as an output bus (left) or as a send destination (right).

HOW TO

Use a group as a monitor mix (for Cubase Studio 4 users):

1. Create a group channel; name it and choose an output bus for this group.
2. In the Project window, select the channel you want to send to the group channel using the send effects.
3. Click the Edit Channel Settings button.
4. In the Channel Settings panel, activate an empty send effect slot.
5. In this empty effect slot, select the appropriate group as the send effect destination. In Figure 33.7, the group is named Headphone Mix.

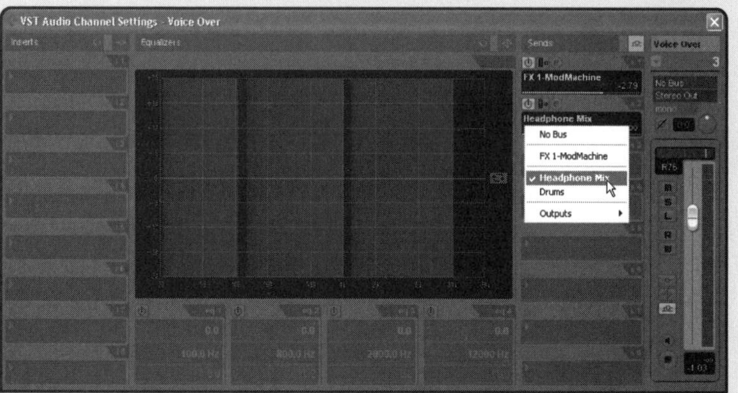

Figure 33.7
Assigning a group as the sends destination.

6. Adjust the level being sent to the send effect (in this case, the group output channel).
7. If you want to send another channel to a send effect assigned to a group, use the Select Channel menu (in the upper-right corner, under the channel's name).

8. Repeat Steps 3 through 6 for each additional channel you want to send to this subgroup mix.
9. Adjust the group's level being sent to its output. You also can adjust the output level of the output bus.

Alternative Submix Technique for Cubase Studio 4 Users

If you don't want to have to assign individual channels to a group through send effects in each channel, you can create a submix group. Let's take our previous example of the DrumKit group. First, you assign the outputs of all channels to this group. Then, you create a second group that you call something like Headphones. All you need to do is assign the send effect for the DrumKit group to the Headphones group output, and then you assign the Headphones group output to another bus, and voilà! (See Figure 33.8 for a diagram of this example.)

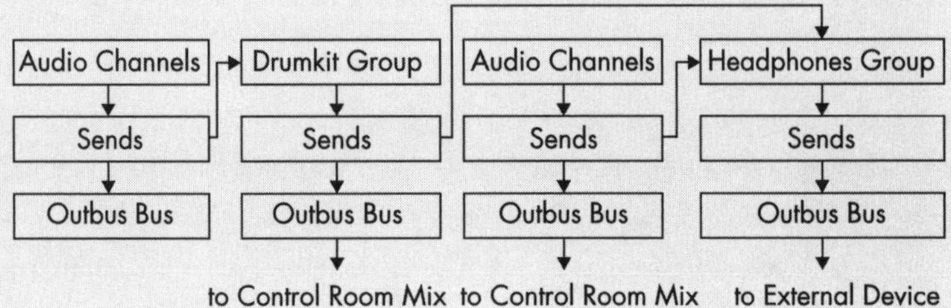

Figure 33.8
Example displaying how the signal travels when using a group as a headphone sub-mix.

34 Writing Automation

Cubase supports two basic automation recording techniques. First, you can create mix automation in real time by writing the volume, pan, and other parameter changes you make in the Mixer window—or anywhere that real-time controls are available in Cubase. For some users, recording automation in real time is especially intuitive when their hardware setup includes a remote control surface. Secondly, you can also create automation by drawing automation curves in the automation subtracks. We will look at these two methods separately. Owning a remote control surface definitely makes it more convenient to automate a mix when compared to using a mouse alone, but either way, the automation subtracks are always easy to access and can be edited at any time. Also, if you're used to the mixer environment, recording automation may feel more comfortable to you when the Mixer window is visible. On the other hand, editing previously recorded automation might be easier if done through the Project window.

Here's a summary of what you will learn in this chapter:

- How to use the Read and Write buttons to record and play back automation
- How to record channel and plug-in parameter automation
- How to change the automation mode
- How to draw channel settings automation values in an automation track
- How to add automation using the Line tools
- How to hide and remove automation subtracks

Using Read and Write Buttons

You can set the levels and pans of audio channels in the Mixer or Inspector without using automation, just as you would on a normal mixer desk. This enables you to adjust the level and position of your tracks in the mix without adding automation to them. As long as the Write or Read Automation buttons (found in the Common panel on the left of the Channel Mixer window) are not activated (not lit), the faders, pan, and any other effect settings stay at the same position.

When the Read Automation button is disabled in the Common panel, Cubase will not read any existing automation in your tracks. However, disabling automation doesn't mean that you lose the automation you previously recorded.

Read and Write Automation buttons are available to record and play back mix automation for each channel in the Mixer window, the Track List, the Channel Settings panel, or the Channel section of the Inspector. Use the Write button to record the automation and the Read button to enable playback of any automation data contained in this track's automation subtracks (whether created in real time with the Write Button or drawn using the mouse). To activate the automation writing process, click the Write Automation button of the desired channel. Clicking this button in any of the mentioned areas activates the same function in all subsequent windows where the channel is represented (the Inspector, the Track List, the Channel Settings panel, and the Mixer window). By clicking the Write Automation button directly in the channel, you activate the writing automation functions for this channel only. If you want to activate the automation writing mode for all channels at once, you can enable the All Automation to Write Status button found both at the top of the Track List and in the Common panel of the Mixer window, as demonstrated in Figure 34.1. Whether you enable writing of automation on one or all channels depends on what you want to achieve. Notice in this figure that the Write or Read Automation buttons do not light up when the Common panel's corresponding button is pressed. That's because this channel has been frozen, which is indicated by the asterisk in the fader's handle. You can change the fader's position when a track is frozen, but you can't change its automation. To find out why the Freeze function exists and how you can use it, take a look at Chapter 39, "Project Optimization."

When you activate the Write button on a channel or in the Common panel of the Mixer, Cubase is ready to record any change you make in parameter settings during playback. This includes all channel controls, insert and send effects, VSTi control panels, and Inspector parameters, for example. Bear in mind that writing of automation is completely independent of the recording function on audio or MIDI tracks. If you don't move a given parameter, Cubase will not record any data for this parameter.

After you have recorded automation, you need to activate or enable the Read Automation button in order for Cubase to read whatever automation you have recorded. Otherwise, the information is present, but your automation is not read during playback. As with the Write Automation button, the Read Automation button is available in several windows inside your project, and enabling it on a channel in one window enables it in all the other windows as well. The All Automation to Read Status button found at the top of the Track List and in the Common panel of the Mixer window also activates the Read option for all channels at once.

Writing Channel Track Automation

This section describes how to record the most common type of automation: track automation. This type of automation is associated with a Mixer channel (also seen as a track in the Project window), as well as MIDI and audio channel settings. Automation is frequently used to change

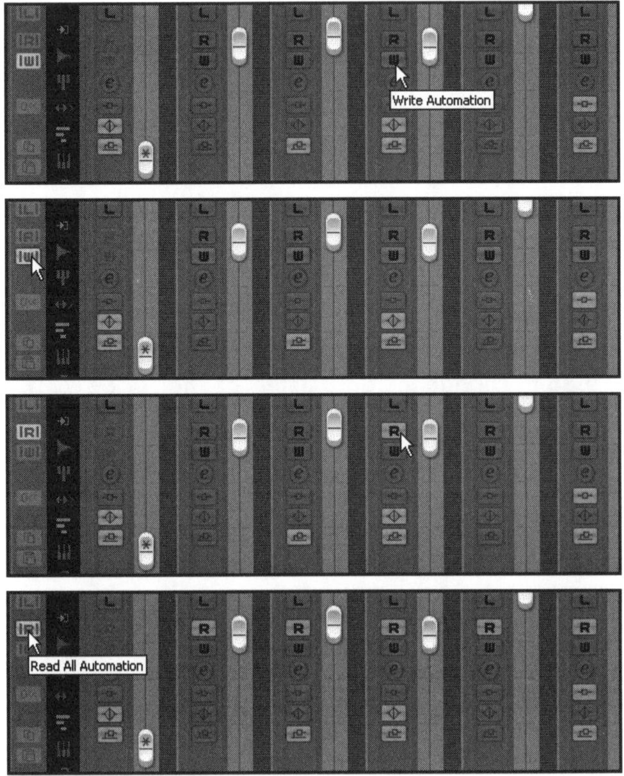

Figure 34.1
Writing automation by using channel and common write functions.

the volume or pan of a track in the course of a project, to alter the parameters of its sends or insert effects, or to mute a track or its effects by enabling the Mute button or bypassing one or several inserts or sends at a time. The actual settings you can write in real time are determined by the track class itself.

Write channel automation in real time:

1. Open the Mixer window. (F3 is the default key command.)
2. Activate the channel's Write Automation button. This button is lit when active.
3. Position your playback cursor and click the Play button on the Transport panel (or press the space-bar) to start playback.
4. Move the appropriate faders, knobs, switches, and so on.
5. Stop playback when done.

After automation has been written, you can listen to it by activating the Read Automation button and bringing the play cursor to the same location where you started writing this automation. Click the Play button to see (and hear) the automation on this channel.

After your automation is written into the track, you can use the channels' automation subtracks to view the automation curves for each setting that was automated. We'll get into this a little later in this chapter.

Writing Parameter Automation

Writing real-time parameter changes in a plug-in effect, such as a VSTi or send effect, is quite similar to automating channel settings in a track. However, automation events for VST effects and software instruments are recorded in separate tracks and subtracks, created automatically by Cubase as soon as you move any of the controls of an effect or VSTi when the Write Automation button is activated inside the plug-in's control panel. (This can be a VSTi or VST effect plug-in.) This type of automation is normally used to change the parameters of effects or a VSTi, creating dynamic changes in the plug-in over time during playback. For example, you can automate the Cutoff frequency by moving this parameter in the VSTi's control panel (provided there is such a parameter on the instrument itself).

HOW TO

Write automation for plug-in parameters in real time:

1. Open the desired effect's control panel.
2. Activate the Write Automation button found inside the panel. This button is lit when active.
3. Position your playback cursor and click the Play button on the Transport bar (or press the spacebar) to start playback.
4. Move the appropriate faders, knobs, switches, and so on. You might need to consult the documentation provided with the effect to find out which parameters are automatable because this varies from one effect to the next. (See an example in Figure 34.2, featuring the Filter Envelope parameters of a VST instrument plug-in.)

Figure 34.2
Moving the Attack parameter in this example, while the Write Automation button is active and the project is playing, records the changes through time to this parameter.

5. Stop the playback when finished.

Once automation has been created in a track, you can listen to it by activating the Read Automation button, as mentioned earlier in this chapter.

About Automation Modes

An automation mode determines how Cubase behaves when you change parameters with the mouse or a remote control surface; different modes can be used depending on the type of automation you want to perform. For example, use the Overwrite mode when you need to replace a portion of an existing automation.

In Cubase 4, there are five automation modes: Touch Fader (default), Autolatch, X-Over, Overwrite, and Trim:

- With **Touch Fader**, the program starts writing automation as soon as you press or move any control for a parameter, such as the Volume fader, and stops writing when you release the mouse button.
- With **Autolatch**, the program starts writing the automation as soon as you press or move any control and stops writing when you stop playback or deactivate the Write Automation button. In other words, the last automation value is continuously written until you turn off the Write Automation button within the channel mixer found in the Inspector area or in the Mixer window. This mode is useful if you want to write over (to replace) a long section containing previously recorded automation. It is also useful when you are using an external control surface to control your mix. Because Cubase has no way of knowing which control you want to rewrite, it starts writing as soon as you move a control and keeps writing the value sent by this control (overwriting any existing automation for the particular parameter) until you stop playback or disable the Write Automation button. Make sure, however, that you don't touch any other controls when doing this; otherwise, you might end up replacing automation by mistake. Note that this also applies for some VSTi and VST plug-in effects parameters.

Locking Automation Once Completed

Once you are happy with a track and its automation, that's a good time to lock it in place with the Lock button found in the Track List area. By locking a track, you can avoid unintentionally overwriting existing automation data.

- **X-Over** works much like the Autolatch mode, with one exception: As soon as your playback cursor crosses a previously recorded automation curve point, the write process is automatically turned off.

- **Overwrite** is also similar to Autolatch mode with the exception that it only affects volume automation. Existing automation will be written over as soon as you start playback, even if you don't touch any controls. Use this mode when you want to clear out any previously recorded volume automation.
- **Trim**, like the Overwrite mode, works only on volume automation. What makes it different, however, is that it does not erase existing automation data; rather, it *offsets* the previously recorded automation. For example, let's say you recorded a volume automation, starting your automation at –10 dB. While you listen to the result, you realize that the automation curves are good, but the whole thing is too soft. After selecting the Trim automation mode, you can place the play cursor a bit before your previous automation, enable the Write Automation button, and raise the fader slightly after pressing Play. As a result, all the following automation will be raised proportionally by this amount. So, if you start your automation at -7 dB instead, the rest of the automation will have shifted proportionally.

Change the automation mode:

1. In the Project window, click the Automation Mode Selection field in the toolbar (see Figure 34.3).

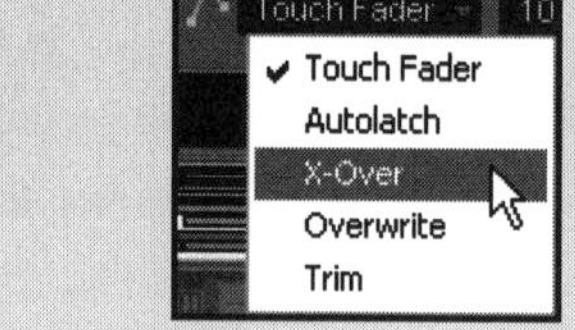

Figure 34.3
The Automation Mode Selection field in the Project window's toolbar.

2. Select the desired automation mode from the drop-down menu.

Drawing Automation

If working with a remote control surface is not for you, or you need to perform some fine-tuning on your automation, or you simply want to set a curve to a specific value using a specific curve shape, then perhaps drawing the automation offers the best solution for you.

This section describes how to add automation curves into an automation subtrack for any channel.

HOW TO

Draw channel settings automation curves in an automation subtrack:

1. In the Project window's Track List area, select the track for which you want to create automation events.
2. In the bottom-left corner of the selected track, click the Show/Hide Automation button (small arrow) to reveal its first automation subtrack.
3. Enable the Read Automation button for this track/channel (and/or the particular automation subtrack).
4. Select the parameter you want to automate from the Parameter field (see Figure 34.4). If the parameter you want to automate doesn't appear in this list, click the More option to display a dialog box revealing additional automatable parameters available for this track. Select the one you want and click OK to return to the subtrack. At this point, the Parameter field should display the parameter you just selected.

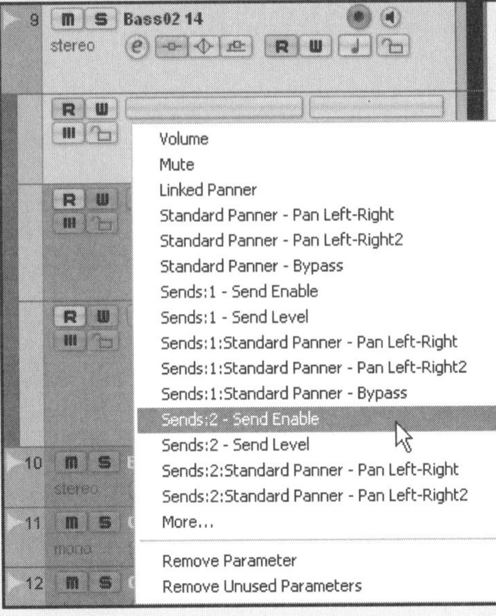

Figure 34.4
Selecting to display an automation parameter.

5. If there is currently no automation for this parameter, a colored flat horizontal line appears within this subtrack in the Event Display area. Select the Draw tool in the Project window toolbar.
6. To add a curve point, click near the location inside this lane where you want to add an automation value. If you want to create a ramp between two points, release the mouse. However, if you want to create a curve, drag your mouse to the next desired location and value (see Figure 34.5).
7. Repeat Step 5 to add more automation curve points along this parameter's subtrack.

Note that an automation curve point is added at each location where you click, as long as you are using the Pencil or Draw tool and stay inside the subtrack's boundaries.

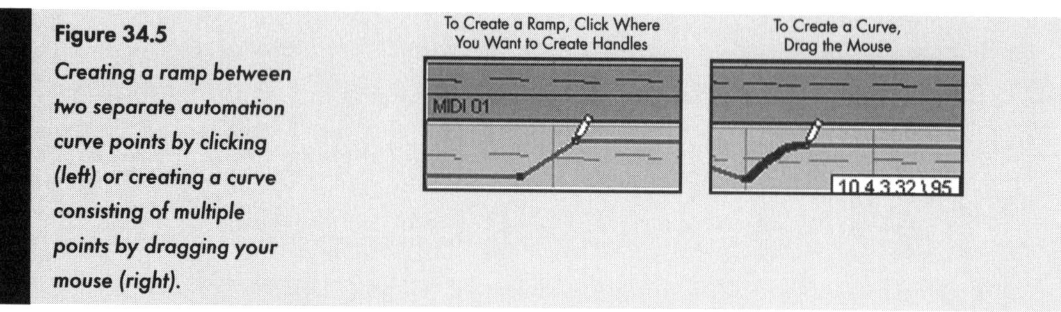

Figure 34.5
Creating a ramp between two separate automation curve points by clicking (left) or creating a curve consisting of multiple points by dragging your mouse (right).

If you want to create automation events to another parameter for the same channel, you can either select another parameter from the Parameter field to display a new parameter in the same subtrack or click the Append Automation Track button as displayed in Figure 34.6. When the new subtrack is visible, repeat Steps 3–6 from the previous list.

Figure 34.6
Appending automation subtracks.

Note that choosing a different parameter in a subtrack that already contains automation does not remove or cancel the automation it holds. When a track contains recorded automation events for a given parameter, an asterisk appears after this parameter's name in the Parameter selector field for the automation subtrack (see Figure 34.7). These asterisks help you quickly spot which parameters already contain automation, thereby making editing and troubleshooting much more efficient.

Figure 34.7
Parameters with recorded automation events appear with an asterisk in the Parameter field.

After you've recorded automation on a track, you can select the Show Used Automation option available in the Track List's context menu (right-click on PC or Control-click on Mac). You can add automation to several parameters by using a single subtrack, changing the parameter's name to view, or adding new automation, and after you are done, reveal all automation subtracks containing events. Remember that each parameter has its own subtrack.

Under the Line tool are several drawing shapes: Line, Parabola, Sine, Triangle, and Square. As described in Chapter 16, these tools can be used to create automation values, such as pan effects. However, using the Parabola and Line tools, you can create consistent automation curves instead of drawing curve points freehand-style, as displayed in Figure 34.8.

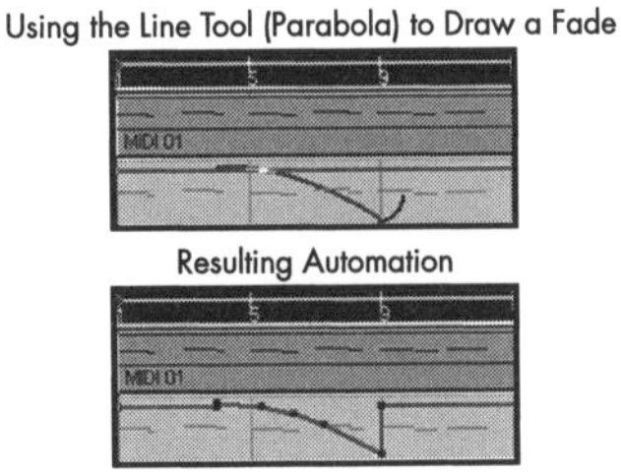

Using the Line Tool (Parabola) to Draw a Fade

Resulting Automation

Figure 34.8
Using the Parabola to create consistent automation curves.

HOW TO

Add automation using the Line tools:

1. Select the drawing shape you want to use for the Line tool.
2. Select the desired track and expand its automation subtracks.
3. From the Parameter selection field, select the parameter for which you want to create some automation curve points. You also may append additional automation subtracks if you want.
4. If the parameter you want to automate doesn't appear in this list, click the More option to display a dialog box revealing additional automatable parameters available for this track (see Figure 34.9), select the one you want, and click OK to return to the subtrack. At this point, the Parameter field should display the parameter you just selected.

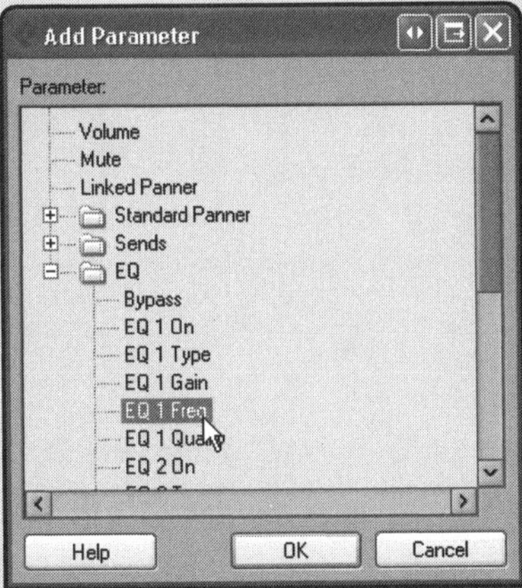

Figure 34.9
The Add Parameter dialog box.

5. Click and drag the cursor in the automation track to add curve points. The options pertaining to the shapes, frequency, amplitude, and starting point of the Line tool are the same as described in Chapter 16.

Hiding and Removing Automation Subtracks

When working with automation, you can hide automation subtracks that you don't need to see in order to clean up your working area. Hiding automation subtracks does not prevent their automation from being read. If you don't want to hear the changes made by automation, simply turn off the Read Automation button for this track—or at the top of the Track List if you want to globally disable reading of *all* automation in this project. At any time, you also can mute only a specific type of automation by clicking the Mute Automation button for the subtrack that is displaying that parameter in the Track List. For example, Figure 34.10 shows the Linked Panner parameter automation as muted (top), whereas the automation for the parameter in the subtrack immediately below it is *not* muted. This means that the track plays one type of automation, but not the other.

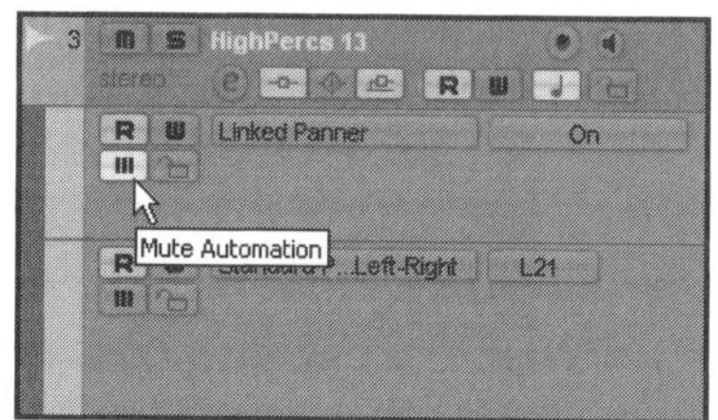

Figure 34.10
The subtrack's Mute Automation button.

HOW TO

Hide automation subtracks:

- To hide all automation subtracks, select the Hide All Automation option from the context menu. This appears after right-clicking (PC)/Control-clicking (Mac) anywhere in the Track List.
- To hide all automation for one track, click the Show/Hide Automation button for this track (the arrow pointing up in the lower-left corner of the track containing the automation subtracks). Note that this button only becomes visible when your mouse cursor rolls over this corner of the track's entry in the Track List.
- To hide only one automation subtrack, click the Show/Hide Automation button of the subtrack above it (the minus sign in the upper-left corner of the subtrack containing the automation you want to hide).

HOW TO

Remove automation subtracks:

- To erase all automation events for a subtrack's parameter, select the Remove Parameter option from the Parameter field of this subtrack. This removes the automation subtrack, as well as all the automation curve points on the selected subtrack.
- To erase some of the automation events on a subtrack, select them by using the Selection tool or Range Selection tool and delete them by pressing the Delete or Backspace key. You also can click on the selected automation events (curve points) using the Eraser tool.
- To remove unused subtracks that might have been left behind after editing, select the Remove Unused Parameters option from the Parameter field in one of the subtracks.

Editing Automation

After you've recorded automation, editing it is not very different. You can use the Mixer window to edit automation in real time through the Write/Read Automation buttons or by editing automation parameters in their respective automation subtracks in the Project window. As mentioned earlier when describing the automation modes, Cubase 4 users can switch between these modes to use the mode that best suits their editing needs.

HOW TO

View the automation previously recorded:

1. In the Project window, right-click (PC)/Control-click (Mac) in the Track List.
2. Select the Show Used Automation option from the context menu. If you want to see all automation recorded on all tracks, select the Show Used Automation for All Tracks instead.

You will probably notice that some parameters do not allow intermediate values. This is the case for switch type parameters, such as a Mute, Bypass, or Sustain Pedal MIDI message. Because these parameters are either on or off, there are only two acceptable values: 0 or 127. When editing their automation, you can only enter these values, and the curve points will automatically jump between these minimum and maximum values.

Using Write Automation

To edit existing automation data using the Write Automation button on a channel, you just need to write over the automation again. If Touch Fader is selected as the automation mode, as soon as you touch a control (by clicking on it and holding it or moving it to a new location), the old automation is replaced by new values, until you release the mouse. At that point, if the Read Automation button is also active, from that point forward Cubase continues reading existing automation on the parameter's automation subtrack. (To ensure that the transition back to the existing automation values is smooth, the Automation Return Time field allows you to specify how long this transition should be after you release the control.)

Using Automation Subtracks

When you open a parameter subtrack containing recorded automation, you will notice that curve points (handles) appear along the automation line. Here's a look at how you can edit the points on this line:

HOW TO

Edit recorded automation in a subtrack:

- **To move an existing curve point.** In the Project window, select the Object Selection tool and move the curve point to a new location by clicking it and dragging. Note that the quantize grid settings, if the Snap is active, influence exactly where in time you can move this automation.
- **To move several automation curve points simultaneously.** With the Object Selection tool, drag a selection box over the points you want to move. The selected curve points become red. Click and drag one of the selected points to the new location. You also can Shift-click on several points if you want to edit non-continuous points instead.
- **To draw over existing automation.** In the Project window, select the Draw, Line, Parabola, Sine, Triangle, or Square tool from the toolbar and click where you want to start drawing over the existing automation and drag your tool until the point where you want to stop replacing the existing automation. The first and last point where you draw this automation automatically creates a connection to the existing automation line. You can use the different options associated with each tool to create different shapes; for example, use the Ctrl (PC)/Command (Mac) key to invert the parabola curve.
- **To erase existing curve points.** Click on the point or drag a range over several automation curve points using the Object Selection tool. After the desired points are red, press Delete, Backspace on your keyboard or use the Eraser tool to erase them.
- **To move or erase all automation curve points on a subtrack.** Right-click (PC)/Control-click (Mac) over the desired subtrack's Track List area and select the Select All Events option from the context menu. After they are selected, you can move or erase these automation curve points. Note that if you want to remove all automation for a parameter, you can also use the Remove Parameter option from the subtrack's Parameter field.

You also can use the Browser window to edit automation, as you would edit any other events in your project (see Figure 34.11). Simply expand the track to reveal the automation events and then select the automation parameter in the Project Structure panel to reveal the list of events it holds in the right panel. Then you can select a value and change it in the list. If the Sync Selection option is checked in the Browser window's toolbar, Cubase displays the event you are editing in the Project window.

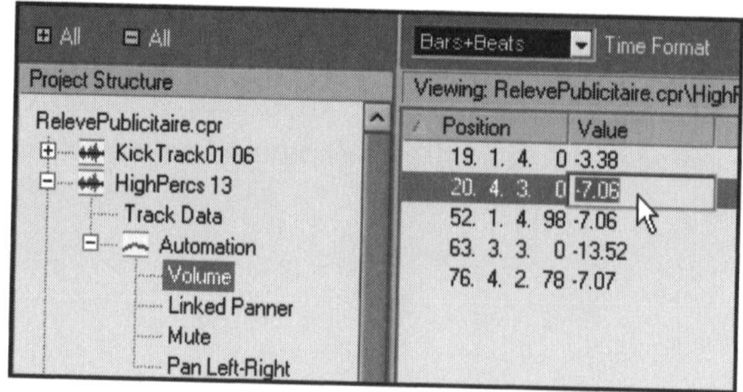

Figure 34.11
Editing automation in the Browser window.

Moving Along Events with Their Automation

Quite often, we start working on a project, record events, and add automation to subtracks below these events. But if you need to move these events, it would be nice if the automation could move along with it. The Automation Follows Events option does exactly that: keeps the automation attached to the event; when you move the event, the automation moves with it. You can enable this option in the Edit menu or in the File (PC)/Cubase(Mac) > Preferences > Editing page.

35 } Automation Techniques

Mixing a recording is an art form unto itself—the art of listening. Being a great musician doesn't mean you're going to be a great mixing engineer, and being a great mixing engineer doesn't mean you will be a great musician. Either way, practice makes perfect, and there's nothing like listening to good performances and good mixes to refine your craft. No matter what your speciality is, the goal is to get everything in perfect balance. Cubase shines through its integration of traditional mixing techniques and the addition of real-time effects processing and automation inside a single application. The mixing process inside Cubase is comparable to the traditional mixing process to the extent that external mixers have many of the same features offered by Cubase. That being said, this chapter does not discuss what makes a good mix or how to achieve this balance. It does, however, look at the tools available in Cubase to achieve this balance. You will find some very good titles that discuss mixing at www.courseptr.com, under the site's Music Technology category.

Here's a summary of what you will learn in this chapter:

- How to view automation tracks
- How to record a SysEx bulk dump from an external MIDI device into Cubase
- How to record parameter changes into Cubase during playback by using SysEx messages
- How to transmit recorded SysEx bulk dumps from Cubase to your external MIDI device
- How to install a MIDI remote control device

Automation in the Mixer

Automation affects the way audio events are played. There are two sets of automation that you can apply: audio channel automation and MIDI channel automation. The computer is responsible for audio processing, whereas MIDI automation is processed by the MIDI instrument (hardware or software) selected as the MIDI output for the track. Table 35.1 displays examples of parameters that you can automate in the Mixer window.

Table 35.1
Examples of Parameters Available for Automation in the Mixer Window

MIDI Channel Settings	Audio Channel Settings (Including ReWire, VSTi, Groups, and FX Channels)
MIDI Volume	Volume
MIDI Pan	Pan and Surround Panner
Mute	Mute
Send effects, bypass switches, and parameters	Send effects, bypass switches, and parameters
Insert effects, bypass switches, and parameters	Insert effects, bypass switches, and parameters
	EQ bypass switches and parameters
	Effect send activation switch
	Effect send levels
	Effect send pre-/post-switch

We have discussed the Mixer window in previous chapters, so its options should be familiar to you by now. Unlike traditional mixers, Cubase allows you to record most of the manipulations you make inside the mixing environment, including effect automation.

Automation Tracks

Automating inside Cubase is not limited to the Mixer window. Parameters in the control panels for VST instruments and send/insert effects can also be automated. You also can record, edit, and draw all automation types in the Project window. Automation data, in the form of automation curve points, can be displayed in the automation subtracks available for each track (see Figure 35.1). Automation parameters can be displayed in several ways:

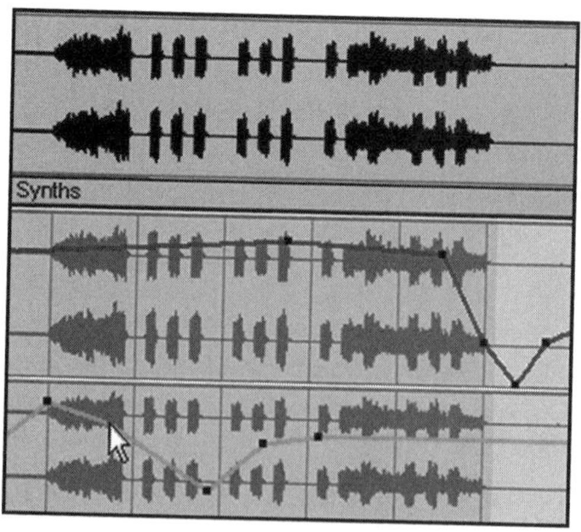

Figure 35.1
Automation subtracks found under the Synths track.

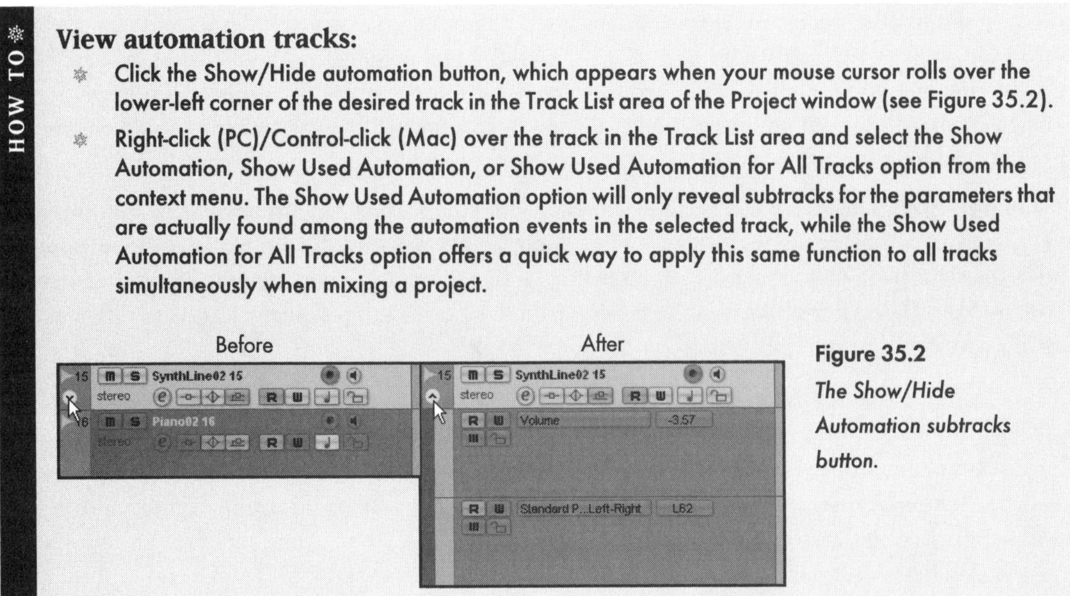

HOW TO

View automation tracks:

- Click the Show/Hide automation button, which appears when your mouse cursor rolls over the lower-left corner of the desired track in the Track List area of the Project window (see Figure 35.2).
- Right-click (PC)/Control-click (Mac) over the track in the Track List area and select the Show Automation, Show Used Automation, or Show Used Automation for All Tracks option from the context menu. The Show Used Automation option will only reveal subtracks for the parameters that are actually found among the automation events in the selected track, while the Show Used Automation for All Tracks option offers a quick way to apply this same function to all tracks simultaneously when mixing a project.

Figure 35.2
The Show/Hide Automation subtracks button.

Automation recorded or drawn into these subtracks of the Project window is no different than the automation recorded in the Mixer window or the control panel of a VST instrument or plug-in. In the Project window, automation is always displayed under the track with which it is associated. For the parameter in question, an automation line (with curve points on it, once any automation has been created) is displayed over a background representation of the content currently playing in the track. The only difference is the way you record these events. When automation is recorded or edited in one window, it is updated in the others as well.

Cubase offers two automation methods: recording the automation in real time using the Read/Write buttons on mixer channels and plug-in control panels or actually drawing automation curve points on the automation subtracks. Both methods offer similar results, and your actions using one method will update the results in the other. For example, you can record automation in the Mixer and then later edit this automation using the Pencil tool on the corresponding automation subtrack in the Project window.

All track classes have their own sets of automation subtracks, depending on what can be automated on them. For example, VSTi tracks can hold as many subtracks as there are parameters and channels available for that particular VSTi. Similarly, a ReWire folder track will appear as soon as you enable the first ReWire channel in your project. If you record automation for this channel, it is stored in additional subtracks, one for each parameter you automated. Even MIDI tracks have automation subtracks for Mixer-related settings, inserts, or send parameter automation. Normally, MIDI will use Control Change messages along with System Exclusive messages to automate MIDI devices, but because certain parameters you can automate for MIDI tracks inside Cubase are not supported by MIDI (such as the status of the channel's Mute button, MIDI plug-in effects, and Track Settings in the Inspector, for example), additional MIDI automation subtrack types pick up where MIDI left off. The more parameters you automate in a single channel, the more automation subtracks are likely to create for this track.

When automating FX channels, each parameter you move while writing automation in real time will generate a subtrack associated with this channel. So you can, for example, progressively make the simulation of a reverberant space bigger by changing (over time) the room size, reverb time, and pre-delay parameters in the control panel for a reverb plug-in just as easily as you can create a fade-out or pan movement on an audio track.

Using SysEx

SysEx (System Exclusive) is used to send data that is specific to a MIDI device, such as a dump of its patch memory, sequencer data, waveform data, or any other information that is particular to a device. In other words, SysEx is used to change MIDI device parameters that no other MIDI message can, because it is the only way MIDI can retrieve parameter data from or send parameter data to a device.

When you are working with Cubase, SysEx can serve two main purposes:

- You can save all the parameters of a MIDI device used in a project using a bulk dump procedure.
- When you can't automate the parameters of an external MIDI device using automation tracks, you can use SysEx to record parameter changes made on your device's front panel into Cubase, and then have Cubase play these back through MIDI.

Whereas the majority of MIDI messages represent events that happen at a particular point in time, SysEx "dumps" of the settings and other data currently stored in the external device may take more or less time, depending on the size of the data to be transferred. However, SysEx can *also* be used in real time to alter parameters on that device (knobs, sliders, effects parameters, filters, effects, envelope generators and other synthesis parameters, for example) that aren't accessible via standard MIDI Control Change messages. You do have some control over how a note is played with MIDI events, such as the control provided by Control Change messages; however, this does not affect how the sound is produced by your MIDI device in most common situations.

It is important that a direct MIDI connection between the sender and the receiver be made. You can work with SysEx messages even with devices in a daisy chain; however, this requires extra precautions, such as making sure a different device ID number is assigned for each device in the chain (rarely a problem if they are from different manufacturers), making sure that the base MIDI channel in your external MIDI device is also different from one device to the next in this chain.

These precautions help make sure that only the MIDI device you intend to communicate with processes the SysEx messages.

Recording SysEx

There are two purposes for recording SysEx. The first purpose is to save all the values that make up one program, or all programs, in the instrument or device, so that when you recall a project, the external device's setup can be restored. This includes how the device's parameters are configured, especially when you've made changes to the original preset sounds provided by the manufacturer, specifically for this project. This allows you to recall the device's parameters as they were when you saved the song. The next time you load your project, you won't have to change anything on your device when you load the project because the parameters were stored with the project file using SysEx. This is called a *bulk dump*.

The second purpose is to store codes that instruct the instrument to change one of its settings, such as the cutoff frequency of a filter or the decay of a reverb during playback or at the beginning of the project. SysEx can be used as a last resort for parameters that can't be accessed using regular MIDI messages. This is done through SysEx parameter changes.

Recording a Bulk Dump

Usually, you will find a function or utility button on the front panel of your MIDI device that allows you to send a bulk dump. This means that you will be sending SysEx messages out through its MIDI Out connector. From that point, you can sometimes choose what kind of information you want to send. For example, you might send user patches, performances, or system settings. If there are no such buttons on your device, there are two workaround solutions:

- Get editor/librarian software that identifies your device and initiates a SysEx bulk dump request from this application. This enables your software to receive the appropriate SysEx information from your external MIDI device.
- Find out what message to send to the device to make it dump its settings via a MIDI output. Use the List editor in Cubase to insert that message in a MIDI track. Writing such a SysEx string is fairly complicated and requires an extensive study of the fine print in the operation manual, so if in doubt, consider sticking with the first method and get an editor/librarian—it'll save you lots of headaches.

Because your MIDI device stores parameter values in its memory, changing these values results in changing the parameter's settings. Usually, your MIDI device can send all or some of these parameters to Cubase using a bulk dump. This action is performed using SysEx messages.

After your device's SysEx has been dumped into Cubase, you can send it back to the device later to reset all the parameters to the way they were when you saved them. Most hardware MIDI devices have specific functions that allow you to send a bulk dump of all or some of your device's parameters. To find out which function or where this function is, you need to consult your device's documentation.

HOW TO

Record a SysEx bulk dump from an external MIDI device into Cubase:

1. Be sure the MIDI Out of your device is connected to the MIDI In of your computer or Cubase.
2. In Cubase, select the File (PC)/Cubase (Mac) menu > Preferences > MIDI > MIDI Filter. This brings up the MIDI Filter preferences page (see Figure 35.3).

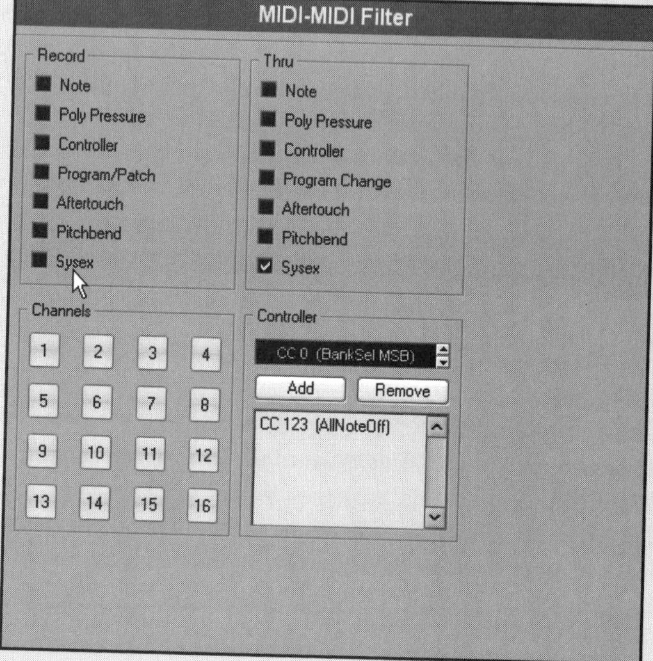

Figure 35.3
The MIDI filtering option in Cubase.

3. Deselect the SysEx check box under the Record section and leave it checked (default) under the Thru section. This enables you to record SysEx data from the MIDI input port, but does not echo these SysEx events through the MIDI output port. Echoing these events back would create a SysEx MIDI loop that could corrupt the transfer.
4. Click Apply, and then click OK to close the dialog box.
5. Create a new MIDI track in your project. This track should be used only for the SysEx events.
6. Assign the MIDI input port appropriately for this track. This should be the port used by the MIDI device to send SysEx to Cubase.
7. Position your cursor at the beginning of your project. Be sure the Metronome Click and Cycle Recording modes are disabled in the Transport.
8. If you already have events recorded in this project, mute all the MIDI, instrument, and ReWire tracks. When recording a bulk dump of your device's parameters, the SysEx messages require a large portion of your MIDI bandwidth.
9. Click the Record button on the Transport panel.

10. Press the appropriate buttons on your MIDI device to initiate the bulk dump. You might notice during the transmission that your device displays a special message on its LCD screen, telling you it's currently transmitting SysEx. When the device is finished with its transmission, you should see a message saying "Done" or "Completed."
11. When the external MIDI device has completed the bulk dump, you can stop recording in Cubase. Depending on the information you transmitted in this bulk dump (it might be just a few parameters or the entire set of parameters in your device), this process can take a few seconds or a few minutes. This creates a single MIDI part, which contains all the SysEx messages sent by the external device.
12. Save the project.
13. Mute this track to avoid having the SysEx retransmitted every time you click Play, or select the Not Connected option from this track's MIDI Output Port selection field in the Inspector or Track List area.

Here are some tips to keep in mind when recording SysEx bulk dumps:

- Only record the parameters you need to record. Usually, you can tell your MIDI device what type of bulk dump you want to perform. This saves space in your sequencer and speeds up the SysEx transfer back to your MIDI device. In a live performance, you don't want to wait a long time when loading up each project file for SysEx to be uploaded to your MIDI devices, so keeping things to a minimum is useful.
- If you only want Cubase to send parameter and patch information to your external MIDI device before a song starts to play, put the SysEx information well before the first bar if possible or before the occurrence of MIDI events in your song. This prevents you from having lags in your actual MIDI performance being sent to your devices, caused by a long SysEx message being sent simultaneously with other MIDI events.
- If all you want to do is change the sound settings (program) during playback, you might be better off creating and saving two different programs on the external device itself, and then using an ordinary MIDI program change message during playback, rather than a SysEx message. Program changes are more efficient in this case, and it takes much less time to update your external MIDI device.
- Avoid sending a SysEx bulk dump from Cubase to several external MIDI devices simultaneously.
- Be sure that when you record a bulk dump you are using the same device ID number that you will use later for sending this bulk dump back to the MIDI device. Otherwise, the device might not accept the SysEx bulk dump.
- Certain sequencers allow you to send a SysEx bulk dump automatically whenever you load a MIDI file. Use this feature to configure your devices appropriately for each song; however, keep the previous tips in mind.

Recording Parameter Automation through SysEx

If you only want to record certain parameter changes, you can proceed in a similar way. This is useful if you want to change a parameter during playback. Remember that MIDI is transmitted over a serial cable, which implies that information is sent sequentially one piece after another, not side by side. In the case of SysEx, the entire SysEx message has to be transmitted before the rest of the MIDI messages can resume their course. So, if you want to record SysEx parameter changes as you are playing notes, the more SysEx messages you are sending, the longer it takes for the other events to be transmitted. Keep your SysEx events as short as possible or, if you can, make sure not to overload a particular port on your MIDI interface with this type of message.

HOW TO

Record parameter changes in Cubase during playback by using SysEx messages:

1. Be sure the MIDI Out of your device is connected to the MIDI In of your computer's MIDI interface.
2. You might need to disable any SysEx filters from your Cubase's MIDI filter options, as mentioned in the bulk dump procedure described earlier.
3. Create a new MIDI track in your project where you want to record the SysEx. You could record SysEx parameter changes in the same track as the other MIDI events being sent to this device as part of your performance, but it is not recommended.
4. Chances are, if you want to update parameters during playback, you probably already have a MIDI track with recorded events. At this point, you'll want to hear this track if you want to update the parameters for the sound used in this track, so be sure this track is not muted.
5. Position your cursor at the appropriate location and click the Record button on the Transport panel.
6. Make the changes to your external MIDI device's parameters when it is appropriate in the project.
7. Stop the recording process when you are finished.
8. Rewind and start playback to hear the result.

Because you recorded the SysEx events on their own track, if you are not satisfied with the result, you can always erase these events and start over without affecting other types of events recorded for the affected part. For example, let's say you have a synth line playing on MIDI port A, channel 1, and you want to change the cutoff frequency of the sound used to play this line as it evolves in the song. You will have one track that contains the notes played by the synth and another track that performs the change in the cutoff frequency using SysEx. Erasing the SysEx events won't affect the notes, because you have kept them on separate tracks.

Transmitting Bulk Dumps

After your bulk dump is recorded in your project, you will probably want to send it back to your MIDI device when the time comes to restore the saved information. This is fairly easy to do because you already know how to do a bulk dump in one direction. The following list describes the steps you should take to transmit the SysEx information back to your external MIDI device.

HOW TO

Transmit recorded SysEx bulk dumps to your external MIDI device:

1. Assign the appropriate MIDI output port for the track containing the SysEx bulk dump events. This should be the output port connected to the MIDI input of your external device.
2. If your MIDI device has the option to deactivate its SysEx reception mode, make sure this is not enabled. In other words, you do want your MIDI device to respond to incoming SysEx information.
3. Solo the track that contains the SysEx data. This might not always be necessary, but it's a good precaution to take because you might have more than one SysEx data track, or you might have other MIDI events that could cause the transfer to interrupt abruptly if transmitted to the same MIDI port from other tracks.
4. Click Play on the Transport panel to begin transmitting a SysEx part to the external MIDI device. You should see some indication on the front panel of your external MIDI device to the effect that it is receiving SysEx.

Just as when your Cubase project is receiving SysEx, you should take the same precautions when sending SysEx from Cubase to your MIDI device. For example, try not to send more data than required. If all you need to recall is a single program's parameters, avoid sending full bulk dumps to your machine. If the bulk dump serves to set up your device for a project, try putting your SysEx in the count-in bars, well before the actual song starts.

Using a Remote Control Mixer

It is possible to use a MIDI remote control device to record and edit automation in a Cubase project. Recording automation using such a device is no different than using the controls inside the Mixer window in Cubase. However, editing recorded automation events is a little different. If your remote control MIDI device does not have touch-sensitive controls, Cubase does not have any way of knowing where a control is until you move it. As a result, if the Touch Fader automation mode is selected, when you activate the Write Automation button in the Mixer window and move a control on your MIDI controller, all the following automation is replaced until the moment you stopped playback or disabled the Write Automation button once again. To avoid recording over automation by mistake, you should only enable the Write Automation button on the specific channels where you want to overwrite automation or avoid moving controllers associated with automation that you want to keep. Note also that it is possible to enable the Lock button on individual automation subtracks–a very good habit that can help you to avoid small disasters during the mixing phase of a project.

To use a remote control surface with Cubase, you have to install it in the Device Setup panel.

HOW TO

Install a MIDI remote control device:

1. Select the Device Setup option from the Devices menu.
2. Click the plus sign above the Devices list in the dialog box (see Figure 35.4).

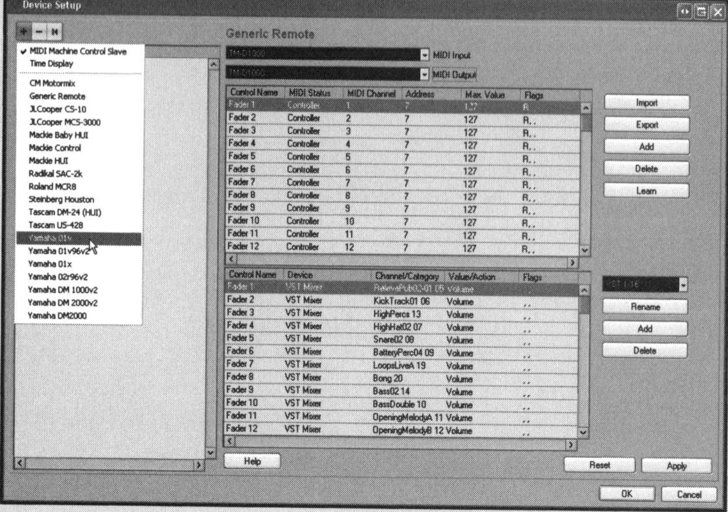

Figure 35.4
Adding a MIDI device controller to your device setup.

3. Select the appropriate device from the Supported Devices list. If your device is not in this list, select the Generic Remote device. The device is added under the Remote Devices folder in the Device Setup dialog.
4. That device will now be highlighted in the Devices list in the left side of the Device Setup dialog box.
5. Select the appropriate MIDI input and output ports connecting the controller to Cubase, and be sure these ports are properly connected to this device. Some remote controllers are connected directly to the computer via USB. In that case, that connection may be listed in these MIDI Input/Output selectors as its "Control Port," even though this isn't technically a MIDI connection.
6. Enable the Auto Select option if your device supports this option. (With this option, a channel is automatically selected when the corresponding fader on the remote is touched.)
7. Click OK when you are finished.

Because remote control surfaces essentially serve as a tactile interface, you can also program a number of key commands that trigger specific functions on the remote device whenever the device supports this. If this is the case, Cubase will display a list below the MIDI port (with Button, Category, and Command columns) where you can associate keys on the remote device with Cubase menu commands and other actions. Otherwise, Cubase only displays the fields with options that are associated with the selected device. When you are selecting a General Remote, Cubase displays two more extensive tables in which you can import existing settings to communicate with the external device or set up your device appropriately to help you perform tasks inside a project.

You can now use your controller with Cubase. How it interacts with Cubase depends greatly on the controller itself. You need to refer to this controller's documentation for further details.

Most remote control devices can control both MIDI and audio channel automation in Cubase 4, even if their parameter setups are different; however, when audio-specific parameters are received by MIDI tracks, such as EQ parameters, they are then ignored by Cubase.

36 Surround Mixing

Cubase 4 offers the possibility of mixing in several surround modes, as well as in stereo mode. *Surround* refers to a multichannel positioning system rather than a standard stereo (left/right) positioning. The advantage of mixing in surround is that beyond the left/right field available in stereo mixes, you can literally place your sound anywhere in space around the listener by using various surround configurations. For example, an LCRS multichannel configuration offers a four-channel setup, and a 5.1 surround configuration offers a six-channel configuration.

Here's a summary of what you will learn in this chapter:

- How to create a child input or output bus
- How to use the Surround Panner
- How to mute speakers in the Surround Panner
- How to edit the routing of an insert effect in a surround output bus configuration
- How to export a surround mix

Multichannel Configurations

How you position the speakers depends on the standard you want to use and the room for which you are mixing. For example, movie theaters often place the left and right channels behind the screen, close to the left and right walls, while the center channel is also behind the screen, but in the center of it. The LFE channel (which stands for *Low Frequency Effects*; that is, a dedicated subwoofer channel) is also behind the screen, while the left and right surround channels are along the other three surfaces of the theater itself.

To use surround mixing in Cubase, you must create a surround output bus that is connected to multi-output audio hardware. You also could create a surround input bus, but your input sources and audio tracks don't have to be multichannel in order to be routed to a surround output bus. When any audio channel is sent to a surround output bus, the Surround Panner appears in the channel's panning area, replacing the pan position value display, offering you control over more than the typical left and right channels in a stereo mix.

You can also choose to route an audio channel (disk-based, VSTi, ReWire, or FX channel) to a specific set of outputs within the surround bus channels. In that case, the Pan control would remain the same as if you were routing the signal through a mono or stereo output bus. Figure 36.1 shows how an audio channel displays the Pan control when it is assigned to a surround output bus on the left and to a stereo output bus on the right.

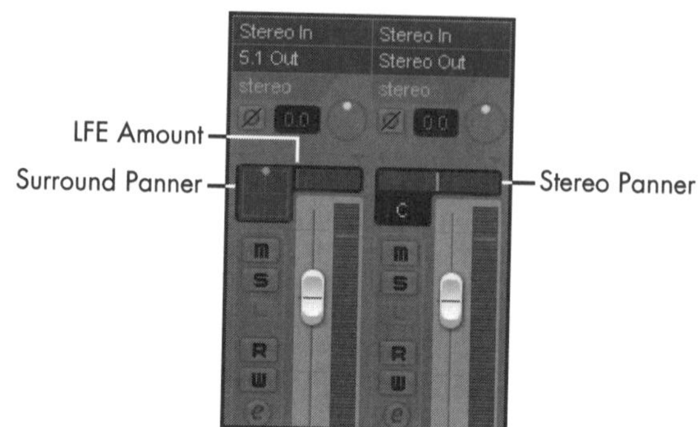

Figure 36.1
An audio channel using surround Pan control (left) and stereo Pan control (right).

Mixing in surround requires multiple-output audio hardware to monitor the signal sent to these additional outputs. It also requires an external multichannel monitoring system to support surround mixes.

Surround Bus

To work with surround configurations, you need to create surround output busses. These are created in the VST Connections panel by selecting one of the multichannel configurations in the Add Output Bus dialog box.

After you have created a surround bus (input or output), you can associate each channel in the bus with an ASIO device port (that is, an individual input or output on your audio interface). How many ASIO device ports you need depends on the surround configuration you choose. For example, a 5.1 configuration will create a six-channel configuration, while an LCRS configuration uses only four (Left, Center, Right, and Surround).

When you want to assign an audio channel to a surround bus, you can decide to route the output directly through one of the individual channels in the surround bus or to all the channels at once, where its exact location will be determined by the position of the Surround Panner. Figure 36.2 displays a channel that is being routed directly to the center channel of the surround bus. When a channel is routed directly to a single channel within the surround bus, the pan area of the channel does not offer a surround panning option.

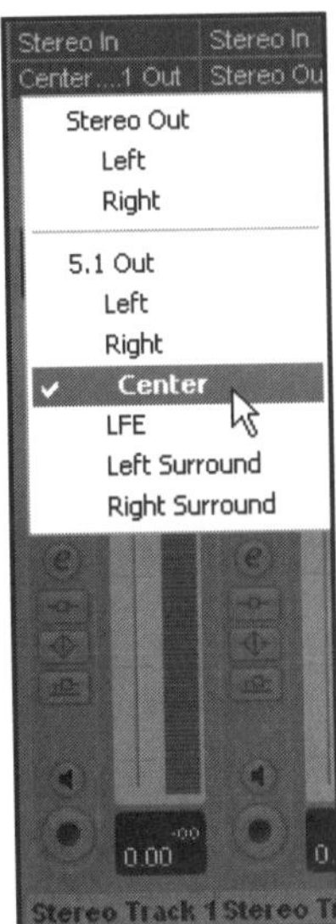

Figure 36.2
An audio channel routed directly to a single channel of a surround output bus.

After a surround bus is created, you can also create child busses. A child bus offers a convenient way of routing an audio channel through a specific set of outputs that forms part of a surround bus. For example, you can create a stereo child bus within a 5.1 surround configuration, where the left and right channels are grouped within the surround bus. Routing an audio channel through a stereo child bus (consisting of two audio outputs on your audio interface) allows you to control where the sound will occur in that child bus, so you will have a stereo Pan control rather than a surround Pan control. In other words, creating a child bus can make it easier to route audio through a surround bus yet keep a stereo control (affecting both channels) when adjusting the pan and volume for this channel. For example, if you are creating a surround input bus to capture a multichannel performance or surround atmosphere, you can create child busses to represent the left/right pair and then a left surround/right surround pair. When adjusting the level of the inputs, changing the volume for the left side will also affect the right side as they are being grouped inside the surround bus configuration.

HOW TO

Create a child input/output bus:

1. Select the surround bus within which you want to create a child bus from the VST Connections window.
2. Right-click (PC)/Control-click (Mac) on the selected surround bus and choose Add Child Bus to [your surround configuration's bus].
3. Select the appropriate Child Bus submenu option that you want to create. In Figure 36.3, selecting Stereo creates a child bus for the left and right channels within this surround output bus.

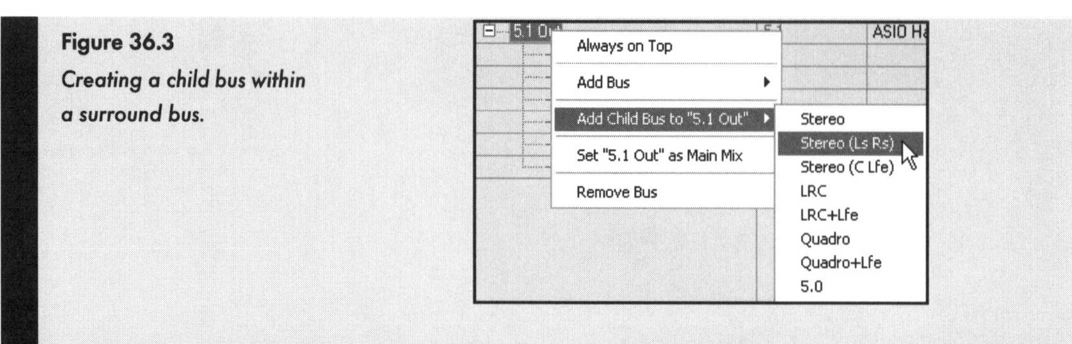

Figure 36.3
Creating a child bus within a surround bus.

Notice that the ASIO device ports assigned to the newly created child bus are also being used by the surround bus. Reassigning these ports in the child bus also changes them in the surround parent bus.

Surround Routing Options

When you are working with surround busses, both as input and output, many routing options are available.

Depending on which routing option you choose, several Pan control options are available. Table 36.1 offers a quick look at the surround signal routing options and the types of Pan control offered by each.

Table 36.1
Surround Signal Routing Options

Source	**Destination**	**Pan Control**
Mono	To single channel inside the surround bus	None. The output channel is mono and is heard through the associated ASIO device port.
Mono	To child bus inside the surround bus	It is handled as a standard stereo or multichannel, depending on the child bus configuration. The pan might affect the surround position or any other location, depending on the current parent bus configuration. For example, if the bus is in 5.1 (six channels) and the child bus set as an LCR subset (three channels), the channel will display the Surround Panner to control the location. On the other hand, if your child bus is stereo (left/right), the mono channel will be panned between left and

Source	Destination	Pan Control
		right (not surround panned, even though it is part of the surround configuration).
Mono	To a surround bus	The Surround Panner positions the signal anywhere within the current surround bus configuration.
Stereo	To stereo child bus inside the surround bus	See above—this is the same as with a mono signal sent to a stereo child bus.
Stereo	To a surround bus	The Surround Panner positions the signal anywhere within the current surround bus configuration.
Surround	Surround	No Pan control; all channels play in the same channel as they came in from. You should avoid sending a multichannel input signal configuration into another multi-input signal configuration or into a mono or stereo output bus. For example, avoid sending a 5.1 multichannel input signal to an LCRS output bus. Doing so results in loss of sound positioning precision.

Surround Panner

The Surround Panner is automatically available in a channel's Pan control area in the Mixer window (and optionally in the Inspector) when mono or stereo audio channels are routed through a surround output bus or a multichannel child bus (but not a stereo child bus). You can position and automate the position of the sound within the surround configuration by dragging the small dot inside the Surround Panner display. Double-clicking on the Surround Panner display opens the full Surround Panner interface, which offers more precision and greater control over the setup and behavior of the panner.

The Surround Panner offers three different modes: standard, position, and angle (see Figure 36.4).

In the upper part, all three modes offer a representation of the speaker placements and the position of this channel's sound in relation to the speakers. The lower part offers a variety of controls over the behavior of the Panner itself. To switch from one mode to the next, you select the desired option from the Mode drop-down menu found in the Panner. Note that the actual number of speakers and how they appear in the upper part depends on the current surround output bus configuration.

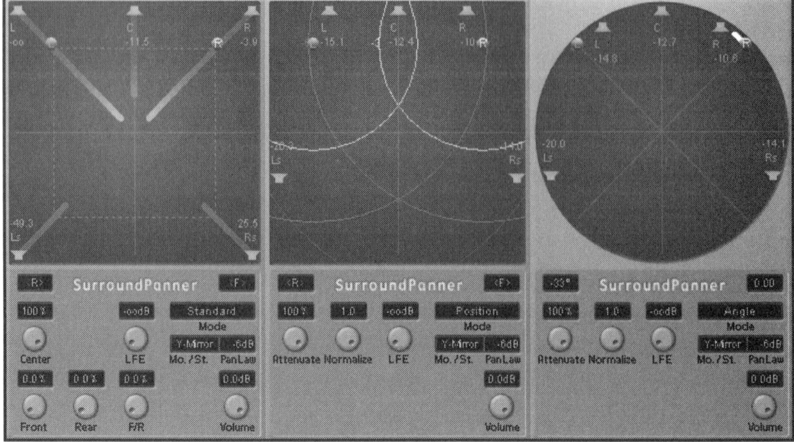

Figure 36.4
Surround Panner modes (from left to right): standard, position, and angle.

Here's a look at the differences between each mode.

- In Standard mode, speakers are aligned to the front and back, similar to a typical movie theater setup. The space between each front speaker in this mode may not be the same in every room because the separation between the left/right speakers depends on the size of the room. This is the default mode and is most appropriate for moving sounds from one channel (position in the surround field) to the next without attenuating the level of this signal as it travels between both positions.
- In Position mode, speakers also are aligned to the front, but not necessarily to the back. Instead, the surround speakers (in a 5.1 or 5.0 setup) are located on the side. Furthermore, the front speakers should be equally spaced from the center as well as the sides. In other words, if you were to divide the front by five, each line would be equally spaced, with lines 1 and 5 representing the left and right walls respectively, and lines 2 and 4 representing the left and right speakers. This mode is also similar to movie theaters. The display also is different, as it depicts concentric circles around the position (or location) of the sound rather than the intensity of the sound emanating from the speakers. Each circle corresponds to a 3-dB decrease in amplitude from the current position of the sound to the previous circle, another 3-dB to the next, and so on.
- In Angle mode, all speakers are considered at equal distance from the center point (the ultimate sweet listening spot). This is probably the most common configuration for 5.1 surround sound, but not a typical movie theater representation. This being said, the Angle mode works well in most surround configurations. In this mode, arcs help you determine the perceived range of a source (see Figure 36.5), and the sound is at its loudest in the middle of the arc and at its weakest toward the ends.

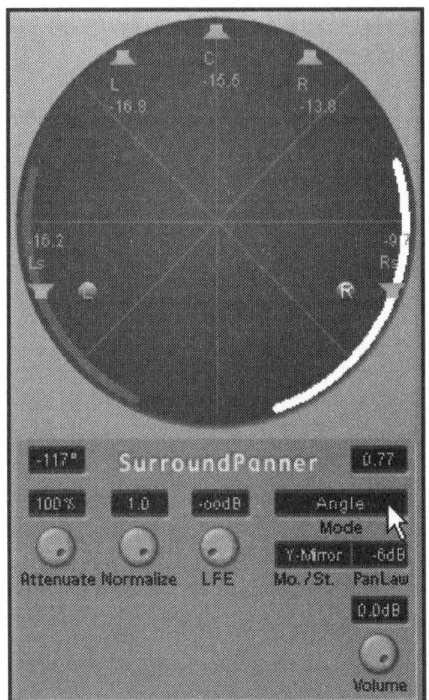

Figure 36.5
The Surround Panner in Angle mode.

In any mode, the speakers represent an optimal speaker setup, and the lines, especially in Standard mode, give you an indication of how loud or soft a sound will be in any given speaker. You might decide, however, to mute a speaker, forcing Cubase to redistribute the sound through the remaining audio channels (hooked to the corresponding speakers) and effectively muting any signal going to that speaker.

HOW TO

Mute speakers in the Surround Panner:

- Alt-click (PC)/Option-click (Mac) on the speaker you want to mute.
- Repeat the operation on the same speaker to unmute it.

In the same display where you found the speakers, you will find either one or two control handles, depending on the mix mode set (see the following list). The control handles allow you to place the source of the sound appropriately in the surround-sound mixing field. In Standard mode, lines emerge from the speakers, indicating the level being sent from this source audio channel to each output. In the example provided in Figure 36.4 (Standard mode), you can see the two controls placed in the upper-left and upper-right portions of the display. Consequently, the front-left and front-right speaker levels are set respectively to minus infinity and −3.9, and the center speaker is set to −11.5 (see the small values next to the speakers in the graphic display), while the left surround and right surround output levels are set to −49.3 and −25.5. These are the levels that determine the apparent positioning of this sound in the current configuration. Consequently, the level of this channel is distributed to each output in the surround output bus by using these levels.

The only speaker that is not represented in this display is the low-frequency sub-bass speaker, which has its own knob (and associated numerical field) in the lower part of the Surround Panner interface.

You can move the source of a signal by dragging the control handle where you want in this display (and in any mode). If the source is stereo and if you are not using the Mono Mix mode (found in the lower part of the Panner), you will find two control handles, labeled L and R. When positioning a stereo sound within the Surround Panner, you will always move the right control handle (labeled R).

The direction the left control handle takes depends on the surround mixer mode set. You have four basic mix modes from which to choose:

- **Mono Mix.** When used on a stereo source, both sources are mixed into a mono channel, and you control where this channel is positioned in the surround field (see Figure 36.6).

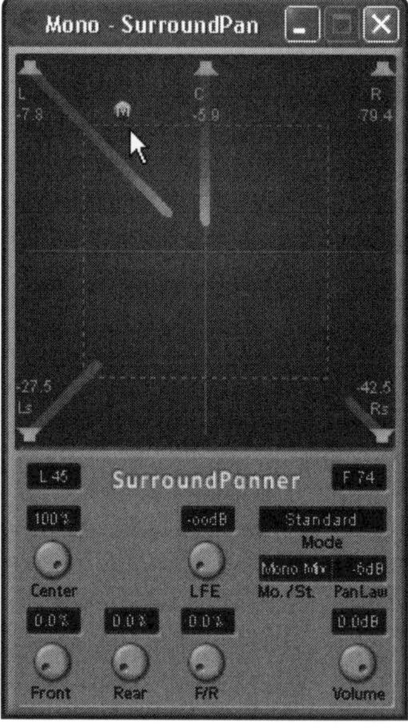

Figure 36.6
A mono channel represented in the Surround Panner's Mono Mix mode.

- **Y-Mirror.** This causes stereo sources to mirror vertically (as shown in Figure 36.5). Moving the right control handle's position to the left or right causes the left field to move in the opposite direction. Moving this control to the front or back causes the left control to move in the same direction. In other words, the position of the right control reflects vertically (the Y axis).

- **X-Mirror.** This causes stereo sources to mirror horizontally. When you move the right control handle's position to the left or right, the left field moves in the same direction. When you move this control to the front or back, the left control moves in the opposite direction. In other words, the position of the right control reflects horizontally (the X axis).
- **X-/Y-Mirror.** This causes stereo sources to mirror both vertically and horizontally. In other words, the left control always moves in the opposite direction of the right control.

In the Standard mode, the Center Level control determines the percentage assigned to the center speaker. When this slider is set to zero percent, the signal that would be positioned in the center speaker is shadowed by the left and right speakers instead, creating a virtual center speaker without using this source. By default, this value is set to 100 percent.

Still in the Standard mode, the following three rings are called Divergence controls, and they determine the attenuation curves used when positioning sound sources for X-axis front (the first ring to the left), X-axis back (the center ring), and Y-axis (the ring on the right). By default, these values are set at zero percent. Raising these values changes the shape of the dotted-line square representation inside the graphic display and can cause the signal to start appearing in other speakers even when you place the source on a single speaker. This occurs because you change the attenuation curve and set the room to react unnaturally, attenuating the sound coming from one source more than the sound coming from another source. As a result, the speakers generate a different level to compensate for this attenuation.

In Position or Angle modes, the Center and Divergence controls are replaced by the Attenuation and Normalize controls. The Attenuation control increases the volume of the source in its current surround position, whereas the Normalize control increases the overall level of all speakers so that the sum of the amplitude from all speakers is at 0dBFS when the Normalize control is set to 1. Note that you should not rely on the Normalize parameter in lieu of a dynamics processor for control over the surround channels because normalizing doesn't prevent peaks from occurring in the signal.

Such peaks could cause one of the surround channels to clip and cause distortion. You should use the Attenuation control when a sound, even when positioned appropriately, still appears to be too loud in the surround mix.

The sub-bass (LFE) speaker control in all modes adjusts the level being sent from this source in the sub-bass channel if such a channel exists in your surround configuration. For example, there are no LFE channels in an LCRS configuration, so this control would not be available. You also can adjust the level of the LFE channel by using the slider next to the Surround Panner display in the mixer channel or by entering a value in the extended portion of the mixer (see Figure 36.7).

You can automate the Surround Panner as you would any other channel automation described in Chapter 13.

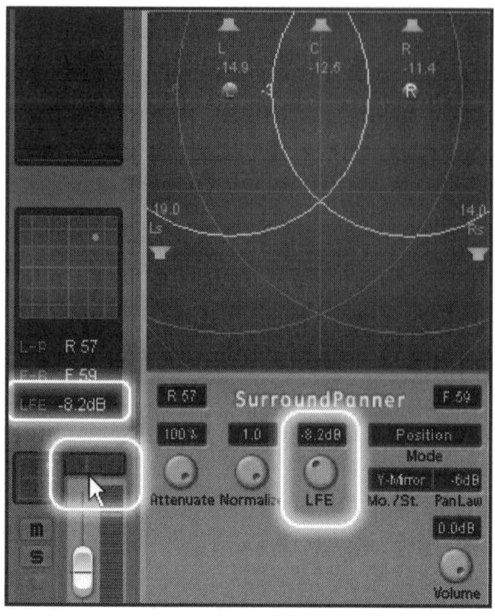

Figure 36.7
Adjusting the amount of signal sent to the LFE channel.

Routing Effects in Surround Outputs

As you might have anticipated, using effects in Surround mode might be a slightly more complex issue because most effects are designed to work on two channels rather than four, five, or six channels. Cubase offers some surround plug-ins and support for surround-compatible plug-ins from third parties, through a special signal path diagram, which is accessible in the Channel Settings panel for the surround output bus (see Figure 36.8). This routing also is available for any stereo or mono channels; however, the surround configuration only shows up when you are editing a multichannel track (recorded from a multichannel input) through a multichannel output bus. By default, the Insert Routing panel shown in Figure 36.8 is not visible. To display it, right-click (PC)/Control-click (Mac) in the window's title bar and select the appropriate panel to display from the context menu's Customize View submenu, as displayed in Figure 36.9. Notice in this image that you can also display the routing for sends and studio sends.

Each vertical line in this display corresponds to a channel (ASIO device port) in the multichannel track, routed to its corresponding output bus channel. By assigning multiple instances of the same effect to different channels in the bus, you can use effects on all channels in the bus. Lines that are interrupted by handles before and after the insert effect indicate that the signal will be processed by this effect on this channel inside the bus. In the example in Figure 36.8, the UV22hr dithering and the MultibandCompressor plug-in effects are the only truly multichannel effects because they affect all channels at once. On the other hand, there are two instances of a third-party reverb, the Waves IR convolution. The first affects the first two channels (left and right); the second affects the left and right surround channels. This enables you to apply the same or different settings to four output channels in this bus.

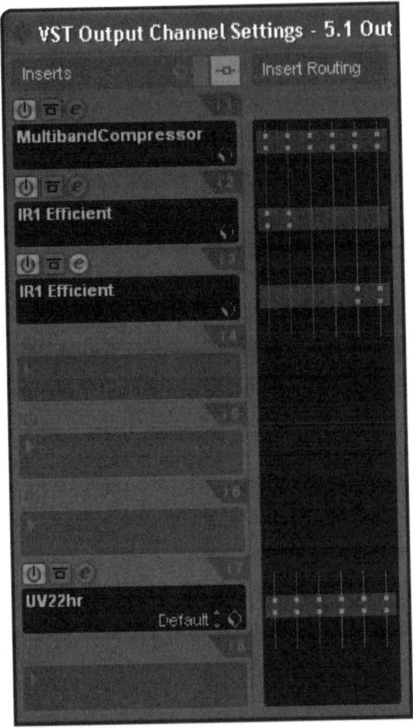

Figure 36.8
Routing insert effects in a surround output bus.

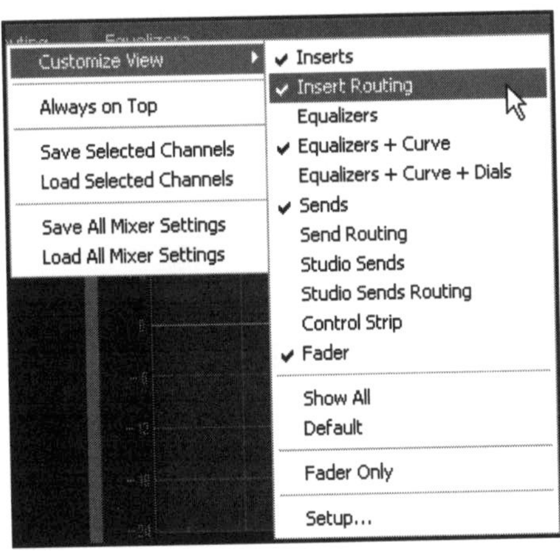

Figure 36.9
Displaying the Insert Routing panel in the VST Output Channel Settings window.

To change the routing of an effect in a multichannel setup, double-click on the routing lines next to the effect you want to route. The Routing editor dialog box, displayed in Figure 36.10, opens and displays three types of paths: broken lines with boxes (L, R), broken lines without boxes (C, LFE), and passing lines (Ls, Rs). The connector at the top represents the input of the insert, and the connector at the bottom represents its output. If a line is broken with a box on each side of the connector, it means that the signal is routed through the effect. In other words, the channel will be routed through that effect. If a line is broken without boxes, the signal is muted from this point on in the signal path. In the same figure, this is the case for the two center lines (channels).

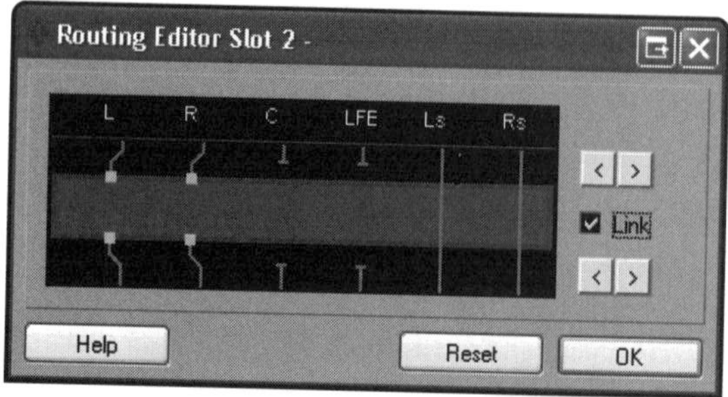

Figure 36.10
The Routing editor: In this example, the left and right channels are processed by the effect.

If the line passes through without breaking, it means that the signal bypasses the effect altogether, as displayed by the Ls and Rs channels in Figure 36.10. You might decide to process a channel with a plug-in yet send the output of this plug-in to another channel. For example, you could process the left and right surround channels with a reverb and send the output of this reverb effect into the left and right channels instead, as is the case in the example in Figure 36.11. In this example, the left and right channels will contain both the source signal bypassing the reverb and the reverb's processed output, which contains the signal originally found on the left and right surround channels.

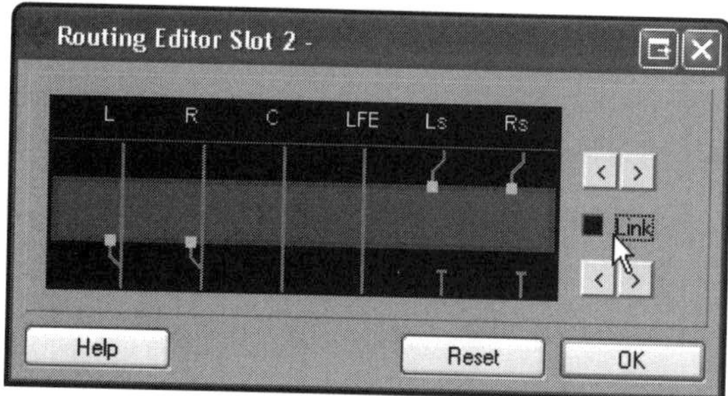

Figure 36.11
Routing the output of an effect into another channel within the surround bus.

The set of arrows separated by the Link check box moves the input channels or the output channels sideways to modify the routing. When the Link check box is active, both the input and output channels will move together.

HOW TO

Edit the routing of an insert effect in a surround output bus configuration:

1. Open the VST Output Channel Settings for the surround bus.
2. Assign the desired effect to the insert effect's slot.

3. Double-click the routing diagram. The Routing editor dialog box will appear.
4. Check or uncheck the Link option, according to your needs (see the description from a moment ago).
5. Click on the input arrows (top pair) to move the connections to the desired channels.
6. Click on the output arrows (lower pair) to move the connections to the desired channels.
7. Click OK when you are finished.

Exporting a Surround Mix

After you have completed your surround mix, you can export it as you would export a normal final stereo mix. The only difference with a surround mix is that you can choose an additional number of output file formats in the File > Export > Audio Mixdown dialog box, as shown in Figure 36.12. The Audio Engine Output field needs to be set to the appropriate multichannel bus output in order for Cubase to render a surround mix properly. The Channels field determines how many files are rendered. For example, if you have a 5.1 surround mix, you can choose to render a mixdown as a single six-channel interleaved file or as six separate channels.

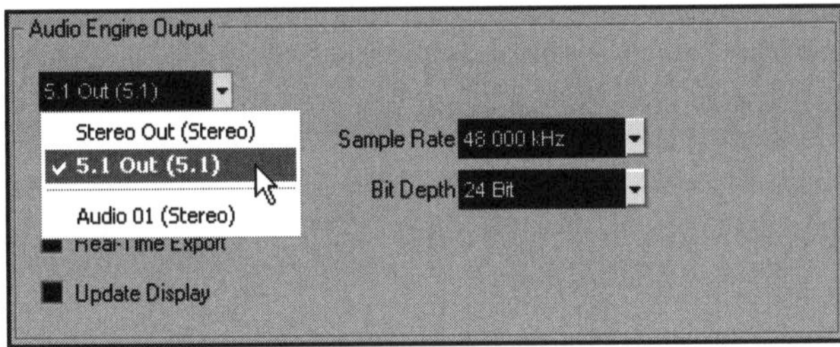

Figure 36.12
Exporting audio files for a surround sound mix.

37 Final Mix Export

Up until now, you have worked entirely inside the Cubase environment, tweaking your project in order to get it just right. You feel you've put enough work into this project and you want others to hear what you have done so far, or you're ready to start distributing your music to the world. For this to happen, you will need to bring the music out of Cubase and into a more user-friendly format.

While most of this chapter discusses how to export a final mix, understand that exporting any track, any part of a track, the audio rendering of an effect to create a sample, or a specific loop inside a project is performed in quite the same way. The same precautions need to be taken to ensure that the quality of the exported mix is good and the same output file format options are available, regardless of the purpose for the export.

Here's a summary of what you will learn in this chapter:

- How to export your final mix as an audio file
- The purpose for lossless and lossy exporting formats
- How to enter information that will be embedded in broadcast wave files
- How to export a project to an OMF format
- Tips on mastering
- Tips on creating an audio compact disc (CD)
- How to set up dithering on your final mixdown
- The importance of backing up your work

Audio Exporting Options

After you are satisfied with your mix and you want to render a final mixdown or just a specific selection, a track containing effects, or a VSTi or ReWire track, you can use the Export Audio

Mixdown function found at File > Export > Audio Mixdown. This function does not export MIDI tracks for non-VSTi devices, such as ReWire devices, unless two conditions are met: the Real-Time Export option must be selected and the external MIDI devices have to be configured using the VST Connections as described in Chapter 9. The following steps assume that you have already configured your VST Connections accordingly and have previously converted your MIDI/ instrument tracks into audio tracks, as described in Chapter 17.

HOW TO

Export your final mix as an audio file:

1. Mute the tracks you don't want to include in your audio mix and unmute those you want to include.
2. Position your left locator where you want to begin the audio mix and the right locator where you want to end the audio mixdown. (If your mix includes reverb and delay effects, be sure to position your right locator *beyond* the last audio and MIDI events in your tracks, leaving enough time for the reverb decay or delay repeats to fade out completely at the end of your mixdown file.)
3. If you want to export the automation when rendering a mixdown, be sure all the appropriate Read Automation buttons are enabled.

Subzero!

The output bus used for the rendering of an audio mixdown should not clip at any time during playback. Clipping causes distortion in your final mixdown. So, be sure your levels stay below zero dBFS (decibels, full scale) at all times and that the clip indicator in this bus does not light up.

4. Select File > Export > Audio Mixdown. The Export Audio Mixdown dialog box will appear, as shown in Figure 37.1.
5. In the File Name field, enter a name for the audio file you want to export.
6. Enable the Use Project Audio Folder check box if you want Cubase to store the exported audio mixdown in this folder. Otherwise, uncheck the option and click the Choose button to select an appropriate folder in which to save this file.
7. Select the appropriate file format for the audio mixdown. Depending on the file format, various additional options will appear in this section. If you are preparing an audio mixdown to burn on a CD, for example, chances are you will select a WAV or AIFF format. For Web distribution, MP3, Ogg Vorbis, RM, or WMA may be more appropriate. The Wave64 format should be selected when you expect the resulting file size will be greater than 2 gigabytes.
8. In the Audio Engine Output section, select the appropriate bus you want to mix down as shown in Figure 37.2. You can optionally choose only a specific channel as the source for your mixdown, such as a VSTi, Group, FX, or audio channel.
9. In addition to creating a stereo mixdown file, you can also check the Mono Export option to render a mono file or select the Split Channels option to split a stereo mix into two files (which will have "Left" or "Right" appended to their file names).

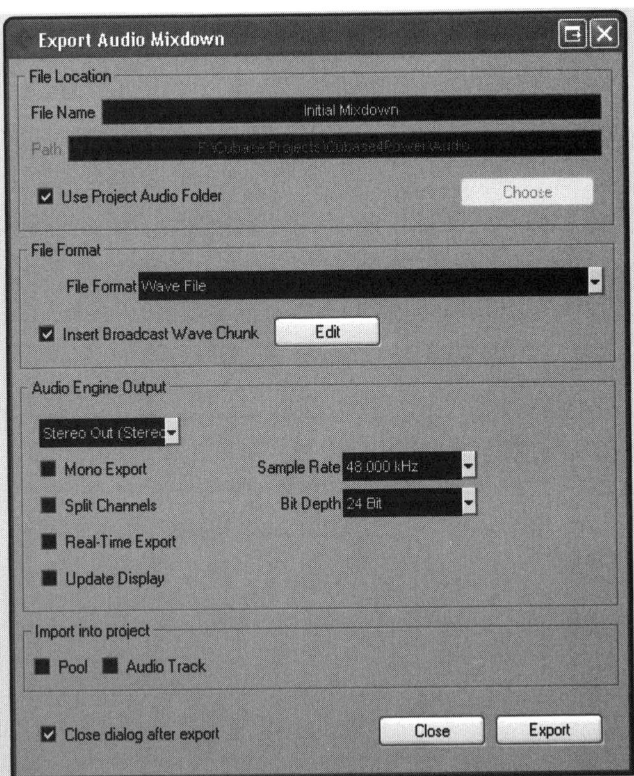

Figure 37.1
The Export Audio Mixdown dialog box.

Splitting Stereo Files

Note that the Stereo Split option in the Channels area of the Export Audio Mixdown dialog box creates a left and a right mono file, rather than a single stereo interleaved file. This might save some steps if you need to use this file in another audio application that doesn't directly support stereo interleaved files, such as Pro Tools.

10. Set the sample rate and bit depth you want to use for your exported file.
11. Check the Real-Time Export option only if needed. Real-time export is particularly useful when you are rendering external MIDI devices, as described in Chapter 17.
12. Check the Update Display option if you want to monitor the levels during mixdown. If a clip occurs, you can see it and adjust the levels appropriately to avoid the problem.
13. If you want to automatically import this file into the Pool or add it as a new track in your project, check the appropriate options in the Import into Project section.
14. Click Save when you are finished.

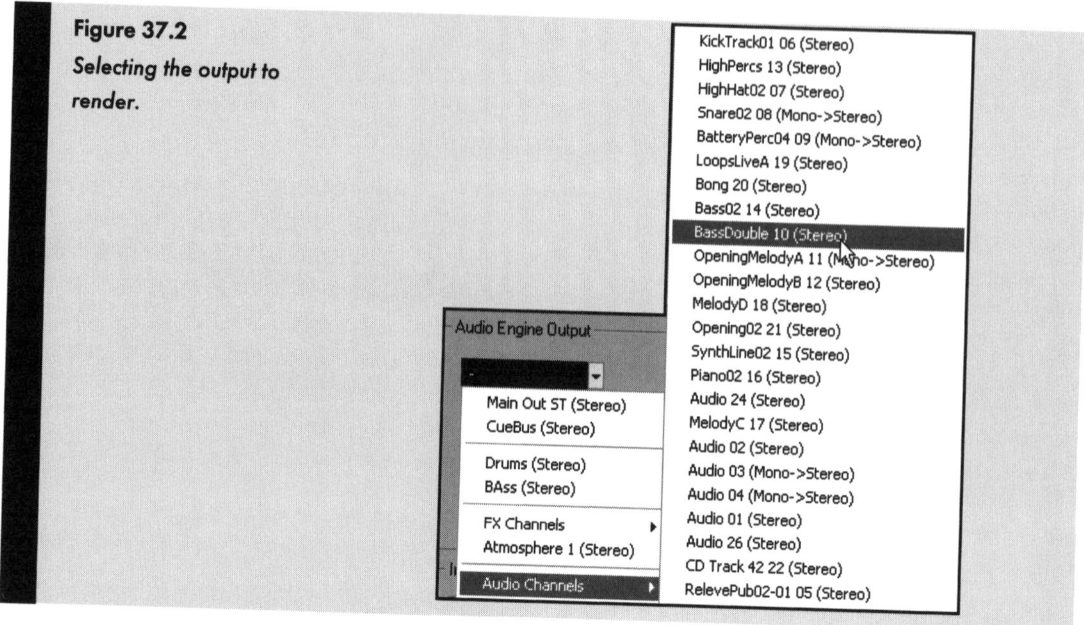

Figure 37.2
Selecting the output to render.

If you have enabled the Import to Audio Track option, Cubase will create a new audio track and name it *Mixdown*. After the newly created track is in place, be sure to mute the source tracks for this new track (containing the audio mixdown). If you have chosen not to import the audio rendering of your mix back into your project, you can proceed with your work as usual, continuing whatever work needs to be done, or save and close your project and start working on the mastering of your album, as discussed later in this chapter.

Lossless versus Lossy Formats

You can export your final mix in two different lossless formats: WAV and AIFF. Both are standard formats and compatible with Mac and PC platforms. Cubase 4 users also can use the Wave64 or .W64 file format, which supports file sizes larger than 2 gigabytes.

The Internet and the Web have been quite helpful to musicians in allowing them to publish their material online, using it as an effective distribution medium and a way to promote their skills. This is one of the reasons why other Web-related exporting formats are now available and are also considered standards in the industry. Among those, Cubase supports Microsoft Windows Media format (PC only), MP3 format (from MPEG 1 Layer 3), and Ogg Vorbis compression format.

What Is Ogg Vorbis?

Ogg Vorbis is an audio compression format that is roughly comparable to other formats used to store and play digital music, such as MP3 and other compressed digital audio formats. It is different from these other compressed formats because it is completely free, open, and unpatented.

Although not all artists realize it, MP3 is what is known as a "lossy" format. Thus, much of the sound data in the original is lost as a result of data compression when MP3 files are created. This results in a file with sound quality inferior to that of a CD. Vorbis also is a "lossy" format, but uses superior acoustic models to reduce the damage. Thus, music released in Vorbis sounds better than a comparably sized MP3 file.

Also, artists should be concerned about licensing terms for formats. If you decide to sell your music in MP3 format, you are responsible for paying Fraunhofer a percentage of each sale because you are using their patents. Vorbis is patent and license-free, so you never need to pay anyone to sell, give away, or stream your own music.

To find out more about this format, you can visit http://www.vorbis.com.

Because these formats were developed with the Web in mind, they make it easy to stream or distribute content over a low-bandwidth system. As a result, a certain amount of audio data compression is applied to these file formats. The more you compress the files, the smaller they are, and this also directly affects sound quality—the smaller the file, the worse the sound quality. All these compression algorithms are lossy, meaning that they irretrievably remove sonic information from the original file when saving it into this new format, and by doing so they reduce sound quality as well.

There is a big difference between data compression, which is used to compress the size of a file, and dynamic compression, which is used to control the dynamics of the audio signal—these two processes should not be confused. Compression of the dynamic range in audio material does not influence the size of the file. You will have a chance to experiment with compression settings for these digital audio file formats and will have to find a compromise that you are comfortable with in the end. Keeping this in mind, remember that there are still many people that don't have high-speed access to the Internet and are using 56K modems to download and listen to music. This is changing rapidly; however, until the time comes when everyone has high-speed access to the Internet, be sure your potential customers will not be discouraged by the size of your file.

Broadcast Wave Properties

Now that your project is ready to be exported, it might be a good time to add information about who created the files. This is done through the Broadcast Wave properties. The information you enter here is embedded in all the digital audio recordings/renderings you create in WAV format, until you decide otherwise. Think of it as a way to protect your property by letting everyone who uses a file you created know you are the owner. Broadcast wave information contains three basic fields: a description, an author, plus a time-stamped reference based on the timeline in your source Cubase project that can be extremely useful when exchanging files with video editors, for example.

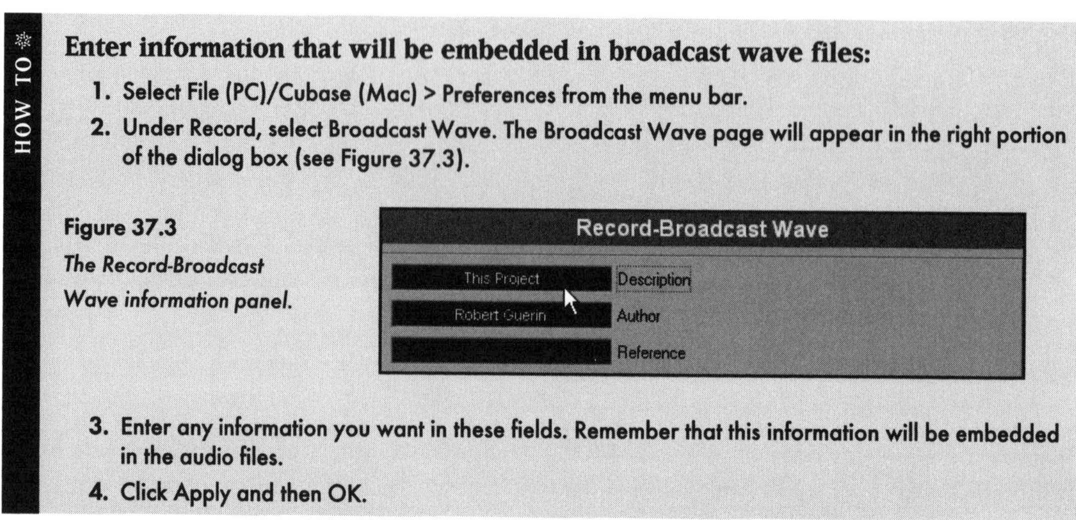

HOW TO

Enter information that will be embedded in broadcast wave files:

1. Select File (PC)/Cubase (Mac) > Preferences from the menu bar.
2. Under Record, select Broadcast Wave. The Broadcast Wave page will appear in the right portion of the dialog box (see Figure 37.3).

Figure 37.3
The Record-Broadcast Wave information panel.

3. Enter any information you want in these fields. Remember that this information will be embedded in the audio files.
4. Click Apply and then OK.

When you export a project using the Export > Audio Mixdown option, the Export Audio Mixdown dialog box offers an option to insert the Broadcast Wave Chunk into the exported audio files. Checking this option will add the information you just added to the files. At that point, you can choose to edit this information further by clicking on the Edit button. This opens the Broadcast Wave Chunk dialog box, where you can change the information embedded into the audio file, as displayed in Figure 37.4.

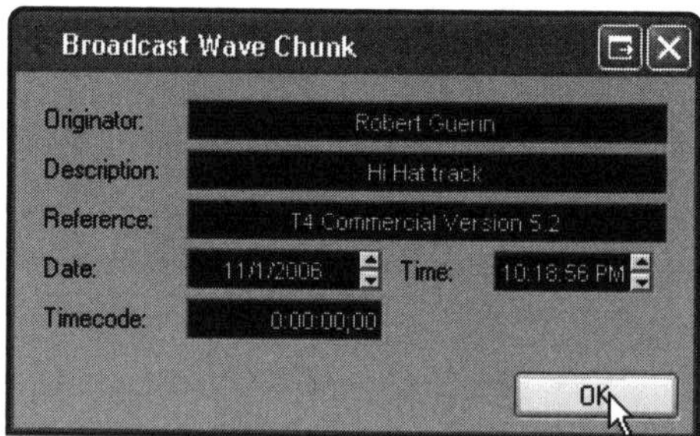

Figure 37.4
The Broadcast Wave Chunk dialog box.

OMF Export Options

As you already saw in Chapter 8, the OMF Export option enables you to save in a platform- and application-friendly format. OMF is friendly in the sense that this is a standard supported by more applications than the current .CPR or Cubase Project file might be. In other words, if you stay within Cubase, you won't need to use the OMF export format, but if your project needs to be added to another application, such as Final Cut Pro or Avid, exporting to OMF format will save everyone lots of time because the volume and fade settings will be retained in the OMF version of your project, as well as the positions of all the audio events within it. This implies that you won't have to re-import and position all your audio content in another application.

Exported OMF files retain references to all audio files that are played in the project (including fade and edit files) and do not include unused audio files referenced in the Pool. They won't contain any MIDI data either, so it's important that you convert all your MIDI parts into audio events and render any tracks with inserts or send effects and include these "flattened" tracks when exporting the project to OMF. If your project contains a video file, the only thing that will be included in the OMF file are the start positions of video events. You will need to manually import video files later in the other OMF application.

HOW TO ❋

Export a project to an OMF format:

1. Select Export > OMF from the File menu. The OMF Export Setup dialog will appear (see Figure 37.5).
2. Check which tracks should be included during the export. Click the Select All button to include all the audio tracks in the project. Because the OMF file interchange format only includes audio and video content, you will need to have exported VSTi, ReWire, and MIDI tracks to audio tracks previously if these need to be included in the OMF export.
3. Select the From Left to Right Locator option if you only want to export a specific section of your project timeline.
4. By default, files being exported will be placed in a subfolder under the location where the OMF file will be saved. If you would like to save the audio assets somewhere else, click the Browse button to specify a location for the exported content.
5. The Copy Media or Consolidate Events options allow you to either copy all the source media into the OMF export document's audio subfolder or consolidate only the portions currently used by the project. Consolidating events requires less space because it does not copy any portion of the source audio file outside an event's boundaries. That being said, if space is not an issue and you would like to have access to the extra audio content later, the choice is there for you. When the Consolidate Events option is checked, you can set the "handle" length in milliseconds. This corresponds to the audio content outside the current event boundaries within the source audio file. Leaving a bit of time before and after will ensure that you can fine-tune or modify the event's boundaries later if necessary, for example, to adjust fade lengths.
6. Select the desired OMF file version, depending on which OMF version is supported by the application in which you plan to import the file later. You might want to check with the studio where you need to bring this file before you make a selection here.
7. Select whether you want to include all audio data used in the project inside one large OMF file (Export All to One File) or use references to external files only (Export Media File References). If you choose the latter option, be sure to include all those source media files, as well as the OMF

file itself, on the backup copy that you bring to the other studio. If you know that everything will fit on a CD or DVD-R (or DVD-RAM), you might be better off creating a self-contained, all-in-one OMF file to ensure that there are no missing files.

8. If you are exporting to a 2.0-compatible OMF file, you will often choose to include the fades and volume settings for each event. To do so, check the Export Clip Based Volume option.
9. By default, the current project's sample size and sample rate are selected for the OMF export, but you can specify another resolution and sample rate for the exported files.
10. Click OK.
11. Type in a name for the exported OMF file.
12. Click the Save button when you are finished.

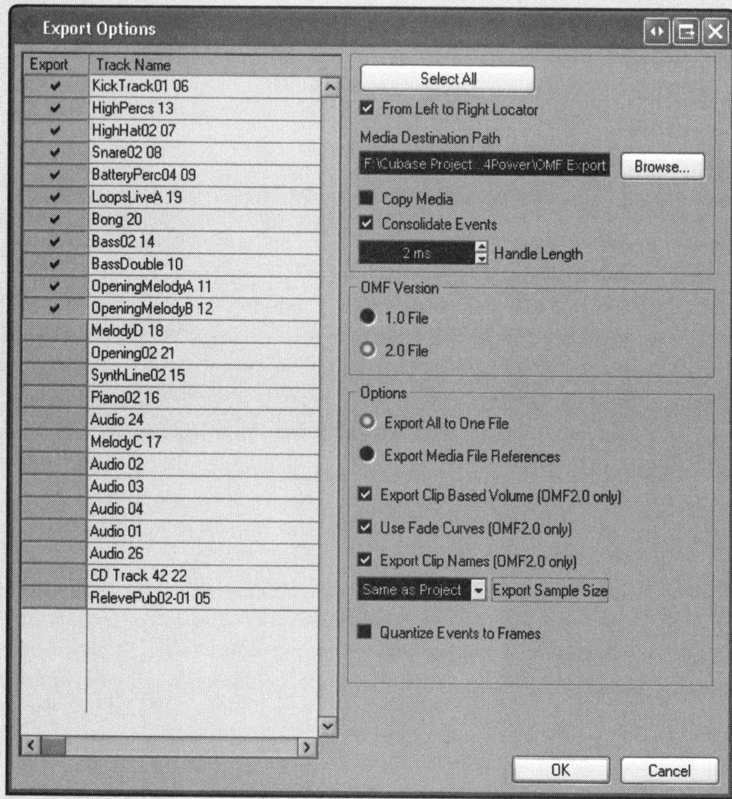

Figure 37.5

The OMF Export Setup dialog box.

With the settings found in Figure 37.5, a single OMF file is created, which includes all the checked tracks. All the files are saved inside the destination folder, as displayed in Figure 37.6.

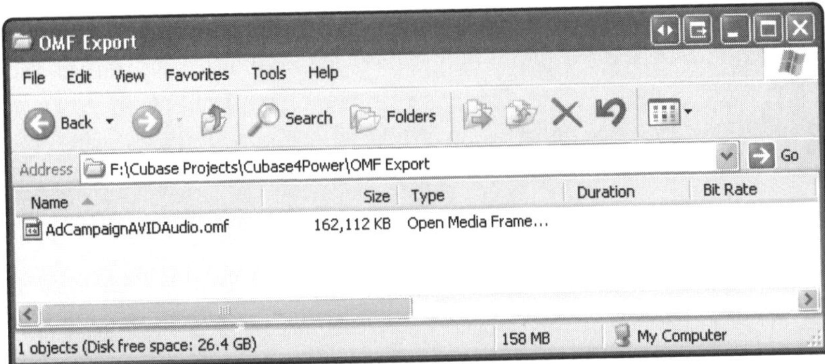

Figure 37.6
A project exported to a single OMF file.

About Mastering

Mastering is the art of subtlety and involves adjusting a collection of final mixes so that they all sound coherent and cohesive when played sequentially. From the first mix you did two months ago to the one you just created at 4:00 a.m. after consuming large amounts of caffeine, they should all have the same quality, sound level, and dynamic intensity. Think of mastering as the art of giving an album its soul.

When preparing an album, mastering is a must before pressing your master copy. The mastering process is used to reduce the aforementioned differences between various mixes by patching together every song in a one- to two-day span—listening to them in the order they will appear on your album and correcting the overall harmonic colors and dynamic range of your songs as necessary.

It is also a good idea not to master your album with the same listening reference as you used for the recording and mixing process because your ears have probably grown accustomed to this sound and may no longer be as critical to some aspects or coloring of the music. Furthermore, if your monitoring system is adequate at best, you will probably benefit from a professional mastering facility rather than a home studio mixing environment because the better facilities provide the best all-around listening and processing equipment to truly isolate problems in the consistency between your songs, not to mention a fresh pair of ears listening to your project. This can add a whole new untapped dimension to your project, which is especially useful if this is to be a commercially distributed album. Probably the *most* valuable asset in the pricey mastering studios is the technical expertise and years of experience that a professional mastering engineer can bring to bear. Mastering engineers have the ability to produce results that are consistent in varied playback environments, which will definitely save you a lot of time on trial and error every time your mix is played on a different system. Finally, there will always be, no matter what the critics of pricey studios might say, a difference in quality between a home studio filled with inexpensive equipment and low-quality components and a quarter-million-dollar mastering facility in which every piece of equipment in the room is meant to optimize your sound.

If you don't have the financial resources or you don't feel the need for a professional mastering because your project is for small and local distribution only, there are no fixed recipes here and no settings that can apply to every situation; rather, there are pointers that should help you get the most out of a mastering session. If you are unsure about how your mix sounds, try listening to music in a similar style, that sounds like how you want your music to sound. Then see whether you can emulate these qualities. Another way of evaluating your mix-in-progress is by listening to it in varied environments, such as on a car stereo, from the room next door, or at a friend's place. Remember that the fresher your mind and ears are, the better it is for the mastering process. So, avoid starting a mastering session after a long day of work or immediately after mixing the last song on your album.

- Mastering is not where you mix your songs. If you are not satisfied with a mix, you should remix it rather than try to fix it at the mastering stage.
- This might be very obvious to most people, but just in case: *Never* master an album using your headphones as a reference. The proximity of headphones gives you false information about depth of field and presence of certain musical events. Also, most people do not listen to music through headphones; they listen to it through speakers.
- When exporting your audio mixes in Cubase for the mastering process, use the highest quality available. If you have worked in 96 kHz, 32-bit stereo format and you have a reliable system that can reproduce these specifications, go for it. You can always convert your final result after the mastering process to 44.1-kHz, 16-bit stereo format.
- Before you start your mastering session, sit down and listen to all the songs in order with your notepad and a pencil in hand. Take notes on inconsistencies between songs.
- Generally, there are two important things that you want to adjust in a mastering session, and these should be kept in mind throughout the entire mastering process of a single album: EQ and dynamics. Both should be consistent from song to song.
- When tweaking the EQ, you are not trying to reinvent the mix, you are just tweaking it. Give the bass more definition, add presence to the vocals and crispness to the high end, and most of all, be sure that all songs have the same equalization qualities.
- Dynamics give punch and life to a mix. Be sure all your tracks come into play at the same level. This doesn't mean they should all be loud or soft, but they should be consistent with the intensity of the song. If a song is mellow, it can come in softer, but the soft intensity in one song has to be consistent in relation to the soft intensity of another song. As with EQ, consistency is the key.
- More and more software packages out there do a pretty good job at EQing and compressing audio. Steinberg's WaveLab, Izotope's Ozone plug-in, various Waves plug-ins, including the famous L1/L2 Maximizer and L3 Multimaximizer, the S1 Spatializer, plus their

Renaissance EQ and Renaissance Compressor, or IK Multimedia's T-Racks are just a few of the tools you can use to help you get the most out of your home mastering session.

Creating an Audio Compact Disc

Creating your CD is often one of the last things you do before having people outside your studio environment listen to your music. After you create an audio mixdown of your MIDI and audio tracks as a premaster file (in whatever format you used to do so), master one or more tracks as discussed earlier, save your files, and convert them into a compact disc–compatible format, you are ready to create a compact disc.

Cubase does not offer any tools to actually burn (record) a CD. But for Windows users Steinberg offers one solution through WaveLab, a very comprehensive program for mastering and recording CDs. This is by no means the only tool available. If you purchased a CD recorder, it might have come with a CD recording application. One thing is certain: You need software capable of creating a CD-DA compatible disc (Compact Disc Digital Audio). This brings us to formats. When you are creating CDs, the two most common types of CDs are CD-ROM and CD-DA. CD-ROMs contain data suitable for your computer. CD-DAs contain audio that is suitable for both your computer and your CD player. There are two variations of this: the Enhanced CD and the Mixed Mode CD formats, which can be created by some software and some CD recorders. The Enhanced CD is a multisession CD containing a series of CD-DA–compatible tracks in the first session, making it compatible with your home CD player, and a second session containing data, which is read by computers only. In Mixed Mode, it's the reverse: The data tracks are at the beginning and the audio tracks follow. This usually means that your conventional audio CD player will not read it. This type of CD is used for multimedia content, such as games, educational software, or multimedia sales presentations. In light of this, understand that you need to select the proper type of CD when creating a CD within the software application. There are a few rules to follow if you want your CD to play back in any CD player.

When recording a CD, there are three aspects that come into play: the format of the CD (CD-ROM, CD-DA, Enhanced CD, Mixed Mode, and so on), the session, and the disc. A *session* is an instance in which you decide to write something on a CD. For example, today you decide to record a WAV file onto a CD. You write a session and, to complete the process, you close the session for the disc to be understood by the CD-ROM drive. A disc is closed when you can't record anything else on it and open when you can still add more sessions to it. In our previous example, if you close the session but leave the disc open, you can record another session on it, making it a multisession disc, each time closing the session but leaving the disc open for another recording. When you want to close the disc because the disc is full, you can do so after the last session you record, disabling it from being recorded anymore. This is called a *multisession CD*, which is common in CD-ROMs, Enhanced CDs, and Mixed Mode CDs, but this method of recording the CD is not compatible with audio CDs.

For an audio CD to play in a consumer CD player, you can only have one closed session and one closed disc in CD-DA format unless you are using the Enhanced CD format. When creating an audio CD, you can use two methods of writing the information to disc: TAO, short for *Track-At-Once*, or DAO, short for *Disc-At-Once*. You probably will want to consult your software and hardware documentation to see whether these features are supported, but for now, understand that TAO records the audio CD one track at a time, leaving a two-second gap between each song that you added to the CD recording session. DAO, on the other hand, does not record this two-second gap between each song you added to the CD recording session (see Figure 37.7). Note that when preparing a duplication master, DAO should always be used.

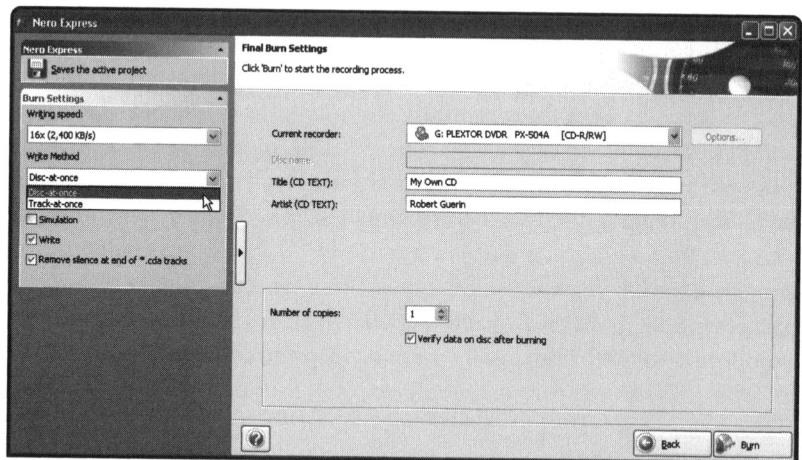

Figure 37.7
Creating a music CD using Nero Express software.

With these basic principles in hand, you can create audio CDs in your own home by using the audio CD creation software of your choice. It is also a good idea to create intermediate audio CDs so that you can listen to your music on other sound systems, confirming that you are pleased with what you hear before you produce the final master. Most new domestic CD players accept an audio disc on rewritable media (CD-RW). Rewritable CDs aren't acceptable as a duplication master, but if your player is compatible they can be a good way to create test mixes. But remember that for your audio CD player to recognize a disc, it has to be in audio CD format (CD-DA) and not in data CD format (CD-ROM).

About Dithering

Using 24-bit resolution and above during the production process helps increase the potential dynamic range of your project, while reducing the possibility of any audible noise being introduced as a result of the digitization process itself. It also increases the signal-to-error ratio, which is the degree of rounding determined by the "resolution" or bit-depth. This error is more noticeable when signals are recorded at low levels or as they fade out to a lower level in reverb, for instance—especially if their levels get significantly boosted later in the mixing process. As you saw earlier in this book, this signal-to-error ratio (in theory) is around 146 dB in a 24-bit recording and 194 dB in a 32-bit recording. Such a ratio suggests that when you record a sound using 32-bit resolution, your theoretical dynamic range is 194 dB, a signal-to-error ratio that is inaudible and negligible by any standards. Of course, in practice, you rarely get such impressive signal-to-noise ratios due to many noise-generating elements before and after the audio hardware's converters, but the ratios are consistently more impressive when you are using higher bit rates. Unfortunately, when you transfer a stereo mixdown to a 16-bit DAT recorder, or you want to record it on a CD that you will burn for compact disc players, you need to bring this precision down to 16-bit.

There are two methods used to accomplish this reduction in bit depth: truncating and dithering. Truncating simply cuts the least significant portion of the digital word that exceeds the 16-bit word length. For example, if you have an audio sample stored in 24-bit, it might look like this:

1110 0111 1100 0111 0011 1100

Now, if this sample were truncated to 16-bit, it would look like this:

1110 0111 1100 0111

The last eight digits were cut off, or truncated. These last eight digits are often more noticeable in reverb trails dying in the noise or harmonics of instruments at low-level intensities. Cutting them off usually adds what is known as *quantization error*. The digital distortion of the original audio waveform produced by quantization error (in essence, a rounding error due to the word length not offering enough amplitude levels to accurately depict the waveform) sounds unnatural to human ears. You are probably familiar with some extreme examples of this, in the 8-bit audio used by certain children's toys and vintage computers or game systems.

The solution is to add a special kind of random noise to the sound when you need to bring down the resolution. This random noise is *dither noise*. What it does is change the last bit in a 16-bit word randomly, creating a noise at –98dB, which is pretty low. Dithering is not needed when you are working in a 24-bit or 32-bit environment, so keep this for the end.

HOW TO ❊

Set up dithering on your final mixdown:

1. Open the Mixer window. (F3 is the default key command.)
2. Because dithering is—and should be—the last step in your mixdown process, it should only be added when you are exporting the final mixdown directly to a 16-bit sound file. Because of this, load the

UV22HR dithering plug-in in the last Insert (Number 8, which, as always with insert slots 7 and 8, is post-fader). The UV22HR plug-ins are located by default in the Earlier VST Plug-ins > Other effects submenu (see Figure 37.8).

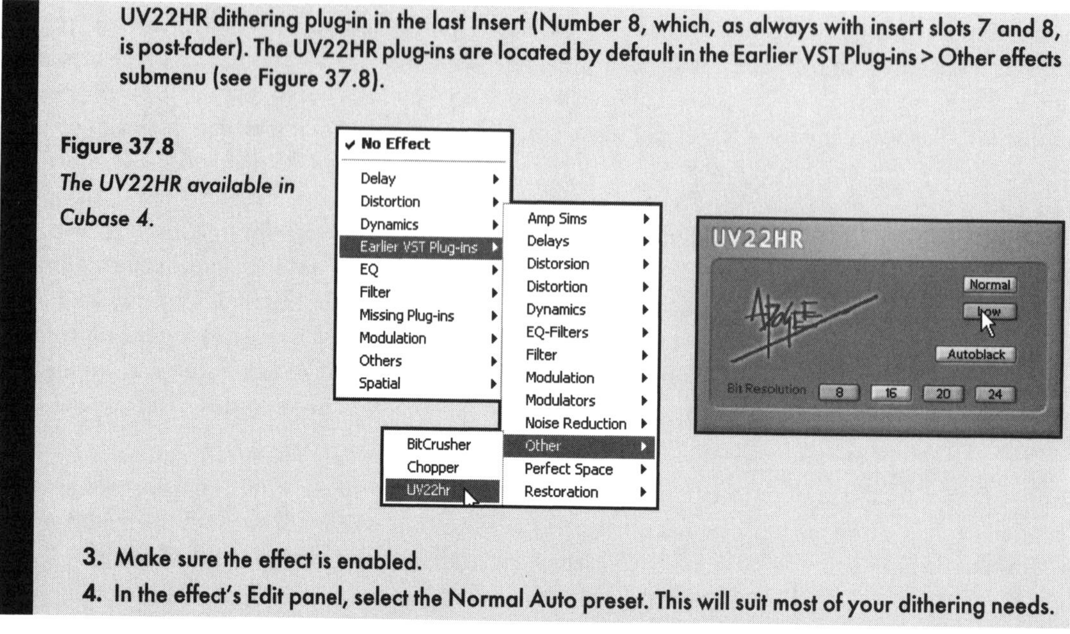

Figure 37.8
The UV22HR available in Cubase 4.

3. Make sure the effect is enabled.
4. In the effect's Edit panel, select the Normal Auto preset. This will suit most of your dithering needs.

With this final option set, you are now ready to export your mix to an audio file. Note that in certain cases, you may want to export your stereo mixdowns at 24-bit resolution. For example, more sophisticated CD creation programs such as WaveLab, CD Architect, Nero, Jam, and others may offer their own tools for fine-tuning mixes, including various dithering algorithms—in which case it is preferable to export your mixes at 24-bit resolution (or higher) for use with these programs. Also, if these mixdowns will be turned over to a mastering engineer, 24-bit files with no dithering (and generally, no EQ or dynamics processing on the main output bus) are the norm.

Backing Up Your Work

Making backup copies of your work as you go is paramount. Not only does it prevent you from having to rerecord your material if you make mistakes and erase files, but it is also a good way to keep source material from being lost because of hard drive crashes. Another good reason to back up files as you are working with them is that you can always go back and change things later in an arrangement or create a new arrangement altogether by using the source material rather than the master two-track recording. If these are not good enough reasons for you, consider this last piece of advice: When you are working on a project for someone else and charging studio time, it's doubtful that your client will be impressed by your work if you lose some of their recordings!

There are many ways to do backups inside and out of Cubase:

- Create an Archive folder containing all the audio present in the Audio Pool of your project by using the Prepare Archive function in the Pool menu, as shown in Figure 37.9. This prompts you to select a destination folder where a copy of all the audio files used in the Pool are copied, making it easy to save this folder on a backup medium, such as a DVD-R or CD-R, DVD-RW or CD-RW, tape backup, or removable media drive. Now that you have consolidated all the audio files this project uses into its Audio subfolder, you can be sure that copying this project folder to an archive medium will include all the files it requires (including the .CPR project file itself). Be sure to also include any video files used by the project in your backup, if applicable.
- Use the Save Project to New Folder command in the File menu and copy the content of this folder to your backup media. This is probably the quickest way, but only once your project is nearly completed, especially if you enable the Freeze Edits and Remove Unused Audio options in this command's dialog box.

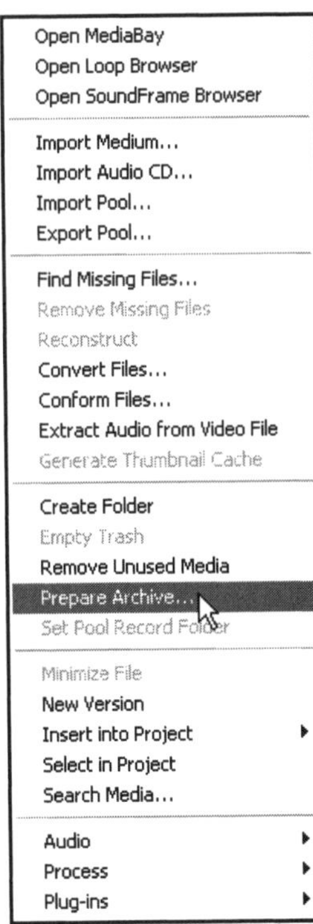

Figure 37.9
Using the Prepare Archive function in the Pool window's context menu or in the Pool menu to save all audio files in a single folder for backup.

- Use your DVD/CD creation software to create a data disc that contains all the source material (audio, arrangements, song, preset, and setting files) used for this project, labeling your DVD/CD accordingly.
- Use backup software or disk imaging software to create a backup image of your files, either to disk or tape.

Keeping in mind that computer crashes occur quite unexpectedly, and that disc failures are not as infrequent as we would wish, making backup copies of your work makes sense—even after each working session. This way, you reduce the amount of time lost if something bad ever happens.

Reading the documentation provided with your DVD/CD burning and backup software to understand how it works and how you can retrieve information from backup discs and tapes might prove useful (especially in a crisis!), so take a little bit of time to familiarize yourself with these options.

VII Managing

38 Project Customization

Once you start getting comfortable with Cubase, working habits will also start settling into place. That's when you'll start wondering whether you can customize where tools are laid out and how you can more efficiently do the actions you perform the most often. This chapter discusses ways that you can customize settings and create reusable documents to suit your working preferences and habits.

Here's a summary of what you will learn in this chapter:

- How to create and organize your Workspaces
- How to create a project template
- How to customize key commands
- How to create a macro and add commands to it
- How to use a macro in a project
- How to change the appearance of a toolbar and save this customization
- How to show/hide Transport panel sections
- How to create customized track controls for the Track List area and select customized settings

Workspaces

Workspaces provide an easy way to recall a particular window layout for your Cubase project, such as a useful view for editing events or a wide Mixer panel for the mixdown phase of a project. Workspaces are saved along with the project file or can be saved as presets that are available for all projects in Cubase. Workspaces and Workspace presets retain the current position and state of windows inside a project, but not the project-specific content within windows, such as a part loaded in a particular editor or the size of the main Cubase window on the desktop.

HOW TO

Create a Workspace:

1. Open the windows you want to display on your desktop. For example, if you always place your Project window in the upper-right corner and the VST Instruments panel on the bottom of your desktop, click and drag these windows into position by their title bars.
2. After you are satisfied with the layout, select Workspaces > New Workspace from the Window menu.
3. Name your Workspace appropriately.
4. Repeat these steps to create additional Workspaces.
5. In the Window menu, select Workspaces > Organize.
6. Next to the newly created Workspaces, check the Locked option to prevent the layout from being overwritten by mistake. You can still move windows around afterwards, but recalling the Workspace returns all windows and panels to their saved states and locations.
7. In the ID column, select the appropriate ID number for this Workspace. An ID number determines the position of the Workspace in the Workspaces submenu. In Figure 38.1, the Recording Workspace is ID #3, placing it at the third spot in the Workspace submenu.
8. Click OK when you are finished.

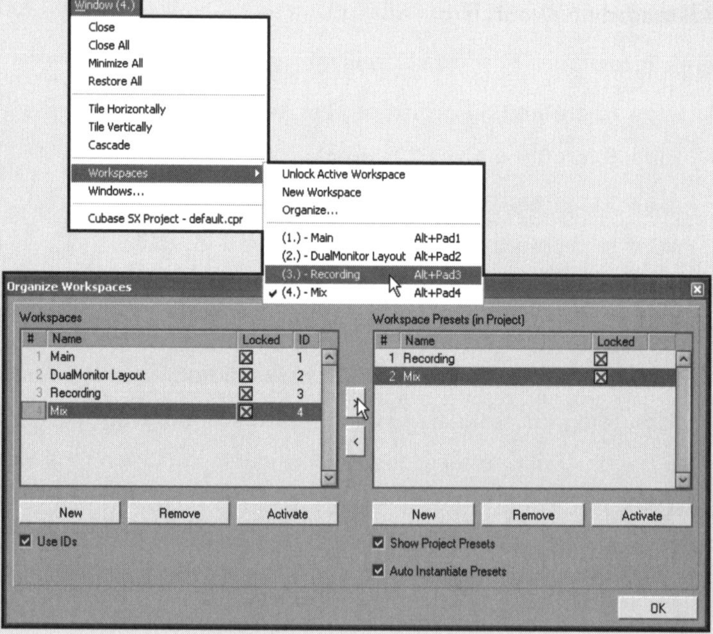

Figure 38.1

The Workspaces submenu options and the Organize Workspaces dialog box.

HOW TO

Organize your Workspaces:

1. Select Workspaces > Organize from the Window menu.
2. Select the Workspace you want to copy as a preset, edit, or remove from the list.
3. Click the Remove button if you want to remove a layout from the list. Click the New button to save the current Workspace, or click Activate Cubase to apply the display attributes of the selected Workspace to your current project.

You can create several Workspaces and recall them through a set of customized key commands. You'll find more on how to customize key commands later in this chapter.

Creating Templates

When we work, we often start with basic settings. For example, if you have a favorite VSTi that you load for drums, a favorite window layout, a typical bus routing, or a number of tracks that you always name the same way, you might consider creating a template. Templates are Cubase project documents that are saved in a Template folder. Saving a project as a template before you start recording events into it allows you to save all these settings, including preferences, output and input settings, and all the previously mentioned settings. To use a template, you simply select Create New Project from the File menu. This opens the New Project dialog box (see Figure 38.2). The options available in the New Project dialog box include all the template files found in the Template folder.

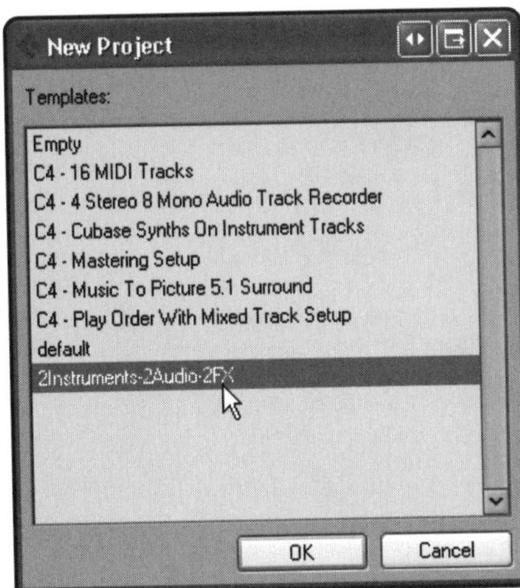

Figure 38.2
Templates appear in the New Project dialog box when you create a new project.

HOW TO

Create a project template:

1. Organize your project as you normally do. For example, if you often start from a guitar, vocal, synth bass, and drum machine setup, create a project with at least two audio tracks and two MIDI/instrument tracks, make the VST Instruments panel visible, set up the appropriate connections, and so on.
2. When you are satisfied that this is a worthy template—in other words, that all the setup steps you just took to get here are worth saving for the next time around—select the Save As Template option from the File menu.
3. Enter a name for your template. The exact name you enter for this saved template file will appear as an option in the New Project dialog box from now on, as shown in Figure 38.2.

Because templates are just like regular project files, you can rename or delete them from your hard drive to rename or remove a file from the template list. This also means that you can save audio and MIDI events within a template file if necessary.

Another way you can customize your environment at startup is by saving your default preferences as the default.cpr file in the templates subfolder under the Cubase Program folder. To edit the default file, open it, make the desired changes, and save it. Once a default.cpr file is saved, you need to select the Open Default Project option in the File (PC)/Cubase (Mac) > Preferences > General > On Startup field, as displayed in Figure 38.3. The On Startup field determines what

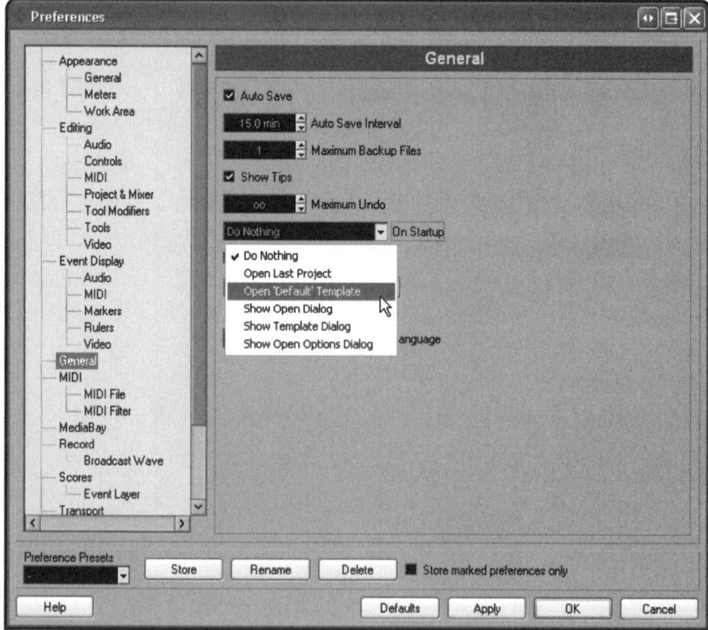

Figure 38.3
Setting up a default behavior on startup.

actually occurs when you launch Cubase, so any selection you make here will affect Cubase's behavior at every startup of the program.

For Mac users, the file location setup for templates is slightly different. User templates are stored in YourUserName > Library > Preferences > Cubase 4 > Templates. If you type in **default** as you save your own new template, this gets stored in this user's Preferences subfolder. Once this new "customized" default project file is saved, setting the Open Default Project option in Preferences will instruct Cubase to load your new default project file. In the New Project Dialog, the user is presented not only with any user-created templates, but also the small collection that was installed with the program.

Customizing Key Commands

Throughout this book, references are made to key commands (more commonly known as keyboard shortcuts). Although Cubase provides a default set of key commands for a number of functions and operations, you can change these default settings to better reflect your working habits and add some of your personal favorites to the existing key commands.

The commands that can be associated with keyboard shortcuts are found under File > Key Commands. This brings up the Key Commands dialog box. At the top of this dialog box, you'll find a Search field, and to the right of this field, you'll see a magnifying glass icon (see Figure 38.4). All the commands are grouped by category in the list area below the Search field. The easiest way to find a command is to type its name in the Search field and then click on the magnifying glass to display the first match in the list below. After a command is found, you can see whether a key command is already associated with this command by looking at the Keys column in the same area.

HOW TO

Customize a key command:

1. In the Key Commands dialog box, select the Cubase function to which you want to assign a key command (keyboard shortcut, for most of us).
2. Click inside the Type in Key field to make it active. If the selected item already has a key command associated with it, the Keys field (above) will display the associated key or key combination.
3. Press the key or key combination (for example, Alt+G on PC or Option+G on Mac) you want to associate with the currently selected item. If the key or key combination is already assigned to another function in Cubase, the name of this function will appear in the Assigned To area below.
4. Click the Assign button to associate the keys you entered with the selected function. The keys should appear in the Keys area above. If another key command was previously assigned to the selected item, it will be replaced by the new one you just created.

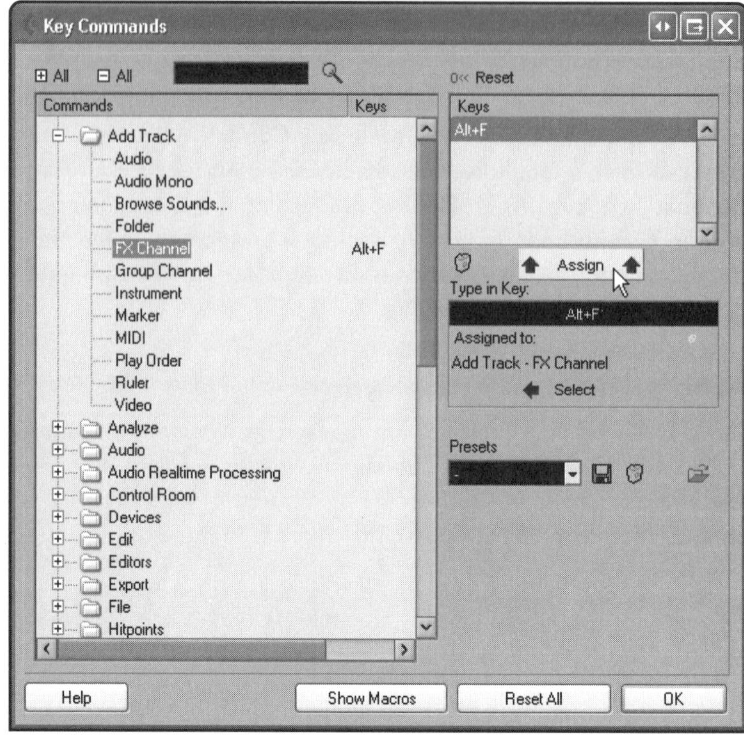

Figure 38.4
The Key Commands dialog box.

The Recycle Bin (Delete) icon below the Keys area removes the keyboard shortcut associated with a selected command, while the Presets field manages the previously saved presets or enables you to save a preset to memory. Note that there are already presets available for Cubase VST or other applications users. Using the same shortcuts to do the same tasks from one software to the next can make sense, so if you're used to working with a specific set of keyboard shortcuts, this dialog box customizes the key command associations to better meet your needs.

Macros

Using Cubase macros is a way to save a sequence of tasks that you perform regularly, one after the other. For example, you might often need to quickly create four audio tracks and a Marker track, select a window layout, and select a zoom level. Performing these tasks can take many steps—or only a single step when programmed as a macro command.

HOW TO

Create a macro:

1. From the File menu, select the Key Commands option.
2. In the Key Commands dialog box, click the Show Macro button. This reveals the Macros section at the bottom of the dialog box (see Figure 38.5).

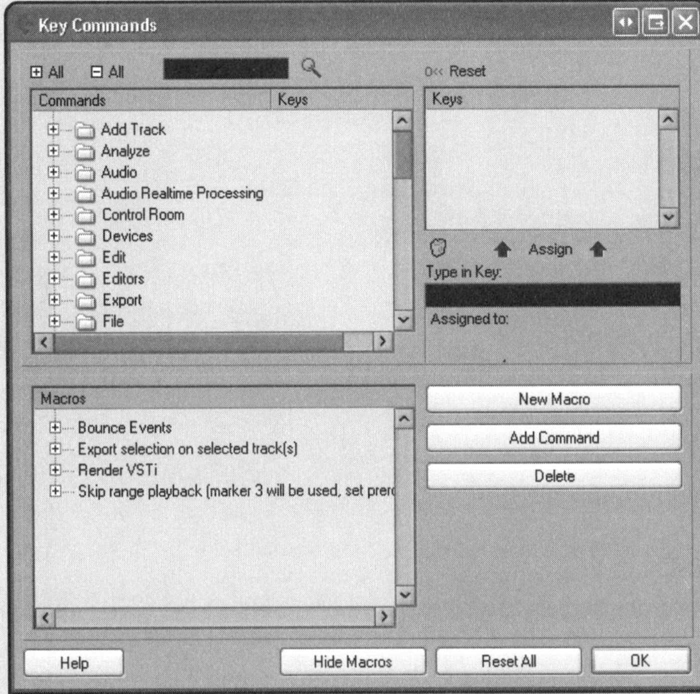

Figure 38.5
Creating macro commands in the Key Commands dialog box.

3. Click the New Macro button to add a new macro in the Macros area.
4. Double-click the new macro's name and type in a new name for it.

Now your new macro is created, but it won't do anything yet. Let's add commands to it.

HOW TO

Add commands to a macro:

1. In the Key Commands dialog box, click on the category of command you want in the Commands area. Categories are represented by little folders. You either double-click to open or close them or click on the plus signs to their left (or their "disclosure triangle" buttons on a Mac) to reveal the actual commands found within the desired category folder.
2. Select the command you want to add to your macro.

3. Click the Add Command button in the Macro section. The selected command now appears in the Commands list area of the Macro section.
4. Repeat the previous steps for each command you want to add to your macro.
5. When you've finished adding commands to your macro, click OK to close this dialog box.

When you launch your new macro, the commands you have just entered will be executed in the order in which you entered them in the macro. Note that as you get more experienced with key commands and macros, not only can you assign a key command to any macro, but you can also launch one macro from within another.

HOW TO

Use a macro in a project:

1. Once any macros have been created in Cubase, they appear in the Edit > Macro submenu (see Figure 38.6).
2. Select the desired macro, to execute the list of commands it contains.

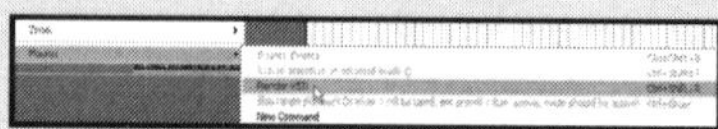

Figure 38.6
Launching a macro that contains a preconfigured sequence of commands.

Customizing Toolbars

You can now change the tools that are displayed in a window's toolbar and save these layouts for further use. This can come in handy when you need certain tools during one part of your creative process, but not during another. Also, depending on the resolution currently selected for your computer's display, you may not have enough space onscreen to display all the tools at once—this may particularly be the case with the Project window toolbar, for example.

HOW TO

Change the appearance of a toolbar:

1. Right-click anywhere in the toolbar. A context menu will display all the options available for this toolbar. The toolbar elements with check marks next to them are currently visible, while the others are not.
2. Select an option with a check mark to hide it from the toolbar, or select an option without a check mark to enable its display in the toolbar.

You can also save these customizations and select them later from the same context menu, as shown in Figure 38.7. This is a very useful technique that you should try to incorporate as soon as possible in your learning process with Cubase.

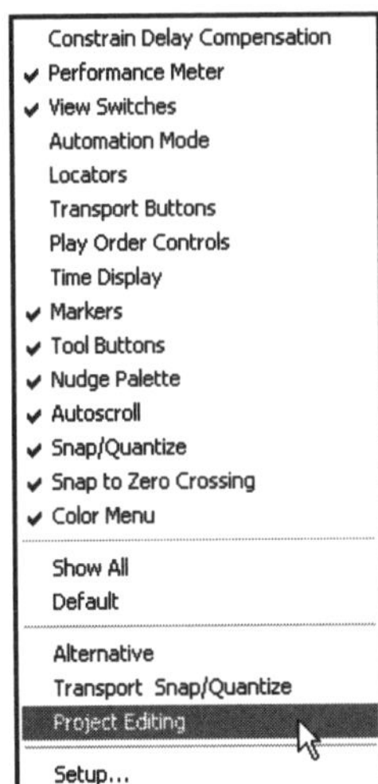

Figure 38.7
Selecting a saved toolbar configuration.

HOW TO

Save a toolbar customization:

1. Right-click anywhere in the toolbar.
2. Select the Setup option at the bottom of the context menu. Items that appear under the Visible Items columns (see Figure 38.8) are currently visible, while the items in the Hidden Items column are not.

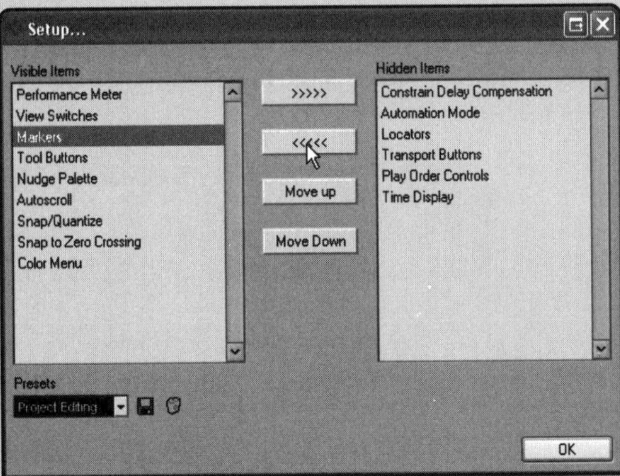

Figure 38.8
The toolbar Setup dialog box.

3. By using the arrow buttons in the center, you can move items between the left and right columns. You can also use the Move Up and Move Down buttons to change the order in which the visible items will appear from left to right in the toolbar.

4. Once you are satisfied with your changes, click on the disk icon at the bottom of this dialog box to save the changes into a preset. Note that clicking on the Recycle Bin (Delete) icon deletes the preset currently displayed in the Presets field.
5. Another dialog box will appear, prompting you to enter a name for your preset. Enter a descriptive name for your preset. The name you enter here will now appear in this dialog box's Presets selection field.
6. Click OK twice to return to the previous window.
7. The newly created preset can now be selected from this toolbar's customization context menu (see Figure 38.7).

If you want to return the toolbar to its default state, you can do so by selecting the Default option in the same context menu, or you can choose to display *all* the available toolbar items by selecting the Show All option instead.

Customizing Your Transport Panel

You can choose to hide certain portions of the Transport panel if you don't need to use them or if you want to free up some valuable desktop space. Also, most of the time, we use certain tools more during certain types of projects or during certain steps in a project. For example, after you've completed the recording session, the Punch-In/Punch-Out buttons won't be of much use.

HOW TO

Show/hide Transport panel sections:

1. Right-click (PC)/Control-click (Mac) anywhere on your Transport panel (except inside value fields that can be changed with your cursor).
2. From the pop-up context menu, check the sections you want to see and uncheck the sections you don't want to see, as shown in Figure 38.9.

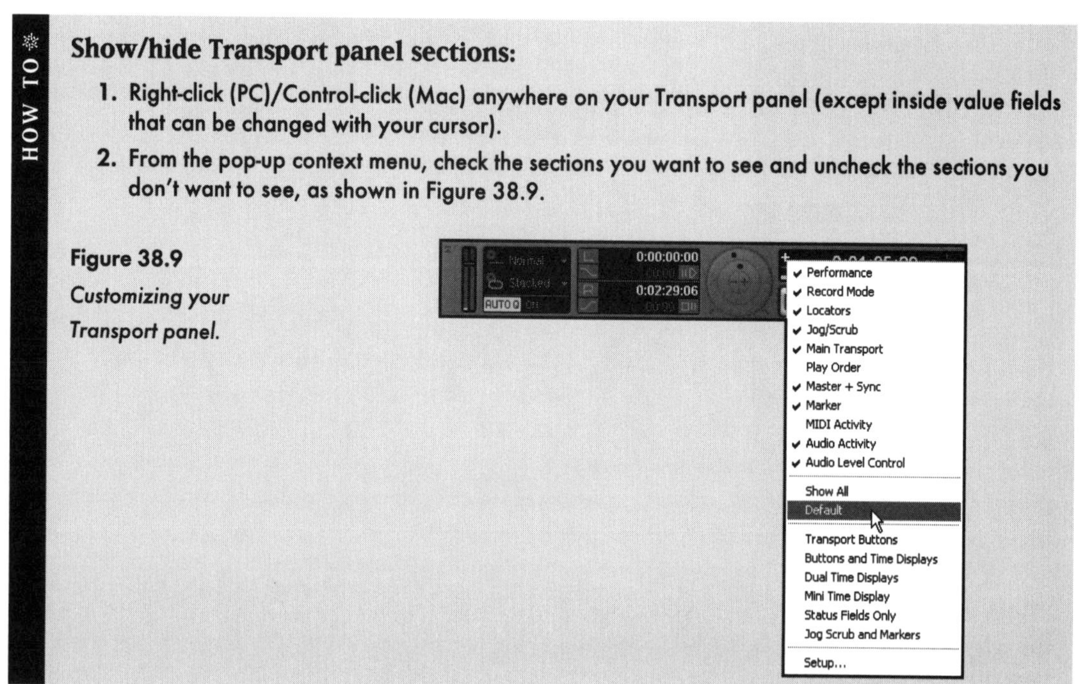

Figure 38.9
Customizing your Transport panel.

Customizing Track Controls

Although working with controls in the Track List is convenient, sometimes dealing with all the controls available might become cumbersome and confusing. Certain controls are used only during the recording process, while others are used only during the editing process. Furthermore, some users might never use a particular control from the Track List, using the Inspector or Mixer panel instead, while others might never use the Mixer panel and only use the Track List.

You can customize the controls that are displayed in the Track List, save these settings for each track class, and recall them later on when you need them.

HOW TO

Create customized track controls for the Track List area:

1. Right-click (PC)/Control-click (Mac) anywhere within the Track List and select the Track Controls Settings option, or select the same option from the Track Controls Settings drop-down menu that can be opened via the button at the top left of the Track List area. The Track Controls Settings dialog box will appear (see Figure 38.10).

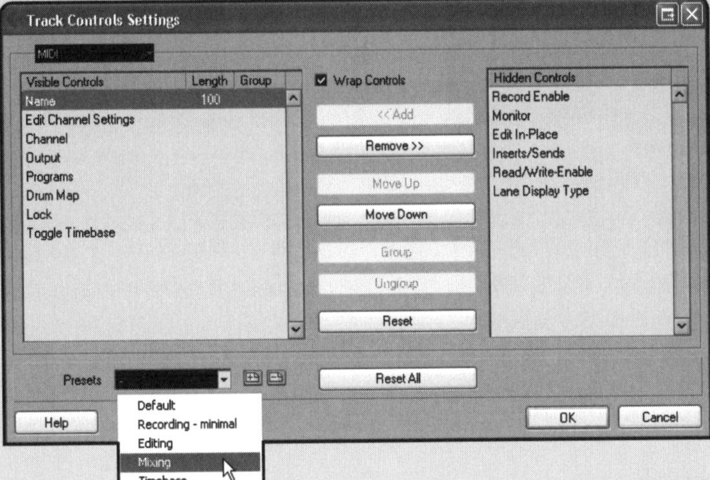

Figure 38.10

The Track Controls Settings dialog box.

2. Select the desired track type from the Track Type drop-down selector in the upper-left corner of this dialog box. The control elements on the left side are currently visible in the Track List. The control elements on the right are available, but not currently visible. Before creating a preset, let's look at an existing one to see whether there's already a preset that would suit your needs.
3. From the Presets menu in this dialog box, select the appropriate preset to see its current track control settings.
4. To add a control to the current preset, select the control under the Available Controls column on the right and then click the Add button.

5. To remove a control from the current preset, select the control under the Used Controls column on the left and then click the Remove button. As you probably noticed, the selected control will move from one side to the other. You can also change the order in which the controls appear in the Track List area.
6. Select the control that you want to modify in the Used Controls area and click the Move Up or Move Down button to move this control to a new position in the list. To make sure two or more controls always stay together on the same line when you resize the Track List area, you can group them.
7. Select the first control you want to group; then Ctrl-click (PC)/-click (Mac) on the other controls you want to group together. Note that if a control is already in a group, you'll need to ungroup it first, before you can group it with another control.
8. Click on the Group button to group the controls.
9. Repeat Steps 4 through 8 until you are satisfied with the results.
10. Click the Add Preset button to create a new preset.
11. Enter the desired name in the field and click OK.
12. Click OK once again to return to the Project window.

Remember that you can always remove unwanted presets by selecting them in this dialog box and clicking on the Remove Preset button.

HOW TO

Select a customized track control setting:

- Select the appropriate preset from the Track Controls drop-down menu found at the top-left corner of the Track List area.

39 Project Optimization

As projects grow in size, so does the real-time processing demand on a computer's CPU, which eventually can cause the project to outgrow the computer's limited resources and require more processing power than what is available. Although this might sound a bit limiting creatively, it doesn't always have to be this way, and you don't always have to spend more to get an even faster computer if you need to get the project done with the resources that are available to you today. This chapter is all about how you can manage the resources you have available and what can be done to optimize a project when these resources are running low.

Here's a summary of what you will learn in this chapter:

- How to disable unnecessary audio tracks to reduce disk access
- How to use offline processing instead of online (real-time) processing to reduce CPU load
- How to optimize audio edits by saving a project to a new folder
- How to use free up resources by freezing audio channels, object edits, real-time processes, and VST instruments
- How to optimize the audio track of a video file by using Cubase
- How to use folder tracks to group and control several tracks together

Disabling Audio Tracks

After you start recording audio inside a project, you will gather more audio takes than needed in the final version, because you will most likely have different takes from which to choose and different versions of the same audio content. You might also create several working tracks along the way that are not used anymore. Simply muting these audio tracks only mutes their output level, but the information on these tracks is still read, causing your media drive to look for them and load them anyway. After a while, these muted tracks might start dragging down your project. To avoid this, you can disable audio tracks that are not currently being used in your project. This offers the advantage of shutting down all disk activity related to the audio content found on these tracks, while the tracks still remain in your project in case you need them later.

HOW TO

Disable audio tracks:

1. Right-click (PC)/Option-click (Mac) in the Track List area.
2. From the context menu, select Disable Track.

You can re-enable a track after it has been disabled by repeating this operation, as displayed in Figure 39.1. The option in the context menu is replaced by Enable Track instead.

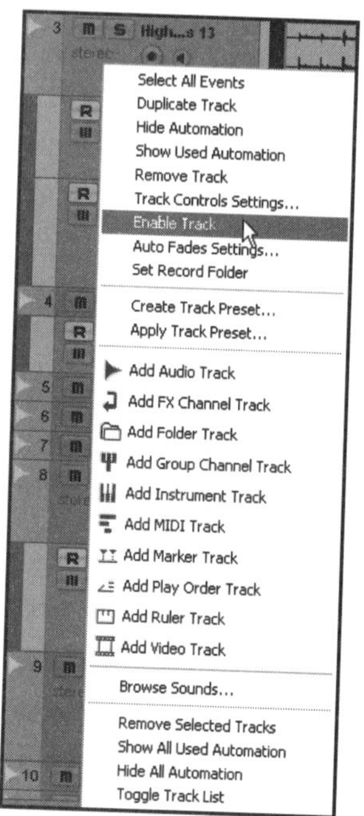

Figure 39.1
Re-enabling an audio track once it has been disabled.

Using VST Plug-Ins

VST plug-in effects, as you saw earlier in this book, can be added as inserts or used as send effects on an FX channel track. When doing so, you are processing the audio in real time, as described in Chapter 20. You also can apply VST plug-in effects available on your computer to a file directly, if you want to affect only a portion of a track or don't want to add an additional real-time processing load on your computer's CPU.

Remember that when you apply one of these *offline process* effects to all or part of a selected object, the processed result is saved in a special file, leaving your original file intact. This new file is seamlessly integrated into your project. In other words, you won't even feel or see it's a different file, other than the fact that this portion is processed.

Because VST plug-in effects vary from one computer to another, we will not discuss the specific settings of these plug-ins, but understand that you can use these effects in an offline process (non-real-time) the same way as you would use them in an online process (real-time). The only difference is that with offline effects you don't have the flexibility to vary their parameters over the range of time that will be affected by this processing.

HOW TO

Add a plug-in effect to a selected object:

1. Select all or part of the desired object in the project's timeline.
2. Select the desired plug-in from the Plug-Ins submenu in the Audio menu (see Figure 39.2). On Windows only, additional DirectX effects may be available under the DirectX submenu.

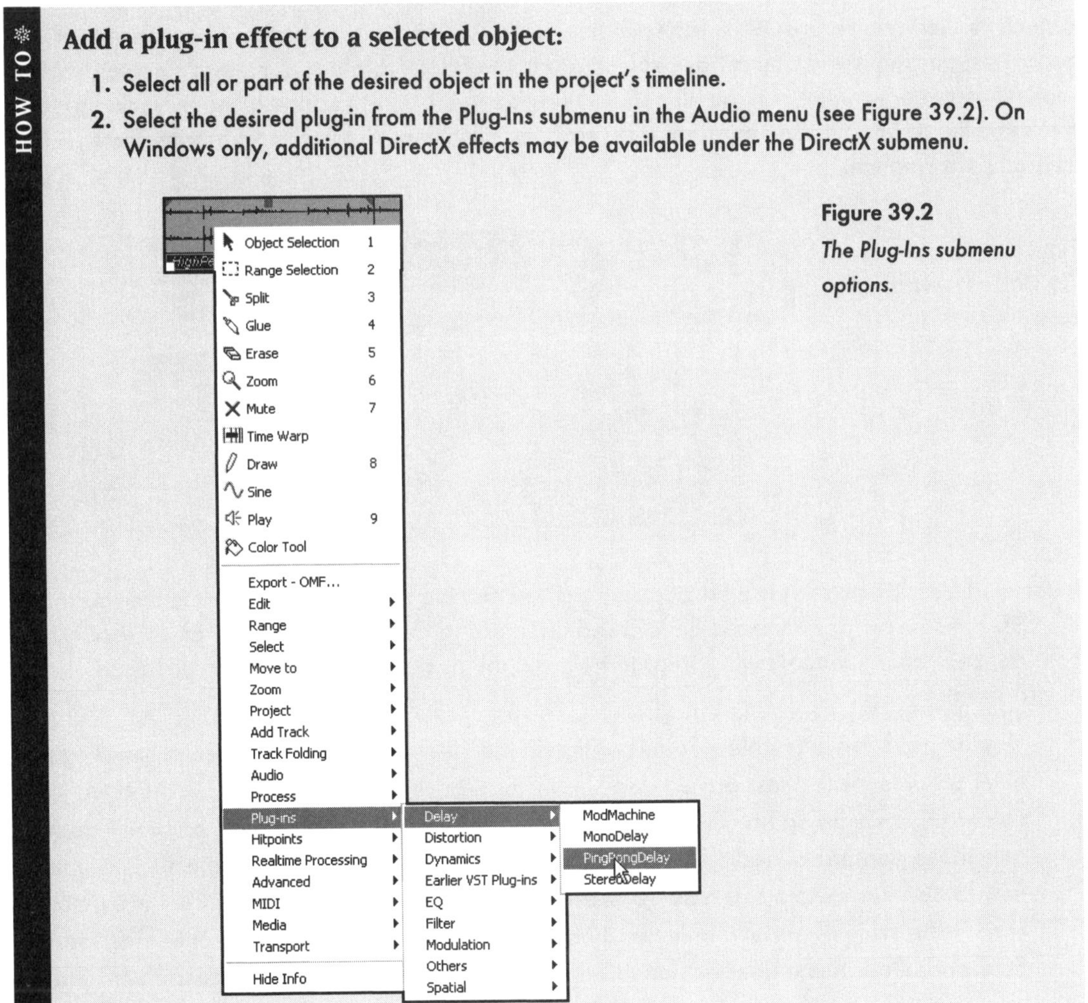

Figure 39.2
The Plug-Ins submenu options.

3. Make the appropriate adjustments in the dialog box. To preview the result, click the Preview button.
4. When you are satisfied with the settings, click the Process button.

Optimizing Projects after Processing

When you perform offline processes in Cubase, the processed audio is rendered to separate files on your media drive, which are stored inside the project's Edits folder. These files are necessary to preserve the original audio clip intact, while still providing the option to change an offline process that has been applied previously. For example, you can change the settings and the parameters of a previous process or even replace it with another type of process entirely. For each offline process, a line is created in the Offline Process History dialog box for a selected object, as shown in Figure 39.3. For each line in the Offline Process History, a rendering of the processed portion of this object has been stored in the Edits subfolder of your project folder. This makes it very convenient, but you also should realize that asking Cubase to move back and forth from one file to another and managing several tracks with multiple edited portions costs you in overall performance.

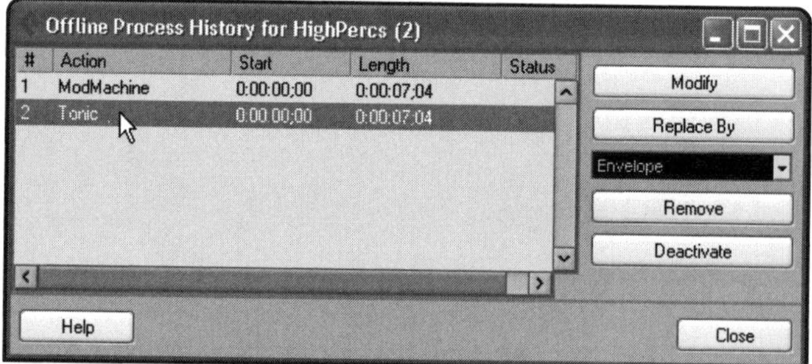

Figure 39.3
The Offline Process History dialog box.

If you start noticing an increased processing activity making the performance meter representing the CPU's resources or the media drive creep up, causing Cubase to feel slow or unresponsive, consider performing the following steps to help get things back to a more fluid working environment:

- Use the Save Project to New Folder option in the File menu. When Cubase prompts you to enter a name for the new project version, be sure to check all the options in the Save to Folder Options dialog box (see Figure 39.4). The Minimize Audio Files option will copy only those portions of audio files actually used in the project from the project's Pool to the new folder. For example, if only 30 seconds of a two-minute source audio file are actually used in the Project window, only this 30 seconds of audio will be copied over. The Freeze Edits option renders a new version of the audio events, reflecting all processing currently shown in the Offline Process History dialog box for each event, while the Remove Unused Files option will not save any audio clips that are not actually used in the Project currently, even if they are found in the Pool.

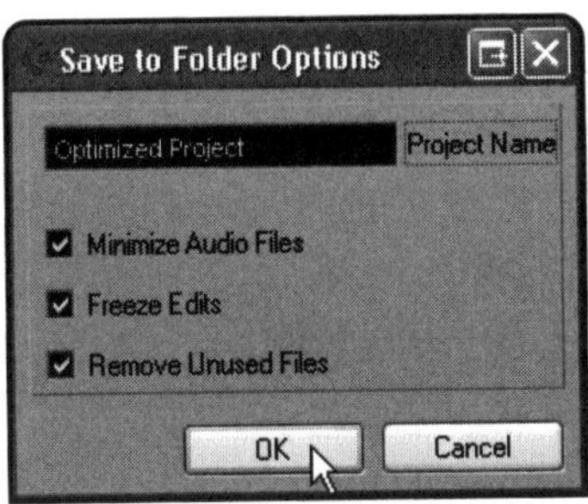

Figure 39.4
The Save to Folder Options dialog box.

- If you don't want to save your entire project to a new folder, you can select those audio events that contain the most offline processing steps and choose the Freeze Edits option from the Audio menu. Cubase will ask you whether you want to create a new file or replace the existing one. Choose the appropriate option. Either way, this improves the performance because Cubase doesn't have to skip from one file to another in order to produce the result of all this processing.
- Be sure that your disk is defragmented regularly to avoid having your computer operate slowly because of inefficient disk reading caused by fragmented files.

About Freeze

Many effects, edits, VST instruments, and automation tasks are occurring whenever you press the Play button with a full project going. When you need more processing juice than your computer can muster, but you don't want to render tracks permanently in case you'd like to change something, think of freezing them.

Freezing renders a new audio event incorporating all that track's processing and loads it up in an invisible audio channel. Then it locks the event, track, VSTi, or plug-in effects, saves their settings, and unloads them from memory until you decide to change something, such as a cutoff frequency parameter on filter, for example.

If you like trying different things while you are composing, chances are you might load up your memory with instances of VST instruments, giving you access to many layers of sound. This layering is what makes using Cubase such a great experience. What's not so great is when you run out of resources and your computer starts its "I've had enough" routine, crackling the sound, jerking playback, and exhibiting other related computer behaviors.

In the following sections, we'll discuss several techniques that let you free up some valuable processing power, while keeping the option of change conveniently close enough that you won't feel like you are spending most of your time dealing with problems during playback.

Freeze an Audio Channel

The Freeze Audio Channel button found in the Audio Settings section of the Inspector renders a temporary audio file of the audio track, including all its pre-fader insert effects in slots 1–6. You can still adjust the track's volume, pan, EQ, and Sends parameters. To unfreeze an audio channel, click on the Freeze Audio Channel once again; this time, the button is orange (see Figure 39.5). A dialog box prompts a selection:

- Unfreeze erases the temporary audio rendering and unlocks the audio channel.
- Keep Freeze Files keeps the temporary audio rendering in case you need to re-freeze. If an error occurs that prevents you from getting the same result you had before you froze, and the freeze file is no longer available, you won't be able to get the same process, even though the original unprocessed file will still be there.

Figure 39.5
The Freeze Audio Channel button.

Freeze Edits

The Freeze Edits option makes it possible to write all the offline processing added to an event in this project to a new file on a media drive or to replace the original file with the new, processed version. When you freeze edits, the original always remains on the drive unless it is used only once in the project. Freezing the edits of an event that's used in more than one place in a project automatically prompts you to save to a new file.

You can access the Freeze Edits option from the Audio menu, as displayed in Figure 39.6, on any selected event in the Pool that has been processed in some way.

Freeze Real-Time Processes

Earlier, we discussed Audio Warp tools and different methods of quantizing audio using warp tabs. We also discussed ways of applying real-time time-stretching and pitch-shifting processes to get loops to play at the project's tempo without altering the pitch or vice versa (altering the pitch and not the tempo). Once you've tied down the tempo of your project and you are pretty sure

Figure 39.6
The Freeze Edits option in the Audio menu.

you aren't going to change the pitch of an event, freeze the processing to free up processing resources. Cubase once again renders a new file to disk and loads the new version in the project, replacing the processing-intensive version. You can think of this as a way to get a better-quality offline process rendered with the audio.

Freeze events that are being time-stretched or transposed in real time:

1. Select the appropriate event. This may be an audio quantized event with warp tabs or a time-stretched musical mode event, for example.
2. From the Audio menu, select Realtime Processing > Freeze Timestretch and Transpose.

Freezing VSTi

Freeze creates a temporary audio render of the VSTi for all MIDI events routed through the selected VSTi you chose to freeze. As a result, the MIDI track becomes locked from editing and muted, the VSTi unloads from memory, and Cubase creates a special audio rendering corresponding to the result of the MIDI events going through the VSTi. This offers the advantage of hearing what you heard before—MIDI events playing through a VSTi without the resource real estate required by VSTi. The frozen audio will not appear in the project as a separate audio channel, but will continue to be controlled in the Mixer panel through its VSTi channel. So, any volume, EQ, or routing will continue to have an effect on the sound. If you want to change something in the MIDI track, you can unfreeze the VSTi, change the MIDI, and refreeze again. Once a VSTi is unfrozen, the freeze file is removed from its special Freeze folder, which can be found inside the project's main folder. Note that parts that are muted will not be frozen. In other words, the result of a freeze, in terms of what you hear, is identical to the VSTi generating the sounds in real time.

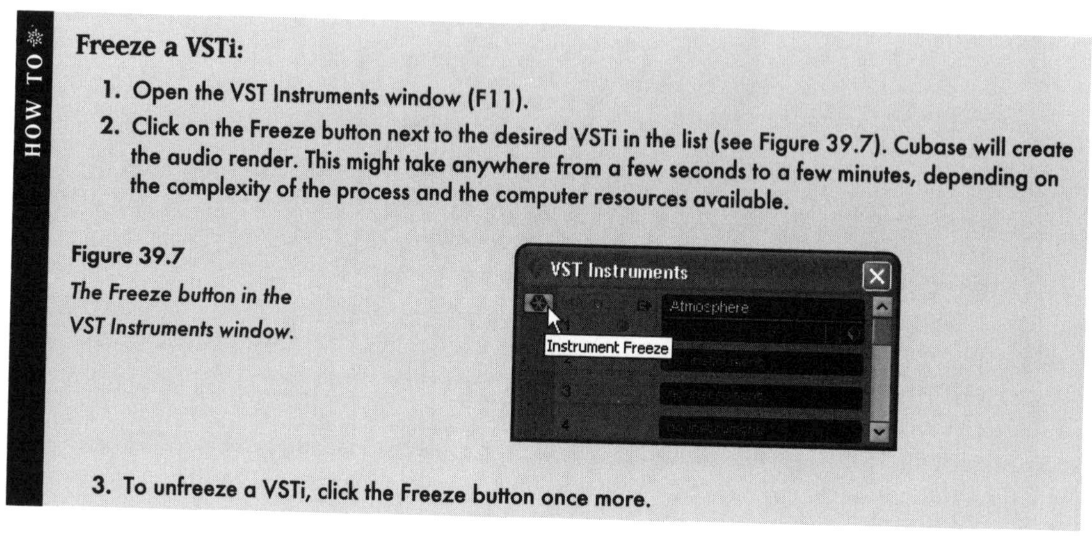

HOW TO

Freeze a VSTi:

1. Open the VST Instruments window (F11).
2. Click on the Freeze button next to the desired VSTi in the list (see Figure 39.7). Cubase will create the audio render. This might take anywhere from a few seconds to a few minutes, depending on the complexity of the process and the computer resources available.

Figure 39.7
The Freeze button in the VST Instruments window.

3. To unfreeze a VSTi, click the Freeze button once more.

When a VSTi is frozen, the Freeze button will appear orange, and you won't be able to make any changes to the MIDI tracks being sent to this VSTi.

Working with Video Files

With the arrival of DV cameras on the market, more and more video enthusiasts are using their computers to edit movies. Cubase allows you to take these video files and add sound to them to create original soundtracks or musical scores.

There are two basic methods of viewing a video inside Cubase—using your computer monitor to display the video, which implies your computer's CPU is processing the video codec in real time, or using a special video card that connects to an external monitor. In the latter case, the video card handles the video codec and frees up the computer's resources, giving you a better-quality image and a bigger image all together while working on the sound.

The PC version of Cubase supports up to four playback engines: Microsoft DirectShow, Microsoft DirectX, Apple's QuickTime format, and Video for Windows. The Mac version supports the QuickTime format, which supports video files in QuickTime (.mov), AVI, MPEG, and DV format and also can use an external device connected to the computer's FireWire port to display the video file. In either platform, this implies that you can open MPEG files or AVI and QuickTime files using the following codecs: Cinepak, Indeo, MPEG, or M-JPEG. To use the QuickTime playback method on a PC, you need to install QuickTime on your computer.

HOW TO

Set up for online video files in a Cubase project:

1. In the Devices menu, select the Device Setup option.
2. In the Device Setup dialog box, highlight the Video Player option to view the corresponding settings in the right side of the dialog box, as shown in Figure 39.8.

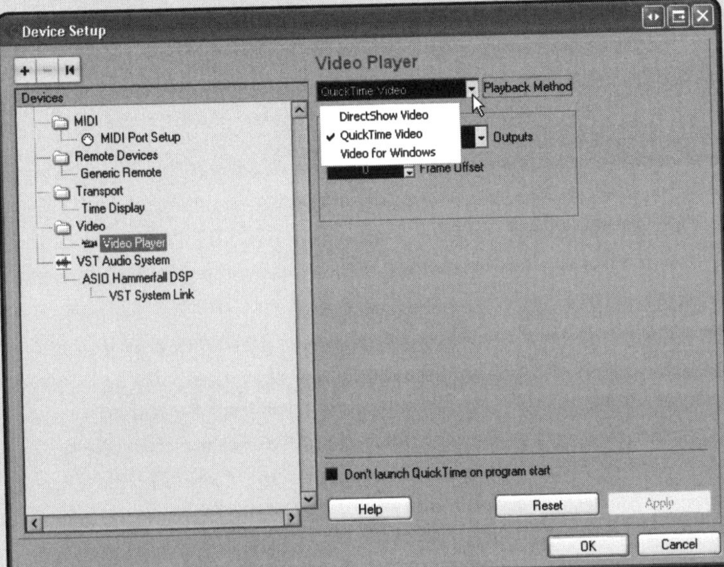

Figure 39.8
The Video Player settings in the Device Setup dialog box.

3. In the Playback Method drop-down menu, select the desired playback method.
4. Under Video Window, select the size of window you want to use. Note that the larger the Video window is, the more processing will be required by your computer.
5. Click the Apply button, and then click OK.
6. In the File (PC)/Cubase (Mac) menu, select Preferences.
7. Under Event Display, select Video. This page offers two options.
8. Click the Show Video Thumbnails to see a thumbnail preview of the video in the video track.
9. The video cache size represents the cache memory reserved to display thumbnails in the video track. If you are using a long video file or you want to stretch the video track to see bigger frames, you need to increase the cache size for the thumbnails to display properly. Otherwise, leave this setting at the default value.
10. Click OK to close the window.

HOW TO

Import an online video file into a Cubase project:

1. Back in the File menu, select Import, and then Video File.
2. Browse to the location of your file, select it, and then click Open. This adds the video file to the Pool.
3. Right-click (PC)/Control-click (Mac) in the Track List area and select Add Video Track from the context menu.
4. From this point, you can use one of two methods to add your video to the video track. First, you can right-click the video in the Pool and select the Insert into Project option in the context menu. Then you can choose whether you want to insert it at the current cursor position or at the video's original time. Second, you can drag the video, as you would for an audio event, into the video track at the desired location.

Note that when the Video window is active, you can right-click (PC)/Control-click (Mac) on it to expand the window to full screen.

Folder Track

Folder tracks, as you might have guessed, are used as folders into which you can put any combination of track classes, including other folder tracks. You can use folder tracks as you would use folders in your computer, grouping related tracks into a single folder that you name appropriately. You can also hide the folder track to give you more working space on your screen, or you can mute or solo its entire contents with a single click. For example, if you have several percussion tracks, you could create a folder, name it "Percussion," and drag all these tracks inside it. When you're not working on your percussion tracks, you can fold up the folder track to minimize the space that these tracks would otherwise use in the Track List. When the time comes to edit these tracks, all you need to do is unfold the folder track to reveal all the tracks and controls inside.

When tracks are moved inside a folder track, a folder part is created in the Event Display area, which graphically represents the contents of the folder track even when it is minimized.

The Inspector for a selected folder track only contains one section. This section contains the name of the tracks you moved inside the folder track. Whenever you click on the name of a track in this section, that track's Inspector area is displayed below the folder section (also in the Inspector area, as shown in Figure 39.9).

Notice in Figure 39.9 that at the top of the Inspector for this folder track, there are some buttons that are also found in other track classes (and were explained previously). These buttons affect all the tracks inside the folder track simultaneously. For example, clicking the Mute button for a folder track in the Inspector or the Track List mutes all the tracks inside the folder track.

Figure 39.9
The Inspector settings for a folder track.

Similarly, clicking the Lock button locks all these tracks from editing. As you would guess, this makes recording, monitoring, muting, soloing, or locking multiple tracks simultaneously very easy.

HOW TO

Move tracks into a folder track:

1. In the Project window's Track List, click and drag the track you want to move to a folder track, as shown in the top part of Figure 39.10.
2. When a green line appears within your folder track, drop your track into it by releasing the mouse button (as shown in the center image of Figure 39.10).

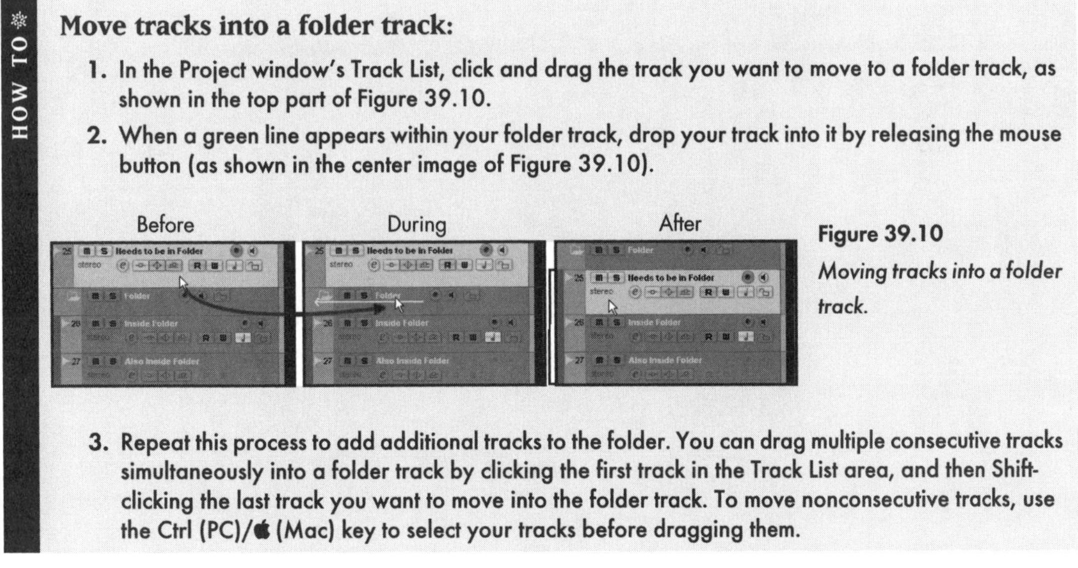

Figure 39.10
Moving tracks into a folder track.

3. Repeat this process to add additional tracks to the folder. You can drag multiple consecutive tracks simultaneously into a folder track by clicking the first track in the Track List area, and then Shift-clicking the last track you want to move into the folder track. To move nonconsecutive tracks, use the Ctrl (PC)/ (Mac) key to select your tracks before dragging them.

To remove tracks from a folder track, simply drag them outside of the folder track in the Track List, just as you moved them inside of it.

When tracks are added to a folder track, a folder part is created, as shown in Figure 39.11 As you can see in the same figure, the folder part displays the position and colors used by the parts on the tracks it contains. In this example, the folder track has been unfolded, showing the details of these tracks. You can click the track's Folder icon (to the left of the Mute button) to toggle the folded/unfolded states of selected folder tracks. You also can rename folder tracks as you would any other tracks through the Inspector area.

Figure 39.11
Folder parts appear in the folder track.

HOW TO

Rename a track by using the Inspector:

1. Click in the name box at the top part of the Inspector for the selected track.
2. Type a new name for your track.

Index

B

C

G

H

I

J–K

L

M

P

Q

R

S

T

THOMSON
COURSE TECHNOLOGY